Handbook of Research on Special Education Teacher Preparation

Compilations of research on teacher preparation often include no more than a cursory mention of the specific roles and needs of special education teachers. Although the work that special education teachers perform does indeed differ from the work of classroom teachers, teacher preparation in the two fields has much in common. The purpose of this seven-part handbook is to expand our knowledge of teacher education broadly by providing an in-depth look at the most up-to-date research on special education teacher preparation. Opening chapters ground the collection in political and economic context, while subsequent sections delve deeply into issues related to the current state of our special education workforce and offer insights into how to best prepare and sustain that workforce. Ultimately, by illuminating the particularities of special education teacher preparation, this landmark handbook addresses the state of current research in the field and sets an agenda for future scholarship.

Paul T. Sindelar is Professor of Special Education, School Psychology, and Early Childhood Studies at the University of Florida, USA.

Erica D. McCray is Associate Professor of Special Education, School Psychology, and Early Childhood Studies at the University of Florida, USA.

Mary T. Brownell is Professor of Special Education, School Psychology, and Early Childhood Studies at the University of Florida, USA.

Benjamin Lignugaris/Kraft is Professor and Department Head of Special Education and Rehabilitation at Utah State University, USA.

Handbook of Research on Special Education Teacher Preparation

Edited by Paul T. Sindelar, Erica D. McCray, Mary T. Brownell, and Benjamin Lignugaris/Kraft

Routledge
Taylor & Francis Group
NEW YORK AND LONDON

First published 2014
by Routledge
711 Third Avenue, New York, NY 10017

and by Routledge
2 Park Square, Milton Park, Abingdon, Oxon OX14 4RN

Routledge is an imprint of the Taylor & Francis Group, an informa business

Library of Congress Cataloging-in-Publication Data
Handbook of research on special education teacher preparation : edited by Paul T. Sindelar, Erica D. McCray, Mary T. Brownell, and Benjamin Lignugaris/Kraft.
pages cm
Includes bibliographical references and index.
1. Special education teachers–Training of–United States. 2. Educational accountability–United States. 3. Special education–United States. I. Sindelar, Paul T.
LC3969.45.H354 2013
371.9–dc23
2013027164

ISBN: 978–0–415–89308–4 (hbk)
ISBN: 978–0–415–89309–1 (pbk)
ISBN: 978–0–203–81703–2 (ebk)

Typeset in Bembo
by Swales & Willis Ltd, Exeter, Devon, UK

FSC
www.fsc.org
MIX
Paper from responsible sources
FSC® C014174

Printed and bound in the United States of America by Sheridan Books, Inc. (a Sheridan Group Company).

Dedication

We dedicate this *Handbook* to the many aspiring teachers in our lives from whom we have learned so much and derived so much inspiration.

Contents

Illustrations

Figures

Tables

Contributors

Peter J. Alter is an Assistant Professor in the Special Education Program in the School of Education at St. Mary's College of California. His research interests and numerous publications are focused on the use of effective instructional practices for working with students with emotional/behavioral disorders.

Alfredo J. Artiles is Associate Dean of Academic Affairs and the Ryan Harris Professor of Special Education at Arizona State University's Teachers College. His scholarship focuses on understanding and addressing educational inequities related to the intersections of disability with sociocultural differences.

Jungah Bae is a doctoral candidate in special education at the University of Florida. Before coming to the doctoral program, she worked with students with disabilities and their families in Korea for over 10 years. Her research seeks to understand teacher qualifications and instructional practices that are linked to student engagement in learning and achievement.

Joshua Barton is a doctoral candidate and instructor in the Department of Special Education at the University of South Florida. His research interests include preservice and in-service special education teacher training and licensure, national standards and accountability, and inclusive service delivery systems, such as collaborative teaching and multitiered systems of support.

Cynthia Coss Baughan, Ph.D., is an Assistant Professor in the Department of Special Education and Child Development at the University of North Carolina, Charlotte. Her areas of expertise are early intervention and early childhood special education. Dr. Baughan's research interests include the transition into school age programs, kindergarten readiness, and culturally responsive teacher preparation.

Amber Benedict is a former special education teacher and a special education doctoral candidate at the University of Florida. Her research interests include a focus on accountability policy reform, providing teachers with effective professional development experiences, and improving the reading-related outcomes of students with high-incidence disabilities.

Elizabeth Bettini is a special education doctoral student at the University of Florida. Her research interests include special education teachers' working conditions, special education teacher quality, and teacher effectiveness for serving students with emotional and behavioral disabilities.

Bonnie S. Billingsley is a Professor in Special Education at Virginia Tech. Her research interests include special education teacher retention and induction and the leadership practices that promote effective and inclusive educational programs for students with disabilities.

Linda P. Blanton is a Professor in the Department of Teaching and Learning at Florida International University. Her areas of expertise and research interests focus on teacher quality, teacher education, and collaborative teacher education programs in general and special education. She has served in numerous national, state, and university leadership positions and was the recipient of the Excellence in Teacher Education Award given by the Teacher Education Division of the Council for Exceptional Children.

Erling E. Boe is a Professor of Education at the Graduate School of Education, the University of Pennsylvania. His general area of scholarship is on research relevant to education policy. Most recently, this research has focused on the demand, supply, qualifications, and turnover of special education teachers.

Mildred Boveda is a doctoral candidate in Exceptional Student Education in the College of Education at Florida International University. She received an M.S. in Exceptional Student Education from Florida International University and an Ed.M. in Education Policy and Management from Harvard Graduate School of Education. Her research interests are in collaboration in teacher education, preparing teachers to teach a growingly diverse student population, and the application of intersectionality theory to teacher education practice.

Brian A. Boyd is an Assistant Professor in the Division of Occupational Science and Occupational Therapy in the Department of Allied Health Sciences at the University of North Carolina at Chapel Hill. He has published numerous articles focused on behavioral intervention strategies to address the challenging behaviors of young children with autism spectrum disorders and related developmental disabilities.

Laura Bozeman is an Associate Professor and the Director of the Vision Studies Program in the School for Global Inclusion and Social Development at University of Massachusetts Boston. Her main areas are visual impairment and multiple disabilities with specific interests in personnel preparation in a low-incidence disability field, orientation and mobility, low vision, self-defense and visual impairment, and innovative teaching through distance education.

Mary T. Brownell is a Professor of Special Education at the University of Florida. She also directs the Collaboration for Educator Effectiveness, Development, Accountability, and Reform (CEEDAR Center). Her areas of expertise include teacher effectiveness and its assessment, teacher preparation, literacy, and professional development as they relate to students with disabilities.

Beth Clavenna-Deane has 20-plus years of experience facilitating successful transitions to adulthood for students with disabilities. Her research has focused on improving transition services for students with autism spectrum disorders and conducting personnel preparation for secondary special education and transition. She currently is an Autism Behavior Specialist in a large Midwestern school district as well as a graduate level instructor at a local university.

Belva C. Collins is Professor and Chair of the Department of Early Childhood, Special Education, and Rehabilitation Counseling at the University of Kentucky. Her research agenda has focused on systematic instruction for persons with moderate and severe disabilities, as well as distance education in teacher preparation. She is the author of both texts and refereed publications on these topics.

Vincent J. Connelly is an Associate Professor in the University of New Hampshire Department of Education. His areas of scholarship include teacher and leadership preparation, and culturally responsive instruction and behavioral support.

Maureen A. Conroy is a Professor of Special Education and Early Childhood Studies in the Department of Special Education, School Psychology, and Early Childhood Studies and Co-Director of the Center for Excellence in Early Childhood Studies at the University of Florida. Dr. Conroy has extensive experience in personnel preparation and conducting research with children who are at-risk for or have social and behavioral disabilities, including children with autism spectrum disorders.

Vivian I. Correa, Ph.D., is a Professor in the Department of Special Education and Child Development at the University of North Carolina, Charlotte. Her areas of expertise are in early intervention and early childhood special education. Dr. Correa's research interests include culturally responsive teacher preparation, early childhood special education, and literacy interventions with Latino parents and their young children.

Jean Crockett, Ph.D., is Professor and Director of the School of Special Education, School Psychology, and Early Childhood Studies at the University of Florida. Her research addresses special education policy and leadership practices that foster effective instruction for students with disabilities.

Lani Florian is a Professor and the Bell Chair of Education at the University of Edinburgh. Dr. Florian has over 20 years' experience in higher education as a teacher educator and researcher. Her research interests include models of provision for meeting the needs of all learners, inclusive pedagogy and teaching practices in inclusive schools.

Peggy A. Gallagher, Ph.D., University of North Carolina at Chapel Hill, is a Professor and Program Coordinator of Early Childhood Special Education at Georgia State University. She is a Past-President of the Teacher Education Division of CEC. Her current research focus is personnel preparation in ECSE and working with families of young children with disabilities.

William L. Geiger is a Professor of Special Education and Vice Provost for Academic Affairs and Dean of the Graduate College at the University of Texas at Tyler. His research interests have been in the areas of the supply and credentialing of special educators.

Katherine B. Green, Ph.D., Georgia State University, is a new faculty member in the Department of Communication Sciences and Special Education at the University of Georgia. Her background in language and literacy, along with an interest in mathematics for young children, has led her to focus on research in the areas of language, literacy, and mathematics for young children with and without disabilities.

Cynthia C. Griffin, Ph.D., is a Professor of Special Education at the University of Florida, Gainesville. Her research interests are in the areas of mathematics learning disabilities, the use of schema-based strategy instruction in mathematics problem solving, and teachers' content knowledge for teaching mathematics in inclusive elementary classrooms.

Shannon Harris is a doctoral fellow in the multidisciplinary Disability Disciplines Doctoral Program in the Department of Special Education and Rehabilitation at Utah State University. Her areas of research include evidence-based language and literacy practices, effective instructional approaches for students with disabilities, and special education personnel preparation.

Beth Harry is a Professor of Special Education in the Department of Teaching and Learning at the University of Miami. A native of Jamaica, she entered the field of special education as a parent of a child with cerebral palsy, an experience that has been chronicled in her memoir, *Melanie, Bird with a*

Broken Wing: A Mother's Story. Inspired by her experience as a parent, Dr. Harry's research and teaching focus on the impact of special education on children and families from diverse cultural and linguistic backgrounds.

Michael Jabot is Professor of Science Education in the Curriculum and Instruction Department of the State University of New York at Fredonia. His research focuses on the conceptual understanding in science and in particular issues around place-based education and sustainability.

Margaret L. Kamman is an Assistant Scholar and Project Coordinator for Collaboration for Effective Educator Development, Accountability and Reform (CEEDAR Center) at the University of Florida. Her research interests include teacher induction, technology applications, beginning teacher effectiveness, and middle school reading instruction for students with disabilities.

Michael J. Kennedy is an Assistant Professor in the Curry School of Education at the University of Virginia. Kennedy's research interests include the use of multimedia to support teaching and learning in teacher education programs and professional development offerings.

Jenna Kimerling is a doctoral candidate at the University of Florida. Her primary research interests include special education teacher quality and the contextual factors that impact it, improving working conditions for special education teachers, and increasing the academic engagement of students with disabilities.

Jeannie Kleinhammer-Tramill, Ph.D., is a professor in the Department of Special Education, University of South Florida. Her interests are personnel preparation policy, and the impact of state and federal policy on students with disabilities.

Victoria Knight is an Assistant Professor in the Special Education Department at Vanderbilt University. Her research agenda has focused on general curriculum access for students with significant disabilities, especially in STEM, and evaluating and disseminating evidence-based practices. She is the author of both book chapters and refereed publications on these topics.

Elizabeth B. Kozleski is Chair and Professor in the Department of Special Education at the University of Kansas. Her scholarship focuses on inclusive teacher education, and on the social construction of equity, culture, and dis/abilities and social justice in education transformation.

Lisa Lacy is a graduate student in the Curriculum and Instruction, emphasis on Special Education doctoral program at Arizona State University. Her research interest focuses on how the use of assistive technology influences the self-concept of adolescent females.

Kristine E. Larson is a Doctoral Fellow in the Special Education Teacher Preparation program at the Johns Hopkins University School of Education. Her areas of research include teacher preparation, professional development, and culturally responsive classroom management.

Christopher D. Leko is a doctoral candidate at the University of Florida. His research interests are special education teacher evaluation and teacher supply and demand.

Melinda M. Leko, Ph.D., is an Assistant Professor in the Department of Rehabilitation Psychology and Special Education and the University of Wisconsin—Madison. Her research interests are in the areas of special education teacher education and reading instruction for secondary students with disabilities.

Susan Lenihan, Ph.D., CED, is Professor and Director of Deaf Education at Fontbonne University in St. Louis, Missouri. Her professional interests include early intervention, the role of the family in communication development, professional collaboration, and literacy. Dr. Lenihan serves on the Board of the Alexander Graham Bell Association.

Timothy J. Lewis is Professor and Chair in the Department of Special Education at the University of Missouri. He conducts research, teaches classes, and works on creating policy related to school-wide positive behavior supports.

Benjamin Lignugaris/Kraft is Department Head of Special Education and Rehabilitation and Professor of Special Education at Utah State University. His areas of research include effective instruction for students with mild/moderate disabilities, preparation of teachers for students with mild/moderate disabilities, and special education leadership preparation.

Miriam Lipsky is the project manager for Project INCLUDE in the University of Miami's School of Education and Human Development. Dr. Lipsky's research interests include undergraduate teacher preparation (with an emphasis on reading), and children's vocabulary development in preschool settings.

Larry Maheady is Professor and Horace Mann Endowed Chair in Exceptional Education at SUNY Buffalo State. Dr. Maheady has authored or coauthored over 80 articles in peer-reviewed journals, 12 book chapters, and two books. His primary areas of interest include evidence-based education, peer-mediated learning, and preparing highly effective teachers for 21st century schools.

Erica D. McCray is an Associate Professor of Special Education at the University of Florida. She teaches at the undergraduate and graduate levels and has experience as a special educator for students with behavioral and learning disabilities in elementary and middle school settings. Dr. McCray's research focuses on teacher quality and faculty development in the context of diversity.

Patricia Alvarez McHatton, Ph.D., is a Professor and Chair of the Department of Inclusive Education at Kennesaw State University. Her research interests include culturally responsive teacher preparation, collaboration, school experiences of diverse youth and families, and the use of arts-based methods for research and reflection.

Debra McKeown is an Assistant Professor in special education at Georgia State University in Atlanta. Her research interests include teacher preparation/quality and effective instructional practices, especially in writing.

James McLeskey is a Professor in the School of Special Education, School Psychology, and Early Childhood Studies at the University of Florida. He has extensive experience in teacher education and professional development activities related to providing high quality, inclusive services for students with disabilities. His research interests include effective methods for achieving school reform/improvement, the role of the principal in developing effective, inclusive schools, and issues influencing teacher learning and the translation of research-based methods into practice.

Ann Mickelson is an Assistant Research Professor at the University of Connecticut where she serves as the project coordinator for the OSEP-funded Early Childhood Personnel Center. Her research centers on interdisciplinary personnel preparation for professionals working with young children with and without disabilities with a particular interest in blended or unified models of early childhood teacher education.

Robert Morgan is a Professor in the Department of Special Education and Rehabilitation at Utah State University, and serves as the Chair of the Undergraduate Teacher Preparation Committee. His research interests include transition from school to adult roles and applied behavior analysis. He has coauthored two books, five book chapters, over 80 journal articles, and 13 educational products.

Mary E. Morningstar is an Associate Professor in the Department of Special Education at the University of Kansas. She is currently the Director of the Transition Coalition that implements research-based professional development in secondary special education and transition. She is coordinator of the KU Online Transition Master's Program and the Transition Certificate Program.

Lauri H. Nelson, Ph.D., is Assistant Professor of Deaf Education at Utah State University in Logan, Utah. Her professional interests include audiological services and the academic achievement of children who are deaf or hard of hearing.

Regina M. Oliver is an Assistant Research Professor in the Center for Child and Family Well-Being in the Special Education and Communication Disorders department at the University of Nebraska—Lincoln. Dr. Oliver has published and conducted research in teacher preparation, evaluation of effective classroom organization and behavior management, and improving teacher use of evidence-based classroom management practices.

Yujeong Park, Ph.D., is an Assistant Professor in the Special Education program at the University of Tennessee. Her research interests include a focus on improving the reading-related outcomes of students with high-incidence disabilities and students who are English language learners. She is also a highly skilled quantitative methodologist.

Marleen C. Pugach is Professor of the Practice of Education at the University of Southern California and Professor Emerita in the University of Wisconsin—Milwaukee School of Education. Her areas of expertise include the reform of teacher education at the intersection of general and special education and the intersections of diversity and disability in the redesign of teacher education. She has been a Fulbright Scholar and has received awards for her research contributions from the American Association of Colleges for Teacher Education and the Teacher Education Division of the Council for Exceptional Children.

Daniel J. Reschly is a Professor of Education and Psychology in Peabody College, Vanderbilt University where he Chaired the Department of Education from 1998 to 2006, gaining the #1 national ranking for the first time in 2003. Dr. Reschly has published on response to intervention, reduction of special education disproportionality, identification of disabilities (high incidence, minority issues), and policy issues in special education. His recent funding and research focuses on teacher quality.

Michael S. Rosenberg is Dean of the School of Education and Professor of Education at the State University of New York at New Paltz. He also is Professor Emeritus in the Johns Hopkins University School of Education. A former coeditor of *Teacher Education and Special Education*, his areas of scholarship include teacher and leadership preparation, and culturally responsive behavior management.

Charles Salzberg is a Professor of Special Education at Utah State University. He is a Past-President of the Higher Education Consortium for Special Education and of the Teacher Education Division of the Council for Exceptional Children. His research and development work has focused on teacher preparation in special education, children and adults with severe disabilities, and transition of individuals with disabilities from public school to employment and postsecondary education.

Paul T. Sindelar is Professor of Special Education at the University of Florida and Co-Director of the CEEDAR Center. Dr. Sindelar's recent research has focused on teacher education policy and the impact of economic conditions on teacher employment and outcomes for students with disabilities.

Cynthia Smith is Associate Professor of Mathematics Education in the Curriculum and Instruction department of the State University of New York at Fredonia. Her interests include working with children/families from poverty, preparing 21st century math educators, and addressing important issues, trends, and research in mathematics education.

Sean J. Smith is an Associate Professor in the Department of Special Education at the University of Kansas. Dr. Smith's scholarship includes the impact of technology innovations on student learning and social/behavioral outcomes, teacher development towards innovation implementation, and teacher and parent engagement towards student outcomes.

Elizabeth A. Steed, Ph.D., University of Oregon, is an Assistant Professor in Early Childhood Special Education at University of Colorado—Denver. Before becoming a professor, Elizabeth was an early childhood special education teacher and then a clinical supervisor for an early intervention program. Her current research focuses on professional development for preschool teachers, positive behavioral interventions and supports, and young children with challenging behavior.

Trisha Steinbrecher is an Assistant Professor of Special Education at the University of New Mexico. Her research interests are special education teacher quality and certification, measuring teacher effectiveness, and teacher evaluation across the service continuum.

Kristina Hernandez Taylor is a doctoral candidate in Exceptional Student Education in the College of Education at Florida International University. She has worked in the field of special education since graduating with her master's degree from the University of Florida in 2005. Her primary research focus is on working collaboratively with immigrant families of individuals with special needs in urban populations.

Cathy Newman Thomas is an Assistant Professor in the Department of Special Education at the University of Missouri. Her research interests are focused on technology-enhanced learning in teacher education and for providing access to the curriculum for diverse learners including students with disabilities.

Rachel A. Thomas is a doctoral candidate in Special Education at the University of Florida. Her recent research has focused on teacher education and writing instruction for secondary students with learning disabilities and from diverse backgrounds.

Tracy G. Ulrich, M.Ed., is a doctoral candidate in the Special Education program at the University of Florida, Gainesville. A former kindergarten teacher, her research is focused on the mathematics learning of young children.

Delinda van Garderen, Ph.D., is an Associate Professor of Special Education at the University of Missouri, Columbia. Her research interests are in the areas of learning disabilities in mathematics, the use of representations in mathematics problem solving, and teachers' use of Universal Design for Learning in science and mathematics.

Leah Wasburn-Moses is Associate Professor of Special Education at Miami University in Oxford, Ohio. Her research focuses on reform in teacher education. Her Campus Mentors model, alternative schools located on college campuses, raises achievement among local youth at-risk and enhances the preparation of teachers.

David L. Westling is the Adelaide Worth Daniels Distinguished Professor of Special Education at Western Carolina University. He is the coauthor of *Teaching Students with Severe Disabilities, Special Education for Today's Teachers: An Introduction*, and *Inclusion: Effective Practices for All Teachers*, and has published more than 50 papers in refereed journals in special education.

Karl R. White, Ph.D., is Professor of Psychology and holds the Emma Eccles Jones Endowed Chair in Early Childhood Education at Utah State University. He is the founding Director of the National Center on Hearing Assessment and Management. His scholarly activities focus on improving early hearing detection and intervention programs.

Kim Zebehazy is an Assistant Professor in the Department of Educational and Counseling Psychology and Special Education at the University of British Columbia. Her area is special education, blindness, and visual impairment and she has particular research interests in preservice teacher reflective practices, orientation and mobility, low vision, and supporting thinking and problem-solving skills of students with visual impairments.

Preface

Special education teachers work hard. Their job is demanding and intense, and doing it well requires knowledge, skill, persistence, resilience, and intelligence. Their caring and patience are taken for granted. (What special education teacher has not been told how patient he or she must be?) Now, with the expectation that teachers will have the knowledge needed to select, implement, and make data-based adjustments to evidence-based practices; the requirement that students with disabilities have access to and make progress in the general education curriculum; and the stipulation that, to be considered highly qualified, teachers demonstrate content mastery, the importancae of effective preparation has been ratcheted up. Oh, yes—policy makers and members of the public have expressed keen interest in teacher preparation and teacher quality, as well.

The Individuals with Disabilities Education Act entitles students with disabilities to a free, appropriate public education, what those of us in the field know as FAPE. If the assumption is made that qualified, competent, and caring teachers are essential to fulfilling this obligation, it can be argued that the promise of FAPE went unrealized for over 30 years. During that time, the field was plagued by teacher shortages, which hovered at 10%. Clearly, thousands and thousands of students were denied FAPE for lack of a qualified teacher. Now, with special education teacher shortages abating and increased demands for improving the achievement of student with disabilities, our attention has focused on the quality of teachers who graduate from our programs. The *Handbook of Research on Special Education Teacher Preparation* is intended to provide an overview of what we have learned about developing competent teachers from the scholarship on effective preparation.

The Office of Special Education Programs has invested substantially in such scholarly work, including the Center on Personnel Studies in Special Education (COPSSE), which two of us directed from 2001 to 2007. Part of that Center's work involved developing a comprehensive set of research syntheses. In those papers, eminent scholars—many of whom have contributed chapters to this *Handbook* —identified key unanswered questions for our research agenda. Judging from the feedback from the field, the authors raised provocative questions and made clear how much we had yet to learn about recruiting, preparing, and retaining special education teachers. Today, special education scholars know much more about effective preparation than they did a decade ago. One purpose of developing this *Handbook* was to exploit the fruits of recent scholarship and to organize and compile what we have learned in the decade since the COPSSE papers first appeared about preparing a competent and caring teacher workforce.

What special education teachers do often differs substantially from what general education teachers do, and, as a result, compilations of research on teacher preparation often include little more than cursory mention of our discipline. A second purpose of this *Handbook* was to complement and extend existing compendia of teacher education research by gathering and organizing scholarship on the preparation of special education teachers. Our hope is that giving voice to scholars in our field will enrich both our understanding about the work we do as well as the general scholarship on the preparation of teachers.

The *Handbook* is organized into seven sections. The four chapters in the introductory section provide political, historical, administrative, and international overviews of the field. In the second section, chapters address persistent problems related to the status of the workforce, including supply and demand, retention, and diversification. The six chapters in section three address critical features in both the design and delivery of special education teacher preparation. The four chapters in section four review aspects of teacher education pedagogy, both generally and with regard to specific content areas. In the two sections that follow, chapters address the highly specialized preparation that a complex field like special education requires, with regard to both different disabilities and the challenges they present to teachers (in section five) and the specialized roles that special educators play (in section six). In the final section, chapter authors discuss teacher quality, the state of qualitative research in the field, and an agenda for advancing scholarship and practice.

We have a number of people to thank for their contributions to this *Handbook*. Lane Akers, now retired from Routledge, was instrumental in recruiting us to undertake this effort, and Alex Masulis, his replacement, has been every bit as helpful, supportive, and encouraging as Lane. Here at UF, we benefited greatly from the contributions of Jenna Kimerling, Amber Benedict, and Rachel Thomas, special education doctoral students, who gave generously of their time. For them, no timeline was impossible, and no task too menial or esoteric. Jane Erin of the University of Arizona, Fred Spooner of University of North Carolina-Charlotte, Jackie Rodriguez, then at the University of Central Florida and now at the College of William & Mary, and Blane Trautwein of the University of Texas Health Science Center at San Antonio all contributed helpful and well-appreciated reviews for chapters we were not comfortable evaluating ourselves. Finally, we are thankful for the opportunity to work with our chapter authors—esteemed colleagues and friends, to whom credit for the success of this *Handbook* belongs.

Paul T. Sindelar, Erica D. McCray, Mary T. Brownell, and Benjamin Lignugaris/Kraft

Note on the Text

In several chapters of this *Handbook*, authors have referred to and cited data tables from ideadata.org. Unfortunately, during the production of the *Handbook*, ideadata.org went off-line. State-level data files from which these "OSEP" tables were created were moved to http://tadnet.public.tadnet.org/pages/712, but the data tables themselves are not available at either site. We decided to retain the original citations and references even though they are no longer working. We regret any inconvenience our decision may cause readers or any questions it may raise regarding the accuracy of assertions in this *Handbook*. However, we have retained a large (but incomplete) set of tables, which we are willing to share with interested readers. Please contact Paul Sindelar (pts@coe.ufl.edu) for more information.

Abbreviations

AACTE	American Association of Colleges for Teacher Education
ABA	Applied Behavior Analysis
AC	Alternative Certification
ACOS-R	Automated Classroom Observation System for Reading
ACVREP	Academy for Certification of Vision Rehabilitation and Education Professionals
AERA	American Educational Research Association
AERBVI	Association for the Education and Rehabilitation of the Blind and Visually Impaired
APH	American Printing House for the Blind
AR	Alternative route to licensure/certification
ARRA	American Recovery and Reinvestment Act
ASD	Autism Spectrum Disorders
ASL	American Sign Language
AT	Assistive technology
AUCD	Association of University Centers on Disabilities
AYP	Adequate Yearly Progress
BAIP	Blending Assessment With Instruction Program
Bi-Bi	Bilingual-bicultural
BIE	"Bug in ear" technology
BIP	Behavioral intervention plan
CAEBER	Center for ASL/English Bilingual Education and Research
CAI	Computer-assisted instruction
CAID	Council of American Instructors of the Deaf
CAP	Content Acquisition Podcast
CASE	Council for Administrators of Special Education
CBA	Curriculum-based assessment
CCSS	Common Core State Standards
CDA	Child Development Associate
CDC	Centers for Disease Control and Prevention
CEASD	Conference of Educational Administrators of Schools and Programs for the Deaf
CEC	Council for Exceptional Children
CED	Council on Education for the Deaf
CENTe-R	Collaborative Early Intervention National Training e-Resource
CEP	Center on Education Policy
CFDA	Catalog of Federal Domestic Assistance
CHAT	Cultural-Historical Activity Theory
CIS	Commonwealth of Independent States
CLASS	Classroom Assessment Scoring System

CLD	Culturally and linguistically diverse
COBM IC	Classroom organization and behavior management innovation configuration
COE	College of education
COPSSE	Center for Personnel Studies in Special Education
CRT	Culturally responsive teaching
CRTIEC	Center for Response to Intervention in Early Childhood
CSPD	Comprehensive system of personnel development
DCDT	Division of Career Development and Transition
DEC	Division of Early Childhood
DfES	Department for Education and Skills (UK)
DHH	Deaf or hard of hearing
DIBELS	Dynamic Indicators of Basic Early Literacy Skills
DLD	Division for Learning Disabilities
DOE	Department of Education
E/BD	Emotional/behavioral disorders
EADSNE	European Agency for Development in Special Needs Education
EBP	Evidence-based practice
ECC	Expanded core curriculum
ECERS-R	Early Childhood Environment Rating Scale-Revised
ECI	Early childhood intervention
ECSE	Early childhood special education
ED	U.S. Department of Education
EFA	"Education for All"
EHA	Education for all Handicapped Children Act
EHDI	Early hearing detection and intervention
EI	Early intervention
ELL	English Language Learners
ELLCO	Early Language Literacy Classroom Observation
ERIC	Education Resources Information Center
ESEA	Elementary and Secondary Education Act
ESOL	English for Speakers of Other Languages
FAPE	Free appropriate public education
FBA	Functional behavioral assessment
FFT	Framework for Teaching
FRL	Free and reduced lunch
FVA	Functional vision assessment
FY	Financial year
GAS	Goal Attainment Scale
GET	General education teacher
GMR	Global Monitoring Report
GPA	Grade point average
HEA	Higher Education Act
HFA	High-functioning autism
HLM	Hierarchical linear modeling
HOUSSE	High, objective, uniform, state standard of evaluation
HQT	Highly qualified teacher
IC	Innovation configuration
ICE	International Conference on Education
ICED	International Congress on Education of the Deaf

IDEA	Individuals With Disabilities Education Act
IEP	Individualized Education Program
IFSP	Individualized Family Service Plan
IHE	Institution of Higher Education
IMH	Infant mental health
INTASC	Interstate New Teacher Assessment and Support Consortium
IRA	International Reading Association
ISE	Individualizing Teacher Effectiveness
ISEI	International Society on Early Intervention
ISTE	International Society for Technology in Education
IT	Instructional technology
ITERS-R	Infant/Toddler Environment Rating Scale-Revised
JCIH	Joint Committee on Infant Hearing
K–12	Kindergarten through 12th grade
LD	Learning disabilities
LEA	Local education agency
LMA	Learning media assessments
LRE	Least restrictive environment
LVT	Low vision therapists
MANOVA	Multivariate analysis of variance
MET	Measuring Teacher Effectiveness
MSIP	Monitoring and State Improvement Planning Division (in OSEP)
MTA	Main teaching assignment
MTP	MyTeachingPartner
MTSS	Multi-tiered system of support
NAD	National Association of the Deaf
NAEP	National Assessment of Educational Progress
NAEYC	National Association for the Education of Young Children
NASDSE	National Association of State Directors of Special Education
NASDTEC	National Association of State Directors of Teacher Education and Certification
NBPTS	National Board for Professional Teaching Standards
NCATE	National Council for Accreditation of Teacher Education
NCCTQ	National Comprehensive Center for Teacher Quality
NCES	National Center for Education Statistics
NCIPP	National Center to Inform Policy and Practice in Special Education
NCLB	No Child Left Behind
NCLID	National Center on Low-Incidence Disabilities
NCSO	National Center on Service Obligations
NCSSD	National Center on Severe and Sensory Disabilities
NCTAF	National Commission on Teaching and America's Future
NCTM	National Council of Teachers of Mathematics
NCTQ	National Council on Teacher Quality
NECTAS	National Early Childhood Technical Assistance System
NETS•T	National Educational Technology Standards for Teachers
NGA	National Governor's Association
NGO	Non-governmental organization
NIDRR	National Institute on Disability and Rehabilitation Research
NMAP	National Mathematics Advisory Panel
NPDCI	National Professional Development Center on Inclusion

NPTARS	National Partnership for Teaching in At-Risk Schools
NPTP	National Plan for Training Personnel to Serve Children With Blindness and Low Vision
NYC	New York City
O&M	Orientation and mobility
OECD	Organisation for Economic Cooperation and Development
OPEPD	Office of Planning, Evaluation and Policy Development
OSEP	Office of Special Education Programs
OSERS	Office of Special Education and Rehabilitative Services
P–12	Prekindergarten through 12th grade
P–16	Prekindergarten through tertiary education
PA	Phonological awareness
PACT	Performance Assessment of California Teachers
PALS	Peer-assisted learning strategies
PBIS	Positive behavioral intervention and supports
PBS	Positive behavior support
PD	Professional development
PDP	Personnel Development Program
PLC	Professional learning community
Pre-K	Prekindergarten
PTRL	Professional Training Resource Library
R & R	Recognition and Response
RD	Reading disabilities
REI	Regular Education Initiative
RF	Reading First
RMLOs	Remembering math learning objects
RSA	Rehabilitation Services Administration
RTI	Response to Intervention
RTP	Research to Practice Division (in OSEP)
SASS	Schools and Staffing Survey
SAT	Scholastic Assessment Test
SE	Special education
SEA	State education agency
SEN	Special educational needs
SES	Socioeconomic status
SET	Special education teacher
SLD	Specific Learning Disabilities
SPDG	State Personnel Development Grant
SPeNSE	Study of Personnel Needs in Special Education
SRSD	Self-regulated strategy development
STEM	Science, Technology, Engineering, and Mathematics
STEP	Secondary Teacher Education Program
STTS	Secondary Teachers Transition Survey
SWD	Students with disabilities
SW-PBIS	School-wide positive behavioral interventions and supports
SW-PBS	School-wide positive behavior support
TAC	The Teacher for All Children Program
TACSEI	Technical Assistance Center on Social Emotional Intervention for Young Children
TBFF	Thomas B. Fordham Foundation

TDSE	Teacher Development and School Empowerment
TEP	Teacher education programs
TES	Teacher Evaluation System
TFA	Teach for America
TFS	Teacher Follow-up Survey
TLC	Teaching and Learning Center
TPA	Teacher Performance Assessment
TPACK	Technological pedagogical content knowledge
TQ	Teacher Questionnaire
TREK	Training Rural Educators in Kentucky project
TSG	Teacher study groups
TSVI	Teacher of students with visual impairments
TTP	Traditional teacher preparation
UDL	Universal Design for Learning
UNCRPD	United Nations Convention on the Rights of Persons with Disabilities
UNESCO	United Nations Educational, Scientific and Cultural Organization
UNICEF	United Nations Children's Fund
UNRWA	United Nations Relief and Works Agency
UPE	Universal primary education
USDB	Utah Schools for the Deaf and Blind
USDE	U.S. Department of Education
VI	Visual impairment
VRT	Vision rehabilitation therapists

Part I
Overview

1

The Policy and Economic Contexts of Teacher Education

Paul T. Sindelar
UNIVERSITY OF FLORIDA

Leah Wasburn-Moses
MIAMI UNIVERSITY

Rachel A. Thomas and Christopher D. Leko
UNIVERSITY OF FLORIDA

Things to Think About

- Linking teacher education to student outcomes is a complex and difficult task.
- Although alternative routes to teacher education are now commonplace, they continue to spur much controversy in the area of teacher education.
- Major differences between general and special education in our nation's schools have significant implications for teacher preparation.
- The recent economic downturn has had significant repercussions for the teacher labor market and is likely to have significant repercussions for teacher education in the future.
- Relatively new but widespread initiatives such as Reading First and Response to Intervention (RTI) may reduce the number of students with disabilities and, as a result, the demand for special education teachers.
- RTI implementation has created new roles for special education teachers that can guide teacher education reform.

Never before has teacher education figured so prominently in the educational policy arena. Traditional teacher preparation has fallen out of favor, and criticisms of it abound. Characterized as overly long, lacking in substance, and burdensome, especially for high ability students, formal teacher preparation is considered by many to be unnecessary. There is widespread and bipartisan support for streamlined alternatives to traditional teacher preparation, such as Teach for America or the New Teacher Project. While supporters of traditional teacher preparation struggle belatedly to establish its warrant, critics assert correctly that proof is lacking. Indeed, most studies have failed to link the nature or extent of teacher preparation to student achievement gain or other valued outcomes. Furthermore, federal policy has supported a proliferation of alternatives to traditional teacher preparation, undermining the authority of the teacher education establishment in the process. It is not surprising that colleges of education (COEs) have been derided as defenders of a lousy status quo (Farkas & Duffett, 2010; Walsh, 2001).

Special education teacher preparation is not immune to this onslaught of criticism, even though it differs in important and relevant ways from general education. In this chapter, we first describe the policy issues that plague teacher education generally. These issues include (a) our failure to link teacher preparation to valued educational outcomes, (b) the proliferation of alternatives to traditional preparation, (c) diminishing respect for the work of colleges of education generally, and (d) the extension of accountability policy to teacher preparation. We describe why we think special education is different, considering in the process both empirical evidence as well as a conceptual analysis of the two disciplines. Finally, we also consider the impact of a second significant contextual factor affecting the field: the economic downturn of 2008. Although its impact on special education teacher (SET) preparation and employment cannot yet be isolated from other factors, the SET employment market is changing dramatically, and the implications of this change are broad and worrisome. We conclude by summarizing the policy and economic backdrops to the remaining chapters in this volume.

Failure to Link Teacher Education to Valued Outcomes

No one would argue with the proposition that teachers should be held accountable for what their students learn. Although this simple and compelling idea belies the complexity involved in linking teachers to student outcomes, simplicity plays well among policy makers, and student achievement gain has become the gold standard with which teacher preparation is judged. In fact, in an October 22, 2009 speech at Teachers College of Columbia University, Arne Duncan, U.S. Secretary of Education, made clear the Department of Education's position on the importance of student outcomes as a measure of preparation quality. He encouraged every "teacher education program today to make better outcomes for students the overarching mission that propels all their efforts" (U.S. Department of Education, 2009). He alluded to the fact that the U.S. Department of Education had required it in the Teacher Quality Partnerships and would require it again in Race to the Top grants. Value-added modeling, a statistical method capable of parsing out a teacher's contribution to student learning, has provided a means for assessing individual teachers' contributions to student achievement growth. Unfortunately, scholars using value-added modeling have rarely found significant links between preparation and achievement, leading Kate Walsh, President of the National Council on Teacher Quality (NCTQ), to conclude that teacher education does not make a difference on variables of importance to policy makers and the public (Walsh, 2001). Why? NCTQ contends that, largely due to ineffectual requirements, most novice elementary teachers and recent graduates from traditional teacher preparation programs are ill-equipped to teach reading and math, and many novice middle school teachers are ill-prepared in the content they teach (NCTQ, 2010). This criticism of traditional preparation is widespread and bipartisan.

Recently, with the aim of improving teacher education, Senators from five states—three Democrats and two Republicans—proposed the Growing Excellent Achievement Training Academies for Teachers and Principals Act. As proposed, state participation in the act would be voluntary, but in participating states the bill provides for the authorization of teacher education academies. These academies would be obligated to adopt rigorous admissions guidelines, emphasize clinical instruction, and tie graduation to improving student achievement (Bennet, Alexander, & Mikulski, 2011). In exchange, academies would be exempted from burdensome regulations that now govern teacher preparation. Traditional programs would be eligible to participate, but so would Teach for America (TFA) and other nontraditional routes. In participating states, programs that failed to produce successful teachers or principals would not be reauthorized (Bennet et al., 2011).

Policy makers and educational organizations are promoting residency programs as another means for bolstering the quality of preparation. In a residency program, teachers apprentice for a year with induction support. In Duncan's October 22, 2009 speech, he suggested residency programs as an antidote to the shortcomings of traditional teacher preparation. Yet, the breadth of support for teacher education reform, in general, and the enhancement of clinical training, in particular, is seen no more clearly than in the National Council for Accreditation of Teacher Education's (NCATE) advocacy for stronger clinical preparation. In its *Report of the Blue Ribbon Panel* (2010), NCATE argued that "teacher education must shift away from a norm which emphasizes academic preparation and course work loosely linked to school-based experiences" (p. ii) and promote an integration of "content, pedagogy, and professional coursework around a core of clinical experiences" (p. 8)—ideas with roots in the work of the National Commission on Teaching and America's Future (NCTAF, 1996). As a cornerstone of the teacher education establishment, NCATE's position on bolstering clinical training has gravitas. It also makes clear that the teacher education status quo has few remaining defenders.

Yet special education may be different. Evidence is accumulating that preparation does make a difference in our field and that more preparation is better than less preparation (Boe, Shin, & Cook, 2007; Feng & Sass, 2012). Boe et al. (2007), for example, found that general and special education teachers with extensive preparation reported being better prepared to teach subject matter and to manage their classrooms than other novices with less preparation. Furthermore, special education teachers (SETs) with extensive preparation were more likely to be fully certified and teaching in-field than SETs with only some or no preparation. Feng and Sass (2012) linked student achievement to preservice preparation. They found that preservice preparation in special education affected the ability of special education teachers to promote achievement for students with disabilities, especially in reading. They also found that teachers with advanced degrees were more effective in promoting achievement in math for students with disabilities than those with only 4-year degrees. Although these studies may be far from conclusive, they are suggestive and encouraging. Special education preparation may indeed make a difference in student outcomes.

Proliferation of Alternatives to Traditional Teacher Preparation

In the current policy context, alternatives to traditional teacher preparation have proliferated in both general and special education. No Child Left Behind (NCLB) encouraged states to develop pathways that move teachers into the classroom on a fast-track basis. Also, TFA and the New York Teaching Fellows, two leading alternative route programs in teacher education, have gained considerable recognition and strong bipartisan political support. Individuals seeking to become teachers have many options, and completing an on-campus preservice program is no longer an exclusive means for entering the profession.

NCLB calls for a provision of "alternative routes to teacher education" (p. 1658) in order "to establish, expand, or enhance a teacher recruitment and retention program for highly qualified mid-career professionals (including highly qualified paraprofessionals), and recent graduates of an institution of higher education" (p. 1657). Proponents argue that certification standards dissuade college graduates and mid-career professionals from entering teaching. In his report on teacher quality, Former Secretary of Education Rod Paige went on: "NCLB gives the green light to states that want to lower barriers to the teaching profession" (U.S. Department of Education, 2003, p. 5). States can "dramatically streamline their processes and create alternative routes to full state certification that target talented people who would be turned off by traditional preparation and certification programs" (U.S. Department of Education, 2003, p. 5). However, in length and credit requirements, most alternative programs are more like traditional routes (Rosenberg, Boyer, Sindelar, & Misra, 2007; Walsh & Jacobs, 2007) than the streamlined alternatives envisioned in NCLB. Concern about whether alternative programs can do what traditional programs can do has been replaced by concern about whether streamlined training can do what more extensive training experiences can do. To date, the answer to that question is unclear.

In preparing its participants for the classroom, TFA requires an intensive 5-week summer institute, including individualized mentoring, professional development, and 4 weeks of student teaching, as well as 2 years of ongoing support in the classroom. Although some studies have shown TFA graduates to be more effective than other novice teachers (Boyd et al., 2010; Raymond, Fletcher, & Luque, 2001; Xu, Hannaway, & Taylor, 2009), others have found the differences between traditional teacher preparation and TFA to be insubstantial. For example, Decker, Mayer, and Glazerman (2004) found statistically nonsignificant differences in reading and math achievement for students in TFA classrooms. Boyd, Grossman, Lankford, Loeb, and Wyckoff (2006) found a positive impact in math favoring TFA graduates but not until the second year of service and beyond, by which time TFA participants had received training and often certification. Additionally, Darling-Hammond, Holtzman, Gatlin, and Vasquez Heiling (2005) found that "rates of attrition for TFA teachers were about twice as high as for non-TFA teachers" (p. 14).

Although questions remain about alternative routes and streamlined training, both are fast becoming fixtures of the policy landscape. Research has demonstrated that competent teachers can be prepared via alternative routes (Humphrey & Wechsler, 2007; Humphrey, Wechsler, & Hough, 2008; Sindelar, Daunic, & Rennells, 2004). Of course, many of the alternatives that have been studied are long and substantive, and more like traditional programs than the NCLB ideal or TFA and others. Furthermore, findings from studies in which TFA graduates have outperformed other novice teachers are not clear-cut. For example, in Raymond et al. (2001), nearly one fifth of the novices with whom TFA teachers were compared lacked bachelor's degrees; in Decker et al. (2004), TFA graduates and the other novices with whom they were compared did not differ substantially on the extent and nature of their preparation. Thus, the studies to date have not involved comparisons of TFA and fully trained and qualified novice teachers. Furthermore, in evaluating TFA and other programs that incur limited obligations to teach, cost effectiveness becomes an important consideration. Although TFA may prepare teachers inexpensively, high attrition inflates costs. In fact, Darling-Hammond (2002) found that TFA programs were more costly than even 5-year, Holmes-type (for more information see Holmes Group, 1986) programs when costs were assessed 3 years out from program completion.

Colleges of Education in the Crosshairs

COEs are in the crosshairs of policy makers committed to a deregulation perspective, and those of us who work in them feel vulnerable. We clearly have failed to persuade the public of the merits of what we do. We cannot reliably link formal preparation to achievement or other outcomes valued by policy makers, and we struggle to compete with alternatives that enjoy strong political support and public respect. In the process, the hegemony that COEs once held over entry to the profession has been significantly weakened. We have become easy targets for critics who complain that traditional preparation costs too much and that its content and practitioners are indifferent to real-world needs. According to *Cracks in the Ivory Tower*, a report of the Thomas B. Fordham Institute, "teacher educators show only modest concern for real-world challenges such as managing classrooms and student discipline, implementing differentiated instruction, and working with state standards—even though K–12 teachers often say these are among the most difficult elements of teaching" (Farkas & Duffett, 2010, p. 8). With regard to faculty, the report asserts, "most professors of education say their field needs no change" (p. 9).

Although there is palpable bias in the Fordham report, COEs are vulnerable to even responsible critics, Art Levine (2006) among them. Levine, former President of Teachers College, noted that

> teacher education has taken on a special urgency because the United States needs to raise both the quantity and quality of our teacher force … To address both demands simultaneously is an enormous challenge, made even more difficult because the nation is deeply divided about how to prepare large numbers of high-quality teachers.
>
> *(p. 5)*

Echoing harsher critics elsewhere, he recommended that COEs focus more on classroom practice, student achievement as the primary measure of program success, extensive 5-year preparation, and "effective mechanisms for teacher education quality control" (p. 109).

Emphasis on Accountability at All Levels

In the contemporary policy context, students, teachers, and teacher educators are all thought to contribute to achievement growth, and all are held accountable for it. For example, the *Growing Excellent Achievement Training Academies for Teachers and Principals Act* proposes that if a program's graduates fail to produce achievement gains, they should not be allowed to graduate and the programs themselves should not be reauthorized (Bennet et al., 2011). The Higher Education Act of 2008, originally intended to provide financial aid for college students, now stipulates that teacher education be held accountable for preparing highly qualified teachers. Race to the Top, a $4.35 billion competitive grant program, has encouraged and rewarded educational reforms, among them linking teacher education to student learning outcomes. Of course, special education is seldom discussed in Race to the Top proposals (U.S. Department of Education, 2011, September), and special education teacher evaluation is rarely discussed separately from general education teacher evaluation. Such one-size-fits-all thinking about teacher evaluation belies the difficulty of assessing the growth of students with disabilities (SWDs), whose needs and abilities are highly diverse.

In sum, traditional teacher preparation and the colleges of education that purvey it have fallen out of favor. After decades of unquestioned authority over who enters the profession, we have lost the confidence and support of policy makers and the public alike. We now endeavor to demonstrate that what we do makes a difference, particularly on outcomes of importance. Meanwhile, alternatives to traditional teacher preparation proliferate, and the questions about preparation have become how little is required and how quickly can it get done? In special education, however, there is some evidence to suggest that teacher preparation is indeed related to student achievement gains and some evidence to suggest that preparation is better than no preparation at all. Regardless, special education is painted with the same policy brushstrokes as general education. In the section to follow, we argue for differentiating policy in special education teacher preparation and describe the important ways in which special education differs from its general education counterpart.

The Distinctiveness of Special Education

Regarding general and special education, Zigmond and Kloo (2011) observed that "from the start, [they] evolved from different premises, with different emphases in teacher preparation, and different research bases to ground their educational practices" (p. 170). Today, these distinctions include differences in licensure structures, student needs, teacher roles, and service delivery systems. Examining such distinctions is crucial when predicting changes in the labor market, outlining the future of service delivery in the schools, designing accountability systems, and ultimately, preparing teachers to reach all students.

Several major systemic elements distinguish special education from general education, characteristics that affect both practice and preparation in the area of special education. First, the structure of teacher licensure differs. In general education, licensure structure traditionally has followed grade bands. Although these bands vary somewhat across states, they are also fairly straightforward (e.g., K–6, 7–12). Special education, however, requires a more complex licensure system. Some states use grade bands, but the majority continue to offer K–12 licenses in at least some areas (Geiger, 2006). Licensure by disability category (also referred to as "categorical" licensure) is also prevalent, with most states adopting a mixture of categorical and noncategorical systems (e.g., licensure in "mild-moderate" disabilities, for example, with separate licenses in specific low-incidence disabilities, such as hearing impairment or multiple disabilities). Specialized licensure for early childhood special education and transition is also common. Additionally, some states require initial licensure in general education before an individual can be licensed in special education (Geiger, Crutchfield, & Mainzer, 2003).

Licensure complexity has a major impact on the field. For example, preparing teachers to work with individuals with such a wide range of ages and needs clearly necessitates broad preparation. However, special education is a field in which specific skill sets related to pedagogy are also at a premium (Zigmond & Kloo, 2011). Thus, teachers are expected to be specialists in many different disability areas, regardless of the age or ability level of the students or the content they teach. In the broader policy context, the complexity of licensure structures impacts many of the issues we introduced above. For example, alternative routes to licensure are more difficult to develop when program content is broadly defined, as in the case of multicategorical certification. Given the breadth of knowledge and skills that a teacher with a K–12, multicategorical certificate must command, preparation can be neither abbreviated nor fast-tracked. By contrast, in other high-need areas like math and science, the content for preparation and licensure requirements are relatively stable and well defined, even across states.

The complexity of teacher roles also plays a large part in distinguishing special education from general education. This issue has a long history that has been documented in the literature on special education teacher attrition (Gehrke & Murri, 2006; Otis-Wilborn, Winn, Griffin, & Kilgore, 2005; White & Mason, 2006). Role complexity can be characterized in a variety of ways. First is the variation in student needs and the standards to which these students are held. Second is the need for special education teachers to work both collaboratively and alone. Third is the wide variation by disability category, student needs, and service delivery model. Fourth is the special education teacher's role as child advocate, which can put special education teachers in conflict with colleagues. Each of these issues validates concerns about the lack of distinction between general and special education in policies affecting all teachers.

The variation of student needs in special education also is well documented. In fact, special education as a field originally developed from the need for additional services for students who fell outside the norm set in general education (Zigmond & Kloo, 2011). Because the roots of special education are in individualized instruction, there is greater opportunity to focus on the whole child in special education than in general education. In addition to academics, special educators are responsible for teaching behavioral skills, social skills, learning strategies, and planning for transition (Billingsley, Griffin, Smith, Kamman, & Israel, 2009). Thus, despite new policy encouraging a single focus on academic achievement for all students, variations in teacher roles in special education still demonstrate commitment to other aspects of students' development.

Second, although special education teachers are pushed to work collaboratively, they also are expected to work alone in developing and implementing plans. McKenzie (2009) argued that "in the last decade, no facets of special education have generated a greater reconstruction of instructional design or more debate than inclusive classrooms and the collaborative relationship between the general and special educators who teach in them" (p. 379). The push for greater inclusion has been spurred further by policies requiring every student be held to general education standards. Additionally, the highly qualified teacher (HQT) mandate has pushed many special education teachers to spend additional time in general education settings. Despite this change, though, a recent study on the use of teacher time in special education found that teachers still engaged in many activities considered "specific to a special educator," including paperwork, Individualized Education Program (IEP) meetings, and consultation and collaboration. Taken together, these activities accounted for nearly one quarter of a teacher's day (Vannest & Hagan-Burke, 2010). Both of these scenarios, working collaboratively and alone, appear to place stress on special educators. For example, implementing inclusion and working with general education teachers represent the largest source of stress for special educators (Billingsley et al., 2009; Griffin et al., 2009; McKenzie, 2009). Conversely, these authors have also shown documenting compliance through IEPs and other paperwork to be another major stressor and area of need identified by novice teachers.

A third major approach that can be used to characterize the complexity of special education teacher roles is to examine task variation. Clearly, teacher roles do vary by disability and severity of disability served, even though licensure structures often translate into one teacher serving students with a variety of disability labels. For example, teachers who serve students with emotional or behavioral disorders must conduct behavioral assessments, write behavior plans, and implement interventions. Landrum, Tankersley, and Kauffman (2006) argued that "the structure, intensity, precision, and relentlessness with which (these) teachers deliver, monitor, and adapt instruction" (p. 21) are what makes this type of education unique. Teachers of students with severe or intensive disabilities match students with augmentative and alternative communication, define assessment appropriate to the individual, and provide for generalization of skills to the real world (Browder & Cooper-Duffy, 2006). Teachers of students with various physical and sensory impairments also have unique roles.

Service delivery is arguably the most visible aspect of special education that differentiates the field from general education. For decades, special education has relied on the continuum of services to place students in their least restrictive environment (LRE). Special education services can be provided in a separate school or classroom, in a resource room, or in the general education classroom. Even schools within the same district can vary in their approach to special education service delivery. Some schools have moved to full inclusion using team-teaching; some retain the pull-out, resource-room model; and some have self-contained classes that may serve students with a variety of disability labels. Many schools use multiple types of service delivery, resulting in Vannest and Hagan-Burke's (2010) finding that "the use of (special education) teacher time is differentially spread across 12 activities and differentially distributed within instructional settings" (p. 140). Even within one service delivery mode, tasks may vary widely. For example, McKenzie (2009) described the multiple ways in which special educators' expertise is utilized (or underutilized) in inclusive settings, concluding that the co-teaching role may be the most ambiguous of all.

Fourth, another traditional role for special educators has been acting as advocates for students with disabilities. This role often requires special education teachers to negotiate with their general education colleagues regarding instructional planning, accommodations, and placement. Unfortunately, though, such interactions have been labeled as one of the greatest sources of stress for special education teachers (Billingsley et al., 2009). Other barriers to acting as student advocates include heavy caseloads and lack of time for collaboration and consultation.

Thus, the roles of special educators are highly complex and evolving, and they are likely to differ from school to school, from teacher to teacher, and from year to year. The large variation in student needs, the settings and service delivery models within which teachers work, and the tensions inherent in focusing on the whole child in an academic-achievement driven atmosphere have plagued the field as a source of stress and role confusion among teachers (Billingsley et al., 2009). These unique issues set special education teachers apart from their general education colleagues.

Amidst this complex backdrop of varying teacher roles and service delivery, a revolution in the interface between special and general education has developed in the form of Response to Intervention (RTI). Fuchs, Fuchs, and Stecker (2010) described this change as a blurring of special education and general education. Under this system, both special and general educators have responsibility for assessing and intervening with students who are at-risk. Although special education teacher roles in this process have not been clearly defined, they may include interpreting assessment data, planning interventions, providing direct instruction of individuals or small groups, evaluating and modifying support systems, and participating in ongoing system-wide evaluation (Cummings, Atkins, Allison, & Cole, 2008). Although the precise impact of RTI on special education service delivery is unknown, it is expected that general and special education will experience the need for even greater collaboration. Some important unknowns include the population, settings, and curricula with which special educators will work. Although the impact of such dramatic change in system-wide service delivery on teacher preparation is unknown (Fuchs et al., 2010), some see it as an opportunity to bring clarity to teacher preparation as roles are further developed (Brownell, Sindelar, Kiely, & Danielson, 2010).

In conclusion, we are entering an era in which "successful teaching (in special education) has been redefined to mean satisfactory progress in the general education curriculum" (Brownell et al., 2010, p. 358). Accountability systems have been built upon these perceived similarities. Although special education teacher roles are evolving with the changing times, special and general education licensure, roles, and functions remain quite different and distinct. Complexities unique to practice in the field of special education include variations in licensure, the variety of student needs, an emphasis on life domains in addition to academics, and the multiplicity of roles and service delivery models under which special education teachers work. Yet, despite these clear and significant differences between general and special education, policy remains undifferentiated.

To this point we have argued that, for the purposes of teacher preparation policy, special education ought not be lumped with general education. The work of SETs is distinct, and preliminary research findings suggest that special education preparation more so than general education preparation has a discernible impact on student outcomes. To make matters interesting, this policy drama is unfolding against a backdrop of serious economic decline. Districts are struggling to provide everything they once provided and to maintain the quality of the educational services they do provide. A poor economic context casts a shadow over every reform: Is RTI, for example, being undertaken because it is in the best interest of children or because it reduces costs? In the sections to follow, we describe the current economic context and its impact on school funding. We consider changes in the special education teacher labor market and the possibility that educational reform (e.g., Reading First and Response to Intervention) may contribute to this change.

Current Economic Context

Recently, the Center on Education Policy (CEP) published a report entitled, "Strained Schools Face Bleak Future: Districts Foresee Budget Cuts, Teacher Layoffs, and a Slowing of Education Reform Efforts" (Kober & Rentner, 2011). In the report, CEP presented findings from a survey it conducted in 2011 of a random and nationally representative sample of school districts (Kober & Rentner, 2011). Respondents were asked to describe their district's fiscal condition during the 2010–2011 school year, how they coped with budget cutbacks, and what they expected its fiscal condition to be for the upcoming 2011–2012 school year. Districts' answers to these questions help explain the report's dreary title.

For schools, the full impact of the economic downturn of 2008 was blunted by stimulus money in both 2009–2010 and 2010–2011. In fact, the U.S. Department of Education invested $80 billion in ARRA (American Recovery and Reinvestment Act) funds alone (Kober & Rentner, 2011). Offsetting the infusion of ARRA funds were substantial losses in state and local revenues. In fact, roughly 70% of the districts responding to the survey had experienced funding cuts in 2010–2011, and even more (84%) anticipated cuts for the upcoming school year. Kober and Rentner (2011) reported that only 30% of U.S. schools anticipated having any ARRA funds available for 2011–2012 and characterized school funding prospects as a grim situation about to get worse.

According to the CEP survey, districts coped with shortfalls by cutting staff or supporting staff positions with stimulus funds. Indeed, 85% of districts whose budgets were cut in 2010–2011 reported eliminating positions, and 75% reported eliminating teachers. In addition, districts were asked whether they anticipated additional cuts in 2011–2012. Although, at the time of the survey, many districts anticipating cuts in 2011–2012 reported being *undecided* about how to reduce spending, 60% had decided to cut positions again. With stimulus money all but spent, U.S. schools are likely to experience a decline in the total employment of teachers and other school personnel in the coming school year.

Shortfalls in state and local revenues along with the loss of ARRA funds have forced districts to make other significant cuts, including investments in equipment and technology, professional development, maintenance, and, notably, instructional time. In 2010–2011, 84% of responding districts either engaged in no reform, or slowed or postponed implementation of existing reforms (Kober & Rentner, 2011). In special education, districts used ARRA supplements to IDEA (Individuals With Disabilities Education Act) funding in much the same ways. In addition to saving or creating jobs (83%), they invested IDEA supplements in providing professional development (66%), purchasing assistive technology (55%), and increasing the numbers of students served (14%) (Kober & Rentner, 2011).

The employment of fewer teachers represents, in effect, a decline in the total demand for teachers. Declining total demand is likely to have an interesting and multifaceted impact on employment patterns. For one thing, because of poor employment prospects in the public sector, fewer teachers are likely to leave the field for employment in other fields. Boe, Cook, and Sunderland (2008) provided estimates of this potential reduction in attrition. With data from three 1990s administrations of the *Schools and Staffing Survey* and the *Teacher Follow-up Survey*, Boe et al. (2008) estimated the number of teachers who left the profession to seek employment in other fields and the number of teachers who retired. They reported that nearly 3% of all SETs and slightly less than 2% of all general education teachers (GETs) left teaching annually for other fields of employment.

Because of the impact that the condition of the economy has had on retirement funds and other investments, some teachers who otherwise might retire may have to put off such plans. Fewer retirements also mean less attrition. Boe et al. (2008) estimated that (during the 1990s) roughly 1% of all SETs and 2% of GETs retired annually. In the current economic context, those percentages are likely to fall. Thus, the 4% of both special and general education teachers who ordinarily would retire or leave the field for other employment represents a small but substantial component of attrition that will be reduced by weak employment prospects outside of teaching and deferred retirements. If, indeed, fewer teachers are leaving teaching and fewer are retiring, the job market for new graduates is certain to tighten.

Especially sobering for teacher education programs are data on newly hired teachers. Although not all states maintain data on new hires, Boe et al. (2013) obtained data from Florida, Maryland, Georgia, Connecticut, and West Virginia. In Florida, from 2005 to 2009, the annual number of newly hired special education teachers dropped by 60%, from 3,438 to 1,374. In Maryland, the recent decline also has been dramatic. From 2005 to 2009, the number of new special education hires dropped from 955 to 417, a decrease of over 56%. In Georgia, over the same years, new hires dropped only 15%, from 2,467 to 2,089. Connecticut showed a similar decline, with a reduction of 19% between 2004 and 2011. On the other hand, West Virginia saw an increase of 31% new special education teachers hired between 2004 and 2010. Because the annual number of new hires represents demand for the product of teacher education, for special education teacher preparation, business is not looking up.

On the other hand, declining demand for teachers has a distinct upside. For one thing, districts stand to benefit from the increased availability of teachers seeking employment. Increased supply may enable districts to address such persistent problems as critical shortages of math, science, and special education teachers or the inequitable distribution of teacher quality across schools. Evidence that the shortage of highly qualified SETs may be easing can be seen in SET employment data: The percent of all SETs employed in U.S. schools who are *highly qualified* has increased substantially over the past several years. In fact, in 2009, the most recent year for which data are available, roughly 93% of SETs were reported to be highly qualified (ideadata.org, n.d.a). In 2006 (the first year the Office of Special Education Programs (OSEP) used *highly qualified* to replace *fully certified*), less than 89% of SETs were so judged (ideadata.org, n.d.b).

Special education occupies an important niche in the teacher labor market. Through the years, many GETs have obtained special education certification as a hedge against layoffs and reductions-in-force. One consequence of this trend is that unemployed GETs may enter the ranks of individuals seeking special education employment. This trend, along with reduced attrition and deferred retirements, may well increase SET supply. Furthermore, GETs' presence in the special education reserve pool may reduce the demand for newly graduated SETs. Given the emergence of these unfavorable market conditions, we are concerned about the impact poor employment prospects will have on the allure of a teaching career in special education. We also are concerned about the consequences for special education teacher preparation programs of reduced demand. Poor employment prospects—and the proliferation of options to traditional, campus-based training—may ultimately lead to enrollment decline. University-based teacher preparation programs, in all likelihood struggling to absorb significant budget cuts of their own, may become vulnerable if enrollment declines—and declines persist. Although the addition of a special education certificate retains appeal for GETs, and their enrollment may offset decline somewhat, special education remains vulnerable in the short run (Boe et al., 2012).

Nationally, the employment of special education teachers declined in 2006 for the first time in 25 years. In 2005, U.S. schools employed 426,493 SETs (ideadata.org, n.d.c); by 2009, the most recent year for which data are available, the number had dropped to 389,133 (ideadata.org, n.d.a), an 8.8% decline. The onset of this decline predates the economic downturn of 2008, which raises the possibility that other forces besides economic downturn have contributed to the decline. One such factor is the reduction in the number of students with disabilities. In 2004–2005, 6.2 million students with disabilities (SWDs) were served under IDEA Part B (ideadata.org, n.d.d); by 2009, that number had fallen to 5.9 million (ideadata.org, n.d.e), a 3.7% decline. This decline is limited to a single disability category—Specific Learning Disabilities (SLD), which decreased from 2.78 million to 2.46 million, a decrease of 11.6% between 2004 and 2008. The decrease in the number of students with SLD is sufficiently large to overcome substantial increases in the low-incidence categories of Autism (76%) and Other Health Impairments (26%). Overall, the decline in the identification of students with SLD has yielded an overall downward trend in the number of SWDs. Why are fewer students being identified with SLD? In the next section, we consider two factors—Reading First implementation and Response to Intervention (RTI). Boe et al. (2012) assessed the impact they have had on SLD identification and the impact they are likely to have on SET employment.

Reading First Implementation

Reading First (RF) was established in NCLB to improve reading achievement in high poverty schools through effective coaching and implementation of scientifically based practices. With federal RF funding, states made approximately 1,809 sub grants to districts that ultimately served approximately 5,880 schools (U.S. Department of Education, 2011, June). If the implementation of RF were associated with a reduction in students identified SLD, then logically a measure of the degree of implementation should correlate with change in the number of students with SLD.

To come up with a reasonable metric of RF's impact on numbers of students with SLD, Boe et al. (2012) first determined the number of RF schools by state, using information available on the RF website.[1] By determining the percentage of schools implementing RF in each state and using OSEP child count data, it is possible to correlate the degree of RF implementation with the decline in SLD identification (from 2004 to 2008). This calculation yields a moderately strong, statistically significant negative correlation of $-.27$ ($p < .05$), such that states with higher percentages of RF implementation have greater reductions in the number of students classified as SLD. Furthermore, in a study done in Florida, Torgesen (2009) reported that the SLD identification fell by 81% in kindergarten and 67% in first grade in the first 3 years of RF implementation. These results suggest either that RF is successful in preventing reading difficulties in young children or that RF teachers are more willing to accommodate struggling readers without referral to special education.

Response to Intervention Implementation

Response to Intervention (RTI) is designed as a method to identify students who need early intervention and supports (Spectrum K–12, 2010). Logically, successful RTI implementation should reduce identification of SWDs, especially students with SLD. Indeed, in a recent survey (Spectrum K–12), over 80% of districts reported that special education referrals were reduced by RTI implementation, with 11% estimating the RTI reduction to exceed 50% and an additional 12% estimating it to be 25% to 49%. It seems clear that there is some connection between RTI and special education referrals, yet this connection is elusive, in part because there is no standard method of measuring RTI implementation and no definitive studies to date. However, based on an analysis of state policy, Zirkel and Thomas (2010) categorized states by the degree of RTI implementation. At the time, SLD identification via RTI was mandatory and had replaced traditional classification based on severe discrepancy (SD) in seven states; in 38 others, RTI implementation was not mandatory. Using OSEP child count data, Boe et al. (2012) estimated RTI's impact on changes in the number of students identified with SLD. SLD counts fell substantially more in states that mandated RTI (21.8%) than in states that did not (11.3%).

Although there seems to be some connection between state RTI policy and the identification of students with SLD, Boe et al. (2012) do not make clear whether RTI caused the reduction. In a closer look at RTI implementation effects on special education referrals, VanDerHeyden, Witt, and Gilbertson (2006) performed an analysis of the effects of RTI on special education identification for five schools in a school district outside of Tucson. Based on their analysis, fewer evaluations were conducted at four of the five schools studied over the school year, and reductions were larger in some schools than in others. One school went from 32 referrals before RTI to 10 referrals in the first year of RTI implementation and seven referrals in the second year. Another school saw an average of 17 referrals/year for the 3 years preceding RTI implantation drop to seven referrals in the first year of implementation.

Referred students in these schools were also far more likely to qualify for special education services with RTI implementation. In the first school, in the year before RTI implementation, 22 of the 32 students referred for assessment qualified for special education services. After RTI implementation, all seven referrals qualified for services. In the second school before RTI implementation, of 17 annual referrals, six students qualified for services. In the first year of RTI implementation, five of seven referrals qualified for services. Overall, the number of students referred for special education evaluation in each of the five schools was reduced below baseline numbers and the percentage of students accepted into special education services rose.

Clearly, more research is needed on this important topic. At this point, what little evidence we do have suggests that RTI implementation is associated with reduced SLD identification rates (VanDerHeyden et al., 2006), and fewer students with SLD means less demand for SETs trained to work with them. To the extent that struggling students—students who once would have been referred to special education—are now succeeding in general education classes, RTI implementation represents a major step forward, and the employment of fewer SETs is a reality the field must come to grips with. The more skeptical perspective—that RTI is implemented poorly, improperly, or overzealously, and that some children who require special education services do not get them—leads to different conclusions. Thus, until data on the success of students in RTI delivery models are available, we will not know with complete confidence how best to understand the reduction of the SET workforce.

Conclusion

In this chapter, we have attempted to describe the current political and economic contexts in which colleges of education exist and teacher educators work. Clearly, our context is turbulent, and hostile policy and a faltering economy constitute a tough one-two punch that has taken its toll on traditional teacher preparation. Policy makers and the public seem to have lost confidence in teacher educators and in our capacity to prepare a competent teaching workforce. Policy makers have endorsed options to traditional preparation that minimize formal preparation and attract more academically well-qualified individuals to the field. They have asked teacher educators to assess the quality of their programs on the basis of their graduates' impact on their students' achievement and have downplayed both the logical and logistical difficulty of doing so. Perhaps the most discouraging facet of the policy context is that it seems bipartisan.

Economic decline adds to our woes, or soon will. Schools are employing fewer special education teachers, and the market for our graduates is tightening. The stimulus funds that have propped up teacher employment since 2008 are nearly exhausted, new stimulus funding seems unlikely, and tax revenues are unlikely to increase in the short-term. Schools are struggling to make ends meet. Poor employment prospects for education majors will sooner or later affect enrollments, particularly given the short-term, fast-track options available to recent graduates. Declining enrollments make teacher education programs vulnerable to budget cutting at the college and institution level, and smaller, relatively expensive programs seem particularly at-risk. Such is the backdrop against which teacher educators currently ply their trade.

By contrast, in the chapters to follow, we see the upside to special education teacher preparation. Our work is evolving in positive directions, thanks to the efforts of scholars generating new knowledge and practitioners applying it in their classes and programs. In this *Handbook*, author teams have reviewed and synthesized research and identified both what we know with confidence and what work holds most promise for advancing us further. Although we may continue to face the problem of low public regard for our work and widespread support for what seem to be glib, oversimplified alternatives, the work described in this *Handbook* communicates a seriousness of purpose, an intellectual rigor, and a strong commitment to improving the lives of students with disabilities, all of which has been lost in the policy debate about teacher preparation.

Note

1 http://www2.ed.gov/programs/readingfirst/performance.html

References

Bennet, M. F., Alexander, L., & Mikulski, B. (2011). GREAT Teachers and Principals Act. Retrieved from http://www.newschools.org/news/bipartisan-bill-seeks-to-remake-teacher-training-programs

Billingsley, B. S., Griffin, C. C., Smith, S. J., Kamman, M., & Israel, M. (2009). *A review of teacher induction in special education: Research, practice, and technology solutions.* Gainesville, FL: University of Florida, National Center to Improve Policy and Practice in Special Education Professional Development. Retrieved from http://education.ufl.edu/grants/ncipp/files_5/NCIPP Induction Exc Summ.pdf

Boe, E. E., Cook, L. H., & Sunderland, R. J. (2008). Teacher turnover: Examining exit attrition, teaching area transfer, and school migration. *Exceptional Children, 75,* 7–31.

Boe, E. E., de Bettencourt, L. U., Dewey, J. F., Rosenberg, M. S., Sindelar, P. T., & Leko, C. (2013). Variability in demand for special education teachers: Indicators, explanations, and impacts. *Exceptionality, 21,* 103–125. doi: http://dx.doi.org/10.1080/09362835.2013.771563

Boe, E., E. Shin, S., & Cook, L. H. (2007). Does teacher preparation matter for beginning teachers in either special or general education? *Journal of Special Education, 41,* 158–170. doi:10.1177/00224669070410030201

Boyd, D., Grossman, P., Hammerness, K., Lankford, H., Loeb, S., Ronfeldt, M., & Wyckoff, J. (2010). *Recruiting effective math teachers. How do math immersion teachers compare?: Evidence from New York City.* Cambridge, MA: National Bureau of Economic Research. Retrieved from http://www.nber.org/papers/w16017

Boyd, D., Grossman, P., Lankford, H., Loeb, S., & Wyckoff, J. (2006). How changes in entry requirements alter the teacher workforce and affect student achievement. *Education Finance and Policy, 1,* 176–216. doi:10.1162/edfp.2006.1.2.176

Browder, D. M. & Cooper-Duffy, K. (2006). What is special about special education for students with severe disabilities? In B. G. Cook & B. R. Schirmer (Eds.), *What Is Special About Special Education*? (pp. 26–36). Denver, CO: Pro-Ed.

Brownell, M. T., Sindelar, P. T., Kiely, M. T., & Danielson, L. C. (2010). Special education teacher quality and preparation: Exposing foundations, constructing a new model. *Exceptional Children, 86,* 357–377.

Cummings, K. D., Atkins, T., Allison, R., & Cole, C. (2008). Response to Intervention: Investigating the new role of special educators. *Teaching Exceptional Children, 40*(4), 24–31.

Darling-Hammond, L. (2002). *Solving the dilemmas of teacher supply, demand, and standards: How we can assure a competent, caring, and qualified teacher for every child.* New York: National Commission on Teaching and America's Future. Retrieved from http://www.stanford.edu/~ldh/publications.html

Darling-Hammond, L., Holtzman, D., Gatlin, S., & Vasquez Heilig, J. (2005). Does teacher preparation matter? Evidence about teacher certification, Teach for America, and teacher effectiveness. *Education Policy Analysis Archives, 13*(42), 1–51.

Decker, P. T., Mayer, D. P., & Glazerman, S. (2004). *The effects of Teach for America on students: Findings from a national evaluation.* Princeton, NJ: Mathematica Policy Research, Inc.

Farkas, S., & Duffett, A. (2010). *Cracks in the ivory tower? The views of education professors circa 2010.* FDR Group/Thomas B. Fordham Institute. Retrieved from http://www.edexcellencemedia.net/publications/2010/201009_cracksintheivorytower/Cracks%20In%20The%20Ivory%20Tower%20-%20Sept%202010.pdf

Feng, L., & Sass, T. R. (2012). *What makes special education teachers special? Teacher training and achievement of students with disabilities.* Working Paper 12-10. Atlanta: Georgia State University, Andrew Young School of Policy Studies. Retrieved from: http://papers.ssrn.com/sol3/papers.cfm?abstract_id=2020714

Fuchs, D., Fuchs, L. S., & Stecker, P. M. (2010). The "blurring" of special education in a new continuum of general education placements and services. *Exceptional Children, 76,* 301–323.

Gehrke, R. S., & Murri, N. (2006). Beginning special educators' intent to stay in special education: Why they like it here. *Teacher Education and Special Education, 29,* 179–190. doi:10.1177/088840640602900304

Geiger, W. L. (2006). *A compilation of research on states' licensure models for special education teachers and special education requirements for licensing general education teachers.* Lanham, MD: Education Resources Information Center. Retrieved from ERIC database (ED491706).

Geiger, W. L., Crutchfield, M. D., & Mainzer, R. (2003). The status of licensure of special education teachers in the 21st century (COPSSE Document No. RS-7). Gainesville, FL: Center on Personnel Studies in Special Education. Retrieved from http://copsse.education.ufl.edu/copsse/docs/RS-7/1/RS-7.pdf

Griffin, C., Kilgore, K., Winn, J., Otis-Wilborn, A., Hou, W., Garvan, C. (2009). First-year special educators: The influence of school and classroom context factors on their accomplishments and problems. *Teacher Education and Special Education, 32,* 45–63. doi: 10.1177/0888406408330870

Holmes Group. (1986). *Tomorrow's teachers.* East Lansing, MI: Author.

Humphrey, D. C. & Wechsler, M. E. (2007). Insights into alternative certification: initial findings from a national study. *Teachers College Record, 109,* 483–530.

Humphrey, D. C., Wechsler, M. E., & Hough, H. J. (2008). Characteristics of effective alternative teacher certification programs. *Teachers College Record, 110,* 1–63.

Ideadata.org. (n.d.a). *Table 3.2. Teachers employed (FTE) to work with children, ages 6 through 21, who are receiving special education Under IDEA, Part B, by qualification status and state: Fall 2009.* Retrieved from https://www.ideadata.org/arc_toc12.asp#partbPEN

Ideadata.org. (n.d.b). *Table 3.2. Teachers employed (FTE) to work with children ages 6 through 21, who are receiving special education services Under IDEA, Part B, by qualification status and state: Fall 2006.* Retrieved from https://www.ideadata.org/arc_toc9.asp#partbPEN

Ideadata.org. (n.d.c). *Table 3.2. Teachers employed (FTE) to work with children ages 6 through 21, who are receiving special education services Under IDEA, Part B, by qualification status and state: Fall 2005.* Retrieved from https://www.ideadata.org/arc_toc8.asp#partbPEN

Ideadata.org. (n.d.d). *Table 1.3. Students ages 6 through 21 served under IDEA, Part B, by disability category and state: 2004.* Retrieved from https://www.ideadata.org/arc_toc6.asp#partbCC

Ideadata.org. (n.d.e). *Table 1.3. Students ages 6 through 21 served under IDEA, Part B, by disability category and state: 2009.* Retrieved from https://www.ideadata.org/arc_toc11.asp-partbCC

Kober, N., & Rentner, D. S. (2011, June). *Strained schools face bleak future: Districts foresee budget cuts, teaching layoffs, and a slowing of education reform efforts.* Washington, DC: Center on Education Policy. Retrieved from http://www.cep-dc.org/publications/index.cfm?selectedYear=2011

Landrum, T. J., Tankersley, M., & Kauffman, J. M. (2006). What is special about special education for students with emotional or behavioral disorders? In B. G. Cook & B. R. Schirmer (Eds.), *What is special about special education?* (pp. 12–25). Denver, CO: Pro-Ed.

Levine, A. (2006). *Educating school teachers.* Washington, DC: The Education Schools Project. Retrieved from http://www.edschools.org/teacher_report.htm

McKenzie, R. G. (2009). A national survey of pre-service preparation for collaboration. *Teacher Education and Special Education, 32,* 397–393. doi:10.1177/0888406409346241

NCTAF (National Commission on Teaching & America's Future). (1996). *What matters most: Teaching for America's future.* New York: Author. Retrieved from http://nctaf.org/teacher-turnover-cost-calculator/nctaf-research-reports/

NCATE (National Council for Accreditation of Teacher Education) Blue Ribbon Panel. (2010, November). *Transforming teacher education through clinical practice: A national strategy to prepare effective teachers.* Report of the Blue

Ribbon Panel on Clinical Preparation and Partnerships for Improved Student Learning. Retrieved from http://www.ncate.org/Public/ResearchReports/NCATEInitiatives/BlueRibbonPanel/tabid/715/Default.aspx

NCTQ (National Council on Teacher Quality). (2010). *2009 state teacher policy yearbook: National Summary*. Washington, DC: Author. Retrieved from http://www.nctq.org/dmsView/2009_State_Teacher_Policy_Yearbook_National_Summary_NCTQ_Report

No Child Left Behind Act of 2001, Pub. L. No. 107–110 (2002).

Otis-Wilborn, A., Winn, J., Griffin, C., & Kilgore, K. (2005). Beginning special educators' forays into general education. *Teacher Education and Special Education, 28*, 143–152. doi:10.1177/088840640502800401

Raymond, M. Fletcher, S. H., & Luque, J. (2001). *Teach for America: An evaluation of teacher differences and student outcomes in Houston, Texas*. Palo Alto, CA: Stanford University, CREDO. Retrieved from http://credo.stanford.edu/downloads/tfa.pdf

Rosenberg, M. S., Boyer, K. L., Sindelar, P. T., & Misra, S. K. (2007). Alternative route programs for certification in special education: Program infrastructure, instructional delivery, and participant characteristics. *Exceptional Children, 73*, 224–241.

Sindelar, P. T., Daunic, A., & Rennells, M. S. (2004). Comparisons of traditionally and alternatively trained teachers. *Exceptionality, 12*, 209–223. doi:10.1207/s15327035ex1204_3

Spectrum K–12 School Solutions. (2010). *Response to intervention (RTI) adoption survey*. Towson, MD: Author. Retrieved from http://rti.pearsoned.com/docs/RTIsite/2010RTIAdoptionSurveyReport.pdf

Torgesen, J. K. (2009). The response to intervention instructional model: Some outcomes from a large-scale implementation in reading first schools. *Child Development Perspectives, 3*(1), 38–40. doi:10.1111/j.1750-8606.2009.00073.x

U.S. Department of Education. (2003). *Meeting the highly qualified teachers challenge: The Secretary's second annual report on teacher quality*. Washington, DC: Author. Retrieved from http://www2.ed.gov/about/reports/annual/teachprep/index.html

U.S. Department of Education. (2009, October). *Teacher preparation: Reforming the uncertain profession*—Remarks of Secretary Arne Duncan at Teachers College, Columbia University. Retrieved from http://www2.ed.gov/news/speeches/2009/10/10222009.html

U.S. Department of Education. (2011, June). *Reading First implementation study 2008–09*. Retrieved from http://www2.ed.gov/rschstat/eval/other/reading-first-implementation-study/report.doc

U.S. Department of Education. (2011, September). *Race to the Top fund*. Retrieved from http://www2.ed.gov/programs/racetothetop/index.html

VanDerHeyden, A. M., Witt, J., & Gilbertson, D. (2006). A multi-year evaluation of the effects of a Response to Intervention (RTI) model on identification of children for special education. *Journal of School Psychology, 45*, 225–256. doi:10.1016/j.jsp.2006.11.004

Vannest, K. J., & Hagan-Burke, S. (2010). Teacher time use in special education. *Remedial and Special Education, 31*, 126–142. doi:10.1177/0741932508327459

Walsh, K. (2001). *Teacher education reconsidered: Stumbling for quality*. Baltimore, MD: Abell Foundation. Retrieved from http://www.nctq.org/p/publications/docs/ed_cert_1101_20071129024241.pdf

Walsh, K. & Jacobs, S. (2007). *Alternative certification isn't alternative*. Washington, DC: Thomas B. Fordham Institute and National Council on Teacher Quality. Retrieved from http://www.nctq.org/dmsStage/Alternative_Certification_Isnt_Alternative_NCTQ_Report

White, M., & Mason, C. Y. (2006). Components of a successful mentoring program for beginning special education teachers: Perspectives from new teachers and mentors. *Teacher Education and Special Education, 29*, 191–201. doi:10.1177/088840640602900305

Xu, Z., Hannaway, J., & Taylor, C. (2009). *Making a difference? The effects of Teach for America in high school*. Washington, DC: National Center for Analysis of Longitudinal Data in Education Research. doi:10.1002/pam.20585

Zigmond, N. P., & Kloo, A. (2011). General and special education are (and should be) different. In J. Kauffman & D. Hallahan (Eds.), *Handbook of Special Education* (pp. 160–172). New York, NY: Routledge

Zirkel, P. A., & Thomas, L. B. (2010). State laws and guidelines for implementing RTI. *Teaching Exceptional Children, 43*(1), 60–73.

2

Federal Support for Personnel Development in Special Education

Where We've Been, Where We Are, and a Look to the Future

Jeannie Kleinhammer-Tramill,
UNIVERSITY OF SOUTH FLORIDA
Ann Mickelson
UNIVERSITY OF CONNECTICUT
Joshua Barton
UNIVERSITY OF SOUTH FLORIDA

Things to Think About

- The U.S. Department of Education Office of Special Education Programs' (OSEP) funding priorities to support personnel development include awards determined using a congressional formula as well as discretionary funds awarded through a competitive process.
- The organizational structure of the Office of Special Education and Rehabilitative Services and OSEP has evolved over time.
- OSEP has a detailed process for soliciting and reviewing applications and funding awards.
- Over the years, the Professional Development Program has been influenced by litigation and legislation and, in turn, influences special educator preparation.

The Personnel Development Program (PDP) in the Office of Special Education Programs (OSEP) at the U.S. Department of Education is one of the nation's oldest federal student financial aid programs, originating in 1958 under P.L. 85-926, the Education of Mentally Retarded Children Act. Today, Section 662 of the Individuals with Disabilities Education Act (IDEA) authorizes, and OSEP manages, funding for grants to support the preparation of personnel to serve children with disabilities.

The purpose of this chapter is to provide an overview of the federal investment in personnel development for careers in the field of special education. The chapter is organized into five sections, the first of which situates the special education personnel development program (PDP) within the context of the U.S. Department of Education. The second section provides an overview of types of priorities. The third section gives a brief history of the PDP and how it has evolved over time. The fourth section outlines current funding priorities and describes their purposes. A look to the future comprises the final section. Our intent with this chapter is to somewhat demystify the OSEP personnel development grant process, particularly for future leaders who are likely to submit proposals to fund preparation of personnel for careers related to special education at colleges or universities, as well as to illustrate how the OSEP PDP has helped to build a profession.

The U.S. Department of Education as a Context

The original Department of Education was established in 1867 and with it began the federal focus on gathering information as to what works in our educational system and to promoting these practices. The year after it was established, the Department was demoted to an Office of Education due to concerns that it would exercise too much control over local schools. Despite the fact that the name and placement of the agency within the Executive Branch has varied considerably over the last 140 years, the emphasis on collecting and analyzing data pertaining to the nation's schools has endured (U.S. Department of Education, 2012).

When the PDP program for special education was first authorized in 1958, the U.S. Office of Education was situated within the U.S. Department of Health, Education, and Welfare (HEW). Congress established the U.S. Department of Education (ED) as a Cabinet-level agency in 1980 through the passage of the Department of Education Organization Act, Public Law 96-88 (U.S. Department of Education, 2010). This law outlined the mission of the ED as to:

- strengthen the federal commitment to assuring access to equal educational opportunity for every individual;
- supplement and complement the efforts of states, the local school systems and other instrumentalities of the states, the private sector, public and private nonprofit educational research institutions, community-based organizations, parents, and students to improve the quality of education;
- encourage the increased involvement of the public, parents, and students in federal education programs;
- promote improvements in the quality and usefulness of education through federally supported research, evaluation, and sharing of information;
- improve the coordination of federal education programs;
- improve the management of federal education activities; and
- increase the accountability of federal education programs to the President, the Congress, and the public (U.S. Department of Education, 2010).

In fulfilling this mission, ED engages in several activities. These include: (a) establishing policies related to federal financial support for education and administration of such funds; (b) supervision of research on American schools and dissemination of results to Congress, educators, and the public; (c) identification of issues in education and drawing national attention to them; and (d) enforcement of federal statutes prohibiting discrimination in activities and programs that receive federal funds to ensure equal access to education for all (U.S. Department of Education, 2010). The ED is currently organized as depicted in Figure 2.1. The Secretary of Education leads the Department and promotes the mission, goals, and objectives. This individual is nominated by the President, confirmed by the Senate, and serves as a member of the President's Cabinet. Under the administrative offices within the Department

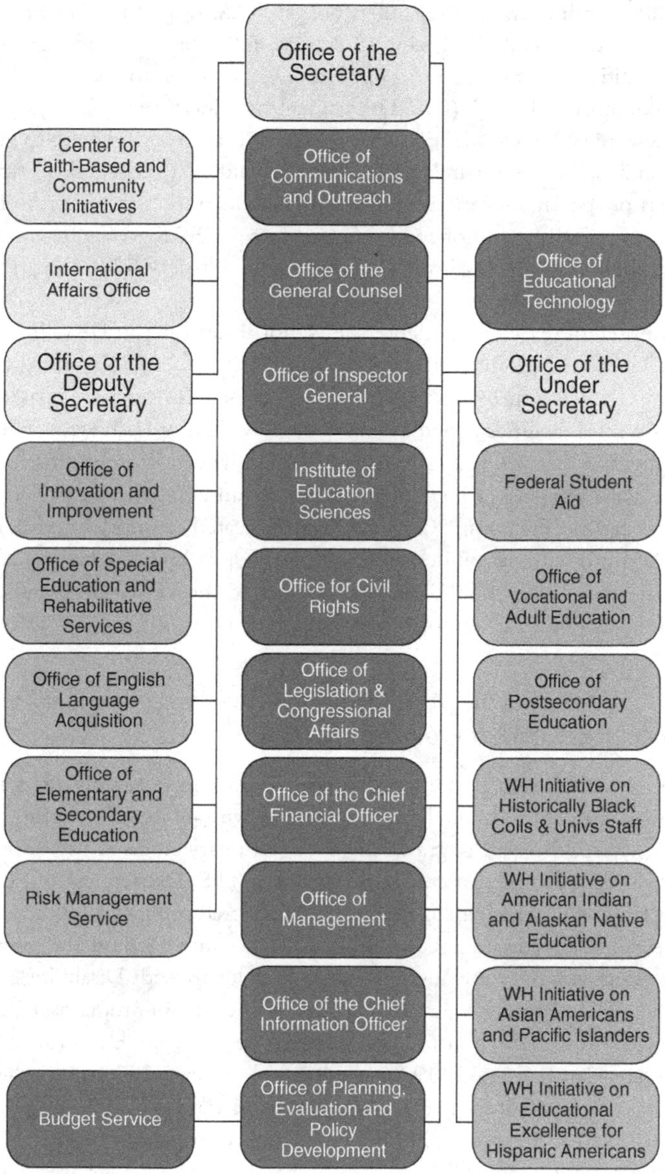

Figure 2.1 U.S. Department of Education Coordinating Structure

(source: U.S. Department of Education, 2011)

there are several program offices including the Office of Special Education and Rehabilitative Services (OSERS; U.S. Department of Education, 2010).

Office of Special Education and Rehabilitative Services (OSERS)

The Office of Special Education and Rehabilitative Services is charged with supporting programs that "meet the needs and develop the full potential of children with disabilities, reduce dependency and enhance the productive capacities of youths and adults with disabilities, and support research to improve the lives of individuals with disabilities regardless of age" (U.S. Department of Education, 2010). The mission of OSERS is to "provide leadership to achieve full integration and participation in society of people with disabilities by ensuring equal opportunity and access to, and excellence in, education, employment and community living" (U.S. Department of Education, 2013). As part of this mission, OSERS supports research efforts to identify what works in education, and helps to guide policy around improving results and outcomes for individuals with disabilities. OSERS also provides a wide array of supports in areas of special education, vocational rehabilitation, and research. Through provision of multiple types of funding, as authorized by federal law, OSERS works to ensure that individuals with disabilities are fully included in school, employment, and society (U.S. Department of Education, 2011d).

OSERS is comprised of three components: the National Institute on Disability and Rehabilitation Research (NIDRR), the Rehabilitation Services Administration (RSA), and the Office of Special Education Programs. NIDRR provides leadership and support for research related to the rehabilitation of individuals with disabilities aimed at improving the lives of individuals with disabilities of all ages (U.S. Department of Education, 2010). RSA oversees grants that support the provision of services to help individuals with physical or mental disabilities obtain employment and live more independently (U.S. Department of Education, 2010). OSEP is dedicated to improving results for infants, toddlers, children, and youth with disabilities ages birth through 21 by providing leadership and financial support to assist states and local school districts as authorized through Parts B and C of IDEA as well as supporting national activities as authorized through Part D of IDEA (U.S. Department of Education, 2010).

The Office of Special Education Programs (OSEP)

The U.S. Department of Education's Office of Special Education Programs offers two types of grants that support the preparation of personnel to serve students with disabilities: (a) formula grants to agencies using formulae determined by Congress; and (b) discretionary grants to organizations, agencies, and individuals that are awarded through a competitive process (U.S. Department of Education, 2011d).

Formula Grant Programs, which are often state-administered programs, are noncompetitive awards based on a congressionally predetermined formula that takes into account the population of students to be served. For example, under the auspices of the Individuals with Disabilities Education Act, the Office of Special Education Programs administers three formula grant programs: (a) the Grants to States program authorized by Part B Section 611 for children ages 3 through 21; (b) the Preschool Grants program authorized by Part B Section 619 for children ages 3 through 5; and (c) the Grants for Infants and Families program authorized by Part C for infants and toddlers, ages birth through 2 and their families (U.S. Department of Education, 2011b). The primary purpose of funds from IDEA Parts B and C is to assist states in covering the additional costs of direct educational services to children and youth with disabilities. A small portion of these funds can be used by states to cover administrative costs. In some cases, states use a portion of their Part B and/or C funds to provide professional development or technical assistance.

Unlike a formula grant, discretionary grants are funded on the basis of a competitive process. The Department reviews applications through a formal peer-review process that takes into consideration the legislative requirements as well as published selection criteria established for a particular grant program. Review panels, typically consisting of three or five professionals who are knowledgeable in particular fields associated with the grant proposals, read and rate their assigned proposals based on the published criteria. Reviewers also provide feedback as to strengths and weaknesses of the proposal. A member of the OSEP staff is assigned to each review panel to observe and assure a fair and equitable review. While the Department does not conduct blind reviews, reviewers must indicate actual or potential conflicts of interest. Following the peer review, the Department reviews the panel process to identify any irregularities. Once scores for each grant in a particular competition have been determined, the proposals are ranked, and the Department of Education develops a slate of potentially fundable proposals under each priority. While the Department typically approves all proposals according to rank and available funding, it has discretion to determine which applications best address the program requirements and are, therefore, most worthy of funding (U.S. Department of Education, 2011a). Discretionary as well as formula grant competitions are announced in the *Federal Register*, which is available in print and online (https://www.federalregister.gov/). The *Federal Register* provides information on rules, deadlines, available funding, and how to apply.

OSEP is composed of two divisions: the Monitoring and State Improvement Planning Division (MSIP) and the Research to Practice Division (RTP). Together, the two administer the formula and discretionary grants discussed above. MSIP is composed of four teams charged with supervising the formula grants. The Research to Practice Division handles the discretionary grants and is also composed of four teams: Early Childhood; Elementary and Middle School; Secondary, Transition and Postsecondary; and National Initiatives (U.S. Department of Education, 2011a). The PDP grant initiatives cut across these teams and are administered by Program Officers representing the four teams.

The Research to Practice Division administers several discretionary grant programs including those under IDEA Part B and IDEA Part D. IDEA Part B discretionary grant programs consist of: (a) State Personnel Development Grants program (SPDG; formerly the State Program Improvement Grants; CFDA: 84.323), and (b) Special Education—Technical Assistance on State Data Collection (CFDA: 84.373; U.S. Department of Education, 2010). IDEA Part D discretionary grant programs include:

- Special Education—Personnel Development to Improve Services and Results for Children with Disabilities (the PDP; CFDA 84.325);
- Special Education—Technical Assistance and Dissemination to Improve Services and Results for Children with Disabilities (CFDA 84.326);
- Special Education—National Activities, Technology and Media Services (CFDA 84.327); and
- Special Education—National Activities, Parent Information centers (CFDA 84.328; U.S. Department of Education, 2010).

The main purposes of the Personnel Development Program are to help address State-identified needs for highly qualified personnel in special education, related services, early intervention, and general education who work with infants, toddlers, and children with disabilities; and to ensure that those personnel have the necessary skills and knowledge, derived from practices that have been determined through scientifically based research and experience, to be successful in serving this population (U.S. Department of Education, 2010). The PDP contains four investment areas: (a) personnel preparation in the form of personnel preparation grants, (b) program improvement grants, (c) national centers, and (d) program evaluation.

In order to help prepare personnel who are highly qualified in areas of identified, critical need to improve outcomes for children with disabilities, the program identifies three objectives. First, the program seeks to improve the curricula of IDEA training programs to ensure that personnel prepared to serve children with disabilities are knowledgeable and skilled in practices that reflect the current knowledge base. Second, the program focuses on increasing the supply of teachers and service providers who are highly qualified for and serve in positions for which they are trained. Lastly, the program strives to enhance the efficiency of the expenditure of federal dollars under this program (U.S. Department of Education, 2011c). These objectives are reflected in the discretionary grant competitions in the form of priorities. The development of priorities guide the focus and purpose of grant applications as described in the section to follow. Figure 2.2 depicts the objectives in a logic model that seeks to show how OSEP expects to impact outcomes for children with disabilities.

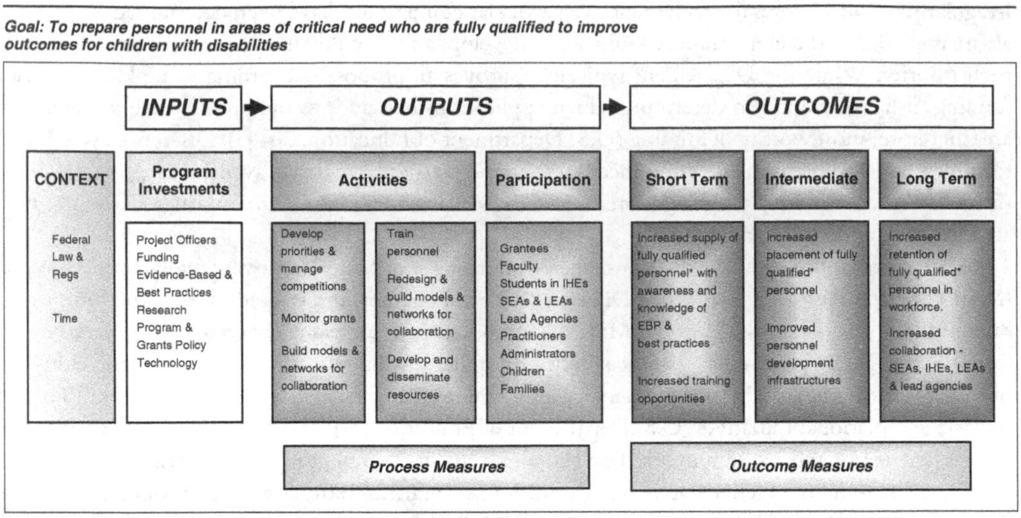

Figure 2.2 Logic Model of OSEP Research to Practice Division's Personnel Development Program

(source: Office of Special Education Programs, 2010)

Note

* Fully Qualified = Highly Qualified for special education teacher; Qualified for paraprofessional/aide; Fully Certified for administrator/coordinator, for related or supportive services in a school setting, or for teacher, related services, or supportive services in early intervention, early childhood.

Types of Grant Priorities

The U.S. Department of Education establishes priorities, authorized by law, that apply to each grant competition. These funding priorities may best be understood as a means of focusing a grant competition on the areas in which the Secretary of the U.S. Department of Education (ED) is interested in receiving applications (U.S. Department of Education, 2010). The three types of priorities defined by ED that pertain to the PDP include *absolute priorities*, *competitive priorities*, and *invitational priorities*.

Applicants must respond to absolute priorities to be eligible for funding, whereas competitive and invitational priorities are optional. In some cases, applicants may receive additional points on the evaluation of their grant applications if they address competitive priorities. An application that addresses an invitational priority, however, receives no preference (additional points) in the application review.[1] Priorities are, thus, an important tool for the government to use in alerting the field to particular policy initiatives.

When Congress passes federal laws regarding education, grant funding is one of the primary policy levers to ensure that the legislation is enacted at the state and local levels. Most education laws include priorities for funding. The administrative offices of the government, or Congress in cases of large government grant programs, have the authority to select which priorities to announce from those allowed by the legislation. All possible grant priorities are listed in the Catalog of Federal Domestic Assistance (CFDA).

Education programs are assigned the CFDA number 84. Particular priorities within Education legislation are then designated by numbers ranging from 84.001 to 84.999. Grant programs for personnel preparation funded through the Office of Special Education Programs under the priority for *Special Education—Personnel Development to Improve Services and Results for Children with Disabilities* are designated as CFDA 84.325. Letters are then used to further specify particular priorities such as:

- Preparation of Special Education, Early Intervention, and Related Services Leadership Personnel (formerly Preparation of Leadership Personnel: CFDA 84.325D)
- Personnel Preparation in Special Education, Early Intervention, and Related Services (formerly Combined Priority for Personnel Preparation: CFDA 84.325K), and
- Special Education Preservice Program Improvement Grants (CFDA 84.325T).

History of Personnel Development Program

The section to follow provides a synopsis of the history of the Personnel Development Program. In describing the history, we describe four phases that characterize the federal initiatives over time, including: (a) early federal support for personnel preparation in special education; (b) the quality initiative; (c) the 1990s and the impact of IDEA; and (d) personnel preparation in the new millennium and revised funding formulae.

Early Federal Support for Personnel Preparation in Special Education

During the late 1950s and early 1960s, new legislation (e.g., P.L. 85-926, P.L. 87-276, and P.L. 88-164) provided access to services including direct support, research, and preparation of new leaders who would build the field of special education. Throughout the first two decades of the federal personnel preparation program, its primary emphases were on increasing the quantity of special education personnel and developing the necessary infrastructure for future special education personnel preparation (Burke, 1976; Harvey, 1980). By the early 1970s, several landmark court cases (e.g., *Mills vs. Board of Education*, 1972; *PARC vs. Commonwealth of Pennsylvania*, 1971) had established legal precedents for the right to education for children with disabilities; moreover, the *PARC* decision laid the groundwork for the adoption of the Least Restrictive Environment (LRE) provisions in later legislation. In 1970, Title VI of the Elementary and Secondary Education Act (ESEA) incorporated all existing legislation related to education of students with disabilities into one authority. In particular, Part D of Title VI supported training for the "Education of the Handicapped" and authorized funding that continued through 1973 for preservice and in-service training for general and special educators to serve students with disabilities. In 1974, appropriations for personnel training were authorized via Public Law 93-380, the Family Educational Rights and Privacy Act of 1974, which authorized funding for personnel preparation through 1977. Part D of P.L. 93-380 included provisions for the preparation of special education teachers and specific provisions for preparation of regular education teachers to serve students with disabilities in the "mainstream" or regular education classroom (Harvey, 1980).

After the passage of Public Law 94-142, the Education for All Handicapped Children Act (EHA) in 1975, states and local schools faced significant challenges in trying to provide educational services for children who had not previously had access to education or who did not receive appropriate educational services (Kleinhammer-Tramill & Fiore, 2003). During this period, the number of special education personnel prepared and the infrastructure for personnel development grew dramatically. Likewise, the number of personnel preparation programs grew from 40 colleges and universities in 1957 (Burke, 1976) to 698 in 1983 (Geiger, 1983).

Concerns About Funding, the Quality Initiative, and the Regular Education Initiative

In the early 1980s, President Reagan sought to reduce the size of government by dismantling the U.S. Department of Education and block-granting a number of previous discretionary education programs to states (Bell, 1993). His initiative raised concern that the federal commitment to support education, and with it, support for the personnel preparation program, was dwindling. In response, the National

Commission on Excellence in Education's *Nation at Risk* report highlighted the need for a strong national effort to improve America's schools (Bell, 1993). Smith-Davis, Morsink, and Wheatley (1984) suggest that the "excellence" movement associated with the National Commission's work spurred a "Quality Initiative" within what was then the U.S. Department of Education's Division of Personnel Preparation.

The plan for implementing the Quality Initiative sought to address concerns that the quality of education was placing the nation at risk and to encourage colleges and universities to demonstrate accountability for quality practices in teacher education for special education. As part of this movement, special education personnel preparation programs were asked to delineate the competencies their preservice educators would acquire and to provide evidence of program accreditation by state and/or national accreditation agencies (Smith-Davis et al., 1984).

The Quality Initiative also facilitated changes in the grant review process to ensure that field readers had expertise relevant to applications under review (Smith-Davis et al., 1984). The system for ranking applications based on numerical scores associated with each criterion was also adopted at this time as a strategy for increasing objectivity in grant reviews and, in addition, the Division of Personnel Preparation was encouraged to engage in long-range planning to highlight and address particular areas of national interest and to identify and disseminate promising practices in personnel preparation for students with disabilities. In the early to mid-1980s, a number of new absolute priorities specific to particular populations were established and funded, including: (a) preparation of personnel for minority children with disabilities; (b) preparation of personnel to provide special education and related services to newborn and infant children with disabilities; and (c) preparation of personnel for the transition to adult and working life (Kleinhammer-Tramill & Fiore, 2003).

In 1986, Madeleine Will, former Assistant Secretary of the U.S. Department of Education, Office of Special Education and Rehabilitation Services (OSERS), issued a call for redesigning special education services to emphasize "shared responsibility" between regular and special education for students with mild disabilities. This spurred the "Regular Education Initiative" (REI; Reynolds, Wang, & Walberg, 1987; Will, 1986). The REI, like the "mainstreaming" movement of the 1970s, encouraged the idea that students with mild to moderate disabilities could best be served in general education classes. Although the REI suggested the need for extensive preparation of regular educators to serve students with disabilities, the only absolute priorities for the preparation of regular educators appeared in grants to State Education Agencies and in invitational priorities (Kleinhammer-Tramill & Fiore, 2003). The REI was met with skepticism on several accounts. Special educators such as Kauffman (1989) worried that, as a Reagan appointee, Ms. Will's intent was to, first, reduce federal funding for special education in general and, second, to shift responsibility for students with mild to moderate disabilities to general education so that funding, resources, and expertise might be focused on students with severe disabilities. During this period of uncertainty about the future of federal support, concern about the quality of education, and advocacy for retaining funds for the personnel preparation program (TED/HECSE, May 12, 1982), the preparation of new special education personnel declined. While 18,545 bachelor's degrees and 14,144 master's degrees were awarded by 1976 (Peters, Fiore, & Kleinhammer-Tramill, 2000), and the number of personnel preparation programs grew from 40 colleges and universities in 1957 (Burke, 1976) to 698 in 1983 (Geiger, 1983), only 6,573 bachelor's degrees and 8,581 master's degrees were awarded in FY 1988, reflecting a considerable drop from the number awarded 18 years earlier (Kleinhammer-Tramill, 2003).

The 1990s and the Impact of the IDEA

During the 1990s, new federal initiatives such as America 2000, Goals 2000: Educate America Act, and reauthorization of the ESEA as Improving America's Schools Act were aimed at improving educational outcomes for all students, including students with disabilities. At the same time, advocacy for the needs of special populations of students with disabilities led to an increase in the number of priorities for personnel preparation during the early 1990s. Kleinhammer-Tramill and Fiore (2003) found that the Final Regulations for the 1990 IDEA included 19 priorities for personnel preparation, and by 1994, the number of personnel preparation priorities had expanded to 21. The broad set of priorities announced for FY 1994 included new directions for promoting personnel quality, priorities to address unique geographic needs (e.g., rural populations), as well as priorities that targeted the needs of specific populations such as personnel preparation for students with Attention Deficit Disorder. The U.S. Secretary of Education selected nine of the possible 21 priorities as absolute priorities for FY 1994.

Following the 1997 reauthorization of IDEA as P.L. 105-17, support for personnel preparation was formally consolidated into four priorities, including: (a) preparation of early intervention personnel to serve infants, toddlers, children, and youth, low-incidence disabilities, and related services; (b) preparation of leadership personnel; (c) preparation of personnel to serve infants, toddlers, and children with high-incidence disabilities; and (d) projects of national significance (Kleinhammer-Tramill & Fiore, 2003). The 1997 reauthorization of IDEA emphasized improving educational outcomes for students with disabilities by promoting high expectations, improving access to the general education curriculum and state standards, increasing participation in state and local assessments, and holding states and local schools responsible for including students with disabilities in their accountability systems (Kleinhammer-Tramill & Fiore, 2003). Another way federal legislation's emphasis on results impacted support for personnel preparation after the 1997 reauthorization of IDEA is reflected in the Service Obligation and Repayment Requirements. As outlined in the Final Regulations of IDEA 1997, persons who receive scholarship and/or stipend support must fulfill a 2-year Service Obligation for each year of scholarship support, or they must repay the government for the assistance they received. The Service Obligation requirement is discussed in more detail in sections to follow.

Personnel Preparation in the New Millennium and Revised Funding Formulae

With the 2004 reauthorization of the IDEA as the Individuals with Disabilities Education Improvement Act (IDEIA), the priority for Projects of National Significance was discontinued and the priorities for High Incidence, Low Incidence, Related Services, Early Childhood, and Minority Institutions appeared as nested absolute priorities under the Combined Priority for Personnel Preparation (Kleinhammer-Tramill, Tramill, & Brace, 2010). Following the 2004 reauthorization, each of the absolute priorities for personnel preparation emphasized the use of "research-based curriculum and pedagogy" and preparation of personnel to improve outcomes for students with disabilities and assist them in accessing the general education curriculum (Kleinhammer-Tramill et al., 2010).

According to Kleinhammer-Tramill et al. (2010), the priorities, the level of funding, and the number of funded grants have changed over time for federal programs in special education personnel preparation. Although the funding for OSEP's personnel preparation program was relatively flat during the late 1990s and early 2000s, when adjusted for inflation, the annual appropriations for personnel preparation have declined since the 1980s (Kleinhammer-Tramill, Tramill, & Westbrook, 2009; Kleinhammer-Tramill et al., 2010). In spite of the decline in funding, the PDP continues to have a significant impact on preparing future generations of teachers, administrators, and scholars.

Current Funding Priorities

The Budgets for FYs 2009 and 2010 were $90.7 million each year and the President's request for FY 2011 was the same. Through the competitive grant process discussed above, Institutions of Higher Education (IHEs) are awarded training grants with a requirement to use 65% of their budget for financial support to scholars. In FY 2010, 451 grantees reported to OSEP in their annual data submission that

6,383 scholars were enrolled in their OSEP-supported programs at the associate's, bachelor's, master's, doctoral, and post-doctoral levels.

A Service Obligation component was established in the 1997 IDEA reauthorization, and since that time, scholarship recipients have been required to work in the field of special education or related services for 2 years for each year of financial support they receive or repay the amount of their scholarship. In the 2004 reauthorization of the IDEA, the responsibility for tracking scholars' employment and service obligations was transferred from IHEs to the Department of Education. While grantees are responsible for tracking scholars' Service Obligations for grants funded between 1999 and 2004, the National Center on Service Obligations (NCSO) is responsible for tracking the service obligations of scholars/obligees funded by PDP grants awarded in FY 2005 and any year thereafter.[2]

Currently, the PDP supports not only training grants, but also national centers that assist the recruitment and retention of persons into the field of special education and related services; improve policy and practice, especially for beginning special education teachers; provide teacher education faculty enhancement on evidence-based practices; assist faculty in minority-serving institutions of higher education; assist states in their data collection efforts on special education teachers and related-service personnel; and support the improvement of personnel training programs of personnel for infants, toddlers, and children with disabilities.

The PDP currently oversees approximately 500 training grants in an active status and 73 program improvement grants.[3] Training grants are funded under two priorities, Personnel Preparation in Special Education, Early Intervention, and Related Services (325K) and Preparation of Special Education, Early Intervention, and Related Services Leadership Personnel (325D). As of FY 2011, training grants were funded to IHEs for up to 5 years and up to $250,000 per year. Nearly 8,000 scholars are enrolled annually in OSEP-supported training grants. Over 55% of those scholars are full-time students, and nearly 50% of those scholars are enrolled in master's level programs.

The Personnel Preparation in Special Education, Early Intervention, and Related Services Priority (325K) increases the number and quality of personnel who are fully credentialed to serve children with disabilities especially in areas of chronic shortage and combines five focus areas of training (FY 2011)—(a) to serve infants, toddlers, and preschool age children with disabilities; (b) to serve children with low-incidence disabilities; (c) to provide related services such as speech/language service and adapted physical education; (d) in Minority Institutions with at least 25% non-White enrollment including Historically Black Colleges and Universities; and (e) secondary transition. The Preparation of Special Education, Early Intervention, and Related Services Leadership Personnel Priority (325D) supports grants that prepare personnel at the doctoral and post-doctoral levels of training; or master's and specialist level programs in special education administration.

A more recent innovation is the improvement of preservice programs so that their graduates would be prepared for the increased rigor of highly qualified teacher (HQT) requirements under the most recent reauthorization of IDEA. OSEP funds two priorities that are exclusively focused on program improvement (FY 2011). These are the Special Education Preservice Program Improvement grants (325T) for teachers, and the Paraprofessional Preservice Program Improvement Grants (325N) priority.

As of FY 2011, 71 Preservice Program Improvement Grants (325T) in over 30 states have been funded to improve the quality of programs that prepare teachers of K–12 students with high-incidence disabilities. These program improvement grants, awarded as cooperative agreements, are required to support improvement activities, such as (a) extensively reviewing and revising courses to assure inclusion of evidence-based practices in the curriculum, (b) partnering with Arts and Sciences faculty to improve the rigor and mastery of the core content and to assure that graduates meet the HQT requirements of their state, and (c) extending the amount of time and depth of experience in clinical and field experiences in local school districts.

OSEP provides support to its 325T grantees in ways that had not been utilized within the program prior to their initial funding in FY 2007, such as monthly webinars for capacity building, administrative updates, and the exchange of exemplary project activities among grantees. Funded at $500,000 over the 5-year project period,[4] these grants are rigorously reviewed after their first planning year by an external review panel.

A second program improvement priority (325N) was initiated with 10 awards being made in FY 2010. Project activities are designed to improve the quality of existing paraprofessional certificate or associate degree programs. An institution receiving support under this priority must enhance or redesign its program curricula so that paraprofessionals are well-prepared to work with children with disabilities and their families. There are two focus areas under this priority: (a) improvement grants for early intervention (EI), early childhood special education (ECSE), and early childhood education (ECE) paraprofessional preservice programs; and (b) improvement grants for K through 12 paraprofessional preservice programs.

As part of the PDP, OSEP also funds a number of strategic national centers that help to build the capacity of states and IHEs so that they can better educate children with disabilities to meet academic standards and other developmental milestones. The centers are designed to provide services and resources beyond their own setting so that programs across the country can benefit as opposed to the discretionary grants described above which are program specific. The following list contains a brief description of national centers funded by this program:

- The ***IRIS Center for Faculty Enhancement*** prepares high quality teaching modules. University faculties, nationwide, use these modules to enhance their knowledge of practices that are evidence-based instructional practices and that improve the education of students with disabilities. This knowledge is integrated into personnel preparation program curriculum (see http://iriscenter.com).
- The ***Personnel Improvement Center*** assists states in strategies to eliminate shortages among special education teachers and related-service personnel by increasing the capacity of states to recruit and retain well-qualified, diverse special educators, early intervention, and related-service providers (see http://personnelcenter.org).
- The ***National Center to Improve Policy and Practice on Special Education Professional Development*** is focused on improving support to beginning special education teachers. NCIPP reports—which are available on its website in the online library—provide insights into issues affecting the quality of beginning special education teachers, such as induction and mentoring, state policies for induction and mentoring, collaboration and partnerships in schools (see http://www.ncipp.org).
- The ***Monarch Center*** is a technical assistance center to increase the capacity of Minority Institutions of Higher Education (MIHEs) to prepare personnel in special education and related services through greater access to OSEP's personnel preparation grants. The intent is that with increased access to these funds, these colleges and universities can develop, enhance, or strengthen special education and related services training programs (see http://www.monarchcenter.org).
- The ***National Professional Development Center for Autism Spectrum Disorders*** is a technical assistance center that promotes the use of evidence-based practice for children with autism spectrum disorders. The Center provides professional development to teachers and practitioners who serve those with autism spectrum disorders, ages birth through school age. The Center selects three states each year to work with its Department of Education, Part C agency, and University Center for Excellence in Developmental Disabilities in their professional development efforts (see http://autismpdc.fpg.unc.edu).

A Look to the Future

In 1995, Secretary of Education Richard Riley suggested that all legislation should be aligned with the standards-based accountability system that is currently embodied in NCLB. Since then, the standards movement has been central to education policy including the 2004 reauthorization of IDEA and, in turn, the PDP priorities. The future seems less certain today on what appears to be the eve of ESEA reauthorization. Currently, NCLB waivers to states as well as concern about the federal debt would seem to suggest that the federal role in education and, with it, federal funding may be dramatically reduced. Likewise, current controversies over how students with disabilities should be included in state assessments when ESEA is reauthorized suggest that those students could be effectively counted out of accountability systems.

New systems for teacher accountability together with continuing controversy over support for alternative routes to teacher licensure likewise suggest that OSEP will face the challenge of promoting new knowledge and skill requirements for both general education and special education teachers and challenges in determining how best to support improvement in both the quality and quantity of special education and related services personnel. In shaping new priorities for personnel preparation, OSEP will also face new challenges in determining whether and how the PDP should support preparation of both general and special educators for the roles they will play in implementing Response to Intervention and in providing inclusive education. The growing population of students who are at-risk for school failure because of poverty, language differences, and immigrant status, and the continuing achievement gap between African-American and Latino students and other racial groups expands the repertoire of essential practices necessary for teaching an increasingly diverse population of students (Correa, McHatton, McCray, & Baughan, Chapter 12, this volume).

Although the PDP has survived a half-century of economic and ideological shifts, the near future may be the most challenging and the most critical. Many special educators who were prepared under the auspices of a personnel preparation grant have already retired or will retire in the near future. While the PDP has never and will never be able to support preparation of all the special education and related services personnel necessary to fully serve students with disabilities, it provides critical incentives for colleges and universities to prepare the next generation of practitioners and leaders and to improve their programs so as to remain responsive to the needs of children and youth with disabilities. We believe that the primary challenge will be to sustain the program that has created a profession. As the nation continues to struggle toward economic recovery, this will require renewed advocacy and evidence of the results we have achieved.

Notes

1 For additional information, see http://www.osepideasthatwork.org/Scholars/index.asp published by ED in 2010.
2 See http://serviceobligations.ed.gov
3 http://www2.ed.gov/programs/osepprep/funding.html
4 Beginning in FY 2010, the grant awards were up to $1.5 million over a five-year project period at up to $300,000 each year.

References

Bell, T. H. (1993). Reflections one decade after A Nation at Risk. *Phi Delta Kappan, 74*, 592–604.

Burke, P. J. (1976). Personnel preparation: Historical perspective. *Exceptional Children, 43*, 144–147.

Geiger, W. (Ed.). (1983). *National directory of special education teacher preparation programs.* Rosslyn, VA: Teacher Education Division, Council for Exceptional Children and National Information Center for Handicapped Children and Youth.

Harvey, J. (1980). *Personnel preparation for the handicapped: Into the third decade.* Washington, DC: U.S. Office of Education, Bureau of Education for the Handicapped.

Kauffman, J. M. (1989). The regular education initiative as Reagan-Bush educational policy: A trickle-down theory of education of the hard-to-reach. *Journal of Special Education, 23*, 256–278. doi:10.1177/002246698902300303

Kleinhammer-Tramill, J. (2003). An analysis of federal initiatives to prepare regular educators to serve students with disabilities: Deans' grants, REGI, and beyond. *Teacher Education and Special Education, 26*, 230–245. doi: 10.1177/088840640302600310

Kleinhammer-Tramill, J., & Fiore, T. A. (2003). A history of federal support for preparing special educators and related personnel to serve children and youth with disabilities. *Teacher Education and Special Education, 26*, 217–229. doi: 10.1177/088840640302600309

Kleinhammer-Tramill, J., Tramill, J., & Brace, H. (2010). Contexts, funding history, and implications for evaluating the Office of Special Education Program's investment in personnel preparation. *Journal of Special Education, 43*, 195–205. doi: 10.1177/0022466908316201

Kleinhammer-Tramill, J., Tramill, J., & Westbrook, A. (2009). Evaluating the federal investment for personnel preparation in special education. *Teacher Education and Special Education, 32*, 150–165. doi:10.1177/0888406409334277

Office of Special Education Programs, Personnel Development Program, Program Logic Model (2010). Washington, DC: U.S. Department of Education.

Peters, J. T., Fiore, T. A., & Kleinhammer-Tramill, P. J. (2000). *Assessment to chart the evolution of the Personnel Preparation Program under IDEA: Document review and funding analysis* (Contract No. H297017001). Durham, NC: Westat.

Reynolds, M. C., Wang, M. C., & Walberg, H. J. (1987). The necessary restructuring of special and regular education. *Exceptional Children, 53*, 391–398.

Smith-Davis, J., Morsink, C., & Wheatley, F. W. (1984). *Quality in personnel preparation for the education of the handicapped: The baseline book.* Vienna, VA: Dissemin/Action.

U.S. Department of Education (2010) U.S. Department of Education, Risk Management Service, *Grantmaking at ED: Answers to Your Questions About the Discretionary Grants Process.* Washington, DC. Retrieved from http://www2.ed.gov/fund/grant/about/grantmaking/grantmaking.pdf

U.S. Department of Education (2011a). Discretionary grants. Retrieved from http://www2.ed.gov/fund/grant/about/discgrant.html

U.S. Department of Education (2011b). Formula grant. Retrieved from http://www2.ed.gov/fund/grant/about/formgrant.html

U.S. Department of Education (2011c). FY 2012 Budget Congressional Justification. http://www2.ed.gov/about/overview/budget/budget12/justifications/index.html

U.S. Department of Education (2011d). Types of grants offered by the U.S. Department of Education. Retrieved from http://www.ed.gov/fund/grants-apply.html

U.S. Department of Education (2012). Overview: The federal role in education. http://www2.ed.gov/about/overview/fed/role.html

U.S. Department of Education (2013). OSERS overview. Retrieved from http://www2.ed.gov/about/offices/list/osers/index.html

Will, M. C. (1986). Educating children with learning problems: A shared responsibility. *Exceptional Children, 32*, 411–416.

3

Patterns of Licensure for Special Education Teachers

William L. Geiger

UNIVERSITY OF TEXAS AT TYLER

Ann Mickelson

UNIVERSITY OF CONNECTICUT

Debra McKeown

GEORGIA STATE UNIVERSITY

Joshua Barton

UNIVERSITY OF SOUTH FLORIDA

Jeannie Kleinhammer-Tramill

UNIVERSITY OF SOUTH FLORIDA

Trisha Steinbrecher

UNIVERSITY OF NEW MEXICO

Things to Think About

- Assurance of the quality of teachers has historically been the responsibility of local or state educational entities. In the 21st century the federal government became involved in the matter of quality assurance through the "highly qualified" teacher provisions of the No Child Left Behind Act of 2001 and the Individuals with Disabilities Education Improvement Act of 2004.
- There is no consistency in the licensure patterns for special educators across the United States.
- A sizable majority of states have licensure systems that are a mixture of categorical and noncategorical options, and prekindergarten/kindergarten/grades 1–12 has been the preferred age/grade option for special education licenses.
- In the final quarter of the 20th century, there was a trend in favor of the adoption of noncategorical licensures options by states.
- At the beginning of the 21st century, only 60% of the states have adopted licensure structures that allow for specialization in secondary special education, transition, and/or special education-related

vocational or adult education; and 80% of the states had licensure for early childhood special education personnel.

- In the face of inconsistency in the licensure of early childhood and early childhood special educators, several national professional organizations have called for uniform and distinct licensure patterns in these areas.
- Federal regulations had a significant impact on who was categorized as a "highly qualified" special education teacher, which in turn affects their licensure patterns. In addition to changes in how these teachers are classified when teaching core subject matter, the ways they become "highly qualified" changed as well.

Overview

The purposes of this chapter are to place the topic of state licensing of special education teachers in an historical perspective and to examine the models of special education licensure[1] that have been adopted by states. The authors will use age/grade structures of licensure of special education teachers to organize the complex and varied patterns of licensure that exist across the United States. The age/grade levels used are: PK/K/1–12, secondary, and early intervention/early childhood special education. The federal requirement for "highly qualified" teachers will be examined, especially as it impacts special education teachers. Suggestions for future studies of patterns of licensure for special education teachers and related aspects of licensure are included at the end of the chapter.

In preparing this chapter the authors completed comprehensive searches of electronic databases, including Education Full Text, Google Scholar, ERIC, ProQuest, WorldCat, and PsychInfo. The authors used the following search terms: certification, licensure, special education teacher, exceptional education, highly qualified, HQT, HQ, NCLB, teacher quality, policy, educational policy, secondary special education, special education transition, early childhood, and early childhood education. Abstracts of identified publications were reviewed, and all relevant articles were considered regardless of publication date. In addition, the reference lists of pertinent publications were examined and citations that were not uncovered in the initial searches were pursued.

Licensure as an Indicator of Teacher Quality

A teaching license is a credential awarded by a state[2] or similar jurisdiction to individuals who have completed mandated requirements such as approved programs of preparation and specialized examinations. Teaching licenses signify that individuals have met state-established minimum requirements designed to assure the quality of individuals hired to teach (Teacher Tools and Advice, 2011).

Mackey and McHenry (1994) observed that credentialing teachers in the United States dates back to the first quarter of the 19th century when local school districts and counties established agencies to examine and license teachers. In the first half of the 19th century, "recruiting and hiring of teachers was a local, private matter" (Sedlak, 1989, p. 259). Teaching appointments were negotiated between a prospective teacher and an individual or group authorized to commit funds on behalf of a school or district. Recruitment practices included active solicitation, and potential teachers were viewed as commodities to be purchased. In this unregulated environment, teaching positions were often used as a form of patronage, and instances of nepotism were not uncommon (Sedlak, 1989).

In the 1830s and 1840s, cities and states recognized the value of free, common schools. Attention was given to the importance of the teaching role, and questions were generated about supplying and selecting teachers (Angus, 2001). There was a growing recognition that many local hiring practices undermined the quality of education. In order to assure the quality of the teaching workforce during the middle decades of the 19th century, there was a substantial shift from local, autonomous practices in hiring teachers to vesting more responsibility with county officials as a means of centralizing authority and assuring more uniform practices (Sedlak, 1989). As the century progressed, the responsibility for licensure of teachers became more centralized at the state level. This shift of responsibility from the local level to the state level continued into the 20th century. Cook reported (as cited in Sedlak, 1989) that by 1926 all states were involved to some degree in the licensure process, and in three fourths of the states, all teaching licenses were awarded *only* at the state level.

Early in the 19th century, no formal preparation was required for teachers. Although some form of examination was commonly administered prior to the formal appointment of a teacher, the rigor of the examinations and the way they were administered varied widely among districts. Examinations were often private events with only the applicant and the examiner(s) in attendance. Consequently, the examination process could be easily abused and result in favoritism or patronage (Sedlak, 1989).

At the close of the 19th century, examinations continued to be the primary means of assuring the quality of the teaching workforce (Angus, 2001). However, in addition to examinations, many superintendents recognized the importance of professional education programs for the preparation of teachers. Gradually, access to teaching positions became controlled through performance on examinations and through favoring applicants who participated in professional education programs, especially those provided by normal schools. By 1900 both professional education credentials awarded by professional education programs and examinations were widely used as bases for awarding teaching licenses. However, between 1870 and 1920 the completion of a preparation program grew to become the preferred form of quality assurance for teachers. Reliance on examinations waned.

In the early 20th century, the mechanism for assuring the quality of teacher candidates was to increase the required period of preparation (Sedlak, 1989). After World War I, many normal schools were converted to 4-year institutions; and there was an expansion of universities, many of which had schools or colleges of education. By 1940, 40 states had set licensure standards for secondary teachers at the bachelor's degree level. Although only 11 states had such a requirement for elementary teachers, there was discernible growth in the number of states that had adopted the bachelor's degree requirement for them.

During the 1930s, states displayed a renewed interest in establishing credible examinations as a means of guaranteeing the quality of teachers. The movement to return to the use of examinations as a measure of teacher quality led to the creation of the National Teacher Examination, which was first administered in 1940 (Sedlak, 1989). From the 1930s until the present, dual criteria—completion of a program of preparation and passing an examination—have been used by states to control entry to the profession of teaching.

At the beginning of the 21st century, state efforts to assure the quality of teachers were strongly influenced by the federal government through the No Child Left Behind Act (NCLB). NCLB "dramatically expanded the role of the federal government in public education by holding states, school districts, and schools accountable for producing measurable gains in students' achievement" (Yell, 2012, p. 57). NCLB provided a definition of a Highly Qualified Teacher (HQT) and required that all teachers be highly qualified by June 30, 2006. The general definition of "highly qualified" follows:

> (A) when used with respect to any public elementary school or secondary school teacher teaching in a State, means that—
>
> (i) the teacher has obtained full State certification as a teacher (including certification obtained through alternative routes to certification) or passed the State teacher licensing examination, and holds a license to teach in such State, except that when used with respect to any teacher teaching in a public charter school, the term means that the teacher meets the requirements set forth in the State's public charter school law; and

(ii) the teacher has not had certification or licensure requirements waived on an emergency, temporary, or provisional basis; (NCLB, 20 U.S.C. § 9101)

NCLB provides clarifying language for new elementary school teachers, and new middle and secondary school teachers, as well as for teachers who are not new to the profession.

In 2004 The Individuals with Disabilities Education Improvement Act (IDEIA) made clear the application of the HQT requirement to special educators. IDEIA continues the "federal involvement in the education of students with disabilities" that began nearly a half-century earlier—in the late 1950s (Yell, 2012, p. 52)—and introduces a federal standard for assuring the qualifications of special education teachers. The law required that new special education teachers have a bachelor's degree, have completed requirements for state licensure in special education, or be enrolled in an alternative certification (AC) program for special education that meets the state requirements. In addition, a special education teacher who teaches a core academic subject must demonstrate subject area competency commensurate with the grade level they teach. This competence must be demonstrated through an objective measure (e.g., coursework, assessments) as determined by each state. Schools can avoid the HQT content-area requirements if they solely utilize consultative or inclusive service delivery models for delivery of content knowledge (34 CFR Parts 300 and 301, Final Rule, 2006). A more in-depth discussion of the HQT expectations for special education teachers is provided later in this chapter. It is important to recognize that the HQT provisions in NCLB and IDEIA mark a shift from more than a century of states' being the source of regulations for quality of teacher to a situation in which the federal government now has noticeable influence on efforts to assure the quality of teachers.

Licensure of Special Education Teachers

Interest in states' models and requirements for licensing teachers of students with disabilities corresponds roughly with federal involvement in the education of students with disabilities. In the early 1950s Mackie & Dunn (1954) published a comprehensive study of special education licensure. Since that time many studies of special education licensure have been conducted, and the picture they present is a complex and confusing one.

As was mentioned in the overview section, an age/grade framework will be used to organize patterns of licensure for special education teachers. The organizational structure will consist of three levels: K–12, secondary/transition personnel, and early intervention and early childhood special education. The levels are not discrete. There is overlap between the K–12 and the other two levels.

Licensure of Special Education Teachers for Students in Grades K–12

Four dimensions of licensure requirements will be examined in this section. The first is whether the state's standards for special education licensure are course-based or competency-based. The second dimension is whether the licensure model is *freestanding* or an *add-on* to a general education teaching license. The third and fourth dimensions focus on the breadth of licensure models—areas/titles of licensure and age/grade ranges.

Course-Based or Credit Hour-Based Versus Competency-Based or Standards-Based

Licensure requirements for teachers tend to be course/credit-hour-based or competency/standards-based. That is, states have adopted standards that either stipulate courses by title or topic or a minimum number of credit hours that must be completed successfully, or they identify competencies that must be demonstrated or content standards that must learned in order for a candidate to be eligible for a license.

At the beginning of the 21st century, more than 60% of the states that award teaching licenses for special educators had course-based requirements (Geiger, 2002).

"'Completion of the curricula of state-approved institutions of higher education' was a basis for issuing a credential in special education" in all states at the beginning of the 21st century (Geiger, 2002, p. 8). In eight states it was the sole basis for issuing a license. For 31 states the completion of courses or credit hours in the curriculum of a state-approved institution of higher education was an additional requirement. About three quarters of the 31 states required a minimum number of credit hours in specific content areas. The number of credit hours required by the states varied noticeably. The lowest was nine credit hours, and the highest was 45. Seven of the 31 states specified a minimum number of credit hours in special education that must be completed, but the content was not prescribed. In those seven states, the number of credit hours in special education ranged from 18 to 30.

In the same study, 16 states required that applicants for special education licensure demonstrate state-adopted standards or competencies for special educators rather than the completion of courses. Three of these states also required applicants to successfully complete performance assessments that involved formal observations of teaching in order to receive a license in special education.

Geiger (2002) also found that 11 states were giving serious consideration to changing the basis for issuing licenses in special education at the beginning of the 21st century. Nearly three fourths of those states planned to shift from requiring a specific number of credit hours in special education to the demonstration of competencies and/or completion of performance assessments.

Freestanding Versus Added to General Education

When the matter of freestanding versus add-on models of special education licensure has been examined since the passage of P.L. 94–142 in 1975, the freestanding model of licensure has consistently been found to be the most commonly adopted. In this model, special education teachers are not required to have licensure in another area of education (for example, elementary or secondary education) prior to being awarded a license in special education.

In 1977, Gilmore and Aroyros found the freestanding model was the most common form of licensure in special education. A few years later Barresi and Bunte (1979) reported that about one third of the states had a free standing model of licensure for special educators, one third had a model that added special education to licensure in general education, and one third offered both options. In the 1990s and into the 21st century, the preference for the freestanding model of special education licensure continued to be reported (Piercy & Bowen, 1993; Putnam & Habanek, 1993; Geiger, 2002).

Since 2002, there have been no studies of the freestanding versus add-on to general education patterns of licensure for special education teachers. In the most recent investigation of this dimension of special education licensure patterns, Geiger (2002) reported that over 80% of the licensing jurisdictions in the United States did not require that special educators be licensed in general education. Seven states reported that licensure in general education was required of special educators. Two other states reported they would move from a freestanding model to one that required licensure in general education. One state reported that it anticipated moving in the other direction.

Geiger's study preceded the *highly qualified teacher* requirement mandated in the 2004 amendments to the Individuals with Disabilities Education Act (IDEA). As a consequence of that legislation, special education teachers who provide direct initial instruction in core academic subjects (e.g., mathematics, reading or language arts, and science) at the secondary level must demonstrate subject-matter competence in each subject taught. At the elementary education level, special education teachers should have subject-matter knowledge appropriate to elementary education content. Although there are a variety of means states can use to assure such competence, one means would be to require that special education teachers be licensed also in general education for the grade level and core subject areas they teach. Additional flexibilities in meeting licensure requirements are discussed later in the chapter.

Areas/Titles of Licensure for Special Educators

States have adopted a wide array of area/titles for licenses in special education. One of the earliest comprehensive studies of special education licensure was conducted by Mackie and Dunn (1954). At that time 32 states and the District of Columbia issued special teaching licenses for teachers of exceptional children, whereas 16 states did not. In their report, Mackie and Dunn presented summaries of licensure requirements across 10 categories of disability. The number of categories of disability for which states issued licenses for special education teachers ranged from one to all 10 categories. In this early study of special education licensure requirements, variety emerged as a hallmark of licensure practices for special educators. Although there have been frequent changes in licensure requirements and configurations since the 1950s, variety has remained a constant characteristic.

A few years prior to the passage of P.L. 94–142, Abeson and Fleury published *State Certification Requirements for Education of the Handicapped* (1972). A purpose of this report was to allow for comparisons of licensure requirements to be made across states. At that time most states had licensure requirements for various categories of disabilities. The number of disability areas for which there were licensure requirements ranged from one to eight. The most common disability categories in which licenses were awarded were mental retardation, hearing impairment, speech/language, visual impairment, and physical disabilities. In the early 1970s, fewer than 10 states reported some form of noncategorical licensure for special educators.

A few years after the passage of P.L. 94–142, Gilmore and Aroyros (1977) published another comprehensive study of special education licensure. This study confirmed that there were many differences across states in the licenses that were issued for special educators. The major differences were in the number and types of disability categories for licenses. In order to analyze the variety of licensure requirements among the states, the authors created a classification system based on the number of categories: those with six or more categories and those with less than six. Thirty-five states had at least six disability categories for which licenses were issued; nine states reported less than six each. The most frequently reported categories for licensure were hearing impairments (43), vision impairments (39), speech/language impairments (37), mental retardation (35), emotional disturbance (33), physical disabilities (33), and learning disabilities (31).

Barresi and Bunte (1979) reported the results of a study similar to that conducted by Gilmore and Aroyros. They also used number of categories as the basis for identifying models of special education licenses. In their system, states with six or more areas of licensure in special education were judged to have a *categorical model*, and those with fewer were classified as a *generic* model. Thirty-five states were found to have categorical models, and 14 had generic models. One state used both. They also discovered that some of the states classified as categorical had a generic license as one of the licensure options.

Since the foundational work of the 1970s, scholars have periodically examined categorical and noncategorical/generic options for licensure of special education teachers. In general the options adopted by states have been able to be classified as categorical, noncategorical/generic, or a mix of the two. Within these three broad structural classifications of special education licensure there is great variability. For example, two states may have primarily a categorical structure for their special education licensure system, but the categories for licensure in State A differ from those in State B. Substantial differences can also be observed across states that have adopted noncategorical systems for licensure as well as in states with systems that include both categorical and noncategorical options for licensure.

In the 1980s, a shift away from states' use of solely categorical models was observed (Chapey, Pyszkowski, & Trimarco, 1985; McLaughlin & Stettner-Eaton, 1988). Growth was seen in the number of states that adopted noncategorical or generic models of licensure for special education teachers, and the practice of states offering a mixture of categorical and noncategorical options was reported with greater frequency. In 1986, McLaughlin, Smith-Davis, and Burke reported that 30 of 56 states had categorical models of licensure, and the remaining 26 had noncategorical models. They also noted that many states offered both options. Noncategorical and mixed models of special education licensure were increasingly popular in the 1990s and into the first part of the 21st century (Berkeley, 1990; National Association of State Directors of Special Education, 1990; National Association of State Directors of Teacher Education and Certification, 2000; Mainzer & Horvath, 2001; Putnam & Habanek, 1993).

The most recent study of this aspect of special education teacher licensure patterns was conducted by Geiger (2002). He reported that only five states had licensure options that were solely categorical, and three had solely noncategorical options. More than 80% of the states offered a mixture of categorical and noncategorical options. One reason for the high percentage of states having mixed options is the fact that nearly all of them retained categorical options in the areas of visual impairment and hearing impairment.

Excluding early childhood special education, the licensure options used most frequently at the beginning of the 21st century were hearing impairment (47), vision impairment (46), emotional disturbance (27), some form of an overall general special education license (27), some form of general special education license based on level of disability (e.g., mild disabilities) (27), specific learning disabilities (23), mental retardation (22), and orthopedic impairments (21). When the options reported in Geiger's study (2002) are compared with those reported a quarter century earlier by Gilmore and Aroyros (1977), it can be seen that categorical licenses in the areas of sensory impairment continue to be the most common, but there have been declines in the use of some other categorical areas. In 1977, the majority of states had six or more categorical areas. In 2002, only five states had licensure models consisting solely of categorical options. In 1977, 13 states were reported as having some form of noncategorical or generic option for certification. In 2002, more than 40 jurisdictions offered some form of noncategorical or generic licensure option in special education.

Since the implementation of P.L. 94–142, "a substantial majority of jurisdictions have adopted licensure structures that include a mixture of categorical and noncategorical licensure options" (Geiger, 2002. p. 21). One explanation for the growth of noncategorical licensure options is that they may provide states and local education agencies with flexibility needed to address chronic shortages of special education teachers. At the beginning of the 21st century, some form of noncategorical special education licensure was the most popular. This conclusion is based on the fact that more than 80% of the degrees awarded in special education were in some form of *general* special education (Mainzer & Horvath, 2001).

Age/Grade Levels of Special Education Licensure

In special education, patterns of licensure vary not only by area/title but also by age/grade levels. Although comprehensive licenses (e.g., K–12) in special education are by far the most common options, some states also offer more restrictive age/grade options.

In the late 1970s, a substantial majority of states had a K–12 or P–12 model of special education licensure. Only 10 states had more restrictive age/grade ranges, e.g., elementary or secondary (Gilmore & Aroyros, 1977).

Putnam and Habanek (1993), in an article on licensure requirements for teachers of students with mild disabilities, reported 11 different age ranges for special education licensure in the 48 states that provided information on this aspect of licensure. The most common age range was K–12. Thirty-one states offered this option, and two more offered grades 1–12. Thirteen states had some grade range for licensure in elementary special education, and a few had middle-grades licensure for special educators. Five states reported secondary licensure that included middle grades, and nine states offered secondary special education licensure options that did not include the middle grades. It is no wonder that Putnam and Habanek included "States of Confusion" in the title of their article.

A few years later, Steffens (1996) reported that some version of a comprehensive age/grade range for special education licensure was in place in more than 60% of the states. In addition 20% of the states offered some version of elementary, middle, or secondary special education licenses, and some states offered options for both comprehensive (e.g., K–12 licenses) and more restricted age/grade licenses in special education (e.g., elementary). At the beginning of the 21st century approximately two thirds of the states offered only comprehensive (e.g., K–12) options for licensure in special education. The other one third offered a mixture that included both comprehensive licenses and age/grade specific options (Geiger, 2002).

Licensure for Secondary Special Educators and Transition Personnel

One age/grade level that has been examined over time is the licensure of secondary special education teachers. In 1973, prior to the passage of P.L. 94–142, Clark and Oliverson conducted a study of the preparation of special education personnel for secondary schools. In one facet of the study, they reported that 14 of the 47 states that responded had 6–12 licensure for secondary and special education, eight states have 6–12 special education licensure only, and seven states had special education 9–12 only. (It was not clear from the manner in which the results were reported whether a single state reported multiple options.) In 1977, Gilmore and Aroyros identified 10 states that had licensure options for secondary special education teachers. There were a few studies in the 1980s that addressed the matter of licensure models for secondary special education teachers. One of these (Bagwell, 1982) focused on teachers of students with learning disabilities and reported that seven states had different requirements for elementary and secondary teachers of students with learning disabilities. In a second study, Fearn (1987) reported that 21 states had some form of secondary special education licensure.

In 1990, the reauthorization of P.L. 94–142, IDEA, included requirements for transition planning for adolescents with disabilities. This requirement contained expectations for special education in secondary schools. A few years after federal legislation mandated transition services in secondary schools, Putnam and Habanek (1993) reported that the most prevalent age range pattern for special education licensure for secondary special educators was K–12. Only nine states had special education licensure options uniquely focused on secondary special education teachers.

In 2003, Kleinhammer-Tramill, Geiger, and Morningstar examined licensure patterns across all states for evidence of special education-relevant vocational education, secondary special education, and transition licenses. At that time, states' licensure systems included the following opportunities for a transition or secondary education credential relevant for personnel who served students with disabilities:

1. Twelve states had licensure or endorsement options of some form for Transition Specialists, Vocational Special Needs, Vocational Education, or Rehabilitation Counselors focused on special education transition.
2. Three states offered Career Technical Education, Adult Education, and Vocational Education credentials that required special education content preparation.
3. Twenty states listed special educator credentials focused on adolescents and/or secondary education services.
4. Four states had licensure options for Transition Specialists, Vocational or Rehabilitation personnel, and Adolescent/Secondary Special Education.
5. Overall, an unduplicated total of 31 states had licensure structures that allowed for specialization in secondary special education, transition, and/or special education-related vocational or adult education.

The authors also examined state licensure systems for evidence of transition-relevant content requirements such as competencies, standards, or required courses. The findings from this second analysis indicated that 35 states, or 70% of all state licensure systems, had some transition-relevant competencies or required courses. However, in some of these states, transition-relevant competencies or courses were included only for certain disability categories (e.g., vision impairment) but not for others.

Licensure in Early Childhood Special Education (ECSE)

Licensure for special education personnel who work with young children with disabilities has been studied more extensively than has licensure for special education personnel who work with adolescents with disabilities. In this section, we present a historical overview of the development of early childhood special education (ECSE) licensure, discuss the complex context of ECSE including the variety of professional roles and settings in which ECSE is provided, and examine patterns of licensure for ECSE teachers that prepare them for these roles and settings in which they will work. Patterns of ECSE licensure are influenced by many factors including degree and other educational requirements, variations in age/grade range, independence from or linkage to other licenses or areas of licensure, and the extent to which models are standards-based/competency-based. Finally the influence of federal policies and regulations on early childhood special education are discussed.

Development of Early Childhood Special Education

When P.L. 94–142, The Education for all Handicapped Children Act (EHA) was enacted in 1975, the right to a Free and Appropriate Public Education (FAPE) for children with disabilities age 3 to 21 years was established. However, the law did not require a FAPE for 3- to 5-year-olds when such a requirement was inconsistent with state law or practice. Also, the EHA did not include provisions related to special education services for children with disabilities under the age of 3. Accordingly, special education licensure for professionals working with young children was not a high priority when the law was first enacted.

In 1986, the EHA was amended by P.L. 99–457, and Section 619 of Part B extended FAPE to all children with disabilities ages 3 through 5. The 1986 amendments also extended provisions to infants and toddlers under what was then Part H of the Act (Saunders, 1995). In addition, states had the option to serve infants and toddlers found to be at-risk for substantial developmental delay. In 1990, further amendments to EHA renamed the legislation as the Individuals with Disabilities Education Act (IDEA), and Part H was reassigned as Part C.

The number of states offering licensure specific to ECSE dramatically increased after 1986. This increase is evident through an historical review of ECSE licensure. In 1980, Trohanis et al. reported that only four states offered licensure in the area of ECSE, and eight more were moving toward putting ECSE licensure structures in place. In 2002, Geiger reported that 80% of 51 states offered licensure in ECSE. Additionally, two states indicated that a credential would be added in the near future. During the two decades that separated these studies, more than 70% of the states created models for licensing early childhood special educators.

Variety of Roles and Settings for Early Childhood Special Education

Within the 1986 amendments to EHA, a family-centered, interdisciplinary, and collaborative framework of services emerged and defined the nature of early childhood services (Klein & Gilkerson, 2000). With that framework came recommendations for personnel preparation and, in turn, the need to credential professionals who would constitute the early childhood special education/early intervention professional community. Twelve professional roles were identified within the Part C early intervention context (Moherek Sopko, 2010). These were: early intervention specialist/developmental specialist/infant toddler specialist; occupational therapist; physical therapist; nurse; speech language pathologist; paraprofessional; audiologist; nutritionist; social worker; counselor; psychologist; and service coordinator.

Many of these same professional roles are involved in the provision of services under Section 619 of Part B in preschool settings.

The physical settings that house ECSE are also highly variable. Kagan, Kauerz, and Tarrant (2008) described the diverse contexts for delivering ECSE services. Among these contexts are private childcare centers, home-based centers, Head Start, state-funded pre-K, and public school early childhood programs. These settings are host to a variety of licensed and nonlicensed professionals, such as early childhood educators, childcare providers, and Head Start staff.

Although this chapter focuses on licensure patterns for special education and will not explore licensure for other professional roles in depth, the brief preceding discussion illustrates the complexity of the context for which early childhood special educators are prepared. Given this context, it is not surprising that great dissimilarity is observed among the states in terms of licensure patterns for ECSE professionals.

Degree and Other Educational Requirements for ECSE Teachers

The educational requirements of states vary widely regarding expectations for providers of early intervention services and early childhood special education personnel. A majority of the states (73%) require Part C early interventionists (early childhood special educators or equivalent instructional personnel) to possess a bachelor degree (Moherek Sopko, 2010). However, only 39% require state licensure, and 9.8% report no requirements at all. Table 3.1 displays degree and licensure requirements for early interventionists (Part C) as reported by Moherek Sopko in 2010.

Table 3.1 Percentage of Responding States[1] and Requirements for Early Interventionists

Associate's degree	*Bachelor's degree*	*Master's degree*	*Professional association certification*	*Additional knowledge and skills specific to EI*	*State licensure*	*No requirement*	*Other*
9.8	73.2	26.8	7.3	46.3	39.0	9.8	43.9

Source: Moherek Sopko, 2010, pp. 2–3.

Note

1 States may have more than one requirement. Therefore, a state may be reported in more than one category in the table.

Similar variation in preparatory requirements has also been reported for Part B contexts. Numerous preschool settings across the states do not require early childhood staff to have college degrees or specific licensure (Stayton et al., 2009). Saracho and Spodek (2006) detail the range of professional requirements for early childhood educators across preschool settings. Public school ECSE teachers in all early childhood programs in all 50 states are required to have at least a bachelor's degree and a state teacher's license. State-funded pre-K programs were reported to have requirements ranging from 24 credit hours to a bachelor's degree with a specific early childhood education endorsement.

Age/Grade Variations of Licensure Applicability

Another aspect of variability within ECSE licensure is the age or grade range to which licenses apply. At least 12 different licensure configurations based on age spans were identified in 1999 by Ratcliff, Cruz, and McCarthy. In 2003, Geiger, Crutchfield, and Mainzer examined states that offered ECSE licensure and highlighted variability across states in terms of age/grade levels. Recently, Lazara et al. (2010) found that licensure requirements for ECSE preschool teachers in 36 states consisted of 13 different age ranges. The range of birth to 5 years was found to be the most prevalent. Ranges of birth to grade 3, birth to kindergarten, and 3 to 5 years were also common. In 2009, Stayton et al. surveyed preschool special education coordinators (Part B 619 of IDEA) in all 50 states, the District of Columbia, and US territories. Their findings are consistent with previous studies (Lazara et al., 2010; Geiger, 2002; Ratcliff, Cruz, & McCarthy, 1999). That is, ECSE licensure requirements vary greatly across states regarding age/grade ranges and the model of licensure. Stayton et al. (2009) identified 11 different age ranges. The most common configurations were birth–5 years (30%), birth–8 years (19%), 3–5 years (15%), and 3 years to grade 12 (8%). The remaining seven configurations are used in only one state each (Stayton et al., 2009).

Freestanding, Add-On, Blended, and Other Models of Licensure

The ECSE licensure landscape is also highly variable regarding the overall design of licensure models for early child special educators. In the Stayton et al. (2009) study, 68% of the Part B 619 coordinators, in response to a question about models of licensure, indicated that there was only one route to ECSE licensure in their state. However, the single routes reflected six different models. These models were: ECSE ($n = 13$, 50%); ECSE endorsement added onto special education or regular education license ($n = 6$, 23.07%); blended ECE and ECSE license ($n = 3$, 11.54%); special education license ($n = 2$, 7.69%); both ECSE and special education endorsement ($n = 1$, 3.85%); and both ECE and special education endorsement ($n = 1$, 3.85%). Twelve states reported having two or more routes to qualify to teach young children with special needs. One state coordinator reported that six different routes to licensure were available.

Licensure Based on Standards or Competencies

Stayton et al. (2009) also investigated whether ECSE licensure guidelines were based on standards/competencies. Twenty-nine (76%) of the 38 states that participated in the study had licensure requirements that were standards/competency-based. Three states had semester or quarter hour requirements for designated content areas, three had specific content requirements and deferred to colleges/universities on how to address these requirements, and three offered options that included standards/competencies among others (Stayton et al., 2009).

Influence of Federal Policy and Regulation

There is no apparent consistency across states' licensure models for early childhood special education teachers and early interventionists. One reason for the variability in ECSE licensing is the fact that IDEA gives states the responsibility to determine requirements for early childhood special educators. IDEA also stipulates that states are responsible for determining licensure requirements for early childhood special educators under Part B, Section 619. In addition to licensure requirements, the 2006 Part B Regulations of IDEIA stipulate that teachers in early childhood or preschool programs that are part of a public school system must meet the highly qualified special education teacher requirements under NCLB (Stayton et al., 2009; Walsh, 2006).

Federal policies have attempted to address teacher qualifications for some ECE settings (Stayton et al., 2009). For example, changes in Head Start teacher requirements reflect the value placed upon teacher education (Blank, 2010). As of October 1, 2011, all Head Start classrooms were required to have a teacher who has an associate, baccalaureate, or advanced degree in early childhood education or an equivalent discipline (Administration for Children and Families, 2008). However, this requirement will have minimal impact on much of the variability that exists in licensure requirements for early childhood special educators.

The National Association for the Education of Young Children (NAEYC) and the Division for Early Childhood of the Council for Exceptional Children (DEC/CEC) have called for the development of freestanding licensure with common standards for all educators (special and general education) working with children birth to 8 years of age to encourage reciprocity across states (Stayton et al., 2009; Hyson, 2003; Sandall, McLean, & Smith, 2000). Within the birth-to-8 age span, there are three distinct age groups: infant/toddler, preschool, and primary. Preparation in two contiguous age groups is recommended by these organizations. NAEYC and DEC are not alone in recommending common standards for all early childhood educators. As reported in Stayton et al. (2009), other organizations, including the Association for Childhood Education International, the National Association of State Boards of Education, and the American Federation of Teachers have issued recommendations for uniform and distinct early childhood licensure. These recommendations are fairly consistent regarding content requirements for ECE and ECSE licensure. Until these or similar recommendations are adopted by states throughout the nation, inconsistency will prevail as a hallmark of licensure for early childhood education personnel.

Licensure of Special Education Teachers and the *Highly Qualified Teacher* Requirement

Previously in the chapter, reference was made to a federal requirement for highly qualified teachers. In 2001, President George W. Bush signed NCLB into law. The regulations for this piece of federal legislation defined a highly qualified (HQ) teacher. In 2004, President Bush reauthorized the IDEIA. This reauthorization contained definitions for HQ special education teachers aligned with NCLB (U.S. Department of Education, 2006). In the reauthorized IDEA, provisions to meet the "highly qualified" standard were made for new special education teachers, for those who were teaching children with disabilities working toward alternative achievement standards, and for those who were teaching multiple subjects to children with disabilities.

At a minimum new special education teachers are required to have a bachelor's degree, have completed requirements for state licensure in special education, or be enrolled in an alternative certification program for special education that meets the state requirements. Teachers may not have special education certification or licensure requirements waived on a temporary, emergency, or provisional basis (34 CFR 300.18(b)(1)).

Although full state licensure is required to be a HQ special education teacher under the regulations for IDEA, a fully licensed special education teacher may not be a HQ special education teacher unless he/she has met the core subject requirements expected for the teaching assignment. It is reasonable to expect that the core subject requirements in the HQ definition have significantly impacted preparation and licensing.

A special education teacher who teaches a core academic subject must demonstrate subject area competency commensurate with the grade level they teach. This competence can be demonstrated in a variety of ways determined by the state. Special education teachers who teach a core academic subject only to children assessed on alternate achievement standards (i.e., children who are not expected to meet grade-level standards even when provided with the best instruction) must meet the general requirements for being a licensed special education teacher and the standards set for HQ elementary school teachers. In cases where a special education teacher is teaching to alternative standards, but a student needs instruction above the elementary school level (e.g., a high school student performs at the seventh grade level in mathematics, but not as high in any other subject area), the special education teacher would need to demonstrate competence in the subject area to the grade level needed to teach effectively to those standards. These changes place new emphasis on subject-matter preparation where the historical emphasis has been on pedagogy.

To help address the need, the Office of Special Education Programs (OSEP) has competitively funded IHEs to redesign special education preparation programs so graduates will be prepared to meet the HQ requirements and to meet the needs of students with high-incidence disabilities. At present 65

IHEs have been awarded 325T grants to improve their special education teacher preparation (National Center to Inform Policy and Practice in Special Education Professional Development, 2012).

High Objective Uniform State Standard of Evaluation (HOUSSE)

Regulations for HQ special education teachers allow states to build multiple pathways to determining a teacher is HQ. States may use content-knowledge assessments; a content-area major, graduate degree, or licensure; or a High Objective Uniform State Standard of Evaluation (HOUSSE) (IDEA, 2004). This flexibility allows states to determine if teachers can meet the definition of HQ in all core areas through one streamlined process (i.e., multisubject HOUSSE) or by completion of several objective measures of core content knowledge in one content area (i.e., single-subject HOUSSE) (Burdette, Laflin, & Muller, 2005). While new special educators must meet HQ special education licensure requirements as well as content requirements in one subject area for initial licensure, single or multisubject HOUSSEs may be used for (a) new special educators who need HQ status for multiple subject areas, provided they are already HQ in one subject area; or (b) experienced special educators hired prior to 2002 who are not HQ in one or more subject areas. This flexibility is particularly pertinent to special educators providing direct instruction in secondary school core content areas assessed at standard levels, and the multisubject HOUSSEs were developed to address both general and special educators teaching in multiple content areas.

Most states' HOUSSE mechanisms use a combination of classroom experience, professional development, and demonstrated knowledge in the content area (Burdette, Laflin, & Muller, 2005). A survey of state-level officials identified course work and course credits as valid and objective indicators of content knowledge and valued them over measures such as professional development workshops and awards (Drame & Pugach, 2010). Concerns over state HOUSSE's rigor and varying procedures have led some educational experts to question HOUSSE assessment validity and reliability (Government Accountability Office, 2005); and some state officials have admitted that special education HOUSSEs typically require fewer content courses that general education HOUSSEs (Drame & Pugach, 2010). However, the majority of state officials indicated that the phase-out of HOUSSE requirements would be detrimental to their state's abilities to meet special education HQ content-area requirements.

Introduction by the federal government of the HQ requirement for special education teachers at the beginning of the 21st century added to the complexity of the crazy quilt of standards and patterns for licensure of special education teachers that already existed in the United States. As a result of the 2004 reauthorization of IDEA, special education teachers must not only meet the licensure standards adopted by the state in which they teach but must also be judged to be highly qualified for the specifics of their teaching assignments.

Summary and Suggestions for Future Research

Licensure is a mechanism by which states assure the quality of teachers. In the public school sector of the United States, responsibility for the assurance of teacher quality has shifted during the last two centuries from immediate employers to state agencies. In the early 21st century, the federal government became involved in quality assurance through NCLB and IDEIA.

States have adopted many patterns of licensure for special educators. In order to study these patterns, core elements or dimensions of licensure have been identified. These dimensions include course- or credit-hour-based and competency-based state standards, freestanding/stand alone special education licenses and models that require adding a license in special education to one in general education or being prepared concurrently for both, areas/titles of licenses, and age/grade ranges for licenses. With regard to the latter dimension, great variability exists even within subsets of ages/grades, such as licenses for secondary and transition personnel and for personnel in preschool special education programs (Section 619) and early intervention programs (Part C).

With the exception of a few studies of patterns of licensure for early childhood special educators, most research on patterns of special education licensure predates the 2004 reauthorization of IDEA, P.L. 108–466, which contained a provision for highly qualified special education teachers. In order to deliver direct initial instruction in a core content area, the special educator is required to demonstrate content knowledge of that subject (e.g., mathematics). Since that requirement was mandated, there have been no studies of patterns of licensure for special education teachers in the elementary and secondary grades. The impact of the highly qualified teacher provision in P.L.108–466 (and in NCLB) on patterns of licensure for special education teachers remains unknown and is an important area for future investigation.

Future research efforts should follow current trends that include dual-enrollment programs (i.e., elementary education or core content plus special education), alternative certification, and programs developed to meet HOUSSE requirements. However, large-scale, national studies on these topics are limited by current state and national data collection systems. First, the current HQT data systems do not appear to be accurate (Steinbrecher, McKeown, & Walther-Thomas, in press). In addition, critical discrepancies exist across national data sets due to inconsistencies among data sources, missing data points, and definitions of HQT. Second, the current HQT data collection systems do not distinguish between teachers who are licensed through traditional or alternate routes: both groups are considered highly qualified.

There is also little research on how HQT requirements have impacted the requirements in traditional university-based special education licensing programs. There is little understanding whether programs have added core content requirements to build candidates' knowledge base, whether more states have adopted licensure models that require licensure in general education prior to or concurrent with licensure in special education as a means of assuring required content knowledge, whether more programs are moving from special education licensing at the bachelors' level to special educator licensing at the masters' level to accommodate the new content knowledge focus, or if more states are moving toward distinct elementary and secondary special education credentials to accommodate the HQ content requirements for endorsements (e.g., requirements for a K–6 math endorsement may be different than requirements for 7–12 math endorsement).

In addition, there is little research on the effects of HQT on special educator attrition or service delivery. One potential impact of the HQT requirement in secondary schools is an increase in co-teaching to serve students with disabilities in content classes. There is little research to verify whether the HQT requirement has had this impact, whether this has resulted in additional professional development and state funding support for implementing a co-teaching model, and most importantly the effect of these changes on outcomes for students with disabilities. While many states now recommend the use of co-teaching in secondary content areas to enable special educators to meet HQT requirements, the capacity (e.g., co-teaching knowledge, special educators, funding) to support increases in this service delivery model is questionable. Finally, is special education service delivery still based on the student's least restrictive environment (LRE) or is it now a combination of student LRE and their assigned special educator HQT qualifications? That is, are students being assigned to certain placements despite the recommendations of the Individualized Education Program team, because their special educator is not highly qualified in that subject? These questions as well as others remain unanswered as we move forward with the implementation of the HQT requirements in the 2004 reauthorization of IDEA.

Significant variance in patterns of special education licensure has been observed for decades. However, there are few attempts to systematically study the impact of different patterns of licensure for special educators on how well special educators are prepared, and the resulting effects on the performance of the students they teach. Until such research is conducted and certain patterns are determined to be more conducive to preparation that results in effective instruction and learning gains by students with disabilities, there is little reason (other than possibly supply and demand) to expect that states will consider adopting more common patterns of licensure for special educators.

Licensure is intended to assure the quality of individuals hired to teach. Effective teaching should promote learning gains by students. At this stage in the evolution of licensure for special education teachers, it cannot be said that any pattern or patterns of special education licensure results in a more effective special education teacher and increased learning by the children they teach.

Notes

1 In this chapter a teaching license and a teaching certificate are considered to be interchangeable.
2 In this chapter "state" is used to represent states or comparable jurisdictions that award teaching licenses/certificates.

References

34 CFR Parts 300 and 301, Final Rule. (2006.) *Highly Qualified Special Education Teachers* (§ 300.15). Discussion to Comment #19 regarding roles and responsibilities of special education teachers who do not teach core academic subjects. P. 46557, column 3. Retrieved from http://idea.ed.gov/download/finalregulations.pdf

Abeson, A., & Fleury, J. B. (1972). *State certification requirements for education of the handicapped.* Arlington, VA: State-Federal Information Clearinghouse for Exceptional Children. (ERIC Document Reproduction Service No. ED 069 063)

Administration for Children and Families, Office of Head Start. (2008). *Information memorandum: Statutory degree and credentialing requirements for Head Start teaching staff.* IM 08-12. Retrieved from http://eclkc.ohs.acf.hhs.gov/hslc/standards/IMs/2008/resour_ime_012_0081908.html

Angus, D. L. (2001). *Professionalism and the public schools: A brief history of teacher certification.* Washington, DC: Thomas B. Fordham Foundation. (ERIC Document Reproduction Service No ED 449 149)

Bagwell, I. (1982). Certification requirements for secondary learning disabilities teachers. *Teacher Education, 5*(4), 56–60. doi:10.1177/088840648200500409

Barresi, J., & Bunte, J. (1979). *Special education certification practices: A summary of a national survey.* Reston, VA: Council for Exceptional Children. (ERIC Document Reproduction Service No. ED 189 800)

Berkeley, T. R. (1990). *Special education certification survey of the states.* Reston, VA: National Clearinghouse for Professions in Special Education. (ERIC Document Reproduction Service No. ED 354640)

Blank, J. (2010). Early childhood teacher education: Historical themes and contemporary issues. *Journal of Early Childhood Teacher Education, 31*, 391–405. doi:10.1080/10901027.2010.523772

Burdette, P., Laflin, B., & Muller, E. (2005, December). HOUSSE: State approaches to supporting special educators to become "Highly Qualified." *inForum*, 1–9. Retrieved from http://www.nasdse.org/publications-t577/housse-state-approaches-to-supporting-special-educ.aspx

Chapey, G. D., Pyszkowski, I. S., & Trimarco, T. A. (1985) National trends for certification and training of special education teachers. *Teacher Education and Special Education, 8*, 203–208. doi:10.1177/088840648500800405

Clark, G. M., & Oliverson, B. S. (1973). Education of secondary personnel: Assumptions and preliminary data. *Exceptional Children, 39*, 541–546.

Drame, E. R., & Pugach, M. C. (2010). A HOUSSE built on quicksand? Exploring the teacher quality conundrum for special education teachers. *Teacher Education and Special Education, 33*, 55–69. doi:10.1177/0888406409356402

Fearn, K. M. (1987). *Report on the status of certification of special educators in the united states and territories.* Reston, VA: The Council for Exceptional Children.

Geiger, W. L. (2002). *Requirements for conventional licensure of special education teachers.* Arlington, VA: ERIC Clearinghouse on Disabilities and Gifted Education. (ERIC Document Reproduction Service No. 460–563)

Geiger, W. L., Crutchfield, M. D., & Mainzer, R. (2003). *The status of licensure of special education teachers in the 21st century* (COPSSE Document No. RS-7). Gainesville, FL: University of Florida, Center on Personnel Studies in Special Education. U.S. Office of Special Education Programs. Retrieved from http://copsse.education.ufl.edu/copsse/docs/RS-7/1/RS-7.pdf

Gilmore, J. T., & Aroyros, N. S. (1977). *Special education certification: A state of the art survey.* Albany, NY: New York State Education Department. (ERIC Document Reproduction Service No. ED 158 447)

Government Accountability Office. (2005). *No Child Left Behind Act: Improved accessibility to education's information could help states further implement teacher qualification requirements* (No. GAO-06-25). Washington, DC: Author. Retrieved from http://www.gao.gov/assets/250/248606.pdf

Hyson, M. (2003). *Preparing early childhood professionals: NAEYC's standards for programs.* Washington, DC: National Association for the Education of Young Children.

Individuals with Disabilities Education Improvement Act of 2004, Pub. L. No. 108–446 (2004).

Kagan, S. L., Kauerz, K., Tarrant, K. (2008). *The early care and education teaching workforce at the fulcrum: An agenda for reform*. New York, NY: Teachers College Press.

Klein, N. K., & Gilkerson, L. (2000). Personnel preparation for early childhood intervention programs. In J. P. Shonkoff & S. J. Meisels (Eds.), *The handbook of early childhood intervention* (2nd ed., pp. 454–484). New York, NY: Cambridge University Press. http://dx.doi.org/10.1017/CBO9780511529320.023

Kleinhammer-Tramill, P. J., Geiger, W., & Morningstar, P. (2003). Policy contexts for transition personnel preparation: An analysis of transition-related credentials, standards, and course requirements in state certification and licensure policies. *Career Development for Exceptional Individuals, 26*, 185–206. doi:10.1177/088572880302600206

Lazara, A., Danaher, J., Kraus, R., Goode, S., Hipps, C. & Festa, C. (Eds.). (2010). *Section 619 profile* (17th ed.). Chapel Hill: The University of North Carolina, FPG Child Development Institute, National Early Childhood Technical Assistance Center.

Mackey, C., & McHenry, V. (1994). *The history of NASDTEC*. Seattle, WA: The National Association of State Directors of Teacher Education and Certification.

Mackie, R. P., & Dunn, L. M. (1954). *State certification requirements for teachers of exceptional children*. Washington, DC: U. S. Department of Health, Education and Welfare. United States Government Printing Office. Bulletin 1954, N. 1.

Mainzer, R., & Horvath, M. (2001). *Issues in preparing and licensing special educators*. Arlington, VA: The Council for Exceptional Children.

McLaughlin, M., Smith-Davis, J., & Burke, P. (1986). *Personnel to educate the handicapped in America: A status report*. College Park, MD: University of Maryland. (ERIC Document Reproduction Service No. ED 305 81)

McLaughlin, M. J., & Stettner-Eaton, B. (1988). *Categorical certification in special education: Does it really make a difference? Policy issues*. Charleston, WV: Appalachia Educational Laboratory. (ERIC Document Reproduction Service No. ED 311 643)

Moherek Sopko, K. (2010, March). Workforce preparation to serve children who receive Part C services. *inForum*, 1–7. Retrieved from http://www.nasdse.org/publications-t577/workforce-preparation-to-serve-children-who-receiv.aspx

National Association of State Directors of Special Education. (1990). *National, regional, and state accreditation and certification standards for special education and related services personnel: A summary*. Washington, DC: Author. (ERIC Document Reproduction Service No. ED 354644)

National Association of State Directors of Teacher Education and Certification. (2000). *The NASDTEC manual on the preparation and certification of educational personnel* (5th ed.). Dubuque, IA: Kendall/Hunt.

National Center to Inform Policy and Practice in Special Education Professional Development. (2012). *About NCIPP*. Retreived from http://ncipp.education.ufl.edu/

Piercy, S. W., & Bowen, M. L. (1993). *Current and projected practices for certification and monitoring of personnel needs in special education*. Normal, IL: Illinois State University. (ERIC Document Reproduction Service No. ED 366 150)

Putnam, M. L., & Habanek, D. V. (1993). A national survey of certification requirements for teachers of students with mild handicaps: State of confusion. *Teacher Education and Special Education, 16*, 155–160. doi:10.1177/088840649301600207

Ratcliff, N., Cruz, J., & McCarthy, J. (1999). *Early childhood teacher certification licensure patterns and curriculum guidelines: A state-by-state analysis*. Washington, DC: Council for Professional Recognition.

Sandall, S., McLean, M. E., & Smith, B. J. (2000). *DEC recommended practices in early intervention/early childhood special education*. Longmont, CO: Sopris West.

Saracho, O., & Spodek, B. (2006). Preschool teachers' professional development. In B. Spodek & O. Saracho (Eds.), *Handbook of research on the education of young children* (2nd ed., pp. 423–439). Mahwah, NJ: Lawrence Erlbaum.

Saunders, E. J. (1995). Services to infants and toddlers with disabilities: IDEA, Part H. *Health & Social Work, 20*, 39–45.

Sedlak, M. W. (1989). "Let Us Go and Buy a School Master": Historical perspectives on the hiring of teachers in the United States, 1750–1980. In D. Warren (Ed.), *American teachers: History of a profession at work* (pp. 257–290). Washington, DC: American Educational Research Association.

Stayton, V. D., Dietrich, S. L., Smith, B. J., Bruder, M. B., Mogro-Wilson, C., & Swigart, A. (2009). State certification requirements for early childhood special educators. *Infants & Young Children, 22*, 4–12. doi:10.1097/01.IYC.0000343332.42151.cd

Steffens, S. (1996). A comparative analysis of state special education certification for working with students with disabilities: Certification practices and teacher competence. (Unpublished manuscript) Department of Professional Education, Northwest Missouri State University, Maryville, MO.

Steinbrecher, T. D., McKeown, D., & Walther-Thomas, C. (2013). Comparing Validity and Reliability in Special Education Title II and IDEA Data. *Exceptional Children, 79*(3), 313–327.

Teacher Tools and Advice. (2011). FAQs attaining your teaching certificate. Retrieved from http://www.teacherssupportnetwork.com/guest/FAQ.do

Trohanis, P., Barker, M., Button, J., Hazen, S., Jackson, E., Karp, J., & Rostetter, D. (1980). *The State Implementation Grant (SIG) Program: Three years in perspective.* Chapel Hill, NC: The University of North Carolina. (ERIC Document Reproduction Service No. ED 193 875)

U.S. Department of Education, Office of Special Education Programs. (2006). *IDEA regulations, highly qualified teachers.* Retrieved from http://idea.ed.gov/explore/view/p/%2Croot%2Cdynamic%2CTopicalBrief%2C20%2C

Walsh, S. (2006). *IDEA 2004 regulations: Implementation guidance for preschool special education.* Teleconference presentation. Washington, DC: Division for Early Childhood.

Yell, M. (2012). *The law and special education.* New York, NY: Pearson.

4

Preparing Teachers to Work With Students With Disabilitiess

An International Perspective

Lani Florian

UNIVERSITY OF EDINBURGH

Things to Think About

- One of the greatest challenges for teacher education is posed by the demands of "Education for All" (EFA), the international movement to ensure access to basic education for every boy and girl by 2015.
- Of the 75 million children in the world who do not have access to education, UNESCO estimates that over one third are children with disabilities.
- Article 24 of the UN Convention on the Rights of Persons with Disabilities (UNCRPD) specifies that persons with disabilities should have equal access to education.
- In the UNCRPD and other international policy documents, the ideals of EFA are widely promoted but they have proved difficult to implement, particularly with regard to the education of students with disabilities, which requires high quality teacher preparation that is not universally accessible, nor standardized across the developed and developing world.
- There are also diverging theories on how best to include students with disabilities in classrooms around the world. Inclusive education, from an international perspective, is grounded in social justice and human rights, and promotes the inclusion of all students, including students from diverse racial, cultural, and linguistic backgrounds, by removing barriers to learning and participation.
- The extent to which special education provision in different parts of the world supports or hinders inclusive education varies widely and is also the subject of debate.
- UNESCO Global Monitoring Reports, and the international literature provide an overview of the global disparities in educational provision for students with disabilities, and differences in approaches to teacher education and teacher qualifications in different regions of the world.
- The challenge for teacher education is to prepare teachers who can respond when students encounter barriers to learning because in all countries there are students who are identified as having additional needs.

Introduction

In the international community today, concern for the education of students with disabilities has been linked with the "Education for All" (EFA) movement, which was launched in 1990 at the World Conference on Education for All in Jomtien, Thailand (see Appendix 1 to this chapter). At this time, delegates from more than 150 countries reaffirmed the long-standing idea of education as a human right (see Appendix 1), and urged all countries to provide for the basic learning needs of all people by the year 2000. Ten years after the Jomtien Conference, at a meeting in Dakar, Senegal, this goal was extended to 2015. In an effort to improve the rate of progress and government accountability toward meeting this goal, the annual Global Monitoring Report (GMR), published by the United Nations Education Scientific and Cultural Organization (UNESCO), has established a reference for tracking the progress toward EFA, including the latest available statistics in eight world regions: sub-Saharan Africa; Arab States; Central Asia; East Asia and Pacific; South and West Asia; Latin America and Caribbean; North America and Western Europe; and Central and Eastern Europe.

While the policy documents, goals, and targets associated with the early EFA efforts did not specifically call attention to the education of students with disabilities, a concurrent international effort coordinated by UNESCO launched at the 1994 World Conference on Special Needs Education in Salamanca, Spain, linked the education of students with disabilities to the EFA agenda by recognizing that all children should be educated within an inclusive education system and stipulating that "a child with a disability should attend the neighborhood school that would be attended if the child did not have a disability" (UNESCO, 1994, p. 17). Subsequently, the idea of *all* children being educated together in an inclusive educational system was adopted in Dakar as a strategy to achieve EFA. In this way, the conceptualization of inclusive education was broadened beyond the education of students with disabilities to encompass Roma children, street children, child workers, child soldiers, and children from indigenous and nomadic groups—in other words, anyone who might be excluded from or have limited access to the general educational system within a country. At the same time, the rights of children with disabilities to have access to and to participate in a country's general education system became firmly established as part of the EFA agenda. This was a significant development because the legislative framework in some countries specifically excludes or restricts access for children with disabilities to the general education system even where education is compulsory and free such as in the countries of the former Soviet Union (UNICEF, 2005). Consequently, the processes of inclusive education are seen to be of particular relevance and importance in creating educational opportunities for students with disabilities; however, because this approach to EFA focuses on reducing barriers to participation in education for marginalized individuals and groups within the regions of the world, inclusive education is defined and enacted in different ways in different areas depending on how schooling is organized and who has access to it (Ainscow & Miles, 2008).

As this chapter will discuss, children with disabilities are less likely than other children to attend school, participate fully in educational opportunities, or do well when they do attend. Efforts to improve access and quality of education receive a great deal of support from the international community. These efforts increasingly require teacher educators to engage with the dual challenges of achieving EFA and inclusive education and to consider common themes. This chapter introduces key issues concerning EFA and students with disabilities. It examines global disparities in educational provision, and teacher preparation quality and supply. The challenge for teacher education presented by the United Nations Convention on the Rights of Persons with Disabilities (UNCRPD) is discussed and some examples of teacher education initiatives in different parts of the world are provided.

Key Issues Relating to Students with Disabilities and Education for All

For the international agencies and nongovernmental organizations (NGOs) that support educational programs for children with disabilities, inclusive education is firmly associated with a human rights based approach to education (Rieser, 2012; UNICEF/UNESCO, 2007). Nonetheless, the historic legacy of exclusion in many regions means that children with disabilities are less likely to attend school than other children. In India, for example, 146.4 million children are of school age (UNESCO, 2005) but 4 million children remain out of school. As India struggles to make good on its legislative promise to provide compulsory education to all children (aged 6–14), it must be noted that fewer than 1% of children with disabilities are thought to be enrolled in school (Mukhopadhyay & Mani, 2002), suggesting that this group is overrepresented in exclusion statistics. The legacy of exclusion from education for children with disabilities is being tackled in India as elsewhere by the establishment of local NGOs, often founded by parents, such as the Spastics Society of India (Hegarty & Alur, 2002), and by international charities such as Save the Children, and World Vision to name but two.

Through linkages and collaborations with international NGOs, coalitions supporting rights-based approaches to education are formed and often become powerful advocacy forces working to overcome discrimination and break down barriers to participation by promoting positive images and messages about disability (Alur & Timmons, 2009; UNICEF, 2007). Such advocacy is an essential ingredient in establishing community-based services for children and families more broadly. It is of particular relevance in regions where families lack support and/or where traditional responses to disability involved lifelong care in large institutions such as "internatus" in the former Soviet Union (UNICEF, 2005).

Where children with disabilities do attend school, concerns that dealing with the difficulties some children experience in learning will interfere with the learning of nondisabled children reinforces negative attitudes and resistance by many teachers to accept responsibility for teaching students with disabilities. Moreover, negative attitudes about disability affect more than education. Writing about attitudes toward disability in the former Soviet Union, Djumagulova (2004) noted:

> Fear, taboo, shame, lack of knowledge, misinformation . . . all encourage negative attitudes towards disability. The impact of such attitudes is evident in the home, school, community, and at the level of national policy making in terms of planning, budgeting and programming. At the household level, children with special needs and their families often develop low self-esteem, hiding away and shunning social interaction, which can lead directly to their exclusion from education. . . . fearing for their safety, or for the respect and honor of the family, parents sometimes lock their children with special needs in the house when they have to go out, or hide them completely so that neighbors may not even know they exist.
>
> *(pp. 128–129)*

Such attitudes, which are apparent to varying degrees in all regions, present major challenges, not least of which is being able to obtain reliable data on the number of children living with disabilities. When parents are reluctant or unable to register the birth of a child, or hide them because of shame, they become invisible. From a rights-based perspective, underreporting of disability is a serious problem for school access because knowing the incidence of children with disabilities is essential to negotiating access for them (Riddell, 2008).

It is estimated that up to 150 million children worldwide have disabilities, with around four in five of these children living in developing countries (World Health Organization and World Bank, 2011). The extent of disability and its concentration in the world's poorest countries contribute significantly to marginalization in education. Children with disabilities are known to be underenrolled in school, as well as overrepresented in out of school statistics in many regions besides India (Peters, 2003; Rieser, 2012). In addition, other factors such as teacher supply, quality, preparation, qualifications, and professional learning opportunities in different regions of the world impact on inclusive education and present various and complex challenges for the education of students with disabilities.

Global Disparities in Educational Provision, Teacher Education, and Teacher Qualifications

Since the first GMR was published in 2002, each of the nine reports has focused on a different theme; for example, the 2006 report (UNESCO, 2006) addressed literacy, while the 2011 report addresses the consequences of armed conflict for education. The report of particular relevance to this chapter is the 2010 report on marginalization. This report elaborated on the finding of the 2009 report that "progress towards the EFA goals is being undermined by the failure of governments to tackle inequality based on income, gender, location, ethnicity, language, *disability* and other markers of disadvantage" (UNESCO, 2009, p. 4, emphasis added). The 2010 GMR extended the exploration of inequality by focusing on the institutional barriers to participation, the threats posed by the global financial crisis, and the forms of marginalization that keep children out of school.

Access to School

As noted above, for children with disabilities, poverty is a significant barrier to schooling. In regions of the world where education is not free, severe poverty means that many families cannot afford school fees, uniforms, or essential materials. In countries such as Cambodia where child labor is an important economic factor for many families, there is evidence that parents carry out a cost–benefit analysis before deciding whether the benefits of education outweigh the costs of sending their child to school (Kim & Rouse, 2011). For children with disabilities, this is unlikely to be the case: UNESCO (2007) estimates that only 2% of children with disabilities in developing countries go to school. Over the past decade there has been a growing recognition that poverty is both a cause and consequence of disability (Department for International Development, 2000). Being poor increases the risk of both congenital and acquired impairments, and having an impairment significantly reduces educational and employment opportunities for individuals with disabilities and their families, thereby increasing the family's level of poverty (Singal, 2007; Yeo & Moore, 2003). Even when the direct economic costs of attending school are removed, as with the abolition of school fees in some countries, the indirect costs such as uniforms and textbooks still have to be taken into account, and many families prioritize the education of boys at the expense of girls and children with disabilities (UNESCO, 2010). Moreover, as is the case with several countries in sub-Saharan Africa, namely Kenya, Ghana, Malawi, and Uganda, another unintended consequence of abolishing fees is overcrowded schools with far fewer resources than in the past when policies to increase universal primary education (UPE) were enacted (Nishimura & Byamugisha, 2011). Thus, decisions about schooling for families of students with disabilities is a complex issue, particularly when those families are also living in poverty.

Although globally comparable data are difficult to obtain, the 2010 GMR estimates there are about 70 million children out of school. While it is important to note that the overall number of children out of school shows a reduction from previous years, the estimate is based on school enrollment data as reported by schools via local education offices to ministries of education and does not capture data on those who may be enrolled but do not attend or have been excluded. In a study of nine developing countries (Burundi, Cambodia, Indonesia, Jamaica, Mongolia, Mozambique, Myanmar, Romania, and Sierra Leone), Filmer (2005) found that

> children with disabilities are less likely to start school, and in some countries have lower transition rates resulting in lower schooling attainment. The order of magnitude of the school participation

> for children with disabilities is often larger than those associated with other characteristics such as gender, rural residence, or economic status differentials.
>
> *(p. 15)*

As the GMRs have consistently documented, most of the world's children who do not attend school reside in South Asia and sub-Saharan Africa where there is a shortage of school places. However, the problem of insufficient school places is not restricted to these regions. Even where there are sufficient places at the national level there may be insufficient places at the regional and local level, especially in rural areas. In China, for example, there are concerns about not only the low enrollment rate for children with disabilities but also the uneven development of provision between urban and rural areas (Yu, Su, & Liu, 2011).

Student Performance and Teacher Quality

The 2010 GMR reports on the millions of children who are not acquiring basic literacy and numeracy skills and suggests that too many education systems are characterized by high levels of inequality, together with low levels of participation and learning, particularly for children with disabilities. It argues that student performance depends on an adequate supply of well-prepared teachers and reasonable pupil/teacher ratios. However, as the 2010 GMR documents, in regions where increasing school enrollments have outpaced teacher supply, class size is high, teachers are often not very well trained or experienced, and achievement gaps are wide. In commenting on why learning outcomes in the Latin American region lag behind the member countries of the OECD (Organisation for Economic Co-operation and Development), Vaillant (2011) noted, "Latin America has shifted from a situation of poor educational coverage and quality to one where coverage is broad, but quality is mediocre, and access is very uneven" (p. 387). Even in the developed world there are challenges in teacher supply and quality. In a review of the world's 25 best performing school systems, McKinsey and Company (2007) concluded that the quality of teachers was a main explanation for the variations in student performance at school.

Helping schools to improve performance of all students requires a strong focus on recruiting, training, deploying, and retaining high quality teachers. However, in countries where the teachers themselves are products of poor education systems and their professional training is meager, this is a tall order. In some countries, many teachers do not receive any initial training and may have only received a few years of secondary schooling. A recent evaluation in Mozambique found that 41% of primary school teachers were untrained (Mulkeen & Chen, 2008, cited in GMR, 2010), while a Green Paper on Teacher Education in Europe (Buchberger, Campos, Kallos, & Stephenson, 2000) found that although not all countries require that teachers be prepared at university level, some (such as Finland) require a master's degree.

Teacher Supply

The 2011 GMR reports that an additional 1.9 million teachers will have to be recruited to provide UPE by 2015. Two thirds of the additional teachers—around 1.2 million—will be needed in sub-Saharan Africa. In the Arab States, where birth rates are high, around 300,000 additional teachers will be required. As evidenced above, the scale of teacher recruitment varies enormously by region and is determined by many factors, including teachers' pay, conditions and status, attrition rates in the workforce, demographics, enrollment rates, and numbers of children still out of school. The above figures take into account recruitment of new teachers, but in addition to increasing recruitment to achieve UPE, governments have to replace teachers expected to retire or leave their posts before 2015. For every additional teacher required to achieve UPE, four more teachers are needed to replace the teachers who will retire or leave the teaching profession worldwide before 2015. Taking into account the need to replace teachers drives up the regional and global recruitment numbers to over 10 million (UNESCO, 2010). Clearly this is a major challenge that will exert pressure on existing systems of teacher education in many countries.

Global disparities in education are in part associated with differences in teacher qualifications and teacher education that exist in different parts of the world. The problem of teacher shortage in many countries puts particular pressures on national systems of teacher education, especially when comparing countries where teaching is a high status profession with good salaries to countries where teaching is a profession of extremely difficult circumstances and salaries are barely enough to subsist (UNICEF, 2005). Therefore, a model of teacher education that works well in Finland is not what is needed in Kenya. Yet little attention has been paid to issues of teacher preparation and development as part of the EFA agenda, other than to note the important disparities in teacher quality, qualifications, supply, and deployment. Reducing these disparities presents a huge challenge to the international community where there also is pressure to improve the quality of the teaching workforce within the financial constraints that many countries currently face. As the 2010 GMR points out,

> While a balance has to be struck between affordability and good teaching, the limits to cost-cutting also have to be recognized. Governments and donors need to ensure that teacher pay and conditions reflect a commitment to delivering good-quality education through a well-qualified and motivated workforce.
>
> *(UNESCO, 2010, p. 117)*

Implications for Teacher Education and Professional Learning

The 2010 GMR (UNESCO, 2010) points out that high quality initial training and professional development for teachers are crucial to effective teaching. The growing consensus that an adequate supply of quality teachers is essential to reducing the disparities in and access to high quality schooling has generated a new interest in the knowledge needed by teachers to be inclusive in their practice. In calling upon the international community "to adopt an inclusive education approach in the design, implementation, monitoring and assessment of educational policies as a way to further accelerate the attainment of EFA goals as well as to contribute to building more inclusive societies" (p. 3), the 48th International Conference on Education (ICE), *Inclusive Education: The Way of the Future* (UNESCO, 2008a), concluded with six recommendations specific to teacher education and development:

> 1 Reinforce the role of teachers by working to improve their status and their working conditions, and develop mechanisms for recruiting suitable candidates, and retain qualified teachers who are sensitive to different learning requirements.
> 2 Train teachers by equipping them with the appropriate skills and materials to teach diverse student populations and meet the diverse learning needs of different categories of learners through methods such as professional development at the school level, preservice training about inclusion, and instruction attentive to the development and strengths of the individual learner.
> 3 Support the strategic role of tertiary education in the pre-service and professional training of teachers on inclusive education practices through, inter alia, the provision of adequate resources.
> 4 Encourage innovative research in teaching and learning processes related to inclusive education.
> 5 Equip school administrators with the skills to respond effectively to the diverse needs of all learners and promote inclusive education in their schools.
> 6 Take into consideration the protection of learners, teachers, and schools in times of conflict.
>
> *(p. 5)*

These recommendations provide new impetus for improving the ways in which teachers are prepared to work with, and take responsibility for, all children. However, a recent review of international trends in teacher education reform efforts (Mitchell, 2010) found that while countries are undertaking reform of teacher education in alignment with the demands of inclusive education, there is considerable variability in how they are responding to initial teacher education, specialist qualifications, paraprofessional training, and continuing professional development. Rieser (2012) provided some examples of this variability by showcasing teacher education reform efforts in Scotland, Brunei, Samoa, and New Zealand that highlight different approaches to preparing classroom and specialist teachers.

The UNCRPD and the Challenge for Teacher Education

The United Nations Convention on the Rights of Persons with Disabilities (UNCRPD) specifically addresses education in Article 24 (United Nations, 2006). This article (see Appendix 2 to this chapter) specifies that States shall ensure "an inclusive education system at all levels" (§ 1) so that "persons with disabilities receive the support required, within the general education system, to facilitate their effective education" (§ 2 (d)). The UNCRPD has broad implications for teacher education and professional development. Some of these are specified in § 4, which calls for staff training to "incorporate disability awareness and the use of appropriate augmentative and alternative modes, means, and formats of communication, educational techniques and materials to support persons with disabilities." Clearly, in Article 24, the availability of specialized support is seen as an important aspect of inclusive education. However, the specialist support demanded by inclusive education requires that it be provided without perpetuating the discriminatory practices that many long-standing critics of special needs education have associated with traditional approaches that depend on disability classification and specialist forms of provision (e.g., Ainscow, 1991; Barton & Tomlinson, 1981; Skrtic, 1991; Thomas & Loxley, 2001). Such challenges will have important implications for teacher education and teacher professional development throughout the world.

These challenges to special needs education are both structural, in terms of the forms of teacher education that prepare different kinds of teachers for different types of students, as well as substantive, in terms of content knowledge. In both cases there are implications for how specialists and general education teachers are prepared to work in schools, but no clear consensus about how to move practice forward. Accordingly, answers to pressing questions about how to meet the challenges for teacher education set out in the ICE recommendations are likely to reflect debates about special and inclusive education that call for increased specialization for some teachers, increased specialist knowledge of general education teachers, and the development of new forms of teacher education based on broad conceptualizations of diversity. Presently, as the variability in the teacher education reform efforts noted above suggest, there are different views about what teachers need to know and how they might be prepared to work in inclusive classrooms. While some recommend more content knowledge about different types of disabilities and difficulties is needed (e.g., Hodkinson, 2005), others (e.g., Slee, 2001) argue for the development of inclusive approaches to teaching and learning that do not depend on the identification of particular forms of disability or difficulty.

Article 24 calls upon States to "ensure that persons with disabilities are able to access general tertiary education, vocational training, adult education and lifelong learning without discrimination and on an equal basis with others" (§ 5). Here the ideals of EFA are widely promoted but there are different views about how best they can be achieved for students with disabilities because schooling itself takes place within particular conceptualizations of special needs education, influenced by cultural perspectives and the kind of preparation their teachers receive. The state of education generally, and teacher education specifically, varies not only by world geographical region but by other important dimensions as well. The United Nations Statistical Division (2011) uses a country classification that divides the world into developing countries, developed countries, and countries in transition. In the transition countries of the former Soviet Union, for example, the legacy of defectology interacts with Soviet traditions of institutionalized care for children with disabilities and a system of teacher education that emphasizes high levels of academic knowledge with little attention to diverse learning needs (Florian & Becirevic, 2011). As a consequence, teachers are prepared for different roles as teachers, pedagogues, and defectologists. An 'inclusive school' in many of the transition countries of the Commonwealth of Independent States[1] (CIS) where universal access to education is well established for nondisabled children, is a specially designated mainstream school that is additionally resourced to include children with disabilities. In the developing world, where universal access to primary education is not assured, separate special education provision may represent the only educational opportunity available to children with disabilities. Thus, although 'special' and 'inclusive' education are different concepts, particularly in many countries of the developed world where inclusive education is seen a part of the larger diversity agenda, rather than a response to a particular group of learners, the terms are used synonymously in other countries. In addition to questions about whether there should be different types of teachers for different types of students (Florian, 2009), there are diverse views about how they might best be prepared to teach students with disabilities (Rouse, 2010).

Preparation of Special Education Teachers

With regard to Article 24, there are two different views about how to prepare special education teachers to respond to the difficulties in learning experienced by students with disabilities. On one hand, as is the case in the USA, the CIS, and many other countries, separate initial teacher education and specialist qualifications for teachers to teach students with different types of disabilities are thought to be needed. This view assumes that specially trained teachers are needed to meet the needs of students with disabilities (Kauffman & Hallahan, 2005). Those who subscribe to this view believe that specialist teaching approaches that respond to the particular learning differences that characterize students with disabilities are essential for effective education and equal opportunity for learning. The question of whether or not there is a *specialist pedagogy* has been debated in the literature (e.g., Cook & Schirmer, 2003; Davis & Florian, 2004; Kavale, 2007; Lewis & Norwich, 2005) and is not repeated here. A consequence of this separate approach, however, is that many general education teachers believe that they do not have the necessary knowledge and skills to teach students with disabilities and therefore rely on experts specially qualified to do this work.

When special education training and support is conceptualized as specialist knowledge, it can be a barrier to the development of inclusion because it absolves the rest of the education system from taking responsibility for all children's learning, even though in many parts of the developed world where students with disabilities do have access to education, they spend most of their time in general education classrooms. Furthermore, in developing countries that do not have a legacy of special education, the rush to achieve universal access to primary education has brought about an increase in the number of students with disabilities who attend regular schools and classes. In this situation, teachers, children, and families are often supported by NGOs with an interest in promoting the UNCRPD. These NGOs are mainly international organizations that participate in the EFA movement and promote a rights-based approach to inclusive education for students with disabilities.

Following the rights-based approach, there is a second view that suggests inclusive education cannot be created through the extension of special education because conceptually and practically special education is seen as part of the problem (Booth & Ainscow, 2002; Slee, 2001). In the 1990s, the UNESCO Special Needs in the Classroom project brought the alternative school improvement approach to special needs education developed in the UK to a wide international audience of practicing special and regular education teachers (Ainscow, 1994). This position calls for an approach to preparing teachers that does not depend on the identification of particular forms of disability or difficulty (Allan, 2006; Booth, Nes, & Strømstad, 2003; Gabel, 2005). Rather than a focus on disability categories, preparing teachers for inclusive education is informed by a social model of disability and proposes an emphasis on removing the barriers to learning and participation as they are encountered by learners. However, this approach has also been problematic insofar as some knowledge about human differences is important—a student who is an English language learner is different from a student with Down Syndrome, and so forth. The problem has been agreeing how to reconcile the differences that matter, with responses that do not ignore or overlook them, with the marginalization that can occur when some students are treated differently. In addition, as the inclusive education approach to preparing teachers to work with students with disabilities has been developed predominately by special educators within university departments of special education in the developed Western world, its reach has been confined mainly to special education teachers in those regions, and to those they have influenced through international consultancies elsewhere.

Preparation of General Education Teachers

When asked, many new teachers state that they do not know enough about specific disabilities such as dyslexia, or autism; they also report feeling unprepared to work in inclusive classrooms (Forlin, 2010; Holdheide & Reschly, 2008; Tait & Purdie, 2000; UNESCO, 2008b). Today, the problem of how to prepare general education teachers to include students with disabilities in inclusive classrooms has taken on a new urgency as international policy documents such as the ICE recommendations and the UNCRPD not only call for preparing teachers for inclusive education but also clearly focus on the link between the quality of teaching and the achievement of EFA. Structurally, many teacher education programs are based on ideas of different types of teachers for different groups of learners: for example, 'primary' or 'secondary,' 'general' or 'special' education teachers. These distinctions have been shown to reinforce teachers' identities in terms of who they are qualified to teach (Young, 2008). In addition, separate teacher education programs have been identified as a barrier to inclusion (Winn & Blanton, 2005), suggesting problems of equity in educational opportunity are structurally linked to the organization of teacher education.

One response to the reported lack of knowledge about disability and belief that there is insufficient content knowledge about different types of difficulty and disability in most teacher education programs (Hodkinson, 2005; Jones, 2006) has been to offer additional courses on special education. Such courses are now widespread in many countries as electives, or required courses. In a cross-regional study (Australia, Hong Kong, Canada, and Singapore), Sharma, Forlin, and Loreman (2008) reported that although both add-on courses and infusion models of embedding content knowledge into teacher education courses were effective in promoting positive attitudes about inclusive education, it was the pedagogical approach taken within the model, rather than the model itself, that appeared to have the greatest impact on attitudes.

Nevertheless, others (Slee, 20007) suggest that special education content knowledge is not adequate to improve inclusive practice in schools because it is not sufficiently linked to the broader pedagogical and curriculum imperatives that trainee teachers have to learn and be able to apply. It is thought that the additional special education knowledge that is added-on to the teacher education course may not be sufficient for student teachers to act upon when teaching. In a study of teacher development for inclusive education in the Western Balkans (Albania, Bosnia and Herzegovina, Croatia, the former Yugoslav Republic of Macedonia, Kosovo, Montenegro, and Serbia), Pantić, Closs, and Ivošević (2011) found that narrow conceptualizations of inclusive education focused only on children with disabilities to be a barrier to social and educational inclusion:

> The unconnected professional education system for all levels of school staff present a challenge to systemic change. The limited concept of inclusive education, if the issue is addressed at all, results in programmes that instruct student teachers in how to remedy deficits rather than on more

> generic, holistic and constructivist educational approaches . . . Although teachers would welcome competence-based teacher standards (currently lacking), their concept of competences is too narrow to achieve inclusive education through the application of such standards.
>
> *(p. 12)*

Preparing Teachers for Inclusive Education: An Emerging International Perspective

As Article 24 of the UNCRPD prompts renewed interest in inclusive education, debates about how to ensure that "persons with disabilities receive the support required, within the general education system" (§ 2 (d)) will no doubt continue, and these debates will influence teacher preparation programs. For teacher educators, it will be important to avoid the polarizing debates about special or inclusive education and to consider developing new ways of preparing both special and general education teachers to work with students with disabilities in ways that promote the underlying human rights approach to education as described in Article 24. Special educators have an important role to play in promoting and supporting the participation and achievement of all students, but this change in practice will need to be supported by teacher education and professional development programs that encourage new collaborative ways of working to support all students. Such a change will not be easy to accomplish because the language of Article 24, which reflects the state of education in many countries, and promotes a policy of educational inclusion while simultaneously supporting policies and practices that rely on separate forms of provision and approaches (i.e., identification and assessment of individual need, individualized education programs (IEPs), and specialist facilities for those who choose them). In England, for example, government guidance was simultaneously based on traditional individualized approaches such as the *SEN [special educational needs] Toolkit* (Department for Education and Skills (DfES), 2001) and inclusive whole school approaches such as *Leading on Inclusion* (DfES, 2005). So, while there are calls for inclusive education as a mechanism to end discrimination, the belief that students with disabilities need special protection and individualized specialist support remains firmly in place. This situation is not unique to the countries of the UK. Indeed the many tensions between special and inclusive education continue to be forcefully debated in academic circles, and the two concepts remain strongly evident in policy and practice in many jurisdictions. The practical implementation of inclusive education worldwide also recognizes the more broadly defined category of children with SEN:

> In many countries today a large proportion of disabled children are in fact educated in institutions of the regular system. Moreover the concept of 'children with special educational needs' extends beyond those who may be included in handicapped categories to cover those who are failing in school for a wide variety of other reasons that are known to be likely to impede a child's optimal progress. Whether or not this more broadly defined group of children are in need of additional supports depends on the extent to which schools are able to adapt their curriculum teaching and organisation and/or to provide additional human or material resources so as to stimulate efficient and effective learning for these pupils.
>
> *(UNESCO, 1997, cited in Organisation for Economic Co-operation and Development, 2007, p. 18)*

The relational definition of special needs education means that the challenge for teacher education in all regions of the world is to prepare teachers who can respond when students encounter barriers to learning. An important common issue in all countries is that there are students who are disabled and who are identified as having additional needs. Across the world, it is common for teachers to encounter a wide range of students who differ in terms of prior experience, language spoken, and other factors that may create difficulties in learning. Moreover, because teachers themselves tend to be trained locally for jobs in their home countries, they may have little experience of diversity. Therefore learning about and knowing how to respond to broad issues of diversity is an important part of teacher education at all levels and across all regions. Understanding the exclusionary pressures associated with migration, mobility, language, ethnicity, and intergenerational poverty, and the reciprocal links between poverty, disability, and underachievement is relevant not only for teachers but also for those who prepare teachers. Smith and Tyler (2011) reported a promising Web-based initiative, the IRIS Center, that responds to this challenge. The IRIS Center's work involves promoting research about effective teaching practices for students with special needs in inclusive school settings. By making resources freely available online, the IRIS Center helps to ensure that cutting edge research is available to educationalists throughout the world.

It is important to note, however, that inter- and intraregional differences also create challenges. Within-region variation is often so significant that cross-regional comparisons can be meaningless. For example, the percentage of children with special educational needs in segregated classrooms and schools in different European countries varies widely from less than 1% (e.g., Italy, Norway, Malta) to more than 4% (e.g., Belgium, Switzerland, Estonia) (European Agency for Development in Special Needs Education (EADSNE), 2003). Yet paradoxically, the issues for teacher preparation are remarkably similar. The issues identified by the Western Balkans study on teacher education for inclusive education (Pantić, Closs, & Ivošević, 2011) include systemic barriers in the education system, unconnected professional education for different levels of school staff, lack of competences for inclusive education, and concern that faculty-based teacher educators lack the knowledge needed to develop effective preservice programs. Clearly these issues are of broad relevance beyond the Western Balkans even though the regional and intraregional responses will reflect cultural and socioeconomic differences as well as differences in national education systems and the role and preparation of teachers. Thus, while international calls to adopt inclusive education are important strategically, they are limited in the guidance they can provide to specific regions. While the advantages of using technology to disseminate information are obvious, sensitivity to context-specific needs is also necessary. In the Arab world, for example, the stability of Jordan enables a very different engagement with Web-based resources than is possible in Gaza where power outages are a significant problem.

It is important to consider what inclusive education means in different regions as well as the implications for preparing teachers in different parts of the world. In countries where specialist pedagogues or special education teachers are part of the general education system, they should be prepared to work in support of efforts to ensure that students who are experiencing difficulties are meaningfully engaged in classroom activities. In countries where specialist training does not exist, the challenge is to ensure that children with disabilities are not excluded by a culture of silence about their learning needs. Sensitivity to the stigma that accompanies disability in many parts of the world is key, and Article 24 specifies awareness training. The hallmark of such practice is to work in ways that respond to individual differences but actively avoid marking some students as different (Florian, 2010). This must not mean that classroom teachers and learners are left on their own without support. Clearly, the ways that teachers respond to individual differences during whole class teaching, the choices they make about group work, and how they utilize specialist knowledge matter. Bringing about this culture shift in thinking about teaching all students is necessary work for those who prepare teachers.

Recently a growing number of teacher educators around the world have begun to describe some initiatives and articulate their ideas about how this work might progress. Two edited books (Forlin, 2010, 2012) document innovative approaches for initial teacher education and professional learning for practicing teachers. In addition, a number of approaches have been discussed in the academic literature. Bartolo (2010) has embedded the lessons learned from a seven-country European-funded study on inclusive education into a rights-based approach to initial teacher education in Malta. Today, courses that formerly focused on handicaps in learning have been replaced with those that focus on removing barriers to learning and responding to student diversity. This development has been described as a "deepening of the understanding of the concept of inclusion in relation to disability . . . and the widening of the application of the inclusion agenda to all marginalised groups" (Bartolo, p. 140). In the United States, efforts to move teacher education toward a more unified or holistic approach to preparing all teachers has focused on the development of collaborative approaches that increase the special education knowledge of general education teachers and ensure that special education teachers have sufficient background in academic content knowledge (Pugach & Blanton, 2009).

In Iceland, the focus is on university–school partnerships in teacher education and professional learning and how these partnerships might develop to support inclusive teacher education (Sigurdardóttir, 2011). McIntyre (2009) described the problems that this might present given current models of partnership in initial teacher education and suggested that the discontinuity between what preservice teachers learn in university and what they learn in school creates serious barriers that will stand in the way of the development of preparing teachers for inclusion. He suggested that teacher educators work more collaboratively with colleagues in schools if they are to do more than promote a theoretical idea. In an example of how this work might proceed, Symeonidou and Phtiaka (2009) described how practicing teachers' prior knowledge could be used to develop relevant university courses for teachers interested in developing inclusive practice in Cyprus.

At a regional level, research in Europe (EADSNE, 2011) has documented a wide range of initial teacher education courses of varying lengths and contents: Whereas the majority of countries require a 3- or 4-year bachelor's degree, some countries require extended initial teacher education of a 4- or 5-years master's program leading to qualified teacher status. Fewer than one in ten European countries offer specialization in special education during initial teacher education. Where this qualification exists, it is generally offered at the postgraduate level for experienced teachers. However, there is also momentum for cross-national work as the European Commission prepares for new initiatives on education and inequality. A European consultation symposium examining measures to combat inequality specifically raised questions about "how to better prepare the professional workforce for diversity, inclusion and individual learning needs" (European Commission, 2011, p. 4).

A review of teacher education for inclusive education in the Arab States (Amr, 2011) found that while the literature recommends both preservice and in-service preparation of mainstream teachers, most university-based courses target preparation efforts on special education teachers only. However, because the research base is scant, it is possible that many emerging initiatives in the region have yet to be documented. For example, the United Nations Relief and Works Agency (UNRWA) provides education services to Palestinian refugee children in the Gaza Strip, the West Bank, Jordan, Lebanon, and the Syrian Arab Republic. The UNRWA has recently developed an education reform strategy for 2011–2015 that includes substantive reform programs in four areas including teacher education and inclusive education (UNRWA, n.d.) The Teacher Development and School Empowerment (TDSE) strategy focuses on supporting teachers to develop interactive pedagogic practices while the Inclusive Education initiative aims to ensure "the rights of all refugee children—regardless of gender, abilities, disabilities, impairments, health conditions and socioeconomic status—to equal access to a meaningful and quality education" (UNRWA, p. 50). In principle, the aims of these two programs are complementary, and linked through outputs that aim to enhance the capacity of teachers through the TDSE program to use tools that will be developed through the Inclusive Education program to support children with diverse needs.

The lack of documentation about existing and emerging programs is an important issue that also affects other regions such as Latin America and parts of Asia. Where teacher education is not a university-based profession, or where the demand for teachers so far outstrips supply, countries are forced to rely on unqualified or underqualified teachers. In such cases, NGOs like UNRWA play an important role in providing professional development opportunities to teachers. Again, the literature is meager but descriptions of initiatives can be found in the publications of international NGOs such as UNICEF (2007), World Vision (2006), and Save the Children (2009).

Conclusion

While the form and structure of teacher education varies within and between countries, the important role that teachers play in providing a good quality education to all students is indisputable. Today important debates about how to best prepare teachers to work with diverse groups of students are raising awareness of the role that teacher education plays in achieving inclusive education at national (e.g., Blanton, Pugach, & Florian, 2011), regional (e.g., EADSNE, 2011) and international levels (Opertti & Brady, 2011). As awareness of the lack of teacher preparedness for the multiple and sometimes conflicting demands of inclusive education becomes linked to issues of teacher quality and achieving a good quality education for all, fundamental questions about what teachers need to know and be able to do in order to implement a policy of inclusion are being raised, and the implications for teacher education are being considered. However, the fundamental work of documenting and mapping current practice has yet to be undertaken. A more robust knowledge base is needed before meaningful cross-national work can be undertaken.

Nevertheless, the importance of holistic approaches to preparing general education teachers to teach students with disabilities is increasingly recognized, and the idea of a single program to prepare all teachers to meet the full range of diverse needs is being promoted in some regions as a more effective use of resources than initiatives designed to close gaps or support particular groups. However, with some notable exceptions, few would agree that existing teacher education courses offer what is needed to achieve inclusive education. There is a need to develop and research new models of teacher education as part of the EFA agenda. There is a case to be made that all teachers, both general and special, at all levels and in all regions should be prepared to work in schools that are increasingly diverse and include students with disabilities. Although teacher education for inclusive education is associated in some countries with special education, innovations that link issues of disability and special educational needs to a broader diversity agenda are needed. All teachers need to be prepared for inclusive education.

Note

1 The Republic of Azerbaijan, The Republic of Uzbekistan, Turkmenistan, The Republic of Tajikistan, The Russian Federation, Republic of Moldova, Kyrgyzstan Republic, The Republic of Kazakhstan, The Republic of Belarus, The Republic of Armenia, Ukraine.

Appendix 1: The International Context of 'Education for All'

1948 UN Universal Declaration of Human Rights—establishes the right to education.

1989 UN Convention on Rights of the Child—affirms education as a human right.

1990 The Education for All movement—launched at the World Conference on 'Education for All' or EFA in 1990 in Jomtien, Thailand initiates a global commitment to provide quality basic education for all children, youth, and adults by agreeing to universalize primary education and massively reduce illiteracy by the end of the decade.

1993 The UN Standard Rules on the Equalization of Opportunities for Persons with Disabilities (1993) says that "where education is compulsory, it should be provided to all boys and girls with all kinds and levels of disabilities." The Rules promote inclusive education and call on States to adopt policies and communities to develop local resources to meet this challenge.

1994 The 1994 UNESCO World Conference on Special Educational Needs attended by 92 governments and 25 international organizations considered the future direction of special education in light of international efforts to ensure the right of all children to a basic education. The Conference produced a Framework for Action, the Salamanca Statement, which called for children with special educational needs to have access to regular schools.

2000 UNDP Millennium Declaration establishes universal access to primary education (UPE) a key goal in the fight to eradicate extreme poverty.

2000 The World Conference on Education meets in Dakar, Senegal, agreeing on a Framework for Action committing governments to provide basic education for all by 2015 and identifying inclusive education as a key strategy to achieve EFA goals.

2008 UN Convention on the Rights of People with Disabilities calls upon States to ensure an inclusive education system at all levels to ensure that persons with disabilities can access an inclusive, qualitative, and free primary and secondary education on an equal basis with others.

2008 UNESCO 48th International Conference on Education chooses inclusive education as its theme and the way of the future. Inclusive education is affirmed as the key strategy for EFA.

Appendix 2: Article 24—Education

1. States Parties recognize the right of persons with disabilities to education. With a view to realizing this right without discrimination and on the basis of equal opportunity, States Parties shall ensure an inclusive education system at all levels and lifelong learning directed to:
   a. The full development of human potential and sense of dignity and self-worth, and the strengthening of respect for human rights, fundamental freedoms and human diversity;
   b. The development by persons with disabilities of their personality, talents and creativity, as well as their mental and physical abilities, to their fullest potential;
   c. Enabling persons with disabilities to participate effectively in a free society.

2. In realizing this right, States Parties shall ensure that:
   a) Persons with disabilities are not excluded from the general education system on the basis of disability, and that children with disabilities are not excluded from free and compulsory primary education, or from secondary education, on the basis of disability;
   b) Persons with disabilities can access an inclusive, quality and free primary education and secondary education on an equal basis with others in the communities in which they live;
   c) Reasonable accommodation of the individual's requirements is provided;
   d) Persons with disabilities receive the support required, within the general education system, to facilitate their effective education;
   e) Effective individualized support measures are provided in environments that maximize academic and social development, consistent with the goal of full inclusion.

3. States Parties shall enable persons with disabilities to learn life and social development skills to facilitate their full and equal participation in education and as members of the community. To this end, States Parties shall take appropriate measures, including:
   a) Facilitating the learning of Braille, alternative script, augmentative and alternative modes, means and formats of communication and orientation and mobility skills, and facilitating peer support and mentoring;
   b) Facilitating the learning of sign language and the promotion of the linguistic identity of the deaf community;
   c) Ensuring that the education of persons, and in particular children, who are blind, deaf or deafblind, is delivered in the most appropriate languages and modes and means of

communication for the individual, and in environments which maximize academic and social development.

4. In order to help ensure the realization of this right, States Parties shall take appropriate measures to employ teachers, including teachers with disabilities, who are qualified in sign language and/or Braille, and to train professionals and staff who work at all levels of education. Such training shall incorporate disability awareness and the use of appropriate augmentative and alternative modes, means and formats of communication, educational techniques and materials to support persons with disabilities.
5. States Parties shall ensure that persons with disabilities are able to access general tertiary education, vocational training, adult education and lifelong learning without discrimination and on an equal basis with others. To this end, States Parties shall ensure that reasonable accommodation is provided to persons with disabilities.

Source: United Nations Enable: Development and Human Rights for All. UNCRPD Article 24: Education http://www.un.org/disabilities/default.asp?id=284

References

Ainscow, M. (1991). *Effective schools for all*. London, United Kingdom: David Fulton.

Ainscow, M. (1994). *Special needs in the classroom: A teacher education guide*. London, United Kingdom: Jessica Kingsley/UNESCO.

Ainscow, M., & Miles, S. (2008). Making Education for All inclusive: Where next? *Prospects, 37*, 15–34. doi:10.1007/s11125-008-9055-0

Allan, J. (2006). The repetition of exclusion. *International Journal of Inclusive Education, 10*, 121–33. doi:10.1080/13603110500221511

Alur, M., & Timmons, V. (Eds.). (2009). *Inclusive education across cultures: Crossing boundaries, sharing ideas*. New Delhi, India: Sage.

Amr, M. (2011). Teacher education for inclusive education in the Arab States: The case of Jordan. *Prospects, 41*, 399–413. doi:10.1007/s11125-011-9203-9

Bartolo, P. (2010). The process of teacher education for inclusion: The Maltese experience. *Journal of Research in Special Educational Needs, 10*(S1), 139–148. doi:10.1111/j.1471-3802.2010.01163.x

Barton, L., & Tomlinson, S. (1981). *Special education: Policy, practice and social issues*. London, United Kingdom: Harper & Row.

Blanton, L. P., Pugach, M. C., & Florian, L. (2011, April). *Preparing general education teachers to improve outcomes for students with disabilities* [White Paper]. Washington, DC: American Association of Colleges for Teacher Education and National Center for Learning Disabilities.

Booth, T., & Ainscow, M. (2002). *The Index for Inclusion: Developing Learning and Participation in Schools* (rev. ed.) Bristol, United Kingdom: Centre for Studies in Inclusive Education.

Booth, T., Nes, K., & Strømstad, M. (2003). *Developing inclusive teacher education*. London, United Kingdom: RoutledgeFalmer.

Buchberger, F., Campos, B. P., Kallos, D., & Stephenson, J. (2000). *Green Paper on teacher education in Europe: High quality teacher education for high quality education and training*. Umeå, Sweden: Thematic Network on Teacher Education in Europe.

Cook, B. G., & Schirmer, B. R. (2003). What is special about special education? Overview and analysis. *Journal of Special Education, 37*, 200–204. doi:10.1177/00224669030370031001

Davis, P., & Florian, L. (2004). *Teaching strategies and approaches for children with special educational needs, a scoping study* (Research Report 516). London, United Kingdom: Department for Education and Skills.

Department for International Development. (2000). *Disability, poverty and development* (DfID policy document). London, United Kingdom: Author.

DfES (Department for Education and Skills). (2001). *SEN Toolkit*. London, United Kingdom: Author.

DfES (Department for Education and Skills). (2005). *Leading on inclusion*. London, United Kingdom: Author.

Djumagulova, C. (2004). *Inclusive education development in Central Asia*. Bishkek, Kyrgyzstan: Save the Children, United Kingdom.

EADSNE (European Agency for Development in Special Needs Education). (2003). *Special needs education in Europe*. Odense, Denmark: Author.

EADSNE (European Agency for Development in Special Needs Education). (2011). *Teacher education for inclusion across Europe: A synthesis of policy and practice in 25 countries*. Odense, Denmark: Author.

European Commission. (2011). *Measures to Combat Educational Disadvantage: A European Consultation Symposium, Brussels, 8–9 December, 2011*. Retrieved from http://www.cardiff.ac.uk/socsi/neset/events/081211neset.html

Filmer, D. (2005). *Disability, poverty and schooling in developing countries: Results from 11 household surveys* (SP Discussion Paper No. 0539). Washington, DC: Social Protection Unit, Human Development Network, The World Bank. Retrieved from http://siteresources.worldbank.org/SOCIALPROTECTION/Resources/SP-Discussion-papers/Disability-DP/0539.pdf

Florian, L. (2009). Preparing teachers to work in 'schools for all.' *Teaching and Teacher Education, 25*, 553–554. doi:10.1016/j.tate.2009.02.004

Florian, L. (2010). Special education in an era of inclusion: The end of special education or a new beginning? *Psychology of Education Review, 34*, 22–27.

Florian, L., & Becirevic, M. (2011). Preparing teachers for inclusive education in CIS/CEE countries. *Prospects, 41*, 371–384. doi:10.1007/s11125-011-9208-4

Forlin, C. (Ed.). (2010). *Teacher education for inclusion: Changing paradigms and innovative approaches*. Abingdon, United Kingdom: Routledge.

Forlin, C. (Ed.). (2012). *Future directions for inclusive teacher education: An international perspective*. Abingdon, United Kingdom: Routledge.

Gabel, S. (Ed.). (2005). *Disability studies in education: Readings in theory and method*. New York, NY: Peter Lang.

Hegarty, S., & Alur, M. (Ed.). (2002). *Education and children with special needs: From segregation to inclusion*. New Delhi, India: Sage.

Hodkinson, A. J. (2005). Conceptions and misconceptions of inclusive education: A critical examination of final year teacher trainees' knowledge and understanding of inclusion. *International Journal of Research in Education, 73*, 15–29.

Holdheide, L. R., & Reschly, D. J. (2008). *Teacher preparation to deliver inclusive services to students with disabilities*. Washington, DC: National Comprehensive Center for Teacher Quality.

Jones, P. (2006). They are not like us and neither should they be: Issues of teacher identity for teachers of pupils with profound and multiple learning difficulties. *Disability & Society, 19*, 159–169. doi:10.1080/0968759042000181785

Kauffman, J. M., & Hallahan, D. P. (2005). *Special education: What it is and why we need it*. Boston, MA: Pearson/Allyn & Bacon.

Kavale, K. (2007). Quantitative research synthesis: Meta-analysis of research on meeting special educational needs. In L. Florian (Ed.). *The Sage handbook of special education* (pp. 207–221). London, United Kingdom: Sage. doi:10.4135/9781848607989.n16

Kim, C. Y., & Rouse, M. (2011). Reviewing the role of teachers in achieving Education for All in Cambodia. *Prospects, 41*, 415–428. doi:10.1007/s11125-011-9201-y

Lewis, A., & Norwich, B. (Eds.). (2005). *Special teaching for special children? Pedagogies for inclusion*. Maidenhead, United Kingdom: Open University Press.

McIntyre, D. (2009). The difficulties of inclusive pedagogy for initial teacher education and some thoughts on the way forward. *Teaching and Teacher Education, 25*, 602–608.

McKinsey & Company. (2007). *How the world's best performing school systems come out on top*. Zwolle, Windesheim University of Applied Sciences, The Netherlands: Identifying-Teacher-Quality Project. Retrieved from http://www.teacherqualitytoolbox.eu/news/4/mckinsey_report_how_the_world_s_best_performing_school_systems_come_out_on_top

Mitchell, D. (2010). *Education that fits: Review of international trends in the education of students with special educational needs*. Final Report *Education Counts*. Retrieved from http://www.educationcounts.govt.nz/publications/special_education

Mukhopadhyay, S., & Mani, M. N. G. (2002). Education of children with special needs. In R. Govinda (Ed.), *India education report: A profile of basic education* (pp. 96–108). New Delhi, India: Oxford University Press.

Mulkeen, A., & Chen, D. (Eds). (2008). *Teachers for rural schools: Experiences in Lesotho, Malawi, Mozambique, Tanzania, and Uganda* (Africa Human Development Series). Washington, DC: World Bank.

Nishimura, M., & Byamugisha, A. (2011). The challenges of universal primary education policy in sub-Saharan Africa. In J. N. Hawkins & W. J. Jacob (Eds.), *Policy debates in comparative, international, and development education* (pp. 225–245). New York, NY: Palgrave Macmillan.

Opertti, R., & Brady, J. (2011). Developing inclusive teachers from an inclusive curricular perspective. *Prospects, 41*, 459–472. doi:10.1007/s11125-011-9205-7

Organisation for Economic Co-operation and Development. (2007). *Students with disabilities, learning difficulties and disadvantages: Policies, statistics and indicators*. Paris, France: Author. Retrieved from http://www.oecd.org/edu/school/studentswithdisabilitieslearningdifficultiesanddisadvantagespoliciesstatisticsandindicators-2007edition.htm

Pantić, N., Closs, A., & Ivošević V. (2011). *Teachers for the future: Teacher development for inclusive education in the Western Balkans*. Luxembourg: European Training Foundation.

Peters, S. (2003). *Inclusive education: An EFA strategy for all children*. Washington, DC: World Bank.

Pugach, M. C., & Blanton, L. P. (2009). A framework for conducting research on collaborative teacher education. *Teaching and Teacher Education*, *25*, 575–582. doi:10.1016/j.tate.2009.02.007

Riddell, S. (2008). The classification of pupils at the educational margins in Scotland: Shifting categories and frameworks. In L. Florian, & M. J. McLaughlin (Eds.), *Disability classification in education: Issues and perspectives* (pp. 109–128). Thousand Oaks, CA: Corwin Press.

Rieser, R. (2012). *Implementing inclusive education: A commonwealth guide to implementing Article 24 of the UN Convention on the Rights of Persons with Disabilities* (2nd ed.). London, United Kingdom: Commonwealth Secretariat.

Rouse, M. (2010). Reforming initial teacher education: A necessary but not sufficient condition for developing inclusive practice. In C. Forlin (Ed.), *Teacher education for inclusion: Changing paradigms and innovative approaches* (pp. 47–55). Abingdon, United Kingdom: Routledge.

Save the Children. (2009). *Policy brief: Inclusive education*. London, United Kingdom: Author. Retrieved from http://www.savethechildren.org.uk/resources/online-library/policy-brief-inclusive-education

Sharma, U., Forlin, C., & Loreman, T. (2008). Impact of training on pre-service teachers' attitudes and concerns about inclusive education and sentiments about persons with disabilities. *Disability & Society*, *23*, 773–785. doi:10.1080/09687590802469271

Sigurdardóttir, A. K. (2011). School-university partnership in teacher education for inclusive education in Iceland. *Journal of Research in Special Educational Needs*, *10*(S1), 149–156. doi:10.1111/j.1471-3802.2010.01160.x

Singal, N. (2007). *Conceptualising disability and education in the south: Challenges for research* (RECOUP Working Paper 10). Cambridge, United Kingdom: University of Cambridge.

Skrtic, T. M. (1991). *Behind special education: A critical analysis of professional culture and school organization*. Denver, CO: Love Publishing.

Slee, R. (2001). Inclusion in practice: Does practice make perfect? *Educational Review*, *53*, 113–123. doi:10.1080/00131910120055543

Slee, R. (2007). Inclusive schooling as a means and end of education? In L. Florian (Ed.), *The Sage handbook of special education* (pp. 160–174). London, United Kingdom: Sage. doi:10.4135/9781848607989.n13

Smith, D. D., & Tyler, N. C. (2011). Effective inclusive education: Equipping education professionals with necessary skills and knowledge. *Prospects*, *43*, 323–339. doi:10.1007/s11125-011-9207-5

Symeonidou, S., & Phtiaka, H. (2009). Using teachers' prior knowledge, attitudes and beliefs to develop in-service teacher education courses for inclusion. *Teaching and Teacher Education*, *25*, 543–550. doi:10.1016/j.tate.2009.02.001

Tait, K., & Purdie, N. (2000). Attitudes toward disability: Teacher education for inclusive environments in an Australian university. *International Journal of Disability, Development and Education*, *47*, 25–38. doi:10.1080/103491200116110

Thomas, G., & Loxley, A. (2001). *Deconstructing special education and constructing inclusion*. Maidenhead, United Kingdom: Open University Press.

UNESCO. (1994). *The Salamanca statement and framework for action on special needs education*. Retrieved from http://www.unesco.org/ulis/cgi-bin/ulis.pl?catno=139394&set=4F703E0F_3_432&gp=1&lin=1&ll=1

UNESCO. (1997). *International standard classification of education*. Paris, France: Author.

UNESCO. (2005). *Children out of school: Measuring exclusion from primary education*. Montreal, Canada: UNESCO Institute for Statistics.

UNESCO. (2006). *Education for all global monitoring report 2006: Literacy for life*. Paris, France: Author.

UNESCO. (2007). *Education for all global monitoring report 2007: Strong foundations: Early childhood care and education*. Paris, France: Author.

UNESCO. (2008a). *Inclusive education: The way of the future. Conclusions and recommendations of the 48th session of the International Conference on Education*. Paris, France: Author. Retrieved from http://www.ibe.unesco.org/en/ice/48th-session-2008/conclusions-and-recommendations.html

UNESCO. (2008b). *Inclusive education: The way of the future. Outcomes and trends in inclusive education at regional and interregional levels: Issues and challenges*. Geneva, Switzerland: UNESCO International Bureau of Education.

UNESCO. (2009). *Education for All global monitoring report 2009. Overcoming inequality: Why governance matters*. Paris, France: Author.

UNESCO. (2010). *Education for All global monitoring report 2010. Reaching the Marginalized*. Paris, France: Author.

UNESCO. (2011). *Education for All global monitoring report 2011. The hidden crisis: Armed conflict and education*. Paris, France: Author.

UNICEF. (2005). *Children and disability in transition in CEE/CIS and Baltic states*. Florence, Italy: UNICEF Innocenti Research Centre.

UNICEF. (2007). *Education for some more than others?* Geneva, Switzerland: UNICEF Regional Office for Central and Eastern Europe and the Commonwealth of Independent States.

UNICEF/UNESCO. (2007). *A human rights-based approach to education for all.* New York, NY: Author.

United Nations. (2006). *United Nations convention on the rights of persons with disabilities.* New York, NY: Author. Retrieved from http://www.un.org/disabilities/default.asp?id=284

United Nations Relief and Works Agency. (n.d.). *UNRWA education reform strategy 2011–2015.* Retrieved from www.unrwa.org/userfiles/2012042913344.pdf

United Nations Statistical Division. (2011) *Composition of macro geographical (continental) regions, geographical sub-regions, and selected economic and other groupings.* Retrieved from http://unstats.un.org/unsd/methods/m49/m49regin.htm

Vaillant, D. (2011). Preparing teachers for inclusive education in Latin America. *Prospects, 41*, 385–398. doi:10.1007/s11125-011-9196-4

Winn, J., & Blanton, L. (2005). The call for collaboration in teacher education. *Focus on Exceptional Children, 38*(2), 1–10.

World Health Organization and World Bank. (2011). *World report on disability.* Geneva, Switzerland: Author.

World Vision. (2006). *Teachers and inclusion: A disability perspective.* Milton Keynes, United Kingdom: Author.

Yeo, R., & Moore, K. (2003). Including disabled people in poverty reduction work: "Nothing about us, without us." *World Development, 31*, 571–590. http://dx.doi.org/10.1016/S0305-750X(02)00218-8

Young, K. (2008). "I don't think I'm the right person for that": Theoretical and institutional questions about a combined credential program. *Disability Studies Quarterly, 28*(4), 1–16.

Yu, L., Su, X., & Liu, C. (2011). Issues of teacher education and inclusion in China. *Prospects, 41*, 355–369. doi:10.1007/s11125-011-9204-8

Part II
Problems

5

Teacher Demand, Supply, and Shortage in Special Education

A National Perspective

Erling E. Boe

UNIVERSITY OF PENNSYLVANIA

Things to Think About

- Chronic shortage of qualified SETs has been a main issue in developing and maintaining the teaching force in special education.
- In analyzing the demand for SETs specifically, it is important and useful to distinguish between *total* demand and *annual* demand.
- Overall, there has been an adequate supply of individuals who are willing to become employed as SETs; however, there has not been an adequate supply of SETs who are *qualified* in their teaching assignments. Nonetheless, the continuing shortage of qualified SETs should not obscure the successes of special education in increasing the supply of qualified SETs over time.
- Two opposing perspectives persist in regards to teacher shortage: the active supply of SETs has been insufficient and the potential supply of teachers is sufficient.
- Teacher turnover has become a major concern in educational research and policy analysis because of the demand it creates for replacement teachers. Additionally, gradually increasing turnover during recent decades is all the more reason to assure a larger supply of qualified SETs, willing and able to assume teaching positions in special education.
- Redistribution of teachers among various school types and locations would not eliminate the shortage problem.
- There are several explanations of teacher shortage, and short-term as well as long-term interventions are necessary to reduce shortage.
- The research field of teacher demand, supply, and shortage in special education needs ongoing attention and nurturing if it is to continue contributing to policy making designed to produce the best attainable outcomes for students with disabilities.

The expression "teacher supply and demand" refers broadly to topics and issues in the study of the teaching profession such as the preparation, qualifications, and turnover of teachers (Boe & Gilford, 1992). As such, teacher supply and demand should be distinguished from "teaching," i.e., the performance of teachers in the classroom. In keeping with this distinction, the purpose of this chapter is to organize and review research on the supply and demand of special education teachers (SETs) at the national level conducted mostly by the author during the past 15 years.

In special education, teacher supply and demand research is directly relevant to the objective of providing all students with disabilities (SWD) with qualified teachers.[1] The numbers of such students by disability classification, along with traditions of sound teaching practice, are used to generate estimates of the numbers for SETs needed to provide instruction by disability classification. Such estimates become operationalized in the *demand* for SETs as defined by the numbers of teaching positions in special education that have been created and funded by policy makers and administrators.

In response to the demand for SETs, the field of special education is responsible for providing an adequate *supply* of qualified SETs to satisfy the demand by disability, instructional level, and geographic location. The supply of SETs can originate in multiple sources (e.g., newly minted graduates and the reserve pool), with requisite qualifications being produced by some combination of initial teacher preparation and continuing professional development. Further and most importantly, SETs are the primary within-school factor[2] responsible for producing the best attainable outcomes for SWD (Rothstein, 2010)—the fundamental goal of special education. Thus, it would be difficult to overemphasize the importance of the supply of qualified teachers for special education.

To the extent that the supply of qualified SETs is insufficient to satisfy the demand for SETs by disability, instructional level, and geographic location, a teacher *shortage* is defined and quantified. Unfortunately, special education has experienced a chronic shortage of qualified SETs for the past several decades in spite of substantial efforts to expand preservice teacher preparation and in-service professional development. As a broad generalization, one of every ten employed SETs has not been fully certified in their teaching assignment (Boe, 2006; Boe & Cook, 2006) during recent decades. This defines the usual extent of the shortage of fully certified SETs.

The shortage of qualified SETs has long been recognized as a major problem in the field of special education (Carriker & Weintraub, 1989; Council for Exceptional Children, 2000; National Clearinghouse on Professions in Special Education, 1992; Office of Special Education Programs (OSEP), 2004). For example, the National Clearinghouse on Professions in Education observed that the shortages of SETs "have now achieved pervasive and critical dimensions" (p. 8). In fact, the shortage problem has been so enduring, so pervasive, and so important that it has provided the driving interest in research on the supply and demand of SETs, including questions such as the relative productivity and qualifications of graduates of various approaches to teacher preparation, the qualifications of SETs hired from various sources of supply, the impact of teacher turnover on the qualifications of the teaching force in special education, and projections of future demand and supply. In short, it is safe to say that if there had been a substantial surplus of qualified applicants seeking to fill teaching positions in special education during the past decades (instead of the chronic and serious shortages that actually existed), there would be little interest in research on supply and demand of SETs.[3]

Because the chronic shortage of qualified SETs has been a main issue in developing and maintaining the teaching force in special education, teacher shortage is the central organizing concept for this chapter on various aspects of teacher supply and demand. That is, to what extent might a topic contribute to shortage and what interventions might reduce shortage? With respect to the demand for SETs, for example, shortage might be reduced by a revised policy that reduces the number of students classified as eligible for special education services, thereby reducing demand. With respect to the supply of SETs, shortage might be reduced by a new policy that provides an incentive to attract unemployed, but qualified, teachers to positions in hard-to-staff urban schools, thereby increasing supply. With respect to the attrition of SETs, there is the possibility of improving the retention of qualified SETs as a way to reduce shortage.

The main data sources for research about public school teachers[4] reviewed here were national sample surveys conducted by the National Center for Education Statistics (NCES). These were four Schools and Staffing Surveys (SASS) during 1990–1991, 1993–1994, 1999–2000, and 2003–2004, and their 1-year longitudinal component, the Teacher Follow-Up Surveys (TFS) during 1991–1992, 1994–1995, 2000–2001, 2004–2005. For detailed information about the 2003–2004 SASS, see Tourkin, et al. (2007); for detailed information about the 2004–2005 TFS, see Cox, Parmer, Tourkin, Warner, and Lyter (2007).

In the sections that follow, the major topics and issues within supply and demand for SETs are considered in turn, beginning with research on demand and followed by research on supply, shortage, turnover, and distribution.

Demand

In general, the demand for teachers in public schools is the "number that school systems want to employ and are prepared to pay for at a given time" (Barro, 1992, p. 133). The demand for teachers occurs at the level of the local school district that has the authority to create and fund teaching positions. Aggregating the demand for teachers at all districts within a state provides the teacher demand in public schools at the state level. Similarly, aggregating the demand in public schools for teachers in the 50 states, the District of Columbia, the Bureau and Indian Affairs, and the five territories, represents the national demand for teachers.

In analyzing the demand for SETs specifically, it is important and useful to distinguish between *total* demand and *annual* demand.

Total Demand for SETs

The *total demand* for SETs is closely approximated in local, state, and national databases by the number of teachers employed with a main assignment in a teaching position in special education. This is usually measured in October of each year. For any year, components of total demand are the number of *employed* SETs during a prior year plus *growth*, or *reduction*, in the total number of funded teaching positions in special education for the current year. The size of this change is the number of new teaching positions created less the number of established teaching positions discontinued.

In using SET demand in the analysis of teacher shortages, it is important to recognize that total demand for SETs is more than just the demand for teachers regardless of qualifications. Rather, it is the demand for *qualified* teachers, such as those with certifications and degree majors relevant to their teaching assignments. This is because all states in the U.S. require, as a minimum, that teaching positions be filled with teachers who are fully certified in their respective positions (National Association of State Directors of Teacher Education and Certification [NASDTEC], 2003).

The long-term trend in the total national demand for SETs is shown in Figure 5.1, an update of the trend in total SET demand beginning in 1967 reported by Boe (2006).[5] The trend of increasing total demand of SETs peaked in fall 2005 at the 426,600 level, and then decreased by 13% from fall 2005 through fall 2010. This decrease even preceded the onset of the severe national economic downturn that occurred in the fall of 2008 and resulted in substantial teacher lay-offs. The total demand in 2009 would have declined substantially from the level seen in Figure 5.1 were it not for federal stimulus funding under the American Recovery and Reinvestment Act (ARRA) that saved or created over 54,000 jobs in special education nationally (U.S. Department of Education, 2010).

It is possible that the gradual increase in the demand for SETs through 2005 and subsequent decline was driven by changes in the numbers of SWD, with the SWD : SET ratio remaining relatively constant. As seen in Figure 5.2, however, the cumulative rate of growth of SETs increased at a higher rate than that of SWD for a period of 6 years, with the difference peaking in 2005. Since then, the cumulative rate of growth of both SETs and SWD declined and reached equivalence by 2007. Throughout the years shown in Figure 5.2, the SWD : SET ratio has remained in the range of 14 : 1 to 16 : 1 (an update of such ratios reported by Boe, 2006). Thus, the demand for SETs has been closely related to the number of students identified with disabilities.

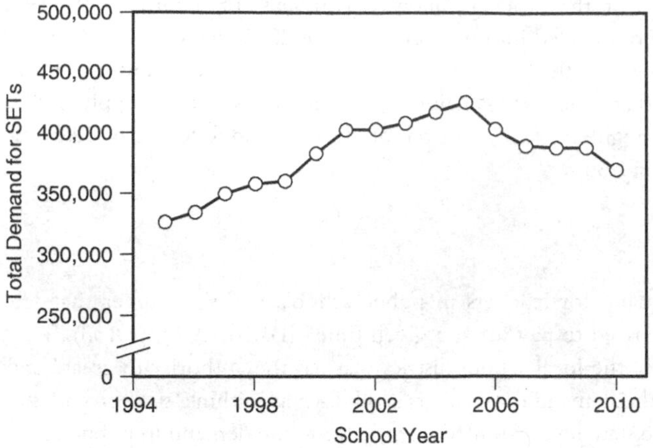

Figure 5.1 Total Demand for SETs at the National Level as of the Fall of Each Year. Total Demand Is the Number of Full-Time Equivalent SETs Employed Each Year for Students Aged 6–21 Years With Disabilities

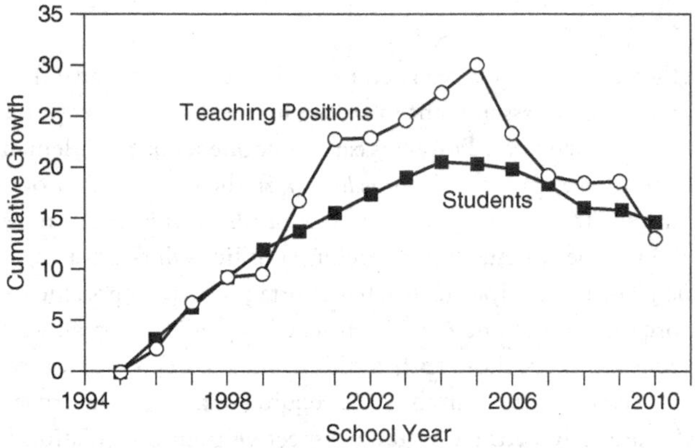

Figure 5.2 Cumulative Percentage of Annual Growth From 1995 Baseline in the Number of Students Ages 6–21 With Disabilities, Compared With the Cumulative Percentage of Annual Expansion of Full-Time Equivalent Teaching Positions in Special Education for These Students as of the Fall of Each Year

(Source of both tables: Data Analysis System of the Office of Special Education Programs)

Therefore, the reduction in total demand for SETs since 2005 can be attributed, in part, to the decline since 2004 in number of SWD identified as learning disabled. However, the decline in SET demand since 2005 was much sharper than the decline in number of SWD (see Figure 5.2). Consequently, other factors are likely to have contributed to lower demand as well, such as increased inclusion of SWD in general education classrooms and reduced funding for teaching positions in special education (Boe et al., 2013).

Annual Demand for SETs

In addition to the total demand for SETs, another indicator of teacher demand is the *annual* demand for SETs. At the national level, the annual demand for SETs is the number of vacant, but funded, teaching positions in special education that needs to be filled annually. The size of the annual demand for SETs is the sum of (a) the number of vacant teaching position due to SETs who *leave* teaching employment (i.e., attrition), (b) the number of vacant teaching positions in special education due to SETs who *switch* to general education, and (c) the *growth*, or *reduction*, in the number of total funded teaching positions in special education from one year to the next.

Based on national data (Boe, Cook, & Sunderland, 2008, 2009c; ideadata.org, 2011), it is possible to estimate the annual national demand for SETs, including the contributions of annual attrition, out-switching, and growth in teaching positions. As seen in Figure 5.3, annual demand increased systematically from 1991 through 2004 to a level of about 90,000 in 2004—representing about 22% of total SET demand for the 2004–2005 school year (i.e., one in every five SET positions). Overall, exit attrition accounted for 40%, out-switching to general education accounted for 46%, and growth accounted for the remaining 14%.

It is not known at the national level whether the annual demand for SETs declined after 2004 as total SET demand did. However, it is reasonable to surmise that it did so, because evidence collected and reviewed by Boe et al. (2013) indicated a dramatic decline in the annual demand for SETs in several states after 2008.

Discussion of Demand

As shown here and in the Annual Reports to Congress by OSEP beginning in 1976 (e.g., OSEP, 2004), the total demand for qualified SETs grew steadily for almost three decades (to 2005). With the backdrop of chronic shortages of qualified SETs, this increasing demand has driven the need for an ever increasing production of novice teachers, originally by traditional teacher preparation (TTP) programs and augmented later (beginning in 1985) by alternative teacher preparation (AR—alternative route) programs (Cook & Boe, 2007; Boe, Cook, & Sunderland, 2009a).

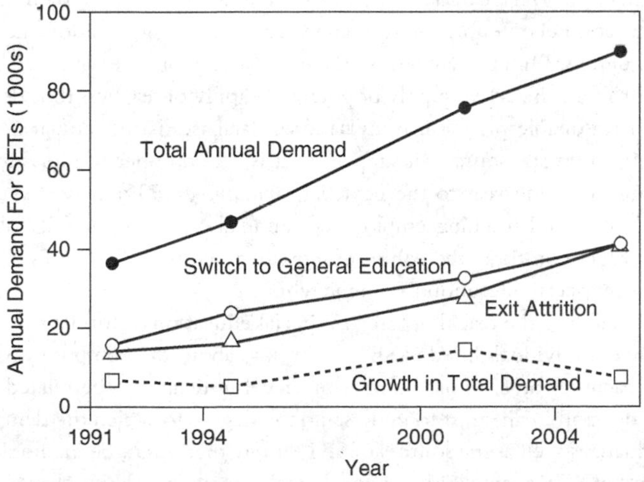

Figure 5.3 Annual Demand for Newly Appointed SETs at the National Level for Each Year

(Data for the Growth in Total Demand From the Data Accountability Center of OSEP, USDE)

Note

Annual demand is the sum of SETs leaving teaching employment after the prior year (exit attrition), SETs switching to general education after the prior year, and the growth in total demand since the prior year. Data for exit attrition and switching from the 1991–1992, 1994–1995, 2000–2001, and 2004–2005 Teacher Follow-Up Surveys, NCES, USDE.

As stated in the introduction, the enduring interest in teacher supply and demand has been due primarily to the serious and chronic shortage of teachers. For decades, the steadily increasing demand for SETs resulted in a shortfall of supply. The recent downturn in SET demand (beginning in 2006) is likely to change this. In the short term, the supply of qualified SETs may well begin to approximate or even exceed the reduced demand. If so, shortages will diminish greatly. Following from this, many teacher education programs may be scaled down or discontinued if the demand for newly minted SETs declines.

Given the historic long-term trend of increasing SET demand, the observed recent decline in the demand has raised questions about what factors contribute to it, whether it is temporary and will reverse in the intermediate future, and its impact on how special education is configured to produce the best attainable outcomes for SWD. In fact, the decline in the size of the teaching force in special education raises uncertainty about whether special education is capable of achieving this goal. Current analyses of and initial research on these issues are reported by Boe et al. (2013).

Although the future impacts of reduced SET demand on the field of special education cannot be predicted with confidence, it is reasonable to expect that they will be profound and therefore worthy of intensive study. The demand for SETs, and its many ramifications, is a topic requiring ongoing systematic analysis and research.

Supply

In general, the total national supply of teachers for public schools in any year is defined as "the number of eligible individuals available from all sources who are willing to supply their services under prevailing conditions" (Boe & Gilford, 1992, p. 24).[6] This definition of teacher supply for public schools can be referred to as the *active* supply, as defined operationally as all eligible individuals who are employed as teachers plus such other eligible individuals who applied for at least one teaching position in a public school within a 1-year period, whether hired or not. In a larger sense, the *potential* supply could be conceived of as all eligible individuals, including members of the reserve pool (former teachers and teacher preparation graduates who have delayed their first teaching employment by more than 1 year), who either are or might later become interested in applying for teaching positions under existing or improved prevailing conditions. Unfortunately, no source of national or state data is capable of providing adequate information about the active supply or potential supply of teachers thus defined.

What is known with reasonable precision from national databases is the annual number of SETs hired in public schools from several sources of supply. That is, the number of individuals continuing in public school teaching from one year to the next (i.e., *continuing* SETs) as well as the number of individuals entering public school teaching employment annually (i.e., *entering* SETs). Collectively, continuing and entering SETs constitute the cohort of individuals employed as SETs (i.e., the national employed teaching force in special education for public schools).

To be useful in understanding the teaching force in special education, information is needed about various sources of supply of individuals hired as SETs, as well as about the composition, qualifications, and distribution of the teaching force. Information at this level of detail can be related to comparable information about SET demand in an effort to understand the degree to which the demand for SETs is met by qualified individuals, as well as the sources of SET supply that might be manipulated by policy. Research on these aspects of SET supply at the national level is reviewed in this chapter.

Continuing Teacher Supply[7]

Of the total teaching force in special education, teachers continuing from one year to the next accounted for between 91% and 93% for the school years 1987–1988 through 2003–2004 (Cook & Boe, 2007; Boe et al., 2009a). The trend the over years in this percentage has been so stable as to give confidence in extrapolating it to more recent years. Obviously, continuing teachers are the predominant source of the supply of SETs, with entering teachers being a vital, but much smaller, source (7%–9%).

Entering Teacher Supply

The size of entering teacher supply in special education, broken down by first-time teachers and experienced teachers, is shown in Table 5.1 for the 1999–2000 school year. A detailed breakdown of the components of entering SET supply is seen in Table 5.2 (data from Boe & Cook, 2006). Some first-time SETs are classified as recent graduates (i.e., within 1 year of graduating), while others are classified as delayed entrants (i.e., 1 or more years since graduating) from the reserve pool. First-time SETs are further subdivided as having extensive teacher preparation (i.e., substantial coursework in teaching methods and a substantial amount of student teaching, as required for full certification), or having some teacher preparation (i.e., less than extensive), or having no teacher preparation.[8]

The predominant source of entering SETs (51.4%) was first-time teachers of all types. The second most productive source of entering SETs was represented by reentering experienced teachers from the reserve pool (41.7%). This source, plus private school migrants (7.0%), indicates that almost half of entering SETs had prior teaching experience. It should also be noted that 5.1% of entering SETs had no preparation for teaching whatsoever.

First-Time Teacher Supply

A more detailed analysis of the preparation of first-time SETs by Cook and Boe (2007) demonstrated that only 46.5% were extensively prepared to teach in special education, whereas another 17.6% of

Table 5.1 The Special Education Teaching Force in Public Schools: National Estimates of the Numbers of Teachers and the Percentages Who Were Partly Certified in Their Main Teaching Assignment, by Four Sources of Supply for the 1999–2000 School Year

	Total SETs		*Partly Certified*[a,b]	
Supply Source	*Number*	*Col %*[c]	*%*	*SE %*
I. Continuing Teachers				
A. Established Teachers[d]	256,489	77.7%	7.4%	0.7%
B. Transitional Teachers[d]	47,890	14.5%	23.2%	2.8%
Subtotal: Continuing	304,379	92.2%	9.9%	0.7%
II. Entering Teachers				
A. First-Time Teachers	13,292	4.0%	60.2%	5.6%
B. Experienced Teachers	12,626	3.8%	27.7%	3.6%
Subtotal: Entering	25,917	7.9%	44.4%	3.9%
Total Teaching Force[e]	330,297	100.1%	12.6%	0.8%

Notes

Data from the 1999–2000 Schools and Staffing Surveys, National Center for Education Statistics, USDE.

a Partly Certified % is the percentage of partly certified SETs *out of* the total number of nationally estimated SETs for each source of supply. SE % is the standard error of the partly certified percentages.

b The supply source by full- vs. part-certification χ^2 (3, N=4,919) =613.4, p <.001.

c Col. % is the column percentages of the nationally estimated number of SETs.

d Established teachers continued in their assignments for 2 or 3 years: transitional teachers entering teaching, switched from general education, and changed assignments within special education, during the prior 2-year period.

e The sample size (N) for total SETs was 4,920.

Table 5.2 Entering Special Education Teachers in Public Schools: Weighted National Estimates of the Numbers of Teachers and the Percentages Who Were Partly Certified in Their Main Teaching Assignment, by Seven Sources of Entering Supply for the 1999–2000 School Year

	Total		*Partly Certified*[ab]	
Supply Source: Entering SETs	*Number*	*Col. %*[c]	*%*	*SE%*
I. First-Time SETs: Recent Graduates				
A. With Extensive Teacher Preparation	6,129	23.7%	35.9%	7.7%
B. With Some Teacher Preparation	–[d]	2.1%	98.6%[d]	2.7%
Subtotal: Recent Graduates	6,668	25.8%	41.0%	7.8%
II. Reserve Pool				
A. First-Time SETs: Delayed Entry Entrants				
1. With Extensive Teacher Preparation	3,706	14.3%	64.9%	9.3%
2. With Some Teacher Preparation	–[d]	6.2%	98.2%[d]	2.7%
B. Reentering Experienced SETs	10,801	41.7%	26.8%	4.0%
Subtotal: Reserve Pool	16,101	62.2%	42.7%	4.7%
III. Other Entering SETs				
A. First-Time SETs without Teacher Preparation	–[d]	5.1%	97.8%[d]	1.5%
B. Private School Migrants	1,824	7.0%	32.9%	11.1%
Subtotal: Other Entering SETs	3,149	12.1%	60.2%	10.9%
Total Entering SETs[e]	25,918	100.1%	44.4%	3.9%

Source: Data from the 1999–2000 Schools and Staffing Surveys, National Center for Education Statistics, USDE.

Notes

a Partly Certified % is the percentage of partly certified SETs out of the total number of nationally estimated SETs for each source of supply. SE % is the standard error of the partly certified percentages.

b For special education teachers, the supply source by full- vs. part-certification χ^2 (6, N=460)=111.1, $p < .001$.

c Col. % is the column percentages of the nationally estimated number of SETs.

d Sample size (n) is less than 30.

e The sample size (N) for total entering SETs was 460.

first-time SETs were extensively prepared to teach in general education. The remaining 35.9% of first-time SETs had lesser levels of preparation for teaching in special education. These findings demonstrate the severe shortage of extensively prepared and appropriately degreed first-time SETs, a shortage so severe that one in every ten first-time SETs had no preparation whatsoever. In the following section, we consider explanations for the shortage of qualified first-time SETs.

Preparation Routes

In the U.S., teacher preparation programs located in colleges and universities have served as the traditional provider of teacher preparation for over 80 years (Schwartz, 1996). Completion of such programs culminates in either a bachelor's or master's degree, and qualifies graduates for full certification. This route to teaching employment is now referred to as TTP (Boe et al., 2009a).

Figure 5.4 shows trends in productivity of degree graduates from teacher preparation programs in special education during the past 18 years (an update of the trend reported by Cook & Boe, 2007). From 1997 through 2007, the production of bachelor's graduates with a special education major gradually declined to the level of about 8,000 per year in 2004 and then increased gradually to the 8,500 level by 2011. This compares with about 17,000 bachelor's graduates in 1977 (Cook & Boe) when the corresponding demand for SETs was much lower (Boe, 2006). The decline in the production of bachelor's

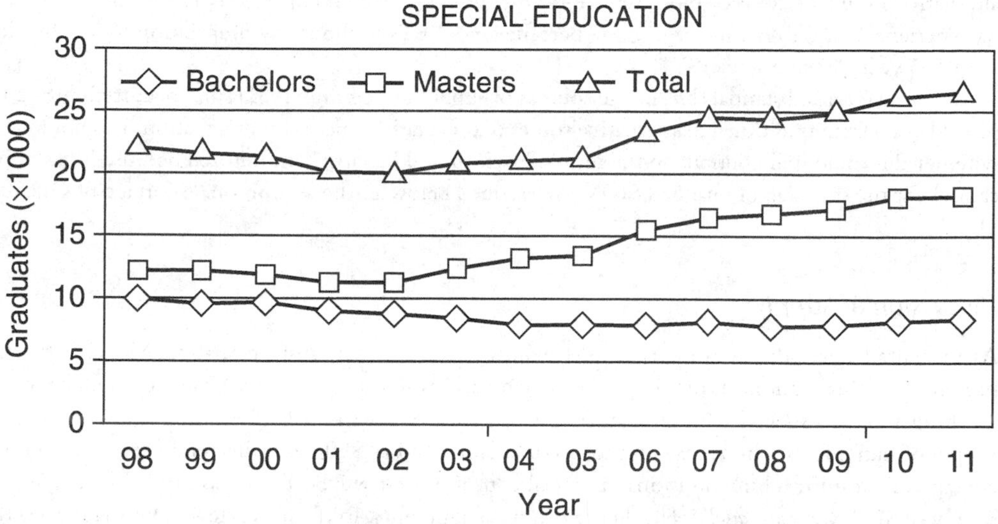

Figure 5.4 Number of Degree Graduates (Thousands) With Majors in Teacher Preparation in Special Education as a Function of Year and Degree Level

(Data from the Integrated Postsecondary Education Data System (IPEDS) of the National Center for Educational Statistics, USDE)

graduates from traditional programs through 2005 occurred in spite of the sharply rising demand for SETs through 2005 seen in Figure 5.1. Then, just as demand has declined since 2005, the production of bachelors graduated in special education teaching began to increase. It these trends continue for some years, the shortage of qualified SETs should gradually be reduced.

The trend of increasing master's degree graduates since 2002 with a variety of majors in special education teaching, as seen in Figure 5.4, might seem to be another reason for expecting reduced shortage of qualified SETs. However, this is not the case because about 89% all such graduates are already employed as teachers (Boe, Sunderland, & Cook, 2006). Although it is constructive for employed SETs to improve their qualifications by earning a relevant advanced degree, this source yields few first-time SETs and does not address the shortage of qualified entering SETs in a substantial way.

As the production of bachelor's graduates from TTP programs declined through 2007, entrants to special education teaching from a second route—AR—have increased (Boe et al., 2009a). Since its inception in 1985, alternative preparation has provided a means by which individuals can secure employment as teachers by circumventing completion of TTP programs. While most traditional programs lead to a degree, some alternative preparation is organized as nondegree programs for individuals who have already earned at least a bachelor's degree. There is great variability in alternative preparation routes (see Feistritzer, 2005, for a description of much of this variation), but much less so in traditional preparation routes.

Boe et al. (2009a) compared the productivity of traditional and alternative preparation routes in preparing employed SETs during the 20 years prior to the 2003–2004 school year. During this period of increasing demand for SETs, the percentage of SETs prepared by traditional means was considerably lower for those with 1–3 years of experience (66.1%) than for those with 11–20 years of experience (82.2%). This decline was compensated for by (a) an increase in the percentage of SETs prepared by alternative means (27.6% for those with 1–3 years of experience compared to 17% with 11–20 years of experience), and (b) an increase in the percentage of SETs without any preparation (6.3% for those with 1–3 years of experience).

In summary, a substantial shift in the sources of supply of beginning SETs has occurred during the past 20 years from traditional to alternative routes of preparation and to no preparation. It is not known whether this trend will continue in the future, but it should be closely monitored because it has implications for the shortage of qualified SETs (as described below in the section on "Shortage of Qualified SETs").

Discussion of Supply

As presented here, the active supply of teachers is not known. Instead, national-level data were presented in this section on the degree to which various sources of supply produce members of the teaching force in special education during a particular year. Overall, there has been an adequate supply of individuals who are willing to become employed as SETs as indicated by a very small percentage of vacant teaching positions in special education. However, there has not been an adequate supply of SETs who are *qualified* in their teaching assignments. Evidence reviewed here indicates that there has been a considerable shortage of qualified first-time SETs. In fact, there has been a large shortage of qualified SETs, the degree of which varies by source of supply. This will be described in the following section.

Increasing the supply of qualified SETs is one major option for reducing the teacher shortage in special education. One such approach has been to expand the production of teachers from AR programs. By 2003–2004, AR programs were producing about 5,000 new hires of first-time SETs annually (compared with a negligible amount 20 years prior). However, this was offset by a decline of almost 5,000 bachelor's degree graduates from AR programs in special education during this period. This has occurred in spite of a substantial commitment during past decades to initial teacher preparation in special education by OSEP, as well as to improving the qualifications of employed SETs through professional development (West & Whitby, 2008).

Nonetheless, the continuing shortage of qualified SETs should not obscure the successes of special education in increasing the supply of qualified SETs over time. As the demand for SETs increased by over 40% from 1988 to 2002, so did the number of fully certified SETs (Boe, 2006). As observed by Boe, "This represents a remarkable achievement by teacher preparation and professional development programs in special education to increase the supply of fully certified SETs" (2006, p. 147).

Shortage of Qualified SETs

A teacher shortage exists when the active supply of *qualified* teachers is insufficient to satisfy total teacher demand. The degree of shortage varies with teaching assignment, grade level, geographic location, and the socioeconomic status of students enrolled in schools. In special education, there has long been a pervasive shortage of qualified teachers across these dimensions, with the exception of a surplus of applicants for positions in schools that rank high in compensation and student academic achievement (Lauritzen & Friedman, 1992).

In contrast with the shortage of qualified teachers, shortage could also be defined in terms of the shortage of *effective teachers*—effective in the sense of producing at least an adequate level of student learning. In fact, teacher qualifications and teacher effectiveness can be subsumed under a multidimensional rubric of *teacher quality* encompassing *qualifications*, *classroom performance*, and *student achievement growth* (Boe, Cook, Sunderland, McGrew, & May, 2005)

Fortunately, good measures of teacher qualifications are available, as represented by the research findings reviewed below about the amount of teacher preparation completed and whether SETs earned a bachelor's degree or higher, were fully certified, and had a degree major in their teaching assignment. Unfortunately, good measures of teacher classroom performance are not available, although the Educational Testing Service, through its "Understanding Teacher Quality Center," is currently embarked on a large-scale effort to develop such measures (Tyler, 2010), and much remains to be learned about dimensions of teacher effectiveness that may be strongly predictive of student achievement.

Bachelor's Degrees

A uniform requirement for teacher certification in all states is that candidates must have earned at least a bachelor's degree (NASDTEC, 2003). Similarly, the No Child Left Behind Act (NCLB) includes this requirement as part of the definition of a highly qualified teacher (HQT). Overall, only a small percentage (about 1%) of public school teachers has not met this standard. This is also true of beginning public school teachers in their first 3 years of teaching experience who completed a TTP. However, 4% of such beginning teachers who completed AR programs had not earned at least a bachelor's degree (Boe et al., 2009a).

Certification Status

Because all U.S. states require that teaching positions be staffed by teachers fully certified in their main teaching assignments (MTAs) (NASDTEC, 2003), SETs should be fully certified in special education. However, NCLB requires only that teachers be fully certified in any subject or disability status (2001). To be defined as *fully certified* using SASS terminology, a teacher must hold either an advanced professional certificate or a regular, standard, or probationary state certificate in their MTA. A probationary certificate is issued after satisfying all requirements for a regular or standard certificate except the completion of a probationary period. To be regarded as *partially certified*, a teacher may hold a provisional, temporary, or emergency certificate, or may have received a waiver of the certificate requirement, or hold no certificate or license of any type in the state of the employing school district. To the extent that SETs are only *partly certified* in their MTA, there is a shortage of fully certified SETs.

As shown in Table 5.1 (Boe & Cook, 2006), only 7.4% of established SETs—teachers who continued in their assignments for 2 or more years—were partly certified, a percentage equivalent to that for established GETs. However, 23.2% of transitional SETs (who, during the prior 2 years, had entered teaching, switched from general education, or switched between MTAs in special education) were only partly certified. Thus, one important factor impacting on the shortage of fully certified SETs has been a fairly high rate of transitional teachers in special education and their higher level of part-certification than in general education.

A second factor impacting the shortage of fully certified SETs has been a fairly high demand for entering teachers to fill open positions, over 44% of whom were partly certified (see Table 5.1). A third major source has been teachers who complete AR programs. Over half of beginning SETs from AR programs were only partly certified (52%) (Boe et al., 2009a).

Degree Major in Assignment

As of the 2003–2004 school year, over half (55%) of SETs in their first 5 years of teaching had not completed a degree major in special education teaching, whereas only 32% of novice GETs had not completed a degree major in general education teaching (Boe, Cook, & Sunderland, 2007). A similar percentage (60%) of beginning SETs had not completed a degree major in their MTA during the 1999–2000 school year (Boe, Shin, & Cook, 2007). Accordingly, there has been a substantial shortage of beginning SETs with degree majors in special education.

Amount of Teacher Preparation

Boe, et al. (2007) defined three levels of amount of teacher preparation (extensive, some, little)[9] with 2003–2004 SASS data. As seen in Table 5.3, less than 80% of SETs in their first 5 years of teaching experience have completed extensive preparation, the level ordinarily expected for candidates to qualify for full certification. The degree of shortage of beginning SETs without extensive preparation is particularly high for those who completed TTP programs (61% without extensive preparation). The shortage of SETs with extensive preparation might have increased since 2003–2004 if AR continues to produce an increasing percentage of individuals entering special education teaching.

Discussion of Shortage

There has been no shortage of individuals willing to accept open positions as SETs. When qualified individuals are not available to accept such positions, unqualified individuals will be hired to fill these positions. To the extent that a shortage of SETs might exist, therefore, it is a shortage of individuals with appropriate qualifications who are willing and able to accept teaching positions under prevailing conditions. It is the extent of the shortage of qualified SETs that has been addressed in this section.

Whether there has been a shortage of qualified teachers generally has been controversial. There are two perspectives—one asserting that there is a teacher shortage, the other asserting that there is not. The first, as stated by the National Governor's Association (NGA) (Curran & Abrahams, 2000), is that "School districts across the country are experiencing shortages of qualified teachers" (p. 1). The second, as stated by the National Commission for Teaching and America's Future (NCTAF) (2003), is that "The common conception is that we just don't have enough good teachers to meet the demand. But,

Table 5.3 Amount of Preservice Teacher Preparation by Type of Teacher Preparation Completed by Beginning Special Education Teachers: Weighted National Estimates for the 2003–2004 School Year

		Amount of Teacher Preparation[a]			
Type of Teacher Preparation[a]	*Statistic*[b]	*Extensive*	*Some*	*None*	*Total*
Traditional Teacher Preparation					
Degree Programs	Nat. Est.	55.9K	2.9K	2.3K	61.1K
	Row %	91.6%	4.7%	3.7%	100.0%
Other Traditional	Nat. Est.	4.4K	0.5K	–[c]	5.3K
	Row %	82.1%	9.5%	–[c]	100.0%
Alternative Teacher Preparation					
Alternative Programs	Nat. Est.	6.8K	5.8K	4.9K	17.5K
	Row %	39.0%	33.1%	27.9%	100.0%
Other Alternative	Nat. Est.	4.1K	0.6K	1.7K	6.4K
	Row %	63.7%	10.4%	25.9%	100.0%
Total	Nat. Est.	71.2K	9.8K	9.3K	90.3K
	Row %	78.8%	10.9%	10.3%	100.0%
	Sample (n)	940	120	80	1,140

Source: Data from the 2003–2004 Schools and Staffing Survey, National Center for Education Statistics, USDE. See Boe, Cook, et al. (2006) for definitions of variables analyzed.

Notes

a The association between the four types of teacher preparation and the three amounts of teacher preparation was statistically significant ($p<.001$) ($4>3$ χ^2 test).

b Nationally weighted estimates (Nat. Est.) of the numbers of full-time and part-time SETs combined at the elementary and secondary levels. Row percentages (Row%) are based on the national estimates. Totals may not sum exactly due to rounding.

c N<30.

the conventional wisdom is wrong" (p. 8). Based on research findings reviewed above, my perspective is that there has been a chronic shortage of qualified SETs in the sense that the *active* supply has been insufficient to meet the demand under prevailing conditions.

The contrary perspective, such as taken by NCTAF, is that the *potential* supply of teachers (i.e., the active supply plus other individuals who are qualified for teaching positions) is sufficient to meet the demand if the prevailing conditions were much improved. This perspective represents a powerful case for improving incentives for teachers to accept less desirable teaching assignments (such as to locate in underserved rural and inner city areas), for improving working conditions, and for increasing compensation. Efforts by policy makers or others to make such improvements to prevailing conditions are constructive and should be encouraged. To the extent that such efforts are effective, the active supply of qualified teachers should increase, thereby reducing shortages. But until the active supply of qualified teachers is sufficient to staff all teaching positions, wherever they occur in every teaching field, teacher shortages will continue.

In summary, there has been a minor shortage of teachers (including SETs) who have earned bachelor's degrees, mostly concentrated in beginning teachers who have completed AR. There has been a considerable shortage of SETs with full certification, especially among those who are new to teaching and who have recently changed teaching assignments. Perhaps of even greater concern has been a large shortage of beginning SETs who have been prepared specifically to teach SWD. The lack of sufficient supply of such SETs has been addressed by the hiring of teachers who have been prepared to teach in general education and by those who have not completed the amount and type of teacher preparation routinely expected of candidates applying for full certification in special education. In short, there has been a substantial shortage of qualified SETs in multiple critical dimensions.

The size and persistence of the shortage of qualified SETs has raised questions about how it can be explained and what can be done about it. These have been enduring problems for policy makers and leaders in the field of special education, problems compounded by the ever increasing demand for a larger teaching force for the field, until recently. However, with the decline in total demand for SETs during the past few years, this issue may be in flux, at least temporarily (Boe et al., 2013). In the sections that follow, various explanations for the shortage of SETs are considered and possible policy responses are discussed.

Turnover[10]

Teacher turnover has become a major concern in educational research and policy analysis because of the demand it creates for replacement teachers (Boe et al., 2008; NCTAF, 2003; Kozleski, Mainzer, & Deshler, 2000; Johnson, Berg, & Donaldson, 2005). For example, Kozleski et al. claimed that "Many special educators leave the profession each year. They leave at almost twice the rate of their general education colleagues" (p. 7). This concern was further dramatized by NCTAF's assertion that "Our inability to support high quality teaching is driven not by too few teachers coming in, but by too many going out, that is, by staggering rates of teacher turnover" (p. 21). These sources attribute the apparent shortage of teachers to exceptionally high demand created by an excessive rate of turnover, rather than insufficient supply. In this sense, teacher shortage is said to be a myth because the supply of teachers is thought to be adequate (Ingersoll, 1997; NCTAF, 2003; Podgursky, 2006). However, this level of concern belies available turnover data.

The contrary and common perspective advanced in this chapter and by others (e.g., Curran & Abrahams, 2000; Boe & Gilford, 1992) is that teacher shortage is due to an imbalance between active teacher supply and demand. Accordingly, a main purpose of this section is to present evidence from research that examines various claims of *excessive* turnover as the predominant factor driving the shortage of SETs. Another purpose is to organize and present research-based information about the extent of, and reasons for, turnover.

Teacher turnover refers to major changes in a teacher's assignment from one school year to the next. Turnover includes three components, the first and third of which have been widely studied: (a) attrition (leaving teaching employment), (b) teaching area transfer (switching from one teaching area to another), and (c) teacher migration (moving to a different school).

Teaching area transfer has been of particular concern to the field of special education because of the switching of SETs to teaching assignments in general education (Kozleski, et al., 2000).

The results of research on teacher turnover have been used to promote major initiatives to improve education policy and practice, all of which were designed to reduce teacher turnover. At the policy level, NCTAF (2003) recommended downsizing schools, offering federal financial incentives for attracting teachers into high shortage areas, and higher teacher compensation. At the practice level, Kozleski et al. (2000) and Billingsley (2005) suggested a number of strategies to enhance teacher retention, including effective professional development and reasonable work assignments. In view of this widespread use of research to advocate changes in policy and practice, it is important to have valid research-based evidence about turnover to assess its impact on SET shortages. Yet, much is not known, and there are several fundamental issues with the reporting, interpretation, and application of teacher turnover statistics to be considered here.

Attrition

The attrition of SETs is a major source of the annual demand for new SET hires. In fact, in 2004–2005, attrition accounted for about 40% of annual demand, or about 41,000 SETs (Boe et al., 2009c). From 1991 through 2004, there has been a steep increase in the annual rate of SET attrition, reaching 10% (see Figure 5.5; Boe et al., 2009c) and thereby increasing demand for new hires of qualified SETs. However, the attrition rates of SETs were not significantly different than that of public school GETs (Boe et al., 2009c).

There has been a long-standing concern about the rate of attrition among novice teachers. However, according to Boe et al. (2008), the average annual attrition rate of SETs in public schools during their first 3 years of teaching employment was 7.9%, a rate comparable to that for beginning GETs and virtually identical to the attrition rate (8%) for all bachelor's degree graduates during their first 3 years of teaching (Presley, 2003). Thus, as shown above with overall attrition rates, the attrition rates of beginning SETs have not been excessive in comparison with those seen in general education. Just as the average attrition of all SETs has increased incrementally since 1991 (see Figure 5.5), so has average attrition for novice SETs (from 7.1% in 1991 to 8.4% in 2000) (Boe et al., 2008).

In addition, the attrition rate of public school teachers has not been higher than that found in other occupations. As reported by Boe et al. (2008), the annual corporate attrition rate for SETs during the 1990s was 10.1%, compared to 13.2% for nonbusiness employees in the U.S. Quite clearly, teacher attrition was not excessively high in comparison with other nonbusiness occupations. With data from the Bachelors & Beyond survey, Presley (2003) reported an annual teacher attrition rate of 8% (from public and private schools combined), a rate no greater than that of the 12 other occupations studied. In addition, Harris and Adams (2007) found that the attrition rate of public school teachers was equivalent to that of nurses and accountants, and lower than that of social workers. Thus, there is *no* evidence that the teacher attrition rates have been excessive in comparison with rates in other occupations.

To investigate the concern that large numbers of teachers leave because they become dissatisfied or for higher paying jobs in other occupations, Boe, Cook, and Sunderland (2005) analyzed the reasons for leaving teaching employment given by public school teachers who left teaching in 1991, 1994, and 2000. The findings are described here for all public school teachers because, overall, SETs and GETs did not differ significantly in these respects (Boe et al., 2008). The reasons for leaving teaching employment were grouped into five major categories: escape teaching, professional

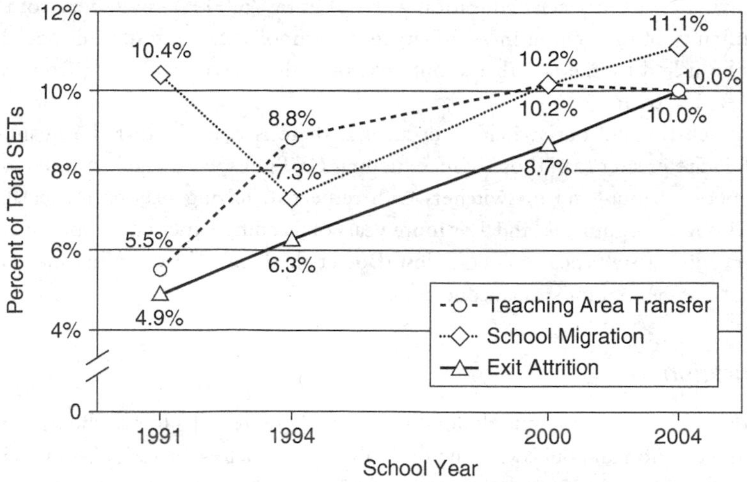

Figure 5.5 Annual Percentage of All SETs Who Left Teaching Employment, Transferred Teaching Areas, or Migrated to Another School by Year

(Data from the 1991–1992, 1994–1995, 2000–2101, and 2004–2005 Teacher Follow-Up Surveys, NCES, USDE)

Note
The trends of increasing exit attrition and teaching area transfer were statistically significant ($p<.001$), whereas the change in school migration over years was not.

development, personal, retirement, and involuntary. Contrary of expectations, only 25% left to escape teaching (i.e., for dissatisfaction or for higher paying jobs in other occupations), whereas 30% left for personal reasons and another 27% retired. Smaller percentages left involuntarily (9%) or for professional development in teaching (9%) (Boe, et al., 2005). Thus, only 25% of teacher attrition would be amenable to policy intervention. For those who leave to escape teaching, it is reasonable to expect that dramatic improvements in induction programs, working conditions, administrative support, and salaries would reduce attrition, but such improvements would likely have only modest impact on the substantial majority of teachers who leave for other reasons (i.e., personal reasons, poor health, job actions, and retirement).

Teaching Area Transfer

Although out-switching of SETs to general education accounts for 46% of annual demand and is as much a loss to the field of special education as attrition, the paucity of research on teaching area transfer contrasts sharply with the wealth of research on teacher attrition. However, as shown in Figure 5.5, Boe et al. (2009c) found that the annual teaching area transfer rate of SETs almost doubled from 5.5% in 1991 to 10% in 2004, and the aggregate annual rates of GETs transferring among 12 teaching areas was not significantly different than the rate of out-switchers from special education. With respect to SETs during their first 3 years of teaching, the average annual rate of teaching area transfer was 12% in 1991, 1994, and 2000 combined, a rate comparable to that of GETs (Boe et al., 2008). In this sense, the rate of teaching area transfer of beginning SETs has not been excessive either.

While out-switching of SETs to general education represents a loss to special education, in-switching of GETs to special education represents a gain. Fortunately, the out-switching of SETs to general education is roughly equivalent in *numbers* to the simultaneous in-switching of GETs to special education (Boe et al., 2008). Overall during the years 1991, 1994, and 2000 combined, the

73,000 out-switchers from special education were offset by 75,000 in-switchers from general education. The difficulty of integrating in-switchers into a school's teaching staff in special education was somewhat diminished by the fact that about 75% of such in-switchers came from within the same school (Boe et al., 2005).

With so much in- and out-switching occurring, there is concern that the qualifications of out-switching SETs are greater than those of in-switching GETs in special education. However, there was equivalency between out- and in-switchers with respect to having majors in special education, full certification, in-area assignments, and 4 or more years of teaching experience. Special education gained more teachers with master's degrees than it lost (Boe et al., 2005). Basically, in- and out-switching has been qualifications-neutral for special education.

School Migration

The migration of SETs to other schools does not routinely represent a loss to the field of special education as does the attrition and out-switching of SETs.[11] Nonetheless, *to a school*, a mover is just as costly as a leaver. At the school level, the migration of SETs requires a supply of replacement teachers. The annual school migration rate of SETs has generally been 10% or greater since 1991 (Boe et al., 2009c). It has been higher than either attrition or teaching area transfer (see Figure 5.5). In 2004, SETs moved to a different school at a significantly higher rate than GETs (11.1% vs. 7.7; Boe et al., 2009c). In this comparison, the migration of SETs appears to have been excessive.

The average annual school migration rate of SETs in public schools during their first 3 years of teaching employment was much higher (19.8%) during 1991, 1994, and 2000 combined (Boe et al., 2008). This rate was substantially higher than the comparable rate for beginning GETs (13.1%). The highest rates of school migration of both SETs and GETs occurred during their first 3 years of teaching, then gradually and substantially declined to well under 10% after 12 years of teaching experience (Boe et al., 2008).

Unfortunately, the specific causes of SET school migration are not known. In prior national research based on all public school teachers, the *main* reason for within-district migration was involuntary on the part of teachers (i.e., 51% was due to school staffing actions by administrative decision) (Boe, Barkanic, & Leow, 1999). In addition, Luekens, Lyter, and Fox (2004) used TFS data for 2000–2001 to compute the percentage of all public school teachers who rated various reasons for all moving (i.e., within- and between-districts combined) as very important or extremely important. By far, the two most important reasons (reported by about 40% of movers) were opportunity for a better teaching assignment (subject area or grade level) and dissatisfaction with administrative support at the previous school.[12]

Total Turnover

As shown in Figure 5.6, the total annual turnover (the sum of attrition, teaching area transfer, and school migration) of SETs increased substantially during the 13-year period from 1991 to 2004 (Boe et al., 2009c).[13] Total annual turnover in special education increased 119% (from 64,100 in 1991–1992 to 118,500 in 2004–2005). This was during a period when the total teaching force in special education (for SWD age 6–21) increased only 35% from 308,900 in 1991–1992 to 417,900 in 2004–2005 (Boe, 2006; ideadata.org, 2005). Thus, the percentage increase in total annual turnover in special education was over 3 times greater than the percentage increase in its teaching force during this 13-year period.

In percentages, the increasing total annual turnover trend seen in general education was virtually the same as in special education. As both the number of public school teachers and the number of public schools increased, the number of teachers turning over per public school increased from 5.66 in 1991–1992 to 8.34 in 2000–2001 (a 47% increase) (Boe et al., 2008).

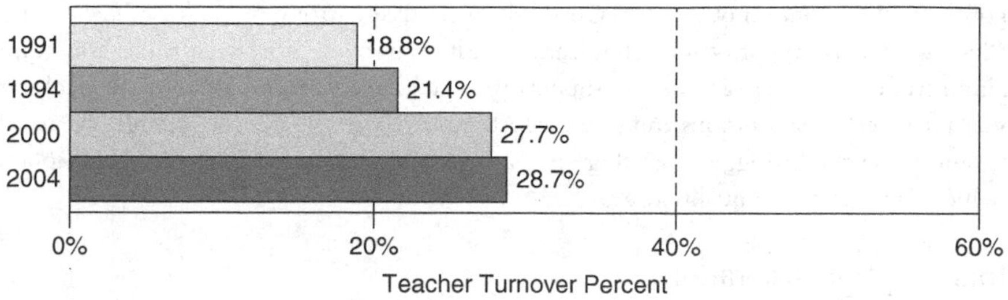

Figure 5.6 Annual Total Turnover of SETs (Attrition, Teaching Area Transfer, and School Migration, Combined) Based on Unduplicated Counts of SETs

(Data from the 1991–1992, 1994–1995, 2000–2001, and 2004–2005 Teacher Follow-Up Surveys, NCES, USDE)

Thus, total annual turnover of public school teachers has grown to what might be considered an alarming level. More than one of every four specific teaching positions in special education was subject to annual turnover by 2004. That is, as positions became open through the departure of incumbent SETs, they were filled with newly recruited teachers. This degree of instability in the teaching staff of individual schools represents a serious problem of filling open teaching positions that educational administrators must, and do, solve each year. Unfortunately as we have seen above, this has been accomplished all too often by appointing unqualified individuals.

Predictors of Turnover

A large and active field of research has been devoted to identifying and analyzing the main predictors of teacher turnover. Because teaching field did not prove to be a statistically significant predictor in two multivariate studies (Boe, Bobbitt, Cook, Barkanic, & Maislin, 1998; Boe, Cook, & Sunderland, 2009b), significant predictors of turnover apply equally well to SET and GET turnover. Accordingly, the discussion of predictors of turnover below pertains to all public school teachers. Some of the highlights of the most recent analyses of turnover with data from the 2004–2005 TFS are reviewed below by turnover component. These analyses have the advantage of being based on the same data and being analyzed by the same multivariate method with the same array of predictor variables, rendering meaningful any differences between the main predictors of each of the three components of turnover.

Predictors of Attrition

The main predictors of *lower* attrition (i.e., higher retention) of teachers in their first 5 years were having extra classroom assistance during the first year of teaching, being well prepared in classroom management, being a racial/ethnic minority, and becoming married during the past year (Boe et al., 2009b). A main value of such multivariate analyses is to identify factors that can be manipulated by policy that promotes the retention of qualified teachers. Two such predictor variables emerged in this analysis—extra classroom assistance and being well prepared in classroom management (Boe et al., 2009b).

Predictors of Teaching Area Transfer

From the only analysis of predictors of out-switching in their first 5 years (Boe, 2009), two fairly strong predictors of *lower* teaching area transfer were identified: having a helpful mentor teacher during their first year of teaching and having a degree major in the teaching area of a teacher's assignment. The latter finding indicates that teachers who do not have a degree major in the area of their assignment are more likely to out-switch to some another area. Curiously, a relatively strong predictor of *higher* out-switching was "having regular supportive communication with a school administrator." This might mean that school administrators provided advice and support in switching to a more appropriate teaching assignment given a teacher's qualifications and interests. All three of these predictor variables are manipulable by policy, and these results suggest that there is a strong tendency for teachers to switch to a teaching area for which they are better qualified.

Predictors of School Migration

For teachers in their first 5 years of teaching employment (Boe et al., 2009b), a very strong predictor of migration was the opportunity for teachers to move to schools in which they would be assigned to teach in an area in which they hold a degree major. As suggested above with the predictors of teaching area transfer, beginning teachers tend to change assignments and schools in order to move into teaching areas for which they are more qualified and perhaps interested (as indicated by the content of their degree majors). This is a benefit of this type of turnover (as well as of teaching area transfer).

Liabilities and Benefits of Turnover

The field of education has allowed high rates of turnover to happen even though it has been recognized that teacher turnover is costly in terms of student achievement, school functioning, and administrative expenditures (see Johnson et al., 2005). Replacement teachers may be less qualified and less effective in producing student learning. Discontinuity in a school's teaching staff may result in loss of valuable institutional memory, diminish staff cohesion, and interrupt program development. And there are high financial costs associated with the preparation, recruitment, and induction of replacement teachers. These high costs represent major liabilities of teacher turnover, and must be paid on a continuing basis.

Nonetheless, there are some benefits of turnover. Regarding teaching area transfer and school migration (as reviewed above), SETs change to areas for which they are more qualified. As to attrition, many who leave teaching are not lost to education. Based on the annual averages of three TFSs during the 1990s for all teachers, about 34% of 173,000 total leavers assumed nonteaching positions in education, whereas only 8% became employed in all noneducation occupations (Boe et al., 2008).

Another consideration is that those who leave teaching employment often reenter teaching from the reserve pool. During the 1990s, approximately 18,500 SETs (on average) left teaching annually. At the same time, approximately 9,000 experienced teachers (on average) reentered teaching in special education annually from the reserve pool (Boe et al., 2008). Furthermore, less than one fourth of reentering SETs (23%) were employed in nonteaching positions in education (K–12 grades) during the year prior to reentry.

Finally, there is the question of qualifications of teachers who leave compared with those who stay. Some are concerned about the teaching profession losing its best and brightest teachers. As described above, there was a somewhat higher rate of attrition of beginning teachers. Some have suspected that those who leave may be lacking in qualifications for the demands of classroom teaching and therefore should leave (e.g., NCES, 2005; Johnson et al., 2005). There is evidence that beginning teachers who leave are about twice as likely as those who stay to be lacking in full certification and to report being less well prepared in pedagogy and in classroom management (Boe, 2008a). No doubt, some of these lesser qualified beginning teachers should have left due to not being qualified for, or suited to, teaching.

Discussion of Turnover

Some (e.g., NCTAF, 2003) contend that excessive teacher attrition is the crux of the teacher shortage problem and that otherwise teacher supply would be sufficient. The evidence reviewed here contradicts this perspective. Attrition rates for public school teachers have been equivalent to, or less than, rates seen in other occupations, and SET attrition rates have been comparable to GET attrition rates. By comparison with other occupations, teacher attrition has *not* been excessive, suggesting that teaching appears to be a reasonably appealing occupation in comparison with others. If teaching were relatively unattractive, initiatives to improve retention would have more promise of success. Even though attrition does contribute substantially to the annual demand for teachers, it does not do so excessively.

However, improvements in the working conditions and compensation for teachers would be constructive and should reduce attrition somewhat. But by how much might attrition be reduced? As of 2004, there was an annual demand for 305,000 newly hired teachers in public education. If even half the 60,000 employed teachers who left in 2004 to escape from teaching could be enticed to remain in teaching by better working conditions and compensation, then the annual demand for new teacher hires would only be reduced from 305,000 in 2004 to 275,000 (Boe, 2008b). Thus, it is not realistic to expect that reducing attrition will result in a major reduction in the shortage of qualified teachers. As Boe et al. (2008) concluded,

> Substantial improvement in teacher retention would require massive systemic changes in the culture of public schooling and even greater allocation of public funds. In spite of enormous efforts to improve public education during the past two decades, teacher attrition has increased. Given this, it is unrealistic to expect a level of sustained national commitment of sufficient scope to reduce substantially teacher attrition.
>
> *(p. 25)*

As the evidence reviewed here demonstrates, the total annual turnover of SETs was very high by 2004 (well over 25%). There is no denying that this poses enormous problems for the field. But these problems are partly offset by the beneficial aspects of turnover reviewed above. There have not been, and no doubt will not be, easy answers to the problem of how to improve the retention of qualified SETs. Gradually increasing turnover during recent decades is all the more reason to assure a larger supply of qualified SETs, willing and able to assume teaching positions in special education.

Teacher Distribution

The topic of teacher distribution refers to ensuring that teachers are placed in teaching positions for which they are qualified in terms of degree major and certification. Teacher distribution has been an active area of research during recent decades. One facet of this topic is out-of-field teaching, meaning the mismatch between a teacher's MTA and degree major (e.g., Hill, 2011). For example, Hill reported out-of-field percentages for high school teachers of 28% for mathematics, 52% for the physical sciences, and 36% for history in 2007–2008.

During the 1999–2000 and earlier SASSs, 15 specializations within special education were defined (such as learning disabilities) for both MTA and degree majors. Using this method of matching MTAs and degree majors, Boe et al. (2005) found that 53% of SETs were teaching out-of-field. Somewhat higher rates of out-of-field teaching were found for the science and bilingual education. It is not surprising that such a large percentage of SETs were teaching out-of-field because a large percentage were hired with degree majors in other fields because of the shortage of candidates with degree majors in special education (Cook & Boe, 2007).

However, Ingersoll (2002) has claimed that

> Out-of-field teaching is not primarily due to a deficit in either the quality or the quantity of teachers. Rather, out-of-field teaching is a common administrative practice whereby otherwise qualified teachers are assigned by school principals to teach classes in subjects which do not match their fields of training.
>
> *(p. 24)*

Apparently, out-of-field teaching was thought to be a product of poor management rather than inadequate supply. Boe et al. (2005) tested this interpretation by determining whether there were enough employed teachers within a state with appropriate degree majors to fill all the MTAs of a particular type within a state (e.g., whether there were enough employed teachers with majors in learning disabilities in a state to fill all the teaching positions in that state for learning-disabled students). Aggregating the 50 state-by-state findings, results showed that, even if all these teachers could be placed in the classrooms for which they held appropriate degree majors, 25% of SETs would still be teaching out-of-field. Applying the same analysis to the entire nation without considering state boundaries, out-of-field teaching in special education then dropped to 18%. Thus, even if all employed teachers in the nation with special education degrees could be placed in classrooms for which they held an appropriate major, there would still be a shortage of qualified SETs. Massive reassignment of qualified teachers throughout the nation to classrooms in special education, even if it were possible, would not eliminate the shortage problem. Similar results were found with most teaching areas.

A second facet of teacher distribution is the distribution of qualified teachers among schools of various types and locations (Boe & Gilford, 1992). This too has been an active area of research showing that qualified teachers have not been equitably distributed to schools in rural and inner city areas, to schools whose students perform at below-average level, to schools whose students tend to come from low-income families, and to schools with high concentrations of minority students (e.g., Lankford, Loeb, & Wyckoff, 2002; Oaks, 1990). Although a review of the literature on this important topic is beyond the scope of this chapter, it should be noted that efforts to engineer more equitable distribution of qualified SETs to disadvantaged schools, though laudable, will only reduce the shortage of qualified teachers in such schools; it will increase the shortage in the schools providing qualified SETs for redistribution. Thus, redistribution is not even a partial solution to the overall shortage of qualified SETs.

Explanations of Shortage

Excessive Demand

It is possible that the shortage of qualified SETs is due, at least in part, to high demand produced by growth in the number of SWDs. As reviewed above, the size of annual demand is closely related to the number of SWD. Presumably, if fewer students were classified as having a disability, there would be less demand for SETs.

Some evidence has been reported of a higher rate of identifying students with learning disabilities than warranted by available diagnostic information (Lyon, 1996; Ysseldyke, Algozzine, Richey, & Graden, 1982). If this were confirmed and quantified nationally, it would suggest that the demand for such SETs was somewhat excessive. However, because research has not been devoted specifically to the possibility of excessive national demand, it is not possible to attribute even part of the shortage of SETs to this potential source.

Excessive Attrition

As some have maintained, the supply of teachers has been adequate. In this view, there just appears to be a teacher shortage because excessive attrition drives up the annual demand for additional teacher hires. The evidence reviewed above demonstrates that this perspective is not valid. The attrition rates of SETs have been comparable to those of GETs, and the attrition of public school teachers has been either equivalent to, or less than, that reported for other nonbusiness occupations. In both senses, the attrition of SETs has not been excessive. This is also true for the attrition rates of beginning teachers in comparison with beginning workers in other professions. Simply stated, attrition is inherent in all occupations; the teaching profession has not been exceptional in this respect. In the absence of research showing that teacher attrition is higher than seen in other occupations, it is not possible to attribute even part of the shortage of qualified SETs to *excessive* attrition, even though attrition itself contributes to the shortage of SETs.

Misassignment and Misdistribution

As reviewed above, much research over recent decades has demonstrated that there is a remarkably high level of out-of-field teaching as defined by a mismatch between teachers' subject matter assignment and their degree majors. Only 47% of first-year SETs had at least one major in their teaching assignment. Nonetheless, some claim that the supply of qualified teachers is actually adequate, and the reason for this high level of out-of-field teaching is misassignment of existing supply.

As demonstrated by other research, however, even if it were possible to reassign to special education all employed teachers in the U.S. with a major in special education teaching, there would still be a large national shortage of SETs. A similar finding applies to most other teaching areas. In addition to what is already done routinely, there is only modest potential to reduce shortage by reassigning teachers to fields in which they are qualified. For example, many teachers with majors in general education teach in special education because of lack of openings in their fields at the locations and under the conditions they are willing to be employed. Likewise, many GETs have degrees in special education but prefer to teach in an area of general education. Few of these are realistic candidates for reassignment, even within a school or within a school district. And of course, no one has the authority to reassign teachers between districts within a state or between states.

With regard to misdistribution, it is widely known that the distribution of qualified teachers among schools is not equitable. There are lower percentages of qualified teachers in rural and inner city schools, in schools serving low-income populations, and in schools with high concentrations of minority students. But redistributing qualified teachers among schools to make assignments more equitable will not reduce the teacher shortage problem; it will simply make shortages more equitable. Thus, although misassignment and inequitable distribution of qualified teachers are genuine problems that should be addressed, misassignment is, at most, a minor determinant of teacher shortages.

Excessive Qualifications Requirements

According to the Thomas B. Fordham Foundation (TBFF) (1999), concerns about the shortage of qualified teachers are irrelevant, because certain traditional qualifications (teacher education, certification, and advanced degrees) are unrelated to student achievement and a barrier to recruiting promising individuals into teaching. Instead, entry to the teaching profession should be deregulated and the focus should be placed on *effective* teachers as defined by student achievement. Only a bachelor's degree in an academic subject and demonstrated expertise in each subject taught (by a degree major or tested knowledge) are regarded as the minimum qualifications required for entering teachers. Effective teaching can best be demonstrated on the job. Successful teachers will be retained, while unsuccessful ones will not.

To the extent that there is deregulation of qualifications (such as full certification) expected for teacher entry, there will no longer be, by definition, a shortage of teachers with such qualifications. Nonetheless, the TBFF view retained two traditional qualifications. As to teachers holding at least a bachelor's degree, research reviewed above indicated that there is negligible shortage. However, there is a considerable shortage of SETs with degree majors in their teaching assignments—a necessary qualification according to TBFF. The TBFF view does not explain the shortage of teachers with subject matter expertise, but only attempts to dismiss from concern shortages of teachers with other qualifications such as full certification.

By specifying that the main criterion for continued teaching employment is the production of satisfactory student achievement, the TBFF position raises the prospect of a shortage of effective teachers, in this sense. Since it is widely recognized that there is a shortage of effective teachers, TBFF has raised a most significant issue. However, the switch from a focus on teacher qualifications to effectiveness does not explain why there is a shortage of either.

Insufficient Supply

Whether the supply of qualified teachers has been sufficient or insufficient in relation to demand has been controversial. According to some, "The nation actually produces far more new teachers than it needs" (Darling-Hammond & Sykes, 2003, p. 4). In this view, the *potential* supply of qualified teachers exceeds demand; it is just that prevailing conditions of teacher employment are not sufficiently attractive to induce enough of them to accept available teaching positions. If only the conditions could be improved sufficiently, a large enough proportion of this potential supply would become employed, thereby eliminating the shortage problem.

The prevailing conditions that are impediments to teaching employment are the geographic location of many positions, the compensation offered, and the working conditions in schools. What are the prospects of improving each of these conditions? As to school location, the least attractive are in remote rural areas and inner cities, and many such schools serve low-income populations. Changing the location of these schools is not an option, of course, but substantial financial bonuses are sometimes offered to induce teachers to accept positions there. Bonus polices of this type could be expanded greatly in amount and scope to address the school location problem, but costs would be prohibitive given the level of funding policy makers are willing to allocate to public education. There is also the reality that novice teachers, by and large, much prefer to become employed in schools close to where they grew up and went to college (Boyd, Lankford, Loeb, & Wyckoff, 2005). Considering all these factors, it will not be possible on a large scale to reduce the school location problem that contributes to the shortage of qualified teachers.

Considering compensation, teacher salaries have been lower in comparison with other occupations requiring comparable investments in higher education and have even been declining when adjusted for inflation. In a cross-national comparison of the salaries of highly experienced teachers with salaries in other occupations requiring college degrees, the Organisation of Economic Co-operation and Development (Schleicher, 2011) reported that teacher pay in the U.S. ranked 22nd out of 27 other countries. In spite of calls by blue ribbon commissions (e.g., The Teaching Commission (2004) and many others over the years) to improve teacher pay substantially, U.S. policy makers have not responded with sufficiently increased appropriations for public education to make this possible. Consequently, it is unlikely that teacher compensation will improve sufficiently in the foreseeable future to reduce teacher shortages.

There is certainly potential to improve teachers' working conditions, the third prevailing condition deterring many from securing teaching employment. Some of the conditions deterring teachers from employment are the need to instruct a considerable percentage of students who do not come to school ready to learn, school reforms that encourage (or require) teachers to perform unwelcome tasks (e.g., teach-to-the-test due to school accountability policies), and increasing scrutiny and accountability of teaching performance. The first of these is a function of socioeconomic policy and family inputs, all well beyond the direct influence of education policy makers. Others of these are the product of well-intentioned education reform policies intended to improve the learning outcomes of students, and are unlikely to be reversed. Other working conditions can be improved, such as steps to promote the collegial collaboration among teachers. In view of all these considerations, it is unlikely that teacher working conditions will improve sufficiently in the foreseeable future to contribute to a reduction in teacher shortage.

If the prevailing conditions of teaching employment cannot be improved substantially, then there is no reason to expect that sufficient numbers of qualified individuals from the *potential* supply of teachers will seek teaching employment to reduce substantially the shortage of qualified SETs. As in the past, the field of special education will only be able to recruit SETs from the active supply of teachers—those able and willing to become employed as teachers under prevailing conditions. As research reviewed in the chapter has shown, this limitation has left special education with a chronic and serious shortage of qualified teachers. Consequently, this shortage is the result of an insufficient active supply of qualified individuals who wish to be employed as teachers in special education. Other explanations considered here have little credibility.

Equilibrating Supply and Demand

Despite the chronic shortage of qualified SETs, a negligible percentage of teaching positions in special education have not been filled. To compensate for the shortage of qualified applicants to fill open teaching positions, three strategies have been used, two manipulating supply and one manipulating demand (see Boe & Gilford, 1992, for an expanded discussion of equilibration). On the supply side, the main strategy is to lower qualifications and hire teachers who are only partly qualified or unqualified for teaching positions in special education (some of whom may be qualified in areas of general education). The large number of teachers employed with emergency certification just before a school year begins illustrates this strategy. In addition, some efforts have been made to enhance teacher supply by offering financial incentives, such as for teaching in shortage areas. With respect to reducing demand, the workloads of employed SETs can be increased by increasing class sizes and the number of SWD assigned to each teacher for individualized instruction. By increasing the SWD : SET ratio, demand for SETs can be reduced.

These methods of equilibrating supply and demand should be short-term measures for addressing the shortage of qualified SETs. Much more difficult and much longer-term interventions are to improve working conditions and compensation. These require much more funding for public education and creativity in improving working conditions, especially under accountability-based school reforms so prevalent today.

Conclusion

As research reviewed in this chapter demonstrates, the increasing total demand for SETs routinely outstripped the supply of *qualified* SETs who were willing and able to accept teaching positions under the prevailing conditions of location, compensation, and working conditions. There has indeed been a chronic and serious shortage of qualified SETs, the extent to which depends on the combination of qualifications used to estimate shortage percentages. At the minimum required by state policies, the shortage of fully certified SETs has long been in the range of 10%–12% of the teaching force in special education. Fortunately, as the demand for SETs has declined in recent years, so has the shortage of highly qualified SETs (from 11.2% in 2006 to 5.8% in 2010 (Boe et al., 2013).

As the size of the total teaching force in special education has risen through 2005 in relation to increasing total demand, so has the size of the qualified component of this force (Boe, 2006). In this respect, efforts by the field to produce increasing numbers of qualified SETs have met with considerable success. With total demand for SETs declining by 13% from 2005 to 2010 since 2005, the size of the qualified component of the SET teacher force has also declined during these years (by 2.7%). But even so, the *percentage* of highly qualified SETs has increased from 88.8% to 94.2% during this recent period (Boe et al., 2013). This is another dimension of success in producing a qualified teaching force. Though the unqualified proportion of the total teaching force has declined considerably, there still remains a considerable shortage of highly qualified SETs available to fill all teaching positions in special education.

The supply–demand dynamics may have changed after 2005 with the beginning of an unprecedented decline in demand for SETs through 2010 (the last year for which national data are available).

This trend has far-reaching implications for the instruction of SWD, for the equitable distribution of SETs, for teacher preparation programs, and for the supply of qualified SETs in relation to total demand. The sources of this decline in demand are poorly understood, but may include the gradual decline in the total number of SWD since 2004 and policy initiatives designed to reduce the proportion of students identified as eligible for special education services (e.g., increased inclusion of SWD in general education classrooms, response to intervention, and the Reading First program). With the onset of the severe economic downturn during fall 2008, it is quite likely that a large number of teaching positions in special education have been eliminated during the past few years because of reduced funding for teaching positions—a circumstance that may or may not be reversed in future years.

In conclusion, the relationship between the total demand for teachers in special education and the total active supply of qualified individuals has been in flux during the past 7 years, and likely will continue in flux for the intermediate future. Though this raises tremendous implications for teacher shortages, no empirical evidence at the national level yet exists to assess the nature of, and extent of, these implications. Just possibly forces are in motion that will result in a substantial reduction in the shortage of qualified SETs. Thus, the research field of teacher demand, supply, and shortage in special education needs ongoing attention and nurturing if it is to continue contributing to policy making designed to produce the best attainable outcomes for SWD.

Notes

1 The specification of a qualified SET is multidimensional concept to be considered later. As a minimum required by state regulation, a qualified SET is fully certified (as distinguished from provisional or emergency certification) in her particular teaching assignment.
2 As distinguished from out-of-school factors such as parental support and peer groups.
3 The same can be said for other fields of teaching such as mathematics and science (Gilford & Tenenbaum, 1990; Ingersoll & Perda, 2010).
4 In this chapter, the focus is on teachers employed in public schools. A teacher is defined as any individual who was employed full-time or part-time at a public school with a main assignment teaching in any specialization of special education at the K–12 grades, including long-term substitutes. Excluded from this definition of a teacher were individuals with a main assignment as a pre-kindergarten teacher, short-term substitute, student teacher, teacher aide, or a nonteaching specialist of any kind.
5 Data on the total demand for SETs (who teach students with disabilities aged 6–21 years) nationally were obtained from the Data Accountability Center website of OSEP (ideadata.org, 2011).
6 In this context, *eligible* individuals are those who hold required qualifications in terms of academic preparation and certification required for teaching positions created and funded (i.e., those for which there is demand). Eligible individuals who are willing to supply their services can be defined as those who apply for positions for which they are qualified. *Prevailing conditions* refers mainly to three aspects of teaching positions—working conditions, compensation, and geographic location.
7 All statistics presented here and in subsequent sections are based on survey data such as SASS, and should therefore be regarded as estimates with a margin of error instead of as exact data points. Most of the references, from which the statistics have been abstracted for this chapter, provide information about the standard errors of these statistics.
8 See Boe, Cook, and Sunderland (2007) for a precise definition of these three levels of the amount of teacher preparation.
9 Approximate definitions of the three levels are: extensive teacher preparation (i.e., substantial course work in teaching methods and at least eight weeks of student teaching), some teacher preparation (less than extensive), and little or no teacher preparation (including no student teaching). See Boe et al. (2007) for a precise definition of these three levels of the amount of teacher preparation.
10 Much of the content of this section is drawn from Boe et al. (2008).
11 The exception is when school migration of SETs is accompanied by out-switching, a combination that occurs in only 16% of the time.
12 In this respect, see the section below on "Predictors of School Migration."
13 These total turnover numbers are unduplicated counts. That is, teachers who both switched teaching area and moved to a different school are counted only once.

References

Barro, S. M. (1992). Models for projecting teacher supply, demand, and quality: An assessment of the state of the art. In E. E. Boe & D. M. Gilford (Eds.), *Teacher supply, demand, and quality: Policy issues, models, and data bases* (pp. 129–209). Washington, DC: National Academies Press.

Billingsley, B. S. (2005). *Cultivating and keeping committed special education teachers: What principals and district leaders can do*. Thousand Oaks, CA: Corwin Press.

Boe, E. E. (2006). Long term trends in the national demand, supply, and shortage of special education teachers. *Journal of Special Education, 40*, 138–150. doi:10.1177/00224669060400030201

Boe, E. E. (2008a). [Qualifications of beginning SETs who leave versus stay in teaching]. Unpublished raw data.

Boe, E. E. (2008b, October). *Teacher turnover: Issues and national research*. Lecture presented in distinguished speaker series, "21st Century Pathways in Education," the College of Education, University of Florida.

Boe, E. E. (2009). [Predictors of teaching area transfer of beginning teachers]. Unpublished raw data.

Boe, E. E., & Cook, L. H. (2006). The chronic and increasing shortage of fully certified teachers in special and general education. *Exceptional Children, 72*, 443–460

Boe, E. E., & Gilford, D. M. (1992). Summary of conference proceedings. In E. E. Boe & D. M. Gilford (Eds.), *Teacher supply, demand, and quality: Policy issues, models, and data bases* (pp. 21–62). Washington, DC: National Academies Press.

Boe, E. E., Barkanic, G., & Leow, C. S. (1999). *Retention and attrition of teachers at the school level: National trends and predictors*. (Data Analysis Rep. No. 1999-DAR1). Philadelphia, PA: University of Pennsylvania, Graduate School of Education, Center for Research and Evaluation in Social Policy.

Boe, E. E., Bobbitt, S. A., Cook, L. H., Barkanic, G., & Maislin, G. (1998). *Teacher turnover in eight cognate areas: National trends and predictors*. (Data Analysis Rep. No. 1998-DAR3). Philadelphia, PA: University of Pennsylvania, Graduate School of Education, Center for Research and Evaluation in Social Policy.

Boe, E. E., Cook, L. H., & Sunderland, R. J. (2005, July). *Turnover of special education teachers: New research on the extent and impact of exit attrition, transfer to general education, and school transfer*. Paper presented at the 2005 OSEP Project Directors Conference, Washington, DC.

Boe, E. E., Cook, L. H., & Sunderland, R. J. (2007). *The prevalence of various aspects of teacher preparation, induction, mentoring, extra support, professional development, and workload factors for beginning teachers in special and general education*. (Data Analysis Rep. 2007-DAR1). Philadelphia, PA: University of Pennsylvania, Graduate School of Education, Center for Research and Evaluation in Social Policy.

Boe, E. E., Cook, L. H., & Sunderland, R. J. (2008). Teacher turnover: Examining exit attrition, teaching area transfer, and school migration. *Exceptional Children, 75*, 7–31.

Boe, E. E., Cook, L. H., & Sunderland, R. J. (2009a). *A comprehensive analysis of the supply of teachers prepared by alternative and traditional methods*. (Data Analysis Report 2009-DAR1). Philadelphia, PA: University of Pennsylvania, Graduate School of Education, Center for Research and Evaluation in Social Policy.

Boe, E. E., Cook, L. H., & Sunderland, R. J. (2009b). *The negligible effects of teacher preparation, induction, mentoring, and professional development on the turnover of beginning teachers in public schools*. (Draft Data Analysis Report No. 2009-DAR2). Philadelphia, PA. University of Pennsylvania, Graduate School of Education, Center for Research and Evaluation in Social Policy.

Boe, E. E., Cook, L. H., & Sunderland, R. J. (2009c). *Trends in the turnover of teachers from 1991 to 2004: Attrition, teaching area transfer, and school migration*. (Data Analysis Rep. 2007-DAR2). Philadelphia, PA: University of Pennsylvania, Graduate School of Education, Center for Research and Evaluation in Social Policy.

Boe, E. E., Cook, L. H., Sunderland, R. J., McGrew, S. P., & May, H. (2005, April). *Three factor framework for understanding chronic teacher shortages: Causes and solutions*. Paper presented at the 2005 CEC Annual Convention and Expo, Baltimore, MD.

Boe, E. E., deBettencourt, L. U., Dewey, J. F., Rosenberg, M. S., Sindelar, P. T., & Leko, C. D. (2013). Variability in demand for special education teachers: Indicators, explanations, and impacts. *Exceptionality, 21*, 103–125. doi: http://dx.doi.org/10.1080/09362835.2013.771563

Boe, E. E., Shin, S., & Cook, L. H. (2007). Does teacher preparation matter for beginning teachers in either special or general education? *Journal of Special Education, 41*, 158–170. doi:10.1177/00224669070410030201

Boe, E. E., Sunderland, R. J., & Cook, L. H. (2006, November). *Special education teachers: Supply and demand*. Paper presented at the meetings of the Teacher Education Division, the Council for Exceptional Children, San Diego, CA.

Boyd, D., Lankford, H., Loeb, S., & Wyckoff, J. (2005). The draw of home: How teachers' preferences for proximity disadvantage urban schools. *Journal of Policy Analysis and Management, 24*, 113–132. doi:10.1002/pam.20072

Carriker, W., & Weintraub, F. J. (1989). *A free appropriate education: But who will provide it?* A statement presented to the Senate Subcommittee on the Handicapped and the House Subcommittee on Select Education on behalf of the American Speech-Language-Hearing Association, Council of Administrators of Special Education, The

Council for Exceptional Children, Council of Graduate Programs in Communication Sciences and Disorders, Higher Education Consortium for Special Education, National Association of State Directors of Special Education, and the Teacher Education Division of CEC.
Cook, L. H., & Boe, E. E. (2007). National trends in the sources of supply of teachers in special and general education. *Teacher Education and Special Education, 30*, 217–232. doi:10.1177/088840640703000402
Council for Exceptional Children. (2000). *Bright futures for exceptional learners: Introduction—an action agenda to achieve quality conditions for teaching and learning*. Reston, VA: Author.
Cox. S., Parmer, R., Tourkin, S., Warner, T., & Lyter, D. M. (2007). *Documentation for the 2004–05 Teacher Follow-Up Survey* (NCES 2007-349). Washington, DC: U.S. Department of Education, National Center for Education Statistics.
Curran, B., & Abrahams, C. (2000, January). *Teacher supply and demand: Is there a shortage?* Washington, DC: National Governors Association. Retrieved from http://www.nga.org/cms/home/nga-center-for-best-practices/center-publications/page-archive/col2-content/title_teacher-supply-and-demand-is-there-a-shortage.html
Darling-Hammond, L., & Sykes. G. (2003). Wanted: A national teacher supply policy for education: The right way to meet the "highly qualified teacher" challenge. *Education Policy Analysis Archives, 11*(33). Retrieved from http://epaa.asu.edu/epaa/v11n33/
Feistritzer, C. E. (2005). *Alternative teacher certification: A state-by-state analysis 2005*. Washington, DC: National Center for Education Information.
Gilford, D. M., & Tenenbaum, E. (Eds.). (1990). *Precollege science and mathematics teachers: Monitoring supply, demand, and quality*. Washington, DC: National Academies Press.
Harris, D. N., & Adams, S. J. (2007). Understanding the level and causes of teacher turnover: A comparison with other professions. *Economics of Education Review, 26*, 325–337. doi:10.1016/j.econedurev.2005.09.007
Hill, J. G. (2011). *Education and certification qualifications of departmentalized public high school-level teachers of core subjects: Evidence from the 2007–08 Schools and Staffing Survey* (NCES 2011-317). U.S. Department of Education. Washington, DC: National Center for Education Statistics. Retrieved from http://nces.ed.gov/pubsearch
ideadata.org. (2005). Table 3.2. *Teachers employed (FTE) to provide special education and related services to students ages 6 to 21 under IDEA, Part B, by certification status and state: Fall 2004*. Retrieved from https://www.ideadata.org/default.asp
ideadata.org. (2011). Retrieved from https://www.ideadata.org/default.asp
Ingersoll, R. M. (1997). Teacher turnover and teacher quality: The recurring myth of teacher shortages. *Teachers College Record, 91*, 41–44.
Ingersoll, R. M. (2002). *Out-of-field teaching, educational inequality, and the organization of schools: An exploratory analysis* (A Research Report). Seattle, WA: University of Washington, Center for the Study of Teaching and Policy.
Ingersoll, R. M., & Perda, D. (2010). Is the supply of mathematics and science teachers sufficient? *American Educational Research Journal, 47*, 563–594. doi:10.3102/0002831210370711
Johnson, S. M., Berg, J. H., & Donaldson, M. L. (2005). *Who stays in teaching and why: A review of the literature on teacher retention*. Cambridge, MA: Harvard University, Harvard Graduate School of Education, The Project on the Next Generation of Teachers.
Kozleski, E., Mainzer, R., & Deshler, D. (2000). *Bright futures for exceptional learners: An agenda to achieve quality conditions for teaching and learning*. Reston, VA: Council for Exceptional Learners.
Lankford, H., Loeb, S., & Wyckoff, J. (2002). Teacher sorting and the plight of urban schools: A descriptive analysis. *Education Evaluation and Policy Analysis, 24*, 37–62. doi:10.3102/01623737024001037
Lauritzen, P., & Friedman, S. J. (1992). *Supply and demand of educational personnel for Wisconsin Public Schools: An examination of data trends*. Whitewater, WI: University of Wisconsin-Whitewater, Wisconsin Educator Supply and Demand Project.
Luekens, M. T., Lyter, D. M., & Fox, E. E. (2004). *Teacher attrition and mobility: Results from the Teacher Follow-up Survey, 2000–01* (NCES 2004-301). U.S. Department of Education, National Center for Education Statistics. Washington, DC: Government Printing Office.
Lyon, G. R. (1996). Learning disabilities. *Special Education for Students with Disabilities, 6*, 54–76.
NASDTEC (National Association of State Directors of Teacher Education & Certification). (2003). *The NASDTEC manual on the preparation and certification of educational personnel 2003* (8th ed.). Sacramento, CA: School Services of California, Inc.
National Clearinghouse on Professions in Special Education. (1992). *Who will teach? Who will serve? A report to the field by the task force on a national personnel agenda for special education and related services*. Arlington, VA: National Association of State Directors of Special Education.
NCES (National Center for Education Statistics). (2005). *The condition of education 2005* (NCES 2005-094). Washington, DC: U.S. Government Printing Office.
NCTAF (National Commission on Teaching and America's Future). (2003). *No dream denied: A pledge to America's children*. New York. NY: Author.

No Child Left Behind Act of 2001, Pub. L. No. 107-110. (2002). Retrieved from http://www2.ed.gov/policy/elsec/leg/esea02/107-110.pdf

Oaks, J. (1990). *Multiplying inequalities: The effects of race, social class, and tracking on opportunities to learn mathematics and science*. (R-3928-NSF) Santa Monica, CA: RAND.

Office of Special Education Programs. (2004). *Twenty-sixth annual report to Congress on the implementation of the Individuals with Disabilities Education Act*. Washington, DC: U.S. Department of Education.

Podgursky, M. (2006). Is there a "Qualified Teacher" shortage? *Education Next*, *6*(2), 27–32.

Presley, J. B. (2003). *Occupational stability of new college graduates* (IERC RN 2003-1). Edwardsville, IL: Illinois Education Research Council.

Rothstein, R. (2010). *How to fix out schools: It's more complicated, and more work, than the Klein-Rhee "Manifesto" wants you to believe* (Issue Brief). Washington, DC: Economic Policy Institute. Retrieved from http://www.epi.org/publication/ib286/

Schwartz, H. (1996). The changing nature of teacher education. In J. Sikula, T. J. Buttery, & E. Guyton. (Eds.), *Handbook of research on teacher education* (2nd ed., pp. 3–13). New York: Simon & Schuster Macmillan.

The Teaching Commission. (2004). *Teaching at risk: A call to action*. New York, NY: Author.

Thomas B. Fordham Foundation. (1999). *Better teachers, better schools*. Washington, DC: Author.

Tourkin, S. C., Warner, T., Parmer, R., Cole, C., Jackson, B., Zukerberg, A., … Soderborg, A. (2007). *Documentation for the 2003–04 Schools and Staffing Survey* (NCES 2007-337). Washington, DC: U.S. Department of Education, National Center for Education Statistics. Retrieved from http://nces.ed.gov/pubs2007/2007337_1.pdf

Tyler, L. (2010, January 27). Measuring teaching effectiveness. *Education Week*. Retrieved from http://www.edweek.org/ew/articles/2010/01/27/19tyler.h29.html

U.S. Department of Education. (2010). *American Recovery and Reinvestment Act, Section 1512 Quarterly reporting through June 30, 2010—by State*. Retrieved from http://www2.ed.gov/policy/gen/leg/recovery/spending/impact4.html

West, J. E., & Whitby, P. J. S. (2008). Federal policy and the education of students with disabilities: Progress and the path forward. *Focus on Exceptional Children*, *41*(3), 1–16.

Ysseldyke, J. E., Algozzine, B., Richey, L., & Graden, J. (1982). Declaring students eligible for learning disability services: Why bother with the data? *Learning Disability Quarterly*, *5*, 37–44. doi:10.2307/1510614

6

Recruiting and Retaining Teachers and Administrators in Special Education

Bonnie S. Billingsley
VIRGINIA TECH

Jean Crockett and Margaret L. Kamman
UNIVERSITY OF FLORIDA

Things to Think About

- Researchers have demonstrated the importance of qualified and experienced teachers, yet there are insufficient numbers of teachers and administrators to meet the demand in the field of special education leading to an increased number of positions vacant or filled by teachers with minimal preparation.
- There are several weaknesses in the literature base in regards to research and theory in recruitment and retention.
- Much of the research on the recruitment and retention of special educators and administrators is not founded on theoretical models that provide possible explanations of what attracts individuals to certain occupations and why individuals remain in (or leave) their jobs.
- Preparation as well as contextual factors related to teachers' entry into the field and work-related conditions matter for teacher and leader retention and turnover.
- More research is needed to examine how new special education leaders are recruited, prepared, and supported in their professional roles.

The need to recruit, hire, and keep effective teachers is emphasized in current policies in the United States, including the Race to the Top Act of 2011. Although the importance of qualified teachers to improving student outcomes is widely accepted, there are insufficient numbers of teachers and administrators to meet the demand in the field of special education. Over two decades ago, researchers and professional organizations began to document the chronic and severe shortage of qualified special education teachers (SETs) (e.g., American Speech-Language-Hearing Association, 1989; Lauritzen, 1990; Smith-Davis, Burke, & Noel, 1984). The need for special educators was widely recognized in the

1980s and early 1990s, yet the teacher shortage continued to grow in subsequent years, and an increased number of positions were filled by teachers with minimal preparation or were left vacant because of an inadequate supply (Boe, 2006; Boe & Cook, 2006; McLeskey & Billingsley, 2008; McLeskey, Tyler, & Flippin, 2004; Smith-Davis & Billingsley, 1993). Today, researchers have demonstrated the importance of qualified and experienced teachers to both student achievement (Feng & Sass, 2012b) and a lower probability of dropping out of school among students with disabilities (Feng & Sass, 2012a).

Although less well documented (Crockett, Becker, & Quinn, 2009), there has also been an inadequate supply of special education administrators creating additional challenges to educational agencies as they considered how to recruit and support these leaders (Muller, 2009). In combination, the shortage of both qualified SETs and administrators is recognized as an obstacle to the provision of high quality instruction and services to students with disabilities.

Numerous factors contribute to the persistent shortages of special education personnel (see Boe, Chapter 5, this volume), and a clear implication of the shortage is the need to increase the supply by recruiting capable individuals into special education teaching and administration. Yet, as Ingersoll (2001) observed, recruitment is not sufficient, particularly if individuals leave after relatively brief careers. Retention is also a critical mediating variable in supply and demand, since a stable workforce reduces the need for new personnel. In this chapter, we review key findings about what is known about both recruiting and retaining SETs and administrators. We organized this chapter in four parts. The first provides an overview of theoretical models and frameworks used to explain teacher and administrator retention. Both the second and third sections include key research findings influencing the recruitment and retention of teachers and leaders, respectively. In these sections, the impact of preparation, entry and working conditions on recruitment and retention are considered. In the final section, we provide suggestions for future research and outline implications for practice.

Research and Theory in Recruitment and Retention

The research base on special education teacher and administrator recruitment and retention provides an incomplete view of the status of personnel needs and provides little in the way of identifying effective long-term strategies to address special education recruitment and retention. Research projects, funded through the U.S. Department of Education's Office of Special Education Programs (OSEP), using the Schools and Staffing Surveys (SASS), which include the Teacher Questionnaire (TQ) and the Teacher Follow-up Survey (TFS) (National Center for Education Statistics) (e.g., Boe & Cook, 2006; Boe, Cook, & Sunderland, 2007a, 2007b, 2008a, 2008b), provide some national data on factors related to teachers' career paths. Another OSEP-funded study, the 1999–2000 Study of Personnel Needs in Special Education (SPeNSE) (e.g., Carlson, Brauen, Klein, Schroll, & Willig, 2002), also provided data on recruitment, entry path, qualifications, and intent to stay from a national sample of special educators. Yet, most of the research from these funded projects is now dated. In addition, most of the SET retention studies, published since 2002, are based on relatively small groups of teachers.

Another weakness in the literature base is the infrequent use of theoretical models to guide research. Theoretical models provide possible explanations of what attracts individuals to certain occupations and why individuals remain in (or leave) their jobs. Some theories focus on the characteristics of individuals and their motivations to enter a particular field, others focus on the organizational context of work, and some theories clearly incorporate both.

Designing policies to recruit and keep teachers is challenging because what is rewarding or motivating differs across individuals. Some individuals focus on financial rewards, others on the opportunities to advance, while still others see work primarily as a calling (Wrzesniewski, McCauley, Rozin, & Schwartz, 1997). Researchers describe (a) teachers' intrinsic motivations to make a difference in students' lives (Lortie, 1975), (b) the "psychic" rewards teachers receive from positive experiences with students (Rosenholtz, 1989), and (c) the need for teachers to have a sense of success with their students

(Johnson & The Project on the Next Generation of Teachers, 2004). Work orientations may overlap and also change over time. For example, a new teacher initially may have been attracted to teaching because of a strong interest in working with students, but later financial pressures associated with having children may force her to seek out higher paying options outside of education.

A broader theory that has been used to frame research on recruitment and retention is the Economic Theory of Supply and Demand. Guarino, Santibañez, and Daley (2006), in applying this theory to teachers, suggested that individuals will enter into and remain in a given position if it is the most "attractive activity to pursue among all activities available to them. By attractive, we mean desirable in terms of ease of entry and overall compensation (salary, benefits, working conditions, and personal satisfaction)" (p. 175). Using their reasoning, the recruitment of special education personnel requires increasing the attractiveness of this work compared to other competing careers. To keep special educators, the work needs to be attractive relative to general education and other occupations.

Similar theories incorporate these perspectives and offer additional explanations. According to Job Choice Theory, job attributes and employment decisions are influenced by "objective factors such as salary and benefits, subjective factors such as how a job meets psychological needs, and the candidate's initial contact with the organization or the work itself" (Orr, 2011, p.119). Using this reasoning, recruiting and retaining special education personnel involves contextual and psychological variables, including first impressions about the very nature of working with special needs learners.

Professional retention and advancement has also been conceptualized as a pipeline that begins with preparation programs and initial positions. From this perspective, candidates need to develop the aspirations as well as the capacities to undertake complex work. Ajzen's (1991) Theory of Planned Behavior, for example, posits that "career intentions are strong predictors of subsequent career pursuits and that, among other factors, attitudes and perceived capacity about the position positively influence intentions" (Orr, 2011, p. 119). Taken together, one's attitudes about a job, what others think about doing the job, and one's perception about having the ability to achieve in the position predict intentions and, in turn, predict whether someone will pursue and persist in a particular position. Models such as these hold promise for strengthening the knowledge base informing the recruitment and retention of both teachers and leaders.

Ingersoll (2001) used a perspective derived from the sociology of organizations to study teacher turnover using SASS data and the TFS. This perspective emphasizes the importance of organizational functioning to job satisfaction, commitment, and turnover. He reported that 42% of all teacher departures were related to some aspect of dissatisfaction, a desire to pursue a better job, or to improve career opportunities in or out of education. Ingersoll criticized the predominant focus on teacher recruitment and emphasized the need to examine the conditions in which teachers work to reduce the high numbers of teachers who leave their schools.

These theories call attention to a range of individual and organizational variables in recruiting and retaining both teachers and administrators. Unfortunately, the research base informing the recruitment and retention of SETs and administrators is limited, although the former group has received more attention than the latter. Many of the recruitment and retention studies of special educators and administrators are not grounded in any theory or model, highlighting the need for a greater focus on explanatory, theoretical perspectives.

Tabulating the numbers of those who stay and those who leave their positions is insufficient without some means of conceptualizing the linkages between features of recruitment, preparation, and induction efforts, and subsequent effects on turnover.

Research on Recruiting and Retaining Special Education Teachers

Available evidence suggests that until at least 2005, an insufficient number of teachers were being recruited into preparation programs and an increasing number of these teachers left the field through this period. Interestingly, new SET graduates made up a modest portion of entering teachers (26%), compared to the reserve pool of delayed entrants and those who returned to teaching (62%) (Cook & Boe, 2007).

At the same time that an insufficient number of teachers were being prepared, turnover rates continued to increase. Turnover is often defined in three ways including leaving for nonteaching activities (e.g., changing occupations, retiring), transferring from special to general education, or migration within special education (teaching in another school, district or state) (Boe et al., 2007b). Across these three types, Boe et al. reported that turnover increased from 18.8% in 1991–1992 to 28.7% in 2004–2005.

Although some turnover is healthy and desirable, an unstable teaching force has high financial costs as districts devote scarce resources to ongoing recruitment and induction as well as the loss of "organizational stability, coherence, and morale" (Smith & Ingersoll, 2004, p. 686). In special education, high turnover may lead to the loss of collaborative relationships and established inclusive programs. Sindelar, Shearer, Yendol-Hoppey, and Liebert (2006) noted that the loss of key teachers was a factor in the demise of a successful inclusive program.

Today the need for new SETs has declined due in part to the economic crisis of 2008 and a decline in the number of students being identified with disabilities (Boe et al., 2013). However, teacher recruitment and retention are important not just during teacher shortages, but during times of teacher surplus as IHEs and districts need to identify, recruit, and keep the best possible candidates. In this section we draw on recent policy initiatives as well as selected research reviews from general education and the special education literature that inform our understanding of teacher recruitment and/or retention (Billingsley, 1993, 2004; Brownell & Smith, 1993; Guarino et al., 2006).

Teacher Recruitment

A wide range of strategies has been used at the federal, state, and district levels to attract high quality SETs. Federal law codified in the Individuals with Disabilities Education Act (IDEA, 2004) requires states receiving special education funds to have plans in place for personnel recruitment. Not surprisingly, a plentiful variety of statewide and district-driven programs exist for the purpose of recruitment, including: (a) providing incentives; (b) reducing barriers related to hiring; (c) attracting local teachers; and (d) creating vehicles for disseminating information related to hiring (Guarino et al., 2006; Hammer, Hughes, McClure, Reeves, & Salgado, 2005; Hirsch, Koppich, & Knapp, 2001; Muller, 2010; NCCTQ, 2007; Putney, 2009; Rice & Goessling, 2005).

Providing incentives is one widely used strategy to entice new teachers to the classroom through long-term or short-term offers. How much a teacher is compensated, with salary and benefits, is typical of any recruitment strategy. In standard salary schedules teachers must climb the ladder annually to receive increases in pay, a slow process. More recently and with the impetus of Race to the Top funds, states are linking teacher salaries to performance pay. New teachers do not have to wait years to gain significant pay increases. Instead, teachers who show merit can receive a salary boost.

In general, districts and states with higher pay are more likely to attract new teachers than their lower paying counterparts (Guarino et al., 2006). Incentives can also be offered in a one-time manner, such as moving expenses or signing bonuses. Hirsch and his colleagues (2001) reported that some districts provide bonuses in specific fields for shortages or in less desirable locations to live and teach. For example, the District of Columbia Public Schools provides the highest bonuses to highly effective teachers who teach in high poverty schools and in high need areas (e.g., special education, mathematics, science) (IMPACTplus for Teachers, 2011). The National Comprehensive Center for Teacher Quality cautions that some short-term strategies have been costly and ineffective (Putney, 2009). The Center recommends providing contingency-based incentives such as a service commitment from the teacher or a reimbursement of the incentive.

Another major strategy is increasing the supply of teachers by providing scholarships, forgivable loans, creating alternate preparation programs and fostering partnerships between districts and universities. Hirsch et al. (2001) found that states developed programs for scholarships or forgivable loans for several reasons. Some scholarships were created to attract high achieving college students, while others were intended to recruit minority teachers. Additionally, since special education is identified as a national shortage area, new teachers can be forgiven a portion of their loans depending on how long they teach in the field (Federal Student Aid, 2008). Over half the states responding to a recruitment survey indicated they used tuition assistance or loan forgiveness to recruit special educators (Muller, 2010). In an effort to ease barriers to the classroom, the Race to the Top Act (2011) also encourages states to create alternative certification programs for teacher licensure. Twenty-four states have some type of alternative to traditional teacher preparation specifically designed for training SETs (National Center to Improve Recruitment and Retention of Qualified Personnel for Children with Disabilities, 2011). Generally, alternate programs differ in some way to traditional campus-based teacher preparation. While there is much variability in programs, they are often abbreviated and have older and diverse participants (Rosenberg & Sindelar, 2005). Teach for America is one example of a program that recruits recent graduates of nonteaching disciplines who complete a summer institute and then commit to serve in high needs schools for a minimum of two years (Dai, Sindelar, Denslow, Dewey, & Rosenberg, 2007). Fostering partnerships between districts and universities can assist in recruitment by creating and implementing alternative programs tailored to specific, local needs; providing more accessible modes of course delivery; collaborating in matching interested individuals to training programs and necessary certification exams; and in cultivating and encouraging an interest in teaching special education (Muller, 2010).

Recruitment is sometimes aimed at local needs, with a focus on recruiting middle and high school students, community college students, paraprofessionals, or convincing retired teachers to return to the classroom (Hirsch et al., 2001). The major benefit is teachers are selected from people who already live in the community and are therefore more likely to remain if they accept a teaching position (Dai et al., 2007). Some rural and urban areas have long-standing difficulties obtaining SETs and have started recruiting as early as middle school (Hammer et al., 2005; Collins, 1999; National Partnership for Teaching in At-Risk Schools (NPTARS), 2005). Rice and Goessling (2005) suggest early recruitment is essential in developing a workforce of male SETs.

Another promising source of new teachers are paraprofessionals who are already working with students with disabilities (Dai et al., 2007). Paraprofessionals bring their knowledge of students with disabilities and their work experience, making it highly probable that they will succeed in both teacher preparation and as future educators. These paraprofessionals are typically long-standing members of the community where the school is located. Teachers who already live in proximity to hard-to-staff schools are much more likely to stay in those positions than ones who are transplanted.

Whether with a comprehensive package or a single strategy, states and districts typically create vehicles for disseminating information related to hiring (McCreight, 2000; Muller, 2010; NPTARS, 2005). More traditional methods include holding job fairs, hiring recruiters, advertising on radio and television, and producing promotional print materials (McCreight, 2000; Muller, 2010; Rice & Goessling, 2005). More recent approaches focus on the use of the Internet to advertise and streamline the hiring process. States are developing online application systems making it easier for potential teachers and employers to find a match (NPTARS, 2005). Designing recruitment websites and capitalizing on the numbers of users on social media sites like Facebook and Twitter also provide new forums for engaging potential special educators (Muller, 2010).

Research on the effectiveness of recruitment tactics is limited. Guarino et al. (2006) only report findings related to salary and retention in their review of research. Similarly, these researchers note the nearly nonexistent rigorous research base on preservice recruitment strategies. States and districts often implement strategies to fill positions quickly and do not evaluate the strategy's long-term effectiveness (Putney, 2009). Tracking the success of varied approaches is important to assessing their effectiveness and the cost-effectiveness. For example, there is some evidence that streamlined alternate programs are more effective in recruitment than monetary incentives (Guarino et al., 2006; Lui, Johnson, & Peske, 2004). Clearly more research is needed regarding recruitment processes that are most successful and cost-effective, particularly with groups of teachers (i.e., early career and minimally prepared teachers) who are at a high risk of leaving the classroom.

Teacher Retention

Defining teacher retention is not a simple matter and may include staying in teaching, the teaching field, or in a particular school or conversely, leaving. Because teacher retention and turnover are rather expensive to measure over time, some researchers have relied on measures of intent to stay and leave (e.g., Gersten, Keating, Yovanoff, & Harniss, 2001). Although this proxy for retention and turnover is obviously not as accurate as looking at actual teacher behavior, Gersten and colleagues (2001) argued that it is a valid predictor of teachers' behavior.

Teachers leave and stay for varied reasons and there are often multiple factors that contribute to their decisions (Billingsley, 2004). Boe and colleagues (2008a) used the SASS and TFS data to provide an overall picture of the reasons SETs give for leaving. About 32% of SETs indicated they left for personal reasons, about 17% for retirement and 37% to "escape" teaching (it should be noted that 23% of general educators also left to "escape" teaching). A number of larger scale, funded studies investigating teacher turnover have considered the relationship of teacher characteristics, preparation factors and working conditions associated with teachers' career decisions or intents (e.g., Boe et al., 2008b; Cross & Billingsley, 1994; Gersten et al., 2001; Miller, Brownell, & Smith, 1999). Several recent investigations have been smaller scale studies that primarily used teacher questionnaires and interviews to determine why teachers left, or why they want to leave or stay (e.g., Fish & Stevens, 2010; Schlichte, Yssel & Merbler, 2005). Assessing both the factors that are associated with career decisions as well as directly asking teachers about their career plans are needed to gain a comprehensive picture of retention factors.

Although much of the research in special education personnel retention does not draw on theory, two conceptual models were identified to help specify factors that influence teachers' career decisions. Billingsley (1993) provided a visual model of three major categories influencing teacher retention including external, employment, and personal factors. The model focuses on factors related to employment, including professional qualifications of the teacher, working conditions, and work rewards, and the teacher's commitments to school, district, teaching field, and teaching profession. Billingsley suggested that teachers with fewer professional qualifications and poorer working conditions would be less likely to experience teaching rewards, and thus have reduced commitment to teaching. Whether a teacher actually leaves depends on a range of variables, including personal, family, and economic circumstances. Brownell and Smith (1993) adapted Bronfenbrenner's ecological systems model to explain how the dynamics of nested, interrelated systems can be applied to the study of retention. They suggested retention is influenced by: (a) the *microsystem* or the teacher's immediate setting and interactions that occur with students in that setting; (b) the *mesosystem*, which includes interrelations among variables in the workplace or school, such as collegiality and administrator support; and (c) the *macrosystem*, or the cultural beliefs and ideologies of the culture as well as economic conditions that impact schools and teachers' career decisions.

In summary, decisions to stay or leave are influenced by a range of variables. The next sections describe research results about the relationship teacher preparation, entry, and work-related factors to turnover and retention.

Preparation

Special education teachers come to the classroom from a variety of preparation avenues. Traditionally, individuals seeking to become teachers attend a 4- or 5-year formal university teacher preparation program. However, the traditional route has not prepared a sufficient number of teachers, leaving districts with little choice other than to hire uncertified teachers or those from abbreviated training programs (Carlson et al., 2002). To study the effect of entry routes on retention, researchers have examined the extent to which teachers from varied retention routes stay in teaching.

Prior to No Child Left Behind (NCLB) (2001), research focused on the relationship between entry path and teacher turnover and retention. Not surprisingly, researchers comparing the retention of certified and uncertified SETs found that teachers with less extensive preparation (Boe et al., 2008b) and uncertified teachers (e.g., Billingsley, 2004; Miller et al., 1999) were more likely to leave the classroom, suggesting the importance of stronger preparation to retention. Unfortunately, this impacts SETs in high poverty districts more since SETs in these districts are less likely to be certified than SETs in more affluent districts (Fall & Billingsley, 2008).

With the enactment of NCLB policy in 2001, certification status was no longer the focus; rather, all teachers were required to be highly qualified. State education agency (SEA) requirements for meeting the highly qualified standard varies; in some states teachers can be designated as highly qualified by completing a brief alternative route program or without formal preparation for teaching, as long as they hold a bachelor's degree and demonstrate sufficient knowledge on a state exam (National Center to Improve the Recruitment and Retention of Qualified Personnel for Children with Disabilities, 2011).

Research findings comparing teacher retention rates from alternate routes and traditional university programs are mixed. For example, Darling-Hammond (1999) found graduates of short-cut alternate routes had much higher attrition rates than graduates of 4- or 5-year teacher preparation programs. However, in a review of the teacher retention literature, Guarino et al. (2006) concluded that alternate route programs have a higher teacher retention rate than traditional programs. One problem with studies comparing alternative and traditional programs is the variability in the length and requirements of these programs. Some alternative programs include only a short summer intensive induction (e.g., Teach for America), while other alternative programs have requirements that look very similar to traditional programs, but may provide coursework through a different mode or schedule. In their 2005 review, Rosenberg and Sindelar were only able to find 10 data-based studies of alternate route programs in special education. Although there was insufficient information to draw conclusions about alternate programs and special education teacher retention, researchers acknowledged the potential of programs to produce competent teachers given collaboration between districts and universities, adequate length, and a diversity of learning activities. A recent study by Robertson and Singleton (2010) extended these findings by comparing two rigorous preparation programs, one traditional and one alternative that had some differences in length and mode of delivery. In this case special education graduates of both programs had similar retention rates, all over 5 years.

The current trend in research focuses on the characteristics of teacher preparation that lead to greater retention. Scholars conclude that well-prepared SETs stay longer (Billingsley, 2004; Boe, Shin, & Cook, 2007; Connelly & Graham, 2009; Thornton, Peltier, & Medina, 2011). For example, Connelly and Graham studied the impact of preservice student teaching on the retention of special educators, finding those teachers with 10 weeks or more of student teaching more likely to remain in the field. Similarly, using SASS and TFS data, Boe, Shin, and Cook reported that teachers with extensive preparation were half as likely to leave teaching in the first three years as teachers with little or no preparation. Extensive teacher preparation was modestly defined as having at least 10 weeks of practice teaching, observations and feedback of instruction, and coursework in teaching theory and methods.

Entry Into the field

Literature on both new special and general educators suggest that they struggle with a range of similar challenges, including student behavior, conflicts with colleagues, state-mandated assessments, and insufficient resources (Billingsley, Griffin, Smith, Kamman, & Israel, 2009). These new teachers are also at high risk of leaving in the early years. In a recent study, new SETs had lower levels of commitment than GETs (Jones & Youngs, 2012), and Smith and Ingersoll (2004) found that SETs left at significantly higher rate than GETs. Unequivocally scholars agree that new SETs need induction for the purposes of retention (Billingsley et al., 2009; Fletcher, Strong, & Villar, 2008; Griffin, Winn, Otis-Wilborn, & Kilgore, 2003; Guarino et al., 2006) as well as continued teacher development and learning support (e.g., Brownell, Sindelar, Kiely, & Danielson, 2010; Thornton et al., 2011). Although induction is often associated with mentoring, it also includes supports such as carefully planned hiring practices, reduced responsibilities, professional development, and meetings with colleagues (Darling-Hammond & Sykes, 2003; Feiman-Nemser, 2001; Smith & Ingersoll, 2004). Most states have policies promoting some form of induction and mentoring (Hirsch et al., 2009). Although evidence suggests that SETs are less likely to have mentors than general educators (Billingsley, Carlson, & Klein, 2004; Wasburn-Moses, 2010), SETs participation in these programs increased from 59% to 67% between 1999–2000 and 2003–2004 (Boe et al., 2007a).

The preponderance of research suggests that induction and mentoring is related to a range of positive outcomes, including increased teacher commitment, retention, instructional practices, and student achievement (Fletcher et al., 2008; Guarino et al., 2006; Ingersoll & Strong, 2011; Smith & Ingersoll, 2004; Wang, Odell, & Schwille, 2008). Unfortunately, research on induction in special education is less robust and only a few studies address the relationship between induction and retention.

No studies were found that specifically addressed the relationship of induction to teacher turnover; however, two studies investigated the impact of mentoring and induction on SETs' intent to stay. Whitaker (2000) found that new teachers, who rated their mentors as effective, were more likely to be satisfied with their jobs and to stay than those who rated their mentors as less effective. Billingsley et al. (2004) did not find that induction support was related to SETs' intent to stay, although SETs who perceived higher levels of induction support viewed their roles as more manageable and reported higher self-efficacy than those receiving less induction support. In a review of nine district mentoring programs for SETs, Billingsley et al. (2009) reported that retention rates were high, although these findings were based on district data and local evaluations that were not peer-reviewed studies.

A major question for researchers and policy makers is whether specific elements of induction that foster retention and effective instructional practices can be identified. Although this question cannot be answered from the available research, some data provide information about what new teachers value in their mentors. New SETs value mentors who are special educators, have strong interpersonal skills (i.e., good communication skills, approachable, patient) and have similar teaching assignments (i.e., age and disability of students and classroom context) (Billingsley et al., 2009). When this type of match is made, new teachers rate mentoring as more effective and more valuable than their colleagues with less accurate matches (Whitaker, 2003). Other important elements include having ready access to a mentor in the same building and more frequent support. In particular, new SETs value emotional support, content area support, and learning about school and special education policies and procedures.

Work-Related Conditions

Researchers in general education emphasize the importance of teachers' work contexts on their commitment to teaching and their subsequent career decisions (e.g., Guarino et al., 2006; Ingersoll, 2001; Johnson & Birkeland, 2003; Rosenholtz, 1989). Ingersoll reported that high teacher turnover is related to elements in school organizations after controlling for both school and teacher characteristics. Factors such as low salaries, insufficient administrative support, lack of opportunity to influence decisions, and problems with student discipline were identified as key contributors to turnover. Guarino et al., in a synthesis of the teacher retention literature, also emphasized that dissatisfaction with salary was associated with decreased commitment and higher turnover and that schools providing more administrative support and autonomy had lower levels of turnover.

One of the challenges in studying working conditions in education is that in general, there is relatively little agreement about what constitutes working conditions or which are most important. Johnson, Kraft, and Papay (2011) constructed measures of nine different areas of work conditions, including collegial relationships, community support, facilities, governance, principal, professional expertise, resources, school culture, and time. Although all nine were important to teacher satisfaction, the interrelated areas of principal, school culture and collegial relationships were most important. Johnson et al. also found that more favorable working conditions were associated with greater academic growth.

Although there is a relatively limited body of literature about SET retention and turnover, researchers have focused on trying to understand the factors that contribute to both SETs' job dissatisfaction and their work-related reasons for leaving (or wanting to leave) their jobs. Billingsley (2004) in a synthesis of SET turnover identified seven work environment variables that contributed to teachers' career decisions or intents, either positively or negatively. These included: (a) salary, (b) school climate, (c) administrative and colleague support, (d) induction and mentoring, (e) professional development, (f) teacher roles, including role problems, paperwork and changing service delivery, and (g) student and caseload issues. Teachers often indicate multiple reasons for leaving, as these factors combine in varied ways to enhance or create barriers to their work.

Although several researchers reported that teachers identified compensation-related issues as contributing to SETs' leaving (Certo & Fox, 2002; Fish & Stevens, 2010; Kaff, 2004), most of the retention/turnover studies focus on teachers' work contexts. Special educators are more likely to stay or desire to stay in schools that are perceived as supportive (Billingsley et al., 2004; Miller et al., 1999). Not surprisingly, SETs indicate that supportive administrators and colleagues are incentives to stay, while less supportive administrators are given as reasons for leaving (Albrecht, Johns, Mounsteven, & Olorunda, 2009; Certo & Fox, 2002; Kaff, 2004; Nance & Calabrese, 2009). Kaff analyzed the results of 341 SETs identifying why teachers wanted to stay or leave. Of those wanting to leave, 57% indicated a lack of support from administrators, general education teachers, and parents. The need for support is especially important for early career teachers as they adjust to the demands of teaching, and a lack of administrative support causes some to reconsider their choice of a career (Schlichte et al., 2005).

Researchers provided examples of what is meant by more versus less supportive administrative behavior. Supportive administrators showed an understanding of and interest in students with disabilities as well as an awareness of legal requirements (Certo & Fox, 2002). Other examples of supportive behavior included ongoing communication between administrators and teachers (beyond crises), listening to SETs and responding to their needs; providing necessary teaching materials and resources, allocating time to prepare and complete paperwork, providing availability of support personnel, and opportunities for professional development (Albrecht et al., 2009; Nance & Calabrese, 2009). Less supportive behavior included not listening to teachers' needs, top-down decision-making, parents' needs placed before teachers' needs, lack of feedback, and not providing necessary resources to teach (Certo & Fox, 2002).

Another clear theme across both older and more recent studies is that chronic role problems have contributed to SETs' frustration, dissatisfaction, and turnover and these role problems reduce SETs' opportunities to teach their students (Billingsley & Cross, 1991; Gersten et al., 2001; Kaff, 2004; Nance & Calabrese, 2009; Paperwork in Special Education, 2003). Many SETs have complex roles given they: (a) work across varied classrooms (often in different grades and subjects), (b) try to find time to collaborate with numerous teachers and service providers, and (c) manage varied nonteaching responsibilities and paperwork (Billingsley, 2004). Kaff indicated teachers are expected to work across multiple roles, while at the same time "running a full service resource/self-contained classroom" (2004, p. 12). Other researchers reported that SETs were overwhelmed with legal documentation, increased requirements of NCLB (Nance & Calabrese, 2009), as well as pressures to complete required IEPs, behavior, and transition plans (DeMik, 2008). Researchers indicated these responsibilities interfered with special educators' time to teach (Nance & Calabrese, 2009), with 48% of those wanting to leave indicating that teaching students with disabilities was not their primary responsibility (Kaff, 2004). According to Certo and Fox, many SETs indicated they were moving to general education because of paperwork resulting from IEPs and state testing requirements. A recent observational study of 36 SETs over 2,200 hours suggests they spend their time in fragmented ways, with paperwork consuming an average of 12% of their time, with some individuals devoting as much as 50% on paperwork (Vannest & Hagan-Burke, 2010).

Teachers also identify high caseloads as reasons for leaving (Connelly & Graham, 2009; DeMik, 2008), with SETs having caseloads approaching those of general educators (McLeskey et al., 2004). The diversity of SETs' caseloads may also contribute to leaving; among those who planned to leave teaching soon, 42% taught students across four or more exceptionality areas (Carlson et al., 2002). Kaff (2004) discussed additional reasons for desiring to leave, which relate to the complexity of students' needs, the wide range of student abilities on teachers' caseloads, and the lack of respect students show teachers.

Unfortunately, research over two decades suggests that specific elements of SETs' work (e.g., lack of administrative support, role complexity, and nonteaching demands) can lead to stress and eventually turnover. It is likely that the longevity of many SETs' careers will be reduced if paperwork takes priority over teaching, if their jobs are structured in ways that reduce their opportunities to teach their students, and if they do not receive the basic supports to do their work. Improving SETs' job design and providing adequate supports should help increase their opportunities to help their students achieve important educational outcomes—a primary motivator for teachers.

Research on Recruiting and Retaining Leaders

Professional turnover is not restricted to instructional personnel, and recent studies suggest that administrators are leaving their positions to assume other posts, or simply leaving the field of education behind. Some 12% of public, private, and charter school principals left the profession in 2008–2009. Retirements accounted for the loss of 45% of public school principals and 22% of private school principals, and in addition, another 6% moved from leading one school to another (Aud et al., 2011). This "churn" (Viadero, 2009, p. 1) in the leadership pool can have negative consequences because leadership is second only to teaching in contributing to what students learn at school (Leithwood, Louis, Anderson, & Wahlstrom, 2004). Successful educational leaders support the performance of teachers as well as students by establishing conditions that focus on instruction; promote a sense of community; and cultivate interactions with families that help students do well in school (Leithwood & Riehl, 2005).

Special Education Leadership

Leadership in schools is exercised primarily by principals and teachers, and is often distributed across other personnel, including those responsible for directing special education. In today's schools, special education leaders serve as advocates for students with disabilities from a diversity of cultural and linguistic backgrounds, and ensure compliance with policies that protect students' rights and ensure their educational benefits. Special education leaders also foster the use of effective instructional practices and assistive technology, and cultivate productive relationships with parents and professionals within the school system and across external agencies. Solving problems, making data-based decisions, and collaborating with others in the complex management of multimillion dollar budgets also comprise their responsibilities (Crockett, 2011; Tate, 2010).

Recent data suggest the demand for personnel well prepared to lead special education exceeds the current supply, and although some states have retained credentialing requirements for special education administrators, many states have elected to fill positions with candidates, not necessarily from the field of special education, who hold generic state leadership licensure (Boscardin, Weir, & Kusek, 2010). As a consequence, many administrators learn about their special education leadership roles and responsibilities from personal or professional experiences instead of from their professional preparation (Crockett, 2012).

The sobering relationship between professional turnover and underpreparation for professional roles established in the teacher retention literature (Billingsley, 2011) raises concerns about the current attrition and retention of special education leadership personnel. Research regarding the career trajectories of educational leaders is sparse compared to research highlighting the numbers of beginning teachers who leave the profession within the first 5 years of their careers. In addition, trends in the attrition and retention of special education leaders is extremely limited and has only been studied sporadically (see Crockett et al., 2009), and mostly in doctoral dissertations. Trends from a national survey, however, conducted by the National Association of State Directors of Special Education (NASDSE), provide recent evidence suggesting turnover among local district directors of special education (Muller, 2009).

Policy analysts at NASDSE's Project Forum distributed an online survey to all state directors of special education to determine how they perceived the attrition and retention of special education directors in local school systems. Responses were received from 75% of the SEAs regarding the number of district director positions filled and vacant. Trends suggest the number of local directors who leave their positions each year varies from state to state, ranging from fewer than five leavers in 10 states, to as many as 30–65 leavers in three states, with most states (16) ranging between 5–20 leavers annually. Fifty-five percent of respondents reported that the attrition of local special education directors posed a significant challenge in their states.

Attrition was ascribed to a variety of causes with most state directors claiming retirements as the prime incentive driving local directors to leave their positions. The second most frequently cited reason was attributed to legal compliance and litigation, and increased demands for data collection and reporting. Attrition was also frequently attributed to working conditions that could compromise the quality of service including (a) assignment of additional responsibilities, such as directing homeless education and coordinating compliance with civil rights provisions of § 504 policy; (b) lack of administrative and school board support; (c) budget constraints and inadequate funding; and (d) increased shortages of qualified SETs. Less commonly reported reasons for attrition included (e) unfamiliarity with the field of special education because local directors are often assigned to their position from other disciplines; and (g) limited knowledge of state and federal legal requirements. Other reasons included (h) the complexity and the overwhelming nature of the local director's job; (i) the isolated nature of the work; and (j) the lack of respect from district level administrators and boards of education (Muller, 2009).

These data are not surprising, and the resulting churn in district leadership aligns with administrative challenges and other trends and issues "that have changed the face of special education in general and special education leadership specifically" (Tate, 2010, p. 113). Special education administrators have traditionally been viewed as experts in implementing disability-related policies and effective instructional practices. Expectations for their competence, however, have increased with heightened demands for accountability under both general and special education policies. As the scope and demand of their responsibilities have expanded, so has their vulnerability to occupational, job-related stress (Wheeler & LaRocco, 2009). Consequently, more needs to be known about how new special education administrators are recruited, prepared, and supported in their professional roles (see Miller & Baker, 2009).

Recruitment and Preparation

Recent federal priorities emphasize the importance of recruiting educational leaders. Provisions of the Elementary and Secondary Education Act, currently reauthorized as NCLB, provide states with professional development funding to improve student achievement by improving the quality of teachers and educational leaders (Yell, 2012). Proposed revisions to the ESEA are designed "to recruit, prepare, place, and support the retention of effective state and district leaders, such as superintendents, chief academic officers, and human resource directors, who are able to lead transformational change in their states and districts" (U.S. Department of Education, 2010, p. 18). Although special education leaders are not specifically mentioned, improving the achievement of students with disabilities is identified as a cross-cutting priority with provisions of the IDEA.

The U.S. Department of Education (USDE) has made the recruitment and development of leadership personnel for special education a priority over the past 11 years (Boscardin et al., 2010). Currently more than 100 graduate students nationwide are federally funded to pursue degrees in special education administration (see http://publicddb.tadnet.org). Preparation is most often provided at the doctoral level with graduates assuming leadership positions in local school districts, and federal and state education departments. To account for this federal investment, more research is needed to determine whether the candidates recruited, selected, and prepared through these projects reduce turnover and strengthen retention rates for special education leadership personnel.

Little is known about exemplary recruitment practices or opportunities to prepare for leadership roles that address special education, and in some states, the percentage of local directors holding advanced degrees in educational leadership (65%) far exceeds the percentage with advanced degrees in special education (18%) (Marsh, 2005). Also, little is known about the organization of leadership development programs, how they address special education issues, or the qualities of the faculty members who educate prospective school leaders for their contemporary roles in educating all learners (Crockett, 2012; Crockett et al., 2009). Rigorous scholarship addressing the recruitment and preparation of educational leaders in general is scant and empirical investigations are derived primarily from surveys, case studies, and qualitative narratives. The literature base is dominated by theoretical or interpretive commentaries highlighting perceived and reported strengths and weaknesses in leadership preparation. More research is needed to determine how candidates are recruited and selected to participate in leadership preparation or development, how they are taught, and how their progress toward accomplishment is monitored and supported (Murphy, Moorman, & McCarthy, 2008).

Although research has yet to demonstrate their worth, local districts have implemented recruitment strategies including programs that assign aspiring leaders to lower-level central office positions. Local districts have also provided monetary incentives that place special education directors on administrative rather than instructional pay scales. Districts have also offered to pay for membership in professional organizations, such as the Council for Administrators of Special Education (CASE), and offered mentors for new local directors. State agencies have also initiated recruitment efforts, including training and technical assistance for new directors; developing online supervisor of special education programs in partnership with state universities; providing tuition assistance to promising candidates; and developing better data systems for tracking the reasons for turnover in leadership positions (Muller, 2009).

The goals of recruiting and preparing leaders include (a) selecting promising candidates, (b) developing their skills and capacities as future leaders, and (c) shaping their aspirations to assume challenging and complex organizational roles (Orr, 2011). To date, there is little research that examines how leadership candidates are prepared for understanding how different children learn; improving the sensitivity of stakeholders to diversity and effectiveness in educating all students, including those with exceptional learning differences; redesigning the organization of schools to address teaching and learning; creating and maintaining an orderly learning environment; and working closely with parents and collaborating with partners outside the school to support student learning (Crockett, 2002; Orr, 2011). Induction and mentoring experiences are often recommended to foster the desire of recruits to assume these challenging roles, as well as to develop their capacity to do so as accomplished educational leaders.

Entry Into the Field

Thoughtful preparation, thorough induction, and ongoing professional learning are considered to be central in addressing problems with turnover and inadequate preparation (Burdette, 2010; Muller,

2009). Over the past three decades, mentoring has been used as a training vehicle for aspiring leaders in many kinds of organizations (Riley, 2009); however, in the field of education, the most widely investigated form of induction is mentoring that supports the practice of beginning teachers. The success of mentoring is frequently supported by testimonials and anecdotes, but more research is needed to inform potential investments in formal, comprehensive induction programs to determine if successful outcomes pertain to educational leaders (Ehrich, Hansford, & Tennent, 2004).

Informal rather than formal mentoring relationships are common practice in school administration, but research on the effectiveness of coaching educational leaders is minimal (Silver, Lochmiller, Copland, & Tripps, 2009). Although the process of induction has been studied more closely than its impact, several factors are associated with perceived success, including adequate resources, sufficient time, and acknowledgment by faculty and staff that senior administrators of the district or region are actively supporting leadership development. Data also suggest that gender matters in mentoring female administrators, especially at the district level, where fewer women hold leadership positions (Gardiner, Enomoto, & Grogan, 2000). Opportunities for initial and ongoing support are limited for special education district leaders, many of whom are female, because of the specialized nature of the position (Collin, 2008).

The number of studies specifically addressing the induction and professional learning of special education directors is very limited and mostly restricted to dissertations (Crockett et al., 2009). In a qualitative study examining the mentoring experiences of eight female special education administrators, Collin (2008) noted that mentor-protégée relationships have both vertical and horizontal properties. Superintendents were most often identified as formal and informal vertical mentors because of their roles in supervising local directors, and ensuring the provision of a free appropriate education to students with disabilities. Others who played a variety of roles in the lives of participants were identified as formal and informal horizontal mentors, including parents, business managers, other district administrators, principals, special educators, and special education attorneys. Mentors provided leadership support "by asking questions, supporting and offering feedback about the administrators' decisions, brainstorming, suggesting situation-specific strategies, and offering information, advice and a different perspective" (pp. 159–160). Horizontal mentors often provided special education leaders with emotional support that served as a buffer against job-related stress, while vertical mentors provided entry into networks and provided feedback that increased their competence as administrators.

Whether mentorship was formal or informal, vertical or horizontal, these special education leaders considered this form of induction as supportive in making difficult decisions and solving complex problems. They expressed concerns, however, that superintendents and other leadership personnel did not understand either special education or the administrator's role in its provision. Similar to findings from research on the induction of SETs, they sought mentors with the expertise to help with the specialized aspects of their professional performance (Billingsley et al., 2009). It is interesting to note that all of the special education administrators who participated in Collin's (2008) study mentioned the need to seek the support of colleagues, sometimes at a distance, who also had experience as a special education administrator. Although gender did not emerge as a feature of Collin's analysis, the importance of developing a network of mentors who could support complex, special education decision-making, reduce isolation, and foster professional confidence was a major emphasis.

Research studies investigating administrative induction and mentoring suggest their primary importance in forming supportive relationships for success, and their secondary importance in supporting continued skill development (Ehrich et al., 2004; Silver et al., 2009). Induction and mentorship appear to ease entry into the practice of leadership by providing collegial supports, but most of the literature addresses the role of the principal, and presumes that outcomes are similar for those who hold more specialized leadership positions. More empirical data are needed about work-related conditions and reasons for turnover across a broader range of administrative personnel to determine if this presumption is, in fact, rebuttable.

Work-Related Conditions

There is relatively little information about the working conditions of special education directors when compared to those in other administrative positions and findings tend to be state specific. However, there does appear to be a convergence of evidence regarding roles, tasks, and concerns across locations. Recent studies have investigated the roles and responsibilities of special education directors (Marsh, 2005); the self-efficacy of public school special education directors (Hubbard, 2009); the job satisfaction of district and regional special education directors (Alexander, 2009); and factors that ameliorate job-related stress for special education administrators (Wheeler & LaRocco, 2009). Marsh's data, collected from 76% of the local directors in Tennessee, indicated that special education directors spend more than half (52.3%) of their time on administrative and supervisory tasks, leaving less time than they preferred for instructional and curriculum leadership. This suggests a need for reworking the demands of the director's position itself so these leaders have more time to support teaching and learning and collaboration with others. Special education directors also expressed desires for increased opportunities for communication and collaboration with members of the district leadership team (Marsh, 2005).

Conclusions

In today's accountability context, improving the quality of both teachers and leaders is viewed as a primary approach to improving student outcomes. The importance of finding and keeping teachers and leaders who can implement research-based practices is widely acknowledged. Unfortunately, over the last decades, an insufficient number of qualified special education personnel have been prepared, hired, and retained to meet the needs of schools and districts. The importance of addressing recruitment and retention of both teachers and administrators is essential to the opportunities of students to achieve critical educational outcomes.

The focus of the special education recruitment and retention research has centered on describing problems, rather than on generating or testing solutions. For example, in terms of the research on SET supply and demand (see Boe, Chapter 5, this volume), we have a better understanding of the overall need for teachers, their entry paths, and the proportion of those leaving over time. Yet, there are few studies directed at understanding the effectiveness of varied recruitment and entry paths, for either SETs or administrators, or the *specific* conditions that will promote retention. While it is likely that competitive salaries, supportive work contexts, and recruitment and hiring incentives will make a difference, they provide little guidance in terms of what salary differentials are needed, what effective role design looks like in special education, and what entry paths (or the nature of those paths) and induction support promote career longevity.

Future research on recruitment and retention also needs to be more theoretical. Overall, much of special education recruitment and retention research is not grounded in theory, emphasizing the need to incorporate explanatory perspectives. Such work might also help to show the relationships among recruitment, preparation, and induction efforts, and the eventual effects on turnover. As an example, theoretical models such as Job Choice Theory and the Theory of Planned Behavior (Ajzen, 1991) help conceptualize how administrative candidates may approach their role development. These models suggest that career interests and advancement are shaped by professional knowledge and beliefs, and are grounded in the premise "that career interests and advancement are modifiable, and that candidates' preparation can positively influence both leadership capacities and interests in career advancement" (Orr, 2011, p. 118). With regard to recruiting and retaining leaders who make a difference for students with disabilities, perhaps this factor is of high importance. If most personnel who assume leadership positions hold advanced degrees from programs in educational leadership, how and from whom are they learning the knowledge and beliefs about assuming positions of leadership that focus on special education students?

In addition, investments are needed in the development of reliable databases that will provide up to date information about the teacher labor market (Guarino et al., 2006). In special education, a comprehensive database would provide researchers with opportunities to study important questions and such data are needed to better inform policy makers so that targeted teacher investments can be made in high need areas (e.g., exceptionality, geographic, district type). More research is also needed to examine the career trajectories of educational leaders who hold a variety of positions in schools, districts, and educational agencies. In addition, data are needed about the needs of new leaders and their recruitment, initial preparation, induction, and retention in today's schools as well as how this information is communicated and disseminated (see Miller & Baker, 2009).

References

Ajzen, I. (1991). The theory of planned behavior. *Organizational Behavior and Human Decision Processes, 50*, 179–211. doi:10.1016/0749-5978(91)90020-T

Albrecht, S. F., Johns, B. H., Mounsteven, J., & Olorunda, O. (2009). Working conditions as risk or resiliency factors for teachers of students with emotional and behavioral disabilities. *Psychology in the Schools, 46*, 1006–1022. doi:10.1002/pits.20440

Alexander, G. H. (2009). *A study of the job satisfaction of special education local plan area (SELPA) directors and local school district special education directors in four counties of southern California*. Unpublished doctoral dissertation, University of La Verne, La Verne, CA.

American Speech-Language-Hearing Association, Council for Administrators of Special Education, Council for Exceptional Children, Council for Graduate Programs in Communication Sciences and Disorders, Higher Education Consortium for Special Education, National Association of State Directors of Special Education, & Teacher Education Division. (1989). *A free appropriate education: But who will provide it?* Unpublished report for the House Subcommittee on Select Education, Reston, VA.

Aud, S., Hussar, W., Kena, G., Bianco, K., Frohlich, L., Kemp, J., & Tahan, K. (2011). *The condition of education 2011* (NCES 2011-033). U.S. Department of Education, National Center for Education Statistics. Washington, DC: U.S. Government Printing Office.

Billingsley, B., Carlson, E., & Klein, S. (2004). The working conditions and induction support of early career special educators. *Exceptional Children, 70*, 333–347.

Billingsley, B. S. (1993). Teacher retention and attrition in special and general education: A critical review of the literature. *The Journal of Special Education, 27*, 137–174. doi:10.1177/002246699302700202

Billingsley, B. S. (2004). Special education teacher retention and attrition: A critical analysis of the research literature. *The Journal of Special Education, 38*, 39–55. doi:10.1177/00224669040380010401

Billingsley, B. S. (2011). Factors influencing special education teacher quality and effectiveness. In J. M. Kauffman & D. P. Hallahan (Eds.), *Handbook of special education* (pp. 391–405). New York, NY: Taylor & Francis.

Billingsley, B. S., & Cross, L. H. (1991). Teachers' decisions to transfer from special to general education. *The Journal of Special Education, 24*, 496–511. doi:10.1177/002246699102400408

Billingsley, B. S., Griffin, C. C., Smith, S. J., Kamman, M. L., & Israel, M. (2009). *A review of teacher induction in special education: Research, practice and technology solutions* (NCIPP Doc. No. RS-1). Gainesville, FL: University of Florida, National Center to Inform Policy and Practice in Special Education Professional Development. Retrieved from http://ncipp.org/reports/rs_1.pdf

Boe, E. E. (2006). Long-term trends in the national demand, supply, and shortage of special education teachers. *Journal of Special Education, 40*, 138–150. doi:10.1177/00224669060400030201

Boe, E. E., & Cook, L. H. (2006). The chronic and increasing shortage of fully-certified teachers in special and general education. *Exceptional Children, 72*, 443–460.

Boe, E. E., Cook, L. H., & Sunderland, R. J. (2007a). *The prevalence of various aspects of teacher preparation, induction, mentoring, extra support, professional development, and workload factors for beginning teachers in general and special education*. Data Analysis Report No. 2007-DAR1. Philadelphia, PA: University of Pennsylvania, Graduate School of Education, Center for Research and Evaluation in Social Policy.

Boe, E. E., Cook, L. H., & Sunderland, R. J. (2007b). *Trends in the turnover of teachers from 1991 to 2004: Attrition, teaching area transfer, and school migration*. Data Analysis Report No. 2007-DAR2. Philadelphia, PA: University of Pennsylvania, Graduate School of Education, Center for Research and Evaluation in Social Policy.

Boe, E. E., Cook, L. H., & Sunderland, R. J. (2008a). Teacher turnover: Examining exit attrition, teaching area transfer, and school migration. *Exceptional Children, 75*, 7–31.

Boe, E. E., Cook, L. H., & Sunderland, R. J. (2008b). *Teacher qualifications and turnover: Bivariate associations with various aspects of teacher preparation, induction, mentoring, extra support, professional development, and workload factors for early career teachers in special and general education*: Data Analysis Report No. 2008-DAR 1. Philadelphia, PA: University of Pennsylvania.

Boe, E. E., deBettencourt, L. U., Dewey, J. F., Rosenberg, M. S., Sindelar, P. T., & Leko, C. D. (2013). Variability in demand for special education teachers: Indicators, explanations, and impacts. *Exceptionality*, *20*, 103–125. doi: http://dx.doi.org/10.1080/09362835.2013.771563

Boe, E. E., Shin, S., & Cook, L. H. (2007). Does teacher preparation matter for beginning teachers in either special or general education? *The Journal of Special Education*, *41*, 158–170. doi:10.1177/00224669070410030201

Boscardin, M. L., Weir, K., & Kusek, C. (2010). A national study of state credentialing requirements for administrators of special education. *Journal of Special Education Leadership*, *23*, 61–75.

Brownell, M. T., Sindelar, P. T., Kiely, M. T., & Danielson, L. C. (2010). Special education teacher quality and preparation: Exposing foundations, constructing a new model. *Exceptional Children*, *76*, 357–377.

Brownell, M. T., & Smith, S. W. (1993). Understanding special education teacher attrition A conceptual model and implications for teacher educators. *Teacher Education and Special Education*, *16*, 270–282. doi:10.1177/088840649301600309

Burdette, P. (2010). *Principal preparedness to support students with disabilities and other diverse learners*. Alexandria, VA: National Association of State Directors of Special Education.

Carlson, E., Brauen, M., Klein, S., Schroll, K., & Willig, S. (2002). *Study of personnel needs in special education: Key findings*. Retrieved from http://education.ufl.edu/spense/files/2013/06/Key-Findings-_Final_.pdf

Certo, J. L., & Fox, J. E. (2002). Retaining quality teachers. *The High School Journal*, *86*(1), 57–75. doi:10.1353/hsj.2002.0015

Collin, P. (2008). *Female special education administrators' perceptions of mentoring relationships*. Unpublished doctoral dissertation, University of Hartford, Hartford, CT.

Collins, T. (1999). *Attracting and retaining teachers in rural areas*. Charleston, WV: ERIC Clearinghouse on Rural Education and Small Schools. (ERIC No. ED438152)

Connelly, V., & Graham, S. (2009). Student teaching and teacher attrition in special education. *Teacher Education and Special Education*, *32*, 257–269. doi:10.1177/0888406409339472

Cook, L. H., & Boe, E. E. (2007). National trends in the sources of supply of teachers in special and general education. *Teacher Education and Special Education*, *30*, 217–232. doi:10.1177/088840640703000402

Crockett, J. B. (2002). Special education's role in preparing responsive leaders for inclusive schools. *Remedial and Special Education*, *23*, 157–168. doi:10.1177/07419325020230030401

Crockett, J. B. (2011). Conceptual models for leading and administrating special education. In J. M. Kauffman & D. P. Hallahan (Eds.), *Handbook of special education* (pp. 351–362). New York, NY: Taylor & Francis.

Crockett, J. B. (2012). Developing educational leaders for the realities of special education in the 21st century. In J. B. Crockett, B. Billingsley, & M. L. Boscardin (Eds.), *Handbook of leadership and administration for special education* (pp. 52–66). New York, NY: Taylor & Francis.

Crockett, J. B., Becker, M. K., & Quinn, D. (2009). Reviewing the knowledge base of special education leadership and administration: 1970–2009. *Journal of Special Education Leadership*, *22*(2), 55–67.

Cross, L., & Billingsley, B. (1994). Testing a model of special educators' intent to stay in teaching. *Exceptional Children*, *60*, 411–421.

Dai, C., Sindelar, P. T., Denslow, D., Dewey, J., & Rosenberg, M. S. (2007). Economic analysis and the design of alternative-route teacher education programs. *Journal of Teacher Education*, *58*, 422–439. doi:10.1177/0022487107306395

Darling-Hammond, L. (1999). *Teacher quality and student achievement: A review of state policy evidence*. Seattle, WA: Center for the Study of Teaching and Policy, University of Washington.

Darling-Hammond, L., & Sykes, G. (2003). Wanted: A national teacher supply policy for education: The right to meet the "highly qualified" teacher challenge. *Education Policy Archives*, *11*(33), 16–19.

DeMik, S. A. (2008). Experiencing attrition of special education teachers through narrative inquiry. *The High School Journal*, *92*(1), 22–32. doi:10.1353/hsj.0.0009

Ehrich, L. C., Hansford, B., & Tennent, L. (2004). Formal mentoring programs in education and other professions: A review of the literature. *Educational Administration Quarterly*, *40*, 518–540. doi:10.1177/0013161X04267118

Fall, A. M., & Billingsley, B. (2008). Disparities in teacher quality among early career special educators in high and low poverty districts. In T. E. Scruggs & M. A. Mastropieri (Eds.), *Advances in learning and behavioral disabilities: Personnel preparation* (Vol. 21, pp. 181–206). Stanford, CT: JAI. doi:10.1016/S0735-004X(08)00007-4

Federal Student Aid. (2008). *Stafford loan forgiveness for teachers*. Retrieved from http://studentaid.ed.gov/PORTALSWebApp/students/english/cancelstaff.jsp

Feiman-Nemser, S. (2001). From preparation to practice: Designing a continuum to strengthen and sustain teaching. *Teachers College Record*, *103*, 1013–1055. doi:10.1111/0161-4681.00141

Feng, L., & Sass, T. R. (2012a). *Competing risks analysis of dropout and educational attainment for students with disabilities.*

Working Paper 12-09. Atlanta: Georgia State University, Andrew Young School of Policy Studies. Retrieved from: http://aefpweb.org/sites/default/files/webform/dropout%20and%20ed%20attainment%20for%20special%20ed%20students%20Feng%20and%20Sass(AEFP)%20updated.pdf

Feng, L., & Sass, T. R. (2012b). *What makes special education teachers special? Teacher training and the achievement of students with disabilities*. Working Paper 12-10. Atlanta: Georgia State University, Andrew Young School of Policy Studies. Retrieved from: http://papers.ssrn.com/sol3/papers.cfm?abstract_id=2020714

Fish, W. W., & Stephens, T. L. (2010). Special education: A career of choice. *Remedial and Special Education, 31*, 400–407. doi:10.1177/0741932509355961

Fletcher, S., Strong, M., & Villar, A. (2008). An investigation of the effects of variations in mentor-based induction on the performance of students in California. *Teachers College Record, 110*, 2271–2289.

Gardiner, M. E., Enomoto, E., & Grogan, M. (2000). *Coloring outside the lines: Mentoring women into school leadership*. Albany, NY: State University of New York Press.

Gersten, R., Keating, T., Yovanoff, P., & Harniss, M. K. (2001). Working in special education: Factors that enhance special educators' intent to stay. *Exceptional Children, 67*, 549–567.

Griffin, C. C., Winn, J. A., Otis-Wilborn, A., & Kilgore, K. L. (2003). *New teacher induction in special education* (COPSSE Document No. RS-5). Gainesville, FL: University of Florida, The Center on Personnel Studies in Special Education. Retrieved from http://copsse.education.ufl.edu/docs/RS-5/1/RS-5.pdf

Guarino, C. M., Santibañez, L., & Daley, G. A. (2006). Teacher recruitment and retention: A review of recent empirical evidence. *Review of Educational Research, 76*, 173–208. doi:10.3102/00346543076002173

Hammer, P. C., Hughes, G., McClure, C., Reeves, C., & Salgado, D. (2005). *Rural teacher recruitment and retention practices: A review of the research literature, national survey of rural superintendents, and case studies of programs in Virginia*. Charleston, WV: Appalachia Educational Laboratory at Edvantia. (ERIC No. 489143).

Hirsch, E., Koppich, J., & Knapp, M. (2001). *Revisiting what states are doing to improve the quality of teaching: An update on patterns and trends*. Seattle, WA: University of Washington, Center for the Study of Teaching and Policy.

Hirsch, E., Rorrer, A., Sindelar, P. T., Dawson, S. A., Heretick, J., & Jia, C. L. (2009). *State policies to improve the mentoring of beginning special education teachers*. (NCIPP Doc. No. PA-1). Gainesville, FL: University of Florida, National Center to Inform Policy and Practice in Special Education Professional Development. Retrieved from http://www.ncipp.org/reports/pa_1.pdf

Hubbard, C. C. (2009). *The self-efficacy of special education directors in the state of Texas*. Unpublished dissertation, Texas Woman's University, Denton, TX.

IMPACTplus for Teachers (2011). The performance-based compensation systems for Washington Teachers' Union (WTU) members. Retrieved from http://www.dc.gov/DCPS/In+the+Classroom/Ensuring+Teacher+Success/IMPACT+%28Performance+Assessment%29/IMPACTplus

Individuals with Disabilities Education Improvement Act of 2004, Pub. L. No. 108-446 (2004).

Ingersoll, R. M. (2001). *Teacher turnover, teacher shortages and the organization of schools* (Document R-01-1). Seattle, WA: University of Washington, Center for the Study of Teaching and Policy.

Ingersoll, R. M., & Strong, M. (2011). The impact of induction and mentoring programs for beginning teachers: A critical review of the research. *Review of Educational Research, 81*, 201–233. doi:10.3102/0034654311403323

Johnson, S. M., & Birkeland, S. (2003). Pursuing a "sense of success": New teachers explain their career decisions. *American Educational Research Journal, 40*, 581–617. doi:10.3102/00028312040003581

Johnson, S. M., Kraft, M. A., & Papay, J. P. (2011). *How context matters in high-need schools: The effects of teachers' working conditions on their professional satisfaction and their students' achievement*. Unpublished manuscript, Harvard University, Cambridge, MA. Retrieved from http://scholar.harvard.edu/mkraft/files/teacher_working_conditions_-_tcr_revision_-_final.pdf

Johnson, S. M., & The Project on the Next Generation of Teachers. (2004). *Finders and keepers: Helping teachers survive and thrive in our schools*. San Francisco, CA: Jossey-Bass.

Jones, N., & Youngs, P. (2012). Daily emotions and their association with the commitment and burnout of beginning teachers. *Teachers College Record, 114*(2), 1–36.

Kaff, M. S. (2004). Multitasking is multitaxing: Why special educators are leaving the field. *Preventing School Failure, 48*(2), 10–17.

Lauritzen, P. (1990, April). *How critical is the special education teacher shortage*? Paper presented at the annual meeting of the Council for Exceptional Children, Toronto, Canada.

Leithwood, K., Louis, K. S., Anderson, S., & Wahlstrom, K. (2004). *How leadership influences student learning*. Minneapolis: University of Minnesota, Center for Applied Research and Educational Improvement. Retrieved from http://www.sisd.net/cms/lib/TX01001452/Centricity/Domain/33/ReviewofResearch-LearningFrom-Leadership.pdf

Leithwood, K. A., & Riehl, C. (2005). What do we already know about educational leadership? In W. A. Firestone & C. Riehl (Eds.), *A new agenda for research in educational leadership* (pp. 12–27). New York, NY: Teachers College Press.

Lortie, D. (1975). *Schoolteacher: A sociological study*. Chicago, IL: University of Chicago Press.
Lui, E., Johnson, S., & Peske, H. (2004). New teachers and the Massachusetts signing bonus: The limits of inducements. *Educational Evaluation and Policy Analysis, 26*, 217–236. doi:10.3102/01623737026003217
Marsh, J. (2005). *A policy analysis of the role of special education directors in Tennessee public schools*. Unpublished doctoral dissertation, University of Memphis, Memphis, TN.
McCreight, C. (2000). *Teacher attrition, shortage, and strategies for teacher retention*. Washington, DC: National Institute of Education. (ERIC No. ED444986)
McLeskey, J., & Billingsley, B. S. (2008). How does the quality and stability of the teaching force influence the research-to-practice gap? A perspective on the teacher shortage in special education. *Remedial and Special Education, 29*, 293–305. doi:10.1177/0741932507312010
McLeskey, J., Tyler, N. C., & Flippin, S. S. (2004). The supply of and demand for special education teachers: A review of research regarding the chronic shortage of special education teachers. *Journal of Special Education, 38*, 5–21. doi:10.1177/00224669040380010201
Miller, M., & Baker, P. (2009). What are the needs of beginning special education administrators? *In Case, 50*(6), 6–10.
Miller, M. D., Brownell, M., Smith, & S. W. (1999). Factors that predict teachers staying in, leaving, or transferring from the special education classroom. *Exceptional Children, 65*, 201–218.
Muller, E. (2009, June). *Retention and attrition of local special education directors: inForum Brief Policy Analysis*. Alexandria, VA: National Association of State Directors of Special Education. Retrieved from http://nasdse.org/DesktopModules/DNNspot-Store/ProductFiles/95_4e8e0c7b-2bcd-47cf-8b6d-8d9d780cf999.pdf.
Muller, E. (2010, October). *State-level efforts to recruit and retain qualified special education personnel including related service providers: inForum Brief Policy Analysis*. Alexandria, VA: National Association of State Directors of Special Education.
Murphy, J., Moorman, H. N., & McCarthy, M. (2008). A framework for rebuilding initial certification and preparation programs in educational leadership: Lessons from whole-state reform initiatives. *Teachers College Record, 110*, 2172–2203.
Nance, E., & Calabrese, R. L. (2009). Special education teacher retention and attrition: The impact of increased legal requirements. *International Journal of Educational Management, 23*, 431–440. doi:10.1108/09513540910970520
National Center to Improve Recruitment and Retention of Qualified Personnel for Children with Disabilities. (2011). *Personnel improvement center*. Retrieved from http://www.personnelcenter.org/
National Comprehensive Center for Teaching Quality. (2007) *Recruiting quality teachers in mathematics, science and special education for urban and rural schools*. Retrieved from www.gtlcenter.org/sites/default/files/docs/NCCTQRecruitQuality.pdf
National Partnership for Teaching in At-Risk Schools. (2005). *Qualified teachers for at-risk schools: A national imperative*. Retrieved from http://www.ecs.org/html/projectspartners/NPTARS/npreport.asp
No Child Left Behind Act of 2001, Pub. L. No. 107-110 (2002). Retrieved from http://www2.ed.gov/policy/elsec/leg/esea02/107-110.pdf
Orr, M. T. (2011). Pipeline to preparation to advancement: Graduates' experiences in, through, and beyond leadership preparation. *Educational Administration Quarterly, 47*, 114–172. doi:10.1177/0011000010378612
Paperwork in special education (SPeNSE Factsheet). (2003). *SPeNSE Factsheet*. Retrieved from http://ferdig.coe.ufl.edu/spense/Paperwork.doc
Putney, L. L. (2009, November). *Key issue: Recruiting special education teachers*. Formerly available at: http://resource.tqsource.org/Search/tqResources.aspx
Race to the Top Act of 2011. (2011). H.R. 1532—112th Congress. In *GovTrack.us* (database of federal legislation). Retrieved from http://www.govtrack.us/congress/bills/112/hr1532
Rice, C., & Goessling, D. (2005). Recruiting and retaining male special education teachers. *Remedial & Special Education, 26*, 347–356. doi:10.1177/07419325050260060501
Riley, P. (2009). The development and testing of a time-limited mentoring model for experienced school leaders. *Mentoring & Tutoring: Partnership in Learning, 17*, 233–249. doi:10.1080/13611260903050163
Robertson, J. S., & Singleton, J. D. (2010). Comparison of traditional versus alternative preparation of special education teachers. *Teacher Education and Special Education, 33*, 213–224. doi:10.1177/0888406409359904
Rosenberg, M. S., & Sindelar, P. T. (2005). The proliferation of alternative routes to certification in special education: A critical review of the literature. *Journal of Special Education, 39*, 117–127. doi:10.1177/00224669050390020201
Rosenholtz, S. J. (1989). Workplace conditions that affect teacher quality and commitment: Implications for teacher induction programs. *The Elementary School Journal, 89*, 420–439. doi:10.1086/461584
Schlichte, J., Yssel, N., & Merbler, J. (2005). Pathways to burnout: Case studies in teacher isolation and alienation. *Preventing School Failure, 50*(1), 35–40. doi:10.3200/PSFL.50.1.35-40
Silver, M., Lochmiller, C. R., Copland, M. A., & Tripps, A. M. (2009). Supporting new school leaders: Findings from a university-based leadership coaching program for new administrators. *Mentoring & Tutoring: Partnerships in Learning, 17*, 215–232. doi:10.1080/13611260903050148

Sindelar, P. T., Shearer, D. K., Yendol-Hoppey, D., & Liebert, T. W. (2006). The sustainability of inclusive school reform. *Exceptional Children, 72*, 317–331.
Smith, T. M., & Ingersoll, R. M. (2004). What are the effects of induction and mentoring on beginning teacher turnover? *American Educational Research Journal, 41*, 681–714. doi:10.3102/00028312041003681
Smith-Davis, J., & Billingsley, B. (1993). The supply/demand puzzle. *Teacher Education and Special Education, 16*, 202–217. doi:10.1177/088840649301600303
Smith-Davis, J., Burke, P. J., & Noel, M. (1984). *Personnel to educate the handicapped in America: Supply and demand from a programmatic viewpoint*. College Park, MD: University of Maryland, Institute for the Study of Exceptional Children and Youth.
Tate, A. (2010). The changing face of special education administration. *Journal of Special Education Leadership, 23*, 113–115.
Thornton, B., Peltier, G., & Medina, R. (2011). Reducing the special education teacher shortage. *The Clearing House: A Journal of Educational Strategies, Issues and Ideas, 80*, 233–238. doi:10.3200/TCHS.80.5.233-238.
United States Department of Education. (2010). *ESEA blueprint for reform*. Washington, DC: Office of Planning, Evaluation and Policy Development.
Vannest, K. J., & Hagan-Burke, S. (2010). Teacher time use in special education. *Remedial and Special Education, 31*, 126–142. doi:10.1177/0741932508327459
Viadero, D. (2009). Turnover in the principalship focus of research. *Education Week, 29*(9), 1–14.
Wang, J., Odell, S. J., & Schwille, S. A. (2008). Effects of teacher induction on beginning teachers' teaching: A critical review of the literature. *Journal of Teacher Education, 59*, 132–152. doi:10.1177/0022487107314002
Wasburn-Moses, L. (2010). Rethinking mentoring: Comparing policy and practice in special and general education. *Education Policy Analysis Archives, 18*(32), 1–25.
Wheeler, D. S., & LaRocco, D. J. (2009). Special education administrators: Who and what helps buffer job-related stress? *Journal of Special Education Leadership, 22*, 85–92.
Whitaker, S. D. (2000). Mentoring beginning special education teachers and the relationship to attrition. *Exceptional Children, 66*, 546–566.
Whitaker, S. D. (2003). Needs of beginning special education teachers: Implications for teacher education. *Teacher Education and Special Education, 26*, 106–117. doi:10.1177/088840640302600204
Wrzesniewski, A., McCauley, C., Rozin, P., & Schwartz, B. (1997). Jobs, careers, and callings: People's relations to their work. *Journal of Research in Personality, 31*, 21–33. doi:10.1006/jrpe.1997.2162
Yell, M. L. (2012). *The law and special education*. Upper Saddle River, NJ: Pearson.

7

Equity Challenges in the Accountability Age

Demographic Representation and Distribution in the Teacher Workforce

Elizabeth B. Kozleski[1]

UNIVERSITY OF KANSAS

Alfredo J. Artiles

ARIZONA STATE UNIVERSITY

Erica D. McCray

UNIVERSITY OF FLORIDA

Lisa Lacy

ARIZONA STATE UNIVERSITY

Things to Think About

- Equity challenges in the United States include: rapidly shifting demographics, a primarily White, middle-class teaching force, and a glacially shifting dominant culture that privileges standardization and assimilation at the expense of contextualization and respect for diversity.
- Attracting, retaining, and developing equity-minded teachers will require structural as well as cultural shifts in how the teacher labor force is conceptualized.
- Teachers must be able to cross cultural borders and connect students to learning by capitalizing on their cultural histories and community experiences.
- Teacher distribution across different contexts often solidifies inequities in opportunities for learning and student outcomes.

This chapter focuses on the equity challenges that are posed by the tightening bonds of accountability at a time when the demographic composition of the United States and particularly that of its school-age population is shifting dramatically. Waves of immigration from Central and South America, India, China, Africa, Southeast Asia, Eastern Europe, the Middle East, and the Pacific Islands are coming to rest not only in major coastal cities but traveling into interior cities and even to small, rural towns in the Midwest, the South, and the West. Old discourses that contributed to the social, political, and economic subordination of indigenous and African-American peoples resurfaced during the immigration tides of the late 19th and early 20th century (Galindo & Vigil, 2006). Those same discourses challenge the status quo today. Whose English is the real English? Whose histories, mores, and geographies are legitimized in schooling? How do teachers navigate the cultural boundaries between and among students, families, and the official school curricula? These are controversial spaces to inhabit, to understand, to mobilize, and to learn in and from. How teachers conceptualize their work, the degree to which they are supported to examine their practices, and grapple with fundamental challenges with what and how we know places the equity challenges in schooling today at the heart of what we mean by education.

For special education, equity issues are most readily connected to the 40-year history of disproportionate representation of students from culturally and linguistically diverse backgrounds in special education (Artiles, Kozleski, Trent, Osher, & Ortiz, 2010). Questions about who is identified for special education services and for what purpose, particularly in the high-incidence categories of emotional/behavioral disorders, learning and intellectual disabilities, continue to trouble the field (Donovan & Cross, 2002; Dyson & Kozleski, 2008). One of the important areas of inquiry surrounding disproportionality in referral, identification, and placement issues has to do with the cultural understandings that teachers in general and special education bring to their knowledge of student development, participation, and performance in schools, and designs for learning that support and acknowledge the cultural histories and experiences of their students (Artiles & Kozleski, 2010).

In this chapter, we explore the cultural, demographic, and historical discontinuities between the teaching force and the current student population. We provide a framework to advance understanding about how these discontinuities influence and produce particular kinds of educational experiences and school performances. The measurement (and mismeasurement) of learning that places responsibility for particular kinds of outcomes on schools and teachers produces particular kinds of local policy environments that can constrain and limit the social and intellectual capital that resides within communities and schools. Such environments impact and influence the ways in which school administrators and teachers perceive their jobs and contribute to attrition in the teacher workforce (Loeb, Darling-Hammond, & Luczak, 2005). Moreover, educational discontinuities are shaped by structural, economic, political, and cultural fissures that give students from nondominant cultures less access to higher education and thus, to teaching careers (Loeb & Reininger, 2004).

Here, we draw from research on the teacher workforce in both general and special education, recognizing that many of the equity issues that teachers, schools, and students face cut across general and special education borders. The final section of this chapter explores the implications of these perspectives on research, policy, and practice.

Foregrounding Context in Teacher Demographic Representation and Distribution

Since the 1965 passage of the first Elementary and Secondary Education Act (ESEA), national education policy has increasingly influenced education policy and practice at the state and local levels. Tying federal funds to the provision of services for students whose family incomes fell below certain thresholds meant that federal educational policy impacted how, when, and where programs to improve literacy as well as other school reforms were delivered. Subsequent reauthorizations of the legislation refined those policies, strengthening particularly the ways in which districts and schools were held accountable for the use and outcomes of federal funding (Kozleski & Huber, 2012). With the 2001 reauthorization of ESEA, the No Child Left Behind Act of 2001 (2002), major shifts in measuring and assessing student outcomes were made. Importantly, the use of whole school improvement gauges to demonstrate Adequate Yearly Progress (AYP) for students caused a sea change in how teachers, principals, and districts conceptualized and organized their roles and actions. NCLB required that schools demonstrate progress of *subgroups* of students who fell into specified racial/ethnic or ability categories. None of this counting and measuring was related to changing structural opportunities to learn, improving access to higher education for individuals from nondominant cultures who then might be available to join the teacher workforce, or justice discourses in the law that addressed segregated neighborhoods and the cultural capital required for success in mainstream curriculum (Zeichner, 2010). Against this background of increasing surveillance and accountability, schools and school districts—where students struggled with inadequate school facilities and material resources, and underprepared teachers—experienced increasing teacher shortages while the teaching force expanded.

Close on the heels of NCLB, the Individuals with Disabilities Education Act (IDEA) (1990) was reauthorized in 2004. With more attention to congruence between NCLB and IDEA, the 2004 version of IDEA focused greater attention on the *outcomes* of special education. States were required to provide data to the federal government that not only demonstrated their compliance with the law but also provided information about changes in how students with disabilities were being served and supported through special education. The tensions created between the premises and practices of these two major policies create inequities for some of the very students the policies intend to benefit (Artiles, 2011). In this section, we explore how these top-down contexts influenced teacher distribution and representation.

Demographic Portraits of the General and Special Education Fields

According to the 2010 U.S. census, 63% of the population is White (not Hispanic), 15% identify as Hispanic or Latino, 13.1% identify as Black, 5% identify as Asian, 2.4% as two or more races, 1.2% identify as American Indian/Alaska Native, and 0.2% as Native Hawaiian and other Pacific Islander. More than 80% of elementary teachers are female, while about 57% of secondary teachers are women. While women have dominated the teaching force for the last 50 years, the labor market in general now offers many more career options for women than in previous decades. The majority of the teaching force identifies as White (83% overall) with 7.2% as Hispanic, 6.9% Black, 1.6% Asian, and 0.8% American Indian/Alaska Native (Aud et al., 2011). These numbers reflect the state of special education personnel as well. According to the SPeNSE database of more than 5,000 special education teachers, more than 8 of every 10 teachers in special education were White (http://education.ufl.edu/spense/). While the overall percentage of White special educators was above 85, in the mid-south and the southeastern regions of the country, White teachers composed about 75% of the special education teaching force with special educators who identified as Black or African American making up around 20% of the population. Special educators who identified as Hispanic constituted about 10% of the population in both the southeastern U.S. and the western states.

In highly populated states like California, New York, and Texas, student demographics have significantly shifted. More than 50% of the students in California are Hispanic, with White students comprising a little more than a quarter of the population (Aud et al., 2011). Aud et al. also found that, in New York, just under half of the population remains White (49%), and Hispanic and Black students comprise 41% of the population combined. Moreover, in Texas, Hispanic students are 48% of the population while White students constitute 34%. Yet even in these states, the teaching population remains majority White. A little over half of the students in the U.S. were White, while Hispanic students represented almost a quarter of all U.S. students. Black students comprised 17% of the school-age population with Asian or Pacific Islander, American Indian/Alaska Native, Native Hawaiian, and students reporting two or more races composing about 8% of the school population. So while students of color across the nation represent 5 of every 10 students, they are most likely to be taught by a White woman.

Teacher Supply and Demand in the Time of Outcomes Equity: A History of the Present

Corcoran, Schwab, and Evans (2004) found that teachers are more likely to select teaching careers when starting wages are high relative to wages in other occupations. Salaries vary based on teaching assignments. For instance, teachers tend to have higher salaries in urban, suburban, and large towns than they do in rural and small towns (Strizek, Pittsonberger, Riordan, Lyter, & Orlofsky, 2006). States vary considerably in terms of the average beginning teacher salaries. To illustrate, in 2006 first year teachers in Connecticut could expect starting salaries around $39,259 while starting teachers in Arizona would receive annual salary offers of around $30,404, although these salaries also vary between school districts. And, where base salaries were at best $30,000 per year, teachers were also likely to move or leave teaching all together (Béteille & Loeb, 2009). Teacher shortages within particular fields also vary region-to-region, state-to-state, and district-to-district. Salary plays a role in this variance, as do several other factors including poor working conditions, racial composition, and income level of students' families (Loeb et al., 2005). In fact, other researchers suggest that race/ethnicity and student achievement play a more significant role than salary in teacher workforce stability (Hanushek, Kain, & Rivkin, 2004).

Where schools serve low-income students, wages can serve an important mediating factor in who chooses to teach where, considering that most teachers prefer to begin their careers near home (Boyd, Lankford, Loeb, & Wyckoff, 2005). While teachers' wages have risen over the last 40 years, they have fallen behind salaries in nonteaching occupations that require similar kinds of qualifications, such as lawyers, doctors, scientists, and engineers (Loeb & Reininger, 2004). Who chooses to become a teacher when both gender boundaries within and among career paths are disappearing and salaries are not competitive with other professional fields is being resolved in a number of ways that have particular long-term consequences for public education. One well-documented example comes from the Teach for America (TFA) initiative. TFA[2] is, by design, meant to attract a cadre of individuals from elite schools and colleges who might not select education as a lifelong career but are willing to invest part of their early wage earning years in teaching (Labaree, 2010). The short- and long-term effects of purposely creating a short-term workforce within a profession in which skill levels impact the lives and opportunities to learn for a generation of students deserves close and careful scrutiny (Cochran-Smith, 2005). Further, TFA tends to attract a higher percentage of White teacher candidates than other teacher education routes (Xu, Hannaway, & Taylor, 2009). While demographics alone do not produce equity, the lack of diversity means that the wide range of cultural histories, experiences, and communities that are increasingly becoming the majority in the school student population are not reflected in the teaching force creating a cultural center that bears little resemblance to the worlds that students inhabit in and out of school.

From 1978 to 2003–2004, the special education teaching ranks grew from 194,802 to 412,750 practitioners (Béteille & Loeb, 2009). Almost a third of the teaching force is over the age of 50, with anticipated retirements coming in the next 10 years, increasing the demand for new teachers. This means that an increasing number of novices will be entering the field in some localities while in others, where populations are declining, teacher hires are also declining. Attracting teachers will be critical to the workforce, particularly in special education since the special education pool appears to be particularly vulnerable (Boe, Cook, & Sunderland, 2008). At a time when schools are intently focused on student progress, having a younger and less experienced workforce brings some concerns. For instance, teacher experience seems to be consistently correlated with higher student test scores with the benefit peaking at 21 to 27 years of experience although more than half of the gain in test scores occurred during the first couple of years of teaching (Clotfelter, Ladd, & Vigdor, 2007; Hanushek et al., 2004; Rockoff, 2003). Thus, teacher retention remains vital to sustain the benefit realized in improving student outcomes in the early years of teaching.

While the number and percentage of teachers who stay in the field has been slightly declining over the past decade, still more than 80% of the teaching force stays each year, remaining in the same school. Less than 10% of teachers with regular or standard certification in their field leave teaching. Teachers with temporary or provisional certificates are more likely to leave. In a study of teachers between 2003 and 2005, special education teachers were the most likely to switch schools as well as leave teaching (Béteille & Loeb, 2009; Boe, Cook, & Sunderland, 2008). Special education teacher turnover appears to follow three tracks: (a) migration from one school to another; (b) transfer from special to general education assignments; and (c) exodus from teaching (Boe, Cook & Sunderland, 2008). Teacher mobility varies by region with the Northeast experiencing the least turnover. Urban areas experience more teacher turnover than suburban areas. Schools with higher proportions of Black and Hispanic students experience more turnover (Béteille & Loeb, 2009). Few studies illuminate tensions that may arise for teachers from dominant and nondominant backgrounds and how those tensions inform teacher turnover. When the teaching force is segregated itself, it offers little opportunity for teachers to build their own intercultural understanding.

The consequences of who chooses to teach and teacher turnover create discontinuities in school histories and cultures, lack of traction for complex school reform, and loss of effort in improving recruiting efforts. Studies suggest while the least effective teachers leave the profession, another group of teachers who are less qualified or experienced than their colleagues are likely to transfer (Aud et al., 2011), moving from school to school over time. Most research on attrition focuses on the ways in which salary, school climate, administrative support, and blurred role assignments contribute to decisions to transfer and/or leave education (Billingsley, 2003; Kozleski, Mainzer, & Deshler, 2000). Billingsley summed up the research on special educator attrition, indicating that a wide range of factors influences attrition, including teachers' personal circumstances and priorities. Younger special educators are more likely to leave than their older, more experienced peers and special educators without certification are more likely to leave than those with certification. Unlike general educators, special educators with higher test scores are more likely to leave than those with lower scores (Béteille & Loeb, 2009). When qualified teachers leave the profession, field, or a school the consequences are greatest for the students and schools needing to replace them. This evidence suggests, therefore, that a host of structural factors mediates the supply and demand patterns in the teacher workforce, often deepening inequalities in the quality of teachers available to various subgroups of students.

NCLB and Teacher Quality Requirements: Assumptions and Consequences

NCLB includes a set of criteria to determine whether teachers are highly qualified. The criteria rely on proxies for quality performance. These proxies entail requiring teachers to hold at least a bachelor's degree, show mastery on a state-designed measure, and demonstrate subject-matter knowledge through certification or an intent-to-earn licensure through an approved program. While a teacher should know content and be able to enact that knowledge, using a test to assess what a teacher knows offers little evidence that the teacher will be able to impart that knowledge, regardless of context, student characteristics, and other factors (Cochran-Smith & Lytle, 2006). The assumption that knowledge itself is sufficient for robust, effective teaching without gauging teachers' abilities to adjust delivery is problematic. Several researchers have noted that teacher knowledge has little purpose separate from pedagogical content knowledge and domain expertise (Ball, Thames, & Phelps, 2008; Hill et al., 2008) and understandings of learner characteristics and needs (Darling-Hammond & Bransford, 2005). These challenges are even more pronounced in special education where teachers are expected to meet NCLB's high-stakes accountability requirements while teaching students with more complex needs (Brownell, Sindelar, Kiely, & Danielson, 2010; Stough & Palmer, 2003).

NCLB's language places limited value on university routes for teacher preparation that require extensive practice in the field under the mentorship of practicing professionals in addition to building a theoretical and research base for practice (Darling-Hammond, 2010). Providing entrée to some underprepared individuals through rapid, often inadequate, preparation programs ignores the developmental nature of a profession that is performance oriented (Darling-Hammond, 2010). Other professional fields (e.g., medicine and law) require extensive preparation and apprenticeships prior to solo practice (Cochran-Smith, 2005). Not only did NCLB remove some of the safeguards to preserving the standards of teacher preparation, it suggested that traditional programs deterred potentially superior candidates from pursuing the field (Zeichner, 2010). Yet, research suggests that the extent and focus of preparation is critically important (Boe, Shin, & Cook, 2007; Feng & Sass, 2012; Gelman, Pullen, & Kaufman, 2004; Goldhaber, 2002; Heck, 2007; Phillips, 2010; Wilson, Floden, Ferrini-Mundy, 2001), particularly when teacher candidates are preparing to teach the most vulnerable students. In fact, Phillips showed the significant impact that a teacher who had gone through a graduate program in her subject area (elementary education) had on reading achievement gains for first graders, even for students identified as at-risk for failure when compared to teachers whose preparation was at the undergraduate level.

Even when teachers are prepared well, the contexts in which they work make a difference (Donovan & Cross, 2002). Schools and districts that consistently perform poorly as measured by state and/or district assessment systems are likely to lose teachers who are highly skilled because they resist having their autonomy and the ability to make sound instructional decisions usurped (Cochran-Smith & Lytle, 2006; Sanders, 2008). Thus, a consequence of NCLB is continued placement of children in targeted subgroups (i.e., low SES, non-White, special needs, emerging bilingual) in schools with higher turnover and less-qualified teachers (Drame & Pugach, 2010). A workforce that is poorly prepared compounds its vulnerabilities. A group of poorly prepared teachers creates a network of poorly designed learning environments. Similarly, a critical mass of high-quality teachers is able to support student-learning gains in schools with high-needs students (Heck, 2007). Not surprisingly, schools that Heck identified as having high levels of teacher quality provided more equitable learning opportunities school-wide.

IDEA and Teacher Shortage: Dimensions and Magnitude of the Problem

Teacher shortages continue to be troubling in special education. The shortage of special educators has hovered around 10% since the field's inception although there has been substantial decline in the last 5 years (Sindelar, Brownell, & Billingsley, 2010). The highest rates of attrition occur during the first 3 years of teaching for both general and special educators, with special educators with 13 to 24 years of experience leaving the field at twice the annual percentage rate of general educators (Boe et al., 2008). Yet, while teachers leave special education at greater rates than their general education counterparts (Boe et al., 2008), teachers, in general, leave the field at lower rates than employees in all occupations (Boe et al., 2008). Teacher attrition data are only part of the shortage story that continues to challenge schools and school systems. When teacher attrition and transfer are combined, special and general education teacher turnover approaches almost a quarter of the teaching force annually (Boe et al., 2008). Teacher turnover leads to localized teacher shortage. In the most recent document from the Department of Education outlining teacher shortages as reported by states, every state reports shortages in special education (U.S. Department of Education, 2011).

Why Context Matters

Increasingly prescriptive and robust federal legislation both in NCLB and IDEA touched the lives of teachers in unprecedented ways. Workforce instability continues—particularly in special education—with schools reeling from turnover rates that approach 25% of their faculties. Such contexts bode poorly for sustained and specific school improvement efforts that rely on shared histories, counternarratives, and networked groups of educators who work collaboratively to design learning environments and opportunities that reach out to students historically marginalized in schools. The contexts in which special and general educators teach are governed by policies that demand more standardization of procedures and practices while the population of students continues to present more and more diversity.

General and Special Education Teacher Distribution: Who Goes Where?

Teachers are produced locally. In one study of teachers in New York State, Loeb and Reininger (2004) found that 61% of teachers started teaching in a school district within 15 miles of the district where they graduated from high school. A full 85% of teachers entered teaching within 40 miles of their high school. Boyd et al. (2005) also reported the same association between distance from college and the location of teaching jobs. One explanation is that teachers sort themselves into locations that resemble socially and racially the schools they attended as children. Because teachers display such a strong preference for staying close to home and/or college, geography preferences may explain some of the attrition that urban schools face. Reininger (2012) found that schools with large populations from nondominant cultures and large percentages of children on free and reduced-price lunch produce far fewer students who go on to earn bachelor's degrees, thus limiting their access to teachers who will want to return to teach. As a consequence and in contrast with many districts, urban districts are forced to import teachers from the suburbs and fringe towns (Boyd et al., 2005). In combination, the preference for home turf and the lower rates of college degrees from urban schools make the job of attracting and keeping teachers in urban schools even more complex.

The distribution of teachers across schools and districts is further constrained because of hiring practices. Often, districts fail to make job offers until late summer, long after many applicants have taken other jobs or withdrawn their applications (Béteille & Loeb, 2009). Studies suggest that applicants who are hired early or withdraw have significantly better qualifications than late hires (Béteille & Loeb, 2009). Budgeting practices, union transfer agreements, and vacancy notification requirements all contribute to late hiring practices. Urban districts often have the most bureaucratic and complex hiring policies making them more vulnerable to beginning school without all teaching positions filled and potentially filling empty positions with teachers whose qualifications are marginal.

Although much of the research on teacher labor markets focuses on the choices that teachers make, some of it also examines the ways in which schools and school districts strategically position themselves to attract and retain teachers who work well with underperforming students. Some of the research suggests self-perpetuating cycles in which schools that produce strong achievement patterns for their students tend to attract more effective teachers who are likely to leave current positions to teach in more effective schools (Loeb, Kalogrides, & Béteille, 2011). Novice teachers in more effective schools tend to be placed in classrooms with a range of student abilities and performances. More effective schools tend to continue to improve over time and retain their more effective teachers. In essence, success garners more successful outcomes and attracts more successful teachers (Loeb et al., 2011).

The distribution of the teaching force by ethnicity seems to be geographically determined (Béteille & Loeb, 2009; Boyd et al., 2005). For urban and rural schools, already considered hard-to-staff, the preference to return home to teach complicates their recruiting capacity. These schools are less likely to have a large pool of teacher education graduates to return and join the teaching ranks. The schools may be forced to hire individuals who are underqualified and lack contextual knowledge to teach students who need well-qualified, effective teachers (Phillips, 2010). Predominantly monocultural communities (represented by predominantly one ethnic group) are likely to have a teaching force that reflects the community demographics. Addressing equity issues in schools could be compromised when the cultural histories of the faculties and administrators are more alike than different. Yet even these distinctions must be nuanced, because within-group differences such as dialect variations or food preferences are often as distinct and deep as between-group differences (Artiles et al., 2010). Difference itself is constructed from a normative center that, because it establishes the conditions for what is contained within the center, also determines difference (Minow, 1990). Thus, if a particular form of English usage, say the pronunciation of a word like "clematis," a type of flowering vine, is deemed to have an emphasis on the second syllable, then pronunciation that varies from this form is seen as different. That is, normative usage determines what is heard as difference. A fluent English speaker, from India, for instance, who places emphasis on the first syllable, might legitimately ask, "Whose English is it?" In other words, a particular cultural preference was declared as the norm from which all other usages would be viewed as different, although the meaning of clematis does not change with the change in syllable emphasis. The more that a center is disturbed and loses its coherence, the more likely it is that multiple notions of equity can be explored and ultimately embraced within a school community. It follows that if a school's faculty and administration come from the same cultural and linguistic backgrounds (i.e., norms, values, assumptions, and cultural practices are shared, and thus, define, what is considered "different"), there is a high probability that the practices, values, and other cultural expressions that do not overlap with school personnel's cultural "center" will be ignored, misunderstood, or worse, suppressed.

Kalogrides, Loeb, and Béteille (2011) examined teacher and student characteristics and apparent sorting practices. They found that schools with high enrollments of students from nondominant cultures have higher numbers of teachers with less than 10 years of experience. Further, schools with high enrollments of students from nondominant cultures have the lowest proportion of teachers teaching in their areas of certification (Kalogrides et al., 2011). The same authors also found that more than a fifth of the non-White student population has teachers who do not hold certificates in any of the areas that they teach compared to the 15% of White students who experience the same condition. While 16% of White students are taught by teachers who failed the general knowledge certification exam, more than a quarter of all non-White students find themselves in classrooms with teachers with similar credentialing histories. Poverty also seems to separate student experiences. For instance, 30% of low-income students had teachers who failed the general knowledge certification compared with only 21% of higher-income students (Kalogrides et al., 2011). Non-White teachers are also more likely to teach in central cities. Differences in teacher distribution occur not only between districts and between schools within districts but also *within* schools. Less experienced, women from nondominant cultures are assigned students with more behavioral problems, more absenteeism, and low achievement profiles. Their students have repeated grades, tend to come from low-income backgrounds, and tend to be students of color (Kalogrides et al., 2011).

Why Teacher Diversity Matters

Teacher diversity matters because teaching is a deeply personal and relational practice (Artiles & Kozleski, 2007). The social, intellectual, and political capital teachers draw from informs the rapid transactions within classrooms between and among teachers and students (Erickson, 2004). Not only do teachers draw on their own rich cultural histories, but also the nuances of their practice are being mediated by the institutional cultures in which they practice. The school cultures reify certain kinds of knowledge sorting, gathering, and predicting—to the neglect of others. The curricula are based on particular epistemological assumptions about what constitutes knowledge, how knowledge is accumulated, and what knowledge is used and for what purposes. Indigenous cultures and other localized cultures such those of the Ojibwe and Navajo nations, as well as cultures that have been deeply reliant on oral histories sort, gather, and predict in very different ways than the dominant pattern prevalent in many U.S. and Western nation schools. The very recent history of Indian Boarding schools is a reminder of the ways in which school may or may not account for and connect to the cultural histories and practices of students. Transactions between and among students and teachers not only shape the accumulation and expansion of transmitted knowledge and discovery, they form the web of cultural practices that determine what is valued, permitted, and suppressed (McDermott & Varenne, 1995). Assumptions made about students' backgrounds, home life, and access to resources and support undergird decisions about who may need special help, who can flourish with a bit of extra attention, and whose needs are too complex to address (Tyler, Yzquierdo, Lopez-Reyna, & Flippin, 2002). The biases that underlie triage decisions (e.g., distinguishing between who needs extra attention or more complex interventions) are often unexamined in the rush and bustle of daily life in classrooms and schools. Moreover, when teachers come up to breathe and reflect, they are buffeted by school processes and procedures that require them to sort and count in particular ways. This social process contributes to the overreferral of students who are culturally and linguistically diverse to special education assessment and decisions to place students in special education.

Cultural diversity in general, where teachers and other practitioners represent a diversity of perspectives, histories, experiences, and cultural histories, offers the possibility of creating institutional contexts that have more flexible boundaries about what counts as knowledge, performance, and discourses of learning. Intercultural ignorance and misunderstanding seeps into the education system via community de facto segregation through a variety of housing, employment, and transportation mechanisms. These institutionalized structures create internalized assumptions about who can learn that both mainstream and nondominant communities absorb. Although we explore diversifying the workforce, attending also to the distribution of teachers across types of schools, aligning students and teachers demographically will not offer a solution to the pernicious and internalized assumptions about who can learn. Rather, understanding structural, political, and economic histories that contribute to patterns of teacher and student distribution and cultural understanding will help readers to deepen their understanding and enrich policy discourse.

Explaining Inequities in Teacher Distribution: A Critique

How is the unequal distribution of teachers explained in the extant literature? Before we answer this question, it is useful to summarize some of the main patterns about unequal teacher distribution described thus far. Although it is generally argued that schools serving nondominant students have less-qualified teachers due to shortages, the research evidence suggests that it is largely produced by distributional inequities, "with surpluses in some areas and shortfalls in others" (Darling-Hammond & Sykes, 2003, p. 14; Lauritzen & Friedman, 1993). Indeed, it would be difficult to argue that the patterns of teacher distribution are serendipitous. As Murnane and Steele (2007) explained,

> the unequal distribution of effective teachers is perhaps the most urgent problem facing American education. Poor children and children of color are disproportionately assigned to teachers who have the least preparation and the weakest academic backgrounds, and this pattern is long-standing. *(p. 36)*

This phenomenon has worsened in the last 15 years (Darling-Hammond & Sykes, 2003). This pattern, in turn, is linked to the demographic discontinuity between teachers (mostly White) and students from nondominant backgrounds, and to the fact that many teacher education programs are only recently placing systematic emphasis on equipping teachers with the dispositions and skills to teach this population (Little & Bartlett, 2010). There continues to be a scarcity of teachers from nondominant cultures. Nevertheless, we must be cautious not to assume that matching the sociocultural backgrounds of teachers and students will resolve the complex conditions that shape the educational performance of students from nondominant backgrounds. Kalogrides et al. (2011) found that, like novice and unqualified teachers, teachers from nondominant cultures are assigned more low-achieving, behaviorally challenged students than their counterparts, especially when the school leadership and the faculty are majority White. This pattern is particularly disturbing because students experience diminished learning benefit *and* the school is more likely to lose the less effective teacher, which contributes to secondary costs of the loss of school history, reform momentum, and disruptions to the school culture. In addition, certified teachers in underresourced schools serving students predominantly from nondominant cultures have a high chance to be assigned to teach out-of-field, and these schools tend to have high teacher turnover rates (Cochran-Smith, 2004). It is not surprising, therefore, that these distribution patterns result in substantial opportunity gaps for nondominant students compared to students from affluent socioeconomic backgrounds; incidentally, this gap is one of the largest in the world (Akiba, LeTendre, & Scribner, 2007).

Little and Bartlett (2010) argued that the opportunity gap is typically explained with research that examines teacher individual factors (e.g., career choices and dispositions) and "state and local policies, practices, and workplace conditions" (p. 300). School location, for instance, plays a substantial role in teacher decisions about where they teach; they tend to favor a site close to where they were raised (Darling-Hammond & Sykes, 2003). Although the research evidence supports the role of personal variables, the research on organizational and policy influences has received less attention in the literature, though the available data are compelling.

Darling-Hammond, Holtzman, Gatlin, and Heilig (2005), for example, examined evidence from Houston that covered a 6-year period and concluded that, "as Houston hired and retained greater numbers of certified teachers, these teachers were disproportionally distributed to higher-income students and white students" (p. 14). Goldhaber, Choi, and Cramer (2007) also documented how distribution of National Board Certified Teachers advantaged the already advantaged learners, and such patterns were observed at the district, school, and classroom levels. Other complex structural factors compound maldistribution patterns. To illustrate, schools serving predominantly nondominant students tend to report large numbers of unfilled teaching positions, have larger class sizes due to funding disparities, have more limited access to higher-level courses, and are more likely to fill job openings with unqualified teachers (Darling-Hammond & Sykes, 2003). Salary differentials, working conditions and dissatisfaction (e.g., class size, facilities, year-round schedules), teacher preparation and support (e.g., strong, explicit, and systematic induction and continued support), and personnel management preferences and practices (e.g., salary caps for experienced teachers, credentialing state reciprocity, pension portability across states, information systems and burdensome paperwork for application and hiring processes) are additional examples of structural and institutional factors that contribute to inequitable distribution of teachers (Darling-Hammond & Sykes, 2003).

To conclude, teacher distribution is one of several factors associated with equity related to the teaching workforce. The research evidence suggests that attention to teacher quality is critical because teacher certification is associated with higher student achievement (Darling-Hammond & Sykes, 2003). However, the notion of *quality* must be examined carefully for there are problematic definitions and uses of this term. For instance, the typical view of *qualified* alludes to the academic backgrounds of teachers—that is, whether a teacher is certified by a credentialing agency—and other indices such as GPA, score on an academic standardized test, or the selectivity of higher education institutions attended. Theory and research about teacher quality that focuses on factors other than teacher individual traits or organizational forces are the exception (Little & Bartlett, 2010). There is an urgent need, therefore, to produce knowledge on maldistribution patterns that sheds light on processes that transcend the teacher as the unit of analysis, particularly at a time when reforms to address this problem privilege the examination of individual variables and rewards, at the expense of social, historical, and institutional contexts of teacher distribution patterns (Little & Bartlett, 2010). This work on quality would be framed

> to be both an individual and a collective characteristic, simultaneously a property (the acquired knowledge, skill, and experience of individuals and groups) and an ongoing accomplishment, manifest in what teachers do, individually and together, and in institutional—and organizational—level developments.
>
> *(p. 315)*

The work of Bryk, Sebring, Allensworth, Luppescu, and Easton (2010) is an example of such an approach. According to Bryk et al., five essential supports mediate school learning impact, namely leadership, instructional guidance, professional capacity, connections with families and communities, and learning-oriented school climate. The model acknowledges individual and organizational factors as well as contextual influences beyond the school (e.g., neighborhood factors). Thus, for example, professional capacity is mediated by the quality of the staff, professional development opportunities, work orientation, and professional community.

Shaping the Teacher Workforce From an Equity Perspective

Too much of our nation's educational history is drawn from narratives that expose the vastly different opportunities to learn that are afforded children from different ethnic, racial, ability, linguistic, and economic backgrounds (Little & Bartlett, 2010). What the analysis of the teacher workforce reminds us is that the path to becoming a teacher begins early in schools where students see teaching and the conditions of teaching valued and supported, or not. Understanding the contexts in which teachers come to practice, for what purpose, and for what outcomes, is a study not only of demographics but of the economic and political conditions that build creative, intellectual, and social capital in some communities while constraining the development of capital in others (Brayboy, Castagno, & Maughan, 2007). This is not to say that communities do not exercise their own agency in creating counternarratives that produce powerful cultural artifacts (e.g., beliefs systems) and practices. They do, in the face of great adversity. It is to say that public education should offer opportunities to create and advance knowledge in and about all communities and value the role of teaching in formal as well as informal settings. Yet, the reviewed data show persistent patterns that constrain educational opportunities in the most vulnerable communities while affording opportunity in others. Overwhelmingly, White teachers continue to stream into the profession while the numbers of teachers from other ethnic and racial groups barely grow in spite of the nation's rapidly shifting demographics.

An examination of the research describing who comes into teaching and stays, particularly in special education, is a reminder of the importance of accounting for structural pathways: (a) a robust P-12 education that provides models for what teaching can be in every community; (b) salaries and conditions for teaching that attract new recruits; (c) preparation programs that are supported through public investment; (d) practice settings that provide robust opportunities to learn, assess, and refine teaching practices *prior* to the first solo years of teaching; (e) mentoring programs that provide assistance to new teachers; and (f) school climates and leaders that embrace and develop their teachers for career-long membership. These six elements must be imbued with cultural responsivity that acknowledges the differences among settings, students, and teachers so that flexibility in approach and pedagogy is optimized while maintaining high performance thresholds for outcomes.

This is no small task since color consciousness requires that educational policy, scholarship, and practice no longer ignore what has been accepted as a neutral stance in terms of culture (Gutierrez, 2005). Culture permeates the policies that govern who is recruited and retained in teaching, how salaries are determined and awarded, and who should go to what kinds of schools. The analysis in this chapter begins to look at those conditions and raises questions about who benefits from the way that we currently recruit, support, and retain teachers. A dominant, White culture permeates the kinds of problem spaces that we research, we question, we fund, and we act upon. Who teaches and why has a historical trajectory based on cultural premises whose arc touches us today. Equity in and among the teaching force cannot be realized without a discourse that acknowledges the cultural biases that lie within the two most powerful pieces of federal educational legislation: NCLB and IDEA.

Notes

1 The first author acknowledges the support of the Urban Professional Learning Schools Initiative (H325T070009) awarded by the U.S. Department of Education's Office of Special Education Programs. The first and second authors acknowledge the support of the Equity Alliance at ASU under OESE's Grant # S004D080027. Funding agency endorsement of the ideas presented in this article should not be inferred. They do not necessarily support the views expressed in this paper. All errors are attributable to the authors.

2 TFA corps members typically work in high poverty schools. About 33% persist in teaching beyond their 2 year TFA commitment. Controversy surrounds TFA's high attrition level since most TFA graduates teach in urban schools that persistently experience high levels of teacher attrition.

References

Akiba, M., LeTendre, G., & Scribner, J. P. (2007). Teacher quality, opportunity gap, and national achievement in 46 countries. *Educational Researcher, 36*, 369–387. doi:10.3102/0013189X07308739

Artiles, A. J. (2011). Toward an interdisciplinary understanding of educational equity and difference: The case of the racialization of ability. *Educational Researcher, 40*, 431–445. doi:10.3102/0013189X11429391

Artiles, A. J., & Kozleski, E. B. (2007). Beyond convictions: Interrogating culture, history, and power in inclusive education. *Language Arts, 84*, 351–358.

Artiles, A. J., & Kozleski, E. B. (2010). What counts as response and intervention in RTI? A sociocultural analysis. *Psicothema, 22*, 949–954.

Artiles, A. J., Kozleski, E. B., Trent, S. Osher, D., & Ortiz, A. (2010). Justifying and explaining disproportionality, 1968–2008: A critique of underlying views of culture. *Exceptional Children, 76*, 279–299.

Aud, S., Hussar, W., Kena, G., Bianco, K., Frohlich, L., Kemp, J., & Tahan, K. (2011). *The Condition of Education 2011* (NCES 2011-033). U.S. Department of Education, National Center for Education Statistics. Washington, DC: U.S. Government Printing Office.

Ball, D. L., Thames, M. H., & Phelps, G. (2008). Content knowledge for teaching: What makes it special? *Journal of Teacher Education, 59*, 389–407. doi:10.1177?0022487108324554

Béteille, T., & Loeb, S. (2009). Teacher quality and teacher labor markets. In G. Sykes, B. Schneider, & D. Plank (Eds.), *Handbook of education policy research* (pp. 596–612). New York, NY: Routledge.

Billingsley, B. S. (2003). *Special education teacher retention and attrition: A critical analysis of the literature* (COPSSE Document No. RS-2). Gainesville, FL: University of Florida, Center on Personnel Studies in Special Education. Retrieved from http://copsse.education.ufl.edu/copsse/docs/RS-2/1/RS-2.pdf

Boe, E. E., Cook, L. H., & Sunderland, R. J. (2008). Teacher turnover: Examining exit attrition, teaching area transfer, and school migration. *Exceptional Children, 75*, 7–31.

Boe, E. E., Shin, S., & Cook, L. H. (2007). Does teacher preparation matter for beginning teachers in either special or general education? *The Journal of Special Education, 41*, 158–170. doi:10.1177/00224669070410030201

Boyd, D., Lankford, H., Loeb, S., & Wyckoff, J. (2005). The draw of home: How teachers' preferences for proximity disadvantage urban schools. *Journal of Policy Analysis and Management, 24*, 113–132. doi:10.1002/pam.20072

Brayboy, B. M. J., Castagno, A. E., & Maughan, E. (2007). Equality and justice for all? Examining race in education. *Review of Research in Education, 31*, 159–194. doi:10.3102/0091732X07300046159

Brownell, M. T., Sindelar, P. T., Kiely, M. T., & Danielson, L. C. (2010). Special education teacher quality and preparation: Exposing foundations, constructing a new model. *Exceptional Children, 76*, 357–377.

Bryk, A. S., Sebring, P. B., Allensworth, E., Luppescu, S., & Easton, J. (2010). *Organizing schools for improvement.* Chicago, IL: University of Chicago Press.

Clotfelter, C., Ladd, H., & Vigdor, J. (2007). *How and why do teacher credentials matter for student learning?* (NBER Working Paper No. 12828). Cambridge, MA: National Bureau of Economic Research.

Cochran-Smith, M. (2004). *Walking the road: Race, diversity, and social justice in teacher education.* New York, NY: Teachers College Press.

Cochran-Smith, M. (2005). The new teacher education: For better or for worse? *Educational Researcher, 34*, 3–17. doi:10.3102/0013189X034007003

Cochran-Smith, M., & Lytle, S. L. (2006). Troubling images of teaching in No Child Left Behind. *Harvard Educational Review, 76*, 668–697.

Corcoran, S., Schwab, R., & Evans, W. (2004). Women, the labor market, and the declining relative quality of teachers. *Journal of Policy Analysis and Management, 23*, 449–470. doi:10.1002/pam.20021

Darling-Hammond, L. (2010). Teacher education and the American future. *Journal of Teacher Education, 61*, 35–47. doi:10.1177/0022487109348024

Darling-Hammond, L., & Bransford, J. (2005). *Preparing teachers for a changing world: What teachers should learn and be able to do*. San Francisco, CA: John Wiley & Sons.

Darling-Hammond, L., Holtzman, D. J., Gatlin, S. J., & Heilig, J. V. (2005). Does teacher preparation matter? Evidence about teacher certification, teach for America, and teacher effectiveness. *Education Policy Analysis Archives, 13*(42), 1–48.

Darling-Hammond, L., & Sykes, G. (2003, September 17). Wanted: A national teacher supply policy for education: The right way to meet the "highly qualified teacher" challenge. *Education Policy Analysis Archives, 11*(33). Retrieved from http://epaa.asu.edu/epaa/v11n33/

Donovan, M. S., & Cross, C. T. (Eds.) (2002). *Minority students in special and gifted education*. Washington, DC: National Academies Press.

Drame, E. R., & Pugach, M. C. (2010). A HOUSSE built on quicksand? Exploring the teacher quality conundrum for secondary special education teachers. *Teacher Education and Special Education, 33*, 55–69. doi:10.1177/0888406409356402

Dyson, A., & Kozleski, E. B. (2008). Disproportionality in special education: A transatlantic phenomenon. In L. Florian & M. McLaughlin (Eds.). *Dilemmas and alternatives in the classification of children with disabilities: New perspectives* (pp. 170–190). Thousand Oaks, CA: Corwin Press.

Erickson, F. (2004). *Talk and social theory*. Malden, MA: Polity Press.

Feng, L., & Sass, T. R. (2012). *What makes special education teachers special? Teacher training and achievement of students with disabilities*. Working Paper 12-10. Atlanta: Georgia State University, Andrew Young School of Policy Studies. Retrieved from: http://papers.ssrn.com/sol3/papers.cfm?abstract_id=2020714

Galindo, R., & Vigil, J. (2006). Are anti-immigrant statements racist or nativist? What difference does it make? *Latino Studies, 4*, 419–447. doi:10.1057/palgrave.lst.8600224

Gelman, J. A., Pullen, P. L., & Kauffman, J. M. (2004). The meaning of highly qualified and a clear road map to accomplishment. *Exceptionality, 12*, 195–207. doi:10.1207/s15327035ex1204_2

Goldhaber, D. (2002, March). The mystery of good teaching. *Education Next, 20*(1). Retrieved from http://educationnext.org/the-mystery-of-good-teaching/

Goldhaber, D., Choi, H. J., & Cramer, L. (2007). A descriptive analysis of the distribution of NBPTS-certified teachers in North Carolina. *Economics of Education Review, 26*, 160–172. doi:10.1016/j.econedurev.2005.09.003

Gutierrez, K. (2005). White innocence: A framework and methodology for rethinking educational discourse and inquiry. *International Journal of Learning, 12*, 1447–9540.

Hanushek, E., Kain, J. F., & Rivkin, S. (2004). Why public schools lose teachers. *Journal of Human Resources, 39*, 236–354. doi:10.2307/3559017

Heck, R. H. (2007). Examining the relationship between teacher quality as an organizational property of schools and students' achievement and growth rates. *Educational Administration Quarterly, 43*, 399–432. doi:10.1177/0013161X07306452

Hill, H. C., Blunk, M. L., Charalmobos, C. Y., Lewis, J. M., Phelps, G. C., Sleep, L., & Ball, D. L. (2008). Mathematical knowledge for teaching and the mathematical quality of instruction: An exploratory study. *Cognition and Instruction, 26*, 1–81.

Individuals with Disabilities Education Act, Pub. L. No. 101-476 (1990).

Kalogrides, D., Loeb, S., & Béteille, T. (2011). *Power play? Teacher characteristics and class assignments*. A working paper. Washington, DC: The Urban Institute.

Kozleski, E., Mainzer, R., & Deshler, D. (2000). Bright futures for exceptional learners: An action agenda to achieve quality conditions for teaching and learning. *TEACHING Exceptional Children, 32*(6), 56–69.

Kozleski, E. B., & Huber, J. J. (2012). System-wide leadership for culturally responsive education. In J. Crockett, B. Billingsley, & M. L. Boscardin (Eds). *Handbook of leadership and administration for special education* (pp. 155–169). Abingdon, United Kingdom: Routledge. doi:10.1177/088840649301600304

Labaree, D. (2010). Teach for America and teacher ed: Heads they win, tails we lose. *Journal of Teacher Education, 61*, 48–55. doi: http://dx.doi.org/10.1177/0022487109347317

Lauritzen, P., & Friedman, S. J. (1993). Meeting the supply/demand requirements of the Individuals with Disabilities Education Act. *Teacher Education and Special Education, 16*, 221–229. doi: http://dx.doi.org/10.1177/088840649301600304

Little, J. W., & Bartlett, L. (2010). The teacher workforce and problems of educational equity. *Review of Research in Education, 34*, 285–328. doi:10.3102/0091732X09356099

Loeb, S., Darling-Hammond, L., & Luczak, J. (2005). How teaching conditions predict teacher turnover in California schools. *Peabody Journal of Education, 80*, 44–70. doi:10.1207/s15327930pje8003_4

Loeb, S., Kalogrides, D. and Béteille, T. (2011) *Effective Schools: Demonstrating Recruitment, Assignment, Development, and Retention of Effective Teachers*. NBER Working Paper No. 17177. Cambridge, MA: National Bureau of Economic Research.

Loeb, S., & Reininger, M. (2004). *Public policy and teacher labor markets: What we know and why it matters*. East Lansing. MI: Michigan State University, The Education Policy Center.

McDermott, R., & Varenne, H. (1995). Culture as disability. *Anthropology & Education*, *26*, 324–348. doi:10.1525/aeq.1995.26.3.05x0936z

Minow, M. (1990). *Making all the difference: Inclusion, exclusion, and American law*. Ithaca, NY: Cornell University Press.

Murnane, R. J., & Steele, J. L. (2007). What is the problem? The challenge of providing effective teachers for all children. *Future of Children*, *17*(1), 15–43. doi:10.1353/foc.2007.0010

No Child Left Behind Act of 2001, Pub. L. No. 107-110 (2002). Retrieved from http://www2.ed.gov/policy/elsec/leg/esea02/107-110.pdf

Phillips, K. J. (2010). What does "highly qualified" mean for student achievement? Evaluating the relationships between teacher quality indicators and at-risk students' mathematics and reading achievement gains in first grade. *The Elementary School Journal*, *110*, 464–493. doi: http://dx.doi.org/10.1086/651192

Reininger, M. (2012). Hometown disadvantage? It depends on where you're from: Teachers' location preferences and the implication for staffing schools. *Educational Evaluation and Policy Analysis*, *34*(2), 127–145. doi:10.3102/0162373711420864

Rockoff, J. (2003). The impact of individual teachers on student achievement: Evidence from panel data. *The American Economic Review*, *94*, 247–252. doi:10.1257/0002828041302244

Sanders, A. (2008). Left behind: Low-income students under the No Child Left Behind Act (NCLB). *Journal of Law & Education*, *37*, 589–596.

Sindelar, P. T., Brownell, M. T., & Billingsley, B. (2010). Special education teacher education research: Current status and future directions. *Teacher Education and Special Education*, *33*, 8–24. doi: http://dx.doi.org/10.1177/0888406409358593

Stough, L. M., & Palmer, D. J. (2003). Special thinking in special settings: A qualitative study of expert special educators. *The Journal of Special Education*, *36*, 206–222. doi:10.1177/002246690303600402

Strizek, G. A., Pittsonberger, J. L., Riordan, K. E., Lyter, D. M., & Orlofsky, G. F. (2006). *Characteristics of schools, districts, teacher, principals, and school libraries in the United States: 2003–2004 Schools and Staffing Survey* (NCES 2006313). Washington, DC: National Center for Education Statistics.

Tyler, N., Yzquierdo, Z., Lopez-Reyna, N., & Flippin, S. (2002). *Diversifying the special education workforce* (COPSSE Document No. RS-3). Gainesville, FL: University of Florida, Center on Personnel Studies in Special Education. Retrieved from: http://copsse.education.ufl.edu/copsse/docs/RS-3/1/RS-3.pdf

U.S. Department of Education (2011). *Teacher shortage areas: Nationwide listing 1990–91 thru 2011–12*. Washington, DC: U.S. Department of Education/Office of Postsecondary Education.

Wilson, S., Floden, R., & Ferrini-Mundy, J. (2001). *Teacher preparation research: Current knowledge, gaps, and recommendations*. Seattle, WA: University of Washington, Center for the Study of Teaching and Policy. Retrieved from: http://depts.washington.edu/ctpmail/publications/reports.shtml

Xu, Z., Hannaway, J., & Taylor, C. (2009). *Making a difference?: The effects of Teach for America in high school*. Washington, DC: Center for Analysis of Longitudinal Data in Education Research.

Zeichner, K. (2010). Competition, economic rationalization, increased surveillance, and attacks on diversity: Neoliberalism and the transformation of teacher education in the U.S. *Teaching and Teacher Education*, *26*, 1544–1552. doi:10.1016/j.tate.2010.06.004

Part III
Program Design and Delivery

8

Examining Indicators of Teacher Education Program Quality

Intersections Between General and Special Education

Linda P. Blanton
FLORIDA INTERNATIONAL UNIVERSITY

James McLeskey
UNIVERSITY OF FLORIDA

Kristina Hernandez Taylor
FLORIDA INTERNATIONAL UNIVERSITY

Things to Think About

- Accreditation and student outcomes in teacher preparation are dominating quality indicators of teacher preparation programs.
- Historically, various stages of teacher education research and accompanying policy mandates have influenced accreditation components.
- Expanding state databases, especially in the last decade, have provided the opportunity to establish the connection between teachers' preparation and the performance of the students they teach.
- Several other indicators of teacher education program quality attempt to broaden the ways in which programs can demonstrate quality and comply with federal mandates, including graduates' job placements, teachers' job retention, graduate and employer satisfaction surveys, and performance assessments.
- For special education, examining effective teaching practices is important given many evidence-based practices that have been developed are rarely used in classrooms and teachers' practices extend beyond teaching content well.

Policy makers have addressed teacher education program quality in federal and state legislation and have substantially shaped approaches currently used to determine the quality of teacher education programs. While educators and education researchers continue to stress the importance of using multiple indicators in determining a teacher education program's quality, policy makers often hold fast to singular notions that the gold standard for judging a teacher education program is the extent to which its graduates improve the performance of the students they teach in K–12 schools on standardized measures of academic content. In the current policy-driven context, what indicators are dominating views of quality in teacher education? How does research inform what we know about the quality indicators dominating teacher education? What other indicators need to be considered in both practice and research? Finally, how is teacher education in special education addressed within these discussions? This chapter addresses these questions.

What counts as indicating quality in teacher education is hotly debated in the current educational policy context, as policy makers emphasize holding teacher educators accountable for their graduates. These debates are fueled in part by different understandings and stances about what quality teaching means, and how teacher quality relates to students' academic achievement. The reasons behind choosing specific indicators of quality in teacher education are often driven by the varying perspectives that different groups bring to the meaning of teacher quality and how these understandings are translated into the components and structures of teacher education. These differences result in perspectives that are more strongly influenced by a teacher's knowledge, a teacher's performance, or the outputs the teacher can achieve with students, or some combination of these factors (Wang, Lin, Spalding, Klecka, & Odell, 2011). Efforts over many years to study and reform teaching in schools underpin the current policy drive to reshape teacher education.

Accreditation is one indicator that has stood the test of time and continues to be viewed by many as denoting a quality teacher education program (Wilson & Youngs, 2005). Accreditation (i.e., a state or national body's process of approving teacher education programs) grew from the earliest calls for reform in teacher education, especially on the heels of massive teacher shortages following World War II (Wilson & Youngs, 2005). The various components (e.g., content knowledge, field experiences) that make up state or national accreditation processes have changed over time as a result of the influence of a growing body of research on teaching and teacher preparation, as well as the expanding role of the federal government in determining the credentials of teachers who enter the nation's classrooms (Imig & Imig, 2008; Wilson & Youngs, 2005). All states implement some type of process for teacher education program approval, some have a partnership with a national accreditation group (e.g., National Council for the Accreditation of Teacher Education [NCATE]), but not all states require programs in the state to acquire national accreditation. Although both state and national accreditation have focused historically on university-based teacher education programs, most have expanded their processes to cover any program (e.g., private providers) preparing teachers for the schools.

A second quality indicator dominating the current landscape—*student outcomes linked to teacher preparation*—has resulted from strong federal involvement in teacher education in the last decade. The federal role in teacher education has grown steadily, but particularly since the early 1990s as a result of amendments to the Elementary and Secondary Education Act (ESEA) in 1994 and 2001 (when the act was renamed the No Child Left Behind [NCLB] Act) and in 1992 and 1998 by amendments to the Higher Education Act (HEA) (Imig & Imig, 2008; Wilson & Youngs, 2005). ESEA placed a priority on teachers holding a bachelor's degree, being certified, and knowing the content they would be teaching. In a related vein, these amendments changed accountability requirements for teachers by mandating that states use student outcome data to evaluate teacher performance. Also contributing substantially to changes in teacher education, the accountability demands of the HEA amendments placed teacher education control in the hands of university presidents, increased accountability expectations, and encouraged alternative pathways to traditional (university-based, full-time programs) teacher education. More recently, the requirements of the American Recovery and Reinvestment Act of 2009 made it even clearer that the evaluation of teacher education will be anchored in assessments showing the extent to which program graduates improve the achievement of the students they teach (Smith, Robb, West, & Tyler, 2010).

One area, teacher certification, that some may argue is an indicator of teacher education program quality was not considered in this review for several reasons. First, it can be argued that state teacher certification does not represent the quality of a teacher preparation *program*, but only of individuals who have met a state's requirements to enter the profession via one of many approaches (e.g., university-based teacher education program, district-based program, passing a test) used to gain entry. Adding to this point, in some states, because of the diversity of routes to certification, the numbers of alternatively certified teachers is very high (e.g., Sass, 2011), resulting in substantially different levels and types of preparation for teachers who are considered "certified." Second, criticisms are common about the criteria (e.g., course counting, knowledge tests) used in states for teacher certification, with some noting that these criteria usually fail to discriminate among those who are good performers in classrooms, and those who are not (Pianta, 2012). In addition, certification criteria vary from one state to the next (Heck, 2007), with some states connecting these criteria directly to the recommendations of the teacher preparers themselves, some accepting expedited routes, while others do not, among many other differences. Given these issues with the definition of "certification" within and across states, we determined that research on this topic did not merit inclusion in this chapter addressing indicators of teacher education program quality.

Even with previously described issues surrounding state teacher certification, it should be noted that a good deal of research has been conducted on teacher certification, to examine first whether holding certification has value by comparing certified, undercertified, and not certified teachers (e.g., Wilson & Youngs, 2005). Findings of these investigations have been mixed, but greater emphasis on this line of inquiry has emerged in recent years with the availability of school district and state databases (e.g., Neild, Farley-Ripple, & Byrnes, 2009; Noell, Porter, Patt, & Dahir, 2008). Two other areas of research on teacher certification have examined, for one, whether teachers who gain certification through different pathways produce better student outcomes by comparing traditional and alternative routes (e.g., Constantine et al., 2009; Seftor & Mayer, 2003) and, for another, the extent to which advanced certification improves student achievement (e.g., Goldhaber & Anthony, 2007).

It is within today's policy-driven environment that we contextualize this review, first to illustrate some of the ways one indicator, *accreditation*, has changed over time and, second, to review current research on another indicator, *student outcomes linked to teacher preparation*, to show how this criterion has begun to dominate what counts as quality in teacher education. Next, we consider other indicators of teacher education program quality that have and are being discussed currently by federal agencies, states, professional organizations, and teacher education programs in attempts to broaden the ways in which programs can demonstrate quality and comply with federal mandates. These include (a) graduates' job placement, (b) graduates' job retention, (c) satisfaction surveys of employers and graduates themselves, and (d) performance assessments either before or after students complete a teacher education program. An overview of research in these areas is provided to show the landscape of this complex and often contentious area of quality indicators in teacher education. Within each of these sections, we address how special education has or has not been considered.

Methods Used to Review Research

Studies on teacher education program quality indicators selected for review ranged from the time period of 1998 to the present and focused only on programs in the United States. The year 1998 was chosen as the starting year for this review because the reauthorization of the HEA marked a turning point in the federal government's stronger entry into teacher education, a shift that some have referred to as "the federalization of teacher education policy" (Imig & Imig, 2008, p. 897).

Complicating the issue of quality indicators in teacher education programs is the subjectivity of what defines a teacher education program. Emphasis is sometimes placed on the location of the program (e.g., university-based, school district-based, company-based), the pathway used to offer the program (e.g., face-to-face, online, long or shorter routes), or whether a program is needed at all (e.g., a prospective teacher with a degree in a content area can simply take a test). Because it is beyond the scope of this chapter to review these issues separately, Cochran-Smith and Fries' (2005) definition of research on teacher education—"refers to studies of aspects of the preparation of K–12 teachers where the learners in question are teacher candidates" (p. 71)—was used to guide the review, and thus included any study that fits this definition, regardless of location or pathway.

Databases and journals in both general and special education were searched. Extensive research was conducted using the ERIC database, while Google Scholar was used to find resources beyond those acquired through ERIC. The terms *teacher education program, special education teacher education program, quality teacher education program indicators, teacher testing, accreditation, student outcomes, special education, value added assessment of teacher education program, VAA-TPP, PRAXIS, teacher certification, performance assessment, teacher preparation, alternative teacher certification*, and *teacher education programs of study* were some of those used in conducting the search.

General education and special education journals were searched both electronically and by hand. Journals searched included: *American Educational Research Journal, American Journal of Education, Economics of Education Review, Education Finance and Policy, Policy Analysis Archives, Educational Researcher, The Elementary School Journal, International Journal of Educational Management, Journal of Human Resources, Journal of Research in Rural Education, The Journal of Special Education, Journal of Teacher Education, Leadership and Policy in Schools, Peabody Journal of Education, Review of Educational Research, Review of Research in Education, Teacher Education and Special Education, Teacher Education Quarterly, The Teacher Educator, Teachers College Record, Teachers and Teaching, Teaching and Teacher Education, Theory into Practice*, and *Urban Education.*

Accreditation: The Changing Landscape of Research

Very few studies have examined teacher education accreditation per se. In their review of this research, Wilson and Youngs (2005) reported no empirical studies. Our search uncovered only two studies addressing accreditation of teacher education. One study conducted by the Educational Testing Service (Gitomer, Latham, & Ziomek, 1999) found that graduates of NCATE accredited colleges of education passed the PRAXIS II test at a greater rate than graduates of unaccredited colleges. In a second study, Darling-Hammond (2000) reported that states with more nationally accredited teacher education programs have more teachers who are fully certified and possess majors in the field in which they teach. The data were gathered from the 1993–1994 Schools and Staffing Surveys (SASS), data provided by the National Assessment of Educational Progress (NAEP), analyses of case studies, and a survey of professionals in all 50 states regarding educational policies. Clearly, this line of research is sparse and has generated little interest on the part of researchers in teacher education.

What has drawn the attention of both researchers and policy makers alike are findings from teaching and teacher education research that have influenced changes in the components (i.e., standards and accompanying indicators) that make up accreditation processes (e.g., NCATE), with many indicators becoming largely outcome focused. Historically, findings from research on teaching and teacher education have influenced specific standards (e.g., candidate learning outcomes; diversity) of state and national accreditation and illustrate the growing role of policy makers in the practice and evaluation of teacher education. Cochran-Smith and Fries (2005, 2008) identify three stages of research on teacher education and although these stages are not sharply divided, overarching themes that influence components of accreditation stand out in each stage. For example, in the earliest stage of research on teacher education (from the 1950s and continuing well into the 1980s) the investigation of specific teacher behaviors (e.g., provide clear explanations and ample classroom time, use a brisk pace) were found to produce positive student outcomes. Known commonly as *process–product* studies, this line of inquiry led to the identification of a number of specific teacher behaviors that were judged to comprise the knowledge and skills needed by teachers to achieve better student performance. Subsequently, these teacher behaviors were translated into state policies and in turn into essential components of teacher education programs (McDiarmid & Clevenger-Bright, 2008).

As research on teacher education shifted in what Cochran-Smith and Fries (2005, 2008) have called a second stage of inquiry beginning in the 1980s, a dominating focus was on examining teachers' learning, thinking, and beliefs. The research of this stage on teachers' belief systems also opened doors to rich discussions about the diversity of learners in schools and influenced many teacher education programs to redirect their curricula toward issues of social justice (McDiarmid & Clevenger-Bright, 2008). During this same time researchers explored the importance of subject matter and pedagogical knowledge, as well as the intersection of these topics, *pedagogical content knowledge*, and sought to codify the knowledge base needed by teachers.

The 1980s was a time when numerous national reports (e.g., *A Nation at Risk* in 1983; *A National Prepared: Teachers for the 21st Century* in 1986) placed greater emphasis on the importance of setting standards for teacher preparation (McDiarmid & Clevenger-Bright, 2008). With this focus on "professionalizing" teacher education, national groups were formed that developed standards for what beginning teachers need to know and be able to do upon entering the profession (i.e., Interstate New Teacher Support and Assessment Consortium—INTASC), and for the performance of experienced teachers who are highly accomplished (i.e., National Board for Professional Teaching Standards—NBPTS). Subsequently, the beginning teacher standards developed by INTASC were used as guides by many states in the program approval process, as well as by NCATE in the national accreditation process (Gollnick, 2008).

The growing emphasis on standards and accountability ushered in a new stage in the history of teacher education research in the 1990s (Cochran-Smith & Fries, 2005, 2008), a stage that influenced accreditation (e.g., NCATE) to shift from a focus on input standards (e.g., number of faculty) to emphasizing output standards (e.g., impact teacher candidates have on their students' learning) (Gollnick, 2008). This stage, which has continued to the present, has been driven strongly by research that calls on the use of large-scale databases, most of which are at the state level. For example, as databases have grown in states such as North Carolina, Florida, and Louisiana, researchers have used these databases to explore a myriad of topics, many with value-added models (i.e., measures that estimate, in the case of teacher education, the effect of graduates of a teacher preparation program on student achievement). This research has not only influenced accreditation, and to some extent state certification, but has also supported what many would say is the current dominant quality indicator promoted by federal policy—*student outcomes linked to teacher preparation*—which will be discussed in the following section of this chapter.

This abbreviated historical review illustrates how teaching and teacher education research and accompanying policy mandates have influenced accreditation components. Although it is beyond the scope of this chapter to provide a critical analysis of the sizeable body of research on teacher education that has contributed to changes in accreditation, the reader is referred to compilations of this research as analyzed in multiple editions of handbooks, as well as in commissioned and professional organization reports. Most recently, these reviews have included the third edition of the *Handbook of Research on Teacher Education: Enduring Questions and Changing Contexts* (Cochran-Smith, Feiman-Nemser, McIntyre, & Demers, 2008) and the American Educational Research Association's compilation, *Studying Teacher Education: The Report of the AERA Panel on Research and Teacher Education* (Cochran-Smith & Zeichner, 2005). Prior to these publications, a review of teacher preparation was commissioned by the U.S. Department of Education (USDE) and published in the *Journal of Teacher Education* (Wilson, Floden, & Ferrini-Mundy, 2002), and another review was published by the Education Commission of the States, *Eight Questions on Teacher Preparation: What Does the Research Say?* (Allen, 2003).

Although research on teacher education has not been a major priority in special education (Sindelar, Brownell, & Billingsley, 2010), studies have typically followed the same stages as teacher education research generally (Blanton, Sindelar, & Correa, 2006). The funding in 2000 of a national center by the

USDE to study teacher education (the Center on Personnel Studies in Special Education [COPSSE]) marked a milestone in acknowledging the area as critically needed in special education. This center and its successor, the National Center to Inform Policy and Practice in Special Education (NCIPP), have provided reviews of the literature on a range of teacher preparation topics.

Two recent reviews (Billingsley, 2011; Sindelar et al., 2010) provide perspective on the areas of teacher education that have been addressed in special education. Billingsley concludes her summary of research on teacher education in special education by stating that teacher education programs vary widely, and that this heterogeneity has made it difficult to identify the "elements of effective teacher preparation" (p. 400). She further states that "research on teacher preparation, broadly defined, is scattered and thin and lacks a strong conceptual base" (p. 400). A key factor that has influenced the heterogeneity of special education programs and the dearth of research on teacher education in special education is the rapidly evolving conceptual frameworks that have undergirded these programs (Brownell, Sindelar, Kiely, & Danielson, 2010). The variability of special education teacher preparation programs has long made it difficult to study these programs systematically.

Student Outcomes Linked to Teacher Preparation: The Surge in Research

Expanding state databases, especially in the last decade, have provided the opportunity to establish the connection between a teachers' preparation and the performance of the students they teach. According to the Data Quality Campaign (2011), 41 states have the capacity to match P–12 data with higher education data; however, Crowe (2011) reports that only three states (Florida, Louisiana, Texas) are currently using value-added models of student achievement as part of the evaluation of teacher education programs. Although a few states are leading the way in holding teacher education accountable with value-added measures, the use of longitudinal databases for this purpose is still emerging in most states (Crowe, 2011). It is clear, however, that the stakes for teacher education have grown significantly in recent years as federal legislation (e.g., Race to the Top requirements) now *requires* states to evaluate teacher preparation programs at least in part based on the achievement of the students their graduates teach (Crowe, 2011; Smith et al., 2010).

Louisiana has produced reports since 2003–2004 showing the K–12 student achievement score results linked to the graduates of the state's teacher preparation programs (e.g., Gansle, Burns, & Noell, 2012; Gansle, Noell, Knox, & Schafer, 2010; Noell & Gleason, 2011). More recently, additional states (e.g., Tennessee) have begun issuing report cards to show K–12 student gains on standardized tests connected to the graduates of all teacher education programs in the state, including teachers certified through traditional and alternative programs (Tennessee Higher Education Commission, 2010). Similarly, one study (Henry et al., 2010) using North Carolina's database reported the P–12 student scores of the graduates of the state's public and private teacher preparation programs, alternative pathways such as Teach for America, as well as with students who enter the state from programs in other states.

Many studies (e.g., Decker, Mayer, & Glazerman, 2004; Kane, Rockoff, & Staiger, 2008; Sass, 2011; Xu, Hannaway, & Taylor, 2011) in recent years have used state and large school district databases to explore the value-added by different types of teacher preparation programs, focusing on the impact of pathways on student achievement. While certainly of high interest to policy makers, a focus primarily on pathways fails to contribute substantially to understanding teacher education program quality because many studies have not examined the components (e.g., coursework, field experiences) of programs that might contribute to graduates' impact on student achievement. Some studies, however, have examined the type and number of courses, and/or the extent of field experiences that teachers had in preparation programs to understand potential links between graduates' experiences and the achievement of the students they teach. These build on earlier studies such as one by Wenglinsky (2002) that used NAEP data to examine the teacher preparation, teacher practices, and student achievement connection. Findings showed that students who performed well on NAEP math assessments were taught by teachers with a major or minor in math, who had preparation in developing higher order thinking skills, and who also had preparation in working with diverse students, including those with disabilities. Current studies using state and school district databases reveal similar trends for teachers' content preparation, and to some extent pedagogy, although the nature of the pedagogical preparation is not always clear.

In one study, Boyd, Grossman, Lankford, Loeb, and Wyckoff (2009) examined traditional and alternative pathway programs and used predominately qualitative methodology (e.g., document analysis, interviews, surveys) to compare the specific program features (e.g., characteristics of field experiences) that teachers experienced to the achievement of their students, both within and between pathways. Boyd et al. (2009) found that teachers in 31 New York City elementary schools whose preparation had been anchored in classroom practice (e.g., many opportunities to practice with the instructional programs they would implement in schools; multiple opportunities to work with students on subject matter) produced greater student achievement in their first year of teaching. Findings also showed positive relationships, particularly in the area of math, between student achievement and teachers' content-focused coursework in the subject area, as well as in pedagogy related to the subject area. Similarly, in their examination of data from Florida's data warehouse, Harris and Sass (2011) found comparable results when teachers' preparation was focused strongly on content, especially in math at the secondary level.

Constantine et al. (2009) also explored the association of teachers' practices and the specific coursework taken by teachers to the achievement of their students. Controlling for program type (alternative and traditional), programs were randomly drawn and stratified based on geography and type of program. Students were randomly assigned to alternatively certified novice teachers and traditionally certified novice teachers in schools where these groups of novice teachers could be matched at the same grade level. Teacher subgroups were also formed based on the amount of coursework (credit hours of content and pedagogy) that had been required in novice teachers' alternative teacher preparation programs. Each teacher pair constituted a mini-experiment to minimize student, classroom, or school characteristics. Overall, the two-year study represented seven states, 2,600 students, 62 schools, and 20 school districts. Findings relating to teachers' preparation programs showed no evidence of relationships either between amount of teacher preparation coursework and teachers' effectiveness or between the content of teacher preparation courses and teacher effectiveness.

Findings by Constantine et al. (2009) demonstrate that merely counting credit hours and content taken, and determining when the content is taken by groups of teachers in teacher education programs, will likely yield little information about what these teachers do to be effective with students. In contrast, in studies such as one by Neuman and Cunningham (2009), the experimental group that received a course on literacy with accompanying coaching (included reflection and practice opportunities) during professional development significantly outperformed (e.g., higher quality practices such as adult and child interactions) other groups, including an experimental group taking the same course without coaching. Such studies offer insight into the specific practices that need to be targeted in content areas in teacher preparation rather than the number of course credits and their general content.

Sass (2011) examined the courses of teacher candidates in both traditional and alternatively certified programs in Florida and found that about half the courses in traditional programs were in education while the alternative pathway programs had one or fewer courses in education. The biggest difference in content courses taken across pathways was in science but, for the most part, courses in content areas were similar. Although the contribution to student achievement differed somewhat across traditional and alternative pathway groups, results were generally insignificant and provided limited conclusions about the value of particular courses. One finding discussed was the difference in the background characteristics of teachers entering the profession through different pathways For example, although some groups of alternatively certified teachers passed certification exams on the first try more than did traditionally certified teachers, value-added findings were generally not significant across pathways.

A study by Kukla-Acevedo (2009) used 3 years of fifth grade students' math score data from a Kentucky school district, and information gathered from the state on teachers' coursework and academic performance, to explore teachers' preparation experiences and student achievement. The investigation controlled for specific teacher, student, and school characteristics and found that teachers' overall math grade point average, both in content and pedagogy math courses, was related to students' math achievement. Kane et al. (2008) also found a relationship between teacher candidates' grade point average and the achievement of students they later taught. However, the issue in both studies is that a gross measure like grade point average provides no information about specific courses or experiences that might have contributed to quality in teacher preparation.

Recent studies exploring the value-added by teachers with advanced degrees have produced mixed findings, although most show little impact of a graduate degree on student achievement (e.g., Aaronson, Barrow, & Sander, 2007; Clotfelter, Ladd, & Vigdor, 2007a, 2007b; Harris & Sass, 2011; Huang & Moon, 2008; Nye, Konstantopoulos, & Hodges, 2004). In one study by Nye et al., these researchers reported results related to randomization effects and teacher effects of a 4-year study, Project STAR, using data from 79 elementary schools (grades K–3) throughout Tennessee. In the analysis of the effects of teachers' education level (master's or higher) on student achievement, significant differences favoring education level were found only for third grade mathematics. When studies have examined the teacher's major or the types of courses taken in a graduate program, the findings of some studies have revealed positive relationships with student achievement, especially in mathematics (e.g., Harris & Sass, 2011; Rowan, Correnti, & Miller, 2002). For example, Harris and Sass reported a relationship between teachers with advanced degrees and achievement in mathematics for students at the middle school level.

In special education, Feng and Sass (2010) used Florida's data warehouse to examine the value-added by special education teachers to the achievement of students with disabilities. These researchers first considered the value-added by special education certification, and then reconsidered the data with other measures of preservice education (e.g., amount of coursework, having a bachelor's degree in special education). Findings suggested that the achievement of students who have disabilities in reading, and to some extent math, are positively influenced by teachers who are prepared in special education, regardless of whether the measure used was certification, coursework in special education, or holding a bachelor's degree in special education. Feng and Sass concluded that teachers who completed traditional preservice special education teacher education programs produced significantly higher student outcomes in reading. These outcomes were characterized as quantitatively substantial. Teachers also produced significantly better student outcomes in mathematics, although these differences were smaller than in reading. In addition, certification in special education, an undergraduate major in special education, and the amount of special education coursework in college were all found to have strong positive correlations with the performance of teachers in improving the reading achievement of students with disabilities.

Although the Feng and Sass (2010) study is a landmark in the examination of a large-scale state database for special education, there are reasons to be concerned about the application of this approach for evaluating the quality of special education teacher education programs. Research has shown that value-added scores are found to correlate with student characteristics, even when these characteristics are accounted for in multilevel analyses (Hill, Kapitula, & Umland, 2011). For example, in a study of math in four schools, Hill et al. found higher value-added scores for teachers who taught higher achieving students and, conversely, lower value-added scores for teachers who taught English Language Learners, students on free and reduced lunch, and students who were labeled for special education. These findings add to concerns that under current high stakes accountability systems, teachers can be rewarded or penalized unfairly (Chetty, Friedman, & Rockoff, 2011) based on the characteristics of the students they teach.

The pressure on teacher education programs to consider the implications of outcomes-focused research is likely to grow stronger as more studies using large-scale databases are reported to policy makers, especially research on teachers who are successful at improving long-term student outcomes. For example, one such study on the long-term impact of high value-added teachers (Chetty et al., 2011) examined school data from a large urban school district and tax records over a 20-year time period to analyze the impact of high value teachers. Findings revealed large impacts in such areas as earnings and college attendance. The results also showed that while some of the improved outcomes faded over time, in some areas the gains stabilized and persisted.

Studies that link P–12 student performance, teachers, and teacher education are on the rise, but suffer from a number of shortcomings needing more extensive examination among teacher education researchers and policy makers, particularly when they are applied to special education teachers. For example, implementing valid and reliable systems to measure teacher effectiveness is a major task facing school districts and states (Data Quality Campaign, 2010; Harris, 2012; National Research Council, 2010). In addition, developing clear causal links (e.g., specific teacher characteristics linked to student achievement) in value-added research is difficult given the many variables contributing to teachers' knowledge and practices by the time they enter classrooms (National Research Council, 2010). The methodologies employed in value-added research have been criticized (Barnett & Amrein-Beardsley, 2011), although recent studies have begun using more sophisticated methods based on student-level scores and larger, more sophisticated databases on teachers' preparation programs (Harris & Sass, 2011). Moreover, recent studies have used randomization or other means to control selection effects (e.g., parents' selection of school districts), although researchers have enumerated concerns about how the results of some studies have been interpreted (Harris, 2012).

It is noteworthy that applying a value-added approach to studying special education teacher education comes with more substantive criticisms. Value-added models generally rely on relatively narrow outcomes and assessments that may not adequately measure growth among students with disabilities. Additionally, there are several statistical challenges associated with applying value-added modeling analyses to special education teachers. These issues are discussed in greater depth in Chapter 26 of this *Handbook*, and they raise serious concerns about the validity of this approach for assessing the impact of special education teacher education.

Other Quality Indicators of Teacher Education: Promising Options

Although reviewing the landscape of research on accreditation and student outcomes linked to teacher education certainly provides insight into the current policy context related to indicators of quality in teacher education programs, these are only two of the indicators that are being considered by teacher educators, researchers, and policy makers. The fact is that what one person, or a group, considers an indicator of quality in teacher preparation, another may not value to the same degree. As already noted, views on teacher quality influence whether indicators may be largely knowledge-based, performance-based, or outcomes-based. Accreditation attempts to include all three, although accreditation does not seem to be of high interest to policy makers. Value-added research generally focuses on one indicator—outcomes—and has gained much attention on the part of policy makers.

Several areas—graduates' job placements, teachers' job retention, and graduate and employer satisfaction surveys—have been proposed at state and national levels as measures demonstrating quality of teacher preparation (Nelson, 2012; Pianta, 2012). These proposed indicators have been the subject of some research on, for example, graduates' satisfaction regarding their preparedness to teach (e.g., Darling-Hammond, 2006; Darling-Hammond, Eiler, & Marcus, 2002) and differences in job retention of teachers prepared through alternative pathways (e.g., Kane et al., 2008; Rosenberg & Sindelar, 2005). From a practical perspective, such indicators may provide useful information to programs because measures such as these are relatively inexpensive to obtain (e.g., student or employer satisfaction surveys), can provide information from large numbers of program completers, and may have great appeal to those concerned with obtaining information quickly and efficiently on a variety of quality indicators.

Unfortunately, while such measures, similar to value-added measures, may carry some weight in today's policy context, they are distal measures of a teacher education program's quality and reveal limited useful information about teachers' practices that improve student learning and behavior. Instead, calling on multiple measures, including those measures examining classroom-based tasks (e.g., observations of teachers' classroom performance) offer an opportunity to more fully understand the practices that teachers use when teaching specific content, and in specific contexts, with targeted groups of students. Using multiple measures is especially important because of the validity and reliability issues that exist for most all measures of teacher effectiveness (Harris, 2012).

With the stakes higher for identifying quality indicators for teacher preparation, performance assessments (i.e., classroom-based tasks, both written and observed) are receiving greater attention by states, professional organizations, and teacher education programs. Performance assessments can be used for both formative and summative purposes in teacher education programs, as well as for certification and accreditation decisions (Pecheone & Chung, 2006). The current interest in performance assessment is driven by the fact that these measures evaluate teachers' actual teaching practices and have the potential to provide a deeper understanding of what contributes to student learning. The use of performance and portfolio assessments as measures of teachers' practices in classrooms has been the subject of research since the 1980s and evidence has accumulated to demonstrate their use in differentiating among teachers' performance (Pecheone, Pigg, Chung, & Souviney, 2005). Much of the research, however, has focused on general education teachers (Brownell, Billingsley, McLeskey, & Sindelar, 2012), with only a few studies using performance assessments specifically with special education teachers (Nougaret, Scruggs, & Mastropieri, 2005; Sindelar, Daunic, & Rennells, 2004). This is an important point given that little is known about the use of such assessments for special education teachers.

Several states (e.g., California and Connecticut) have used performance assessments for certification and/or for induction programs, although research on these specific uses is sparse (Pecheone et al., 2005). Although performance assessments require substantial time, effort, and considerable costs, the Performance Assessment of California Teachers (PACT) is an example of how a large-scale system of performance assessments, with both formative and summative purposes, can be implemented (Pecheone & Chung, 2006). Research being conducted on the implementation of PACT is limited, but some investigations have examined how the system informs the teacher education programs in California about needed changes in, for example, curriculum (e.g., Pecheone & Chung, 2006), and one study was identified that analyzed the impact of implementing PACT on a single teacher education program (Peck, Gallucci, & Sloan, 2010). The PACT in California has been the impetus for the launch of a national effort by the American Association of Colleges for Teacher Education (AACTE) and Stanford University—the Teacher Performance Assessment (edTPA)—to provide states and teacher education programs a system similar to PACT with embedded signature assessments and portfolios including teaching events (http://edtpa.aacte.org/faq#17). Developed and piloted, the edTPA involves over 20 states and offers an assessment that is nationally accessible.

Applying performance assessment systems such as PACT and edTPA to special education teachers needs cautious consideration. In particular, working from an assumption that general and special education teachers do similar instructional work can be faulty. Research has not definitively supported such an assumption. In addition, research using performance assessment systems with special education teachers as participants is sparse (Brownell et al., 2012).

Examining effective teaching practices has been the subject of much interest among teacher educators and education researchers. This interest has grown in teacher education policy as evidenced by the recent report of NCATE's Blue Ribbon Panel (National Council for Accreditation of Teacher Education, 2010) calling on teacher education to anchor programs more squarely in teaching practice. The role of practice has guided the work of Ball and her colleagues (e.g., Ball & Forzani, 2009) who have produced a line of research analyzing the content that teachers need to teach and suggests that teacher education should carefully examine elements of instruction related to content, and then engage their candidates in highly skilled preparation related to these "high leverage strategies." This trend is important for special education, given the consensus among researchers that many of the evidence-based practices that have been developed are rarely used in classrooms (Cook & Schirmer, 2003). In addition, teachers' practices extend well beyond teaching content and teaching it well, and also encompasses teacher dispositions contributing to learning for students representing diverse cultural and racial backgrounds in which special education students are nested. While only touched on in research (e.g., Wenglinsky, 2002), this critical component is not as likely to be overlooked if the examination of teachers' classroom practices are central to measures of a teacher education program's quality.

Conclusion

Research examining indicators of teacher education program quality is likely to grow and continue emphasizing the extent to which a teacher education program's graduates can make a difference in the achievement of the students they teach. At present, however, although research is making the connection from student achievement to the teacher and then to the teacher's preparation program, distal measures (e.g., value-added paradigms) are dominating what counts as a quality indicator of a teacher education program. While useful for determining a program's effectiveness, this research is limited in the examination of the actual practices that teachers use that, in turn, contribute to outcomes for students. Understanding such practices is critical in both general and special education and has potential for supporting quality in teacher education that goes beyond students' achievement in basic content areas, but also in all the areas (e.g., behavior) of a child's growth and development that support them as contributing adults in society.

To fully capture these practices, multiple lines of research on teacher education need to be considered and valued so that the contributions of both large- and smaller-scale studies support a variety of indicators used to determine quality in teacher education. For example, exploring the link between teacher preparation and teachers' classroom practices (e.g., Borko, Whitcomb, & Byrnes, 2008; Good et al., 2006; Konold et al., 2008) and the link between teachers' classroom practices and student achievement (e.g., Desimone & Long, 2010; Goe, 2007; McDiarmid & Clevenger-Bright, 2008; Stronge, Ward, & Grant, 2011) has contributed to better understanding the importance of both the content and pedagogical content knowledge needed in teacher education programs. In short, the field needs both well-designed smaller-scale studies that have the capacity to examine closely the content and practice of teaching and the link to student achievement, as well as studies drawing on large-scale databases to show what components of a teacher's preparation contribute to student learning and behavior. It is only through the design of high quality research addressing this broad range of variables that we will achieve a thorough understanding of how to better prepare teachers who use effective practices in classrooms that improve outcomes for all of their students, including those who have disabilities.

References

Aaronson, D., Barrow, L., & Sander, W. (2007). Teachers and student achievement in the Chicago public high schools. *Journal of Labor Economics, 25*, 95–135. doi:10.1086/508733

Allen, M. B. (2003). *Eight questions on teacher preparation: What does the research say?* Denver, CO: Education Commission of the States.

Ball, D. L., & Forzani, F. M. (2009). The work of teaching and the challenge for teacher education. *Journal of Teacher Education, 60*, 497–511. doi:10.1177/0022487109348479

Barnett, J., & Amrein-Beardsley, A. (2011, January 13). Evaluating teacher education programs in the accountability era. *Teachers College Record*, http://www.tcrecord.org/content.asp?contentid=16290

Billingsley, B. (2011). Factors influencing special education teacher quality and effectiveness. In J. M. Kauffman & D. P. Hallahan (Eds.). *Handbook of special education* (pp. 391–405). Abingdon, United Kingdom: Routledge.

Blanton, L. P., Sindelar, P. T., & Correa, V. I. (2006). Models and measures of beginning teacher quality. *The Journal of Special Education, 40*, 115–127. doi:10.1177/00224669060400020201

Borko, H., Whitcomb, J. A., & Byrnes, K. (2008). Genres of research in teacher education. In M. Cochran-Smith, S. Feiman-Nemser, D. J. McIntyre, & K. E. Demers (Eds.), *Handbook of research on teacher education: Enduring questions in changing contexts* (3rd ed., pp. 1017–1049). New York, NY: Routledge.
Boyd, D. J., Grossman, P. L., Lankford, H., Loeb, S., & Wyckoff, J. (2009). Teacher preparation and student achievement. *Educational Evaluation and Policy Analysis, 31*, 416–440. doi:10.3102/0162373709353129
Brownell, M. T., Billingsley, B. S., McLeskey, J., & Sindelar, P. T. (2012). Teacher Quality and effectiveness in an era of accountability: Challenges and solutions in special education? In J. B. Crockett, B. S. Billingsley, & M. L. Boscardin (Eds.), *Handbook of leadership and administration for special education* (pp. 260–280). New York. NY: Routledge.
Brownell, M. T., Sindelar, P. T., Kiely, M. T., & Danielson, L. C. (2010). Special education teacher quality and preparation: Exposing foundations, constructing a new model. *Exceptional Children, 76*, 357–377.
Chetty, R., Friedman, J. N., & Rockoff, J. E. (2011). *The long-term impacts of teachers: Teacher value-added and student outcomes in adulthood*. Cambridge, MA: National Bureau of Economic Research, Working Paper No. 17699.
Clotfelter, C. T., Ladd, H. F., & Vigdor, J. L. (2007a). Teacher credentials and student achievement: Longitudinal analysis with student fixed effects. *Economics of Education Review, 26*, 673–682. doi:10.1016/j.econedurev.2007.10.002
Clotfelter, C. T., Ladd, H. F., & Vigdor, J. L. (2007b). Teacher-student matching and the assessment of teacher effectiveness. *The Journal of Human Resources, 41*, 778–820.
Cochran-Smith, M., Feiman-Nemser, S., McIntyre, D. J., & Demers, K. E. (2008). *Handbook of research on teacher education: Enduring questions in changing contexts* (3rd ed.). New York, NY: Routledge.
Cochran-Smith, M., & Fries, K. (2005). Researching teacher education in changing times: Politics and paradigms. In M. Cochran-Smith & K. M. Zeichner (Eds.), *Studying teacher education: The report of the AERA panel on research and teacher education* (pp. 69–109). Mahwah, NJ: Erlbaum.
Cochran-Smith, M., & Fries, K. (2008). Research on teacher education: Changing times, changing paradigms. In M. Cochran-Smith, S. Feiman-Nemser, D. J. McIntyre, & K. E. Demers (Eds.), *Handbook of research on teacher education: Enduring questions in changing contexts* (3rd ed., pp. 989–999). New York, NY: Routledge.
Cochran-Smith, M., & Zeichner, K. (2005). *Studying teacher education: The report of the AERA panel on research and teacher education*. Mahwah, NJ: Erlbaum.
Constantine, J., Player, D., Silva, T., Hallgren, K., Grider, M., & Deke, J. (2009). *An evaluation of teachers trained through different routes to certification*. Washington, DC: U.S. Department of Education. Retrieved from http://nces.ed.gov/Pubsearch/pubsinfo.asp?pubid=NCEE20094043
Cook, B., & Schirmer, B (2003). What is special about special education: Overview and analysis. *The Journal of Special Education, 37*, 200–205. doi:10.1177/00224669030370031001
Crowe, E. (2011). *Race to the Top and teacher preparation: Analyzing state strategies for ensuring real accountability and fostering program innovation*. Washington, DC: Center for American Progress. Retrieved from http://www.americanprogress.org/issues/education/report/2011/03/01/9329/race-to-the-top-and-teacher-preparation/
Darling-Hammond, L. (2000). Teacher quality and student achievement: A review of state policy evidence. *Education Policy Analysis Archives, 8*. Retrieved from http://epaa.asu.edu/ojs/article/view/392
Darling-Hammond, L. (2006). Assessing teacher education: The usefulness of multiple measures for assessing program outcomes. *Journal of Teacher Education, 57*, 120–138. doi:10.1177/0022487105283796
Darling-Hammond, L., Eiler, M., & Marcus, A. (2002). Perceptions of preparation: Using survey data to assess teacher education outcomes. *Issues in Teacher Education, 11*(1), 65–84.
Data Quality Campaign. (2010). *Strengthening the teacher-student link to inform teacher quality efforts*. Washington, DC: Author. Retrieved from http://www.dataqualitycampaign.org/resources/details/947
Data Quality Campaign. (2011). *State analysis by essential element: 10 essential elements*. Washington, DC: Author. Retrieved from http://www.dataqualitycampaign.org/your-states-progress/10-essential-elements
Decker, P. T., Mayer, D. P., & Glazerman, S. (2004). *The effects of Teach for America on students: Findings from a national evaluation*. Princeton, NJ: Mathematica Policy Research, Inc.
Desimone, L., & Long, D. A. (2010). Teacher effects and the achievement gap: Do teacher and teacher quality influence the achievement gap between Black and White and high- and low-SES students in the early grades? *Teachers College Record, 112*, 3024–3073.
Feng, L., & Sass, T. R. (2010). *What makes special education teachers special? Teacher training and achievement of students with disabilities*. Working Paper 12-10. Atlanta: Georgia State University, Andrew Young School of Policy Studies. Retrieved from: http://papers.ssrn.com/sol3/papers.cfm?abstract_id=2020714
Gansle, K. A., Burns, J. M., & Noell, G. H. (2012). Do student achievement outcomes differ across teacher preparation programs? An analysis of teacher education in Louisiana. *Journal of Teacher Education, 63*, 304–317. doi:10.1177/0022487112439894
Gansle, K. A., Noell, G., Knox, M., & Schafer, M. (2010). *Value added assessment of teacher preparation in Louisiana: 2005–2006 to 2008–2009*. Baton Rouge, LA: Louisiana Board of Regents. Retrieved from http://regentsfiles.org/

assets/docs/TeacherPreparation/200910ValueAddedAssessmentOverviewofPerformanceBandsFINAL82610.pdf

Gitomer, D. H., Latham, A. S., & Ziomek, R. (1999). *The academic quality of prospective teachers: The impact of admissions and licensure testing*. Princeton, NJ: Educational Testing Service.

Goe, L. (2007). *The link between teacher quality and student outcomes: A research synthesis*. Washington, DC: National Comprehensive Center for Teacher Quality.

Goldhaber, D., & Anthony, E. (2007). Can teacher quality be effectively assessed? National Board Certification as a signal of effective teaching. *The Review of Economics and Statistics, 89*, 134–150. doi:10.1162/rest.89.1.134

Gollnick, D. M. (2008). Teacher capacity for diversity. In M. Cochran-Smith, S. Feiman-Nemser, D. J. McIntyre, & K. E. Demers (Eds.), *Handbook on teacher education: Enduring questions in changing contexts* (3rd ed., pp. 249–257). New York, NY: Routledge.

Good, T. L., McCaslin, M., Tsang, H. Y., Zhang, J., Wiley, C. R. H., Bozack, A. R., & Hester, W. (2006). How well do 1st-year teachers teach: Does type of preparation make a difference? *Journal of Teacher Education, 57*, 410–430. doi:10.1177/0022487106291566

Harris, D. N. (2012, October 15). *How do value-added indicators compare to other measures of teacher effectiveness?* Carnegie Knowledge Network. Retrieved from http://carnegieknowledgenetwork.org/briefs/value-added/value-added-other-measures

Harris, D. N., & Sass, T. R. (2011). Teacher training, teacher quality and student achievement. *Journal of Public Economics, 95*, 798–812. doi: http://dx.doi.org/10.1016/j.jpubeco.2010.11.009

Heck, R. H. (2007). Examining the relationship between teacher quality as an organizational property of schools and students' achievement and growth. *Educational Administration Quarterly, 43*, 399–432. doi:10.1177/0013161X07306452

Henry, G. T., Thompson, C. L., Bastian, K. C., Fortner, C. K., Kershaw, D. C., Purtell, K. M., & Zulli, R. A. (2010). *Portal report: Teacher preparation and student test scores in North Carolina*. Chapel Hill, NC: Carolina Institute for Public Policy. Retrieved from http://publicpolicy.unc.edu/research/Teacher_Portals_Teacher_Preparation_and_Student_Test_Scores_in_North_Carolina_2.pdf/view

Hill, H. C., Kapitula, L., & Umland, K. (2011). A validity argument approach to evaluating teacher value-added scores. *American Educational Research Journal, 48*, 794–831. doi:10.3102/0002831210387916

Huang, F. L., & Moon, T. R. (2008). Is experience the best teacher? A multilevel analysis of teacher characteristics and student achievement in low performing schools. *Education, Assessment, Evaluation, and Accountability, 21*, 209–234. doi:10.1007/s11092-009-9074-2

Imig, D. G., & Imig, S. R. (2008). From traditional certification to competitive certification: A twenty-five year retrospective. In M. Cochran-Smith, S. Feiman-Nemser, D. J. McIntyre, & K. E. Demers (Eds.), *Handbook on teacher education: Enduring questions in changing contexts* (3rd ed., pp. 886–907). New York, NY: Routledge.

Kane, T. J., Rockoff, J. E., & Staiger, D. O. (2008). What does certification tell us about teacher effectiveness? Evidence from New York City. *Economics of Education Review, 27*, 615–631. doi:10.1016/j.econedurev.2007.05.005

Konold, T., Jablonski, B., Nottingham, A., Kessler, L., Byrd, S., Imig, S., Berry, R., & McNergney, R. (2008). Adding value to public schools: Investigating teacher education, teaching, and pupil learning. *Journal of Teacher Education, 59*, 300–312. doi:10.1177/0022487108321378

Kukla-Acevedo, S. (2009). Do teacher characteristics matter? New results on the effects of teacher preparation on student achievement. *Economics of Education Review, 28*, 49–57. doi:10.1016/j.econedurev.2007.10.007

McDiarmid, G. W., & Clevenger-Bright, M. (2008). Rethinking teacher capacity. In M. Cochran-Smith, S. Feiman-Nemser, D. J. McIntyre, & K. E. Demers (Eds.), *Handbook on teacher education: Enduring questions in changing contexts* (3rd ed., pp. 134–156). New York, NY: Routledge.

National Council for Accreditation of Teacher Education. (2010, November). *Transforming teacher education through clinical practice: A national strategy to prepare effective teachers*. Report of the Blue Ribbon Panel on Clinical Preparation and Partnerships on Improved Student Learning. Washington, DC: NCATE. Retrieved from http://www.ncate.org/Public/ResearchReports/NCATEInitiatives/BlueRibbonPanel/tabid/715/Default.aspx

National Research Council. (2010). *Preparing teachers: Building evidence for sound policy*. Washington, DC: Author.

Neild, R. C., Farley-Ripple, E. N., & Byrnes, V. (2009). The effect of teacher certification on middle grades achievement in an urban district. *Educational Policy, 23*, 732–760. doi:10.1177/0895904808320675

Nelson, L. A. (2012, April 5). Far from consensus. *Inside Higher Education*. Retrieved from http://www.insidehighered.com/news/2012/04/05/us-panel-negotiates-over-rules-teacher-preparation-programs

Neuman, S. B., & Cunningham, L. (2009). The impact of professional development and coaching on early language and literacy instructional practices. *American Educational Research Journal, 46*, 532–566. doi:10.3102/0002831208328088

Noell, G. H., & Gleason, B. (2011). *The status of the development of the value added assessment model as specified in Act 54: A report to the Senate Education Committee and the House Education Committee of the Louisiana Legislature.*

Retrieved from http://www.regentsfiles.org/assets/docs/TeacherPreparation/LegilsativeValueAddedReport-Feb2011FINAL.pdf

Noell, G. H., Porter, B. A., Patt, R. M., & Dahir, A. (2008). *Value added assessment of teacher preparation in Louisiana: 2004–2005 to 2006–2007.* Retrieved under Year Five (2007–08) technical report, from http://regents.louisiana.gov/value-added-teacher-preparation-program-assessment-model/

Nougaret, A., Scruggs, T., & Mastropieri, M. (2005). Does teacher education produce better special education teachers? *Exceptional Children, 71*(3), 217–229.

Nye, B., Konstantopoulos, S., & Hodges, L. V. (2004). How large are teacher effects? *Educational Evaluation and Policy Analysis, 26*, 237–257. doi:10.3102/01623737026003237

Pecheone, R. L., & Chung, R. R. (2006). Evidence in teacher education: The Performance Assessment for California Teachers (PACT). *Journal of Teacher Education, 57*, 22–36. doi:10.1177/0022487105284045

Pecheone, R. L., Pigg, M. J., Chung, R. R., & Souviney, R. J. (2005). Performance assessment and electronic portfolios: Their effect on teacher learning and education. *The Clearing House, 78*, 164–176. doi:10.3200/TCHS.78.4.164-176

Peck, C. A., Gallucci, C., & Sloan, T. (2010). Negotiating implementation of high-stakes performance assessment policies in teacher education: From compliance to inquiry. *Journal of Teacher Education, 61*, 451–463. doi:10.1177/0022487109354520

Pianta, R. C. (2012, May 6). Stop complaining about teacher assessments: Find alternatives. *The Chronicle of Higher Education.* Retrieved from http://chronicle.com/article/Tired-of-Debating-Teacher/131803/

Rosenberg, M. S., & Sindelar, P. T. (2005). The proliferation of alternative routes to certification in special education: A critical review of the literature. *Journal of Special Education, 39*, 117–127. doi:10.1177/00224669050390020201

Rowan, B., Correnti, R., & Miller, R. J. (2002). What large-scale survey research tells us about teacher effects on student achievement: Insights from the Prospects Study of Elementary Schools. *Teachers College Record, 104*, 1525–1567. doi:10.1111/1467-9620.00212

Sass, T. (2011). *Certification requirements and teacher quality: A comparison of alternative routes to teaching.* Working Paper 64. Washington, DC: National Center for Analysis of Longitudinal Data in Education Research. Retrieved from www.caldercenter.org/upload/Sass_Certification-Requirements.pdf

Seftor, N. S., & Mayer, D. P. (2003). *The effect of alternative certification on student achievement: A literature review.* Princeton, NJ: Mathematica Policy Research, Inc.

Sindelar, P. T., Brownell, M. T., & Billingsley, B. (2010). Special education teacher education research: Current status and future directions. *Teacher Education and Special Education, 33*, 8–24. doi:10.1177/0888406409358593

Sindelar, P. T., Daunic, A., & Rennells, M. S. (2004). Comparisons of traditionally and alternatively trained teachers, *Exceptionality, 12*, 209–223. doi:10.1207/s15327035ex1204_3

Smith, D. D., Robb, S. M., West, J., & Tyler, N. C. (2010). The changing education landscape: How special education leadership preparation can make a difference for teachers and their students with disabilities. *Teacher Education and Special Education, 33*, 25–43. doi:10.1177/0888406409358425

Stronge, J. H., Ward, T. J., & Grant, L. W. (2011). What makes good teachers good? A cross-case analysis of the connection between teacher effectiveness and student achievement. *Journal of Teacher Education, 62*, 339–355. doi:10.1177/0022487111404241

Tennessee Higher Education Commission. (2010). *Report card on the effectiveness of teacher training programs.* Retrieved from http://www.tn.gov/thec/Divisions/fttt/report_card_teacher_train/Report%20Summary.pdf

Wang, J., Lin, E., Spalding, E., Klecka, C. L., & Odell, S. J. (2011). Quality teaching and teacher education: A kaleidoscope of notions. *Journal of Teacher Education, 62*, 331–338. doi:10.1177/0022487111409551

Wenglinsky, H. (2002). How schools matter: The link between teacher classroom practices and student academic performance. *Educational Policy Analysis Archives, 10.* Retrieved from http://epaa.asu.edu/ojs/article/view/291

Wilson, S. M., Floden, R. E., & Ferrini-Mundy, J. (2002). Teacher preparation research: An insider's view from the outside. *Journal of Teacher Education, 53*, 190–204. doi:10.1177/0022487102053003002

Wilson, S. M., & Youngs, P. (2005). Research on accountability processes in teacher education. In M. Cochran-Smith & K. M. Zeichner (Eds.), *Studying teacher education: The report of the AERA panel on research and teacher education* (pp. 591–643). Mahwah, NJ: Erlbaum.

Xu, Z., Hannaway, J., & Taylor, C. (2011). Making a difference: The effects of Teach for America in high school. *Journal of Policy Analysis and Management, 30*, 447–469. doi:10.1002/pam.20585

9

Working Together

Research on the Preparation of General Education and Special Education Teachers for Inclusion and Collaboration

Marleen C. Pugach
UNIVERSITY OF SOUTHERN CALIFORNIA

Linda P. Blanton and Mildred Boveda
FLORIDA INTERNATIONAL UNIVERSITY

Things to Think About

- To respond to the challenge of improving educational outcomes for students with disabilities, general and special education teacher preparation have undergone reform to improve collaboration.
- In order to prepare general teachers for inclusion and collaboration, teacher education programs have either redesigned components of preservice programs or undertaken full preservice program redesign.
- Scholars studying program redesign have used a variety of measures, including evaluations of candidates' performance, learning gains of students taught by candidates during field experiences, analysis of program curricula, and exploration of candidates' socialization and identity development.
- Using *intentionality* as a lens for developing future research offers a more consistent opportunity to address complex questions about the structure and outcomes of teacher education for inclusion.
- Scholars can improve the overall quality of research by coming to some agreement about the definitions and concepts applied in research on collaborative teacher education.

How the education system responds to the persistent low achievement of students who have disabilities is directly related to efforts to improve the quality of their teachers. It is within the daily decisions and acts of teachers, those in both what has come to be called "general education" and those in special education alike, that students with disabilities are either included and can succeed—both socially and academically—or are excluded. On the part of teacher education, one of the principal responses to the challenge of improving educational outcomes for students with disabilities has been to create preservice programs that bring together the preparation of general and special education teachers in a variety of curricular and practice configurations, spanning a range of certification options that can include both general and special education licensure (Blanton & Pugach, 2011). While efforts to redesign the preparation of general and special education teachers in relationship to each other actually have a long history, there has been a marked expansion of this activity in recent years (Pugach, Blanton, & Correa, 2011). The goal of these programs is to (a) improve the preparation of general education teachers to increase their ability to be successful with students who have disabilities and (b) build on the improved preparation of general education teachers as a way of redefining the roles and preparation of specialists (Blanton & Pugach, 2011).

Underlying these two goals is an assumption that by working together across general and special education at the preservice level, graduates will be better prepared to address the wide diversity of students they will teach, including those who have disabilities (Pugach & Blanton, 2012b). A second assumption is that the redesign of teacher preparation in general education for students with disabilities depends upon joint effort across general and special education to adequately retool the preservice curriculum. Further, such joint efforts have an important contribution to make in informing the redesign of teacher education in special education, helping to establish role redefinition (Blanton, Pugach, & Florian, 2011) and to identify reciprocal job parameters of general and special education teachers. In other words, without a deep consideration of what is developed to constitute the preparation of general education teachers, it is difficult to redefine the roles of special educators and how best to prepare them.

The purpose of this chapter is to describe and critique research on teacher education programs in which general and special educators are brought together to redesign preparation, either of an entire program or segments of a program, for general and special education teachers. The history of these efforts has recently been described (Pugach et al., 2011). But in view of the trending activity level in programs that claim a commitment to restructuring teacher education to foster inclusive educational practice by engaging in joint activity across general and special education, it seems timely to document the scope and characteristics of the empirical base, particularly research on redesigned teacher education, either partial or total, that includes general and special educators working together.

Scope and Method

Guided by these assumptions, this chapter does not include studies in which special education faculty were asked to speak on behalf of, and/or represent the views of, their general education colleagues on various issues related to program redesign and collaboration. Among those that were not included were studies that had as participants special education faculty only, who were then asked to identify perceptions regarding collaboration in teacher education not only for themselves, but also for their general education peers (e.g., McKenzie, 2009; Smith & Edelen-Smith, 2002; Voltz, 2003). Other studies have addressed how special education preservice teachers learn to collaborate, but in the absence of any interaction with their general education counterparts (Bradley & Monda-Amaya, 2005). The point is not that it is problematic to engage in research on perceptions and practices regarding teacher education in special education in isolation, but rather that when the salient issue is collaboration, it is important to consider how collaborators, in this case general and special educators, approach or participate in research in teacher education together.

Because this chapter is focused on the *practice* of preservice education, studies that used surveys exclusively were excluded, even when participants represented both general and special education. Studies were also excluded that relied exclusively on preservice teachers' attitudes toward inclusive education and collaboration as dependent measures. Although attitude studies are important and deserve the attention of those who engage in the redesign of preservice programs, the scope of this review is to illustrate the landscape of research conducted by general and special educators working together on problems of practice in teacher education. As noted above, studies were included only if they engaged teacher educators and/or preservice students in both general and special education. Further, if student participants were enrolled in programs of dual certification, those studies were included.

This review was anchored in 1997; in that year in the United States, the general education curriculum was emphasized in the legislative reauthorization of the Individuals with Disabilities Education Act as the appropriate curriculum goal for most students who have disabilities. The earlier, international *Salamanca Statement and Framework for Action* (UNESCO, 1994) was also a critical anchor point with regard to inclusive education, one with important implications for teacher education, such that by 1997 studies regarding inclusive teacher education would likely have begun to surface outside of the US.

The following databases were searched: Academic Search Complete, EBSCO Host, Education Full Text, Education Research Complete, ERIC, Google Scholar, Psych Abstracts, Taylor & Francis Online, and Wiley Online, using the following keywords: *co-teaching, collaboration, cooperation, faculty, inclusion, teacher education, university*, and *partnerships*. Next, searches were conducted of all tables of contents for the following journals from the years 1997–2011: *Action in Teacher Education, British Journal of Special Education, Disability Studies, European Journal of Special Needs Education, European Journal of Teacher Education, Exceptional Children, International Journal of Inclusive Education, International Journal of Special Educational Needs, Journal of Research in Special Educational Needs, Journal of Teacher Education, Remedial and Special Education, Teacher Education and Special Education, Teacher Education Quarterly, Teachers College Record, Teaching and Teacher Education, The Teacher Educator*, and *Theory into Practice*. Finally, ancestry searches were conducted for all articles identified.

Studies included in this chapter were peer-reviewed, had a relatively complete discussion of methodology, and had a clear sense of purpose with regard to inquiring into some aspect of exploring the practice of the preparation of general and special education teachers. Studies that added special education content to general education teacher preparation without further attention to collaboration were eliminated. The 30 empirical studies identified as meeting these criteria fell into two main clusters: (a) studies of redesigned components of collaborative preservice programs, including co-teaching; and (b) studies of full preservice program redesign.

Studies of Program Components

Sixteen studies targeted specific program components, such as methods courses or field experiences, to improve preservice teachers' knowledge and skills for inclusive practice; in most cases, general and special education faculty conducted the research together. These studies clustered into two groups: (a) those where program components were designed to improve preservice teachers' instructional knowledge and competence for inclusive practice, and (b) those that examined methods within-program components to develop collaboration skills among general and special education candidates. More studies were identified on collaboration and the development of collaboration skills than on preservice teachers' development of instructional skills. The methods used to conduct these 16 studies ranged from quasi-experimental designs to qualitative methods using thematic analysis, to descriptive studies; the use of surveys and questionnaires were included as part of the data in most studies.

We initially assumed that the rationale for the focus on program components was that these studies represented early steps toward more broad-based curriculum redesign, and/or that studies of program components lent themselves more easily to using quasi-experimental designs. However, the reasons offered by specific authors for examining and reporting on targeted program components often seemed to be that this approach was viewed as being preferable to, or at least more realistic to accomplish, than redesign that involves entire teacher education programs. For example, Van Laarhoven, Munk, Lynch, Bosma, and Rouse (2007) suggest that partial program redesign may be more reasonable because of the multiple barriers that can stand in the way of more comprehensive redesign. Although such additive approaches are not as likely to result in real or sustained transformation of teacher education programs (Pugach & Blanton, 2009), conducting research on a variety of redesigned program components can illustrate important aspects of preservice preparation that might be included in subsequent, comprehensive program redesign.

Studies of Preservice Candidates' Instructional Knowledge and Skills

Six studies examined the impact of redesigned courses and/or field experiences on candidates' instructional knowledge and competence for inclusive practice. Although the approaches used to redesign courses and/or experiences varied, the most common element was adding content, an activity, or an experience to the curriculum. Two of the studies used quasi-experimental designs, two were largely descriptive, and two used qualitative methodology.

Brown, Welch, Hill, and Cipko (2008) and Van Laarhoven et al. (2007; also reported in Van Laarhoven et al., 2006) used quasi-experimental designs to compare candidates' performance across course sections. In Van Laarhoven et al. (2007), experimental course sections were enhanced in three ways: a 10-hour institute, addition of targeted content (i.e., functional behavioral assessment, curricular accommodations, and assistive technology), and a clinical experience. Teacher candidates from special, elementary, and secondary education volunteered to participate in both the experimental and control course sections. Curricular probes and attitude surveys were used to collect data; of interest to this review are the curricular probes administered as pre/posttests to assess candidates' knowledge and competence in the three new content areas. Data included written responses to three vignettes about classrooms, one for each of the targeted content areas. Results indicated that all groups showed growth, but growth for experimental groups was significantly greater than for control groups. Effect sizes for the general education majors in the experimental group were largest (e.g., $d = 1.42$ using Cohen's d for probes on assistive technology as compared to $d = 0.95$ for the same probes with the special education majors in this group), suggesting that that this group benefitted most from the addition of projects and experiences. Brown et al. (2008) explored the knowledge acquired by all teacher education majors in experimental and control sections of an assessment course; the experimental intervention included knowledge and activities on understanding and adapting assessments for students with learning disabilities. Pre/postsurvey data were collected from 99 teacher education candidates in the experimental group and 109 in the control group; 21% of these were special education candidates. Results indicated that adding content and activities significantly increased the experimental group candidates' knowledge about working with and adapting assessments and instruction for students with learning disabilities, for example, discussing specific interventions in more depth.

In two primarily descriptive studies (Maheady, Jabot, Rey, & Michelli-Pendl, 2007; Golder, Norwich, & Bayliss, 2005), content and experiences were added to the curricula. In Maheady et al., faculty from general and special education, educational administration, and a science teacher collaborated to add projects to a four-semester sequence. Four hundred and twenty-two undergraduate participants from general education programs in early childhood, elementary, and secondary education worked with peers to plan and teach lessons; candidates collected pre and post data, using teacher-developed assessments, on the performance of their students. Results revealed improvements in candidates' use of evidence-based practices and increases in student outcomes on the teacher-developed assessments for a majority of students they taught. Similarly, Golder et al. added a school-based activity to the program of 320 secondary preservice candidates focused on working with a student identified as having special educational needs. Faculty provided a framework for candidates to use in working with and reporting on the progress of their assigned student. Analysis of semistructured questionnaires and progress reporting showed that candidates gained a greater understanding of students with special educational needs.

In a recent study by Frey, Andres, McKeeman, and Lane (2012), faculty from general and special education used universal design for learning (UDL) principles to redesign a semester block of pedagogy and special education courses for all secondary education majors. Faculty also team-taught courses in the block. Redesigned courses were evaluated two semesters later, during student teaching, by collecting data from candidates' lesson plans, teaching philosophy statements, and observational records. Findings showed that candidates used UDL principles such as multiple formats for teaching content and demonstrated the use of instructional adaptations. Although outcomes varied across majors, many of the students with disabilities achieved the goals that candidates had set for them in lesson plans.

Andrews (2002) added case-based instruction during student teaching to better prepare teacher candidates for inclusive classrooms. Among the questions that guided the research, two focused on the use of online collaboration and developing student teachers' confidence for working in diverse classrooms. Forty candidates in elementary, secondary, and a new dual degree program participated. The researcher developed the case with a fifth-grade teacher whose classroom included several students with disabilities and whose primary language was not English. After analyzing the case, candidates worked in cooperative learning groups to develop a lesson plan. Data were collected from an analysis of lesson plans, themes drawn from written reflections, and candidate responses to a survey about their abilities. Results, which were not disaggregated by group membership, suggested that candidates were able to adjust instruction to include students with disabilities, especially after receiving feedback on lessons from the cooperating teacher. Their confidence in adjusting instruction also increased, although many also reported concern about their ability to adapt instruction.

Studies of Preservice Candidates' Collaboration Skills

Ten studies focused on building preservice candidates' collaboration skills for inclusive practice. These studies clustered into three groups: teaching collaboration skills through projects and assignments in courses and experiences, organizing candidates to co-teach and organizing faculty into co-teaching arrangements to examine the impact on both faculty and candidates' collaboration skills.

Teaching Collaboration Skills in Courses and Experiences

Four studies explored experiences within courses and/or field experiences to develop collaboration skills; three (Geer & Hamill, 2007; Jeffs & Banister, 2006; Kurtts, Hibbard, & Levin, 2005) used technology as the medium for these collaborative experiences. These researchers all concluded that technology seemed to play a beneficial role in supporting the development of collaboration skills (e.g., learning from each other; supporting each other). Kurtts et al. examined how collaborative problem solving between elementary and special education undergraduates from two teacher education programs in different states, using a specific problem-solving model, was supported by online teaching, especially the synchronous chat feature. One activity was on prereferral of students to special education and one was on co-teaching. Data were collected from transcripts of online meetings, candidate responses to pre/post problem-based learning probes, reactions to the projects, and an end-of-semester survey of half of the candidates. Geer and Hamill, and Jeffs and Banister examined experiences related to methods courses taken by general and special education teacher candidates within their own preservice programs. Geer and Hamill used the field experience component of methods courses for online discussions and conducted a thematic analysis of their content. In Jeffs and Banister, students in a methods course for general education students and students in a methods course for special education students used technology to teach the other section a lesson on a topic (e.g., assistive technology) that was not ordinarily included; data were collected via pre- and postactivity survey.

Griffin, Jones, and Kilgore (2006) examined how 20 preservice candidates in the 5-year Unified Elementary and Special Education Program at the University of Florida perceived a collaborative project required for student teaching in which special education candidates in that program worked with other colleagues to support students with disabilities in a general education classroom. Results from a thematic analysis of written assignments indicated five areas that facilitated collaboration (frequent, even if informal, opportunities for communication; concern for the student; similar goals; involvement of family; and a school climate supporting collaboration) and six obstacles (differences in the knowledge base about students with disabilities; perceived lower role status of the student teacher; different expectations of the student held by the student teacher and colleagues; conflicting goals between professionals and parents; limited communication; and no follow through by the person with whom the student teacher was collaborating). These findings suggest that the ability to learn collaborative skills is mediated by the specific school context that preservice teachers enter.

Organizing Candidates to Co-teach

Four studies focused on supporting preservice students as co-teachers during field experiences; one study included faculty participants. Three studies used qualitative methodology; one used mixed methods. Generally these studies were concerned either with roles, or with the structure of the co-teaching experience itself.

Kamens and Casale-Giannola (2004) explored how teacher candidates and cooperating teachers viewed candidates' roles during student teaching placements in inclusive, co-taught classrooms. Five student teachers (four in a dual-certification program and one in elementary education), two university supervisors, five cooperating teachers, and co-teaching partners participated. Themes derived from an analysis of observation notes, interviews, focus groups and open-ended surveys were related to support, planning, modeling and awareness of elements of co-teaching. For example, student teachers reported that having more than one cooperating teacher made it possible for someone to always be there in the classroom to answer their concerns; this also enhanced the planning experience and provided practical experiences that extended their understanding of co-teaching. Disadvantages included the added pressure of building relationships with two cooperating teachers, difficulty in finding common planning time, and creating a state of constant vigilance for the student teacher. Student teachers and cooperating teachers alike noted that the dyad experience reinforced the values of collaboration and varied teaching styles, but diminished opportunities for student teachers to create a sense of independence and autonomy. This lack of independence included difficulty in negotiating and balancing general education and special education roles.

In a study that also explored the experiences of preservice teachers and their cooperating teachers when co-teaching, Kamens (2007) paired preservice teachers, one from general education and one from a dual certification program, with teams of collaborating cooperating teachers. Data sources included notes, observations, and reports, including e-mail communications, from researchers, university supervisors, student teachers, and cooperating teachers. Findings showed that student teachers noted the benefits of having a partner to provide continual feedback, technical support, and encouragement while student teaching, but cooperating teachers expressed concerns that when student teachers share the workload, this may not prepare them for the "realities of teaching alone in the classroom" (Kamens, 2007, p.160). Both student teachers and cooperating teachers noted the importance of having compatible personalities. Collaborating teachers identified an element of competition when student teachers were not of equal ability in specific areas. Overall, participants' perceptions of the co-student teaching structure on the children were positive.

McHatton and Daniel (2008) described the collaboration of two professors, one in special education and one in English education, to engage preservice students in collaborative and consultative relationships through an early practicum experience. Eight special education majors were randomly assigned to partners in secondary English for a co-teaching experience. The results from both quantitative (i.e., survey) and qualitative (i.e., reflections and open-ended questions) measures revealed that both groups grew in their understanding of the roles and responsibilities of general and special educators in schools. Pre- and posttest survey results analyzed using a MANOVA revealed that both English education and special education students improved significantly on each of three areas in the survey: awareness, knowledge of meeting the needs of diverse learners, and knowledge of content. Findings gleaned from reflections and open-ended questions also indicated favorable results in each of the three areas. Researchers noted their concern about how often host teachers relegated special education candidates to the status of assistants rather than full partners in co-teaching, even though host teachers had prior experience in co-teaching.

Goodnough, Osmond, Dibbon, Glassman, and Stevens (2009) used a student teaching triad model in which pairs of preservice teachers worked with cooperating teachers in a semester-long field experience to investigate co-teaching models. From semistructured interviews, e-journal entries, observations, and transcripts of reflection and debriefing meetings, the researchers described co-teaching and documented benefits and challenges experienced by the triads. Preservice teachers and cooperating teachers reported several strengths of co-teaching: learning from each other, professional support, outcomes for P–12 students, comprehensive feedback about teaching and classroom practice, and preservice teacher confidence. Limitations and concerns identified by both groups included dependence, confusion with classroom management issues, loss of individuality, and competition between preservice teachers.

Organizing Faculty to Co-teach

Two studies focused on faculty organizing themselves to co-teach to determine the impact on their own work and on preservice teachers' understanding of collaboration. Both studies employed qualitative methodology.

To better understand the professional and institutional realities of team teaching for general and special education faculty teams, York-Barr, Bacharach, Salk, Hinz Frank, and Benick (2004) invited all 40 general and special education faculty at one university to engage in team-teaching preservice courses. Eighteen were selected as having adequate background knowledge to teach designated courses (e.g., Learning Disabilities Methods II) in the experimental undergraduate program; six of the 18 participated and made up four teaching teams, each with a general education and special education faculty member. Data were collected using an interview protocol. With one exception, faculty views about the effects of team teaching on the preservice teacher education students were positive and included, among others, that students gained broader perspectives on teaching and learning. In addition, faculty noted that students benefitted both from engaging in co-teaching themselves and from observing their instructors model co-teaching. Benefits for faculty were also dominated by positive comments, with effects such as professional development and increased understanding of "other disciplines" (p. 79) and "the other profession" (p. 82) noted, although faculty expressed some concerns about workload issues and negotiating roles and responsibilities. The challenges for one team that had struggled arose primarily from philosophical and instructional differences.

Arndt and Liles (2010), one a special education instructor and the other a social studies instructor, designed collaborative opportunities focused on co-teaching in inclusive classrooms for two classes of preservice students—one in elementary and special education and one in secondary social studies. The two instructors provided individual class projects and cross-class projects on collaboration and co-teaching, as well as combining their classes periodically to model co-teaching themselves. Data were analyzed from transcriptions of student reflections, oral presentations, and focus groups. One key finding suggested that students were open to co-teaching as an effective method; however, they voiced a number of concerns, one of which was not being comfortable teaching the content of another field. Further, the second key finding revealed that student concerns about not knowing the content of another field may lead them to think of co-teaching as merely two persons teaching together occasionally. Researchers attributed this perception by students to be the fault of the way the experience was structured and that "the structure and design of our program shape our students' perceptions in a way that can later interfere with their ability to develop and put into practice effective coteaching models" (p. 22). Several considerations were discussed for how teacher preparation programs might overcome such unintended outcomes.

Studies of Complete Program Redesign

Eleven studies of complete program redesign met the criteria for this review, a small number given the rapid growth in recent years of such programs. Seven studies reported evaluation data, predominantly on teacher education candidate performance. Further, most of these studies were limited in the sophistication of the evaluation design and used small numbers and self-report instruments, among other methodological weaknesses. Only one study reported on learning gains of students taught by candidates while enrolled in a collaborative program. Two studies analyzed the curricula of collaborative programs and one study explored how teacher candidates in a dual licensure program are socialized and develop an identity as both a general educator and a special educator. Although multiple approaches to the study of collaborative teacher education programs are emerging, the few studies available may say more about the difficulty of conducting this type of research than about the interest of faculty in conducting it.

Evaluation Studies: Candidate Performance

Six of the seven programs in this section were elementary education (one included licensure covering early education) and three were secondary education programs; two of the secondary studies reported data for both elementary and secondary education. Some programs were undergraduate, some postbaccalaureate, and some culminated in a master's degree (or offered the option to do so). All studies were conducted by faculty in the programs and often by pairs or groups of general and special educators.

Two studies (Jenkins, Pateman, & Black, 2002; Lesar, Benner, Habel, & Coleman, 1997) focused on evaluating initial cohorts of redesigned programs. In the Lesar et al. study, a group of general and special education faculty redesigned the elementary (K–5) education program for inclusive settings; this represented a comprehensive curricular reform effort in that the structure and delivery of the program was reconceptualized and comprised a three-phase training model, a year-long internship accompanied by local school monitoring, and instructional approaches anchored in constructivist theories of learning. Data collected over 2 years included retention and graduate degree attainment; candidate responses to the model and the interdisciplinary constructivist approach; and perspectives of teachers, administrators, and candidates. Thematic analysis of candidate responses indicated that they developed a better understanding how to work with different learners; findings were attributed to the model and constructivist approach guiding the program. Consistent themes also emerged related to the perspectives of teachers, administrators, and candidates around outcomes such as the value of a year-long internship and the fact that the program prepared candidates for the realities of the population of diverse students in schools.

The program evaluated by Jenkins et al. (2002) was collaboratively redesigned with a local school district, anchored in field experiences, and offered dual licensure in elementary education and special education. Multiple formative assessments (e.g., e-mail journals, conferences with mentor teachers) and a summative assessment based on questionnaires and focus groups were collected over the 2 years of the program. Among the findings was that students recommended a stronger integration of the elementary and special education programs. In a more comprehensive program evaluation of the Teach for All Children Program (TAC), Stoddard, Braun, Hewitt, and Koorland (2006) gathered formative assessments over 3 years, as well as summative data from an annual survey of graduates. The redesigned elementary education undergraduate program, combined with graduate courses in special education, culminates in a master's degree and dual licensure. Multiple formative assessments (e.g., interviews) were collected and although limited data were actually reported based on these assessments, Stoddard et al. summarized several findings, one of which was that teachers reported that TAC candidates were better prepared for inclusive classrooms than traditional teacher education candidates. Data from the summative evaluation for 3 years of TAC graduates were reported in greater detail; results from two questions on the survey, which were focused on working with colleagues in general and special education and using inclusive practices, indicated that the majority of graduates reported that they used inclusive practices either somewhat or to a great extent.

Sobel, Iceman-Sands, and Basile (2007) also relied on surveys to assess the extent to which 88 candidates in both elementary and secondary education in a redesigned collaborative program reported meeting competencies related to working with diverse students in inclusive school programs. The authors also reported results of a follow-up survey of 30 randomly selected graduates in their first year of teaching. Candidates rated themselves on their competence to adapt instruction, create learning environments, and provide activities that increase the self-confidence of diverse students. Candidates rated themselves highly on two of the three items, but reported difficulty in adapting instruction. Four items focused on working with colleagues in both general and special education and on program experiences that supported them in working with diverse students. Respondents commented positively on the program, emphasizing the importance of practicing collaboration and their confidence and skill development for working with diverse students, but suggested the need for more modeling of inclusive classroom practices.

Fullerton, Ruben, McBride, and Bert (2011) reported results of an evaluation of the STEP program in secondary and special education, where candidates exit with licensure in a secondary content area, special education secondary education, and an M.Ed. Forty-four candidates and graduates from two cohorts participated, as well as two faculty members, seven student teaching supervisors, and three principals. The evaluation included: candidate self-assessment of competency (e.g., adapting lesson plans) after student teaching, at program completion, and 1 year later; candidate responses to the school of education's survey of all teacher education candidates at program completion and again 1 year later; candidate work samples as judged by faculty near the end of the program; and interviews of university supervisors, principals, and graduates midway through the first year of teaching. Three questions were directed at candidates' ability to accommodate diverse learners; engage in differentiated planning, assessment, and instruction; and whether candidates initiate collaboration with parents and school personnel. Findings for each of the questions were positive and suggested that graduates made accommodations for diverse students, used differentiated approaches in their planning, assessment, and instruction, and were collaborative.

Although not a full-scale evaluation, a study by Corbett, Kilgore, and Sindelar (1998) examined data from a small subgroup of the first cohort of Project PART, an experimental elementary education program designed and implemented by special and general education faculty in which candidates could elect additional coursework to gain a second license in special education. As part of a seminar associated with three continuous semesters of field experience, data were collected through interviews, observations, and document analysis. Major themes were that students appreciated the additional knowledge they gained, were more willing to take responsibility for and manage instruction for all students they taught, and developed increased confidence in managing classrooms for all learners.

Outcome Studies

Only one study (Utley, 2009) reported data on the learning gains of P–12 students of candidates enrolled in what was described as a unified general and special education program. Data were gathered from a performance assessment that required candidates to develop a curriculum unit, lesson plans, teacher-made pre/post assessments, and scoring rubrics. Two products were used for data analysis: a comparison of results of pre and post assessments after implementing the unit, and elements of the lesson plan showing how candidates designed instruction.

Results for all students taught by candidates were analyzed, including students with disabilities. A comparison of pre and post assessments indicated that for 14 of the 20 curriculum units, across grade levels and for multiple assessments, students with disabilities demonstrated learning performance similar to peers without a disability. In examining the elements of lesson plans for units where the learning of students with disabilities was similar to their peers, cooperative learning and graphic organizers were used most frequently, followed by the use of two forms of Universal Design for Learning (i.e., multiple means of representation and multiple means of expression), and extended time for assessments.

Studies Analyzing Program Curricula

Two studies drew on analyses of websites and course syllabi to describe the content and dynamics of general education, some with dual certification options, as they relate to preparing teachers for working with students who have disabilities. By inquiring into the curricular content of collaborative teacher education, these studies shift the conversation from a focus on describing content within a single program to a focus on analyzing curricular structures across several programs.

Holland, Detgen, and Gutekunst (2008) investigated the curricula of 36 general education elementary programs in the southeastern United States to identify the extent to which they reflected seven strategies for integrating content related to disability. Data from this stratified random sample were drawn primarily from program websites and included course catalogues, syllabi, and other relevant program documents, with follow-up interviews with six chairs of elementary education programs. Consistent with past practice, the most common approach to addressing disability issues, in 86% of programs, was requiring one or more courses in special education. Disability-related content was required in 38% of multicultural education courses, 37% of reading courses, 17% of mathematics courses, and 23% of general methods courses, and was embedded in field experiences for 63% of programs. An analysis of program mission statements indicated that disability was mentioned as a priority in 58% of programs, and disability was related to diversity in 28% of mission statements. Although disability and diversity were often connected in these statements, "seldom was the relationship between disability and diversity clearly articulated" (Holland et al., 2008, p. ii). Within the courses themselves, for example, in reading methods courses, teaching students who have disabilities was typically covered under how "to address the individual needs of diverse learners" (p. 14)

Pugach and Blanton (2012b) studied three long-standing merged programs, in which all graduates earned both a general and special education license, to determine the relationship between disability and other social identity markers of diversity. Using website-based program information, course catalogues, and a complete set of course syllabi for each program, this study examined how concepts of diversity, inclusivity, and the boundaries between general and special education were defined. At least one third of the titles of all courses across programs referenced special education and/or inclusion. The analysis of syllabi indicated that course topics and assignments did not necessarily align with the emphasis in course titles, for example, a traditional learning and development course that includes the words "for Inclusive Schooling" in the title but does not look substantially different than most such courses. Additionally, 59% of required textbooks were oriented toward specific subjects in general education (e.g., science, reading), 44% toward special education, 9% toward diversity of race, class, culture and/or language but not disability; an additional 9% represented a broad definition of inclusive education across diversities, but written by authors generally identified with some aspect of special education. Surprisingly, collaboration was addressed relatively infrequently (ranging from one to four class sessions), and primarily in relationship to working with families.

A diversity profile was created for each program to document the different ways diversity was addressed within and across programs. Over the 44 semester courses analyzed, a total of 8.5% of class topics/sessions, or 45 topics/sessions, included reference to diversity other than disability; 27 of these were in one program. A total of six class topics/sessions, or 1%, on English Language Learners was identified across all programs. One program included two assignments on diversity other than disability, one offered four, and one offered over 10. Upwards of 120 class topics/sessions, or 23% of all class topics/sessions, focused specifically on disability across the three programs. Pugach and Blanton (2012b) argued that the need to meet external state and national standards might contribute to program curricula being disproportionately weighed toward special education, at least as identified in program documents, syllabi and assignments.

Studies of Candidate Socialization and Identity Development

Young (2011) examined how teacher candidates experienced professional socialization and developed identities as both general *and* special educators, as well as the norms and values associated with a program that combines general and special education. Seventeen participants from a cohort of 20 students in a combined credential program that culminated in licensure in both elementary and special education completed questionnaires; 18 participated in semistructured interviews.

Frequency counts and content analysis were used to analyze the data; results indicated that candidates were aware of the negative perceptions the public holds of persons with disabilities, but varied in how those perceptions influenced them. Regarding why the university offered a dual licensure program, most candidates spoke about inclusion in schools and the fact that the practice is here to stay. Personal histories of candidates regarding students with disabilities were varied and ranged from recalling no one to having someone with a disability in their families. Findings indicated that societal, institutional, and personal influences all contribute to professional socialization in a dual licensure program. The question posed about the type of teacher identity that develops from a dual licensure program was left essentially unanswered. However, candidates who entered the program seeking to be special education teachers left the program still seeking to be special educators. Candidates entering with a goal of being a general education teacher experienced some shift in willingness to work with students with disabilities. Young concludes that because societal and personal influences appear so powerful, the norms and values of specific dual licensure programs may not necessarily change candidates in dramatic ways.

Interpreting Trends and Gaps in Research on Preparing Teachers for Inclusion and Collaboration

The most extensive body of research located for this review is represented by the study of specific program components, ranging from individual courses, to specially designed field experiences that emphasize co-teaching, to adding multiple new program components simultaneously. Approaching collaborative teacher education from the perspective of research on specific program components has both benefits and limitations. If the study of such components has been successful on some reasonable outcome measure of student learning (e.g., Maheady et al., 2007), these results could suggest directions to be used in developing more complete program redesigns. As noted above, however, if faculties are satisfied with making changes only at the level of specific program components, they may reason that a comprehensive redesign of teacher education is not possible—without ever trying to achieve it. Such a stance implicitly diminishes the potential for program redesign from the outset. Further, with regard to research on components, greater clarity is needed in distinguishing between what is viewed as a redesigned *component* and a fully redesigned *program*. For example, in the Frey et al. (2012) study, a redesigned semester around UDL for secondary general education majors was often referred to as a redesigned program.

Some studies of program components, particularly those focused on co-teaching, point to ongoing difficulties with how special education teachers' roles are defined (e.g., Arndt & Liles, 2010; McHatton & Daniel, 2008). The confusion over what exactly it is that special education teachers should know and be able to do indicates how essential it is for special education as a field to take up this issue and clearly differentiate the relative roles of general and special education teachers, particularly for mild to moderate disabilities. This issue has direct implications for research and practice; without resolution, it will be difficult to set parameters for what takes place programmatically at the preservice level, and thus, for what it is reasonable to study. Further, in component and program evaluation studies alike, participants were often asked about preparation for their future roles. In a context where role definition is uncertain, the value of asking such questions of preservice teachers represents a limitation in the research process because the very roles they are being asked about being prepared for are likely to be unstable as the work of general and special educators is being redefined. An additional issue related to role definition is how group membership is assigned for research purposes. For example, in the Kamens and Casale-Giannola (2004) and Kamens (2007) studies, students who were enrolled in a dual certification program were viewed as the special education partner in the co-teaching team. In the Andrews (2002) study, participants were enrolled in elementary, secondary, and dual degree programs, but results were not disaggregated. As the field shifts and as certification options change, the question of the professional identity of dually certified candidates is an emerging and fertile area for study (see Naraian, 2010; Pugach & Blanton, 2012a). Role redefinition itself could be identified as a construct for research on preservice collaboration.

The dominant mode of study for redesigned programs is program evaluation, which relies heavily on follow-up surveys and other self-report measures. Only one study, by Utley (2009), linked a full program to data on P–12 student learning, but even this particular study would be considered a program evaluation given that there was no comparison group. The preponderance of program evaluation studies suggests that research on program redesign is limited not only by the kinds of data that typical follow-up surveys afford, but also by the scope of the studies themselves. For example, program evaluations have not focused on student identity development as a result of program completion, or the relationships between various parts of the curriculum such as those between teaching English Language Learners and teaching students who have disabilities, or the specific ways that strands of content about disability have been integrated into the content.

Likewise, when program evaluations report that graduates feel well prepared for differentiated planning (e.g., Fullerton et al., 2011), or that they feel well enough prepared for creating learning environments and providing activities that increase the self-confidence of diverse students, but not for adapting instruction (Sobel et al., 2007), it is not possible to determine what precisely in the program accounts for these results, nor how the program's curriculum specifically defined these various terms and constructs. Similarly, when Stoddard et al. (2006) report that graduates who completed dual certification were reportedly better prepared for inclusive classrooms than traditional teacher education candidates, whether this was a result of the redesigned elementary program as a whole or the specific special education coursework that was added onto that program is not clear. When Corbett et al. (1998) report that graduates value the additional skills they acquired in their special education courses, how those skills may build on or interact with the skills they gained in their elementary education coursework was not explored. Interestingly, in the Utley (2009) outcome study, the instructional strategies that program graduates most often reported using were cooperative learning and graphic organizers, strategies that are often taught in elementary programs that do not include an extensive special education component.

It is certainly encouraging to see that teacher educators are often working together across general and special education to conduct these studies. In light of the willingness to engage in such joint inquiry, however, as noted above, more complex designs could be developed and more complex issues problematized around this important preservice program trend. Program evaluation may be the predominant mode of inquiry because it provides the field with what it really wants to know about programs. On the other hand, as Zeichner (2005) has noted about teacher education research more generally, reliance on program evaluation may represent a lack of time and resources to engage in a more complex, sophisticated study of teacher education.

Another gap is the way these studies address social identity markers in addition to disability. Several authors frame the concern for fostering collaborative teacher education not only in terms of disability, but also in terms of preparing teachers for the increasing cultural and linguistic diversity of students. For example, York-Barr and her colleagues (2004) often refer to the increasingly culturally and linguistically diverse population of students. Little in the description of the study, however, indicates that faculty or their students tackled this topic. Further, in York-Barr et al. (2004), diversity does not appear as one of the four areas of inquiry that formed the interview protocol, although faculty participants did speak of the value of "multiple perspectives" (p. 80) when teaming. Therefore, even when researchers express interest in issues of equity in terms of race, culture, and language in addition to disability, this body of research appears to be focused primarily on equity in terms of disability, suggesting a lack of attention to how diversity is actually embedded into the study of redesigned teacher education practice. Referencing multiple social markers of diversity, but choosing not to address them in any depth, represents a constraint rather than an affordance with respect to the opportunity program redesign offers. Only the curriculum analysis studies (Holland et al., 2008; Pugach & Blanton, 2012b) overtly mention diversity other than disability in any significant way. Specifically, Pugach and Blanton (2012b) examine how diversity is addressed in relationship to disability throughout the curriculum of the three programs they studied, eventually raising concerns about whether there could be a curricular imbalance that is tipped toward special education in relationship to other social identity markers.

Additionally, participant demographics are referenced inconsistently. In most of the co-teaching studies, for example, participants' gender is included, but only three make mention of participants' race or cultural background (i.e., Arndt & Liles, 2010; Griffin et. al., 2006; Kamens, 2007). When gender was described, no discussion about how gender dynamics came into play was included, even when a gender divide existed among participants (e.g., predominantly female special education preservice teachers and predominantly male preservice social studies teachers in the 2010 Arndt and Liles study). In the three articles that discuss faculty teaming, no mention of the faculty/participants' or researchers' race is made. When there is silence on the racial composition of participants, is it appropriate to infer, for example, that the majority of the participants were White women? Typically if the term "diverse" arose in these studies, it was usually to reference the diversity of academic or department backgrounds of the participants, or the diverse learning needs of the P–12 learners.

Intentionality as a Lens for Developing a Future Research Agenda

To better understand research on teacher education where general and special educators have worked together, it may be useful to think about the level of *intentionality* these studies represent. The initial assumption we made was that any study focused on rethinking the relationship between teacher educators in general and special education could be viewed as intentional in its attempt to try to shed light on some aspect of collaborative teacher education. However, as we read and analyzed the 30 studies reviewed here, it was difficult to ascertain the extent of intentionality on the parts of special and general education faculty beyond a very basic level of joint commitment and joint action.

In general, the research described here represents a group of rather modest studies, where faculty members may have identified opportunities in their programs to gather data for purposes of gaining some understandings about how their work might improve teacher education for inclusion. But beyond this broad goal, what the faculty intended to accomplish in their programs is often not discussed in any depth, nor is it clear how the authors came together to conceptualize and design the research. In addition, little evidence is provided regarding how faculty considered their own roles as part of the project of reshaping teacher education for inclusion. As a result, it seems reasonable to ask whether research on teacher education for inclusion could be conducted more intentionally such that it might offer a more consistent opportunity to address more complex questions about the structure and outcomes of teacher education for inclusion—questions that expand, rather than limit, the vision of what is possible. In other words, a commitment to joint action is a necessary but insufficient starting point for reframing how we think about the relative preparation of general and special educators.

For example, as noted above, faculty coming together to redesign a particular program component as a program revision goal is vastly different from faculty coming together to intentionally place that program component into a larger, more comprehensive program redesign effort. It would seem important at the outset of a study for researchers to clarify whether the long-term goal is to develop new practices that place special education content into an existing elementary or secondary teacher education program, based on the assumption that the central problem is the absence of existing special education content in the general teacher education curriculum (which appears to be the case in most of these studies), or whether, more intentionally, they are using the opportunity to fundamentally redesign the preservice curriculum.

Using intentionality as a lens, a more complex redesign goal might take into account, for example, the complicated intersections of disability, race, class, culture, and language in relationship to organizing classroom communities for maximum student learning. Few studies in this review appeared to interrogate the relationship between disability and other social markers of diversity in any depth. Related, it may be possible that program redesign efforts that have their origins in responding only to students who have disabilities, and remain focused on doing so, whether implicitly or explicitly, are fundamentally different enterprises than program redesigns that are conceptualized from the outset as significant and overarching reform opportunities within which the needs of students with disabilities are considered. In both cases the education of children who have disabilities continues to be a critical concern, but framed in different ways depending on the perspective.

Another set of questions that might emerge should researchers use intentionality as a prominent lens could be focused on the kinds of interactions and discourses that might take place when different configurations of faculty participate in the research. For example, does the participation of heterogeneous faculty with respect to race, class, and language change the way topics related to disability are taken up in methods classes? Would this make a difference is how program graduates rate their preparation?

The question of intentionality as a departure point is likewise critical because redesigning the base preparation of general education teachers has the potential to support redefining the roles of special education teachers (Pugach & Blanton, 2009). For example, in the Kamens and Casale-Giannola (2004) and Kamens (2007) studies, the researchers chose not to problematize the fact that the special education member of the co-teaching team was enrolled in a dual certification program. As role definition continues to be an ongoing challenge, studies of dual certification provide an opportunity for asking more complex questions about not only roles, but identity development of the next generation of teachers who come to their work having taken different pathways to gain special education expertise. From a different perspective, Arndt and Liles (2010) assumed that the problem of modeling co-teaching was primarily the responsibility of what occurred in university classes. In both the Arndt and Liles (2010) and the McHatton and Daniel (2008) studies, the researchers chose not to discuss the prospect of developing different configurations of clinical experience, configurations that might maximize the ability to draw on the best modeling of co-teaching by teachers in practice. With clinical experience at the forefront of reform (National Council for Accreditation of Teacher Education, 2010), pushing the boundaries of how we study the dynamics related to developing roles in practice settings seems timely. Further, in the Sobel et al. (2007) study, the assumption was made that graduates' roles upon completion of a dual certification program were not problematic. This contrasts with how Naraian (2010) documented the identity development of a graduate of an integrated dual certification program. Further, comparative research has not yet been undertaken, for example, on how graduates of the two dominant models of dual certification, those that completely merge the curricula of general and special education, and those where special education builds on redesigned general education in an integrated fashion (Blanton & Pugach, 2011), function in their practice in schools upon program completion.

In designing the studies that have been located for this review, teacher educators seem to have imagined a limited view of what is possible to inquire into as a means of moving the field ahead. The absence of focused intentionality limits rather than expands current discourse about and opportunities for new teacher education practices for inclusion. Further, the studies are limited in number and have widely varying purposes. Taken together, this makes it difficult for cumulative learning about teacher education for inclusion to take place.

Marker Variables as a Consideration for Moving Research on Teacher Education for Inclusion Forward?

When a field of research is relatively new, but is growing quickly, its rapid growth may outweigh the ability to learn by looking across studies. One way of improving the overall quality of research on collaborative teacher education is for scholars to come to some level of agreement about definitions and concepts that can be applied in the conduct of their research. This increases the potential for knowledge to be accumulated across study results to more efficiently inform the field about directions in which it might advance. The studies identified for this chapter were widely disparate, often depending on exit surveys and questionnaires with little documentation offered regarding their quality.

This review suggests that research on teacher education that brings together general and special education might be at just such a juncture—in need of common agreements about what descriptive information to include and what concepts to use in framing this area of research in order to create the potential for learning more about this phenomenon by looking across studies. To determine the possibility of such agreements, we revisit the concept of *marker variables* from the work of Barbara Keogh and her colleagues (Keogh, Major, Reid, Gándara, & Omori, 1978; Keogh, Major, Omori, Gándara, & Reid, 1980) several decades ago. The goal of that project was to create some level of common understanding of and comparability in sample characteristics across studies to advance more meaningful research on the definition of learning disabilities—that is, to move toward a identifying a more common population of study. Marker variables, Keogh and her colleagues argued, could serve as "empirical anchors" (1978, p. 10) to provide common understandings across many unique studies:

> It is important to note that the utilization of marker variables in no way restricts the initiative and originality of the individual researcher or program innovator. In addition to whatever else the individual investigator chooses to collect, marker variables provide information and a common frame of reference within which a comprehensive data base can be built. Rather than restricting investigation and innovation, the use of markers may well serve to encourage increasingly insightful individual work.
>
> *(1978, p. 7)*

It may be timely for research on collaborative teacher education to adapt the idea of marker variables to be reported in descriptions of research in order to benefit this area of study and to encourage researchers to think in more complex ways about the meaning of collaborative teacher education. Proposing such a set of marker variables at this point in time might serve two purposes. First, it could begin to foster discussion about some of the gaps in how the research is conceptualized. Asking researchers to think about variables that have been relatively absent to date might foster intentionality, or as Keogh and her colleagues (1978) note in the above quotation, encourage increasingly insightful work. Next, as researchers move into designs that are more consistently concerned with outcomes measures across program designs, greater comparability might be possible. A starting set of such marker variables might include, for example:

- Identifying researchers with regard to their primary work as being in either general or special education, and also whether general education faculty participants are from curriculum areas or foundational areas such as multicultural education.

- Identifying participants (preservice students and/or faculty) as being either in special or general education, or clearly defining new professional identity categories based on new program conceptions and designs, for example, developments based on identities related to dual certification.
- Identifying the demographics of researchers, faculty, and student participants.
- If applicable, identifying the type of redesigned program (*integrated* or *merged*), or at least a complete enough description of the programs underpinnings to enable the reader to understand the program's structure.
- Collecting data from both general and special education preservice students and/or faculty or from general education students and/or faculty when collaboration is a central dynamic in the research.
- Defining how the authors are using the terms "diversity" or "diverse learners" and/or "inclusive education" and the specific relationship in the research between diversity defined as disability and diversity related to social identities, including race, class, culture, language, and gender.
- Addressing the role definition of general education teachers as compared with special education teachers.
- Defining a study as program components change versus full program redesign.

Markers such as these can be viewed as a transitional stage in research on collaboration for inclusive practice. Some of the proposed markers necessitate locating researchers and participants within the current structures and definitions of special or general education, but the goal is to work toward redefinition within program reform, with the end goal of improving how teachers are prepared to work with students who have disabilities in the context of today's classrooms.

Conclusion

Program transformation that is at the heart of the meaning of collaborative teacher education (Pugach & Blanton, 2009) depends upon renegotiating the roles of general and special educators alike in an effort to raise the bar for the quality of work each practices. Research on preservice preparation for collaboration and inclusion, however, still seems to be in the early stages of development. Methodologically, dependent measures more often reflect what appear to be weakly constructed self-report and follow-up surveys in a program evaluation context, and less often attend to outcomes beyond the preservice program itself. Further, several studies reviewed here, including but not limited to those on program components, illustrate attempts, in various ways, to include special education content within existing programs. While the additive approach (e.g., adding components only to existing curricula) may allow scholars in teacher education to understand how specific content about special education can be learned and used during preservice preparation, it is less helpful in contributing to a robust understanding of how to frame the redesign of teacher education in ways that fundamentally alter the relationship between faculty and candidates in general and special education toward improving the practice of both. In other words, an unintended consequence of adopting an additive approach may be to defer, or avoid completely, the larger challenge of addressing how specific components contribute to the goal of redefining the roles of general and special education teachers to reach a more effective practice of inclusive education.

Research on collaborative teacher education has the potential to move the field toward transcending the long-standing divide between general and special education that, to date, has often functioned as an obstacle to reform. But in so doing, a different narrative should be emerging, one that takes into account, in fundamental ways, the needs of students who have disabilities, but that situates special education within the broad contours of diversity such that teachers are clear about the relationship between their views about the cultural, linguistic, and socioeconomic diversity of their learners and the specific actions they may need to take instructionally to help them learn. This analysis suggests that the distance between the traditional narrative that divides general and special education and any new narrative that must emerge to achieve long-standing success for students who have disabilities is still quite wide.

But altering the relationship is not an end in and of itself. Rather, designing research that intentionally takes these relationships into account provides the opportunity—as yet not fully mined—to ask substantially more complex questions about what it means to teach in diverse "general education" classroom, within which the needs of students who have disabilities should be a major consideration. The progress that has been made to date documents the field's ongoing interest, but also suggests a need for greater imagination in what that relationship could be.

References

Andrews, L. (2002). Preparing general education pre-service teachers for inclusion: Web-enhanced case-based instruction. *Journal of Special Education Technology*, *17*(3), 27–35.

Arndt, K., & Liles, J. (2010). Preservice teachers' perceptions of coteaching: A qualitative study. *Action in Teacher Education*, *32*(1), 15–25. doi:10.1080/01626620.2010.10463539

Blanton, L. P., & Pugach, M. C. (2011). Using a classification system to probe the meaning of dual licensure in general and special education. *Teacher Education and Special Education*, *34*, 219–234.

Blanton, L. P., Pugach, M. C., & Florian, L. (2011, April). *Preparing general education teachers to improve outcomes for students with disabilities*. Washington, DC: American Association of Colleges for Teacher Education and The National Center for Learning Disabilities. Retrieved from www.aacte.org/pdf/Publications/Reports_Studies/AACTE%20NCLD%20Policy%20Brief%20May%202011.pdf

Bradley, J. F., & Monda-Amaya, L. (2005). Conflict resolution: Preparing preservice special educators to work in collaborative settings. *Teacher Education and Special Education*, *28*, 171–184. doi:10.1177/088840640502800404

Brown, K. S., Welsh, L. A., Hill, K. H., & Cipko, J. P. (2008). The efficacy of embedding special education instruction in teacher preparation programs in the United States. *Teaching and Teacher Education*, *24*, 2087–2094. doi:10.1016/j.tate.2008.02.013

Corbett, N. L. Kilgore, K. L., & Sindelar, P. T. (1998). "Making sense" in a collaborative teacher education program: Lessons from Project PART students. *Teacher Education and Special Education*, *21*, 293–305. doi:10.1177/088840649802100405

Frey, T. J., Andres, D. K., McKeeman, L. A., & Lane, J. J. (2012). Collaboration by design: Integrating core pedagogical content and special education methods courses in a preservice secondary education program. *The Teacher Educator*, *47*, 45–66. doi:10.1080/08878730.2011.632473

Fullerton, A., Ruben, B. J., McBride, S., & Bert, S. (2011). Evaluation of a merged secondary and special education program. *Teacher Education Quarterly*, *38*(2), 45–60.

Geer, C., & Hamill, L. (2007). An online interdisciplinary discussion: Promoting collaboration between early childhood and special education preservice teachers. *Journal of Technology and Teacher Education*, *15*, 533–553.

Golder, G., Norwich, B., & Bayliss, P. (2005). Preparing teachers to teach pupils with special educational needs in more inclusive schools: Evaluating a PGCE development. *British Journal of Special Education*, *32*, 92–99. doi:10.1111/j.0952-3383.2005.00377.x

Goodnough, K., Osmond, P., Dibbon, D., Glassman, M., & Stevens, K. (2009). Exploring a triad model of student teaching: Pre-service teacher and cooperating teacher perceptions. *Teaching and Teacher Education*, *25*, 285–296. doi:10.1016/j.tate.2008.10.003

Griffin, C. C., Jones, H. A., & Kilgore, K. L. (2006). A qualitative study of student teachers' experiences with collaborative problem solving. *Teacher Education and Special Education*, *29*, 44–55. doi:10.1177/088840640602900106

Holland, D., Detgen, A., & Gutekunst, L. (2008). *Preparing elementary school teachers in the Southeast Region to work with students with disabilities* (Issues & Answers Report, REL 2008-No. 065). Washington, DC: U.S. Department of Education, Institute of Education Sciences, National Center for Education Evaluation and Regional Assistance, Regional Educational Laboratory Southeast. Retrieved from http://ies.ed.gov/ncee/edlabs

Jeffs, T., & Banister, S. (2006). Enhancing collaboration and skill acquisition through the use of technology. *Journal of Technology and Teacher Education*, *14*, 407–433.

Jenkins, A. A., Pateman, B., & Black, R. S. (2002). Partnerships for dual preparation in elementary, secondary, and special education programs. *Remedial and Special Education*, *23*, 359–371. doi:10.1177/07419325020230060601

Kamens, M. W. (2007). Learning about co-teaching: A collaborative student teaching experience for pre-service teachers. *Teacher Education and Special Education*, *30*, 155–166. doi:10.1177/088840640703000304

Kamens, M. W., & Casale-Giannola, D. (2004). The role of the student teacher in the co-taught classroom. *The Teacher Educator*, *40*, 17–32. doi:10.1080/08878730409555349

Keogh, B. K., Major, S. M., Omori, H., Gándara, P., & Reid, H. P. (1980). Proposed markers in learning disabilities research. *Journal of Abnormal Child Psychology, 8*, 21–31. doi: http://dx.doi.org/10.1007/BF00918159

Keogh, B. K., Major, S. M., Reid, P., Gándara, P., & Omori, H. (1978). Marker variables: A search for comparability and generalizability in the field of learning disabilities. *Learning Disability Quarterly, 1*, 5–11. doi: http://dx.doi.org/10.2307/1510932

Kurtts, S., Hibbard, K., & Levin, B. (2005). Collaborative online problem solving with preservice general education and special education teachers. *Journal of Technology and Teacher Education, 13*(3), 397–414.

Lesar, S., Benner, S. M., Habel, J., & Coleman, L. (1997). Preparing general education teachers for inclusive settings: A constructivist teacher education program. *Teacher Education and Special Education, 20*, 204–220.

Maheady, L., Jabot, M., Rey, J., & Michelli-Pendl, J. (2007). An early field-based experience and its impact on pre-service candidates' teaching practice and their pupils' outcomes. *Teacher Education and Special Education, 30*, 24–33. doi:10.1177/088840640703000103

McHatton, P. A., & Daniel, P. L. (2008). Co-teaching at the pre-service level: Special education majors collaborate with English education majors. *Teacher Education and Special Education, 31*, 118–131. doi:10.1177/088840640803100205

McKenzie, R. G. (2009). A national survey of pre-service preparation for collaboration. *Teacher Education and Special Education, 32*, 379–393. doi:10.1177/0888406409346241

Naraian, S. (2010). General, special, *and* inclusive: Refiguring professional identities in a collaboratively taught classroom. *Teaching and Teacher Education, 26*, 1677–1686. doi:10.1016/j.tate.2010.06.020

National Council for Accreditation of Teacher Education. (2010). *Transforming teacher education through clinical practice: A national strategy to prepare effective teachers.* Report of the Blue Ribbon Panel on Clinical Preparation and Partnerships on Improved Student Learning. Washington, DC: Author. Retrieved from http://www.ncate.org/Public/ResearchReports/NCATEInitiatives/BlueRibbonPanel/tabid/715/Default.aspx

Pugach, M. C., & Blanton, L. P. (2009). A framework for conducting research on collaborative teacher education. *Teaching and Teacher Education, 25*, 575–582. doi:10.1016/j.tate.2009.02.007

Pugach, M. C., & Blanton, L. P. (2012a). *Advancing conceptual thinking on the meaning of dual certification in general and special education: An autoethnographic approach.* Paper presented at the Annual Meeting, American Educational Research Association, Vancouver, Canada.

Pugach, M. C., & Blanton, L. P. (2012b). Enacting diversity in dual certification programs. *Journal of Teacher Education, 63*, 254–267. doi:10.1177/0022487112446970

Pugach, M. C., Blanton, L. P., & Correa, V. (2011). A historical perspective on the role of collaboration in teacher education reform: Making good on the promise of teaching all students. *Teacher Education and Special Education, 34*, 183–200. doi:10.1177/0888406411406141

Smith, G. J., & Edelen-Smith, P. J. (2002). The nature of the people: Renewing teacher education as a shared responsibility within colleges and schools of education. *Remedial and Special Education, 23*, 336–349.

Sobel, D. M., Iceman-Sands, D., & Basile, C. (2007). Merging general and special education teacher preparation programs to create an inclusive program for diverse learners. *The New Educator, 3*(3), 241–262. doi:10.1080/15476880701484113

Stoddard, K., Braun, B., Hewitt, M., & Koorland, M. A. (2006). Teacher for all children: A combined elementary and special education teacher preparation program and three year evaluation. *International Journal of Special Education, 21*, 87–97.

UNESCO. (1994). *The Salamanca Statement and Framework for Action on Special Needs.* Paris, France: UNESCO.

Utley, B. L. (2009). An analysis of the outcomes of a unified teacher preparation program. *Teacher Education and Special Education, 32*, 137–149. doi:10.1177/0888406409334204

Van Laarhoven, T. R., Munk, D. D., Lynch, K., Bosma, J., & Rouse, J. (2007). A model for preparing special and general preservice teachers for inclusive education. *Journal of Teacher Education, 58*, 440–455. doi:10.1177/0022487107306803

Van Laarhoven, T. R., Munk, D. D., Lynch, K., Wyland, S., Dorsh, N., Zurita, L., Bosma, J., & Rouse, J. (2006). Project ACCEPT: Preparing pre-service special and general educators for inclusive education. *Teacher Education and Special Education, 29*, 209–212. doi:10.1177/088840640602900401

Voltz, D. L. (2003). Collaborative infusion: An emerging approach to teacher preparation for inclusive education. *Action in Teacher Education, 25*(1), 5–13. doi:10.1080/01626620.2003.10463287

York-Barr, J., Bacharach, N., Salk, J., Hinz Frank, J., & Benick, B. (2004). Team teaching in teacher education: General and special education faculty experiences and perspectives. *Issues in Teacher Education, 13*(1), 73–94.

Young, K. S. (2011). Combined credential programs: Pedagogic, practical, and ideological concerns. *Teacher Education Quarterly, 38*(2), 7–26.

Zeichner, K. M. (2005). A research agenda for teacher education. In M. Cochran-Smith & K. M. Zeichner (Eds.), *Studying teacher education: The report of the AERA Panel on Research and Teacher Education* (pp. 737–759). Mahwah, NJ: Lawrence Erlbaum Associates.

10

Field Experiences and Instructional Pedagogies in Teacher Education

What We Know, Don't Know, and Must Learn Soon

Larry Maheady
SUNY BUFFALO STATE

Cynthia Smith
SUNY FREDONIA

Michael Jabot
SUNY FREDONIA

Things to Think About

- What effects do field experiences and instructional pedagogies have on prospective teachers' cognition, affect, and instructional practice?
- What impact can clinically rich field experiences have on prospective teacher knowledge, practice, dispositions, and student learning?
- How can we understand the effects of teacher preparation on pupil learning without fully understanding teaching practice and its relationship to student learning?
- What roles, if any, might evidence-based practices play in the design, implementation, and evaluation of clinically rich teaching experiences?
- Which instructional pedagogies lend themselves most readily to the needs of P–12 students and how might we use them to meet important student needs?
- What roles can hot instructional technologies play in linking evidence-based teaching practices to important pupil outcomes?

Too many American children are plagued by adverse educational outcomes (Duncan, 2009). Almost one third of students drop out or fail to complete school on time and only 60% of African-American and Latino pupils graduate when expected. In many large cities, half or more low-income teens drop out of school. Children who attend our neediest schools are more likely to have less-qualified teachers and over the next decade more than one million teachers will retire and be replaced by 1.6 million new teachers. Secretary of Education Duncan argued that this situation poses both an enormous challenge and extraordinary opportunity for our educational system; an opportunity to transform public education and deliver an excellent education for all children (U.S. Department of Education, 2011).

Unacceptable educational outcomes and inequities, however, are not new. Indeed, countless others have lamented our academic decline, persistent achievement gaps, and increases in disruptive and destructive student behavior (Abell Foundation, 2001; Ballou & Podgursky, 2000; Carnine, 2000; Coalition for Evidence-Based Educational Policy, 2002; U.S. Department of Education, 2002; Walker, Ramsey, & Gresham, 2003–2004). Educators were warned as well that persistent educational failure may lead ultimately to societal questioning of teacher education's efficacy and its sole right to prepare teachers (Greenwood & Maheady, 1997). Secretary Duncan (2009) commented soberly on this situation by noting that 62% of recent teacher education graduates do not feel adequately prepared to work in 21st century classrooms. He cited specific shortcomings in classroom and behavior management, working with high needs students, and using data to improve instruction and student learning. A clear gap exists between the educational realities of P–12 schools and preparation efforts in many teacher education programs (Cibulka, 2009).

To address the gap between how teachers are prepared and what P–12 schools need, the National Council for Accreditation of Teacher Education's (NCATE) Blue Ribbon Panel on Clinical Preparation and Partnerships for Improved Student Learning (NCATE, 2010) argued that teacher preparation in the United States must be "turned upside down" (p. ii). They recommended an immediate and substantive shift from an emphasis on academic preparation and coursework linked loosely to school-based experiences to "programs that are fully grounded in clinical practice and interwoven with academic content and professional courses" (p. ii). The proposed *clinically based* approach places instructional practice and student learning at the center of teaching preparation and requires more extensive partnerships with P–12 schools. The proposal also rekindles attention around the potential roles that field experiences and instructional pedagogies (e.g., microteaching, computer simulations, video technology and hypermedia, case studies, portfolios, and practitioner research) can play in teacher preparation, and how teacher educators might deliver, monitor, and staff such clinically rich programs. This chapter contributes to the dialogue by: (a) summarizing and analyzing research on field experiences and instructional pedagogies, (b) describing the state of the art regarding extant research efforts, (c) identifying controversies and trends in the use of these instructional methodologies, and (d) discussing implications and recommendations for future research and practice. The chapter also examines the potential role that evidence-based practices may play in shaping teacher educators' responsiveness to the clinically rich reform agenda.

We offer a brief historical perspective on the roles of field experiences and instructional pedagogies in teacher education followed by an examination of the research on such practices. Research findings are analyzed in terms of their credibility, comprehensiveness, and utility. The state of the art on field experience-related research is discussed in terms of what is known and unknown and particular attention is focused on controversies, trends, and implications for future research and practice. Hopefully, the chapter can provide direction for future inquiry around clinically based programs in general and special education.

The following caveats are offered related to our discussion. First, there are other important facets of clinically rich programming that are beyond the scope of this chapter (e.g., developing and sustaining meaningful partnerships with schools, revamping curricula, incentives, and staffing patterns in higher education and P–12 schools, improving candidate recruitment, selection, and retention practices, developing and refining system- and state-wide data collection procedures, and improving induction services). Second, our analyses, interpretations, and discussion are framed by the experiences of a mathematics, a science, and a special educator who have prepared preservice and in-service general education teachers in an *integrated* preparation program (Blanton, Pugach, & Florian, 2011) for the past two decades (Maheady, Harper, Karnes, & Mallette, 1999; Maheady, Harper, Mallette, & Karnes, 1993; Maheady, Jabot, Rey, & Michielli-Pendl, 2007). SUNY-Fredonia, has never had separate general and special education programs; instead, special education faculty is included fully in the general education curriculum. Third, the chapter focuses primarily on the impact that preparation programs have on teaching practice and pupil learning, the center-pieces of the Blue Ribbon Panel's clinically rich reform agenda (NCATE, 2010). This emphasis is not intended to diminish the important roles that cognitive (e.g., thoughts, reasoning, and professional reflections), affective (e.g., beliefs, attitudes, and predispositions), contextual (e.g., cooperating teacher and supervisor characteristics, length and nature of placements, and types of settings and students), and sociological (e.g., socialization into the profession) variables play in teacher development, but rather to highlight areas that have received insufficient attention in extant teacher education research (Goe & Coggshall, 2007; Wilson, Floden, & Ferrini-Mundy, 2002). Fourth, the research summary is illustrative rather than comprehensive. Readers are referred to relevant literature reviews on selected topics throughout the document.

Nature of Field Experiences and Instructional Pedagogies in Teacher Education

Field experiences have been integral components of general and special education preparation programs for a very long time (Hixon & So, 2009; McIntyre, Byrd, & Foxx, 1996; NCATE, 2010). They are planned opportunities for prospective teachers to work with real students, teachers, and curriculum in natural settings (Huling-Austin, 1992). Much like medical residencies, field experiences provide future teachers with opportunities to play active participatory roles in their professional development. The culminating field experience in most teacher preparation programs is student teaching during which prospective educators gradually assume total instructional responsibility under the joint supervision of cooperating teachers and university supervisors. The rationale for field experience in teacher education emanated from the work of John Dewey (1938), who pioneered the progressive movement and emphasized learner-centered instruction. Zeichner (1985) noted that the inclusion of field experiences in teacher education makes sense because of their high degree of face validity. Individuals who are planning to become teachers *should* have first-hand experiences in classrooms before they assume full instructional responsibility. Zeichner argued further, however, that while some form of applied experience in classrooms is necessary and desirable, the *quality* of such experiences is more important.

More recently, Zeichner and Conklin (2008) noted that field experiences in teacher education programs vary substantially along a number of important dimensions. Some programs, for instance, require one-semester student teaching experiences, while others offer full-year internships. In some programs, student teaching or internships are completed as "teachers of record" while in others they are not. Some preparation programs intersperse applied teaching experiences throughout their curriculum while others require only a capstone experience. Teacher education programs also vary in how closely connected field experiences are with required coursework (e.g., methods classes), program visions and goals, and P–12 school needs. Finally, programs differ in the nature and amount of instructional responsibilities that are assigned to prospective teachers. Programs can vary, for example, in terms of the explicitness of expectations, clarity of decision-making responsibilities (e.g., university only or university and P–12 schools), and the extent to which subsequent field experience build upon one another (Zeichner & Conklin, 2008). The Blue Ribbon Panel (NCATE, 2010) concluded recently that, "clinical preparation is poorly defined and inadequately supported" (p. 4) in too many contemporary teacher education programs.

In addition to field experiences, teacher educators use a variety of instructional pedagogies to prepare prospective teachers for the classroom. Grossman (2005) described six common pedagogical methodologies used in teacher education: (a) microteaching, (b) computer simulations, (c) video technology and hypermedia, (d) case methods, (e) portfolios, and (f) practitioner research. Table 10.1 summarizes

Table 10.1 Research Methods and Findings Derived From Six Instructional Pedagogies in Review by Grossman

Instructional Pedagogy	*Number of Studies*	*Common Research Methods*	*Important Findings*
Microteaching	N=4	Experimental vs. control groups with random assignment; quasi-experimental designs, no random assignment	Experimental group placed greater value on supervision; feedback helped candidates learn to teach; no significant differences between groups on knowledge of teaching measure, direct observations, and/or tests of reflection; training in instructional clarity produced higher ratings on clarity measures; experimental teachers expressed higher satisfaction.
Computer simulations	N=4	Quasi-experimental design, no random assignment; experimental study; mixed methods	Different kinds of learners benefitted from different instructional methods; working alone and textual presentations helped those with higher formal reasoning skills; experimental subjects showed significantly higher knowledge of concepts and self-efficacy; simulations supported student evaluation and modification of ideas and facilitated model building; improved acquisition and maintenance of specific teaching skills, and positive social validity assessments.
Video technology and hypermedia	N=9	Quasi-experimental, no random assignment and/or no control group; qualitative studies; mixed methods	Experimental subjects scored higher than controls on four of five teaching competences; students who learned about cooperative learning via videodisc performed better on measures of content knowledge; over one third of discussion topics were adopted, changed, or created by discussing video cases; technology was viewed favorably by participants; improved content knowledge and displays of greater pupil involvement and on task behavior in classrooms.
Case studies	N=6	Qualitative studies	Prospective teachers' entering beliefs were resistant to change through case interpretation; candidates could do five elements of reasoning; improved critical reflection; greater reflection and meta-cognition; increased candidates reception to instruction; changes in teacher thinking.
Teacher portfolios	N=5	Qualitative research; surveys and interviews; mixed methods	Portfolios enhanced reflection and candidate abilities to link theory and practice; most candidates felt that tasks were valuable but for different reasons; preservice teachers who used portfolios were more likely to reflect about content and teaching; two thirds of candidates felt they learned from portfolios and one third reported frustrations with their use.
Practitioner research	N=8	Qualitative studies; interpretative case studies	Placing student teachers with reform-minded teachers was effective way to foster reform-mindedness; action research helped candidates become more aware of their practice, but did not foster critical reflection; student teachers placed with teacher-researchers felt more welcomed and supported; student teachers used action research to pursue their pedagogical interests.

the number of empirical studies completed on each approach, common methodologies, and brief synopses of findings as summarized by Grossman (2005).

Evolution of Research on Field Experiences and Instructional Pedagogies in Teacher Education

Clift and Brady (2005), Grossman (2005), and Pugach (2005) provide in-depth descriptions of research on field experiences and instructional pedagogies in general and special education. These authors note that research in these areas has evolved considerably over the years from a search for discrete, observable, and measurable teaching behaviors that could impact student learning to more recent investigations of the complex interactions among teacher thinking, intention, belief, attitudes, and the social and institutional contexts in which they occur. These conceptual and empirical changes coincided with the movement from behavioral to cognitive perspectives on teaching and learning and resulted in fewer empirical studies that examined *directly* the impact of field experiences and instructional pedagogies on teaching practice and even fewer that measured effects on pupil learning.

In an early review of field experience research, Guyton and McIntyre (1990) reported that, in most teacher preparation programs, student teaching was rarely related to program goals, and that there was insufficient support for supervision and collaboration among higher education and school-based partners. The authors noted as well that research focused more on what different individuals (student teachers, cooperating teachers, and supervisors) did to fulfill their professional roles than what they learned from field experiences. In a later review, McIntyre et al. (1996) suggested that as a result of earlier research, progress was made in clearly defining program goals and aligning field experiences with curricular purposes. The authors noted, however, that insufficient quantitative and qualitative data existed to determine if teacher educators were, in fact, preparing more thoughtful reflective teachers. Most of the empirical studies McIntyre et al. reviewed adopted a cognitive psychological framework and examined teacher beliefs and intentions. McIntyre et al. concluded that the instruction provided within most teacher education programs was influenced by prospective teachers' prior and current beliefs and that these beliefs, in turn, helped to shape the instruction provided within their preparation programs.

In a subsequent literature review, Wideen, Mayer-Smith, and Moon (1998) commented further on teacher beliefs and their interactions with field experiences and related coursework. The authors reported that prospective teachers' beliefs were often resistant to practices advocated by teacher educators because the practices were incompatible with the teachers' beliefs. Wideen et al. noted further that some evidence indicated that teacher beliefs do change, although not always in ways deemed desirable by researchers and/or practitioners. The authors criticized those who conducted programmatic research in this area for assuming that knowledge alone would lead to desirable changes in teaching behavior and urged researchers to adopt an ecological perspective for understanding how individuals, institutions, programs, and ideas were interrelated in field experience research. In two subsequent reviews, Munby, Russell, and Martin (2001) and Sleeter (2001) summarized the inherent complexities of teacher knowledge and practice and warned against descriptions that ignored or diminished that complexity. Interestingly, Sleeter also noted that ongoing debates in teacher education about the limitations of positivism may have produced "generations of scholars who have not learned to use tools of positivist research such as gathering quantitative data" (p. 240). She went on to recommend more longitudinal studies that tracked prospective teachers through teacher education programs and into actual classroom teaching.

More recently, Clift and Brady (2005) summarized findings from 105 empirical studies on field experiences and related coursework. They reiterated the importance of teacher beliefs and argued that field experiences can impact prospective teachers' thoughts about instruction and in some cases even their actual teaching practice. Clift and Brady noted, however, that there were still only a few studies that examined the impact of student teaching into initial years of teaching and almost none that were conducted jointly by university researchers and classroom teachers. They reported that qualitative methods (e.g., case studies involving a small number of participants) dominated the literature and as such any causal claims and/or generalizations of findings were quite limited. The quantitative studies that were cited (e.g., Bowman & McCormick, 2000; Dinkelman, 2000; Gill & Hove, 2000; Knight, Wiseman, & Cooner, 2000; Worthy & Patterson, 2001) typically examined the effects of field experiences on immediate instructional practice, however, virtually none evaluated the long-term impact on practice and/or pupil learning.

In contrast to research on field experiences, more quantitative (e.g., quasi-experimental and experimental designs) and mixed methods studies have appeared in the instructional pedagogies literature (Grossman, 2005). The range of empirical methods and outcomes associated with the use of all six instructional pedagogies is depicted in Table 10.1. As seen, studies ranged from surveys to quasi-experimental and experimental investigations of select instructional strategies, to qualitative studies of others' and one's own teaching practice. Grossman reported that most research on microteaching was completed in the 1960s and 1970s and was reviewed extensively elsewhere (e.g., Copeland, 1982; MacLeod, 1987; McIntyre et al., 1996; Vare, 1994; Wilkinson, 1996; Winitzky & Arends, 1991). Early research on microteaching focused on the development of discrete teaching skills primarily through the use of videotape analysis and the provision of feedback. Grossman concluded that research on microteaching provided a compelling example of both the promise and pitfalls of research on instructional pedagogies. On the positive side, microteaching research provided the closest approximation to an extended line of programmatic research on instructional pedagogies. Investigators conducted multiple studies from different theoretical perspectives (behavioral and cognitive), attempted to tease out the effects of subject matter, grade levels, types of feedback and models on selected outcomes, and engaged in some well-controlled comparative studies (e.g., Winitzky & Arends, 1991). At the same time, most microteaching research was atheoretical, underrepresented in the peer-reviewed literature, and generally lacking in definitive conclusions. As MacLeod (1987) noted, "despite the enormity of the research endeavour, there are few definite conclusions which can be drawn about the effects and effectiveness of microteaching" (p. 538).

Research on computer simulations includes experimental, quasi-experimental, and mixed methods designs and focuses primarily on teaching preservice teachers to use specific skills that are related to effective teaching (e.g., giving feedback, instructional pacing, and managing classroom disruptions). Two studies indicated that computer simulations can help prospective teachers develop targeted skills within the simulations; however, neither study examined teaching practice in actual classroom settings (Strang, Badt, & Kaufmann, 1987; Strang, Landrum, & Lynch, 1989). Like microteaching studies, computer simulations focused more on teaching behavior, although cognitive outcomes are assessed in more recent investigations (Grossman, 2005).

Empirical findings on the use of video technology and hypermedia were derived from qualitative, quasi-experimental, and mixed methods research designs. For the most part, these studies focused more on cognitive (e.g., reasoning, thinking, and professional reflections) than behavioral outcomes. A number of studies indicated that preservice teachers were positive about the use of video technology and hypermedia materials (e.g., Daniel, 1996; Lambdin, Duffy, & Moore, 1997), and that viewing videotapes can improve their understanding of teaching strategies and instructional concepts (e.g., Carlson & Falk, 1989, 1990; Overbaugh, 1995). While the data suggest that videotapes can be as effective as other instructional methods (e.g., role plays, live observation, or written materials) in helping prospective teachers' understand instructional approaches, there was no evidence that they impacted actual teaching practices in classroom settings. Grossman (2005) reported as well that video technology research lacks a strong theoretical framework, is relatively silent on the features of video materials that contribute to learning, and/or has not examined what prospective teachers learn from watching videos of their own practice, a somewhat surprising outcome given current increases in the use of teaching videos for certification and licensure.

Case methods research has focused almost exclusively on improving preservice teachers' ability to reason and reflect on teaching and have utilized qualitative research methods. According to Grossman, despite the enthusiasm for case methods, there is relatively little empirical research on its uses in teacher education. Like microteaching, many case methods studies are not included in the peer-reviewed literature and there appears to be little evidence that they, in fact, improve preservice teachers' reasoning skills and there is no evidence that case-based pedagogy affects their actual teaching practice.

The use of teacher portfolios appeared about the same time as case-based pedagogy and despite the numerous claims made about the potential benefits of this methodology, there have been few systematic studies regarding their use for either assessment or developmental purposes (Grossman, 2005; Zeichner & Wray, 2001). For the most part, researchers studied portfolio usage in their own educational settings and focused attention on helping prospective teachers reflect on their practice and assess their own learning. Despite the challenges of using portfolios, most preservice teachers saw value in the process of developing them. Again, there were no studies that indicated that portfolio development and/or use impacted prospective teachers' practice or pupil learning.

Critical Analysis of the Literature

High-quality research, albeit qualitative or quantitative, is designed to rule out alternative explanations for a study's results (Odom et al., 2005). In general, the higher the quality of research methodology, the more confidence practitioners and researchers can place in study findings. Researchers have delineated quality indicators for both quantitative (i.e., experimental, quasi-experimental, and correlational designs) (Gersten et al., 2005; Horner et al., 2005; Thompson, Diamond, McWilliam, Snyder, & Snyder, 2005) and qualitative research (e.g., case studies, action research, narrative research, content, conversational and discourse analyses, and interpretive research) (Brantlinger, Jimenez, Klingner, Pugach, & Richardson, 2005) methodologies. These indicators were used as guidelines for assessing the credibility, comprehensiveness, and potential utility of extant research on field experiences and instructional pedagogies.

Credibility speaks to the believability or trustworthiness of research findings and is often linked to the rigor with which studies are conceptualized, implemented, evaluated, and interpreted. Quantitative studies typically report measures of validity and reliability to establish credibility, while qualitative research often employ strategies such as triangulation, disconfirming evidence, member checks, external auditors, and prolonged field engagement to produce trustworthy outcomes (Brantlinger et al., 2005). It is safe to say that most, if not all, literature reviews on field experiences and instructional pedagogies indicate that rigor is lacking in too many empirical studies. This lack of rigor is attributed to the relative youth of research endeavors in these domains, the complexity and multidimensional nature of teaching and learning, and the challenges inherent in working in applied educational settings.

Clift and Brady (2005) note, for example, that many studies conducted on field experiences often lack well-developed theoretical frameworks for studying their short- and long-term impact on teaching practice and pupil learning. There is also an absence of quantitative analyses of the relationships among teacher education programs, teaching practice, and pupil learning. More troubling is the scarcity of information on participants, settings, field experience, and pedagogical activities, as well as data collection and analysis procedures. According to Clift and Brady, descriptions of empirical procedures are, "often so sparse that repeating the studies would be impossible" (p. 333). There is also an overreliance on conclusions generated from short-term case studies that are often conducted within the confines of the researchers' institutions.

Grossman (2005) noted similar shortcomings among empirical studies on instructional pedagogies. Efforts to make claims about particular pedagogical approaches, for example, are hampered by a general lack of information on instructional context (e.g., little information on teaching practices that surrounded use of case methods and portfolios, time allotted to the use of particular pedagogies, and/or relationships among teachers and pupils in educational settings), a failure to make research methods explicit (e.g., which data were collected, relationships between researchers and students, and manner in which data were analyzed), and a lack of a common tradition for conceptualizing and assessing study outcomes. Of particular importance, is Grossman's conclusion that few, if any, empirical studies investigated the difficult problem of the relationships among instructional pedagogies, teaching practice, and pupil learning (Wilson et al., 2002). The fact that teaching practice and pupil learning are the *least studied* outcomes raises serious questions regarding the credibility of assertions regarding their use in teacher education.

Comprehensiveness refers to the extent to which research on field experiences and instructional pedagogies address important issues across diverse populations, context, and outcomes impacted by those findings. For example, how representative are research questions, study participants and settings, research methodologies, and empirical outcomes of the issues and concerns that confront practitioners, teacher educators, and educational researchers? A perusal of both literatures suggests wide variations in representation across constituencies, topics, and outcomes. These variations range from large numbers of qualitative studies to very few and mostly dated quantitative investigations. High degrees of visibility are found for preservice educators and their college instructors, but there are considerably fewer practicing teachers and pupils. Empirical outcomes are predominantly cognitive and affective in nature (e.g., teacher thinking, beliefs, and reflections) and impact on teaching practice and student learning is almost nonexistent.

Regarding participants in research on field experiences, Clift and Brady (2005) report that most subjects are often described simply as male or female, undergraduate or graduate, and elementary or secondary. Teacher educators, cooperating teachers, and educational researcher descriptions are even more limited with occasional references to novice or experienced. Perhaps more troubling is the finding that pupils are rarely, if ever, mentioned no less described in the field-experience literature. Research questions focusing on teacher cognition and affect are well-represented and qualitative studies (e.g., participatory observations, self-studies, and focused interviews) are clearly the designs of choice. There is an absence of empirical studies that directly addressed issues of teaching practice and pupil learning.

Grossman (2005) reports similar and varying levels of comprehensiveness among studies conducted on the six instructional pedagogies. In general, these studies included more quantitative and mixed methods investigations, larger sample sizes, and a broader array of outcome measures, including more direct measures of teaching practice (e.g., direct observations and pupil work samples) and pupil learning (e.g., curriculum-embedded and standardized achievement measures) than field-experience studies. Study interpretations are hampered, however, by insufficient information on study participants and context, empirical methods, and data collection and analysis procedures. The author recommended increasing the representativeness of practitioners and P–12 students in future studies, making research methods more explicit, and collecting outcomes that reflected cognitive, affective, and behavioral outcomes.

Utility refers to the usefulness or applicability of research findings for different "audiences." In the case of research on field experiences and instructional pedagogies, there are numerous potential audiences, including but not limited to prospective and practicing teachers, teacher educators, educational researchers, university supervisors, P–12 administrators, and policy makers. The question here is, to what extent can this diverse range of educational professionals apply the available research on field experiences and instructional pedagogies? Obviously, utility is impacted to varying degrees by both the credibility and comprehensiveness of existing findings. Overall applicability, therefore, is affected adversely by the generalized lack of rigor and representativeness discussed previously. It appears as well that the primary audiences for research on field experiences and instructional pedagogies are educational researchers and teacher educators, particularly those who hold cognitive perspectives and use qualitative research methods. There does not seem to be much applicability, however, for those with specific interests in teaching practice, pupil learning, and how to impact both outcomes.

Clift and Brady's (2005) review on field experiences provides useful information, for example, for teacher educators who are interested in assessing and impacting prospective teachers' thinking, beliefs, and professional reasoning and decision-making skills. They are provided with a number of theoretical perspectives and assessment procedures for examining their candidates' knowledge, beliefs, and attitudes, as well as a few different methodologies for studying these outcomes. Qualitative researchers as well are exposed to a variety of measures and methods for studying these variables and are provided with some potentially fruitful recommendations for future research in these areas. In contrast, there is very little applicable information for P–12 administrators, policy makers, and educational researchers who are interested in studying and impacting teaching practice and pupil learning. The complete absence of attention to both variables speaks volumes about their perceived importance in extant research.

Grossman's (2005) review on instructional pedagogies also provides useful information for teacher educators and educational researchers, particularly those interested in cognitive and affective outcomes. The utility of this information seems to vary as well across the six instructional pedagogies. For instance, quasi-experimental and experimental studies conducted on microteaching, video technologies, and computer simulations examine the impact of these technologies on measures of teaching practice and student learning, albeit to insufficient degrees. As such, practitioners and those interested in using these technologies to impact teaching practice and pupil achievement can apply some of those findings. Teacher educators and educational researchers interested in cognitive and affective outcomes can find useful information to inform both their practice and research. Once more, there does not appear to be many definitive findings that are particularly relevant for P–12 administrators and educational policy makers.

State of the Art on Research on Field Experiences and Instructional Pedagogies

There are clearly more unanswered than answered questions regarding the use of field experiences and instructional pedagogies in teacher education. These questions are conceptual, theoretical, and methodological in nature and require significantly more attention than can be provided here. Instead, we summarize what is known and unknown about field experiences and instructional pedagogies, highlight some of the more salient controversies and trends in the field, and provide a few general guidelines for future research and practice. Knowledge related to field experiences and instructional pedagogies is discussed in terms of its applicability to research and practice.

What We Know

At the level of practice, we know that field experiences in general and student teaching in particular can be found in most teacher education programs, yet there appears to be little consistency in the nature and function of these experiences from institution to institution. This variability in purpose and implementation, in turn, makes it difficult to consider field experiences as common forms of practice. We also know that some instructional pedagogies (e.g., video technology, case studies, and portfolios) are used more often than others (i.e., microteaching and practitioner research) in contemporary programs and that the former are well-represented at our institution. Again, there appears to be variability in how instructional pedagogies are being used (e.g., to inform cognition, beliefs, and/or practice) and even less consistency in how their use is being assessed. Finally, we know that practice in teacher education programs like our own is influenced significantly by current reform movements, the most notable of which calls for a clinically rich reform agenda (Cibulka, 2009; NCATE, 2010). Such reform efforts will require extensive reconceptualization and restructuring at the program level and more substantive empirical knowledge about the impact of field experiences and instructional pedagogies on teaching practice and student learning.

Current research suggests that field experiences *can* impact teacher thinking, beliefs, and reflections in ways that are deemed positive, although these changes are not always predictable or easy to achieve.

We know as well, however, that a number of research studies in both domains lack empirical rigor and representativeness which, in turn, limits their utility. We also know that field experiences in general and some instructional pedagogies (e.g., computer simulations, video technology, and portfolios) are viewed quite favorably by prospective and cooperating teachers, and that field experiences in particular are used to socialize educators into the profession. Finally, we know that research on field experiences and instructional pedagogies is relatively silent with regard to impact on teaching practice and student learning. While teacher cognition and affect obviously influence what candidates do in classrooms, how they do so is not clearly articulated nor is it linked directly to student learning (Goe & Coggshall, 2007; Shulman, 2002; Wilson et al., 2002).

What We Don't Know

There is obviously much we don't know about the use of field experiences and instructional pedagogies in teacher education. At the level of practice, we have insufficient information, for example, on how to select, design, implement and evaluate "high-quality" field experiences. While educators agree that prospective teachers should only be assigned to high-quality placements, there are few documented criteria for identifying such placements. Similar questions remain about the nature of field-based experiences, practices for assessing candidate and pupil learning, and overall program evaluation. We also don't know what impact, if any, field experiences and instructional pedagogies have on candidates' teaching practice and pupil learning. A decade ago, Wilson et al. (2002) concluded that valid methodologically rigorous research that linked the content and structure of teacher preparation programs to student outcomes was scant, inconclusive, and aggregated at a level that was not particularly useful. It does not appear that much has changed in the ensuing decade. The generalized failure to measure teaching practice makes it virtually impossible to determine the impact of field experiences and instructional pedagogies on pupil learning (Goe & Coggshall, 2007).

Among the many other unanswered questions facing teacher educators and researchers alike are: (a) Which teaching practices, if any, produce improved pupil outcomes? (b) How might these practices be taught so that prospective teachers can use them as intended? (c) What types of learning outcomes should be assessed and how might they be captured and analyzed in an effective, efficient, and socially acceptable manner? (d) What kinds of knowledge and dispositions must prospective teachers possess to use those practices well? (e) How might we prepare prospective teachers to choose practices that promote positive student outcomes over those that fail to do so? and (f) To what extent can teaching practices be adapted to meet diverse students' needs and setting demands? The questions among many others provide a robust agenda for future educational research.

Controversies and Trends

There are a myriad of controversies surrounding the use of field experiences and instructional pedagogies in teacher education. These controversies include conceptual (e.g., what is the nature of teaching and learning, what roles do teacher educators play in teacher preparation, and what roles can teacher education play in resolving inequitable educational outcomes) and methodological (e.g., which research questions are most important to address, how to design applied studies to test researchers' hypotheses and that rule out alternative explanations, and how to disseminate findings in ways that improve practice for teachers and pupils) issues that represent long-standing disagreements in education, psychology, and related fields and which cannot be resolved here. Our discussion, therefore, highlights two particular controversies and three important trends in the use of field experiences and instructional pedagogies.

Perhaps the most salient controversy confronting teacher educators and educational researchers is how to conceptualize the basic nature of teaching and learning in our respective disciplines. As reiterated often in the literature, psychology and education moved away from behavioral explanations for human learning because they were perceived as too simplistic and mechanistic to address the complexity of teaching and learning. As a result, researchers stopped examining teaching practice and pupil learning as important outcomes and instead focused on teacher thinking, beliefs, and reflections. Shulman (2002) cautioned, however, that "to study teaching without reference to students was unethical self-indulgence" (p. 251). He suggested further that the shift to cognitive and affective outcomes may have made the study of teaching and learning more complicated than it needed to be. The hallmark of scientific progress in most disciplines, for example, is increased simplification not complication. Moreover, if research findings are to be disseminated to practitioners and policy makers, then they must be both simple and clearly connected to easily understood indicators of student achievement. Shulman (2002) argued as well that there was a moral message in early process–product research; that our bottom-line obligation as teachers and teacher educators was to pupils and their learning. A failure to address issues of teaching practice and pupil learning would not be a constructive professional response in an era of increased accountability and scrutiny for teacher education.

A second related controversy is how to respond to the fundamental mismatch that exists between the goals of the clinically rich reform agenda and the nature of research and practice in teacher education. While NCATE's Blue Ribbon Panel (2010) placed teaching practice and student learning at the center of the reform agenda, there is little research that examines the relationship between teacher preparation practices and pupil learning. It is highly unlikely that researchers will learn more about influencing teacher preparation, practice, and/or learning without studying them more directly and persistently. Elevating improved student learning to the forefront of research on field experiences and instructional pedagogies is a necessary first step in this regard. It is equally clear, however, that research methodologies must expand beyond those that describe, explain, interpret, and/or make predictions about human behavior. Models that can actually change behavior in a systematic and rigorous manner would be particularly welcome in this regard.

There are also at least three important trends that may shape the roles that field experiences and instructional practices play in teacher education: (a) clinically rich reform movement, (b) mandated use of scientifically or evidence-based instructional practices, and (c) technological advances in professional development. The emergence of the clinically rich reform agenda provides a golden opportunity for teacher educators and educational researchers to refocus their attention on improving teaching practice and pupil learning. The Blue Ribbon Panel outlined 10 key principles to follow when designing more effective clinically based experiences. These principles include: (a) making P–12 student learning the focal point for designing, implementing, and evaluating clinically based programs, (b) integrating clinical experiences throughout every facet of the program in a dynamic way, (c) using data to monitor teacher candidate and student progress in clinical experiences, (d) preparing teachers who are experts in content and how to teach it effectively, (e) providing ample opportunities for feedback on candidate and pupil performance in a collaborative learning culture, (f) selecting and preparing clinical instructors rigorously to ensure that they model effective practices, (g) developing intensive clinical-based experiences that are structured, staffed, and financed to support candidate learning and student achievement, (h) using state-of-the-art technologies to promote enhanced productivity, greater efficiency, and collaborations through learning communities, (i) developing a rigorous research and development agenda and using data to support continuous program improvement, and (j) creating and/or strengthening strategic partnerships with P–12 schools. These principles provide clear directions for future research and practice on field experiences and instructional pedagogies.

A second important trend in teacher education involves the use of scientifically or evidenced-based practices (see for example, Cook, 2011; Cook & Cook, 2010; Cook, Landrum, Tankersley, & Kauffman, 2003; Detrich, Keyworth, & States, 2008) in education. While this movement appears to be more visible in special than general education, it has been reflected clearly in federal education policies (e.g., No Child Left Behind, 2002; Individuals with Disabilities Education Improvement Act, 2004), professional ethics codes (e.g., American Psychological Association, Council for Exceptional Children, and National Association of School Psychologists), and critiques of teacher education research and practice (e.g., Carnine, 2000; Walker, 2004). Detrich et al. (2008) define evidence-based practices as a decision-making process that emphasizes the use of data to guide decisions about which teaching practices to select and use and how to evaluate the effects of any interventions on student learning. Ultimately, the evidence-based practice movement is about consumer protection; it assumes that evidence-based practices are more likely to improve pupil learning than nonevidence-based approaches, and that they should be selected and used whenever possible, particularly with our most vulnerable learners (e.g., students with special needs, culturally and linguistically diverse pupils, and those from poverty, abuse, or neglect environments).

Even if selected practices are identified as "evidence-based," there are no guarantees that they will have similar effects when practitioners apply them in more naturalistic settings. (Issues related to generalizing research from laboratory to applied settings have been discussed in length in the professional literature; see for example, Chorpita, 2003; Detrich et al., 2008; Kazdin, 2008.) It may be more important, therefore, to monitor and evaluate the effects of evidence-based practices when they are applied in naturalistic settings; a process referred to as "practice-based evidence" (Detrich et al., 2008). Practice-based evidence studies appear to be compatible with some existing instructional pedagogies (e.g., practitioner research and portfolios) and have been used to align teacher research efforts with the demands of the clinically rich reform agenda (see, for example, Maheady & Jabot, 2011). Studies involving prospective teachers' uses of evidence-based practices in naturalistic settings may be a productive avenue for studying both teaching practice and pupil learning.

A third important trend in teacher education involves the expanding role of instructional technologies. Odom (2008) described these technologies as "the tie that binds" evidence-based practices, implementation science, and important educational outcomes for children. Emerging instructional technologies may be used to facilitate teacher understanding and use of more effective teaching practices (e.g., evidence-based practices), which, in turn, may be applied to meet important P–12 student needs. Odom also described a variety of "wired" or hot topics in emerging technologies that may have particular relevance for field experiences and instructional pedagogies. Hot topics included practice-based reviews of evidence, an expansion of implementation science, and the use of "enlightened" instructional approaches (e.g., peer coaching, web-based video and visual access, and communities of practice) to improve teaching practice. Combining evidence-based practices with scientifically validated professional development strategies provides a potentially constructive framework for impacting teaching practice and student learning at the classroom, building, and system levels.

Recommendations for Future Research and Practice

The clinically rich and evidence-based practice movements provide excellent opportunities for teacher educators and educational researchers to have a more visible impact on teaching practice and student learning. However, to do so will require substantive changes in how teaching and learning are conceptualized, how clinical experiences are designed and evaluated, and how instructional pedagogies are applied to promote such developments. Five recommendations are offered to guide such efforts (see Table 10.2).

First, teacher educators and educational researchers must make teaching practice and pupil learning the overarching goals of both field experience and instructional pedagogies research and practice. Minimally, this will require new and improved measures of practice and student learning. In the interim, we may need to improve pupil performance on existing measures (e.g., curriculum-based assessments and standardized tests) even though they may leave much to be desired. Elevating improved teaching practice and student learning to the forefront of research and practice is a necessary first step in this regard.

Table 10.2 Guidelines for Improving Research and Practice on Field Experiences and Instructional Pedagogies

1. Make improved teaching practice and pupil learning the overarching goals of field experiences and instructional pedagogies research and practice.
2. Adopt an evidence-based practice approach to the selection, identification, and evaluation of teaching practices.
3. Use wired instructional technologies (e.g., practice-based reviews, interactive technologies, and communities of learning) to enhance prospective teachers' understanding and use of evidence-based practices.
4. Select research-to-practice and related designs to establish causal relationships among teaching practice and student learning.
5. Work collaboratively with P–12 schools in long-term relationships to design, implement, evaluate, and refine clinically rich programs.

Second, teacher educators and educational researchers should adopt an evidence-based practice approach to the selection, implementation, and evaluation of teaching practices that are used in P–12 classrooms. Research suggests that not all teaching practices are equally effective in promoting student learning. Teacher educators and educational researchers must make a concerted effort to identify those that are unusually effective while simultaneously adapting or discarding those that fail to improve pupil learning. Clinically rich experiences provide an authentic vehicle for studying the effects of selected practices on important measures of student performance.

Third, teacher educators and educational researchers should use wired instructional technologies to facilitate prospective teachers' use of evidence-based practices. Odom (2008) noted that substantive improvements have been made in our understanding of how to foster teachers' professional growth. We know, for example, that lecture-based training does little, if anything, to change practice. In contrast, in-class assistance in the form of modeling, coaching, and performance-based feedback does help teachers improve their instruction (Buysse, Sparkman, & Wesley, 2003; Buysse & Wesley, 2006: Joyce & Showers, 2002). In addition, peer coaching, web-based video and visual access, and communities of practice can be used to refine and sustain teacher use of effective teaching practices. Combining evidence-based practices with scientifically validated collaborative assistance provides a potentially constructive framework for changing practice at the classroom, building, and system levels.

It is also obvious that teaching practice and pupil learning will not improve until the amount and quality of research that undergirds it improves as well. Currently, the literature is dominated by qualitative studies many of which lack rigor and do not address directly or adequately the issues of practice and pupil learning. A fourth recommendation, therefore, is to use more rigorous research methodologies, preferably those that measure practice and learning more directly and reliably. Single-case research designs, for example, provide one powerful way for practitioners to demonstrate the effects of teaching practice on educationally important and reliably measured instructional outcomes (Kennedy, 2005). The value of these designs lies in their sensitivity to behavioral change, the rigor of their measurement systems, and the flexibility with which they can be applied (Kennedy, 2005).

The final recommendation is that teacher educators and educational researchers should work collaboratively with P–12 schools to create evidence-based decision-making cultures in our schools. The Blue Ribbon Panel (NCATE, 2010) outlined a number of important steps in this regard. Teacher educators might, for example, create seamless transitions between preservice and in-service education, wrap their university coursework around P–12 educational needs, and establish more functional clinical experiences. Those clinically rich experiences, in turn, should be more intensive, offered in our most needy schools, and accompanied by data collection efforts that show prospective teachers' impact on pupil learning.

Summary and Conclusions

The state of the art on field experiences and instructional pedagogies is not pretty; at least, not in terms of its documented impact on teaching practice and student learning. This does not mean, however, that these educational variables cannot impact practice and learning. Rather, a more concerted effort must be made to do so. Teaching practice and pupil learning can no longer remain secondary variables of interest for teacher educators and educational researchers. Instead, improvements in pupil learning must be viewed as the gold standard for determining if field experiences, instructional pedagogies, or any professional development activities are, indeed, effective (Greenwood & Maheady, 1997). Similarly, field experiences and instructional pedagogies must be reconceptualized as components of a larger evidence-based culture that is dedicated to the improvement of all teaching practice. To do this, a roadmap for building an evidence-based culture will be required (Detrich et al., 2008). Finally, teacher educators and applied researchers must work collaboratively with P–12 schools to identify common educational needs and to develop effective, efficient, and socially acceptable strategies for preventing and/or ameliorating these challenges. Given the increasing role of science in education, the rise of federal policies mandating evidence-based practices, and the urgent need to improve educational outcomes in the U.S., there may be no better time for such revolutionary changes to occur. Clinically rich field experiences and selected instructional pedagogies may serve as vehicles for making such sweeping changes a reality.

References

Abell Foundation. (2001, October). *Teacher certification reconsidered: Stumbling for quality*. Baltimore, MD: Author. Retrieved from http://www.abell.org/publications/detail.asp?ID=59

Ballou, D., & Podgursky, M. (2000). Reforming teacher preparation and licensing: What is the evidence? *Teachers College Record, 102*(1), 5–27. doi:10.1111/0161-4681.00046

Blanton, L. P., Pugach, M. C., & Florian, L. (2011). *Preparing general education teachers to improve outcomes for students with disabilities*. Washington, DC: American Association of Colleges for Teacher Education (AACTE) and National Center for Learning Disabilities (NCLD). Retrieved from http://aacte.org/research-policy/recent-reports-on-educator-preparation/preparing-general-education-teachers-to-improve-outcomes-for-students-with-disabilities.html

Bowman, C. L., & McCormick, S. (2000). Comparison of peer coaching versus traditional supervision effects. *Journal of Educational Research, 93*, 256–261. doi:10.1080/00220670009598714

Brantlinger, E., Jimenez, R., Klingner, J., Pugach, M., & Richardson, V. (2005). Qualitative studies in special education. *Exceptional Children, 71*, 195–207.

Buysse, V., Sparkman, K., & Wesley, P. W. (2003). Communities of practice: Connecting what we know with what we do. *Exceptional Children, 69*, 263–277.

Buysse, V., & Wesley, P. W. (2006). Evidence-based practice: How did it emerge and what does it really mean for the early childhood field? In V. Buysse & P. W. Wesley (Eds.), *Evidence-based practice in the early childhood field* (pp. 1–34). Washington, DC: Zero to Three.

Carlson, H. L., & Falk, D. R. (1989). Effective use of interactive videodisc instruction in understanding and implementing cooperative group learning with elementary pupils in social studies and social education. *Theory and Research in Social Education, 17*, 241–258. doi:10.1080/00933104.1989.10505591

Carlson, H. L., & Falk, D. R. (1990). Effectiveness of interactive videodisc instructional programs in elementary teacher education. *Journal of Educational Technology Systems, 19*, 151–163. doi:10.2190/FJX7-Y5NC-WH44-GHRK

Carnine, D. (2000, April). *Why education experts resist effective practice: Report of the Thomas B. Fordham Foundation*. Washington, DC: The Thomas B. Fordham Foundation.

Chorpita, B. F. (2003). The frontier of evidence-based practice. In B. F. Chorpita (Ed.), *Evidence-based psychotherapies for children and adolescents* (pp. 42–59). New York, NY: Guilford Publishers.

Cibulka, J. G. (2009). *Meeting urgent national needs in P–12 Education: Improving relevance, evidence, and performance in teacher preparation*. Washington, DC: National Council for Accreditation of Teacher Education.

Clift, R. T., & Brady, P. (2005). Research on methods courses and field experiences. In M. Cochran-Smith & K. Zeichner (Eds.), *Studying teacher education: The report of the AERA Panel on Research and Teacher Education* (pp. 309–424). Mahwah, NJ: Lawrence Erlbaum Associates, Inc.

Coalition for Evidence-Based Educational Policy Report. (2002). *Rigorous evidence: The key to progress in education: Lessons from medicine, welfare, and other fields.* Washington, DC: The Council for Excellence in Government. Retrieved from http://evidence-basedmanagement.com/wp-content/uploads/2011/11/Final_Online_Version_-_November_18_Forum_Transcript.pdf.

Cook, B. G. (2011). *Evidence-based practices and practice-based evidence: A union of insufficiencies.* President's Message, Fall 2011. Alexandria, VA: Council for Exceptional Children, Division for Research. Retrieved from http://www.cecdr.org/message.cfm?id=4718D087-FCDF-ECFA-9A6225F09F6FB06A

Cook, B. G., & Cook, S. C. (2010). Evidence-based practices, research-based practices, and best and recommended practices: Some thoughts on terminology. *Savage Controversies, 4*(1), 2–4.

Cook, B. G., Landrum, T. J., Tankersley, M., & Kauffman, J. M. (2003). Bringing research to bear on practice: Effecting evidence-based instruction for students with emotional or behavioral disorders. *Education and Treatment of Children, 26*, 345–361.

Copeland, W. (1982). Laboratory experiences in teacher education. In *Encyclopedia of Educational Research* (5th ed., Vol. 2, pp. 1008–1019). New York, NY: Free Press.

Daniel, P. (1996). Helping beginning teachers link theory and practice: An interactive multi-media environment for mathematics and science teacher preparation. *Journal of Teacher Education, 47*, 197–204. doi:10.1177/0022487196047003006

Dewey, J. (1938). *Experience and education.* New York: Macmillan.

Detrich, R., Keyworth, R., & States, J. (2008). A roadmap to evidence-based education: Building an evidence-based culture. In R. Detrich, R. Keyworth, & J. States (Eds.), *Advances in evidence-based education (Vol. 1): A roadmap to evidence-based education* (pp. 3–19). Oakland, CA: The Wing Institute.

Dinkelman, T. (2000). An inquiry into the development of critical reflection in secondary student teachers. *Teaching and Teacher Education, 16*, 195–222. doi:10.1016/S0742-051X(99)00055-4

Duncan, A. (2009, October). A call to teaching: Secretary Arne Duncan's Remarks at the Rotunda at the University of Virginia. Retrieved from http://www2.ed.gov/news/speeches/2009/10/10092009.html

Gersten, R., Fuchs, L. S., Compton, D., Coyne, M., Greenwood, C., & Innocenti, M. S. (2005). Quality indicators for group experimental and quasi-experimental research in special education. *Exceptional Children, 71*, 149–164.

Gill, B., & Hove, A. (2000, February). *The Benedum collaborative model of teacher education: A preliminary evaluation.* Santa Monica, CA: RAND. Retrieved from http://www.rand.org/pubs/documented_briefings/DB303.html

Goe, L., & Coggshall, J. (2007). *The teacher preparation→teacher practices→student outcomes relationship in special education: Missing links and necessary connections.* NCCTQ Research and Policy Brief. Washington, DC: National Comprehensive Center for Teacher Quality. Retrieved from http://ea.niusileadscape.org/docs/FINAL_PRODUCTS/LearningCarousel/may2007brief_newconnections.pdf

Greenwood, C. R., & Maheady, L. (1997). Measurable change in student performance: Forgotten standard in teacher preparation? *Teacher Education and Special Education, 20*, 265–275. doi:10.1177/088840649702000307

Grossman, P. (2005). Research on pedagogical approaches in teacher education. In M. Cochran-Smith & K. Zeichner (Eds.), *Studying teacher education: The report of the AERA Panel on Research and Teacher Education* (pp. 425–476). Mahwah, NJ: Lawrence Erlbaum Associates, Inc.

Guyton, E., & McIntyre, D. J. (1990). Student teaching and school experience. In W. R. Houston, M. Haberman, & J. Sikula (Eds.), *Handbook for research on teacher education* (pp. 514–534). New York, NY: Macmillan.

Hixon, E., & So, H. (2009). Technology's role in field experiences for preservice teacher training. *Educational Technology & Society, 12*, 294–304.

Horner, R. H., Carr, E. G., Halle, J., McGee, G., Odom, S. L., & Wolery, M. (2005). The use of single subject research to identify evidence-based practices in special education. *Exceptional Children, 71*, 165–179.

Huling-Austin, L. (1992). Research on learning to teach: Implications for teacher induction and mentoring programs. *Journal of Teacher Education, 24*, 173–180. doi:10.1177/0022487192043003003

Individuals with Disabilities Education Improvement Act of 2004, Pub. L. No. 108-446 (2004).

Joyce, B., & Showers, B. (2002). *Student achievement through staff development* (3rd ed.). Alexandria, VA: Association for Supervision and Curriculum Development.

Kazdin, A. E. (2008). Evidence-based treatments: Challenges and priorities for practice and research. In R. Detrich, R. Keyworth, & J. States (Eds.), *Advances in evidence-based education* (pp. 157–170). Oakland, CA: The Wing Institute.

Kennedy, C. H. (2005). *Single-case designs for educational research.* Boston, MA: Allyn & Bacon.

Knight, S. L., Wiseman, D. L., & Cooner, D. (2000). Using collaborative teacher research to determine the impact of professional development school activities on elementary students' math and writing outcomes. *Journal of Teacher Education, 51*, 26–38. doi:10.1177/002248710005100104

Lambdin, D. V., Duffy, T. M., & Moore, J. A. (1997). Using an interactive information system to expand preservice teachers' visions of effective mathematics teaching. *Journal of Technology and Teacher Education, 5*, 171–202.

MacLeod, G. (1987). Microteaching: End of a research era? *International Journal of Educational Research, 11*, 531–541. doi:10.1016/0883-0355(87)90013-9

Maheady, L., Harper, G. F., Karnes, M., & Mallette, B. (1999). The Instructional Assistants Program: A potential entry point for behavior analysis in education. *Education and Treatment of Children, 22*, 447–469.

Maheady, L., Harper, G. F., Mallette, B., & Karnes, M. (1993). The Reflective and Responsive Educator (RARE): A training program to prepare preservice general education teachers to instruct children and youth with disabilities. *Education and Treatment of Children, 16*, 474–506.

Maheady, L., & Jabot, M. (2011). Using research-to-practice studies to increase general educators' use of evidence-based practices. *Savage Controversies, 4*(2), 2–4.

Maheady, L., Jabot, M., Rey, J., & Michielli-Pendl, J. (2007). An early field-based experience and its impact on pre-service candidates' teaching practice and their pupils' outcomes. *Teacher Education and Special Education, 30*, 24–33. doi:10.1177/088840640703000103

McIntyre, D. J., Byrd, D., & Foxx, S. M. (1996). Field and laboratory experiences. In J. Sikula, T. Buttery, & E. Guyton (Eds.), *Handbook of research on teacher education* (2nd ed., pp. 171–193). New York, NY: Macmillan.

Munby, H., Russell, T., & Martin, A. K. (2001). Teachers' knowledge and how it develops. In V. Richardson (Ed.), *Handbook for research on teaching* (4th ed., pp. 877–904). Washington, DC: American Educational Research Association.

National Council for Accreditation of Teacher Education. (2010, November). *Transforming teacher education through clinical practice: A national strategy to prepare effective teachers*. Washington, DC: Author. Retrieved from http://www.ncate.org/Public/ResearchReports/NCATEInitiatives/BlueRibbonPanel/tabid/715/Default.aspx

No Child Left Behind Act of 2001, Pub. L. No. 107-110 (2002).

Odom, S. L. (2008). The tie that binds: Evidence-based practice, implementation science, and outcomes for children. *Topics in Early Childhood Special Education, 29*, 53–61. doi:10.1177/0271121408329171

Odom, S. L., Brantlinger, E., Gersten, R., Horner, R. H., Thompson, B., & Harris, K. R. (2005). Research in special education: Scientific methods and evidence-based practices. *Exceptional Children, 71*, 137–148.

Overbaugh, R. C. (1995). The efficacy of interactive video for teaching basic classroom management skills and pre-service teachers. *Computers in Human Behavior, 11*, 43–74. doi:10.1016/0747-5632(95)80014-Y

Pugach, M. C. (2005). Research on preparing general education teachers to work with students with disabilities. In M. Cochran-Smith & K. Zeichner (Eds.), *Studying teacher education: The report of the AERA Panel on Research and Teacher Education* (pp. 549–590). Mahwah, NJ: Lawrence Erlbaum Associates, Inc.

Shulman, L. S. (2002). Truth and consequences: Inquiry and policy in research in teacher education. *Journal of Teacher Education, 53*, 248–253. doi:10.1177/0022487102053003009

Sleeter, C. E. (2001). Epistemological diversity in research on preservice teacher preparation for historically underserved children. In W. G. Secada (Ed.), *Review of research in education* (Vol. 25, pp. 209–250). Washington, DC: American Educational Research Association.

Strang, H. R., Badt, K. S., & Kauffman, J. M. (1987). Microcomputer-based simulations for training fundamental teaching skills. *Journal of Teacher Education, 38*, 20–26. doi:10.1177/002248718703800105

Strang, H. R., Landrum, M. S., & Lynch, K. A. (1989). Talking with the computer: A simulation for training basic teaching skills. *Teaching and Teacher Education, 5*, 143–153. doi:10.1016/0742-051X(89)90012-7

Thompson, B., Diamond, K. E., McWilliam, R., Snyder, P., & Snyder, S. W. (2005). Evaluating the quality of evidence from correlational research for evidence-based practice. *Exceptional Children, 71*, 181–194.

U.S. Department of Education. (2002). *Meeting the highly qualified teachers challenge: The Secretary's annual report on teacher quality*. Washington, DC: U.S. Department of Education, Office of Post-secondary Education, Office of Policy, Planning, and Innovation. Retrieved from http://www2.ed.gov/about/reports/annual/teachprep/2003title-ii-report.pdf

U.S. Department of Education. (2011). *Our future, our teachers: The Obama Administration's plan for teacher education reform and improvement*. Washington DC: Author. Retrieved from http://www.ed.gov/teaching/our-future-our-teachers

Vare, J. W. (1994). Partnership contrasts: Microteaching activity as two apprenticeships in thinking. *Journal of Teacher Education, 45*, 209–217. doi:10.1177/0022487194045003007

Walker, H. M. (2004). Commentary: Use of evidence-based interventions in schools: Where we've been, where we are, and where we need to go. *School Psychology Review, 33*, 398–408.

Walker, H. M., Ramsey, E., & Gresham, F. M. (2003–2004). Heading off disruptive behavior: How early intervention can reduce defiant behavior and win back teaching time. *American Educator, 27*(4), 6–21.

Wideen, M., Mayer-Smith, J., & Moon, B. (1998). A critical analysis of learning to teach: Making the case for an ecological perspective on inquiry. *Review of Educational Research, 68*, 130–178. doi:10.3102/00346543068002130

Wilkinson, G. A. (1996). Enhancing microteaching through additional feedback from preservice administrators. *Teaching and Teacher Education, 12*, 211–221. doi:10.1016/0742-051X(95)00035-I

Wilson, S., Floden, R., & Ferrini-Mundy, J. (2002). Teacher preparation research: An insider's view from the outside. *Journal of Teacher Education, 53*, 190–204. doi:10.1177/0022487102053003002

Winitzky, N., & Arends, R. (1991). Translating research into practice: The effects of various forms of training and clinical experience on preservice students' knowledge, skill, and reflectiveness. *Journal of Teacher Education, 42*, 52–65. doi:10.1177/002248719104200108

Worthy, J., & Patterson, E. (2001). "I can't wait to see Carlos!" Preservice teachers, situated learning, and personal relationships with students. *Journal of Literacy Research, 33*, 303–344. doi:10.1080/10862960109548113

Zeichner, K. M. (1985). The ecology of field experience: Toward an understanding of the role of field experiences in teacher development. *Journal of Research and Development in Education, 18*(3), 44–52.

Zeichner, K. M., & Conklin, H. G. (2008). Teacher education programs as settings for teacher education. In M. Cochran-Smith, S. Feiman-Nemser, & J. McIntyre (Eds.), *Handbook of research on teacher education* (3rd ed., pp. 270–316). New York, NY: Routledge.

Zeichner, K. M., & Wray, S. (2001). The teaching portfolio in U.S. teacher education programs: What we know and what we need to know. *Teaching and Teacher Education, 17*, 613–621. doi:10.1016/S0742-051X(01)00017-8

11

Technology and Teacher Education

Sean J. Smith

UNIVERSITY OF KANSAS

Michael J. Kennedy

UNIVERSITY OF VIRGINIA

Things to Think About

This chapter discusses interrelated applications of technology within teacher education programs, including:

- Successful technology use in classrooms is related to how well teacher preparation programs and educators incorporate specific coursework and experiences related to technology into teaching.
- Structural and procedural barriers in P–12 schools that can inadvertently hinder the implementation and utilization of various technology applications.
- Effects of limited coursework during teacher preparation programs on the knowledge and readiness of P–12 educators to provide students with disabilities the individualized education required by law.
- The use of technology as a tool that teacher educators can use to present content and create engaging learning environments.
- The role of technology in distance education and other remote learning situations, including e-mentoring and bug-in-the-ear coaching.

Technology is everywhere in the field of special education. Most special educators use technology in assistive and instructional roles on a daily basis to support the individualized needs of students with disabilities (Okolo & Bouck, 2007). This includes the use of technology in assistive (Edyburn, 2008) and instructional roles (Kennedy & Wexler, in press), depending on the individualized need of the student with a disability. A large portion of university faculty members use technology in one form or another to help convey content and provide engaging learning opportunities to teacher candidates and in-service educators (Kennedy, Hart, & Kellems, 2011; Ludlow & Duff, 2007). Also, technology can provide a pathway for initial training and ongoing professional development to people who live and work in rural or secluded areas through distance education and other technology-based supports such as e-mentoring or bug-in-the-ear coaching (e.g., Jung, Galyon-Keramidas, Collins, & Ludlow, 2006; Rock et al., 2009). In this chapter we present and discuss evidence related to how practitioners and teacher educators (struggle to) utilize technology in their respective roles.

We believe that additional research, and renewed attention to how technology interfaces with teacher preparation programs will generatively spur emergence of measurable gains in educator quality and student performance. To that end, the purpose of this chapter is to review existing research that can spur new thinking with respect to the need to embed substantial technology training within teacher preparation coursework. This research reflects what we know in the field of special education teacher education, but also includes cues from our colleagues in general education. While this literature base is not extensive, it is growing, and on course to address concerns levied by Sindelar, Brownell, and Billingsley (2010) and Leko, Brownell, Sindelar, and Murphy (2012) who summarily called for increases in the quantity and quality of research in the field. With this said, our review of the research focuses on teacher education and technology for students with disabilities. Included in this review are studies that focus primarily on special education (e.g., assistive technology) but also include general education initiatives (e.g., technology, pedagogy, and content knowledge) that are representative of technology integration efforts across teacher education, special and general education. We conclude the chapter with recommendations for researchers and practitioners that aim to break existing cycles of frustration and limited implementation of instructional tools that may have important effects on outcomes for students with disabilities.

Technology in Teacher Education: Technology as Content

An argument can be made that in the 21st century nearly all technology-based tools and devices will become second nature in schools, and thereby be used by students with and without disabilities. Although this vision appears to have merit, research in technology—including educational technology integration—suggests, at least for now, that unless technology tools are tied directly to a student's Individualized Education Program (IEP), technology may not be integrated into learning in a meaningful and purposeful manner (e.g., Kennedy & Deshler, 2010; King-Sears, 2009). This is problematic, as the purpose of special education is to provide students with specially designed instruction in their specific area of difficulty (Hallahan, Kauffman, & Pullen, 2012). However, simply including the need for assistive or instructional technology within an IEP only increases the likelihood that students will receive these services, and is far from a guarantee.

Coursework for Using Technology in Teacher Preparation Programs

The 1997 Amendments to the Individuals with Disabilities Education Act (IDEA) (1997) required IEP and Individualized Family Service Plan (IFSP) teams to consider assistive technology (AT) devices and services to help support students; the reauthorization of IDEA (2004) continues this requirement. Therefore, it is logical to expect that teacher education programs would emphasize numerous and diverse applications of technology when preparing preservice educators. However, graduates of special education certification programs annually matriculate from these programs in large numbers with limited knowledge and skills in technology (Abner & Lahm, 2002; Hutinger, Johanson, & Stoneburner, 1996; Lesar, 1998; McGregor & Pachuski, 1996). Thus, it is logical to expect that many incoming teachers are unfamiliar with, and unprepared to implement evidence-based applications of technology to support the individualized needs of students with disabilities, regardless of instructional placements. As noted in the previous discussion, students with disabilities require individualized supports; thus, this limitation of practitioners' knowledge creates a mismatch between what students need to be successful and what they actually receive in many classrooms (Kennedy, Lloyd, Ely, & Cole, in press).

To illustrate, Judge and Simms (2009) found that barely a third of undergraduate special education programs require a specific course in AT for degree or licensure attainment. Graduate licensure programs are even less likely to require an AT course. In addition, the majority of AT-specific courses are tied to degree and certificate programs in severe or moderate disabilities. Thus, when students receive

AT coursework, the course frequently emphasizes functional development and issues of access. This focus includes AT relevant to communication, seating, positioning, mobility, and other sensory or physical disabilities, but does not extensively include the needs of a majority of students with learning, behavioral, attention, and related disability challenges. Indeed, a sample of special educators recently agreed they had inadequate training in AT and believed that AT should be a required area of study, and not be limited to a single class or a small portion of an educational technology course (Bauder, 1999; Lee & Vega, 2005).

One result of limited preservice teacher education coursework in the area of technology is that school districts must either provide professional development to teachers and related service personnel (Bausch & Hasselbring, 2004) or establish and maintain systems that work around this limitation. Studies indicate that special education teachers and their professional peers are interested in additional training in technology (Wahl & Buzolich, 2001), yet districts' professional development budgets are limited and teachers can ill-afford the time away from their classrooms even when professional development is available (Smith & Allsopp, 2005). The National Assistive Technology Research Initiative suggests that most AT specialists gain their expertise and related certificates outside of their school districts.

General Education Technology Solutions

Effective pathways for how best to prepare special educators to meaningfully integrate AT solutions may lie in the general education literature. In 2005, Koehler and Mishra first described an instructional design framework that seamlessly integrates technology, content, and pedagogy for design and delivery of various types of content, known as technological pedagogical content knowledge (TPACK). TPACK is a framework for designing and delivering instruction that reflects the interaction among (a) the pedagogical needs of specific content areas, (b) the specific demands of the content being learned, and (c) the role technology can play in making content easier to learn and teach (Koehler & Mishra, 2005). For nearly a decade, general educators have sought to utilize the TPACK framework when considering meaningful technology integration across P–12 and higher education. Koehler and Mishra (2005) described TPACK as an extension of Shulman's (1987) construct of pedagogical content knowledge (PCK). TPACK is a potentially helpful construct for conceptualizing and organizing the role of technology for delivering instruction when teaching students with disabilities across a variety of instructional settings.

TPACK can be a guiding theoretical framework for college and P–12 teaching. Educators who benefit from the TPACK framework recognize that technology is not a tool that can or should be carelessly added to existing instruction (Kennedy & Deshler, 2010; Koehler & Mishra, 2005). Instead, when educators select pedagogies for instruction that are a logical match to enhance and enrich the content being presented (e.g., PCK; Shulman, 1987), technology should then be considered if able to uniquely interface with the selected pedagogy to help shape and deliver content in a way not possible without the use of technology.

Given the aforementioned limitations of how many teachers are minimally prepared to use technology in their classrooms, the use of the TPACK framework may seem beyond the reach of many educators. Yet, well-designed special education teacher preparation is grounded in the instruction of evidence-based practices for students with disabilities (Sindelar et al., 2010). TPACK would extend this pedagogy through the integration of technology innovations within the relevant content being addressed.

Designing high-quality instruction that includes technology for students with disabilities requires educators to reflect comprehensively with respect to how the technology application will interface with the pedagogical principles, the structure of the content, and the individual learning needs of each student (Smith & Okolo, 2010). In general education teacher preparation efforts, TPACK has expanded as a conceptual framework to be an integrated method accompanied by ways in which to measure TPACK (Archambault & Crippen, 2009; Schmidt et al., 2009). Given the relative recent emergence of the TPACK framework, it is not surprising that much remains to be learned about how this framework can further technology integration efforts at the preservice teacher education level. In special education, for example, Marino, Sameshima, and Beecher (2009) are the first to consider TPACK within the context of AT and teacher preparation. By providing examples of how AT and instructional technology (IT) are distinct, yet overlapping constructs to TPACK, Marino and his colleagues offer initial steps in integrating AT within the TPACK framework. Specifically, through purposeful planning across a series of semester-long cycles, AT and IT development can be achieved in special education preparation. With this said, TPACK and the ability to measure technology connections to content and pedagogy within teacher preparation offers exciting considerations for what might prove to be an essential framework for technology integration. In addition, TPACK may serve as a strategy in supporting the inclusion of technology practices within teacher preparation (Marino et al., 2009).

It is not unreasonable to draw parallels between teachers' limited preservice training in the use of technology for students with disabilities and many IEPs being drawn without specific mention of technology devices and materials. An important issue to be addressed is the extent to which the field can expect adherence to IDEA requirements for technology integration when professional standards, research, and teacher education programs are all limited in terms of practical guidance to educators. Fortunately, our colleagues in general education teacher preparation offer a framework for consideration (e.g., TPACK); however, the limited empirical evidence currently available suggests we have a ways to go in the incorporation of such a model. Thus, it may be possible to seek guidance for incorporating technology into instruction from various professional standards.

Specific Standards for Technology Integration

In this increasingly digital age, teachers must integrate technology into instruction. For teacher education programs, professional standards dictate coursework, assessments, program measurements, and preservice teacher outcomes. Not surprisingly, there are specific standards aligned with technology integration. These standards recognize the importance of teachers possessing skills and behaviors inherent in the digital age, and stress the need to infuse these skills into classroom instruction. Forty-eight of the 50 states and the District of Columbia have adopted, referenced, or aligned their state technology plans, teacher education certification or licensure requirements, and curriculum plans and/or assessment plans with the National Educational Technology Standards for Teachers (NETS•T) developed by the International Society for Technology in Education (ISTE). Furthermore, the National Council for Accreditation of Teacher Education (NCATE), an accrediting organization for schools, colleges, and departments of education in U.S. colleges and universities, views the NETS•T as an important component of their Conceptual Framework.

NETS•T Standards

The NETS are the standards for learning, teaching, and leading in the digital age and describe expected competencies for students, administrators, coaches, computer science teachers, and teachers in general. The NETS•T articulates five distinct standards, each with four subcomponents and a set of teacher behaviors that demonstrate compliance with the standard, that is, 25 statements about technology integration with instruction. Although the NETS•T standards are essential in guiding teacher education programs, they are limited in application for special education teachers. To illustrate, the only NETS•T statement that even indirectly addresses students with disabilities is found in Standard 4 (b), which states, "Address the diverse needs of all learners by using learner-centered strategies providing equitable access to appropriate digital tools and resources." This reference to diverse learners could imply special education, but also includes culturally and linguistically diverse learners as well as a host of other students with diverse learning needs.

CEC Standards Related to Technology

Since the NETS•T do not directly address competencies within special education, one might logically expect that the Council for Exceptional Children's (CEC) Knowledge and Skill Standards would provide explicit guidance for the field of special education in the domain of technology integration. While CEC's standards make reference to technology experiences, upon closer examination, they are few and far between when compared with other professional expectations (e.g., reading, behavior, assessment).

CEC's Knowledge and Skills framework reinforces an educational model that is fraught with challenges. Rather than empowering all special educators, CEC continues to support advanced content standards, which in the area of AT involves the specialists in the domain of AT. The specialist, as the name implies, contains its own expectations for knowledge and skills that extend beyond typical teacher preparation requirements. Thus, a limited number of professionals receive an endorsement to be a technology specialist, and even fewer teacher education programs offer the coursework (see California State University, Northridge, for a notable exception). As a result, school districts seek to employ an AT specialist/expert to direct all technology-related efforts across hundreds, if not thousands of students with disabilities and their respective IEP teams. This systemic problem of practice contributes to the challenges raised in the previous sections.

In summary, based on the NETS•T and CEC standards, neither the special or general educator on the IEP team are required to have minimal technology-specific knowledge, or are required to develop basic technology skills specific to the unique needs of the student with disabilities. Without extensive support and guidance from the district AT specialist, nor the ability to turn to standards, educators must rely on the knowledge and practices they obtained during their preparation coursework.

Technology in Teacher Education: Technology as a Tool

Research on Technology Use in Teacher Preparation Programs

Currently there is an influx of multimedia-supported approaches being utilized in teacher preparation pedagogy (U.S. Department of Education, Office of Educational Technology, 2004, 2010). Despite this influx, empirical evidence to support many applications of technology in teacher preparation is either absent, or in short supply (Lawless & Pellegrino, 2007; Mayer, 2004). Frequently, the evidence presented to support the use of technology in higher education takes the form of satisfaction reports from users (Clark, 2009). Many technology-based teaching methods do not specify a theoretical framework that provides the basis and justification for why interventions contain specific design features and should be used during critical coursework (Clark, 2009; Mayer, 2004). In addition, while the majority of studies of technology in higher education focus on user perceptions (Heilson, 2010), for those that do report student learning, the great majority evaluate student learning with technology in comparison to student learning without technology (Schmidt et al., 2009).

Each study reviewed in this section uses multimedia to provide instruction or support student learning. In addition, the quality of the respective studies addresses the need noted by Sindelar and his colleagues (2010) to augment the rigor and overall quality of empirical research in our field. It is expected that the quality and quantity of research will continue to improve in the coming years, especially in distance education, and other applications of technology in teacher preparation coursework and professional development.

Existing Research in Special Education Teacher Education

Sindelar and colleagues (2010) call for the development and experimental testing of specific pedagogical approaches and methods that deliver content including the need for systematic programs of research to emerge from theoretical and conceptual frameworks, and utilization of high-quality research designs, such as random assignment. In the field of special education teacher education, a number of research teams describe innovative uses of theory-grounded technology within the traditional curriculum in their respective programs. This is accomplished through the simulation of various scenarios that teacher candidates will face during practicum experiences and upon graduation (i.e., Dieker et al., 2009; Mitchem et al., 2009), and also by using technology to provide core content and background knowledge (i.e. Gormley & Ruhl, 2007; Kennedy et al., 2011; Kennedy & Thomas, 2012). To illustrate these points, we review eight studies that employed aspects of strong research design and implications for future research and practice (Anderson & Lignugaris/Kraft, 2006; Dieker et al., 2009; Gormley & Ruhl, 2007; Mitchem et al., 2009; O'Neal, Jones, Miller, Campbell, & Pierce, 2007; Kennedy et al., 2011; Kennedy & Thomas, 2012; and Kennedy et al., 2012). This discussion will integrate information regarding the standards set for research methods and paradigms by professional organizations such as the American Educational Research Association (AERA, 2006).

Clear Description of Research Methods and Production Steps

Dieker and her colleagues (2009) created a series of streaming, scripted videos that show teachers modeling evidence-based practices (EBPs). The content of the videos created for this research reflect EBPs and were vetted by content experts to ensure fidelity and other benchmarks of quality. In addition to the meticulous description of the intervention, the researchers also provide clear, detailed and well-defined descriptions of participants, interventions, procedures, and measures. The generative nature of this program of research provides valid implications for future research and practice given the criticisms on lack of generalizability levied by Grossman (2005). Although this study is one of the first of its kind, researchers concluded that teacher candidates who watched the videos showed improvement in their knowledge regarding effective teaching practices. In addition, this study and others by this research team (see Dieker, Hynes, Hughes, & Smith, 2008) address the concern noted by Sindelar et al. (2010) in that the researchers are taking steps to develop, test, and introduce new pedagogical methods to the field.

Use of Theory

Fitzgerald and her colleagues (2011; Mitchem et al., 2009; Miller et al., 2009) lead a line of research that addresses another key criticism levied by Sindelar et al. (2010) and Grossman (2005): the atheoretical nature of many studies in teacher preparation. This work provides an excellent example of how theory should guide a program of research, and is also grounded by a high-quality review of relevant literature. In an exemplar study, Mitchem et al. (2009) used the theoretical principle of practice fields to create a series of multimedia-based case studies to engage students in authentic learning activities related to understanding students with emotional and behavioral disorders. Teacher candidates received instruction using authentic multimedia case-based learning materials designed using a thorough review of the relevant literature. Although participants were nested within classrooms and settings rather than randomly assigned, researchers collected credible qualitative and quantitative data. Their results and conclusions suggest authentic multimedia instruction can improve learning for preservice educators on measures of knowledge and perceived readiness to work with this population of students.

Addressing Generalizability

O'Neal et al. (2007) address the problem of generalizability in their research. The researchers compared learning outcomes for students who either learned content for a course introducing special education during a traditional face-to-face section, or using an online format. The researchers did not detect significant differences in student performance on an end-of-semester examination and concluded that online instruction can be as effective as traditional methods. In this study, the professional standards for experimental design were not achieved. Students volunteered for the type of instruction they received; yet the findings have positive and helpful implications for our field. Clearly, future research should strive to implement experimental design to evaluate the capacity of online instruction to replicate the efficacy of face-to-face instruction across different courses and content areas. Continuation of this type of research would address Sindelar and colleagues' (2010) concern and their call for rigorous examinations of types of special education teacher education programs.

Use of Experimental Design

Gormley and Ruhl (2007) implemented experimental design principles in their study, randomly assigning participants to either a treatment or control condition. These researchers created, implemented, and evaluated the efficacy of a multimedia-based training module for teaching candidates about the alphabetic principle. Using a pre- and posttest design, researchers measured whether teacher candidates could apply and generalize content knowledge presented within researcher-created online training videos and learning materials following 2–6 hours of supplemental online instruction compared to students who only received the typical in-class instruction. Results showed teacher candidates who participated in the multimedia-based instruction ($n=17$) made significant gains in their knowledge of the alphabetic principle compared with students in the control group ($n=20$), but significant gains were not detected in the ability of either group to generalize knowledge of the alphabetic principle during a novel task. Researchers partially attributed the lack of significance to limited dosage of the intervention and the number of participants. Despite these limitations, the use of an experimental design adds credibility to this study's findings and contribution.

Anderson and Lignugaris/Kraft (2006) used strong experimental design features, including randomly assigning participants to conditions, and replicating positive and significant results of the experimental group with the control group following posttest. This study investigated the efficacy of a video-based program for learning about function and antecedent-based behavior management strategies. Participants were exposed to three cases of typical problem behaviors teachers experience in their classrooms, and given multiple and repeated opportunities over a 7-week period to learn about and practice decision-making for proactive, antecedent-based intervention. However, a theoretical framework for the development and use of the multimedia, video-based interactive materials was not presented. Furthermore, the rationale provided for use of such multimedia materials was solely a recommendation from experts in the field as a potential but unproven method for professional development to improve knowledge and skills about the functional behavioral assessment process (Scott & Nelson, 1999).

Using Technology to Augment Presentation Options

Kennedy and his colleagues (Kennedy et al., 2011; Kennedy & Thomas, 2012, Kennedy et al., in press) are engaged in a program of research using Content Acquisition Podcasts (CAPs) to present core course content to teacher education students. CAPs are a form of enhanced podcasts that adhere to Mayer's cognitive theory of multimedia learning (2009). Whereas generic enhanced podcasts do not reflect any particular theoretical paradigm for addressing student learning needs, CAPs combine vivid images, occasional text, and clear narration to reduce users' respective cognitive load and help support active processing (Kennedy, 2011). The researchers originally created CAPs to address the common problem of practice in teacher education coursework: there is limited face-to-face instructional time to provide students with all of the content they need to be successful teachers of students with various disabilities (Kennedy et al., 2011). Thus, CAPs can be assigned as an advance organizer prior to course meetings in order to provide students with key information needed to participate in hands-on learning activities, such as case studies.[1]

Conclusions and Connections

Even if university instructors use multimedia-based instructional materials of the highest quality in all instruction, this will not automatically transfer to the readiness of teacher candidates to use technology in their future teaching. The professional literature in the field of special education and teacher education offers little empirical guidance with respect to methods for training teacher candidates to create, select, implement, and evaluate the effects of technology on student learning (Marino et al., 2009). These limitations of the existing literature base leave many important questions unanswered with respect to effective methods for integrating technology into instruction. Therefore, it is critical for researchers to conduct studies using qualitative and quantitative methods that investigate the extent to which teacher candidates: (a) can learn to create multimedia-based instructional materials; (b) can select evidence-based materials; and (c) are prepared to implement the technology with fidelity when working with students. Dissemination of this research will help augment the existing base of studies shaping our current thinking on these important topics.

Teacher Education and Technology: Distance and Online Learning

Descriptive Overviews and Emerging Research

Distance and online teacher preparation has a rich history in special education. While empirical studies are increasingly expanding upon its effectiveness in comparison to traditional face-to-face programs, the bulk of the literature concentrates on descriptive institution and/or state programs offering insight to the field as well as lessons learned. Much of the literature represents descriptive overviews illustrating university and/or state programs to develop, implement, and extend distance learning (see Glomb, Lignugaris/Kraft, & Menlove, 2009 for a review). Founded to address rural special education licensure concerns, especially in the categorical areas of moderate to severe disabilities, the literature offers distance education program descriptions including efforts in design, development, and applicable technology tools (Canter, Voytecki, & Rodríguez, 2007; Mercer, 2004; Sebastian, Egan, & Mayhew, 2009).

Descriptive Program Overviews

Reports, program descriptions, and the limited research of the late 20th century reinforce that distance education for special education preparation was originally conceived and delivered to increase the number of special educators, especially those to work with students with low-incidence disabilities (Bullock, Gable, & Mohr, 2008; Cegelka & Alvarado, 2000; Cooke & deBettencourt, 2001; Knapczyk, Chapman, Rodes, & Chung, 2001; Spooner, Agran, Spooner, & Kiefer-O'Donnell, 2000). Spooner and his colleagues' (Spooner, Spooner, Algozzine, & Jordan, 1998) reflections on the initial distance education efforts testify to this fact in that they describe current distance education to be synchronous communication (e.g., two-way audio, two-way video in real time, or two-way audio, one-way video in real time) with the program's function to increase special education personnel in remote locations.

Larwood's (2005) description of the evolution of the deaf education alternative program at San Jose State University embodies much of the distance/online literature (Steinweg, Davis, & Thomson,

2005; Ferrell, Persichitte, Lowell, & Roberts, 2001; Ludlow, 2003; Forbush & Morgan, 2004). Like many rural as well as low-incidence special education areas (Ludlow, Foshay, Brannan, Duff, & Dennison, 2002), San Jose State faced long distances between certification programs, limited technologies due to resources and outdated equipment at rural facilities, cost limitations, and an immediacy in need to address the recruitment, training and retention of qualified teachers for students with disabilities across the state of California. The descriptive article, like many of its counterparts, shares information on program planning (Norton & Hathaway, 2008), course modifications (Egbert & Thomas, 2001), support for faculty and K–12 teachers (Delfino & Persico, 2007), technology needs (e.g., skill building, access; Ludlow, Galyon-Keramidas, & Landers, 2007), general program evaluation (Rowlison, 2006; Schweizer, Hayslett, & Chaplock, 2008), and future steps being considered. What these descriptive pieces do not include are data on outcomes, beyond limited perceptions of graduates that measure the effectiveness of these efforts in comparison to face-to-face or other instructional mediums (Bargerhuff, Dunne, & Renick, 2007; Canter et al., 2007; Ajuwon & Craig, 2007).

Descriptive Historical Reports

Recently, programs with an extensive history (e.g., West Virginia, Utah, Kentucky) have enhanced these descriptive reports with historical retrospectives sharing lessons learned. Glomb, Lignugaris/Kraft & Menlove (2009), for instance, discuss the development of the distance education program at Utah State University. Intermixed among this historical overview are lessons learned, questions to be answered, and the ongoing need to prepare special education teachers in remote and rural localities. Similarly, Collins, Baird, and Hager (2009) describe two decades of evolution in the moderate and severe disabilities distance education program at the University of Kentucky. Their intent is to offer a historical perspective from faculty members present during its inception who continue to develop and expand online learning options along with faculty peers new to the program efforts. Data on core courses required, the manner in which they are delivered, and the external funding needed to develop and maintain the program are grounded by personal narratives from the senior faculty. Finally, Ludlow and Duff (2009) offer a historical narrative of West Virginia University's efforts, describing the program's critical role in the delivery of distance education for special education preparation highlighting initial delivery systems (e.g., broadcast television, telephone bridge) and essential partnership building.

While descriptive program overviews represent a majority of online teacher preparation publications, critical elements, including the nature of clinical experiences and reducing student isolation within the learning process, can be found in aspects of the literature (Beattie, Spooner, Jordan, Algozzine, & Spooner, 2002; Bore Korir, 2008). Jung et al. (2006), for instance, highlight models for providing practicum experiences in rural and remote districts. Extending the distance education experience, the article highlights efforts at two universities, West Virginia and Kentucky (known for their efforts in distance special education teacher preparation), highlighting coursework and community partnerships. The article offers the critical elements of community mentors (e.g., teachers with at least 3 years' experience), technical assistance teams, and methods for meaningful direct observation and supervision of teacher education students at remote locations. Likewise, Glomb, Midenhall, Mason, and Salzberg (2009) discuss professional isolation and the role of online-based learning communities to promote learning while combatting program attrition. Building on the research in learning communities (Andrade, 2008), Glomb and her colleagues (2009) describe face-to-face and online teacher mentoring that is purposeful, involves graduates of the distance education licensure program, and is systematic to ensure embedded supports for rural and remote teacher education students in need of professional connections. Findings indicate graduation rates prior to teacher mentoring were as low as 36%. Upon the implementation of regional learning communities, graduation rates rose to 75%. Likewise, respondents to a postgraduation online survey (4 = extremely helpful, 3 = adequate, 2 = somewhat helpful, and 1 = not helpful at all) to determine the benefit of the mentoring/learning community, shared annual averages of 3.7 and 3.8 in consecutive years. However, indicative of this strand of literature, data are limited, if presented at all, concentrating, as illustrated above, on student retention and the number of graduates.

Johnson, Humphrey, and Allred (2009) summarize a promising model in the state of Idaho, specific to the recruitment and retention of special education teachers in rural areas. Their overview adds to previous descriptive studies offering critical elements of strong partnerships (e.g., state and university, university and local education agency), extending the teacher education program into the early induction years, and discussing the development and implementation of completely online programs identifying key considerations from previous hybrid, online, and distance education programs. For example, their efforts include the development of strong partnerships between the universities and partnering districts (something included in other state initiatives), continued engagement (e.g., face-to-face and/or online mentoring) into the teacher induction years beyond the teacher preparation program, and the issues relevant to developing and implementing an entirely online program that extends beyond real-time (e.g., synchronous) instruction but instead, incorporates innovative asynchronous models and tools to support the instructor while engaging the learner.

Distance Education to Provide Alternative Certification

McDonnell and his colleagues (McDonnell et al., 2011) report that distance education and online learning increasingly plays a role in teacher education through alternative routes to certification. For example, they report that as of 2008, there were 201 online alternative certification coursework opportunities across the country. Of those, 65 are paths to special education online teacher certification or certification programs. Furthermore, these reports indicate that at least 20% of all undergraduates have taken at least one distance education course as part of their preparation program. As universities further develop and deliver alternative routes to certification, distance learning appears to be an integral part. That is, technology often is relied upon for course delivery (Jung et al., 2006; Ludlow et al., 2007), clinical experiences, direct supervision, and similar components of teacher education (e.g., Falconer & Lignugaris/Kraft, 2002). Nearly five years ago, Rosenberg, Boyer, Sindelar, and Misra (2007) identified over 200 alternative routes to certification in 35 states. Their findings suggest over two thirds use distance education tools for course, if not, program delivery.

The proliferation of alternative route to licensure (AR) programs in special education teacher preparation led Wasburn-Moses and Rosenberg (2008) to present a series of guidelines intended to assist teacher educators as they develop and improve upon AR programs. The sixth of these seven priority guidelines seeks to integrate instruction in technology. Foremost, distance and online technologies should be developed and integrated in AR programs to connect students (e.g., teachers seeking certification) involved in the teacher development process (Smith & Meyen, 2003). Wasburn-Moses and Rosenberg identify these connections as student-to-student, student-to-mentor, and student-to-coworker (fellow teacher). Accordingly, chat rooms, video-conferencing (e.g., Skype), blogs, discussion boards, and similar tools can help facilitate relationships in AR programs.

Emerging Evidence

O'Neal and her colleagues (2007) lead a line of research that seeks to address the effectiveness of the online experience when compared to face-to-face instruction. Relying on student achievement and student satisfaction (representative of the majority of these studies), findings indicate no significant difference in student achievement or student satisfaction when courses are offered in the web-based or traditional formats. Caywood and Duckett (2003) concentrated on a graduate course on behavior management where a total of 140 students self-selected either an online or traditional face-to-face class. Outcomes were measured through standard multiple-choice tests along with a behavior management observation conducted as part of the students' clinical internship. Similar to prior and subsequent online versus traditional face-to-face studies, no significant difference between these two groups were found (Beattie et al., 2002; Mercer, 2004; Steinweg et al., 2005). McDonnell and colleagues (2011) again found no significant differences between online and on-campus teacher education cohorts, but extend previous research by employing a variety of measures used to assess teacher candidates' acquisition of content and their ability to apply the knowledge and skills in the classroom experience. Finally, Skyler and colleagues (2005) compared distance learning with traditional face-to-face as well as CD-ROM packaged modules. Across three interventions, findings indicated no significant difference in student achievement or satisfaction.

As distance and online teacher preparation has grown and evolved, so has some of the research. For example, Bore Korir (2008) sought to understand student accessibility to online learning resources and their perceptions of the difficulty of assignments, user-friendliness of the technology, and whether online tools enhanced or hindered content comprehension. Convenience was also surveyed while learning outcomes were associated with the degree to which the 88 participants believed they achieved anticipated learning goals. For Scheeler, McKinnon, and Stout (2012), technology innovation in the form of webcams and Bluetooth ear pieces (e.g., bug-in-the-ear) have led to immediate feedback for student clinicians at remote locations. Here, immediate feedback via the technologies increased practicum student behavior allowing them to meet criteria in a shorter period of time. Furthermore, wireless, virtual, video, and Internet-based technology advancements are extending online teacher preparation possibilities as well as initial career development (e.g., e-mentoring; Billingsley, Israel, & Smith, 2011; Johnson et al., 2009; Smith & Israel, 2010). Hager's (2010) preliminary investigation of regularly scheduled web conferencing, where self-reports and completed questionnaires found student satisfaction, represents the potential benefits and next stages in online learning and the evolving tools.

Conclusions and Connections

Considering the history of distance education and online learning in special education teacher preparation, the empirical evidence to support these initiatives is quite limited (McDonnell et al., 2011). There is a need for continued research in the area of distance and online teacher preparation, especially when considering the advancements in technology tools that extend previous online efforts and potentially alter what previously was not possible, or at least feasible (e.g., e-mentoring, virtual instruction).

As online tools advance, the melding of technology-based and online-based tools for teacher education will ultimately become indistinguishable. That is, the use of multimedia (e.g., podcasts), video, or audio tools as independent from the online environment will soon be a thing of the past. Instead, the professional literature indicates a combination of the two tools blended in teacher preparation, face-to-face and/or online that extends the experience for the instructor and preservice student. What is needed, however, is further study (qualitative and quantitative methods) on the impact of these tools investigating the extent to which teacher educators can: (a) extend content knowledge; (b) include more and more potential teacher education candidates in either remote locations and/or on-the-job environments for just-in-time learning; and (c) examine how this technology infusion will not only improve instruction but extend the use of these technology-based tools into the lives of the student with disabilities—the main priority. As we stated above, dissemination of this research will help inform many of the systemic limitations and problems of practice noted throughout this chapter.

Summary

In conclusion, technology and teacher education is a complex issue easily divided across three primary considerations: (a) technology skill development across preservice teacher education, (b) technology-based tool development and implementation across teacher education instruction to advance preservice special educator learning, and (c) distance and online learning innovations to expand teacher preparation capacity and flexibility within the ever-increasing societal and professional demands. Unfortunately, as we discussed, there is no uniformity in addressing the technology challenges associated with teacher preparation. That is, in addressing the first, teaching special educators to further integrate AT into the lives of students with disabilities, is not necessarily achieved through the further integration of technology tools to teach special educators and/or advancements in distance and online learning teacher preparation.

With this said, innovations in technology-based solutions, especially tools to be used in online learning (e.g., podcasts, virtual reality), appear to be blending teacher tools and online learning respective to teacher education. Fortunately, the integration of these tools are increasingly associated with high-quality teacher preparation programs that increase the knowledge and skills of future and current educators to meet the needs of students with disabilities. While technology as a tool for teacher preparation may not directly develop preservice special education competency in AT and IT, expanded use should drive technology expectations across higher education as well as P–12 classrooms and thus, further technology considerations for all learners. Fortunately, the ever-changing technology environment is fostering further integration. The challenge is to develop effective tools and conduct additional empirical research that will foster further technology development and subsequent integration across teacher preparation and hopefully, student learning.

Note

1 A sample CAP is available at https://vimeo.com/40105175. Instructions on how to create a CAP can be viewed electronically at: http://vimeo.com/24179998 (part 1) and http://vimeo.com/24182724 (part 2). Written steps are available at: www.people.virginia.edu/~mjk3p.

References

Abner, G. H., & Lahm, E. A. (2002). Implementation of assistive technology with students who are visually impaired: Teachers' readiness. *Journal of Visual Impairment & Blindness, 96*, 98–105.

Ajuwon, P. M., & Craig, C. J. (2007). Distance education in the preparation of teachers of the visually impaired and orientation and mobility specialists: Profile of a new training paradigm. *Re:View, 39*, 3–14. doi:10.3200/REVU.39.1.3-14

American Educational Research Association. (2006). Standards for reporting on empirical social science research in AERA publications. *Educational Researcher, 35*(6), 33–40. doi:10.3102/0013189X035006033

Anderson, D. H., & Lignugaris/Kraft, B. (2006). Video-case instruction for teachers of students with problem behaviors in general and special education classrooms. *Journal of Special Education Technology, 21*(2), 31–45.

Andrade, M. S. (2008). Learning communities: Examining positive outcomes. *Journal of College Student Retention: Research, Theory & Practice, 9*, 1–20. doi:10.2190/E132-5X73-681Q-K188

Archambault, L., & Crippen, K. (2009). Examining TPACK among K–12 online distance educators in the United States. *Contemporary Issues in Technology and Teacher Education, 9*, 71–88.

Bargerhuff, M., Dunne, J. D., & Renick, P. R. (2007). Giving teachers a chance: Taking special education teacher preparation programs to rural communities. *Rural Special Education Quarterly, 26*(1), 3–12.

Bauder, D. K. (1999). *The use of assistive technology and the assistive technology training needs of special education teachers in Kentucky schools* (Unpublished doctoral dissertation). University of Kentucky, Lexington.

Bausch, M. E., & Hasselbring, T. S. (2004). Assistive technology: Are the necessary skills and knowledge being developed at the preservice and inservice levels? *Teacher Education and Special Education, 27*, 97–104. doi:10.1177/088840640402700202

Beattie, J., Spooner, F., Jordan, L., Algozzine, B., & Spooner, M. (2002). Evaluating instruction in distance learning classes. *Teacher Education and Special Education, 25*, 124–132. doi:10.1177/088840640202500204

Billingsley, B., Israel, M., & Smith, S. (2011). Supporting new special education teachers: How online resources and Web 2.0 technologies can help. *TEACHING Exceptional Children, 43*(5), 20–29.

Bore Korir, J. C. (2008). Perceptions of graduate students on the use of web-based instruction in special education personnel preparation. *Teacher Education and Special Education, 31*, 1–11.

Bullock, L. M., Gable, R. A., & Mohr, J. D. (2008). Technology-mediated instruction in distance education and teacher preparation in special education. *Teacher Education and Special Education, 31*, 229–242. doi:10.1177/0888406408330644

Canter, L., Voytecki, K. S., & Rodríguez, D. (2007). Increasing online interaction in rural special education teacher preparation programs. *Rural Special Education Quarterly, 26*(1), 23–27.

Caywood, K., & Duckett, J. (2003). Online vs. on-campus learning in teacher education. *Teacher Education and Special Education, 26*, 98–105. doi: http://dx.doi.org/10.1177/088840640302600203

Cegelka, P. A., & Alvarado, J. (2000). A best practices model for preparation of rural special education teachers. *Rural Special Education Quarterly, 19*(3/4), 15.

Clark, R. E. (2009). Translating research into new instructional technologies for higher education: The active ingredient process. *Journal of Computing in Higher Education, 21*, 4–18. doi:10.1007/s12528-009-9013-8

Collins, B. C., Baird, C. M., & Hager, K. D. (2009). The University of Kentucky distance education program in moderate and severe disabilities. *Rural Special Education Quarterly, 28*(3), 30–40.

Cooke, N. L., & deBettencourt, L. (2001). Using distance education technology to train teachers: A case study. *Teacher Education and Special Education, 24*, 220–228. doi:10.1177/088840640102400306

Delfino, M., & Persico, D. (2007). Online or face-to-face? Experimenting with different techniques in teacher training. *Journal of Computer Assisted Learning, 23*, 351–365. doi: http://dx.doi.org/10.1111/j.1365-2729.2007.00220.x

Dieker, L., Hynes, M., Hughes, C., & Smith, E. (2008). Implications of mixed reality and simulation technologies on special education and teacher preparation. *Focus on Exceptional Children, 40*(6), 1–20.

Dieker, L. A., Lane, H. B., Allsopp, D. H., O'Brien, C., Butler, T. W., Kyger, M., Lovin, L., & Fenty, N. S. (2009). Evaluating video models of evidence-based instructional practices to enhance teacher learning. *Teacher Education and Special Education, 32*, 180–196. doi: http://dx.doi.org/10.1177/0888406409334202

Edyburn, D. L. (2008). A new paradigm for instructional materials. *Journal of Special Education Technology, 23*(4), 62–65.

Egbert, J., & Thomas, M. (2001). The new frontier: a case study in applying instructional design for distance teacher education. *Journal of Technology And Teacher Education, 9*, 391–405.

Falconer, K. B., & Lignugaris/Kraft, B. (2002). A qualitative analysis of the benefits and limitations of using two-way conferencing technology to supervise preservice teachers in remote locations. *Teacher Education and Special Education, 25*, 368–384. doi:10.1177/088840640202500406

Ferrell, K. A., Persichitte, K. A., Lowell, N., & Roberts, S. (2001). The evolution of a distance delivery system that supports content, students, and pedagogy. *Journal Of Visual Impairment & Blindness, 95*, 597–608.

Fitzgerald, G., Mitchem, K., Hollingsead, C., Miller, K., Koury, K., & Tsai, H. H. (2011). Exploring the bridge from multimedia cases to classrooms: Evidence of transfer. *Journal of Special Education Technology, 26*, 23–38.

Forbush, D. E., & Morgan, R. L. (2004). Instructional team training: Delivering live, internet courses to teachers and paraprofessionals in Utah, Idaho and Pennsylvania. *Rural Special Education Quarterly, 23*(2), 9–17.

Glomb, N., Lignugaris/Kraft, B., & Menlove, R. (2009). The USU mild/moderate distance degree and licensure program: Where we've been and where we're going. *Rural Special Education Quarterly, 28*(3), 18–22.

Glomb, N., Midenhall, T., Mason, L. L., & Salzberg, C. (2009). Reducing isolation through regional mentors and learning communities: A way to support rural learners. *Rural Special Education Quarterly, 28*(4), 31–35.

Gormley, S., & Ruhl, K. L. (2007). Language structure knowledge of preservice teachers: Connecting speech to print. *Teacher Education and Special Education, 30*, 83–92. doi:10.1177/088840640703000203

Grossman, P. (2005). Research on pedagogical approaches in teacher education. In M. Cochran-Smith & K. M. Zeichner (Eds.), *Studying teacher education: The report of the AERA panel on research and teacher education* (pp. 425–476). Mahwah, NJ: Lawrence Erlbaum.

Hager, K. D. (2010). Web conferencing with distant alternate certificate student teachers. *Rural Special Education Quarterly, 30*(1), 49–50.

Hallahan, D. P., Kauffman, J. M., & Pullen, P. C. (2012). *Exceptional learners—An introduction to Special Education* (12th ed.). Boston, MA: Pearson.

Heilson, S. B. (2010). What is the academic efficacy of podcasting? *Computers & Education, 55*, 1063–1068.

Hutinger, P. L., Johanson, J., & Stoneburner, R. (1996). Assistive technology applications in educational programs of children with multiple disabilities: A case study report on the state of the practice. *Journal of Special Education Technology, 13*, 16–35.

Johnson, E. S., Humphrey, M. J., & Allred, K. W. (2009). Online learning and mentors: Addressing the shortage of rural special educators through technology and collaboration. *Rural Special Education Quarterly, 28*(2), 17–21.

Judge, S., & Simms, K. A. (2009). Assistive technology training at the pre-service level: A national snapshot of teacher preparation programs. *Teacher Education and Special Education, 32*, 33–44. doi:10.1177/0888406408330868

Jung, L., Galyon-Keramidas, C., Collins, B., & Ludlow, B. (2006). Distance education strategies to support practica in rural settings. *Rural Special Education Quarterly, 25*(2), 18–24.

Kennedy, M. J. (2011). *Effects of content acquisition podcasts on vocabulary performance of secondary students with and without learning disabilities* (Doctoral dissertation). Retrieved from UMI Proquest Dissertations & Theses (3458221).

Kennedy, M. J., & Deshler, D. D. (2010). Literacy instruction, technology, and students with learning disabilities: Research we have, research we need. *Learning Disability Quarterly, 33*, 289–298.

Kennedy, M. J., Ely, E., Thomas, C. N., Pullen, P., Newton, J. R., Lovelace, S., Ashworth, K., & Cole, M. (2012). Using cognitive learning theory to create multimedia tools to support teacher candidates' learning. *Teacher Education and Special Education, 35*, 243–257. doi: http://dx.doi.org/10.1177/0888406412451158

Kennedy, M. J., Hart, J. E., & Kellems, R. O. (2011). Using enhanced podcasts to augment limited instructional time in teacher preparation. *Teacher Education and Special Education, 34*, 87–105. doi:10.1177/0888406410376203

Kennedy, M. J., Lloyd, J. W., Ely, E., & Cole, M. (2012). Specially designed vocabulary instruction in the content areas: What does high quality instruction look like? *Teaching Exceptional Children, 45*(1), 7. Retrieved from http://tecplus.org/articles/article/1/0

Kennedy, M. J., & Thomas, C. N. (2012). Effects of content acquisition podcasts to develop preservice teachers' knowledge of positive behavioral interventions and supports. *Exceptionality, 20*, 1–19. doi:10.1080/09362835.2011.611088

Kennedy, M. J., & Wexler, J. (2013). Improving literacy achievement in STEM fields: Roles and applications of instructional technology. *Teaching Exceptional Children, 45*(4), 26–33.

King-Sears, M. (2009). Universal design for learning: Technology and pedagogy. *Learning Disability Quarterly, 32*, 199–201.

Knapczyk, D., Chapman, C., Rodes, P., & Chung, H. (2001). Teacher preparation in rural communities through distance education. *Teacher Education and Special Education, 24*, 402–407. doi:10.1177/088840640102400415

Koehler, M. J., & Mishra, P. (2005). What happens when teachers design educational technology? The development of technological pedagogical content knowledge. *Journal of Educational Computing Research, 32*, 131–152. doi:10.2190/0EW7-01WB-BKHL-QDYV

Larwood, L. (2005). A promising practice: Low incidence teacher education in rural and remote California. *Rural Special Education Quarterly, 24*(3), 25–29.

Lawless, K. A., & Pellegrino, J. W. (2007). Professional development in integrating technology into teaching and learning: Knowns, unknowns, and ways to pursue better questions and answers. *Review of Educational Research*, 77, 575–614. doi:10.3102/0034654307309921

Lee, Y., & Vega, L. A. (2005). Perceived knowledge, attitudes, and challenges of AT use in special education. *Journal of Special Education Technology, 20*(2), 60–63.

Leko, M. M., Brownell, M. T., Sindelar, P. T., & Murphy, K. (2012). Promoting special education preservice teacher expertise. *Focus On Exceptional Children, 44*(7), 1–16.

Lesar, S. (1998). Use of assistive technology with young children with disabilities: Current status and training needs. *Journal of Early Intervention, 21*, 146–159. doi:10.1177/105381519802100207

Ludlow, B. L. (2003). An international outreach model for preparing early intervention and early childhood special education personnel. *Infants and Young Children, 16*, 38–248.

Ludlow, B. L., & Duff, M. C. (2007). Copyright law and content prediction mechanisms: Digital rights management for teacher educators. *Teacher Education and Special Education, 30*, 93–102. doi:10.1177/088840640703000204

Ludlow, B. L., & Duff, M. C. (2009). Evolution of distance education at West Virginia University: Past accomplishments, present activities, and future plans. *Rural Special Education Quarterly, 28*(3), 9–17.

Ludlow, B. L., Foshay, J. D., Brannan, S. A., Duff, M. C., & Dennison, K. E. (2002). Updating knowledge and skills of practitioners in rural areas: A web-based model. *Rural Special Education Quarterly, 21*(2), 33–43.

Ludlow, B. L., Gaylon-Keramidas, C., & Landers, E. J. (2007). Project STARS: Using desktop conferencing to prepare autism specialists at a distance. *Rural Special Education Quarterly, 26*(4), 27–35.

Marino, M. T., Sameshima, P., & Beecher, C. C. (2009). Enhancing TPACK with assistive technology: Promoting inclusive practices in preservice teacher education. *Contemporary Issues In Technology & Teacher Education, 9*, 186–207.

Mayer, R. E. (2004). Should there be a three-strikes rule against pure discovery learning. *American Psychologist, 59*(1), 14–19.

Mayer, R. E. (2009). *Multimedia learning* (2nd ed.). New York: Cambridge University Press.

McDonnell, J., Jameson, J. M., Riesen, T., Polychronis, S., Crockett, M. A., & Brown, B. E. (2011). A comparison of on-campus and distance teacher education programs in severe disabilities. *Teacher Education and Special Education, 34*, 106–118. doi:10.1177/0888406410380424

McGregor, G., & Pachuski, P. (1996). Assistive technology in schools: are teachers ready, able, and supported? *Journal of Special Education Technology, 13*, 4–15.

Mercer, D. (2004). Project VISION: An experiment in effective pedagogy for delivering preservice training to professionals in visual impairment through distance education. *Teacher Education and Special Education*, 27, 68–74. doi:10.1177/088840640402700107

Miller, K. J., Koury, K., Fitzgerald, G. E., Hollingsead, C., Mitchem, K. J., Tsai, H. H., & Park, M. K. (2009). Concept mapping as a research tool to evaluate conceptual change related to instructional methods. *Teacher Education and Special Education, 32*, 365–378. doi:10.1177/0888406409346149

Mitchem, K., Koury, K., Fitzgerald, G., Hollingsead, C., Miller, K., Tsai, H., & Zha, S. (2009). The effects of instructional implementation on learning with interactive multimedia case-based instruction. *Teacher Education and Special Education, 32*, 297–318. doi:10.1177/0888406409343520

Norton, P., & Hathaway, D. (2008). Exploring two teacher education online learning designs: A classroom of one or many? *Journal of Research On Technology In Education, 40*, 475–495.

Okolo, C. M., & Bouck, E. C. (2007). Research about assistive technology: 2000–2006. What have we learned? *Journal of Special Education Technology, 22*(3), 19–33.

O'Neal, K., Jones, W. P., Miller, S. P., Campbell, P., & Pierce, T. (2007). Comparing web-based to traditional instruction for teaching special education content. *Teacher Education and Special Education, 30*, 34–41. doi:10.1177/088840640703000104

Rock, M. L., Gregg, M., Thead, B. K., Acker, S. E., Gable, R. A., & Zigmond, N. P. (2009). Can you hear me now? Evaluation of an online wireless technology to provide real-time feedback to special education teachers-in-training. *Teacher Education and Special Education, 32*, 64–82. doi:10.1177/0888406408330872

Rosenberg, M. S., Boyer, K. L., Sindelar, P. T., & Misra, S. K. (2007). Alternative route programs for certification in special education: Program infrastructure, instructional delivery, and participant characteristics. *Exceptional Children, 73*, 224–241.

Rowlison, T. (2006). Meeting the needs for special education teachers in New Mexico. *Rural Special Education Quarterly, 25*(2), 13–17.

Scheeler, M. C., McKinnon, K., & Stout, J. (2012). Effects of immediate feedback delivered via webcam and bug-in-ear technology on preservice teacher performance. *Teacher Education and Special Education, 35*, 77–90. doi: http://dx.doi.org/10.1177/0888406411401919

Schmidt, D. A., Baran, E., Thompson, A. D., Mishra, P., Koehler, M. J., & Shin, T. S. (2009). Technological pedagogical content knowledge (TPACK): The development and validation of an assessment instrument for preservice teachers. *Journal Of Research On Technology In Education, 42*, 123–149.

Schweizer, H., Hayslett, C., & Chaplock, S. (2008). Student satisfaction and performance in an online teacher certification program. *Journal Of Continuing Higher Education, 56*(2), 12–25. doi:10.1080/07377366.2008.10400149

Scott, T. M., & Nelson, C. M. (1999). Functional behavioral assessment: Implications for training and staff development. *Behavioral Disorders, 24*, 249–252.

Sebastian, J. P., Egan, W. M., & Mayhew, J. C. (2009). From two-way television to the internet: The evolution of a rural distance education program. *Rural Special Education Quarterly, 28*(3), 5–8.

Shulman, L. (1987). Knowledge and teaching: Foundations of the new reform. *Harvard Educational Review, 57*, 1–22.

Sindelar, P. T., Brownell, M. T., & Billingsley, B. (2010). Special education teacher education research: Current status and future directions. *Teacher Education and Special Education, 33*, 8–24. doi:10.1177/0888406409358593

Skyler, A. A., Higgins, K., Boone, R., & Jones, P. (2005). Distance education: An exploration of alternative methods and types of instructional media in teacher education. *Journal of Special Education Technology, 20*(3), 25–33

Smith, S. J., & Allsopp, D. (2005). Technology and inservice professional development: Integrating an effective medium to bridge research to practice. In D. Edyburn, K. Higgins, & R. Boone (Eds.), *Handbook of special education technology research and practice* (pp. 777–792). Whitefish Bay, WI: Knowledge by Design.

Smith, S. J., & Israel, M. (2010). E-Mentoring: Enhancing special education teacher induction. *Journal of Special Education Leadership, 23*, 30–40.

Smith, S. J., & Meyen, E. L. (2003). Applications of online instruction: An overview for teachers, students with mild disabilities, and their parents. *Focus On Exceptional Children, 35*(6), 1–15.

Smith, S. J., & Okolo, C. (2010). Response to intervention and evidence-based practices: Where does technology fit? *Learning Disability Quarterly, 33*, 257–272.

Spooner, F., Agran, M., Spooner, M., & Kiefer-O'Donnell, R. (2000). Preparing personnel with expertise in severe disabilities in the electronic age: Innovative programs and technologies. *Research and Practice for Persons with Severe Disabilities, 25*, 92–103.

Spooner, F., Spooner, M., Algozzine, B., & Jordan, L. (1998). Distance education and special education: Promises, practices, and potential pitfalls. *Teacher Education and Special Education, 21*, 121–131. doi:10.1177/088840649802100206

Steinweg, S. B., Davis, M. L., & Thomson, W. S. (2005). A comparison of traditional and online instruction in an Introduction to Special Education course. *Teacher Education and Special Education, 28*, 62–73. doi:10.1177/088840640502800107

U.S. Department of Education, Office of Educational Technology. (2004). *Toward a new golden age in American education: How the Internet, the law and today's students are revolutionizing expectations*. Washington, DC: Author. Retrieved from http://www2.ed.gov/about/offices/list/os/technology/plan/2004/index.html

U.S. Department of Education, Office of Educational Technology. (2010). *Transforming American education: Learning powered by technology*. Washington, DC:Author. Retrieved from http://www.ed.gov/sites/default/files/NETP-2010-final-report.pdf

Wahl, L., & Buzolich, M. (2001, December). [Consultant's Report to the Mt. Diablo Unified School District AT/AAC Taskforce]. Concord, CA: Author.

Wasburn-Moses. L., & Rosenberg, M. S. (2008). Alternative route special education teacher preparation programs guidelines. *Teacher Education and Special Education, 31*, 257–267. doi:10.1177/0888406408330647

12

Preparing Teachers to Work With Diverse Populations

Vivian I. Correa

UNIVERSITY OF NORTH CAROLINA, CHARLOTTE

Patricia Alvarez McHatton

KENNESAW STATE UNIVERSITY

Erica D. McCray

UNIVERSITY OF FLORIDA

Cynthia Coss Baughan

UNIVERSITY OF NORTH CAROLINA, CHARLOTTE

Things to Think About

This chapter addresses the following key concepts:

- Diversity of the student population and its impact on the teaching workforce.
- Synthesis of the literature on preparing preservice and in-service teachers to work with students from diverse backgrounds.
- Challenges and controversies associated with preparing professionals to address issues of diversity.
- Recommendations for teacher education practice and the implications for future research.

Introduction

Today's schools are increasingly diverse. The diversity is expressed in various ways and is no longer solely concerned with issues of race, ethnicity, or language. Also present are differences in socioeconomic class, immigrant status, geographic location, language backgrounds, religion, sexual orientation, family structure, and abilities. Suffice it to say that in today's school environments, educators are more frequently interacting with a diverse student body (Renzulli, Parrott, & Beattie, 2011). The diversity in students and families requires teachers and staff to understand and become competent in working with diverse students and their families. It is not surprising, then, that preparing preservice and in-service teachers for the growing diversity of students has become a critical area of attention in teacher education and professional development. Yet, little is known about how to best address these issues in general and special education teacher preparation.

This chapter addresses this issue by providing a synthesis of the literature on preparing teachers to work with students from diverse backgrounds. The chapter addresses preservice and in-service preparation of culturally responsive teachers and associated challenges. Lastly, we present recommendations for teacher education practice and implications for future research.

Changing Demographics

According to the National Center on Education Statistics (NCES), the population in 2025 will be 58% White, 21% Hispanic, 12% Black, 6% Asian, and 1% American Indian/Alaskan Native (Aud, Fox, & KewalRamani, 2010). Associated with this diversity are data that often alarm stakeholders. According to the NCES report, 18% of children and youth are living in poverty with higher rates among Blacks (34%); American Indians/Alaska Natives (33%); Hispanics (27%); and Native Hawaiians or Other Pacific Islanders (26%) (Aud, Fox, & KewalRamani, 2010). Poverty can put these students at risk for unfavorable educational outcomes. For example, dropout rates for all students aged 16–24 years is 9%, yet among Hispanic students as many as 21% do not earn a high school credential (Aud, Hussar et al., 2010). Issues surrounding emerging bilingual students in schools are also cause for alarm if those students do not receive a highly effective education that supports multiple languages and embraces their rich cultural backgrounds. In 2007, 21% of all students spoke a language other than English at home, with 5% reporting difficulty speaking English (Aud, Hussar et al., 2010). Lewis (2009) reports that there are 364 different languages spoken in the United Sates. Thus, the challenges educators face as students acquire English can be overwhelming, especially if they lack strategies for teaching English to emergent bilinguals.

Lastly, the issue of disproportionality of students receiving special education services continues to be perplexing to educators. Several researchers have reported overrepresentation of African-American, Latino, and American Indian students in special education (Artiles, Harry, Reschly, & Chinn, 2002; Artiles, Kozleski, Trent, Osher, & Ortiz, 2010; Oswald, Coutinho, Best, & Singh, 1999; Skiba, Poloni-Staudinger, Gallini, Simmons, & Feggins-Azziz, 2006; Skiba et al., 2008). The causes of the overrepresentation are complex, but the critical importance of preparing general and special education teachers in nonbiased assessment, culturally relevant instruction, and culturally responsive classroom management practices (Blanchett, 2006; Waitoller, Artiles, & Cheney, 2010) cannot be overstated. One of the dilemmas we face, however, is that the demographics of the workforce are dramatically different than the growing diversity among the students and families they serve (see Chapter 7, this volume, for a more detailed discussion).

Demographics of the Workforce

Despite efforts to recruit and train teachers who reflect the diversity of the student population, the teacher workforce continues to be predominately White, female, young, and middle class (Renzulli et al., 2011; Sindelar, McCray, Kiely, & Kamman, 2008; Tyler, Yzquierdo, Lopez-Reyna, & Flippin, 2004). Schools and Staffing Survey (SASS) data for public schools (2007–2008) indicate that White teachers make up 83.1% of the workforce, while only 7% of teachers are Black, and 7.1% are Hispanic (Aud, Hussar et al., 2010). The numbers are even more dramatically disparate when it comes to other groups. Only 0.5% of teachers are American Indian, 1.2% Asian, and 0.2% Native Hawaiians. With only minimal shifts in the demographic complexion of the teaching force, ensuring cultural understanding and competence among the predominantly White teaching force is even more imperative (Hollins & Guzman, 2005).

Cultural Mismatch

The demographic realities of public schools today are forcing cross-cultural interactions between teachers, students, and families (Gay, 2010; Sleeter, 2001). Educators' satisfaction with their jobs and commitment to the diverse needs of their students may be influenced by these interactions, which could lead some teachers to leave the profession if they are unprepared for these cultural interactions (Renzulli et al., 2011). If we do not address this reality, educators will also continue to struggle with meeting students' needs. Today's teachers require cultural competence, an understanding of multicultural education, and knowledge of culturally responsive teaching (CRT) practices to address the continued disproportional representation in special education. Moreover, teachers will need to serve as cultural brokers and advocates for some of the most vulnerable learners and developing these skills should begin in teacher preparation.

Methodology

To identify relevant literature on diversity preparation for preservice and in-service educators, the following databases were searched: Academic Search Premier, Education Research Complete, ERIC, Psych INFO, Teacher Reference Center, Wilson Omnifile Full Text, Education Full Text, and EBSCO. Key terms included combinations of diversity, in-service teachers, multicultural education, preservice teachers, teacher preparation, special education, cultural diversity, multiculturalism, professional development, teacher education, and school leadership. Some searches led to previous syntheses (e.g., *The Report of the AERA Panel on Research and Teacher Education*). The majority of the papers returned focused on preservice teacher education. Further, many of the papers focused on in-service professional development, provider perceptions, participants' attitudes toward professional development (PD), and program descriptions.

Preparation of Preservice Teachers and Professionals

Multicultural education has been described as:

> an idea, an educational reform movement, and a process whose major goal is to change the structure of educational institutions so that male and female students, exceptional students, and students who are members of diverse racial, ethnic, language, and cultural groups will have an equal chance to achieve academically in school.
>
> *(Smith, 2009, p. 46)*

A critical component of this process is the preparation of teachers who are culturally competent and thus equipped to facilitate the success of all students (Ladson-Billings, 1995, 2002) and to act as change agents (Abbate-Vaughn, 2006). To meet this challenge, many teacher education programs (TEP) have incorporated diversity preparation in an effort to promote changes in the knowledge, pedagogical skills, attitudes, and beliefs of preservice teachers (Smith, 2009).

A substantial amount of literature examines the preparation of preservice teachers for CRT and diversity. Syntheses of the literature reveal that the discussion of teacher preparation for diversity generally includes: (a) the dispositions of preservice teachers toward diversity, multicultural education, and social justice; (b) the curricular and instructional approaches incorporated by TEPs; and (c) the effects of TEPs strategies to prepare preservice teachers (e.g., Artiles, Trent, & Kuan, 1997; Castro, 2010; Jennings, 2007; Trent, Kea, & Oh, 2008; Webb-Johnson, Artiles, Trent, Jackson, & Velox, 1998). The following sections discuss the research related to preparing preservice teachers across these three themes. Although the primary focus of this discussion is the preparation of teachers in special education, some articles related to teacher preparation in general education are included to provide context.

Dispositions of Preservice Teachers

A significant portion of the literature related to preparing preservice teachers for diversity focuses on the cultural mismatch between the student and teacher populations (Gay, 2010; Renzulli et al., 2011; Sleeter, 2001). This mismatch has led to extensive study of the dispositions of preservice teachers toward diversity.

Sleeter (2001) described several perspectives toward diversity that White preservice teachers often exhibit. Specifically, these teachers tend to avoid differences through colorblindness (e.g., Valli, 1995); are often naïve, holding stereotypical beliefs about students from culturally and linguistically diverse backgrounds (CLD; e.g., Larke, Wiseman, & Bradley, 1990; Schultz, Neyhart, & Reck, 1996); and demonstrate a superficial level of acceptance of learning about diversity (Sleeter, 2001). Additionally, these teachers demonstrate a lack of awareness and understanding about the depth of the issues related to diversity, including racism and institutional inequalities (e.g., King, 1991; Su, 1996), viewing multicultural education as simply adding to the existing curriculum (e.g., Vavrus, 1994). Furthermore, these teachers express a lack of confidence in the ability to effectively teach CLD students (e.g., Pang & Sablan, 1998). Castro (2010) identified similar findings. In his review of general education research from 1985–2007, he examined themes related to the views of preservice teachers toward diversity, multicultural education, and social justice. Findings from this analysis suggest contemporary preservice teachers may be entering TEPs with more positive views toward diversity than their counterparts 20 years prior. These views, however, tend to be superficial and do not indicate a deeper understanding of multicultural issues such as institutional inequality and the effects of "privilege on the potential life outcomes of students from marginalized groups" (Castro, 2010, p. 201).

Strategies for Preparing Teachers for Diversity

To address the issues related to the cultural mismatch between students and teachers and the detrimental dispositions and beliefs of many preservice teachers, the majority of TEPs have incorporated strategies to promote teachers' cultural competence. According to Sleeter (2001), these strategies typically fall within two categories: (a) recruiting and training more culturally diverse preservice teachers, and (b) developing critical knowledge and attitudes in White preservice teachers.

Professional organizations have shown interest in the diversity of the teaching force and offered recommendations for recruitment and preparation (see Darling-Hammond, Dilworth, & Bulmaster, 1996; King, & Castenell, 2001). One approach that has been found to increase the diversity of the teacher workforce is alternative teacher education programs (Shen, 2000 as cited in Suell & Piotrowski, 2007). Research on alternative route preparation suggests that when programs are located in diverse communities they attract diverse participants (Rosenberg, Boyer, Sindelar, & Misra, 2007; Tyler et al., 2004). In her review, Sleeter (2001) included several descriptions of TEPs in the literature that increased the diversity of the preservice teachers in their programs. Other programs have been described in more recent papers related to recruiting and training CLD special education candidates, such as Native American teachers in rural areas through web-based distance education (Peterson & Showalter, 2010), CLD teachers through campus and community efforts (Prater, Wilder, & Dyches, 2008), and Latino bilingual teachers for urban schools through grant-funded cohorts (Sakash & Chou, 2007). Two of these papers (see Prater et al., 2008 and Sakash & Chou, 2007) included descriptive data to demonstrate the increase in CLD preservice teachers matriculating through programs. Although efforts to increase the diversity of the teacher workforce continue, the current demographics require an intensive effort to prepare White preservice teachers for the diversity of public school classrooms.

The primary focus of the research on preparing preservice teachers for diversity appears to be the development of critical knowledge and attitudes, primarily in White preservice teachers. A number of reviews examining general and special education preservice programs (e.g., Artiles et al., 1997; Sleeter,

2001; Trent et al., 2008; Webb-Johnson et al., 1998) identified strategies TEPs have typically used in this process. These strategies represent a spectrum of activities with varying levels of intensity and include: (a) offering coursework related to diversity (e.g., Bennett, 2008; Correa, Hudson, & Hayes, 2004; Mullen, 2001; Trent, Pernell, Mungai, & Chimedza, 1998; Zetlin, Beltran, Salcido, Gonzalez, & Reyes, 2011); (b) combining coursework and field experiences (e.g., Frye, Button, Kelly, & Button, 2010; Schrum, Burbank, & Capps, 2007; Wright, Calabrese, & Henry, 2009); (c) incorporating short- and long-term cultural immersion experiences (e.g., Ference & Bell, 2004; Wiggins, Follo, & Eberly, 2007); and (d) implementing program-level strategies to infuse diversity throughout the curriculum (e.g., Alvarez McHatton, Keller, Shircliffe, & Zalaquett, 2009; Artiles, Barreto, Peña, & McClafferty, 1998; Burnstein, Cabello, & Hamann, 1993; Prater et al., 2008; Salend & Reynolds, 1991; West & Hudson, 2010).

Although the approaches used to prepare preservice teachers for diversity vary across TEPs, consistent trends in the priorities of TEPs related to the aspects of diversity that are emphasized have been identified. Specifically, TEPs tend to address diversity in a compartmentalized fashion, focusing on particular characteristics of CLD students. For example, Jennings (2007) used an Internet-based survey to examine the primary areas of diversity being addressed in 142 TEPs across the country. Findings indicated similar priorities across programs with the most emphasized topic being race/ethnicity, followed by exceptionality, language, socioeconomic status, gender, and sexual orientation. Only one exception was noted: in California, language diversity received greater emphasis and exceptionality received less, indicating that regional concerns, in addition to imposed requirements and faculty values and beliefs, may influence the priorities of TEPs. Findings from this investigation indicated an apparent consensus among TEPs that preparing preservice teachers for racial/ethnic diversity is a high priority for teacher educators; however, the continued institutional inequalities experienced by historically marginalized groups in the public schools suggest the need to closely examine the effectiveness of the strategies being used to prepare teachers for diversity (Jennings, 2007).

Effectiveness of Approaches to Prepare Preservice Teachers for Diversity

The literature is replete with descriptions of the problematic attitudes and dispositions toward diversity often held by preservice teachers, which shape the conceptual understanding of teaching and subsequent actions (Gay, 2010). To reach the goal of preparing preservice teachers to promote cultural diversity and social justice (Jennings, 2007; Nieto, 2005; Smith, 2009), the strategies used by TEPs must effectively change underlying attitudes and beliefs that prohibit some preservice teachers from developing a critical consciousness of how attitudes and beliefs shape behaviors and ultimately affect teaching–learning interactions (Gay, 2010; Smith, 2009). It appears, however, that diversity preparation often fails to focus on moving preservice teachers along the continuum from basic awareness to promoting social justice. Building on the work of Jenks, Lee, and Kanpol (2001) and Grant and Sleeter (2006), through a qualitative examination of 45 syllabi from multicultural education courses across the United States, Gorski (2009) concluded that the majority of courses focused on preparing preservice teachers to be aware, sensitive, tolerant, and culturally competent, with few courses focused on preparing teachers to promote social justice and educational equality.

The majority of the research related to the effectiveness of TEPs to prepare preservice teachers for diversity examines the effects of approaches and strategies on the attitudes and dispositions of preservice teachers (Sleeter, 2001; Trent et al., 2008; Webb-Johnson et al., 1998). In general, these studies have typically included small sample sizes, incorporated qualitative or mixed methodology, and been implemented by instructor-researchers (Sleeter, 2001; Trent et al., 2008; Webb-Johnson et al., 1998). Furthermore, reviews of the effects of preparing preservice teachers for diversity have revealed mixed results: some studies indicating powerful effects, some positive effects that were temporarily sustained, and some little or no effect. In fact, in some studies stereotypic attitudes and biases appeared to be reinforced (Sleeter, 2001).

Coursework

For the purpose of this discussion, coursework refers to experiences that occur primarily within the college classroom. One strategy related to coursework involves the infusion of content related to diversity within a course designed primarily to address other content (e.g., foundations of education). This strategy often incorporates group-specific studies (e.g., individuals with disabilities) or a dedicated lesson or unit on the topic of diversity (Alvarez McHatton et al., 2009). Few studies were identified in the general education literature that have examined the effectiveness of the infusion of diversity content within a single course (e.g., Mullen, 2001; Bennett, 2008). Findings from these studies indicated that course participants, in general, demonstrated an increase in awareness, respect, and open-mindedness toward diversity.

A second approach related to coursework is the use of stand-alone courses specifically designed to address issues related to diversity. Several examinations of the effects of stand-alone courses are described in the general education literature, but only three related to special education were identified. For example, Trent et al. (1998) examined the effects of an introductory multicultural/special education course focused on teaching CLD students and students with special needs on 30 randomly selected preservice teachers. Data collected through student pre- and postcourse conceptual maps, explanatory paragraphs, and essays indicated increases in the number and depth of multicultural concepts on the postcourse measures. Furthermore, students developed a broader definition of diversity, revealed a greater understanding of the complexities of teaching diverse students, and incorporated more specific statements about techniques and strategies to implement with diverse students.

Correa et al. (2004) found similar results in their examination of the effects of a one-semester multicultural education course focused on developing cultural competence in 45 preservice teachers in a unified early childhood program. Qualitative and quantitative analysis of data collected through pre- and postcourse concept maps and explanatory paragraphs indicated positive changes in conceptual understanding of multicultural education and beliefs immediately following the course.

In a more recent paper, Zetlin et al. (2011) described and evaluated the piloting of learning modules designed to prepare preservice teachers to work with students from diverse language backgrounds. The modules were integrated within an introductory special education course and included strategies such as media-based demonstrations of classroom instruction, classroom-based assignments, and written reflections to promote knowledge and culturally appropriate pedagogy. Although no specific discussion of a systematic analysis of student outcomes was provided, the authors described increases in the awareness of issues and special education processes related to English Language Learners (ELL).

Findings from these studies suggest that coursework, including focused studies and stand-alone courses designed to address issues of diversity, can promote conceptual changes in preservice teachers immediately following the coursework. The level of change, however, appears to be commensurate with the focus of the course. For example, Mullen (2001) identified changes in awareness and sensitivity consistent with the objectives of the infused focused course. Likewise, findings from Trent et al. (1998) and Correa et al. (2004) indicated changes in basic awareness and acceptance in preservice teachers, but also indicated a movement toward culturally appropriate pedagogy (e.g., strategies and classroom methods) and recognition of the need for social justice (e.g., antibias approach), consistent with the objectives of these courses.

Combinations of Coursework and Field Experience

Combined coursework and field placements are often implemented through service learning, practica, and internships. Several examinations of the effects of coursework and field experiences are described in the general education literature (e.g., Frye et al., 2010), but only one that specifically included special education preservice teachers was identified (e.g., Wright et al., 2009). These authors examined the effects of an urban service learning experience with 16 freshman preservice teachers (six special education, six elementary, two early childhood, two secondary) enrolled in a children's literature course. The 10-hour service-learning requirement for the course included sharing multicultural literature and activities in a diverse urban classroom. Qualitative analysis of the data collected through pre and post surveys and reflective papers suggested that, generally, the preservice teachers believed the experience was valuable. Furthermore, findings indicated the preservice teachers developed a greater awareness and sensitivity toward diversity.

Combining coursework and field experiences may also help develop feelings of competence in preservice teachers. For example, Frye et al. (2010) examined the beliefs of 55 elementary education preservice teachers related to their self-efficacy and outcome expectancies for CRT. Students completed two self-rating scales, the Culturally Responsive Teaching Self-Efficacy and the Outcomes Expectancies Scales (Siwatu, 2007), at the beginning and at the end of a one-semester elementary literacy methods course in which faculty infused culturally responsive pedagogy using literature, art, and history, and provided experiences with CLD students at professional development sites. Throughout the semester, the preservice teachers maintained journals to reflect on their teaching practices, the attitudes and responses of the clinical teachers in the professional development sites, and on lessons and the classroom climate. Analysis of the mean scores on the pre and post rating scales demonstrated an increase in feelings of efficacy and expectations for positive outcomes from CLD students. Specifically, preservice teachers indicated confidence in their ability to develop positive relationships with students.

Including field placements also appears to be an important component of online courses in the preparation of preservice teachers for diversity. Schrum et al. (2007) examined student perspectives related to participating in an online diversity course that incorporated a classroom placement. Analysis of pre- and post-course surveys and open-ended student responses indicated that several of the preservice teachers demonstrated more positive views of diversity and developed a greater sensitivity to the need for culturally responsive practices following participation in the field placement than demonstrated before the placement.

Similar to the findings related to coursework, including a field experience in combination with coursework can increase awareness, cultural sensitivity, and the development of cultural competence in preservice teachers. Additionally, the opportunities to put theoretical knowledge into practice in a field placement may have also contributed to perceived self-efficacy in the preservice teachers and higher expectations of outcomes for CLD students.

Immersion

Another strategy used by TEPs is short- or long-term cultural immersion experiences within a school (e.g., Wiggins et al., 2007) or community context (e.g., Ference & Bell, 2004). Although no studies specifically related to cultural immersion in special education TEPs were identified, several descriptions are available in the general education literature. For example, Ference and Bell (2004) examined the effects of a 2-week cross-cultural immersion project on the knowledge, skills, and dispositions of preservice teachers related to Latino ELL. Before students began the immersion experience, they participated in six preparatory seminars that included readings, basic instruction in conducting ethnographic studies, and discussion of cultural differences and similarities in Latino students. Subsequently, preservice teachers lived with a Latino host family for 13 days, participating in family and community life, as well as a formal school experience at an educational center that served recent immigrants. Preservice teachers were required to complete a portfolio with artifacts reflecting the experience, including three written products: a written philosophy for teaching ELL, journal entries, and an experience summary paper. Qualitative analysis of researcher field notes and student papers indicated positive changes related to awareness, attitudes and misconceptions, culturally responsive pedagogy, and social justice.

Research suggests that immersion experiences of varying length and depth can promote positive changes in preservice teachers' cultural competence. However, upon close examination of immersion experiences, the complexity of factors (e.g., level of involvement beyond the classroom, faculty members on site, preparation for the experience) that are involved makes it difficult to isolate specific characteristics that are likely to develop cultural competence.

Program-Wide Infusion

The potential for combining and infusing diversity related content and experiences across TEPs is of interest to many teacher education researchers (e.g., Alvarez McHatton et al., 2009; Kidd, Sanchez, & Thorpe, 2008; Potts, Foster-Triplett, & Rose, 2008; Prater et al., 2008; West & Hudson, 2010). Individual and focus group interviews with faculty, doctoral students, and in-service and preservice teachers have helped to identify the types of strategies used to infuse diversity content and experiences throughout TEPs' curricula. For example, Potts et al. (2008) examined the perspectives of faculty and doctoral students regarding which strategies were important to include. Interview data revealed that community-based and school-based experiences that included opportunities for reflection through dialogue, aesthetic experiences (e.g., music, drama, poetry), and storytelling (e.g., faculty sharing stories of their own experiences in developing cultural awareness) were perceived to be important strategies for infusing diversity across a 5-year elementary education program.

Alvarez McHatton et al. (2009) also used focus group interviews to examine the efforts of faculty across one college of education to infuse diversity within their courses. A variety of strategies were again identified, including focused units or lessons within courses, capitalizing on teachable moments, field experiences, service learning projects, relevant readings, diverse guest speakers, classroom discussions, immersion experiences, and cross-cultural simulations. Several of these strategies also incorporated opportunities for preservice teachers to reflect and apply their learning through activities such as planning units or lessons that included culturally responsive methods and accommodations for students with disabilities. Furthermore, variation in the foci of the strategies was identified with some focusing on awareness, understanding of self, and the identification of both educational inequalities and the need to address them.

Three papers specifically related to the infusion of diversity content across programs that prepare special educators were identified. In one example, Prater et al. (2008) described how one program began infusing ELL content across a special education program. In a second paper, Salend and Reynolds (1991) described a master's-level migrant special education teacher training program. In the final paper, West and Hudson (2010) used focus groups to examine the perceptions of in-service special education teachers regarding the effectiveness of their TEPs. Several themes related to being prepared to work with CLD students and families were identified. Specifically, in-service teachers reported the need for TEPs to include more coursework related to ELLs and authentic representations of diversity, diverse field experiences that include interactions and opportunities to establish relationships with families, and opportunities to observe home visits. In summary, simply including diversity content within a TEP is no guarantee that preservice teachers will develop the cultural competence required to effectively address the needs of a diverse student population. TEPs must include a variety of strategies that are specifically designed not only to develop awareness and sensitivity, but also to develop competence in CRT and a willingness and ability to serve as institutional change agents.

In our judgment, preparing culturally competent teachers requires multiple strategies including structured delivery of authentic content related to diversity (i.e., coursework and relevant readings); well-designed opportunities for personal encounters with CLD students, families, and culturally competent mentor teachers (i.e., guest speakers, service learning, field experiences, and immersion) within school and community contexts; authentic opportunities to apply theoretical learning; and forums for critical reflection and dialogue. Additionally, TEPs must include multiple courses with a variety of approaches to move students from a simplistic awareness of diversity to cognizance of attitudes and biases that impede the success of CLD students.

The work related to cultural competence does not end at graduation from a TEP. Induction, professional development, and support from school administrators are critical for sustaining and promoting CRT once special educators enter the classroom.

Preparation of In-Service Teachers/Professionals and Administrative Support for Promoting CRT

It is widely accepted that preservice candidates graduate from their programs with knowledge and skills that will need to be honed and cultivated once they enter the profession. Their development will greatly depend on the school in which they work and the culture and climate established by the school's leadership and the surrounding community. The literature reviewed in this section includes studies conducted in the United States that focused on in-service teachers and school leaders with the explicit goal of providing more culturally relevant experiences to K–12 students and their families.

Professional Development for In-Service Educators

The demographics of the teaching force and student population have been discussed, but the impact of the cultural mismatch is most felt at the building level. School and district leaders are under immense pressure to meet federal progress guidelines, which encourage a focus on testing and test scores with less attention given to the actual needs of students and teachers. Educator preparation continues well into the early career years and school leaders are primarily responsible for continued professional development (Griffin et al., 2009).

The need for PD is greater in schools with diverse student populations, including students with disabilities, emergent bilinguals, and those living in poverty. Without proper support, teachers are less likely to be effective and more likely to leave the school, if not the field (Rogers et al., 2005).

Professional development can come in various forms and through different modalities. Recent syntheses have identified varying levels of effectiveness based on the site-specific nature, length, and format of PD (McLeskey, 2011; Vescio, Ross, & Adams, 2008). Most often, unfortunately, CRT and diversity workshops are isolated incidents provided with little understanding of participants' background, needs, or context (Colombo, 2004). In other instances, PD is provided on site, but may still present some of the same challenges with minimal follow-up or ongoing support. Other more supportive options include lesson study, book study, professional learning communities, and consultation or coaching. More recently, technology use has increased as a way to provide synchronous and asynchronous PD to individuals or groups across sites.

Cozart, Cudahy, Ndunda, and VanSickle (2003) and Henze, Lucas, and Scott (1998) discussed off-site PD offered for teachers and administrators to increase cultural awareness and sensitivity. Cozart et al. described the facilitators' perspectives on providing PD with colleagues and overcoming their own challenges and those of the participants. Taking somewhat of an outsider's perspective, Henze and her colleagues conducted a discourse analysis of a particular panel session on race, power, and privilege. The viewpoints of both the panelists and the teacher-participants provided valuable insights on some of the drawbacks of decontextualized training. Off-site PD on sensitive topics requires even more deliberate planning and rules of engagement to create a safe space.

Lesson study is attributed to a practice in Japan that emphasizes the collaborative examination of instructional practice. In one study, researchers worked with early childhood educators and a master teacher to understand how they would use lesson study after receiving training on a mediated format involving support from the other teacher-collaborators, the master teacher, and the researchers (West-Olatunji, Behar-Horenstein, Rant, & Cohen-Phillips, 2008). The researchers used confirmatory analysis and case study methodology to assess participants' knowledge and implementation of culturally relevant strategies. Perhaps, most interesting was that the three teachers were African American, the same cultural background as their students, but were in different settings—one was a master's-prepared teacher in a faith-based setting, one was a stay-at-home mom and home school teacher with a law degree, and the third was a childcare provider with a high school diploma. Even though they shared cultural congruence with their students, they did not take culture into account until prompted through the lesson study. As a result of the process and collaborative inquiry, the participants felt more culturally aware, reflective, and empowered.

Book study is used to engage educators on a topic while providing a third-point focus for discussion (Guerra & Nelson, 2008). Having an external focus allows participants to become more comfortable with the issue, build trust with other participants, and have an opportunity to reflect and make personal connections (Honigsfeld & Dove, 2008). Further, principals have used book study as a springboard to empower teachers to lead groups of their peers (White-Hood, 2007). In one Maryland school with a greater than 90% Black student population, the principal engaged her faculty in a teacher-led book study of *Teach with Your Heart: Lessons I Learned From the Freedom Writers* by Erin Gruwell (2007). The book study experience was enriched through journaling, a parent survey, and a cultural activity.

Professional Learning Communities (PLCs) are another configuration commonly used for teacher development (Blanton & Perez, 2011). PLCs provide a structure for professionals to grow and hold each other accountable. Voltz, Brazil, and Scott (2003, 2004) implemented Project CRISP (Culturally Responsive Instruction for Special Populations) as teacher-directed PD for teams of professionals. Each team had to include at least one special educator as the focus was on reducing disproportionality in special education. As part of their study of the process, participants took part in interviews, responded to questionnaires, completed concept maps and lesson plan analyses, kept journals, and developed their own goals. Voltz and her colleagues learned from participants that they appreciated the collaborative, self-directed nature of the work, but they would have liked more balance in the form of structure (e.g., specific outlines and timelines for tasks) and individual accountability (e.g., equal contributions of team members). Probably the most promising outcome was that teachers shared what they learned with others in their schools and encouraged them to engage in similar activities.

In one highly innovative approach, Mahn, McMann, and Musanti (2005) provided on-site PD for teachers of CLD learners in five elementary schools. The Teaching and Learning Centers (TLC) classroom model created a model second-grade demonstration classroom at each site with an experienced ELL teacher and a trained cofacilitator. Other teachers were invited to observe and participate as guest teachers for a week at a time to work with the expert in the classroom, while the cofacilitator covered the guest teacher's classroom. The teachers greatly valued the peer interaction and learning. Further, this project was resource-intensive initially, but it was viewed as an investment because it built capacity within the school by improving teacher practice.

PD within the context of a subject area is viewed as ideal. Some researchers' efforts to provide PD that promoted cultural relevance within science content did not see the changes they anticipated. Lee, Lukyx, Buxton, and Shaver (2007) developed an intensive PD with curricular materials to encourage culturally relevant science instruction that attended to students' home culture, language, and socio-economic status. They conducted a mixed-method study of implementation and found that the diverse group of teachers believed students' backgrounds were important but some had difficulty seeing the role of culture in their science teaching. The researchers believed the lack of appropriate materials, the school-wide (involuntary) nature of the project, and high-stakes climates may have negatively impacted teacher buy-in. After the first year of the project they noted no significant increase in the use of student home language or culture in instruction.

In some instances, locale can prohibit access to quality PD, although technology has made knowledge and collaboration more accessible. Teemant, Smith, Pinnegar, and Egan (2005) described a program developed to support teams of teachers to earn ESOL/bilingual education endorsement.

Web-based instruction was the primary format with supplemental instruction from an on-site facilitator. The authors noted that distance education technologies do not always encourage sociocultural perspectives, which are essential to meeting the needs of second-language learners. Their goal was to create such a space that could meet distance learning needs while effectively addressing the specific content. The comprehensive program combined activities, readings, video-based models, and student portfolios to create authentic learning experiences even from a distance. Participants appreciated the program and all they learned, but some felt the learning was too compressed and allowed little time for them to reflect on and incorporate their new knowledge.

As evident as diversity is in society, it is not always reflected in what is taught and how it is taught. Even with good intentions, educators can teach a monocultural reality and unintentionally dismiss CLD learners and families. Preservice and in-service teacher development will improve to the extent that research can show evidence of the value of diversity and cultural relevance in instruction.

Challenges and Controversies in the Field

There are several challenges and controversies along the teacher preparation pipeline associated with preparing professionals to address issues of diversity. The challenges associated with teacher beliefs, field experiences, professional development, the role of context, the standardization of teaching, and preparation of faculty are addressed in this section.

Teacher Beliefs

The role of teacher beliefs relative to diverse learners is an important one to consider. As previously discussed, teacher educators place great emphasis on ensuring candidates possess the necessary knowledge, skills, and dispositions to effectively instruct all learners. This raises questions regarding the relationship between what teacher candidates have mastered (knowledge and skills) and the likelihood that they will consistently engage in the desired behavior (dispositions). In other words, does having the knowledge and skill to teach diverse students enhance candidates' dispositions to engage in culturally responsive pedagogy? Should the focus of teacher preparation be solely on enhancing knowledge of diverse learners and culturally responsive practices while providing opportunities for applied experiences within diverse settings? Or, should more emphasis be placed on examining and attempting to change teacher beliefs that are contrary to a multicultural perspective? Are there ethical dilemmas associated with attempts to transform teacher beliefs?

Bandura (1982) and others (e.g., Pajares, 1992; Tillema, 1998) posit that teacher beliefs function as a mediator to the acquisition of knowledge. While an expansive discussion on teacher beliefs and our role in changing them is beyond the purview of this chapter, the function of teacher beliefs in teaching diverse students requires examination. Specifically, how do—or how can—teacher educators change teacher beliefs in the short duration of a program? Is it possible to affect beliefs to the extent that the change resists external factors (e.g., toxic environments, negative colleagues, and challenging students and families)?

Clark-Goff (2008) notes discrepancies within existing research regarding the ability of teacher preparation programs to affect teacher beliefs. While there is existing research that indicates teacher beliefs are "highly tenacious and resistant to change" (p. 35), there is also research demonstrating change in beliefs after completing a course or participating in an applied experience. Clark-Goff's own work examining change in teacher beliefs about ELLs and teaching supports the latter, albeit with a caveat. Although participants reported increased confidence in their ability to effectively teach ELLs, several still expressed concern over their ability to meet the needs of these learners. This is an important consideration as without further intervention (e.g., additional coursework in instructional strategies and opportunities to apply what they learn), there is a possibility that positive beliefs may revert to a deficit perspective upon entering the classroom.

We propose that changing stereotypical beliefs is possible and essential if issues of disproportionality and student achievement are to be substantively addressed. Doing so requires engendering a sense of disequilibrium in teacher candidates that propels them to examine their preconceived beliefs in light of new information (McFalls & Cobb-Roberts, 2001; Schein, 1999) within a safe environment. Additionally, opportunities to observe pockets of positive deviance (Patterson, Grenny, Maxfield, McMillan, & Switzler, 2008)—those settings that contradict stereotypical expectations (e.g., high-performing, high-poverty schools)—are essential to assist teacher candidates in reframing their own perceptions of diverse learners and communities.

Finding High-Quality Field Experiences and Implications of the Accountability Movement

The Blue Ribbon Panel (National Council for Accreditation of Teacher Education, 2010) highlighted the importance of clinical practice in teacher preparation. Existing research points to the benefits of high-quality field experiences including teacher retention (Connelly & Graham, 2009; Graziano, 2009) and increased student gains (American Association of Colleges for Teacher Education, 2009). Teacher candidates often identify their field experiences as the most powerful of their learning experiences noting they provide opportunities to learn from veteran teachers and to work with P–12 learners (O'Brian, Stone, Appel, & House, 2007).

There is an increased demand to provide teacher candidates with opportunities to work with diverse populations (e.g., NCATE Standard 4), but providing high-quality field experiences with CLD learners can be problematic. For example, although the student population is becoming increasingly diverse, there are many teacher preparation programs in geographic locations that lack the diversity more common in urban settings. A lack of diversity in the local area requires innovative initiatives that span beyond the institution's geographical boundaries.

In locations with high numbers of low-performing and high-poverty schools, there are multiple dilemmas. Research indicates that these settings contain higher percentages of undercredentialed or beginning teachers (Aud, Hussar et al., 2010) and have higher turnover (Lankford, Loeb, & Wyckoff, 2002). Further, the increased scrutiny and control due to low performance limit what teacher candidates may be able to do. While there is a demand for teacher preparation programs to place teacher candidates in these settings, there may be an insufficient number of appropriately credentialed teachers to serve as mentors or supervising teachers to support candidates' development. One initiative that has been touted as a possible solution is the Professional Development School. The problem for special education is that there are insufficient numbers of special education teachers in any one setting to support the numbers of teacher candidates needing placements in any one semester (McCray et al., 2011).

Additional concerns that might affect identification of high-quality field placements are the dismantling of tenure systems, value-added teacher evaluation, and the move toward merit pay. These changes are relatively recent, yet the effects are beginning to emerge. Specifically, there is some reluctance on the part of teachers to turn over their classroom to a novice if their pay and continued employment is based in part on student performance.

Diversity-Focused PD

Even with the good intentions at the root of diversity-focused PD, there are inherent challenges in such efforts. Often, PD opportunities are disjointed and fail to provide support after the fact, such as mentoring or coaching, to assist with implementation of what has been learned (Cohen & Hill, 2000). Haycock and Robinson (2001) pointed to the fact the PD is not always research based or of sufficient depth to prompt change. Superficial coverage of content and the lack of continuing support can trivialize the importance of meeting the needs of CLD learners.

Cozart and her colleagues (2003) indicated specific challenges to providing PD to teachers in South Carolina including: developing trust, moving teachers beyond a Heroes and Holidays approach to diversity, and addressing the variability of participants' backgrounds and needs. Skilled facilitators are required to move participants beyond what is comfortable without causing them to retreat (Leistyna, 2001). Henze et al. (1998) also experienced some of the difficulties presented by different developmental needs and perspectives. They found that participants and panelists dealt with conflict and withdrawal during difficult conversations, different perceptions of power, and participants needing different structures for interaction.

Even when PD is appropriate and designed to meet participant needs, Lawrence (2005) found that context moderates its effects. In her follow-up study, professionals working in a supportive district that was advancing an antiracist agenda were much more engaged in changing their practice. Conversely, teachers in other districts felt silenced and discouraged. This study underscores the importance of culture and climate to change teachers' beliefs and practices.

The Role of Context

Teaching and learning occur within complex nested ecological systems, each informing and affecting the other. Thus, context is important in understanding teacher development. If positive school contexts can be a protective factor for children (Donovan & Cross, 2002), it can be presumed that the same holds true for adults within that setting. Flores and Day (2006) examined how context shaped new teachers' identities. Their teacher identity is refined as they become socialized into their teaching environment and attempt to negotiate their lived experience with their previously established perceptions of teaching. Their findings reveal three factors impacting the development of teacher identity: (a) prior influences; (b) initial teacher training and teaching practice; and (c) contexts of teaching. The disconnect between what was learned in their courses and what they were experiencing in their setting resulted in "strategic compliance" (p. 225), whereby participants assumed behaviors exhibited by their supervisors while holding conflicting beliefs about the practices. In their study, the majority of participants (71%) noted their teaching became more teacher-directed over time. Flores and Day's (2006) findings are especially important for special education teacher educators. The field is experiencing an identity crisis. The roles and responsibilities of special educators are diverse, complex, and constantly shifting. Special educators may find themselves in inclusive classrooms, resource rooms, self-contained settings, or consulting as support facilitators (Griffin et al., 2009). Each of these roles requires specific skill sets, and each may or may not be implemented with fidelity. Attempting to address each of these possibilities is a challenge in itself. Doing so in a way that helps teacher candidates make sense of each configuration is doubly so.

The Standardization of Teaching

The standardization of teaching is another challenge. Special education teacher educators provide instruction that highlights the individual, the importance of data-driven problem solving, and the role of the professional in making instructional decisions to meet students' needs. Yet, increasingly, teachers are provided with scripted curricula and pacing guides that discourage deviation. Anecdotal information obtained from the authors' graduates reveals being reprimanded or receiving lower scores when evaluated if they were not in lockstep with the pacing guide. Curriculum maps are essential in ensuring an understanding of the content to be addressed within one school year, but there must be opportunities for instructional decisions based on the needs of all learners in classrooms.

The emphasis on pacing guides and scripted curricula runs contrary to much of what is taught in teacher preparation programs; thus, beginning teachers experience tensions when attempting to reconcile what they were taught with the reality of their setting. The challenge for teacher educators is how to provide teacher candidates with not only a full understanding of best practices but also an honest appraisal of the system they are entering. This also requires teacher educators to equip candidates with knowledge, skills, and dispositions to not simply survive but thrive in what may be toxic environments and to foster resiliency and strategies for advocating for what is in the best interest of students without jeopardizing their position. In other words, teacher educators cannot open candidates' eyes and then fail to provide them with the skills and coping strategies to address what they see.

Preparing Higher Education Faculty

As previously noted, preparing culturally responsive teachers able to meet the academic and affective needs of diverse learners requires a concerted effort by teacher educators and districts. Field experiences in diverse settings coupled with opportunities to reflect on and debrief these experiences are essential. Further, engaging teacher candidates in introspection and examination of worldviews requires that teacher educators facilitate a sense of comfort in discomfort. Schein (1999) notes a change in beliefs is based on three factors: (a) new information that is contrary to personal beliefs and results in a sense of disequilibrium; (b) acceptance of this disconfirming information as relevant and valid; and (c) a safe environment in which to reconcile what is learned and reframe responses. The ability to foster an environment in which "dangerous discussions" (Cobb-Roberts, 2005) result in disequilibrium requires a particular skill set that is not necessarily inherent in all teacher educators.

In a longitudinal self-study examining student resistance to diversity content, Cockrell, Placier, Cockrell, and Middleton (1999) found that students held "different, sometimes opposing" (p. 362) beliefs about diversity. Although teacher candidates enter training programs with varying levels of intercultural sensitivity (Cockrell et al.), there is a lack of literature discussing differentiation of diversity content to foster growth and expertise in teaching diverse learners. Many teacher educators teach about differentiated instruction but may not necessarily model it within their own classrooms. In considering the preparation of culturally responsive educators, designing instruction and applied experiences using a developmental framework is rarely discussed. For the most part, course readings, assignments, and field experiences are standardized rather than strategically designed. For example, all candidates read Peggy McIntosh's (1989) *White Privilege* without an understanding by teacher educators of whether students are developmentally ready to respond constructively to the content. As a result, intentional efforts may be all for naught under these circumstances.

Existing research (Alvarez McHatton et al., 2009; Jennings, 2007) indicates that many instructors express trepidation at addressing sensitive subjects, fearful of eliciting emotions or creating conflict that they may not be able to contain. Student resistance that may result in poor evaluations is a significant concern for tenure-earning faculty. Further, lack of knowledge on diversity topics and on how to infuse these topics into existing courses may impede the depth and breadth at which the content is addressed. This is especially relevant in special education where disproportionality and disparate outcomes persist.

The majority of doctoral programs recruit from the teacher and leadership workforce; thus, teacher educators for the most part reflect the teacher demographics found in P–12 settings leading to what Ladson-Billings (2005) calls the "homogeneity of the teacher education faculty" (p. 230). It is perhaps idealistic to expect teacher educators to prepare culturally competent educators when they themselves may not have been afforded structured opportunities to enhance their own cultural competence or their ability to foster cultural competence in others.

Vescio, Bondy and Poekert (2009) posit the need for purposeful preparation of teacher educators that provides "opportunities for critical self-reflection and for deconstructing frames of reference with regard to schooling" (p. 7). Quite likely, most doctoral preparation programs follow a similar process for addressing diversity topics including infusion, a stand-alone course, and applied experiences in diverse settings (schools and communities)—or some combination of the three. Like the literature on teacher preparation, there is a lack of research documenting the effectiveness of these efforts across time. Another consideration is the fact that developing and sustaining cultural competence is a never-ending process; thus, opportunities must be provided to faculty for continued development in this area.

Although sparse, there is a literature base describing the implementation of professional development programs addressing diversity in higher education (e.g., Devereaux, Prater, Jackson, Heath, & Carter, 2010; Keehn & Martinez, 2006; O'Hara & Pritchard, 2008). Several of these initiatives were multiyear efforts, and these authors detail bridges and barriers that provide important information to the field. In each of these efforts, time was allotted for faculty to participate in the professional development activities, instructional approaches utilized active learning, and activities provided opportunities for dialogue and reflection. Results indicated participants in all three studies enhanced their understanding of diversity and were able to apply what they learned in their courses.

In sum, the research on preparing the workforce for diversity is relatively sparse; there are critical needs to be met. Schools are becoming increasingly diverse and teachers and teacher educators must be prepared to address the needs of CLD learners and their families. From the literature, it is evident that most studies examine perceptions and attitudes rather than the behaviors of preservice and in-service teachers and their impact on student achievement. The current accountability climate and increased attention to teacher value-added measurements make it even more imperative for teachers to understand student diversity in its myriad forms.

Recommendations for Teacher Education Practice and Future Research

The purpose of this review has been to identify issues raised in the literature related to preparing teachers for diverse populations—specifically, preparation practices that can contribute to a more culturally competent special education workforce. The implications from the literature for teacher educators and school leaders were clear. In order to prepare preservice and in-service teachers' with the knowledge, skills, and dispositions for educating students who come from diverse backgrounds, principals, administrators, and IHE faculty must possess an adequate level of expertise in the areas of multiculturalism, CRT, and social justice. Overcoming the challenges and controversies outlined in this chapter also will require highly skilled and committed leadership at all levels of the educational system. Faculty, for example, may feel unprepared to infuse issues of diversity into courses and abdicate diversity content to colleagues. The pressures from external constituents (e.g., state education agencies) to supply more teachers quickly can force IHEs to reduce the number of credits in preparation programs and cut content related to diversity that may be perceived as unnecessary.

The literature addressed in this review focused on the preparation of preservice and in-service teachers and the challenges faced by faculty and school administrators when doing so. From these analyses, several recommendations for preparing special educators for teaching diverse populations are outlined in Table 12.1. Most of the recommendations are supported by the research reviewed in this chapter. However, in areas where there is little research, such as preparing faculty and doctoral students to teach CRT content in college coursework, recommendations are based on ideas that hold promise.

Several areas of importance for future research have also been identified. Little is known about how preservice graduates use CRT in their first years of teaching. Longitudinal studies are needed of teachers who have completed preparation programs that emphasized culturally responsive pedagogy to determine what factors affected their long-term use of the practices. A study that focuses on the role of school culture and climate on preservice graduates' implementation of CRT practices would help teacher educators better understand how to prepare students for a variety of school settings.

Additional research is needed to learn which of the specific components (e.g., service learning, coursework, field placements) of diversity preparation have a greater impact on the development of cultural competence in preservice teachers. Similarly, we believe it is important to determine how different professional development formats and levels of intensity influence in-service teacher practices.

Table 12.1 Recommendations for Preparing Special Educators for Teaching Diverse Populations

For Preservice Teacher Educators

1. Support more opportunities to infuse CRT/diversity into courses across the curriculum.
2. Continue to find ways to deepen the understanding of CRT/diversity by moving preservice teachers beyond superficial understanding to examining their attitudes and beliefs toward diversity.
3. Adopt models of co-teaching in preservice coursework with partnerships between faculty with expertise in CRT and faculty with content expertise.
4. Scaffold experiences with diverse populations each semester starting with service learning projects and ending in rigorous and immersed field experiences in diverse schools.
5. Assure that preservice teachers are thinking critically about diversity through student autobiographies and field-based reflections.
6. Design evaluation measures for assessing the impact of preparation on CRT/diversity practices.
7. Continue efforts to recruit preservice teachers from diverse backgrounds by creating partnerships with local community colleges and feeder high schools from diverse communities.

For In-Service Teachers and School Leaders

1. Provide administrators with knowledge and skills for creating and sustaining a school culture that values diversity.
2. Ensure that administrators and other school leaders hire and mentor committed teachers and support teachers through PD and coaching.
3. Provide a variety of approaches to PD that includes lesson study, book study professional learning communities, and consultation or coaching.
4. Encourage school leaders to recruit and retain teachers from diverse backgrounds.
5. Support sustained PD activities in CRT/diversity through technical assistance, modeling, and ongoing annual workshops.
6. Establish learning communities that focus on the issues of diversity (e.g., culturally responsive response to intervention, nonbiased assessment, culturally responsive pedagogy, emergent bilinguals).
7. Create partnerships between TEPs and local schools to prepare teachers and provide ongoing PD opportunities in CRT/diversity.

For Faculty and Doctoral Students at IHEs

1. Provide ongoing professional development activities for faculty (e.g., brown bag (lunchtime) lectures, shared readings, and discussion groups).
2. Find ways to engage faculty in self-reflection of values and beliefs so they become knowledgeable and less resistant or uncomfortable with diversity issues.
3. Create opportunities for faculty and doctoral students to interact with nationally renowned leaders in the field of CRT/diversity (e.g., webinars, college lecture series, conference presentations).
4. Create doctoral seminars that focus on CRT/diversity and teacher education.
5. Encourage doctoral students to infuse CRT/diversity content in their co-teaching and college teaching internships.
6. Develop stand-alone modules that can be infused into courses with support from faculty developers.
7. Encourage faculty at IHEs to infuse internet training modules into course content, including resources from IRIS (http://iris.peabody.vanderbilt.edu/index.html), the CLAS Early Childhood Research Institute (http://clas.uiuc.edu/aboutclas.html), the Center to Mobilize Early Childhood Knowledge (http://community.fpg.unc.edu/connect-modules), and the Equity Alliance (http://www.equityallianceatasu.org/pl/modules).

Much more research is needed on the design and evaluation of faculty and doctoral student professional development activities in the area of diversity. What PD formats are most effective with faculty and doctoral students? How much PD is necessary to create concrete actions by faculty and successful infusion of diversity content into coursework and field experiences?

In summary, we believe that research is needed on the preparation of preservice and in-service special education teachers as well as IHE faculty. TEPs and school administrators need to move teachers toward a critical consciousness and assist them in making connections between identifying their own biases and the larger context in which institutional biases continue to produce educational inequity for CLD students (Gorski, 2009). Teacher educators and school leaders must work to scaffold the experiences of teachers (Potts et al., 2008) by guiding them to become "students of culture" instead of viewing culture as sets of stable ethnic traits (Seidl & Pugach, 2009). Special education teachers must develop an understanding of and appreciation for the diversity of the students they teach and function as change agents and advocates for all students.

References

Abbate-Vaughn, J. (2006). "Not writing it out but writing it off": Preparing multicultural teachers for urban classrooms. *Multicultural Education, 13*(4), 41–48.

Alvarez McHatton, P., Keller, H., Shircliffe, B., & Zalaquett, C. (2009). Examining efforts to infuse diversity within one college of education. *Journal of Diversity in Higher Education, 2*, 127–135. doi:10.1037/a0016190

American Association of Colleges for Teacher Education. (2009). *Teacher preparation makes a difference.* Retrieved from http://aacte.org/pdf/Publications/Resources/Teacher%20Preparation%20Makes%20a%20Difference.pdf

Artiles, A. J., Barreto, R. M., Peña, L., & McClafferty, K. (1998). Pathways to teacher learning in multicultural contexts: A longitudinal case study of two novice bilingual teachers in urban schools. *Remedial and Special Education, 19*, 70–90. doi:10.1177/074193259801900203

Artiles, A. J., Harry, B., Reschly, D. J., & Chinn, P. (2002). Over-identification of students of color in special education: A critical overview. *Multicultural Perspectives, 4*(1), 3–10. doi:10.1207/S15327892MCP0401_2

Artiles, A., J., Kozleski, E. B., Trent, S. C., Osher, D., & Ortiz, A. (2010). Justifying and explaining disproportionality, 1968–2008: A critique of underlying views of culture. *Exceptional Children, 76*, 279–300.

Artiles, A. J., Trent, S. C., & Kuan, L. (1997). Learning disabilities empirical research on ethnic minority students: An analysis of 22 years of studies published in selected refereed journals. *Learning Disabilities Research and Practice, 12*, 82–91.

Aud, S., Fox, M., & KewalRamani, A. (2010). *Status and trends in the education of racial and ethnic groups* (NCES 2010-015). U.S. Department of Education, National Center for Education Statistics. Washington, DC: U.S. Government Printing Office.

Aud, S., Hussar, W., Planty, M., Snyder, T., Bianco, K., Fox, M., Frohlich, L., Kemp, J., & Drake, J. (2010). *The Condition of Education 2010* (NCES 2010-028). Washington, DC: National Center for Education Statistics, Institute of Education Sciences, U.S. Department of Education.

Bandura, A. (1982). Self-efficacy mechanism in human agency. *American Psychologist, 37*, 122–147. doi: 10.1037/0003-066X.37.2.122

Bennett, M. M. (2008). Understanding the students we teach: Poverty in the classroom. *The Clearing House, 81*, 251–256. doi:10.3200/TCHS.81.6.251-256

Blanchett, W. J. (2006). Disproportionate representation of African American students in special education: Acknowledging the role of white privilege and racism. *Educational Researcher, 35*(6), 24–28. doi:10.3102/0013189X035006024

Blanton, L. P., & Perez, Y. (2011). Exploring the relationship between special education teachers and professional learning communities: Implications of research for administrators. *Journal of Special Education Leadership, 24*(1), 6–16.

Burnstein, N., Cabello, B., & Hamann, J. (1993). Teacher preparation for culturally diverse urban students: Infusing competencies across the curriculum. *Teacher Education and Special Education, 16*, 1–13. doi:10.1177/088840649301600103

Castro, A. J. (2010). Themes in the research on preservice teachers' views of cultural diversity: Implications for researching millennial preservice teachers. *Educational Researcher, 39*, 198–210. doi:10.3102/0013189X10363819

Clark-Goff, K. (2008). *Exploring change in preservice teachers' beliefs about English language learning and teaching.* Retrieved from http://repository.tamu.edu/bitstream/handle/1969.1/ETD-TAMU-2705/CLARK-GOFF-DISSERTATION.pdf?sequence=1

Cobb-Roberts, D. (2005). *Dangerous discussions: Anonymity, intimacy, & identity.* Retrieved October 25, 2012 from http://www.tltgroup.org/ProFacDev/DangerousDiscussions/Anonymity/CtE%20Dec%201.wma

Cockrell, K. S., Placier, P. L., Cockrell, D. H., & Middleton, J. N. (1999). Coming to terms with "diversity" and "multiculturalism" in teacher education: Learning about our students, changing our practice. *Teaching and Teacher Education, 15*, 351–366. doi:10.1016/S0742-051X(98)00050-X

Cohen, D., & Hill, H. (2000). Instructional policy and classroom performance: The mathematics reform in California. *The Teachers College Record, 102*, 294–343.

Colombo, M. (2004). Literacy for all students: Professional development for cultural continuity. *New England Reading Association Journal, 40*(2), 50–54.

Connelly, V., & Graham, S. (2009). Student teaching and teacher attrition in special education. *Teacher Education and Special Education, 32*, 257–269. doi:10.1177/0888406409339472

Correa, V. I., Hudson, R. F., & Hayes, M. T. (2004). Preparing early childhood special educators to serve culturally and linguistically diverse children and families: Can a multicultural education course make a difference? *Teacher Education and Special Education, 27*, 323–341. doi: 10.1177/088840640402700401

Cozart, A. C., Cudahy, D., Ndunda, M., & VanSickle, M. (2003). The challenges of co-teaching within a multicultural context. *Multicultural Education, 10*(3), 43–45.

Darling-Hammond, L., Dilworth, M. E., & Bulmaster, M. (1996, January). *Educators of color.* A Background paper for the invitational conference, "Recruiting, Preparing, and Retaining Persons of Color in the Teaching Profession" of the National Association of Black School Educators, Inc., Detroit, MI.

Devereaux, T. H., Prater, M. A., Jackson, A., Heath, M. A., & Carter, N. J. (2010). Special education faculty perceptions of participating in a culturally responsive profession al development program. *Teacher Education and Special Education, 33*, 263–278. doi:10.1177/0888406410371642

Donovan, M. S., & Cross, C. T. (Eds.). (2002). *Minority students in special and gifted education.* Committee on Minority Representation in Special Education. Washington, DC: National Academy Press.

Flores, M. A., & Day, C. (2006). Contexts which shape and reshape new teachers' identities: A multi-perspective study. *Teaching and Teacher Education, 22*, 219–232. doi:10.1016/j.tate.2005.09.002

Ference, R. A., & Bell, S. (2004). A cross-cultural immersion in the U.S.: Changing preservice teacher attitudes toward Latino ESOL students. *Equity & Excellence in Education, 37*, 343–350. doi:10.1080/10665680490518605

Frye, B., Button, L., Kelly, C., & Button, G. (2010). Preservice teachers' self-perceptions and attitudes toward culturally responsive teaching. *Journal of Praxis in Multicultural Education, 5*, 6–22. doi: http://dx.doi.org/10.9741/2161–2978.1029

Gay, G. (2010). Acting on beliefs in teacher education for cultural diversity. *Journal of Teacher Education, 61*, 143–152. doi:10.1177/0022487109347320

Gorski, P. C. (2009). What we're teaching teachers: An analysis of multicultural teacher education coursework syllabi. *Teaching and Teacher Education, 25*, 309–318. doi:10.1016/j.tate.2008.07.008

Grant, C., & Sleeter, C. (2006). *Turning on learning: Five approaches to multicultural teaching and plans for race, class, gender, and disability*. Upper Saddle River, NJ: Prentice Hall.

Graziano, C. (2009). Public education faces a crisis in teacher retention. *Edutopia*, Retrieved from http://www.edutopia.org/schools-out

Griffin, C. C., Kilgore, K. L., Winn, J. A., Otis-Wilborn, A., Hou, W., & Garvan, C. W. (2009). First-year special educators: The influence of school and classroom context factors on their accomplishments and problems. *Teacher Education and Special Education, 32*, 45–63. doi:10.1177/0888406408330870

Gruwell, E. (2007). *Teach with your heart: Lessons I learned from the Freedom Writers.* New York, NY: Broadway.

Guerra, P. L., & Nelson, S. W. (2008). Use book studies to generate frank talk about beliefs and practices. *Journal of Staff Development, 29*(3), 43–44.

Haycock, K., & Robinson, S. (2001). Time-wasting workshops? *Journal of Staff Development, 22*(2), 16–18.

Henze, R., Lucas, T., & Scott, B. (1998). Dancing with the monster: Teachers discuss racism, power, and white privilege in education. *The Urban Review, 30*, 187–210. doi:10.1023/A:1023280117904

Hollins, E., & Guzman, M. T. (2005). Research on preparing teachers for diverse populations. In M. Cochran-Smith & K. Zeichner (Eds.), *Studying teacher education: The Report of the AERA panel on research and teacher education* (pp. 477–548). Mahwah, NJ: Lawrence Erlbaum Associates.

Honigsfeld, A., & Dove, M. (2008). Poetry in professional development. *Delta Kappa Gamma Bulletin, 75*(1), 10–13.

Jenks, C., Lee, J. O., & Kanpol, B. (2001). Approaches to multicultural education in preservice teacher education: Philosophical frameworks and models for teaching. *Urban Review, 33*, 87–105. doi:10.1023/A:1010389023211

Jennings, T. (2007). Addressing diversity in US teacher preparation programs: A survey of Elementary and secondary programs' priorities and challenges from across the United States of America. *Teaching and Teacher Education, 23*, 1258–1271. doi:10.1016/j.tate.2006.05.004

Keehn, S., & Martinez, M. G. (2006). A study of the impact of professional development in diversity on adjunct faculty. *Action in Teacher Education, 28*(3), 11–28. doi:10.1080/01626620.2006.10463416

Kidd, J. K., Sanchez, S. Y., & Thorpe, E. K. (2008). Defining moments: Developing culturally responsive dispositions and teaching practices in early childhood preservice teachers. *Teaching and Teacher Education, 24*, 316–329.

doi:10.1016/j.tate.2007.06.003

King, J. E. (1991). Dysconscious racism: Ideology, identity, and the miseducation of teachers. *Journal of Negro Education, 60*, 133–146. doi:10.2307/2295605

King, S., H., & Castenell, L. A. (2001). *Racism and racial inequality: Implications for teacher education*. Washington, DC: American Association of Colleges for Teacher Education.

Ladson-Billings, G. (1995). Toward a theory of culturally relevant pedagogy. *American Educational Research Journal, 32*, 465–491. doi: http://dx.doi.org/10.3102/00028312032003465

Ladson-Billings, G. (2002). But that's good teaching! The case for culturally relevant pedagogy. In S. J. Denbo & L. M. Beaulieu (Eds.), *Improving schools for African American students: A reader for educational leaders* (pp. 95–102). Springfield, IL: Charles C. Thomas.

Ladson-Billings, G. J. (2005). Is the team all right? Diversity and teacher education. *Journal of Teacher Education, 56*, 229–234. doi:10.1177/0022487105275917

Lankford, H., Loeb, S., & Wyckoff, J. (2002). Teacher sorting and the plight of urban schools: A descriptive analysis. *Educational Evaluation and Policy Analysis, 24*, 37–62. doi:10.3102/01623737024001037

Larke, P., Wiseman, D. L., & Bradley, C. (1990). The minority mentorship project: Changing attitudes of preservice teachers for diverse classrooms. *Action in Teacher Education, 12*(3), 23–29.

Lawrence, S. M. (2005). Contextual matters: Teachers' perceptions of the success of antiracist classroom practices. *Journal of Educational Research, 98*, 350–365. doi:10.3200/JOER.98.6.350-365

Lee, O., Lukyx, A., Buxton, C., & Shaver, A. (2007). The challenge of altering elementary school teachers' beliefs and practices regarding linguistic and cultural diversity in science instruction. *Journal of Research in Science Teaching, 44*, 1269–1291. doi:10.1002/tea.20198

Leistyna, P. (2001). Extending the possibilities of multicultural professional development in public schools. *Journal of Curriculum and Supervision, 16*, 282–304.

Lewis, M. (2009). *Ethnologue: Languages of the world* (16th ed.). Dallas, TX: SIL International. Retrieved from http://www.ethnologue.com/

Mahn, H., McMann, D., & Musanti, S. (2005). Teaching/learning centers: Professional development for teachers of linguistically and culturally diverse students. *Language Arts, 82*, 378–387.

McCray, E. D., Rosenberg, M. S., Brownell, M. T., deBettencourt, L., Leko, M., & Long, S. (2011). The role of leaders in forming school-university partnerships for special education teacher preparation. *Journal of Special Education Leadership, 24*(1), 47–58.

McFalls, E. L., & Cobb-Roberts, D. (2001). Reducing resistance to diversity through cognitive dissonance instruction implications for teacher education. *Journal of Teacher Education, 52*, 164–172. doi: http://dx.doi.org/10.1177/0022487101052002007

McIntosh, P. (1989). *White privilege: Unpacking the invisible knapsack.* Retrieved from http://www.isr.umich.edu/home/diversity/resources/white-privilege.pdf

McLeskey, J. (2011). Supporting improved practice for special education teachers: The importance of learner-centered professional development. *Journal of Special Education Leadership, 24*(1), 26–35.

Mullen, C. A. (2001). Disabilities awareness and the pre-service teacher: A blueprint of a mentoring intervention. *Journal of Education for Teaching, 27*(1), 39–61. doi:10.1080/02607470120042537

National Council for Accreditation of Teacher Education. (2010). *Transforming teacher education through clinical practice: A national strategy to prepare effective teachers:* Report of the Blue Ribbon Panel on clinical preparation and partnerships for improved student learning. Washington, DC: NCATE. Retrieved from http://www.ncate.org/Public/ResearchReports/NCATEInitiatives/BlueRibbonPanel/tabid/715/Default.aspx

Nieto, S. (Ed.). (2005). *Why we teach*. New York, NY: Teacher's College Press.

O'Brian, M., Stone, J., Appel, K., & House, J. J. (2007). The first field experience: perspectives of preservice and cooperating teachers. *Teacher Education and Special Education, 30*, 264–275. doi:10.1177/088840640703000406

O'Hara, S., & Pritchard, R. H. (2008). Meeting the challenge of diversity: Professional development for teacher educators. *Teacher Education Quarterly, 35*, 43–61.

Oswald, D. P., Coutinho, M. J., Best, A. M., & Singh, N. N. (1999). Ethnic representation in special education: The influence of school-related economic and demographic variables. *The Journal of Special Education, 32*, 194–206. doi: http://dx.doi.org/10.1177/002246699903200401

Pajares, M. F. (1992). Teacher beliefs and educational research: Cleaning up a messy construct. *Review of Educational Research, 62*, 307–332. doi:10.3102/00346543062003307

Pang, V. O., & Sablan, V. A. (1998). Teacher efficacy. In M. E. Dilworth (Ed.), *Being responsive to cultural differences* (pp. 39–58). Thousand Oaks, CA: Corwin Press.

Patterson, K., Grenny, J., Maxfield, D., McMillan, R., & Switzler, A. (2008). *Influencer: The power to change anything*. New York, NY: McGraw-Hill.

Peterson, P., & Showalter, S. (2010). Meeting the need for special education teachers for culturally linguistically

diverse students with disabilities. *Journal of College Teaching & Learning*, 7(10), 7–10.
Potts, A., Foster-Triplett, C., & Rose, D. (2008). An infused approach to multicultural education in a pre-service teacher program: Perspectives of teacher educators. *International Journal of Multicultural Education*, *10*(1), 1–15.
Prater, M. A., Wilder, L. K., & Dyches, T. T. (2008). Shaping one traditional special educator preparation program toward more cultural competence. *Teaching Education*, *19*, 137–151. doi:10.1080/10476210802040765
Renzulli, L., Parrott, H., & Beattie, I. (2011). Racial mismatch and school type: Teacher satisfaction and retention in charter and traditional public schools. *Sociology of Education*, *84*, 23–48. doi:10.1177/0038040710392720
Rogers, R., Kramer, M. A., Mosley, M., Fuller, C., Light, R., Nehart, M., Jones, R., … & Thomas, P. (2005). Professional development as social transformation: The literacy for social justice teacher research group. *Language Arts*, *82*, 347–358.
Rosenberg, M. S., Boyer, K. L., Sindelar, P. T., & Misra, S. (2007). Alternative route programs for certification in special education: Program infrastructure, instructional delivery, and participant characteristics. *Exceptional Children*, *73*, 224–241.
Sakash, K., & Chou, V. (2007, Fall). Increasing supply of Latino bilingual teachers for Chicago public schools. *Teacher Education Quarterly*, *34*(4), 44–52.
Salend, S., & Reynolds, C. (1991). The migrant/special education training program. *Teacher Education and Special Education*, *14*, 235–242. doi:10.1177/088840649101400404
Schein, E. H. (1999). Kurt Lewin's change theory in the field and in the classroom: Notes toward a model of managed learning. *Reflections*, *1*(1), 59–74. doi:10.1162/152417399570287
Schrum, L., Burbank, M. D., & Capps, R. (2007). Preparing future teachers for diverse schools in an online learning community: Perceptions and practice. *Internet and Higher Education*, *10*, 204–211. doi:10.1016/j.iheduc.2007.06.002
Schultz, E. L., Neyhart, K., & Reck, U. M. (1996). Swimming against the tide: A study of prospective teachers' attitudes regarding cultural diversity and urban teaching. *Western Journal of Black Studies*, *20*, 1–7.
Seidl, B., & Pugach, M. C. (2009). Support and teaching in the vulnerable moments: Preparing special educators for diversity. *Multiple Voices for Ethnically Diverse Exceptional Learners*, *11*(2), 57–75.
Shen, J. (2000). The impact of alternative certification policy. In J. McIntyre & D. Byrd (Eds.), *Research on effective models for teacher education* (pp. 235–237). Thousand Oaks, CA: Corwin.
Sindelar, P. T., McCray, E. D., Kiely, M. T., & Kamman, M. (2008). The impact of No Child Left Behind on special education teacher supply and the preparation of the workforce. In T. E. Scruggs & M. A. Mastropieri (Eds.), *Advances in learning and behavioral disabilities, Vol. 21* (pp. 89–123). Bingley, United Kingdom: Emerald Group Publishing Limited.
Siwatu, K. O. (2007). Preservice teachers' culturally responsive teaching self-efficacy and outcome expectancy beliefs. *Teaching and Teacher Education*, *23*, 1086–1101. doi:10.1016/j.tate.2006.07.011
Skiba, R. J., Poloni-Staudinger, L., Gallini, S., Simmons, A. B., & Feggins-Azziz, R. (2006). Disparate access: The disproportionality of African American students with disabilities across educational environments. *Exceptional Children*, *72*, 411–424.
Skiba, R. J., Simmons, A. B., Gibb, A. C., Rausch, M. K., Cuadrado, J., & Chung, C. (2008). Achieving equity in special education: History, status, and current changes. *Exceptional Children*, *74*, 264–288.
Sleeter, C. E. (2001). Preparing teachers for culturally diverse schools: Research and the overwhelming presence of whiteness. *Journal of Teacher Education*, *52*, 94–106. doi:10.1177/0022487101052002002
Smith, E. B. (2009). Approaches to multicultural education in preservice teacher education: Philosophical frameworks and models for teaching. *Multicultural Education*, *16*(3), 45–50.
Su, Z. (1996). Why teach: Profiles and entry perspectives of minority students as becoming teachers. *Journal of Research and Development in Education*, *29*(3), 117–133.
Suell, J. L., & Piotrowski, C. (2007). Alternative teacher education programs: A review of the literature and outcome studies. *Journal of Instructional Psychology*, *34*, 54–58.
Teemant, A., Smith, M. E., Pinnegar, S., & Egan, M. W. (2005). Modeling sociocultural pedagogy in distance education. *Teachers College Record*, *107*, 1675–1698. doi:10.1111/j.1467-9620.2005.00538.x
Tillema, H. H. (1998). Stability and change in student teachers' beliefs about teaching. *Teachers and Teaching: Theory and Practice*, *4*, 217–228. doi:10.1080/1354060980040202
Trent, S. C., Kea, C. D., & Oh, K. (2008). Preparing preservice educators for cultural diversity: How far have we come? *Exceptional Children*, *74*, 328–350.
Trent, S. C., Pernell, E., Mungai, A., & Chimedza, R. (1998). Using concept maps to measure conceptual change in preservice teacher enrolled in a multicultural education/special education course. *Remedial and Special Education*, *19*, 16–31. doi:10.1177/074193259801900103
Tyler, N. C., Yzquierdo, Z., Lopez-Ryan, N., & Flippin, S. S. (2004). Cultural and linguistic diversity and the special education workforce: A critical overview. *The Journal of Special Education*, *38*, 22–38.

doi:10.1177/00224669040380010301
Valli, L. (1995). The dilemma of race: Learning to be color blind and color conscious. *Journal of Teacher Education, 46*, 120–129. doi:10.1177/0022487195046002006
Vavrus, M. (1994). A critical analysis of multicultural education infusion during student teaching. *Action in Teacher Education, 16*(3), 45–57. doi:10.1080/01626620.1994.10463208
Vescio, V., Bondy, E., & Poekert, P. E. (2009). Preparing multicultural teacher educators: Toward a pedagogy of transformation. *Teacher Education Quarterly, 36*(2), 5–24.
Vescio, V., Ross, D., & Adams, A. (2008). A review of research on the impact of professional learning communities on teaching practice and student learning. *Teaching and Teacher Education, 24*, 80–91. doi:10.1016/j.tate.2007.01.004
Voltz, D. L., Brazil, N., & Scott, R. (2003). Professional development for culturally responsive instruction: A promising practice for addressing the disproportionate representation of students of color in special education. *Teacher Education and Special Education, 26*(1), 63–73. doi:10.1177/088840640302600107
Voltz, D. L., Brazil, N., & Scott, R. (2004). Professional development for multicultural education: A teacher-directed approach. *Action in Teacher Education, 26*(3), 10–20. doi:10.1080/01626620.2004.10463328
Waitoller, F. R., Artiles, A. J., & Cheney, D. A. (2010). The miner's canary: A review of overrepresentation research and explanations. *The Journal of Special Education, 44*(1), 29–49. doi:10.1177/0022466908329226
Webb-Johnson, G. C., Artiles, A., Trent, S., Jackson, C. W., & Velox, A. (1998). The status of research on multicultural education in teacher education and special education: Problems, pitfalls, and promises. *Remedial and Special Education, 19*(1), 7–15. doi:10.1177/074193259801900102
West, E. A., & Hudson, R. F. (2010). Using early career special educators voice to influence initial teacher education. *International Journal of Whole Schooling, 6*(1), 63–74.
West-Olatunji, C. A., Behar-Horenstein, L., Rant, J., & Cohen-Phillips, L. N. (2008). Enhancing cultural competence among teachers of African American children using mediated lesson study. *The Journal of Negro Education, 77*(1), 27–38.
White-Hood, M. (2007). Becoming culturally proficient. *Principal Leadership, 8*(1), 35–36.
Wiggins, R. A., Follo, E. J., & Eberly, M. B. (2007). The impact of a field immersion program on pre-service teachers' attitudes toward teaching in culturally diverse classrooms. *Teaching and Teacher Education, 23*, 653–663. doi:10.1016/j.tate.2007.02.007
Wright, A., Calabrese, N., & Henry, J. J. (2009). How service and learning come together to promote Cura Personalis. *International Journal of Teaching and Learning in Higher Education, 20*(2), 274–283.
Zetlin, A., Beltran, D., Salcido, P., Gonzalez, T., & Reyes, T. (2011). Building a pathway of optimal support for English Language Learners in special education. *Teacher Education and Special Education, 34*(1), 59–70. doi:10.1177/0888406410380423

13

Alternative Routes to Special Education Teacher Preparation

Context, Outcomes, and Implications

Vincent J. Connelly

UNIVERSITY OF NEW HAMPSHIRE

Michael S. Rosenberg and Kristine E. Larson

JOHNS HOPKINS UNIVERSITY

Things to Think About

- A prior examination of the research on ARs to special education teacher preparation and certification led to conclusions that AR programs are heterogeneous and their benefits or drawbacks are largely uncertain.
- Since then, there have been changes in AR programs in terms of prevalence, purpose, and participants.
- A reexamination of the research on general education AR programs has indicated there are important differences between traditional and alternative programs, and certain factors are associated with successful outcomes of AR programs graduates.
- A reexamination of the research on special education AR programs has prompted evaluations of single programs and comparisons between and among programs.
- Challenges in the study of AR programs in special education teacher preparation include the persistent limited research base and changes in the demand for and role of special education teachers in schools.
- Conclusions of the research show the debate between traditional and alternative programs is not as important as examining and promoting how best to prepare quality special education teachers.

Reflecting upon the methods, context, and outcomes of over 20 years of preparing special education teachers, Bauer, Johnson and Sapona (2004) concluded their review by restating an observation made a decade earlier. Johnson (1996), in a similar effort, asserted that the most pressing concern within our field is "the same challenge that faced us in the mid 70s, that is, how do we define ourselves, and how do we fit into a broader educational, social and economic context" (p. 204). Nonetheless, Bauer et al. (2004) noted two differences: First, the stakes became much higher, and second, research in teacher education has greatly improved over the past decade.

How valid are these observations today? Clearly, the stakes in special education teacher preparation remain high. The rhetoric from policy makers remains sharp and combative. Arne Duncan, for example, called for "revolutionary change, not evolutionary tinkering" within the nation's colleges of education (Field, 2009), characterizing them as "underperforming cash cows" doing "a mediocre job" of preparing teachers while investing little in rigorous educational research and clinical testing. At the same time, research in special education teacher preparation is limited in quantity and quality. As a whole, it is considered incomplete, relatively scarce, scattered, and lacking a coherent conceptual framework (Sindelar, Brownell, & Billingsley, 2010). Credible outcome measures are lacking and the defining characteristics of what constitutes special education teacher education practice are variable and diverse (Rosenberg, Boyer, Sindelar, & Misra, 2007; Sindelar et al., 2010).

Criticism and challenges such as these demand that the profession rethink (and in doing so possibly redefine) what is a quality special education teacher and how best to prepare many such individuals. In response to these criticisms, alternative route (AR) programs leading to licensure and certification in special education have emerged, arguably, as significant and viable supplements for traditional campus-based preservice teacher preparation programs. During the past two decades AR programs have experienced unprecedented growth. In large part, this proliferation is a function of unmet demand for teachers in hard-to-staff schools and continued disenchantment with traditional modes of teacher preparation.

Beyond meeting unmet need for teachers, a number of education policy makers (e.g., Hassel & Sherburne, 2004) view the growth AR programs as an essential element of school reform. Specifically, AR programs are seen as a dynamic, diverse, and expanding portfolio of creative recruitment and training approaches that leads to improved teacher quality. In sharp contrast, traditional approaches to teacher preparation are viewed as being anachronistic, self-serving, overregulated, and ineffective.

Rosenberg and Sindelar (2005) conducted an examination of the research on ARs to special education teacher preparation and certification. The authors drew five conclusions from this review:

1. There is large heterogeneity among AR programs, and, like an iceberg, there is a small visible portion of the enterprise evidenced in published research, while the vast majority of ARs lie unrevealed below the surface.
2. AR programs can produce competent teachers, but not all AR programs are alike. The limited research base indicates that successful AR programs are planned and delivered collaboratively by institutions of higher education (IHEs) and local education agencies (LEAs), often with policy support from state education agencies (SEAs). Effective programs are of adequate length and employ a variety of learning activities.
3. Successful AR programs make use of IHE supervision and building-based mentor support.
4. It is difficult to judge the efficacy of AR programs due to inadequate outcome variables. Researchers have not examined attrition and retention, as well as teacher performance and student outcome measures. In fairness, this is a criticism that pertains to the field at large.
5. Little is known regarding whether the proliferation of AR programs has affected the professionalization of special education teaching, and if abbreviated training has diminished the role of the teacher and IHEs.

There is general agreement that the political, economic, and service delivery contexts for special education and teacher preparation have changed greatly in the past 10 years (e.g., Fuchs, Fuchs, & Stecker, 2010; Sindelar et al., 2010), and it is essential to have a current review of AR programs in light of changing contexts. For example, Boe et al. (2013) examined how changes in educational and economic contexts are influencing the demand for special education teachers. Due in large part to declining numbers of students identified with disabilities, changes in modes of service delivery such as response to intervention (RTI), and an unprecedented national economic contraction, demand for special education teachers is declining. If these trends hold, newly graduated individuals from special education teacher preparation programs may have difficulty securing teaching positions, and the pipeline of entrants into special education teacher programs is likely to constrict, increasing competition between traditional and AR programs.

In this chapter, we revisit and update what the research has shown about the efficacy of AR programs in special education since the initial Rosenberg and Sindelar (2005) review. First, we reexamine changes in AR programs in terms of prevalence, purpose, and participants. Next, we summarize the current research in general education AR programs. Then we synthesize and analyze the available empirical research in special education, including a wide array of outcome variables. We finish by focusing on the challenges that confront the study of AR programs, and present a series of conclusions.

The Proliferation and Diversity of AR Programs in Special Education

Numerous studies (e.g., Boe, 2006; Brownell, Hirsch, & Seo, 2004), support the need for special education teachers, and the proliferation of AR programs in special education is seen as a response to a significant and broader national teacher shortage. AR programs have become ubiquitous. In 2010 for instance, 48 states reported having one or more AR teacher education programs in place (Feistritzer, 2010). Researchers estimate that over a half a million teachers have been certified via alternative routes in the past 20 years, with nearly one third of all new teachers coming from AR programs (Feistritzer, 2010). Specifically, AR programs in special education now operate in at least 35 states and the District of Columbia (Rosenberg et al., 2007). These programs are differentiated from their traditional peers in that they are generally shorter in duration, involve candidates in teaching immediately or shortly after beginning the program, have an emphasis on field-based training, and are extended to a more diverse candidate population.

Because teacher educators are challenged with the task of designing and delivering effective AR programs that meet the needs of nontraditional learners in a content rich and streamlined fashion, AR programs are characterized by a heterogeneity of programmatic components. In their review, Rosenberg and Sindelar (2005) concluded that this heterogeneity, along with "unbridled program development and the scarcity of existing literature to guide it have created a situation that cries out for additional research" (p. 124). To this end, Wasburn-Moses and Rosenberg (2008) developed guidelines for AR special education program components that incorporate indicators of best practices, including (a) promoting classroom survival, (b) integration of instructor and student developed topics, (c) a requirement of collaboration and teaming, (d) an emphasis on skills needed to improve practice, (e) assignments tailored to professional standards, (f) the integration of instruction in technology, and (g) the promotion of a professional orientation toward teaching. Subsequent analyses of critical features of special education teacher preparation stress this need to determine specific programmatic features that make a difference in how teachers learn, rather than research that stresses a simple comparison between AR programs and more traditional routes (Brownell, Ross, Colón, & McCallum, 2005).

AR Programs: A Critical Review of the Literature

In this section we begin with an overview of current research on general education AR programs. This is followed by a comprehensive and detailed review of recent empirical work conducted on special education AR programs.

General Education AR Programs

Today, nearly one third of all teachers hired by the United States' school districts participated in some type of AR program (Constantine et al., 2009; Feistritzer, 2010) with the majority trained and employed in large urban centers such as New York City, Baltimore, and Washington DC. Geographic factors associated with AR teachers and programs are most striking when comparing central city area hiring practices with those of their close suburban peer districts. In New York City (NYC), for example, the majority of math teachers are products of the fast-track NYC Fellows Math Immersion Program, a program designed for nonmath majors interested in teaching math. However, in the wealthy, teacher rich suburb of Scarsdale, less than 15 miles from NYC, most math teachers hired received their training through more traditional routes (Grossman & Loeb, 2010).

As noted earlier, many school reformers view AR programs as creative recruitment and training approaches that lead to improved teacher quality. Once viewed primarily as a means of addressing unmet demand for teachers, these programs are now viewed as a means of bringing vitality to comprehensive efforts for improving teacher quality (Cohen-Vogel & Hunt, 2007; Gatlin, 2009). However, the high levels of rhetoric and enthusiasm for general education ARs in teacher education reform has exceeded the evidence found in the professional literature. Efficacy research is limited in terms of quantity and has barely addressed the important question of teacher quality. Summarizing the pre-2005 literature (e.g., Hawley, 1992; Wilson, Flodden, & Ferrini-Mundy, 2001; Zeichner & Schulte, 2001), Rosenberg et al. (2009) could not determine if AR programs are effective in supplementing teacher supply, promoting teacher retention, attracting talented candidates from outside education, and contributing to student achievement. They did find that AR programs recruited higher percentages of men, older students, and persons from culturally and linguistically diverse (CLD) groups than traditional programs and that these participants tended to come from areas near their high-needs schools. However, retention of these teachers was mixed and often mediated by the subject specialties of the teachers. Little was found regarding the impact of these efforts on student outcomes.

Recently, a limited database linking AR programs to specific performance outcomes has emerged. In particular, reports are available that examine how well AR programs recruit high-quality candidates and how preparation activities in various types of programs affect student outcomes. For example, analyzing data from the School and Staffing Survey, Cohen-Vogel and Smith (2007) found no significant differences between first year AR and traditionally trained teachers in terms of (a) the percentage who attended selective undergraduate institutions, (b) academic qualification, and (c) the likelihood of assignment to hard-to-staff schools, calling in to question several of assumptions underlying the advocacy for AR programs. In a large-scale study of 174 general education elementary grade teachers, Constantine et al. (2009) investigated whether having an AR or traditionally developed teacher affected the reading and math achievement of 2,600 students in 63 schools across seven states. No differences in student outcomes were found as a function of their teachers' preparation status. Moreover, there were no differences among students who had teachers who had high coursework AR programs (averaging 432 hours) or low coursework AR programs (averaging 179 hours). Similarly, Tournaki, Lyublinskaya, and Carolan (2009) reported comparable levels of teacher effectiveness and efficacy across three teacher preparation routes—one traditional and two AR—offered by one university in New York.

Good et al. (2006), investigating a series of questions on the quality of beginning teachers, only found differences in terms of classroom management; teachers who completed traditional programs were more skilled than those who participated in AR programs. However, Xu, Hannaway, and Taylor (2011) found that disadvantaged high school students taught by Teach for America (TFA) teachers had higher standardized test scores than students taught by non-TFA teachers. Their findings show that TFA status more than offset any experience effects, particularly in teaching high school science subjects. These results may be tempered, however, by the nontraditional aspect of the TFA pool. TFA candidates are recruited from selective universities, and they are likely to only teach for a few years. Taken together, the limited empirical data on general education AR candidates indicate that these programs have not fulfilled their promise as a general means for improving teacher quality. At best, they appear no different than traditional programs in terms of recruiting high-quality teacher candidates and influencing student academic performance.

Researchers suggest (e.g., Boyd, Grossman, Lankford, Loeb, & Wyckoff, 2009; Goldhaber, 2004; Humphrey & Wechsler, 2007) that the lack of empirical evidence showing major differences between general education AR and traditional programs may be a function of variability among AR programs. For example, programs like Teach for America have highly competitive entry requirements while other district- and state-sponsored programs are more inclusive in their admission policies. Moreover, some programs allow rapid entry to classroom teaching with little training while others require some level of preparation prior to assuming the role of teacher of record (Humphrey, Wechsler, & Hough, 2008; Rosenberg et al., 2007). Investigating seven high profile programs (e.g., Teach for America, NYC Teaching Fellows) Humphrey and colleagues (Humphrey & Wechsler, 2007; Humphrey et al., 2008) investigated program and participant factors on teacher outcomes. Regardless of program type and variation among the programs, the school context in which participants were working had the most powerful influence on all outcomes. Participants in schools with strong leaders and a collegial work environment were more likely to be confident in their abilities and planned to stay in teaching. In sharp contrast, AR candidates assigned to unruly schools with weak leadership and isolated teachers were likely to exit teaching. Humphrey and colleagues also found that teacher preparation coursework and education backgrounds of participants were associated with teacher knowledge and self-efficacy. However, mentoring contributed little to the confidence that participants expressed in their ability or whether they planned to stay in teaching. The authors attributed this to low quality mentoring in the programs examined.

So what can be concluded about general education AR programs? The available, albeit limited, literature indicates few important differences between traditional and alternative programs. Moreover, factors associated with successful outcomes of AR program graduates center more on participant recruitment and selection, school placement context, and teacher preparation activities, findings that, arguably, can be generalized to all types of teacher preparation (Humphrey et al., 2008).

Special Education Research

In this section we summarize the results of a search of the empirical literature on special education AR programs. We first discuss what we know generally about the characteristics of these programs, and then summarize program outcomes. In updating Rosenberg and Sindelar's (2005) effort, we report program outcomes from 2004 to the present in two ways: evaluations of single programs, and comparisons between and among programs. Traditional search procedures were used to identify the relevant literature. First, building on descriptors used in previous reviews (e.g., Rosenberg et al., 2009; Rosenberg & Sindelar, 2005), a comprehensive list of search terms was developed. Using various iterations of these terms, an online search of Google Scholar and ERIC databases was conducted. Second, we completed hand searches of four journals: *Teacher Education and Special Education*, *Exceptional Children*, the *Journal of Special Education*, and the *Journal of Teacher Education*. Recognizing that the available research literature is limited in scope, selection criteria for inclusion were purposefully broad. To be included empirical data on important program outcomes (e.g., learner outcomes, completion rates, participant demographics) needed to be presented.

Special Education AR Program Characteristics

In response to the persistent shortage of credentialed personnel, AR programs in special education have proliferated considerably in the past decade (Rosenberg & Sindelar, 2005). Virtually every state offers some type of option or program for individuals seeking to become special education teachers. These programs facilitate entry of underrepresented CLD groups to teaching and provide midcareer changers lacking undergraduate training in education a tangible cost-effective way to enter the classroom (Rosenberg et al., 2007). Moreover, a significant number of special education AR participants (22.8%) are recently graduated general educators, indicating that these programs may be used as a method of entering teaching in a depressed general education marketplace (Dai, Sindelar, Denslow, Dewey, & Rosenberg, 2007; Rosenberg et al., 2007).

Although state policies for AR programs do not usually differentiate special from general education in terms of certification, licensure, and program approval procedures, special education AR programs are considerably different than the streamlined, fast-track approaches typical of general education (Sindelar et al., 2010). In their survey of over 101 programs Rosenberg et al. (2007) found that in addition to requiring full-time teaching in schools, most AR programs (69%) provide a considerable amount of time—18 months or more—for teacher education-based instructional activities. Moreover, unlike general education where a number of organizations (e.g., Teach for America, Troops for Teachers, NYC Teaching Fellows), design and implement programs, the vast majority of special education AR programs are designed and administered by IHEs often in partnership with SEAs and LEAs.

Program Evaluations

We found six program evaluations (deBettencourt & Howard, 2004; Esposito & Lal, 2005; Keller, Brady, Duffy, Forgan, & Leach, 2008; Kurtts, Cooper, & Boyles, 2007; McCray, 2012; Rowlison, 2006) and review them in this section. Table 13.1 highlights those involved in the design of the programs, critical instructional features, and the findings of each of the program evaluations. Four of the programs are considered internship programs in that employment as a teacher is a condition of admission to and continuation in the program. One program is a distance program in that coursework is delivered predominantly online with intermittent face-to-face support. Finally, one program is a step-up program designed for special education paraprofessionals to acquire the skills and credentials to assume the role of teacher of record.

Esposito and Lal (2005) described an IHE/LEA partnership program designed to accelerate certification for 58 in-service teachers working in multiethnic, multilinguistic, and economically disadvantaged schools. The cohort program was similar to its traditional professional development school model of teacher preparation (i.e., collaboration between schools and university, district/university teams providing instruction), however candidates completed the program in three semesters and fieldwork was completed in their own classrooms. Although completion rates were lower than anticipated—only 72% of the participants completed the program in three semesters—candidates who exited the program perceived their preparation to be highly effective and believed they could meet the demands of teaching in high-needs schools. Although no specific figures were provided, the authors noted that AR program costs were greater those than of traditional programs.

DeBettencourt and Howard (2004) described a similar 2-year internship partnership program designed to equip career changers with the skills to become confident and well-prepared special education teachers of students with learning disabilities. Coursework paralleled offerings of the traditional program but was provided at an accelerated pace at night and on weekends, allowing rapid entry to teaching. Modest financial support, counseling, and professional materials were also provided by the partners, a school district, and a nonprofit organization. The authors surveyed the 59 participants each year to ascertain teaching experiences, mentoring experiences, and professional development experiences. Participants rated their teaching higher when first entering classroom than at the end of the year, a trend that the authors attribute to early idealism. Participants also indicated that they found the mentoring helpful, yet they stated they needed more than they received. Although no retention data are provided, approximately 77% of survey respondents projected that they would be teaching special education in 5 years.

Table 13.1 AR Program Evaluations

Source	*Participants*	*Program Providers*	*Program Type*	*Learning Activities*	*Findings*
deBettencourt & Howard (2004)	Career changers with a minimum of a bachelor's degree (n=59)	IHE, LEA, nonprofit organization	Internship	2 year, 29 credit program plus counseling, mentorship, professional development experiences.	Self-report of increased teaching confidence; mentorship seen as helpful; 77% of participants felt they would still be special educators in 5 years.
Esposito & Lal (2005)	Uncertified in-service special education teachers (n =58)	IHE, LEA, DOE	Internship	3 semesters, 44 unit post-baccalaureate degree; in-service fieldwork in own classes.	Participants felt effectively prepared to meet demands of K–12 diverse settings; 72% completed the program.
Rowlison (2006)	In-service teachers with BA and internship license or substandard license (waiver) (n=410; 518)	IHE	Distance	19 special education courses offered online; technical assistance & support during monthly meetings.	Program contributed to the reduction of unlicensed teachers in the state. Participants reported that they liked working on their own schedule.
Kurtts, Cooper, & Boyles (2007)	Paraprofessionals, older than 24 years, away from schooling at least for a year (n=12)	IHE	Step-Up	127 credit hours over 4 years; novel setting for internship, academic skill mentoring.	All participants subsequently employed as special educators; limited outcome data.
Keller, Brady, Duffy, Forgan, & Leach (2008)	Out of field special education teachers (n=78)	SEA/IHE	Internship/ field based	12 courses, 16 credits.	Attrition rate of 86% largely attributable to a certification-by-test option enacted by the state. Completers rated the program as effective.
McCray (2012)	Case study of 3 students 5 years after completing program	IHE	Internship/ MA in Teaching	48 hour program completed in 4 semesters; students are the teacher of record during second semester of program.	Personal backgrounds, program features, work contexts, and professional practice partners contributed to success.

Keller et al. (2008) described a regional internship partnership between an IHE and several LEAs. A program development team composed of IHE and LEA staff designed a 12-course standards-based program to meet the needs of out-of-field special education teachers. All assignments associated with the 12 courses were completed in the participants' classrooms. Although the program was effective in terms of participant ratings of standards of professional preparation (see Brownell, Rosenberg, Sindelar, & Smith, 2004), the authors viewed the effort as a failure because the program did not ultimately increase the number of certified special education teachers. Furthermore, the overall attrition rate among four cohorts was 86%. The authors contend that a new state policy initiative, a test-only route to certification, resulted in AR program participants dropping out of an already customized and streamlined program.

One program evaluation (McCray, 2012) used a case-study methodology to investigate factors that contributed to the success of three teachers, with no prior education background, who remained in the field for 5 years. The author analyzed a variety of data sources (e.g., application records, interviews, efficacy scales, mentor teacher evaluations) to determine how program components, teacher background, and teaching context contributed to each teacher's longevity and self-reported success. Although it was noted that the teachers' personal history influenced choice of and commitment to special education, an individual's background was not a major factor contributing to persistence and perceptions of efficacy. The teachers reported that having a mentor in their building who taught the same population of learners, taking specific courses and completing projects, particularly in the area of behavior management, and having a cohort of supportive peers were most influential in their professional development. They also reported that school context, defined as having administrators and colleagues supportive of their efforts and students, influenced their levels of satisfaction.

Rowlison (2006) described an online special education AR program developed at New Mexico State University in the College of Education through the Office of Licensure and Endorsements for Alternative Preparation in Education. This was a 21-credit program for uncertified in-service teachers holding a bachelor's degree. Participants had the option of earning a master's degree in special education if they completed an additional 15 credit hours. Coursework was supplemented with technical assistance and support during monthly meetings. The program was popular, with semester enrollments ranging from 86 to 518. Although specific program completion data are not provided, the author reported that the program contributed considerably to the reduction in the number of special educators not fully certified, from 539 in 2002–2003 year to 58 in 2004–2005. No program efficacy data are provided, other than evaluations indicating that participants reported that the course required reasonable amounts of effort and that they liked having opportunities to work on their own schedule.

Kurtts et al. (2007) described Project RESTART: Recruitment and Retention: Students on Alternative Routes to Teacher Training, a step-up teacher preparation program. To be part of the program, participants were required to be at least 24 years of age and away from formal schooling for at least a year. Over a 4-year period, 12 paraeducators completed 127 credit hours during the late afternoons, allowing for continued employment in their classrooms. However, these paraeducators were moved to novel settings for student teaching assignments. Mentoring in academic skill areas such as writing and research was also provided. Although outcome data are limited, the authors noted that all of the paraeducator participants were employed as special education teachers.

The available program evaluation literature suggests that internship programs tend to be the most prevalent AR program type. Four of the six programs reviewed required employment as a teacher as a condition of admission to and continuation in program activities. The one distance program reviewed was designed to allow in-service uncertified teachers to earn their credentials, and the one step-up program found required a lengthy program of study prior to one becoming the teacher of record. Still, regardless of differences in type, the programs share several key characteristics. Similar to what was reported by Rosenberg and Sindelar (2005), all six AR programs serve nontraditional populations of students, provide flexibly scheduled instruction in a diverse range of settings, and typically supplement instruction with academic mentoring and field-based support. Moreover, most of the reports of these programs provide data on teacher satisfaction and completion rates. Unfortunately, unlike general education efforts, none of these program evaluations have substantive measures of teacher performance or program costs, indicating that we still know little about the efficacy of special education AR programs. What we have learned, however, is how state policy context influences program enrollments. Specifically, Florida's move to a test-only route to certification resulted in large numbers of participants dropping out of a standards-based, streamlined special education AR program, leaving Keller et al. (2008) to wonder whether participants will come even if teacher educators build customized programs containing convenient and effective professional development activities.

Comparative Studies

We found three comparative studies (McDonnell et al., 2011; Robertson & Singleton, 2010; and Sindelar et al., 2012) and summarize them in this section. Table 13.2 highlights the authors, comparisons conducted among program type, outcome measures examined, and findings for each of the program comparison studies. In the first study, researchers compared the employment and demographics of the University of Memphis's alternative special education institute to a traditional certification program. In the second study, researchers compared the effectiveness of a distance and on-campus teacher education program for teachers of students with severe disabilities. Finally, in the third study, Sindelar et al. (2012) interviewed 31 AR special education program directors and 224 AR program graduates to compare four AR program types on length, content, employment status, and cost.

In a comparison of a long-standing AR special education preparation program to its traditional counterpart at the University of Memphis, Robertson and Singleton (2010) compared rates of job retention and graduate demographics of ethnicity and gender across programs. The authors reported

Table 13.2 AR Program Comparisons

Source	*Comparisons*	*Outcome Measures*	*Findings*
Robertson & Singleton (2010)	Comparison of one university's traditional to a streamlined alternative program (i.e., one with fewer credit hours, courses in no particular order, and no student teaching).	Job retention rate and demographics of individuals who remained in field.	Higher number of alternatively trained teachers remain in field compared to traditional graduates, although those who stay the longest are traditionally trained. No differences in gender (mostly female) and only slight differences in ethnicity with more African Americans remaining in alternative programs than traditional programs. Authors view their AR program as being beneficial for filling vacant jobs with no detrimental attrition effects beyond those experienced by traditional programs.
McDonnell, Jameson, Riesen, Polychronis, Crockett, & Brown (2011)	Participants in preparation program for severe disabilities trained in either traditional on-campus cohort (n=17) or through a distance education cohort (n=15).	Participant demographics; Candidate knowledge of specific instructional processes; GPA in specialization courses; PRAXIS II performance; Student evaluations.	Although differences on several demographic variables, no meaningful differences in amount learned, application of skills, GPA, or Praxis II scores. Authors suggest that distance education programs via interactive video are at least as effective as on-campus programs.
Sindelar, Dewey, Rosenberg, Corbett, Denslow, & Lotfinia (2012)	Comparison of four different AR program types: internship, step-up, distance, and LEA.	Participant demographics; Costs; Program Content.	LEA programs are shorter, larger, and less expensive than other program types, however, these programs provide less special education content and completers tend to migrate to general education. As all program types do not attract midcareer changes from high status positions, step-up programs appear best in terms of recruitment and retention.

that, of the special education teachers from the two programs employed by four local districts (N = 373), over 50% were prepared by the AR program, and 33% were prepared by the traditional program. The AR program graduates remained teaching for a shorter period (M = 4.1 years) than the traditionally certified teachers (M = 6.0 years). These findings likely have more to do with the demographics of the sample and the relationships that the programs enjoy with the local districts than with the aspects of each program. The results are confounded by the fact that the traditional program was completed at the undergraduate level, and the AR program was conducted at the graduate level. In addition, some of the AR program graduates, who brought in prior years of teaching experience, quickly moved into school administration after program completion, while it was speculated that the traditionally prepared undergraduates had more years to teach before moving on to other career aspirations. Lastly, many of the undergraduate, traditionally trained teachers graduated from the university to migrate to other districts to begin their careers, while the alternatively prepared graduates remained in the local districts in which they were working. While the authors did not present any evidence of teacher quality or the abilities of either group to handle the stressors of teaching, they maintained that their alternative pathway is a viable method to adequately fill special education teaching positions that were not being filled by traditionally prepared teachers.

McDonnell et al. (2011) examined the effects of videoconferencing technology and other online teaching tools within an AR program for teachers of students with severe disabilities. Comparing an on-campus cohort (n = 17) to a distance teacher education cohort (n = 15) at the University of Utah, the authors found that the distance education cohort differed in terms of gender (higher numbers of males), age (older), and highest degree held. The older distance education cohort expressed a higher level of comfort with technology, even though most of the participants in the on-campus cohort were younger undergraduates. The authors found no meaningful difference between the groups in measures of: (a) knowledge of IEP development, (b) knowledge of the conceptualization and implementation of instruction, and (c) their PRAXIS II scores. Although no data on long-term retention were collected, the authors reported that all participants, regardless of cohort, were licensed and remained employed in their field of preparation.

In their analysis of the cost-effectiveness of AR programs, Sindelar et al. (2012) conducted structured interviews with program directors of AR programs identified in a previous study (Rosenberg et al., 2007) and identified four AR program types (internship, step-up, distance, and local) that vary by length, employment status, and cost (although all cost less than a traditional program). In all program types, participants were older, expressed an intent to remain in the field, and, on average, made more money teaching than in previous employment. Although hampered by limitations in the sample and databases that constrain the ability to fully represent AR program graduates, most alternative programs studied here were found to be similar to their traditional counterparts, being offered by colleges and universities, requiring over 2 years to complete, incorporating an internship, and leading to advanced degrees. The authors concluded that AR programs are similar to regular program offerings. The authors found that although few in number and with relatively small enrollments, step-up alternative programs tend to fit the context of special education better than those designed to recruit midcareer changers from other more lucrative professions. In addition to providing a better salary, step-up programs attract candidates that tend to persist in the profession.

The available program comparison literature suggests that the AR programs examined are institutionalized as viable, programmatically similar counterparts to their traditional counterparts. What we have learned though, is that while traditional and alternative programs may be structurally similar, studies that employ direct comparisons between them are limited by the differences present in the demographics of each cohort. In the first two comparisons, traditional programs served more students at the undergraduate level, while the AR cohorts were composed mostly of older graduate students with prior experience. These basic differences affect the interpretation of certain outcome measures, namely, teacher persistence in the field in the first study, and student report of comfort with distance technology in the second. In the last comparative study, the authors conveyed the importance of examining the differences in participant demographics within different AR programs. The authors found that while AR program participants were older, expressed an intent to remain in the field, and made more money teaching than in previous employment, specific step-up AR programs are more effective in preparing unique cohorts of candidates that persist in the field because they better fit the context of special education. Although none of the comparison studies reviewed directly examined measures of teacher performance, our review suggests that any future examinations of the efficacy of AR programs take into account the variance in participant demographics both between and within programs of preparation.

Challenges

In this section, we analyze two broad areas that presently challenge the study of AR programs in special education teacher preparation. These challenges for future research concern the persistent limitations in the research base in the field and the changes in the demand for and role of special education teachers in schools.

The Persistent Limited Research Base

There are daunting challenges in designing research that addresses the efficacy of programs of teacher preparation. Arriving at even the most basic definitions of the variables can be problematic. Examined at the programmatic level, the independent variable of teacher preparation is hardly uniform either within or across types of programs of preparation. We lack valid and practical outcome measures of both teacher effectiveness and teacher quality. More broadly, we are challenged within the field to expand our knowledge base of three essential components of alternative special education teacher preparation. First, as detailed in Sindelar et al. (2010), we need to learn more about what constitutes effective teacher education pedagogy. Several practices have been advocated in the above literature (e.g., distance learning), but the effectiveness and these practices for deepening and enhancing teachers' knowledge and practice remains unknown. Sindelar et al. encourage this extension of the research base in alternative routes by asking the salient questions that have yet to be examined, much less answered conclusively: How long must a program be to prepare minimally competent teachers? What features enhance the development of teachers' knowledge and skill? What factors mediate the effectiveness of alternative programs?

Second, we need to be able to better define both the individual and contextual variables within the field that account for variation in outcomes between and within AR programs. As we have seen in the research base in general education, factors associated with success of AR programs center on aspects of participant recruitment and selection, school placement context, and mentoring. By isolating and demonstrating the individual effects of personal attributes, aspects of school placement, and aspects of school-based mentor support on a beginning teacher's efficacy and resiliency, for example, research could better inform AR programs to mitigate teacher failure and attrition.

Third, we need to further identify the essential aspects of specific coursework, induction, placement, and mentoring that help beginning teachers apply their knowledge in the complex and varied settings they encounter in schools. Just as participant demographics of AR programs are unique, more research is needed to help inform AR programs to build unique, relevant, and useful programs that develop competency and confidence within these teachers in the critical beginning years.

Ultimately, the most meaningful measures of the outcomes of teacher preparation in special education are those that contain, at a minimum, valid measures of teacher behavior that are linked to student learning (Brownell et al., 2005). Such measures are difficult to obtain, given the complex nature and embedded organizational structures within special education teaching, most notably (a) the wide variation of individual student needs, (b) the wide variation of content instruction, and (c) the wide variation in teacher contact hours and instructional roles special educators perform with students. In addition, any research must utilize measures that reflect what teachers can do (and cannot do) within any given classroom. These structural challenges exist parallel to a confounding national debate over teacher certification, quality, and effectiveness. A central tenet of the H.R. 1532, The Race to the Top Act (S. 844—112th Congress, 2011), requires that states develop viable approaches based on multiple inputs to measure the effectiveness of teachers (including, most importantly, student growth) and provide an effectiveness rating to each individual teacher. Using this metric, the limited research base in special education AR programs does not examine with precision which routes prepare the most effective teachers, or if any differences even exist in effectiveness among graduates between routes. Given the lack of any viable measure of teacher quality in these reviewed studies, we can only conclude that the field continues to require the support necessary to address the complexities inherent in linking student outcomes to the type and content of special education teacher preparation programs.

Changes in Context

AR programs in special education have grown dramatically in number as part of a national need to increase the number and diversification of the special education teacher workforce (Dai et al., 2007). Federal policy (as codified in No Child Left Behind) has encouraged the development of nontraditional routes to preparation to the point where the line is blurred between traditional, formal, routes to special education teacher preparation and their alternative analogues. Throughout this period of growth, the number of *fully certified* (or most recently, *highly qualified*) special educators has failed to meet demand. Recently, however, the trend of increasing demand for special education teachers has begun to abate (Boe et al., 2013). Boe et al. explain the declining demand for special education teachers as a response to a decrease in the number of students identified with disabilities, particularly learning disabilities; the emergence of tiered models of service delivery; and perhaps most of all, a severe and persistent national economic recession. The stagnant economy provides less funding for jobs, and as more candidates are available to compete for these jobs, fewer special education teachers are likely to leave the profession for other jobs, or to retire. This dramatic and recent shift in the demand for special education teachers upends the status quo and demands that we carefully reconsider what we had taken for granted for decades. That is, that there will always be an unmet demand for special education teachers in U.S. schools. Given this assumption, we need to carefully reexamine AR programs and judge them not only on their ability to alleviate the demand for new special educators, but on the extent to which they produce qualified special education teachers. While alternative programs have noted some success in increasing the overall numbers of teachers certified, we remain unsure if these programs can effectively supplant more intensive traditional preparation routes to providing qualified special educators.

Special educators, more than ever, must be prepared to add value to their students' education. The mandate to provide students with disabilities access to the general education curriculum as well as the increased adoption of multitiered RTI teaching models within schools have combined to clarify the expected roles that general and special educators play in the instruction of all students. RTI's effectiveness lies in the ability of general and special educators to designate responsibility for targeted tiers of instruction to students within the classroom (Vaughn & Fuchs, 2003) as well as for how this instruction is conceptualized and adapted. In this model, the diagnostic and pedagogical knowledge of special educators must be closely integrated with content domain knowledge taught by the general education teacher. In this capacity, special educators can no longer afford to claim their knowledge of methods of adaptive pedagogy as their sole content area. They must integrate their expertise in assessing, supporting, and remediating literacy skills with content knowledge so that students with learning difficulties can access the general education curriculum (Brownell, Sindelar, Kiely, & Danielson, 2010).

This nexus of a limited research base, a sudden decline in teacher demand, and an increasing demand for the relevancy of the special educator within an RTI framework has forced a new discussion and a new opportunity for the field, resonating in the call for a new model of special education teacher quality and preparation:

> In this sense, special education is at a critical juncture—we can no longer afford to be unclear about who high-quality special education teachers are and how they should be prepared. Our future as a field depends on our capacity to upgrade the quality of teacher preparation and influence policies that govern teacher incentive systems.
>
> *(Brownell et al., 2010, p. 374)*

Conclusions

Fueling the housing boom that peaked in 2006, investments that bundled the varied risks of mortgage holders were a popular speculation; everyone was happy to take a dividend from these ventures until the housing bubble burst, necessitating bailouts of banks and a restructuring of the mortgage lending system. Similarly, we are challenged today to assess the risk and rewards associated with various methods of special education teacher preparation in times of economic and demographic change. Given the range, ubiquity, and variability of AR programs offered in special education teacher preparation, along with the blurring of distinctions between traditional and alternative routes, teacher preparation in special education is similar to a bundled speculative investment. Initially conceived as a way to redistribute opportunities of entrance into the profession in response to a growing market of need, our initial embrace of ARs to special education teacher preparation may have hidden potential risks from view. Unfortunately, our research base remains insufficient to gauge the risk that is present within the field of special education teacher preparation. We have seen how the context has begun to change for the demand for special education teachers; AR programs that have grown through the boom years of teacher shortages have become bundled into the fabric of teacher preparation in special education. Now that our market has begun to decline, what are the lasting effects of such variability, replete with potential risks, promises and challenges? With this in mind, this is what we can conclude from our review of the literature.

The efficacy of alternative routes to special educator preparation is still hampered by a limited research base. Current political pressures are demanding that preparation programs establish indicators of their graduates' effectiveness. As these calls for accountability increase, a research agenda within the field must be pursued that moves beyond self-reports of teacher preparation and incorporates objective analyses of teachers' abilities to diagnose and programmatically respond to the needs of students with disabilities as they struggle to acquire content knowledge. Moreover, programs should move beyond conducting basic outcome measures of teacher persistence within the field and examine whether and how their graduates play roles in professional development and leadership within their districts and school communities, and how these roles are mediated by aspects of preservice preparation and in-service context. By establishing more robust outcome measures, the field will benefit from a broader understanding of what makes an effective special education teacher for an array of contexts.

Although alternative routes to special education teacher preparation have become mainstream, the programs reviewed suggest that there is considerable variation within the demographics, needs, and school placements of the cohorts recruited into these programs. These factors must be taken into account in program development, research, and evaluation. Career changers, both from other fields and as step-up candidates from paraprofessional positions, are discrete categories of unique learners that do not contrast neatly to younger, more homogenous candidates more commonly found in traditional programs. Similarly, alternatively prepared candidates tend to serve in areas of need and in schools where the effects of context are more dramatic and extreme than those of their traditional counterparts. Research in AR special educator preparation must not be considered a homogenous whole; the particular nature of each cohort studied limits the external validity and generalizability of the results and expected outcomes for the teachers prepared. Rather than emphasizing the *alternative* nature of the program, future research should clearly describe the candidates studied, the programmatic interventions, and situational variables that result in specific outcomes for each program.

The existence and quality of the teaching internship, coursework and practice in methods of behavior management, mentoring, and induction continue to play a critical role in alternatively prepared teachers' views of the quality of their preservice program, in their perceptions of subsequent effectiveness, and in their likelihood to persist within the profession. Effective programs still need to be of adequate length and incorporate a variety of learning and support activities. As the lines between alternative and traditional routes to preparation intersect, the field must remain focused on implementing what we know works within programs of preparation.

As alternative routes to special education teacher preparation continue to recruit nontraditional candidates to serve in areas of need, the local, state, and national contexts may change quickly and dramatically in ways that challenge the efficacy and viability of these routes. As noted by Keller et al. (2008) the introduction of a state test-only route to certification during the implementation of their alternative program dramatically increased attrition from the program, negating the impact of an otherwise effective program. Teacher educators who devise and commit to programs of preparation must consider how fast-track changes in policy can obviate the need for their programs in students' eyes. Boe et al. (2013) have introduced how the recent decline in demand for special educators may increase competition within the job market. As the reserve pool of teachers increases, teachers considered un- or underqualified to teach are unlikely to be hired over a candidate that is perceived to hold a fuller preparation. In this light, pursuing any expeditious alternative route may not be a strategic benefit for the beginning special education teaching candidate. In a buyer's market, schools are likely to choose new hires more carefully, which may have implications for how competitive any alternative certification route is perceived in the hiring marketplace.

As past special education teacher shortages have encouraged innovation in teacher education, AR programs in special education have emerged and been incorporated into the mainstream of preparation. Past reviews (e.g., Rosenberg & Sindelar, 2005) have called for a cautious examination of the efficacy of these routes and have discouraged adoption and propagation of low cost and low quality programs. In our reexamination of the issue, we see no reason to discount this call for continued vigilance. Although the benefits of a fuller research base would empower the field to draw better conclusions, we have also seen how dramatic shifts in context and the need for special education teachers have pushed the debate past a simple alternative/traditional comparison. As ARs have become more embedded into the fabric of special education teacher preparation, we encourage the field to examine and promote how best to prepare quality special education teachers as a whole, and how to provide them with the expertise and support they need to become relevant, competent instructional leaders in an increasingly competitive market.

References

Bauer, A. M., Johnson, L. J., & Sapona, R. H. (2004). Reflections on 20 years of preparing special education teachers. *Exceptionality, 12*, 239–246. doi:10.1207/s15327035ex1204_5

Boe, E. (2006). Long-term trends in the national demand, supply, and shortage of special education teachers. *Journal of Special Education, 40*, 138–150. doi:10.1177/00224669060400030201

Boe, E., deBettencourt, L. U., Dewey, J., Rosenberg, M. S., Sindelar, P. T., & Leko, M. (2013). Variability in demand for special education teachers: Indicators, explanations, and impacts. *Exceptionality, 21*, 103–125. doi: DOI:0.1080/09362835.2013.771563

Boyd, D., Grossman, P., Lankford, H., Loeb, S., & Wyckoff, J. (2009). Teacher preparation and student achievement. *Educational Evaluation & Policy Analysis, 31*, 416–440. doi:10.3102/0162373709353129

Brownell, M. T., Hirsch, E., & Seo, S. (2004). Meeting the demand for highly qualified special education teachers during severe shortages: What should policymakers consider? *Journal of Special Education, 38*, 56–61. doi:10.1177/00224669040380010501

Brownell, M. T., Rosenberg, M. S., Sindelar, P. T., & Smith, D. D. (2004). Teacher education. In A. D. Sorrels, H. J. Rieth, & P. T. Sindelar (Eds.), *Issues in special education: Access, accountability, and diversity* (pp. 243–257). Boston, MA: Allyn & Bacon.

Brownell, M. T., Ross, D., Colón, E., & McCallum, C. (2005). Critical features of special education teacher preparation: A comparison with exemplary practices in general education. *Journal of Special Education, 38*, 242–252. doi:10.1177/00224669050380040601

Brownell, M. T., Sindelar, P. T., Kiely, M. T., & Danielson, L. C. (2010). Special education teacher quality and preparation: Exposing foundations, constructing a new model. *Exceptional Children, 76*, 357–377.

Cohen-Vogel, L., & Hunt, H. (2007). Governing quality in teacher education: Deconstructing federal text and talk. *American Journal of Education, 114*, 137–163. doi:10.1086/520694

Cohen-Vogel, L., & Smith, T. M. (2007). Qualifications and assignments of alternatively certified teachers: Testing core assumptions. *American Educational Research Journal, 44*, 732–753. doi:10.3102/0002831207306752

Constantine, J., Player, D., Silva, T., Hallgren, K., Grider, M., & Deke, J. (2009). *An Evaluation of Teachers Trained Through Different Routes to Certification, Final Report* (NCEE 2009-4043). Washington, DC: National Center for Education Evaluation and Regional Assistance, Institute of Education Sciences, U.S. Department of Education.

Dai, C., Sindelar, P. T., Denslow, D., Dewey, J., & Rosenberg, M. S. (2007). Economic analysis and the design of alternative-route teacher education programs. *Journal of Teacher Education, 58*, 422–439. doi:10.1177/0022487107306395

deBettencourt, L. U., & Howard, L. (2004). Alternatively licensing career changers to be teachers in the field of special education: Their first-year reflections. *Exceptionality, 12*, 225–238. doi:10.1207/s15327035ex1204_4

Esposito, M., & Lal, S. (2005). Responding to special education teacher shortages in diverse urban settings: An accelerated alternative credential program. *Teacher Education and Special Education, 28*, 100–103. doi:10.1177/088840640502800203

Feistritzer, C. E. (2010). *Alternative teacher certification: A state-by-state analysis 2010*. National Center for Education Information. Retrieved from http://www.ncei.com/

Field, K. (2009, October 21). Duncan urges "revolutionary change" in nation's teacher training programs. *The Chronicle of Higher Education*. Retrieved from http://chronicle.com/article/Duncan-Urges-Revolutionary/48896/

Fuchs, D., Fuchs, L., & Stecker, P. M. (2010). The "blurring" of special education in a new continuum of general education placements and services. *Exceptional Children, 76*, 301–323.

Gatlin, D. (2009). A pluralistic approach to the revitalization of teacher education. *Journal of Teacher Education, 60*, 469–477. doi:10.1177/0022487109348597

Goldhaber, D. (2004). Why do we license teachers? In F. Hess, A. Rotherham, & K. Walsh (Eds.), *A qualified teacher in every classroom: Appraising old answers and new ideas* (pp. 81–100). Cambridge, MA: Harvard Education Press.

Good, T. L., McCaslin, M., Tsang, H. Y., Zhang, J., Wiley, C. R. H., Bozack, A. R., & Hester, W. (2006). How well do 1st-year teachers teach? Does type of preparation make a difference? *Journal of Teacher Education, 57*, 410–430. doi:10.1177/0022487106291566

Grossman, P., & Loeb, S. (2010). Learning from multiple routes. *Educational Leadership 67*, 22–27.

Hassel, B. C., & Sherburne, M. E. (2004). Model 2: Cultivating success through multiple providers: A new state strategy for improving the quality of teacher preparation. In F. M. Hess, A. J. Rotherham, & K. Walsh (Eds.), *A qualified teacher in every classroom? Appraising old answers and new ideas* (pp. 201–222). Cambridge, MA: Harvard Education Press.

Hawley, W. (1992). The theory and practice of alternative certification: Implications for the improvement of teaching. In W. D. Hawley (Ed.), *The alternative certification of teachers* (pp. 3–34). Washington, DC: ERIC Clearinghouse on Teacher Education.

Humphrey, D. C., & Wechsler, M. E. (2007). Insights into alternative certification: Initial findings from a national study. *Teachers College Record, 109*, 483–530.

Humphrey, D. C., Wechsler, M. E., & Hough, H. J. (2008). Characteristics of effective alternative teacher certification programs. *Teachers College Record, 110*, 1–63.

Johnson, L. J. (1996). Evolving transitions? *Teacher Education and Special Education 19*, 202–204. doi:10.1177/088840649601900304

Keller, C. L., Brady, M. P., Duffy, M. L., Forgan, J., & Leach, D. (2008). If you build it and they still don't come: Playing the game of alternative certification. *Education Forum, 72*, 228–244. doi:10.1080/00131720802046032

Kurtts, S. A., Cooper, J. E., & Boyles, C. (2007). Preparing nontraditional adult teacher education candidates to become special education teachers. *Teacher Education and Special Education, 30*, 233–236. doi:10.1177/088840640703000403

McCray, E. D. (2012). Learning while teaching: A case study of beginning special education teachers completing a masters of arts in teaching. *Teacher Education and Special Education, 35*, 166–184.

McDonnell, J., Jameson, J. M., Riesen, T., Polychronis, S., Crockett, M., & Brown, B. E. (2011). A comparison of on-campus and distance teacher education programs in severe disabilities. *Teacher Education and Special Education, 34*, 106–118. doi:10.1177/0888406410380424

Robertson, J. S., & Singleton, J. D. (2010). Comparison of traditional versus alternative preparation of special education teachers. *Teacher Education and Special Education 33*, 213–224. doi:10.1177/0888406409359904

Rosenberg, M., Boyer, K., Sindelar, P., & Misra, S. (2007). Alternative route programs for certification in special education: Program infrastructure, instructional delivery, and participant characteristics. *Exceptional Children, 73*, 224–241.

Rosenberg, M. S., Brownell, M., McCray, E. D., deBettencourt, L. U., Leko, M., & Long, S. (2009). *Development and sustainability of school–university partnerships in special education teacher preparation: A critical review of the literature* (NCIPP document number RS-3). Retrieved from University of Florida, National Center to Inform Policy and Practice in Special Education Professional Development, http://ncipp.education.ufl.edu/files_6/NCIPP_Partner_010310.pdf

Rosenberg, M. S., & Sindelar, P. T. (2005). The proliferation of alternative routes to certification in special education: A critical review of the literature. *Journal of Special Education, 39*, 117–127. doi:10.1177/00224669050390020201

Rowlison, T. (2006). Meeting the needs for special education teachers in New Mexico. *Rural Special Education Quarterly, 25*(2), 13–17.

S. 844-112th Congress: Race to the Top Act of 2011. (2011). In GovTrack.us (database of federal legislation). Retrieved from http://www.govtrack.us/congress/bills/112/s844

Sindelar, P. T., Brownell, M., & Billingsley, B. (2010). Special education teacher education research: Current status and future directions. *Teacher Education and Special Education, 33*, 8–24. doi:10.1177/0888406409358593

Sindelar, P. T., Dewey, J. F., Rosenberg, M. S., Corbett, N. L., Denslow, D., & Lotfinia, B. (2012). Cost effectiveness of alternative route special education teacher preparation. *Exceptional Children, 79*, 25–42.

Tournaki, N., Lyublinskaya, I., & Carolan, B. (2009). Pathways to teacher certification: Does it really matter when it comes to efficacy and effectiveness? *Action in Teacher Education, 30*, 96–109.

Vaughn, S., & Fuchs, L. S. (2003). Redefining learning disabilities as inadequate response to instruction: The promise and potential problems. *Learning Disabilities Research and Practice, 18*, 137–146. doi:10.1111/1540-5826.00070

Wasburn-Moses, L., & Rosenberg, M. S. (2008). Alternative route special education teacher preparation programs guidelines. *Teacher Education and Special Education, 31*, 257–267. doi:10.1177/0888406408330647

Wilson, S., Floden, R., & Ferrini-Mundy, J. (2001). *Teacher preparation research: Current knowledge, gaps, and recommendations* (Document R-01-3). Seattle, WA: University of Washington, Center for the Study of Teaching and Policy. Retrieved from http://depts.washington.edu/ctpmail/PDFs/TeacherPrep-WFFM-02-2001.pdf

Xu, Z., Hannaway, J., & Taylor, C. (2011). Making a difference? The effects of Teach for America in high school. *Journal of Policy Analysis and Management, 30*, 447–469. doi:10.1002/pam.20585

Zeichner, K., & Schulte, A. (2001). What we know and don't know from peer-reviewed research about alternative teacher certification programs. *Journal of Teacher Education, 52*, 266–282. doi:10.1177/0022487101052004002

Part IV
Teacher Education Pedagogy

14

Teacher Preparation

Principles of Effective Pedagogy

Benjamin Lignugaris/Kraft and Shannon Harris

UTAH STATE UNIVERSITY

Things to Think About

- There is a critical relationship between teachers' content knowledge and their pedagogical skills.
- The special educator's role in schools differs in distinct ways from the general educator's role, which is reflected in preparation.
- Research has revealed core instructional skills required of special educators and there is a clear relationship between these skills and student outcomes.
- Prospective teachers must be taught to apply their pedagogical skills in a broad range of instructional contexts.
- There is a continuing effort to establish linkages between teachers' ability to implement specific evidence-based practices and student outcomes.

Introduction

Teachers have a substantial effect on student outcomes regardless of students' achievement level (Goldhaber, 2002; Hanushek & Rivkin, 2010; Rivkin, Hanushek, & Kain, 2005; Sanders & Rivers, 1996). Moreover, students who are regularly assigned to highly effective teachers have a distinct advantage over students assigned to teachers who are less effective (Wright, Horn, & Sanders, 1997). In a review of teacher value-added research, Hanushek and Rivkin report that this impact is consistent across studies conducted in a range of school districts. In math, disparities between a highly effective or a low-performing teacher equates to the difference in moving a student in the middle of an achievement distribution to the 59th percentile (or approximately 0.2 standard deviations in one year). This is comparable to the effect estimated from a 10-student reduction in class size (Hanushek & Rivkin, 2010).

Research that links student outcomes to teacher behavior, based on value-added analyses, is just now emerging. In two studies, Stronge and colleagues (Stronge, Ward, & Grant, 2011; Stronge, Ward, Tucker, & Hindman, 2007) conducted value-added analyses of third-grade and fifth-grade teachers using third-grade students' scores in English, math, social studies, and science, and fifth-grade students' scores in reading and math. In both studies, teachers were rank-ordered from most to least effective based on students' growth scores. The teachers in the top and bottom quartiles were then observed to determine if there were practices that differentiated them. In the third-grade study (Stronge et al., 2007), the teacher observation data were reported descriptively because of the small number of teachers, while Stronge et al. (2011) conducted a statistical analysis to determine if the fifth-grade top and bottom quartile teachers' practices were significantly different. In both studies, top quartile teachers scored higher than the bottom quartile teachers on each teacher effectiveness dimension. Further, Stronge et al. reported statistically significant differences favoring the top quartile teachers in classroom management and classroom organization. Stronge et al. suggest that perhaps there is not one behavior that distinguishes effective from ineffective teachers; rather, effective teachers engage in a variety of behaviors, instructional strategies, and management approaches that fit the learning context and result in higher student achievement.

Teachers' experience with various student populations and curricula also influences their effectiveness. In general, experienced teachers are more adept practitioners than novices (Educational Testing Service, 2004; Harris & Sass, 2010; Kane, Taylor, Tyler, & Wooten, 2010; Prince, Koppich, Azar, Bhatt, & Witham, 2010). While there is some consensus that teachers' skills improve with experience, how long teachers continue to improve is unclear (Goldhaber, 2002; Prince et al., 2010). A number of researchers indicate that teachers continue to improve during their first three years of teaching and then the effectiveness stabilizes or decreases (Gordon, Kane, & Staiger, 2006; Hanushek, Kain, O'Brien, & Rivkin, 2005; Harris & Sass, 2010; Kane et al., 2010; Milanowski, Kimball, & White, 2004; Rockoff, 2004). For example, in a recent analysis of teachers' practices based on the Teacher Evaluation System (TES) in Cincinnati, Kane et al. reported that teachers' TES scores increased more on average in the first three years of teaching than after the third year. Interestingly, they also found that the average increase in TES scores within a given school year for beginning teachers was greater than the average increase in the average TES scores for teachers after their third year of teaching.

There are few studies that compare the instructional skills of experienced and novice teachers of students with disabilities (Stough & Palmer, 2001). Stough and Palmer asked 19 student teachers and 19 experienced special education teachers to provide a running narrative of their thoughts and emotions while viewing two hours of videotape of themselves teaching. The experienced teachers commented more than the novice teachers on students' prior knowledge, students' response to instructional strategies, and their collaboration with general educators to resolve students' instructional problems. In another study, Podell and Tournaki (2007) examined experienced (teaching 4 to 29 years) and inexperienced (teaching 1 to 3 years) general and special education teachers' predictions of student success. Participants were presented case studies of students with disabilities who varied on reading achievement, social behavior, and class attentiveness. The participants were asked to rate the likelihood of academic and social success for each student. Overall, experienced teachers made significantly better predictions of academic and social success than inexperienced teachers. A post hoc analysis yielded no meaningful academic differences, but comparisons of ratings of social success revealed that experienced teachers made more positive social predictions for cooperative students than inexperienced teachers, while there was no difference in experienced and inexperienced teachers' prediction for uncooperative students.

Implications for Special Education

It is clear from the available research on teacher quality that a teacher's instructional and decision-making skills regarding student performance matter relative to student outcomes and these skills continue to develop after a teacher's initial preparation. Teacher preparation programs that provide content knowledge linked to pedagogical skills in different subjects lay a critical foundation for further skill development. Content-focused professional development and experience in classrooms can then help novice teachers become accomplished, exemplary practitioners. The purpose of this chapter is to describe:

(a) a conceptual framework for analyzing special education teachers' pedagogical skills, (b) the foundation pedagogical practices that teachers need to acquire and then situate within content domains to become effective, and (c) how teacher educators use field experiences to prepare special educators to apply their pedagogical practice.

A Conceptual Framework for Understanding How to Prepare Effective Special Education Teachers

Several researchers suggest that teacher effectiveness is composed of two dimensions: teacher knowledge and classroom practice (Brownell et al., 2009; Carlisle, Correnti, Phelps, & Zeng, 2009; Piasta, Connor, Fishman, & Morrison, 2009). Figure 14.1 provides a conceptual framework for how these dimensions contribute to developing effective practitioners. Implicit in this model is the reciprocal relationship between a teacher's content knowledge and understanding of effective instructional practice. That is, a teacher's effectiveness results from the application of pedagogical principles to a content domain, taking into account the instructional context that includes learners' skills and previous knowledge.

Teacher knowledge may be divided into content knowledge and pedagogical knowledge. Content knowledge reflects an understanding of a content domain while pedagogical knowledge is an understanding of critical effective teaching skills. Foorman and Moats (2004) surveyed the language knowledge related to early reading of third- and fourth-grade teachers. Their survey emphasized teachers' knowledge of both oral and written language (e.g., morphology, phonics) and examined the relationships between teacher knowledge, classroom instruction, and student outcomes. The researchers reported small but significant relationships between teacher knowledge scores, instructional effectiveness scores, and student outcomes in one site, but not in a second site where many teachers scored close to the ceiling on the test. This may indicate that content knowledge alone is insufficient for promoting effective reading instruction and maximizing student achievement. In a similar study, Carlisle et al. (2009) examined the direct relationship between teachers' reading knowledge and student achievement and found no direct relationship between level of reading knowledge and improved student outcomes.

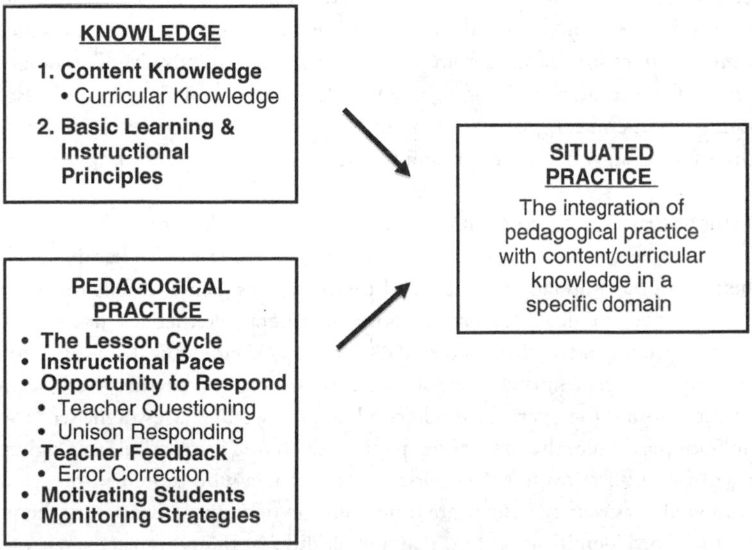

Figure 14.1 A Conceptual Framework Illustrating the Integration of Teacher Knowledge and Foundation Pedagogical Practice to Yield Effective Practice in Specific Content Domains

Carlisle et al., as well as several other researchers, suggest that how teachers enact or situate their knowledge in the classroom, at least in terms of reading instruction and perhaps within other instructional contexts, is critical for producing changes in student achievement (Brownell et al., 2009; Goe & Coggshall, 2007; McCutchen et al., 2002; McCutchen, Green, Abbott, & Sanders, 2009). Simply, teachers must understand the critical concepts and content in a knowledge domain and must know how to apply evidence-based instructional practices to that content to improve student outcomes (Piasta et al., 2009; Skinner, 2010).

In two studies with elementary teachers, McCutchen and colleagues (2002, 2009) examined the link between content knowledge, classroom practice, and student outcomes. In both studies, teachers participated in a two-week instructional institute that focused on intensive study of phonology and explicit comprehension instruction (McCutchen et al., 2002), or word reading, comprehension, and composition (McCutchen et al., 2009). At the end of the institute, each teacher received a compilation of teacher-generated lessons with grade-level appropriate content and a set of integrated reading and writing activities, and researchers provided three follow-up sessions in all classrooms. McCutchen et al. (2002) reported mixed student outcomes with the kindergarten through second-grade teachers. Student data showed no condition effect for children's phonological awareness with the kindergarten teachers. In the first-grade classrooms, the experimental teachers produced significantly more phonological awareness growth than control teachers. For orthographic fluency, kindergarteners in the experimental condition averaged 50% more letter production than children in the control classrooms, while there was no effect for children in the first-grade classrooms. On the reading comprehension measure, there was a significant difference in growth between children in the first-grade experimental classrooms and children in the first-grade control classrooms.

With third-, fourth-, and fifth-grade teachers, McCutchen et al. (2009) conducted a separate student outcome analysis on 140 students who were performing at or below the 50th percentile on the Woodcock Reading Mastery Test—Revised word identification subtest. On all measures (comprehension, vocabulary, composition, spelling, and writing fluency) low-performing students of teachers assigned to the institute intervention group outperformed low-performing students of teachers assigned to the control classrooms. McCutchen et al. also compared student outcomes of teachers whose linguistic knowledge was at least one standard deviation higher than their group mean performance on a linguistic knowledge test. Students of teachers in the high linguistic knowledge group scored significantly higher on vocabulary, word attack, and word identification measures than students of teachers who scored at their group mean (effect sizes ranged from 0.32 to 0.52). Importantly, McCutchen et al. could not separate the effect of the institute training to increase declarative knowledge and classroom consultation, and in both studies, control group teachers and experimental group teachers showed a great deal of overlap in their use of suggested strategies and the frequency with which they used strategies in their classrooms.

In a recent study, Piasta et al. (2009) attempted to clarify the relationship between teacher knowledge, teacher practice, and student achievement in reading. Piasta et al. examined teachers' literacy knowledge, their amount of literacy practice, and their students' achievement in 49 first-grade classrooms within 10 socioeconomically diverse schools. In general, neither teacher knowledge, nor the amount of explicit decoding instruction predicted children's word identification gains from fall to spring assessments. Moreover, teacher knowledge assessment scores did not predict the amount of decoding instruction in a classroom. However, for teachers whose knowledge assessment score was equal to or greater than the 50th percentile, the more time spent on decoding instruction, the higher their students scored on the word identification test. Conversely, for teachers who scored in the 25th percentile or lower on the knowledge assessment, the more time spent on decoding instruction, the worse their students scored on the word identification test. Piasta et al. did not indicate exactly what knowledge was critical for producing the positive outcomes with the high-knowledge teachers, but they did observe that low-knowledge teachers provided more inaccurate examples and responded less frequently to student errors than high-knowledge teachers. In addition, high-knowledge teachers tended to use a larger variety of decoding and word identification activities than low-knowledge teachers. These results suggest, at least in the area of reading and literacy instruction, that student achievement may be a function of teacher knowledge and how that knowledge is enacted or situated within the instructional context presented in a classroom. (see Brownell et al., Chapter 25, this volume, for a more expansive discussion of teacher knowledge and its relationship to student achievement).

Special Educator Roles and Implications for Pedagogical Knowledge and Skills

Special educators and general educators have different roles in schools and thus their preparation is uniquely different (Blanton, Blanton, & Cross, 1994; Brownell, Ross, Colón, & McCallum, 2005; Gilberts & Lignugaris/Kraft, 1997). Blanton et al. presented 20 special educators and 20 general educators with video depicting a teacher conducting a reading lesson with four third-grade students, one of whom had a learning disability. For this student, teachers were asked to rate (from less important to more important) various aspects of instruction, feedback regarding the strengths and needs of the student, and instruction or management strategies that might help this student succeed. The instructional factors the teachers rated were derived from the available literature on effective instruction and included items pertaining to how teachers use assessment data, modify instruction, and implement strategies such as peer tutoring. The special educators' ratings focused on the importance of tailoring instruction (e.g., extra time for reading instruction, small group instruction) to an individual student's needs more than the general educators. Special educators' narrative responses also emphasized the need to provide an organized and structured learning environment (e.g., organize learning, provide clear steps) more than general educators. Gilberts and Lignugaris/Kraft reviewed studies of elementary and special education teacher preparation competencies in classroom management and instruction. Similar to Blanton et al., they reported that special education teacher preparation programs emphasized structured presentation competencies (e.g., provide an organizational framework for students, give rationale for seatwork) while general education teacher preparation programs emphasized preservice teachers' knowledge of subject matter and breadth in ways to deliver that knowledge to students. In a more recent study, Brownell et al. compared the characteristics of 15 AACTE (American Association of Colleges for Teacher Education) and IRA (International Reading Association) exemplary teacher preparation programs, with descriptions and evaluations of special education teacher preparation programs. Similar to previous research, Brownell et al. noted that the general education programs focused on subject matter knowledge and content-specific pedagogy while special education programs tended to focus on generic pedagogical skills for instructing students at various ability levels in a broad range of subjects.

The rationale for the difference in instructional focus between general and special education teacher preparation programs may be found in the differing roles that general educators and special educators have in schools. General education elementary teachers learn skills required to instruct and monitor large groups of students. Their primary focus is to meet state content standards (Blanton et al., 1994; Gilberts & Lignugaris/Kraft, 1997) and the primary focus of their preparation programs is to provide deep content knowledge along with content-specific applications of effective pedagogy when teaching a large number of students (Brownell et al., 2005; Gilberts & Lignugaris/Kraft, 1997). In contrast, the special educator's role is to solve individual instructional and behavioral problems whether students are situated in an inclusive classroom, a resource classroom, or a self-contained classroom. Historically, special educators work with the most challenging students in a school and must address a broad range of content and instructional contexts. The instructional needs of students with disabilities are often more explicit and intensive than instruction that is typically provided in a general education classroom (Fuchs, Fuchs, & Compton, 2012; Fuchs, Fuchs, & Stecker, 2010; Torgesen, 1996). Dingle, Falvey, Givner, and Haager (2004) surveyed general educators, special educators, and administrators to identify the essential competencies that should be taught in inclusive preservice preparation programs as well as specific competencies needed by special educators. While the respondents identified a number of competencies for all teachers, they also identified specific competencies that reflect the special educator's role in providing intensive instruction for students with disabilities. These competencies include developing, implementing, and evaluating behavior change plans, developing individualized educational programs (IEP), and developing and implementing systems for monitoring student progress and determining individual student needs. In essence, the special educator's role is individualized and clinical, and involves an iterative cycle of individualized assessment, instructional planning, and teaching. Special educators are expected to systematically problem solve to adjust instruction for an individual child's needs across several content domains (Fuchs et al., 2012). As a result, special education teacher preparation programs typically focus on foundation instructional pedagogy that has been found to be effective when working with students with disabilities (Gilberts & Lignugaris/Kraft, 1997; Zigmond, 2006). The challenge for these preparation programs is providing teacher candidates with sufficient content knowledge and practice applying the foundation instructional pedagogy within key content domains (e.g., reading, writing, math) so that graduates have the instructional tools needed to adapt and design instructional programs that meet students' individual needs in these domains as well as other domains (e.g., science, social studies). These foundation pedagogical skills serve as building blocks that are refined through experience and professional development in specific content areas. In the next section of this chapter we will describe these generic instructional skills and summarize the evidence base that supports these skills. Finally, we will examine how special education teacher educators provide opportunities for teacher candidates to apply these skills in varied contexts.

Effective Instructional Pedagogy

The process-product research undertaken in the 1970s and 1980s was one of the first attempts to focus on the relationship between instructional pedagogy and student outcomes (Borich & Fenton, 1977; Dickson & Wiersma, 1982; Medley, 1977). Medley suggested that teacher preparation programs should provide quality training experiences that produce teacher performance competencies related to student outcomes. To determine the relationship between how a teacher behaves and how much students learn, Medley reviewed 289 studies. Reported studies were required to (a) have clearly defined teacher behaviors, (b) be based on long-term pupil gains in math and reading achievement, and (c) include results that were statistically and practically significant (i.e., $p > .05$;.40 or higher correlation). Medley found that effective teachers of low-performing students from kindergarten to third grade were distinctive in how they engaged students and used classroom time, organized their instruction, asked questions and responded to students, managed their classroom, and addressed individual learning needs. The teaching behaviors Medley identified are the core teaching behaviors special education researchers continue to study when examining effective methods for working with students with disabilities (Ellis & Worthington, 1994; Englert, Tarant, & Mariage, 1992; Goodman, 1990; Hall, 2002; MacGregor, 2007; Medley, 1977; Rosenshine, 1983). That is, effective special education teachers focus on using instructional time efficiently, organize instruction in small teacher-directed groups, and provide numerous opportunities to respond to confirm content understanding. They continuously monitor student performance, frequently review, adjust and reteach content as needed, and provide immediate corrective feedback (Miller & Hudson, 2007; Morsink, Soar, Soar, & Thomas, 1986). Special education researchers have developed numerous checklists, rating forms, and evaluation tools to assess these skills (e.g., Englert et al., 1992; Haycock, 1988; Holdzkum & Stacey, 1991; Jordan, Mendo, & Weerasinghe, 1997; MacGregor, 2007; Medley, Coker, & Soar, 1984; Sanders & Horn, 1994; Sikorski, Niemiec, & Walberg, 1996; Sindelar, Espin, Smith, & Harriman, 1990; Wright et al., 1997; Ysseldyke & Christenson, 1988). In the following section, we will briefly review the database that supports the foundation pedagogical skills that are effective when working with students with disabilities.

Effective Lesson Structure

The foundation for teaching practice is the lesson cycle (Hudson, Lignugaris/Kraft, & Miller, 1993). The first phase in the lesson cycle includes a learning set or anticipatory set where prerequisite knowledge for the lesson or other familiar material is reviewed (Bickel & Bickel, 1986; Ellis & Worthington, 1994; Englert et al., 1992; Hofmeister & Lubke, 1990; Hudson et al., 1993; Rosenshine, 1983). The second phase includes new material and guided practice (Berliner, 1984; Englert, 1984; Good, Grouws, & Ebmeier, 1983; Hofmeister & Lubke, 1990; Hunter, 1984; Rosenshine & Stevens, 1986). Finally, students engage in independent practice where they participate in activities that align with the content and skills taught (Englert, 1984; Rosenshine & Stevens, 1986). Also, through independent practice, students develop fluency and learn how to apply their new knowledge in various contexts (Hudson et al., 1993). This sequence has been found effective in math and reading instruction (Good et al., 1983; Hofmeister & Lubke, 1990; Rosenshine & Stevens, 1986) as well as content instruction (e.g., science, social studies; Hudson, 1997b).

In a series of studies, Hudson (1996, 1997a, 1997b) demonstrated the necessity of each phase of the lesson cycle when delivering social studies instruction to middle school students with learning disabilities. In study 1, Hudson (1996) compared an experimental condition in which students actively responded to teacher review questions to a control condition in which students silently reviewed their own notes from the previous day's lesson and previewed the current lesson (e.g., skimmed headings in the text). Students in the experimental condition scored higher on unit and maintenance class measures. In study 2, Hudson (1997b) implemented an experimental condition in which guided practice, that included active student responding to teacher questions, followed each social studies lecture. This was compared with a control condition where students silently studied their notes following each lecture. Students in the experimental group performed better on both unit and maintenance assessments, suggesting that guided practice characterized by active student responding helps students with disabilities acquire and retain content information more effectively than when students study individually. In study 3, Hudson (1997a) compared an independent practice condition in which the teacher circulated and provided praise and corrective feedback to a control condition in which students silently studied their notes from that day's lecture. No significant differences were found between the groups on pretest, unit, or maintenance tests, suggesting that a teacher's active participation in independent practice may not be critical to facilitate learning. Finally, in study 4 (Hudson, 1997a), students in the experimental group engaged in all phases of the lesson cycle, while those in the control group were directed to silently review notes, attend to the lecture, and silently review notes again. Students in the experimental group performed better on unit and maintenance tests, but the differences between the groups were not statistically significant because of the small sample size ($n = 16$). Effect sizes using Cohen's d indicated practically important differences favoring the lesson cycle participants (unit test $d = 0.93$; maintenance test $d = 1.03$).

Effective Practices

Within an effective lesson cycle, teachers make many decisions regarding the delivery of instruction and student performance (Borko, Shavelson, & Stern, 1981). Elements such as instructional pace, how teachers provide opportunities to respond, whether teachers provide feedback for accurate responding or to correct errors, how teachers motivate and manage students, and how teachers monitor student responding and use this information to adjust instruction are interrelated elements of lessons that determine the extent to which a lesson yields positive student outcomes.

Instructional Pace

Instructional pace is composed of two components. The first component is the pace with which teachers move through the curriculum and the second component is lesson pace (Hofmeister & Lubke,

1990). Essentially, an effective teacher achieves the balance required between movement through content and the high level of mastery required for each lesson to ensure success in a curriculum (Barr, 1973; Bickel & Bickel, 1986; Cartledge & Kourea, 2008; Engelmann, 2007; Englert, 1984).

Within the lesson cycle, effective teachers present material at a brisk pace (Hofmeister & Lubke, 1990; Ross & Blanton, 2004). Student attention, accuracy of student work, and the quantity of completed lessons are used to indicate the extent to which an instructional pace is appropriate. Carnine and Fink (1978) found that elementary classroom teachers who maintained a brisk pace covered more content and produced more student responses and stronger student outcomes than teachers with a slow instructional pace. Similarly, Heward (1994, 2003) determined that a brisk instructional pace produces stronger student outcomes than a slow pace. While Carnine and Fink, and Heward (1994, 2003) favor a rapid presentation rate, Skinner, Smith, and McLean (1994) suggest that presentation rates may vary based on student responding within a lesson. Variables such as task difficulty and the newness of the task may influence what presentation rate is optimal (Hall, 2002). In general, the lesson pace may be slower when teachers are presenting new, difficult material. Conversely, students require less "think time" and can respond to teacher questions more rapidly when material is familiar. Ultimately, effective teachers balance the pace of their instruction to maintain lesson momentum. An instructional pace that maintains momentum is a powerful tool for maximizing student attention, correct responding, and on-task behavior (Anderson, Evertson, & Brophy, 1979; Lignugaris/Kraft & Rousseau, 1982).

Opportunity to Respond

Opportunity to respond consists of a teacher question or cue, followed by an observable student response (Greenwood, Delquadri, & Hall, 1984: Rismiller, 2004). Providing students with frequent opportunities to actively respond is one of the most powerful means for increasing academic achievement (Greenwood et al., 1984; Heward, 1994; Heward et al., 1996; Hudson, 1997b; Medley, 1977; Morsink et al., 1986; Skinner, Fletcher, & Henington, 1996; Skinner & Shapiro, 1989; Sutherland & Wehby, 2001). Increasing opportunities to respond can also have positive effects on students' social behavior (Rismiller, 2004; Sutherland, Adler & Gunter, 2003; Sutherland & Wehby, 2001). The structure of teacher questions and teacher's use of unison responding are two variables that influence student response opportunities.

Teacher Questions

Through strategic questioning teachers assess readiness for new learning, create interest and motivation to learn, check students' understanding, and redirect student behavior (Levin & Nolan, 2004). The content of a teacher's question depends on the teacher's intent (e.g., assessing student understanding of foundation knowledge vs. synthesizing and analyzing information) and understanding of the subject matter (Carlsen, 1991). Bloom and Krathwohl (1956) developed a hierarchal system of six learning objectives, Bloom's Taxonomy, that teachers may use to guide their questions. The system includes six major categories from concrete or low-level recall objectives, to abstract or high-level synthesis and analysis objectives. Teachers can align their questioning sequence either from low- to high-level objectives, or from high- to low-level objectives.

A low- to high-level questioning sequence might be characterized as a preventative approach. Teachers begin by asking low-level questions and move up through the levels contingent on correct student responding. This direction ensures that students have the foundation knowledge needed to respond thoughtfully to high-level questions (Pressley et al., 1992), which typically results in fewer student errors and increases instructional/behavioral momentum. In contrast, teachers may focus on a high- to low-level questioning sequence by starting with a high-level question and, if students respond incorrectly, move toward low-level questions to diagnose underlying misunderstandings. When teachers use multiple questioning levels they can evaluate student understanding and determine whether to proceed with expanded questioning or to reteach material (Ellis & Worthington, 1994; Sindelar, Smith, Harriman, Hale, & Wilson, 1986; Stronge, 2010).

In one study, Bulgren, Lenz, Marquis, Schumaker, and Deshler (2002) explored teachers' application of a low- to high-level questioning sequence to improve the performance of 134 ninth-grade students in inclusive content classrooms. The researchers used the Question Exploration Guide, a graphic organizer that helps teachers explore and answer high-level questions (e.g., "What is Shakespeare's message about prejudice in *Romeo and Juliet*?) by developing smaller supporting questions (e.g., What is prejudice?). Initially, teachers asked students in the experimental condition to provide written responses to six low-level questions to ensure understanding of the topic prior to answering high-level questions at the end of the sequence. Teachers in the control condition were asked to teach the main idea of the story using their typical procedure. Students instructed using the Question Exploration Guide correctly answered a higher percentage of test questions than those who received traditional instruction, suggesting that moving from low-level questioning to confirm basic content knowledge to high-level questioning that expands that knowledge is effective for increasing student learning. Unfortunately, teachers rarely sequence their questions across levels. Researchers consistently report that as many as 60% of all teacher questions require simple recall (Ellis & Worthington, 1994; Gall, 1984; Redfield & Rousseau, 1981; Wilen and Clegg Jr., 1986).

Unison Responding

One reason large classes are challenging is because teachers have fewer individual opportunities for responding and teaching interactions (Morsink et al., 1986). Unison responding is an effective way to increase opportunities to respond, gain student attention, and reduce off-task behavior, which promotes increased student outcomes. In unison responding all students actively respond, verbally or nonverbally, to teacher-directed questions (e.g., choral unison responding, hand-raising, thumbs up, guided notes, and response cards), thus increasing the number of student response opportunities (Cartledge & Kourea, 2008; Heward, 1994; Lambert, Cartledge, & Heward, 2006; Rosenshine, 1983; Skinner et al., 1996; Wood & Heward, 2005). Unison responding is more efficient than individual responding because it increases students' active participation, allows teachers to monitor students concurrently and address correct or incorrect responding, and continue with new content in an efficient manner.

Sainato, Strain, and Lyon (1987) compared a mixed-response condition with a unison-response condition with 10 preschool children with behavioral and developmental disabilities. In the mixed-response condition, teachers started the lesson by calling on students individually and then prompted unison response opportunities later in the lesson where teachers produced an average of three opportunities to respond per minute. In the unison-response condition, teachers only prompted group responses, which increased opportunities to respond to an average of five per minute. Unison responding alone produced higher rates of correct responding and on-task behavior than the mixed-response condition for all participants. Similarly, Sterling, Barbetta, Heward, and Heron (1997) demonstrated that increasing opportunities to respond through unison responding resulted in more effective learning than an on-task condition with five students with developmental disabilities. Health facts were written on cards that were presented randomly during instruction in both conditions and students took a daily test five hours after receiving instruction. All students provided more correct responses during the unison response condition than during the on-task condition on daily tests and on a maintenance test administered two weeks following the instructional sessions. Simply, unison responding is an effective way to increase active student responding for students with disabilities, especially to confirm student understanding of the basic knowledge needed to respond to high-level questions.

Teacher Feedback

Feedback on academic responses provides teachers and students with information about the task or learning at hand and is an essential pedagogical skill for increasing student achievement (Hattie, 2009). Importantly, students should receive immediate feedback to both correct and incorrect responses (Hall, 2002). Feedback for correct responding allows teachers to maintain instructional momentum/pace and increase student motivation. Similarly, to maintain instructional momentum, error corrections should be direct, positive and immediate, and should give students another opportunity to emit the correct response.

Error Correction

There are a variety of error correction procedures. The procedure with the most empirical support is a *model/test/delayed test* procedure in which the teacher models the correct response (e.g., This word is cat.), followed by a representation of the question (e.g., What word?), a correct student response, and a delayed test on that item later in the lesson (Barbetta, Heron, & Heward, 1993; Barbetta & Heward, 1993; Barbetta, Heward, Bradley, & Miller, 1994; Drevno et al., 1994; Jones, Lignugaris/Kraft, & Peterson, 2007). Other procedures include a *cue/test/delayed test* procedure in which the teacher provides a prompt to help the student derive the correct response (e.g., "Sound out the word, /c/ /a/ /t/."), followed by a representation of the question (e.g., "What word?"), a correct student response and a delayed test later in the lesson, as well as a variety of other procedures that include an explanation why an answer is incorrect (Hofmeister & Lubke, 1990). Critical error correction variables that affect student correct responding are (a) prompting students to emit the correct response following a correction (Barbetta & Heward, 1993; Barbetta et al., 1994), (b) the immediacy with which students emit a correct response (Barbetta et al., 1994), and (c) the interaction between the difficulty of the instructional material and the error correction procedure (Jones et al., 2007).

Barbetta and colleagues (Barbetta & Heward, 1993; Barbetta et al., 1994; Drevno et al., 1994) conducted a series of error correction studies that explored the importance of having students emit a correct response after a teacher model and the immediacy with which teachers corrected student responses. In the first two studies (Barbetta & Heward, 1993; Barbetta et al., 1994), the effects of a *model/test* error correction procedure and a *model-only* error correction procedure were examined on the acquisition of geography facts and sight words with students with learning disabilities. Students learned more geography facts and read more sight words correctly during the *model/test* error correction condition than during the *model-only* correction condition on same- and next-day assessments, as well as 1-week maintenance tests. Drevno et al. (1994) replicated Barbetta et al.'s (1994) study while teaching science to five elementary students. In this study, students in the *model/test* error correction condition produced nearly 50% more correct responses during instruction, confirming the importance of producing active student responses during error corrections with students with disabilities.

Barbetta et al. (1994) examined the importance of the immediacy of error corrections on sight words with five students with developmental disabilities. Unknown words were printed on cards for each condition. During immediate error correction, the teacher modeled the word and prompted the student to provide the correct response before moving on. During delayed error correction, the teacher responded to errors by saying "No, we'll try this word later," set that card aside, and repeated instruction for all incorrect words later in the lesson. The immediate error correction procedure produced better student outcomes than delayed error correction for all students on same- and next-day assessments, as well as 1- and 2-week maintenance tests.

In another study, Pany and McCoy (1988) evaluated the immediacy of corrections on oral reading errors and whether every student error should be corrected. The treatment conditions consisted of (a) feedback given on all oral reading errors, (b) feedback selectively applied to errors that were judged to alter the meaning of the sentence, and (c) no feedback on any oral reading errors. Before reading, students were told whether or not they would receive feedback from the teacher. Both the feedback on all errors and selective feedback conditions resulted in fewer errors overall on oral reading fluency and reading comprehension than when students were in the "no feedback" condition. On a delayed measure given three days after treatment, students in the "feedback on all errors" condition made the fewest errors. Overall, error correction procedures that are direct, immediate, and end with students actively emitting correct responses improve student outcomes.

Motivating Students

Students are more likely to engage in tasks when they expect to do well and when the task is interesting and enjoyable (Brophy, 2010; Meece, Anderman, & Anderman, 2006). Motivation is especially critical when working with low-performing students, as they generally tend to be less motivated and have a history of being frustrated in learning situations (Collins, 1996). Brownell et al. (2009) report that beginning teachers who engage students and motivate them to participate in more intensive, continuous reading instruction influence student achievement gains more than teachers with less skill in this area.

One of the primary practices used to motivate students and manage the classroom is praise (Shores, Cegelka, & Nelson, 1973). Praise increases appropriate behavior and students' academic learning time (Hall, Lund, & Jackson, 1968; Hofmeister & Lubke, 1990). Brophy and Good (1986) indicate that praise should be varied, specific, and contingent on performance of the target behavior. Several researchers have demonstrated the positive effects of teacher praise on students with disabilities (Brophy & Good, 1986; Ferguson & Houghton, 1992; Sutherland, Wehby, & Copeland, 2000). Ferguson and Houghton examined the effects of teachers' contingent praise on eight elementary students with disabilities. Students' on-task behavior was measured prior to the intervention and baseline data were gathered on teachers' praise rate. After viewing three hours of video training on praise, the teachers returned to their classrooms and provided instruction. All teachers significantly increased praise rate and all students increased their mean level of academic learning time. In another study, Sutherland et al. (2000) measured the effects of praise for on-task behavior with fifth-grade students with emotional/behavioral disturbance. When praise was implemented, on-task behavior increased to a mean of 85.6% of the observation intervals compared to a mean of 62.2% during the withdrawal phase. The authors concluded that high rates of praise might serve to increase student on-task behavior.

In general, incorporating these effective practices within an effective lesson structure provides the framework to motivate students and manage the classroom. As teachers become more adept at delivering instruction, they generate more active student responding and devote more attention to student learning and less attention to classroom management (Bents & Gardner, 1992; Espin & Yell, 1994). In essence, when students are actively engaged in a lesson, teachers have more opportunities to provide positive feedback and create a positive learning atmosphere where they spend little time correcting or reprimanding. Successful teachers keep students engaged in lessons and activities, monitor the classroom continually, and intervene as needed, in ways that do not disrupt lesson momentum (Brophy, 2010; Stronge et al., 2011).

Monitoring Strategies

Progress monitoring is essential for helping students with disabilities meet their IEP goals and continue moving toward desired learning outcomes (Stronge, 2010). Well-designed progress monitoring strategies produce information about students' learning that is critical for data-based decision making (Fuchs et al., 2012; Waymen, 2005), and provides information on the effectiveness of teachers' instruction (Cook, Tankersley, & Harjusola-Webb, 2008; Stronge, 2010; Ysseldyke & Christenson, 1988).

Curriculum-based assessment (CBA) is one evidence-based strategy for selecting instructional goals, and monitoring student progress (Deno, Espin, & Fuchs, 2002; Fuchs, 2003; Fuchs, Deno, & Mirkin, 1984; Ysseldyke & Christenson, 1988). The CBA model was designed to help teachers make judgments about meeting students' needs through individualized instruction (Deno, 2006; Deno et al., 2009; Heward, 2003). Frequent assessments help teachers focus on improving skills that are of immediate and critical importance to individual students and evaluate the relationships between instructional interventions and student performance (Jones, Southern, & Brigham, 1998). Curriculum-based assessment data can be used to demonstrate annual progress and are predictive of how students might perform on high-stakes standardized tests (Deno et al., 2009).

Stecker and Fuchs (2000) examined the importance of using individual progress monitoring data to individualize instruction in math for 42 students with mild to moderate disabilities. Teachers administered CBAs twice weekly and adjusted instruction over 20 weeks. Students performed better on a standardized math operations test when teachers adjusted their instruction based on curriculum-based measurement data. In another study, Fuchs et al. (1984) randomly assigned 39 special education teachers to a CBA condition or a conventional special education evaluation condition. In the CBA condition, the teachers wrote IEP goals and objectives and then developed curriculum-based measurements that aligned with the goals. Following instruction, daily performance data were collected and graphed and program changes were implemented whenever a student made benchmark gains. Teachers assigned to the conventional condition wrote IEP goals and objectives based on methods such as informal observation and workbook samples. The teachers in the CBA condition made decisions that were more reflective and responsive to student progress, improved their overall instruction, and their students were more aware of goals and progress than those in the conventional condition. Importantly, student outcomes for these teachers were higher than those students in the conventional condition.

The pedagogical behaviors discussed in this section make up the foundation skills needed to teach effectively. Neither the process-product research (e.g., Medley, 1977) nor recent research comparing highly effective teachers and less effective teachers using value-added analyses (e.g., Stronge et al., 2011) identified exactly how these skills should be applied to maximize outcomes for all learners. Rather, these skills are interrelated and poor performance on one skill may affect other areas of practice. For example, when teachers provide few meaningful opportunities to respond or have a slow instructional pace there are fewer opportunities to praise students, and students are more likely to learn less material and engage in disruptive behavior (Gable, Hester, Rock, & Hughes, 2009; Sutherland, Wehby, & Yoder, 2002). As Brownell et al. (2009) noted, teachers who motivated and engaged students in continuous reading instruction produced stronger student achievement than teachers who did not motivate and engage students in continuous instruction. Similarly, teachers who effectively correct student errors produce more opportunities for students to respond correctly and learn targeted content, than teachers who do not complete error corrections with students emitting the correct response. Simply, the pedagogical skills discussed in this section are the foundation instructional units that preservice special educators must learn to adjust for different learners, content, and instructional contexts.

How Do We Teach Teachers to Apply Their Pedagogical Skill in a Broad Range of Instructional Situations?

Teacher educators have continuously struggled with the problem of how to link preservice teacher preparation to teacher performance in schools (Allsopp, De Marie, Alvarez-McHatton, & Doone, 2006; Goe & Coggshall, 2007; Rosenberg, Jackson, & Yeh, 1996). This problem is exacerbated in special education because most teachers are certified to address students with disabilities in grades K–12 (Geiger, Crutchfield, & Mainzer, 2003). These teachers must have the ability to use their skills across a range of content areas as well as grade-level contexts. The principle tool used to help preservice teachers develop these foundation skills is field-based experiences that start slowly and progress to more challenging teaching contexts (Brownell et al., 2005; Ruhl & Hall, 2002).

Special education teacher preparation has a long history of relying on field experiences to situate teachers' content knowledge and pedagogical practice. Soon after the implementation of the Education for All Handicapped Children's Act (PL 94–142), Reynolds (1979) called for "all teachers to have at least minimal competencies in 'clinical' studies of individual students, including those with special needs" (p. 10). By the late 1970s, competency or performance-based teacher preparation in field settings emerged as the prominent model in special education teacher preparation (Berdine, Moyer, & Suppa, 1978; Buck, Morsink, Griffin, Hines, & Lenk, 1992; Ross & Blanton, 2004; Schuster & Stevens, 1991; Turner, Ludlow, & Wienke, 1987).

Competency-based teacher education (CBTE) grew from the process–product literature and shifted the teacher preparation focus from developing a body of content knowledge to establishing a performance link between knowledge and practice (Lilly, 1979). In a review of special education teacher preparation programs, Brownell et al. (2005) noted that at least one third of the special education teacher preparation program descriptions they reviewed provided a clear integration between field experiences and courses. As noted earlier, special education researchers developed numerous checklists and rating forms in the 1980s and 1990s to evaluate preservice and in-service teacher competencies (Berdine et al., 1978; Sikorski et al., 1996; Ysseldyke & Christenson, 1988). These competency checklists served as important components in the development and planning of both preservice and in-service teacher education programs (Espin & Yell, 1994). Amid growing criticism of reductionist approaches to teacher preparation in special education, Englert et al. (1992) suggested an expanded focus on the quality of teacher–student interactions and designed a rating scale that teacher educators might use to evaluate the extent to which preservice teachers provide students with meaningful instructional activities, promote classroom dialogue, are responsive to the knowledge base students bring to the learning context, and the extent to which teachers build a classroom community. The CBTE movement and Englert et al.'s expanded framework spawned a number of studies that showed a clear, measureable link between teachers' coursework and field-based practice (Maheady, Mallette, & Harper, 1996; Morgan, Gustafson, Hudson, & Salzberg, 1992; Scruggs & Mastropieri, 1993).

In several studies, researchers describe early field experiences where preservice teachers develop foundation skills needed for later field experiences (Lignugaris/Kraft & Marchand-Martella, 1993; Scruggs & Mastropieri, 1993; Skinner, 2010; Trautwein & Ammerman, 2010). Lignugaris/Kraft and Marchand-Martella (1993) demonstrated the systematic development of foundation skills such as instructional presentation, error correction, praise, and instructional pacing. During initial observations, 74% of the trainees met the performance criterion for presentation skills and 32% of the trainees met the criterion for response error correction. At the end of the practicum all the trainees demonstrated criterion performance on presentation skills, and 78% of trainees met criterion performance on error correction skills. This was the first practicum in a sequence of field experiences during which preservice teachers were expected to assume increasing responsibility for lesson design and curriculum organization.

Skinner (2010) suggests that an apprenticeship model in which preservice teachers learn from expert practitioners should encourage preservice teachers to make links between teaching and learning theory and classroom practice. Similar to Lignugaris/Kraft and Marchand-Martella's (1993) approach, preservice teachers' pedagogical skill development is carefully sequenced from mentor-teacher demonstrations followed by short teaching episodes by preservice teachers, to full lessons that incorporate multiple aspects of teaching. For example, cooperating teachers might model specific techniques for managing distribution and collection of materials or managing transitions between lesson activities. Following the demonstration, trainees then construct a plan for incorporating the technique into a lesson. After each teaching episode, trainees might reflect on their teaching with their cooperating teachers. This cycle is repeated weekly within each field experience and across two or more field experiences. Skinner described the implementation of this model over a 1-year period with 44 preservice science teachers and documented a systematic decrease in cooperating teacher modeling of instructional techniques and an increase in preservice teacher classroom responsibilities. Trainees also reported that their discussions with their primary cooperating teacher were the most influential factor affecting their development as practitioners. While this model effectively situated practice and scaffolded learning to teach, linkages between learning theory and practice taught in university classes to public school contexts were unclear. In a recent study, Allsopp et al. (2006) described a teacher preparation model in which candidates take their courses and complete their field experience in the public school setting. In this professional development partnership, course content was integrated into the experiences the candidates were having within the school. Preservice teachers evaluated their experience at the end of the semester and nearly 70% indicated that the linkage between practica and courses was facilitated more with the site-based course and practica model than with the traditional field-based arrangement the participants experienced in previous semesters. While these experiences suggest that field-based practica can help facilitate the performance of desired teaching skills, it is not clear that the experiences were implemented with sufficient fidelity to produce changes in student outcomes.

Brownell et al. (2005) indicated that about one fourth of the special education teacher preparation programs they reviewed used student outcomes as part of their program evaluations. For example, Maheady et al. (1996) showed how a structured early field-based experience could be linked to student outcomes. Maheady et al. provided preservice general educators with opportunities to tutor children with exceptional learning needs in reading. Each pair of preservice teachers was assigned one tutee. The tutors typically implemented an effective lesson cycle appropriate for a reading activity at the elementary or secondary level. Maheady et al. analyzed oral reading fluency data from 72 tutor pairs and 30 individual tutors. Most of the tutored students showed increased oral reading fluency and increased comprehension during the 10-week study. This field experience provided opportunities for preservice teachers to apply what they were learning in their university classes and confirm, based on student outcomes, the effectiveness of these strategies. However, it is not clear how the content taught in the university course aligned to the practices students applied in their field placements. Moreover, it is not clear if this experience influenced these teachers' instructional performance in subsequent field experiences or student teaching.

In several recent studies, researchers demonstrated how university coursework might be linked to preservice teacher skill attainment and student outcomes (Alexander, Lignugaris/Kraft, & Forbush, 2007; Hawkins, Kroeger, Musti-Rao, Barnett, & Ward, 2008; Maheady, Harper, Mallette, & Karnes, 2004; Maheady, Jabot, Rey, & Michielli-Pendl, 2007). Maheady et al. (2007) reported the impact of an early field experience with 422 preservice teachers placed in kindergarten through third-grade settings across five semesters. In the practicum seminar, university instructors taught preservice teachers strategies for implementing a curriculum-based assessment and demonstrated within-group activities for increasing opportunities to respond. The preservice teachers were required to design, implement, and evaluate two lessons in which they collected pre and post student data and used one or more of the evidence-based practices demonstrated in class. The researchers randomly selected 225 preservice teacher lessons and examined the fidelity of implementation of the evidence-based practice included in the lesson, and the student pre/post assessment data to assess the impact on student learning. The researchers reported that the preservice teachers implemented the evidence-based practices with high fidelity. Moreover, across semesters, they reported an accelerating trend in student performance in 50%–66% of preservice teachers' lessons, a marginal effect on student performance in 10%–26% of preservice teachers' lessons, and no effect in 2%–11% of preservice teachers' lessons. Importantly, the preservice teachers were required to design appropriate measures to evaluate student performance and consider the contextual variables (e.g., age of students, students' skills, content area, and instructional objectives) when selecting what evidence-based practice might be most appropriate for maximizing opportunities to respond within their lesson. This demonstration however, provided only a brief evaluation of preservice teachers skills and their ability to produce meaningful student outcomes. Moreover, there was no analysis to determine why some preservice teachers produced marginal or no effects with their students.

In an extended application, Alexander et al. (2007) demonstrated a link between instructional planning strategies taught in an early program university class and then applied to math in an online class, field implementation of the planning strategies, and student outcomes. In the initial university class, preservice teachers were taught to implement an eight-step planning process that included designing curriculum-based assessments, writing instructional objectives, developing a monitoring system, and principles of effective instruction (e.g., an effective lesson structure, general strategies for increasing active student responding, error correction procedures). In the online class, preservice teachers applied the planning process to case study students at various math performance levels and discussed how to apply the general principles of effective instruction to math content. The preservice teachers' implementation of the planning process was then evaluated in a field placement and their students' performance was evaluated using teacher-designed pre- and post-CBAs.

The preservice teachers implemented 79% or more of the curriculum-based planning steps when they applied the planning process in their field placements. On the curriculum-based pretests the preservice teachers identified math skills that students had already mastered (students demonstrated 80% or higher correct performance) and skills that required additional instruction. On the posttests, the preservice teachers' students continued to score higher than 80% correct on problems that were identified as mastered on the pretest. Moreover, their students maintained low performance levels on skills that were not addressed during the practicum. On skills that the preservice teachers identified that their students had mastered during the field placement, posttest scores averaged 84% and all preservice teachers showed increased student scores from pre- to posttest on skills that students were continuing to work on. These studies clearly show how teacher educators might evaluate the relationship between the practices they are teaching preservice teachers in university classes, the preservice teachers' ability to apply those practices in public schools, and the effect on preservice teachers' students. However, in these studies researchers provide only descriptive accounts of preservice teacher applications and student outcomes. Additional experimental studies are needed to understand precisely what university training is necessary to produce robust preservice teacher applications in the field that are maintained and generalize to new instructional contexts. It is also necessary to refine methodology used to establish the linkage between university instruction, preservice teacher practice, and student outcomes. For example, in the available studies the student outcome data are obtained indirectly from the preservice teachers' records. To ensure data are accurate and reliable, it is important to collect interrater reliability on student outcome measures. Moreover, it is important to collect student outcome data using standardized curriculum-based measures (e.g., KeyMath3 Diagnostic Assessment to assess math progress over a semester-long practicum).

Given the problem-based clinical nature of special education, it is critical that researchers examine the extent to which foundation skills such as the effective lesson cycle and effective practices, such as appropriate instructional pacing, producing active student responding, keeping students motivated, and data-based decision making, demonstrated in one field experience are maintained over time and generalize to new field experiences in a different content area. Morgan et al. (1992) provided one such demonstration in which a peer coaching intervention was used to teach five low-performing preservice teachers foundation instructional skills in a reading field placement and examined concurrently in a math field placement. The target foundation instructional skills included a clear presentation of material from a reading curriculum that required students to say sounds and blends, and read words and sentences; correct application of CBA strategies in reading; correct application of a *model/test* error correction procedure; correct delivery of points for appropriate student behavior; and provide general and specific praise statements contingent on students' correct responding. All the preservice teachers improved their teaching performance in reading during the peer coaching intervention. In addition, preservice teachers' instructional performance in math field placements improved concurrent with their reading performance without additional peer coaching. Importantly, the instructional context in math was quite similar to the instructional context in reading (e.g., same class, similar students). It is not clear if these preservice teachers could have adapted their instructional routines to fit a more diverse instructional context or a more diverse array of students.

Clearly, becoming a skillful teacher takes time, continued professional development, and practice (Brownell et al., 2009). Additional research is needed that links preservice preparation to student performance in field experiences and to teacher practices during their first year teaching. Research is needed that examines the extent to which the development of foundation instructional skills enhances the development of more complex instructional repertoires later in teacher preparation programs and, more importantly, as special education teachers gain experience and advance from novice to more experienced veterans. Finally, given the unique role of special educators, we must examine how they adapt their skills to meet the instructional demands in various content areas and the extent to which content knowledge enhances special education teacher practice. Simply, as Feiman-Nemser (2008) stated "teachers need a repertoire of skills, strategies, routines and the judgment to figure out what to do when" (p. 699). The available research suggests that we can prepare special education teachers who know how to implement the necessary foundation evidence-based practices, can implement those practices with fidelity, and at least in the short term, can demonstrate positive student outcomes. It is not clear, however, the extent to which we systematically prepare special education teachers who can adapt their practices to the myriad array of contextual variations found when working with students with disabilities.

References

Alexander, M., Lignugaris/Kraft, B., & Forbush, D. (2007). Online mathematics methods course evaluation: Student outcomes, generalization, and pupil performance. *Teacher Education and Special Education, 30*, 199–216. doi:10.1177/088840640703000401

Allsopp, D., DeMarie, D., Alvarez-McHatton, P., & Doone, E. (2006). Bridging the gap between theory and practice: Connecting courses with field experiences. *Teacher Education Quarterly, 33*(1), 19–35.

Anderson, L. M., Evertson, C. M., & Brophy, J. E. (1979). An experimental study of effective teaching in first-grade reading groups. *The Elementary School Journal, 79*, 193–223. doi:10.1086/461151

Barbetta, P. M., & Heward, W. L. (1993). Effects of active student response during error correction on the acquisition and maintenance of geography facts by elementary students with learning disabilities. *Journal of Behavioral Education, 3*, 217–232. doi:10.1007/BF00961552

Barbetta, P. M., Heron, T. E., & Heward, W. L. (1993). Effects of active student response during error correction on the acquisition, maintenance, and generalization of sight words by students with developmental disabilities. *Journal of Applied Behavior Analysis, 26*, 111–119. doi:10.1901/jaba.1993.26-111

Barbetta, P. M., Heward, W. L., Bradley, D. M., & Miller, A. D. (1994). Effects of immediate and delayed error correction on the acquisition and maintenance of sight words by students with developmental disabilities. *Journal of Applied Behavior Analysis, 27*, 177–178. doi:10.1901/jaba.1994.27-177

Barr, R. C. (1973). Instructional pace differences and their effect on reading acquisition. *Reading Research Quarterly, 9*, 526–554. doi:10.2307/747001

Bents, M., & Gardner, W. (1992). Good teaching: Some views and prototypes. *Action in Teacher Education, 14*(2), 38–42. doi:10.1080/01626620.1992.10462809

Berdine, W. H., Moyer, J. R., & Suppa, R. J. (1978). A competency-based student teaching supervision system. *Teacher Education and Special Education, 1*, 48–54. doi:10.1177/088840647800100208

Berliner, D. C. (1984). The half-full glass: A review of research on teaching. In P. L. Hosford (Ed.). *Using what we know about teaching* (pp. 51–77). Alexandria, VA: Association for Supervision and Curriculum Development.

Bickel, W. W., & Bickel, D. D. (1986). Effective schools, classrooms, and instruction: Implications for special education. *Exceptional Children, 52*, 489–500.

Blanton, L. P., Blanton, W. E., & Cross, L., S. (1994). An exploratory study of how general and special education teachers think and make instructional decisions about students with special needs. *Teacher Education and Special Education, 17*, 62–74. doi:10.1177/088840649401700107

Bloom, B. S., & Krathwohl, D. R. (1956). *Taxonomy of educational objectives: The classification of educational goals, by a committee of college and university examiners. Handbook 1: Cognitive domain.* New York: Longman.

Borich, G. D., & Fenton, K. S. (Eds). (1977). *The appraisal of teaching: Concepts and process.* Reading, MA: Addison-Wesley.

Borko, H., Shavelson, R. J., & Stern, P. (1981). Teachers' decisions in the planning of reading instruction. *Reading Research Quarterly, 16*, 449–466. doi:10.2307/747411

Brophy, J. E. (2010). *Motivating students to learn.* New York: Taylor & Francis.

Brophy, J. E., & Good, T. L. (1986). Teacher behavior and student achievement. In M. C. Wittrock (Ed.), *Handbook of research on teaching* (3rd ed., pp. 328–377). New York: Macmillan.

Brownell, M. T., Bishop, A. G., Gersten, R., Klingner, J. K., Penfield, R. D., Dimino, J., Haager, D., Menon, S., & Sindelar, P. T. (2009). The role of domain expertise in beginning special education teacher quality. *Exceptional Children, 75*, 391–411.

Brownell, M. T., Ross, D. D., Colón, E. P., & McCallum, C. L. (2005). Critical features of special education teacher preparation: A comparison with general teacher education. *Journal of Special Education, 38*, 242–252. doi:10.1177/00224669050380040601

Buck, G., Morsink, C., Griffin, C., Hines, T., & Lenk, L. (1992). Preservice training: The role of field-based experiences in the preparation of effective special educators. *Teacher Education and Special Education, 15*, 108–123. doi:10.1177/088840649201500206

Bulgren, J. A., Lenz, B. K., Marquis, J., Schumaker, J. B., & Deshler, D. D. (2002). *The effects of the use of the question exploration routine on student performance in secondary content classrooms* (Research Report #10). U.S. Department of Education, Office of Special Education Programs.

Carlisle, J., Correnti, R., Phelps, G., & Zeng, J. (2009). Investigating teachers' knowledge of language structure and its relation to students' reading achievement. *Reading and Writing: An Interdisciplinary Journal, 22*, 457–486. doi:10.1007/s11145-009-9165-y

Carlsen, W. S. (1991). Questioning in classrooms: A sociolinguistic perspective. *Review of Educational Research, 61*, 157–178. doi:10.3102/00346543061002157

Carnine, D. W., & Fink, W. T. (1978). Increasing the rate of presentation and use of signals in elementary classroom teachers. *Journal of Applied Behavior Analysis, 11*, 35–46. doi:10.1901.jaba.1978.11-35

Cartledge, G., & Kourea, L. (2008). Culturally responsive classrooms for culturally diverse students with and at risk for disabilities. *Exceptional Children, 74*, 351–371.

Collins, N. D. (1996). Motivating low performing adolescent readers. *ERIC Digest.* Bloomington, IN: ERIC Clearinghouse on reading and communication skills. ED 396 265.

Cook, B. G., Tankersley, M., & Harjusola-Webb, S. (2008). Evidence-based special education and professional wisdom: Putting it all together. *Intervention in School and Clinic, 44*, 105–111. doi:10.1177/1053451208321566

Deno, S. L. (2006). Developments in curriculum-based measurement. In Bryan G. Cook & Barbara R. Schirmer (Eds.), *What's special about special education?: Examining the role of evidence-based practices* (pp. 100–112). Austin, TX: Pro-ed.

Deno, S. L., Espin, C., & Fuchs, L. (2002). Evaluation strategies for preventing and remediating basic skill deficits. In M. R. Shinn, H. M. Walker, & G. Stoner (Eds.), *Interventions for achievement and behavior problems II: Preventive and remedial approaches.* Bethesda, MD: National Association of School Psychologists.

Deno, S. L., Reschly, A. L., Lembke, E. S., Magnusson, D., Callender, S. A., Windram, H., & Stachel, N. (2009). Developing a school-wide progress monitoring system. *Psychology in the Schools, 46*, 44–55. doi:10.1002/pits.20353

Dickson, G. E., & Wiersma, W. (1982). *Measurement of teacher competence: Research and evaluation in teacher education.* Toledo, OH: Center for Research and Services, College of Education and Allied Professions, University of Toledo.

Dingle, M., Falvey, M. A., Givner, C. C., & Haager, D. (2004). Essential special and general education teacher competencies for preparing teachers for inclusive settings. *Issues in Teacher Education, 13*, 35–50.

Drevno, G. E., Kimball, J. W., Possi, M. K., Heward, W. L., Gardner, R., & Barbetta, P. M. (1994). Effects of active student response during error correction on the acquisition, maintenance, and generalization of science vocabulary by elementary students: A systematic replication. *Journal of Applied Behavior Analysis, 27*, 179–180. doi:10.1901/jaba.1994.27-179

Educational Testing Service (ETS). (2004) *Where we stand on teacher quality: An issue paper from ETS.* Teacher Quality Series. Princeton, NJ: ETS.

Ellis, E. S., & Worthington, L. A. (1994). *Research synthesis of effective teaching principles and the design of quality tools for educators* (Tech Rep. No. 5). Eugene, OR: National Center to Improve the Tools of Educators, University of Oregon.

Engelmann, S. (2007). Student–program alignment and teaching to mastery. *Journal of Direct Instruction,* 7(1), 45–66.

Englert, C. S. (1984). Effective direct instruction practices in special education settings. *Remedial and Special Education, 5*(2), 38–47. doi:10.1177/074193258400500208

Englert, C. S., Tarrant, K. L., & Mariage, T. V. (1992). Defining and redefining instructional practice in special education: Perspectives on good teaching. *Teacher Education and Special Education, 15*, 62–86. doi:10.1177/088840649201500203

Espin, C. A., & Yell, M. L. (1994). Critical indicators of effective teaching for preservice teachers: Relationship between teaching behaviors and ratings of effectiveness. *Teacher Education and Special Education, 17*, 154–169. doi:10.1177/088840649401700303

Feiman-Nemser, S. (2008). How do teachers learn to teach. In M. Cochran-Smith, S. Feiman-Nemser, D. J. McIntyre, & K. E. Demers (Eds.). *Handbook of Research on Teacher Education* (pp. 697–705). New York: Routledge.

Ferguson, E., & Houghton, S. (1992). The effects of contingent teacher praise, as specified by Canter's Assertive Discipline. *Educational Studies, 18*(1), 83–93. doi:10.1080/0305569920180108

Foorman, B. R., & Moats, L. C. (2004). Conditions for sustaining research-based practices in early reading instruction. *Remedial and Special Education, 25*, 51–60. doi:10.1177/07419325040250010601

Fuchs, D., Fuchs, L. S., & Compton, D. (2012). Smart RTI: A next generation approach to multilevel prevention. *Exceptional Children, 78*, 263–279.

Fuchs, D., Fuchs, L. S., & Stecker, P. M. (2010). The "blurring" of special education in a new continuum of general education placements and services. *Exceptional Children, 76*, 301–323.

Fuchs, L. S. (2003). *Using curriculum-based measurement for progress monitoring.* U.S. Department of Education: Strategies for Making Adequate Yearly Progress. Retrieved from http://www2.ed.gov/admins/lead/account/aypstr/edlite-slide001.html

Fuchs, L. S., Deno, S. L., & Mirkin, P. K. (1984). The effects of frequent curriculum-based measurement and evaluation on pedagogy, student achievement, and students awareness of learning. *American Educational Research Journal, 21*, 449–460. doi:10.3102/00028312021002449

Gable, R. A., Hester, P. H., Rock, M. L., & Hughes, K. G. (2009) Back to basics: Rules, praise, ignoring, and reprimands revisited. *Intervention in School and Clinic, 44*, 195–205. doi:10.1177/1053451208328831

Gall, M. (1984). Synthesis of research on teachers' questioning. *Educational Leadership, 42*(3), 40–47.

Geiger, W. L., Crutchfield, M. D., & Mainzer, R. (2003). *The status of licensure of special education teachers in the 21st century* (COPSSE Document Number RS-7E). Gainesville, FL: University of Florida, Center on Personnel Studies in Special Education.

Gilberts, G. H., & Lignugaris/Kraft, B. (1997). Classroom management and instruction competencies for preparing elementary and special education teachers in the United States. *Teaching and Teacher Education, 13*, 597–610. doi:10.1016/S0742-051X(97)80003-0

Goe, L., & Coggshall, J. (2007). *The teacher preparation→teacher practices→student outcomes relationship in special education: Missing links and new connections.* Washington, DC: National Comprehensive Center For Teacher Quality. Retrieved from http://eric.ed.gov/?id=ED520770

Goldhaber, D. D. (2002). The mystery of good teaching. *Education Next: A Journal of Opinion and Research, 2*(1), 50–55.

Good, T., Grouws, D., & Ebmeier, H. (1983). *Active mathematics teaching.* New York: Longman.

Goodman, K. (1990). Whole-language research: Foundations and developments. *Elementary School Journal, 90*, 207–221. doi:10.1086/461613

Gordon, R., Kane, R. J., & Staiger, D. O. (2006). *Identifying effective teachers using performance on the job* (Hamilton Project). Washington, DC: Brookings Institute.

Greenwood, C. R., Delquadri, J. D., & Hall, R. V. (1984). Opportunity to respond and student academic achievement. In W. L. Heward, T. E. Heron, D. S. Hill, & J. Trap-Porter (Eds.), *Focus on behavior analysis in education* (pp. 58–88). Columbus, OH: Merrill.

Hall, R. V., Lund, D., & Jackson, D. (1968). Effects of teacher attention on study behavior. *Journal of Applied Behavior Analysis, 1*, 1–12. doi:10.1901/jaba.1968.1-1

Hall, T. (2002). *Explicit instruction.* [Electronic version]. Wakefield, MA: National Center on Accessing the General Curriculum. Retrieved from http://aim.cast.org/learn/historyarchive/backgroundpapers/explicit_instruction#.UmqeMxDEeZ0

Hanushek, E. A., & Rivkin, S. G. (2010). *Using value-added measures of teacher quality.* Washington, DC: National Center for Analysis of Longitudinal Data in Education Research. Retrieved from http://www.urban.org/publications/1001371.html

Hanushek, E. A., Kain, J. F., O'Brien, D. M., & Rivkin, S. G. (2005). *The market for teacher quality.* NBER Working Paper No. 11154. Cambridge, MA: National Bureau of Economic Research. Retrieved from http://www.nber.org/papers/w11154

Harris, D., & Sass, N. (2010). Teacher training, teacher quality and student achievement. *Journal of Public Economics, 95*, 798–812. doi:10.1016/j.jpubeco.2010.11.009

Hattie, J. (2009). *Visible learning: A synthesis of over 800 meta-analyses relating to achievement.* New York: Routledge.

Hawkins, R. O., Kroeger, S. D., Musti-Rao, S., Barnett, D. W., & Ward, J. E. (2008). Preservice training in response to intervention: Learning by doing an interdisciplinary field experience. *Psychology in the Schools, 45*, 745-762. doi:10.1002/pits.20339

Haycock, K. (1988). Good teaching matters: How well qualified teachers can close the gap. *Thinking K–16, 3*(2), 1–14.

Heward, W. L. (1994). Three "low-tech" strategies for increasing the frequency of active student response during group instruction. In R. Gardner, III & D. Sainato (Eds.), *Behavior analysis in education: Focus on measurably superior instruction* (pp. 283–320). Pacific Grove, CA: Brooks/Cole.

Heward, W. L. (2003). Ten faulty notions about teaching and learning that hinder the effectiveness of special education. *The Journal of Special Education, 36*, 186–205. doi:10.1177/002246690303600401

Heward, W. L., Gardner, R., Cavanaugh, R. A. Courson, F. H., Grossi, T. A., Barbetta, P. M. (1996). Everyone participates in this class: Using response cards to increase active student engagement. *Teaching Exceptional Children, 28*(2), 4–10.

Hofmeister, A. M., & Lubke, M. (1990). *Research into practice: Implementing effective teaching strategies*. Needham Heights, MA: Allyn & Bacon.

Holdzkum, D., & Stacey, D. (1991). *The limits of generic skills evaluation: Using the NCTPAS to evaluate special teaching assignments*. Paper presented at the Annual Meeting of the American Education Research Association, Chicago, Ill. Retrieved from Eric Document Reproduction Service ED331 892.

Hudson, P. (1996). Using a learning set to increase learning disabled students' performance in social studies classes. *Learning Disabilities Research & Practice, 11*, 78–85.

Hudson, P. (1997a). *Research on the effective teaching approach and visual display enhancement to improve the content learning of adolescents with learning disabilities*. Final report. Logan, UT: Utah State University. Retrieved from Eric Document Reproduction Service ED305 919.

Hudson, P. (1997b). Using teacher-guided practice to help students with learning disabilities acquire and retain social studies content. *Learning Disability Quarterly, 20*, 23–32. doi:10.2307/1511090

Hudson, P., Lignugaris/Kraft, B., & Miller, T. (1993). Using content enhancements to improve the performance of adolescents with learning disabilities in content classes. *Learning Disabilities Research and Practice, 8*, 106–126.

Hunter, M. (1984). Knowing, teaching, and supervising. In P. L. Hosford (Ed.), *Using what we know about teaching* (pp. 169–193). Alexandria, VA: Association for Supervision & Curriculum Design.

Jones, E. D., Southern, W. T., & Brigham, F. J. (1998). Curriculum-based assessment: Testing what is taught and teaching what is tested. *Intervention In School and Clinic, 33*, 239–249. doi:10.1177/105345129803300407

Jones, M. M., Lignugaris/Kraft, B., & Peterson, S. M. (2007). The relation between task demands and student behavior problems during reading instruction: A case study. *Preventing School Failure, 51*, 19–28. doi:10.3200/PSFL.51.4.19-28

Jordan, H. R., Mendo, R., & Weerasinghe, D. (1997). *Teacher effects on longitudinal student achievement: A preliminary report on research on teacher effectiveness*. Paper presented at the National Evaluation Institute, Indianapolis, IN.

Kane, T. J., Taylor, E. S., Tyler, J. H., & Wooten, A. L. (2010). *Identifying effective practices using student achievement data*. NBER Working Paper No. 15803. Cambridge, MA: National Bureau of Economic Research. Retrieved from http://www.nber.org/papers/w15803.

Lambert, M. C., Cartledge, G., & Heward, W. L. (2006). Effects of response cards on disruptive behavior and academic responding during math lessons by fourth-grade urban students. *Journal of Positive Behavior Interventions, 8*, 88–99. doi:10.1177/10983007060080020701

Levin, J., & Nolan, J. (2004). *Principles of classroom management: A professional decision-making model* (4th ed.). Boston, MA: Pearson.

Lignugaris/Kraft, B., & Marchand-Martella, N. (1993) Evaluation of preservice teachers' interactive teaching skills in a Direct Instruction practicum using student teachers as supervisors. *Teacher Education and Special Education, 16*, 309–319. doi:10.1177/088840649301600404

Lignugaris/Kraft, B., & Rousseau, M. K. (1982). Instructional pacing: Definition and research needs. *Journal of Special Education Technology, 5*, 5–10.

Lilly, M. S. (1979). Competency-based training. *Teacher Education and Special Education, 2*, 20–26. doi:10.1177/088840647900200308

MacGregor, R. R. (2007). *The essential practices of high quality teaching and learning*. Bellevue, WA: The Center for Educational Effectiveness, Inc.

Maheady, L., Harper, G. F., Mallette, B., & Karnes, M. (2004). Preparing preservice teachers to implement class wide peer tutoring. *Teacher Education and Special Education, 27*, 408–418. doi:10.1177/088840640402700408

Maheady, L., Jabot, M., Rey, J., & Michielli-Pendl, J. (2007). An early field-based experience and its impact on pre-service candidates' teaching practice and their pupils' outcomes. *Teacher Education and Special Education, 30*, 24–33. doi:10.1177/088840640703000103

Maheady, L., Mallette, B., & Harper, G. F. (1996). The pair tutoring program: An early field-based experience to prepare preservice general educators to work with students with special needs. *Teacher Education and Special Education, 19*, 277–297. doi:10.1177/088840649601900402

McCutchen, D., Abbott, R. D., Green, L. B., Beretvas, S. N., Cox, S., Potter, N. S., Quiroga, T., & Gray, A. L. (2002). Beginning literacy: Links among teacher knowledge, teacher practice, and student learning. *Journal of Learning Disabilities, 35*, 69–86. doi:10.1177/002221940203500106

McCutchen, D., Green, L., Abbott, R. D., & Sanders, E. A. (2009). Further evidence for teacher knowledge: Supporting struggling readers in grades three through five. *Reading and Writing: An Interdisciplinary Journal, 22*, 401–423. doi:10.1007/s11145-009-9163-0

Medley, D. M. (1977). *Teacher competence and teacher effectiveness: A review of process-product research.* Washington, DC: American Association of Colleges for Teacher Education.

Medley, D. M., Coker, H., & Soar, R. S. (1984). *Measurement-based evaluation of teacher performance: An empirical approach.* New York: Longman.

Meece, J. L., Anderman, E. M., & Anderman, L. H. (2006). Classroom goal structure, student motivation, and academic achievement. *Annual Review of Psychology, 57*, 487–503. doi:10.1146/annurev.psych.56.091103.070258

Milanowski, A. T., Kimball, S. M., & White, B. (2004). *The relationship between standards-based teacher evaluation scores and student achievement: Replication and extensions at three sites.* Paper presented at American Education Research Association annual meeting, San Diego, California.

Miller, S. P., & Hudson, P. J. (2007). Using evidence-based practices to build mathematics competence related to conceptual, procedural, and declarative knowledge. *Learning Disabilities Research & Practice, 22*, 47–57. doi:10.1111/j.1540-5826.2007.00230.x

Morgan, R. L., Gustafson, K. J., Hudson, P. J., & Salzberg, C. L. (1992). Peer coaching in a preservice special education program. *Teacher Education and Special Education, 15*, 249–258. doi:10.1177/088840649201500403

Morsink, C. V., Soar, R. S., Soar, R. M., & Thomas, R. (1986). Research on teaching: Opening the door to special education classrooms. *Exceptional Children, 53*, 32–40.

Pany, D., & McCoy, K. M. (1988). Effects of corrective feedback on word accuracy and reading comprehension of readers with learning disabilities. *Journal of Learning Disabilities, 21*, 546–550. doi:10.1177/002221948802100905

Piasta, S. B., Connor, C. M., Fishman, B. J., & Morrison, F. J. (2009). Teachers' knowledge of literacy concepts, classroom practices, and student reading growth. *Scientific Studies of Reading, 13*, 224–248. doi:10.1080/10888430902851364

Podell, D. M., & Tournaki, N. (2007) General and special educators' predictions of student success as function of learner characteristics and teacher experience. *Teacher Education and Special Education, 30*, 249–263. doi:10.1177/088840640703000405

Pressley, M., Wood, E., Woloshyn, V. E., Martin, V., King, A., & Menke, D. (1992). Encouraging mindful use of prior knowledge: Attempting to construct explanatory answers facilitates learning. *Educational Psychologist, 27*, 91–109. doi:10.1207/s15326985ep2701_7

Prince, C. D., Koppich, J., Azar, T. M., Bhatt, M., Witham, P. J. (2010). *General compensation questions.* Washington, DC: Center for Educator Compensation Reform. Retrieved from http://cecr.ed.gov/guides/researchSyntheses/Research%20Synthesis_Q%20A2.pdf

Redfield, D. L., & Rousseau, E. W. (1981). A meta-analysis of experimental research on teacher questioning behavior. *Review of Educational Research, 51*, 237–245. doi:10.3102/00346543051002237

Reynolds, M. C. (1979). A look to the future in teacher education. *Teacher Education and Special Education, 2*, 9–11. doi:10.1177/088840647900200203

Rismiller, L. L. (2004). *Effects of praise training and increasing opportunities to respond on teachers' praise statements and reprimands during classroom instruction.* (Doctoral dissertation). Retrieved from OhioLink, Ohio State University, http://rave.ohiolink.edu/etdc/view?acc_num=osu1100293893

Rivkin, S. G., Hanushek, E. A., & Kain, J. F. (2005). Teachers, schools, and academic achievement. *Econometrica, 73*, 417–458. doi:10.111/j.1468-0262.2005.00584.x

Rockoff, J. E. (2004). The impact of individual teachers on student achievement: Evidence from panel data. *American Economic Review, 94*, 247–252. doi:10.1257/0002828041302244

Rosenberg, M. S., Jackson, L., & Yeh, C. (1996). Designing effective field experiences for nontraditional preservice special educators. *Teacher Education and Special Education, 19*, 331–341. doi:10.1177/088840649601900405

Rosenshine, B. (1983). Teaching functions in instructional programs. *The Elementary School Journal, 83*, 335–351. doi:10.1086/461321

Rosenshine, B., & Stevens, R. (1986). Teaching function. In M. C. Wittrock (Eds.) *Handbook of research on teaching* (3rd ed., pp. 376–391). New York: Macmillan.

Ross, D. D., & Blanton, L. (2004). Inquiry communities in special education teacher education. *Teacher Education and Special Education, 27*, 15–23. doi:10.1177/088840640402700103

Ruhl, K. L., & Hall, T. E. (2002). Continuum of special education and general education field experiences in the preservice special education program at Penn State. *Teacher Education and Special Education, 25*, 87–94. doi:10.1177/088840640202500109

Sainato, D. M., Strain, P. S., & Lyon, S. R. (1987). Increasing academic responding of handicapped preschool children during group instruction. *Journal of the Division for Early Childhood, 12*, 23–30.

Sanders, W. L., & Horn, S. P. (1994). The Tennessee Value-Added Assessment System (TVAAS): Mixed-model methodology in educational assessment. *Journal of Personnel Evaluation in Education, 8*, 299–311. doi:10.1007/BF00973726

Sanders, W. L., & Rivers, J. C. (1996). *Cumulative and residual effects of teachers on future student achievement*. Knoxville, TN: University of Tennessee Value-Added Research and Assessment Center.

Schuster, J. W., & Stevens, K. B. (1991). Supervising practicum students: Establishing competencies. *Teacher Education and Special Education, 14*, 169–176. doi:10.1177/088840649101400303

Scruggs, T. E., & Mastropieri, M. A. (1993). The effects of prior field experience of student eacher competence. *Teacher Education and Special Education, 16*, 303–308. doi:10.1177/088840649301600403

Shores, R. E., Cegelka, T. T., & Nelson, C. M. (1973). Competency-based special education teacher training. *Exceptional Children, 40*, 192–197.

Sikorski, M. F., Niemiec, R. P., & Walberg, H. J. (1996). A classroom checkup: Best teaching practices in special education. *Teaching Exceptional Children, 29*(1), 27–29.

Sindelar, P. T., Espin, C. A., Smith, M. A., Harriman, N. E. (1990). A comparison of more and less effective special education teachers in elementary level programs. *Teacher Education and Special Education, 13*, 9–16. doi:10.1177/088840649001300102

Sindelar, P. T., Smith, M. A., Harriman, N. E., Hale, R. L., & Wilson, R. J. (1986). Teacher effectiveness in special education programs. *The Journal of Special Education, 20*, 195–207. doi:10.1177/002246698602000206

Skinner, C. H., Fletcher, P. A., & Henington, C. (1996). Increasing learning rates by increasing student response rates: A summary of research. *School Psychology Quarterly, 11*, 313–325. doi:10.1037/h0088937

Skinner, C. H., & Shapiro, E. S. (1989). A comparison of taped words and drill interventions on reading fluency in adolescents with behavior disorders. *Education and Treatment of Children, 12*, 123–133.

Skinner, C. H., Smith, E. S., & McLean, J. E. (1994). The effects of intertribal interval duration on sight-word learning rates in children with behavioral disorders. *Behavioral Disorders, 19*, 98–107.

Skinner, N. (2010). Developing a curriculum for initial teacher education using a situated learning perspective. *Teacher Development, 14*, 279–293. doi:10.1080/13664530.2010.504007

Stecker, P. M., & Fuchs, L. S. (2000). Effecting superior achievement using curriculum-based measurement: The importance of individual progress monitoring. *Learning Disabilities Research & Practice, 15*, 128–134. doi:10.1207/SLDRP1503_2

Sterling, R. M., Barbetta, P. M., Heward, W. L., & Heron, T. E. (1997). A comparison of active student response and on-task instruction on the acquisition and maintenance of health facts by fourth grade special education students. *Journal of Behavioral Education*, 7, 151–165. doi:10.1023/A:1022836907599

Stough, L. M., & Palmer, D. J. (2001). *Teacher reflection: How effective special educators differ from novices*. Paper presented at the Annual Meeting of the Council for Exceptional Children, Kansas City, MO. Retrieved from Eric Document Reproduction Service ED463279

Stronge, J. H. (2010). *Evaluating what good teachers do: Eight research-based standards for assessing teacher excellence*. Larchmont, NY: Eye On Education.

Stronge, J. H., Ward, T. J., & Grant, L. W. (2011). What makes good teachers good? A cross-case analysis of the connection between teacher effectiveness and student achievement. *Journal of Teacher Education, 62*, 339–356. doi:10.1177/0022487111404241

Stronge, J. H., Ward, T. J., Tucker, P. D., & Hindman, J. L. (2007) What is the relationship between teacher quality and student achievement? An exploratory study. *Journal of Personnel Evaluation in Education, 20*, 165–184. doi:10.1007/s11092-008-9053-z

Sutherland, K. S., & Wehby, J. H. (2001). Exploring the relationship between increased opportunities to respond to academic requests and the academic and behavioral outcomes of students with EBD: A review. *Remedial and Special Education, 22*, 113–121. doi:10.1177/074193250102200205

Sutherland, K. S., Adler, N., & Gunter. P. L. (2003). The effects of varying rates of opportunities to respond to academic requests on the classroom behavior of students with EBD. *Journal of Emotional and Behavioral Disorders, 11*, 239–248. doi:10.1177/10634266030110040501

Sutherland, K. S., Wehby, J. H., & Copeland, S. R. (2000). Effects of varying rates of behavior-specific praise on the on-task behavior of students with EBD. *Journal of Emotional and Behavioral Disorders, 8*, 2–8. doi:10.1177/106342660000800101

Sutherland, K. S., Wehby, J. H., & Yoder, P. (2002). Examination of the relationship between teacher praise and opportunities for students with EBD to respond to academic requests (emotional and behavioral disorders). *Journal of Emotional and Behavioral Disorders, 10*, 5–13. doi:10.1177/106342660201000102

Torgesen, J. K. (1996). Thoughts about intervention research in learning disabilities. *Learning Disabilities*, 7(2), 55–58.

Trautwein, B., & Ammerman, S. (2010). From pedagogy to practice: mentoring and reciprocal peer coaching for preservice teachers. *The Volta Review, 110*, 191–206.

Turner, M., Ludlow, B., & Wienke, W. (1987). *Training field-based personnel to supervise on-the-job practicum experiences in rural areas.* Proceeding of the Annual National Conference of the American Council on Rural Special Education. Eric Document Reproduction Service ED 295 354.

Waymen, J. C. (2005). Involving teachers in data-driven decision making: Using computer data systems to support teacher inquiry and reflection. *Journal of Education for Students Placed at Risk, 10*, 295–308. doi:10.1207/s15327671espr1003_5

Wilen, W., & Clegg Jr., A. (1986). Effective questions and questioning: A research review. *Theory and Research in Social Education, 14*, 153–161. doi:10.1080/00933104.1986.10505518

Wood, C. L., & Heward, W. L. (2005). *Good noise! Using choral responding to increase the effectiveness of group instruction.* Unpublished manuscript, School of Physical Activity and Educational Services, The Ohio State University, Columbus.

Wright, S. P., Horn, S. P., & Sanders, W. L. (1997). Teachers and classrooms context effects on student achievement: Implications for teacher evaluation. *Journal of Personnel Evaluation in Education, 11*, 57–67. doi:10.1023/A:1007999204543

Ysseldyke, J. E., & Christenson, S. L. (1988). Linking assessment to intervention. In J. L. Graden, J. E. Zins, & M. J. Curtis (Eds.), *Alternative educational delivery systems: Enhancing instructional opportunities for all students* (pp. 91–110). Washington, DC: National Association of School Psychologists.

Zigmond, N. (2006). Reading and writing in co-taught secondary school social studies classrooms: A reality check. *Reading and Writing Quarterly, 22*, 249–268. doi:10.1080/10573560500455711

15

Preparing Special Educators to Teach Literacy

Mary T. Brownell

UNIVERSITY OF FLORIDA

Melinda M. Leko

UNIVERSITY OF WISCONSIN—MADISON

Things to Think About

- Helping students with reading disabilities (RD) become literate individuals is a complex endeavor. To assist these students, educators need to understand how literacy develops in students with and without RD while concomitantly learning how to implement effective instructional practices and assess results.
- RD, which may result from inabilities in cognitive processing, is one of the most common diagnoses for students with disabilities. No matter what issues students with RD present, explicit and systematic instruction in key areas of reading and writing is critical to helping them access the general curriculum and succeed.
- Special educators' ability to implement research-based literacy interventions for students with RD is often complicated by students' diverse cultural, linguistic, developmental, and affective needs; complex service delivery models and the multiple roles they play within schools; and the need to collaborate with general education teachers to help students achieve standards.
- Teacher educators should consider crafting special education teacher preparation in literacy so that preservice teachers develop well-integrated knowledge bases that characterize the practice of experts. This may involve the use of strategies that increase special education teachers' content knowledge, providing practice-based approaches for integrating content and pedagogy (such as coursework combined with well-structured field experiences, coaching, and opportunities to receive support during implementation), and allowing preservice teachers to develop the ability to apply their knowledge strategically to solve problems in practice.
- Studies of initial preparation and professional development provide evidence that preservice teachers can acquire conceptual and procedural content knowledge, and, with sufficient training, can situate that knowledge in the classroom. Research is needed, however, to identify the most effective and efficient models for teaching teachers the relevant knowledge for teaching literacy and how to structure practica and student teaching that fosters application of that knowledge

base in a diverse array of contexts. The knowledge we need to inform effective special education teaching and ensure its effective implementation in schools will require research in three major areas: (a) increased knowledge about how to improve the literacy skills of students with disabilities; (b) additional understanding about how knowledge and practice for literacy teaching develop and how to assess that knowledge and practice; and (c) research on effective teacher education practice that is founded in theoretically sound models of adult learning.

Helping students with reading disabilities (RD) become literate individuals is a complex endeavor. To become literate, students with RD must develop connected skills of reading, listening, writing and speaking and use these skills successfully in technology-rich environments. Yet, the majority of students with RD demonstrate significant limitations in these areas that inhibit the development of literacy. To assist these students, educators need to understand how literacy develops in students with and without RD while concomitantly learning how to implement effective instructional practices and assess results. Special educators face the additional challenge of teaching students in varied settings that call for frequent interaction with teams of school personnel, including general educators and therapists. Furthermore, more than ever before, general and special educators are required to demonstrate that students with RD reach high levels of proficiency in reading and writing that include higher-order thinking skills. The Common Core State Standards, recently adopted by 46 states, requires students to have sophisticated literacy skills that allow them to "actively seek wide, deep, and thoughtful engagement with high quality literary and informational texts that that builds knowledge, enlarges experience, and broadens worldviews" (Common Core State Standards Initiative, 2010).

Helping students with RD achieve such high standards is especially difficult given limitations of our current knowledge base. At present this research base, though substantive in some areas (e.g., early literacy instruction), is lacking in others. Teachers, and in particular special educators providing intervention instruction, will be placed in situations where they must use their knowledge of effective practices in adaptive ways to adjust to specific teaching circumstances. Teacher educators then face great challenges in constructing curriculum and instruction to prepare special educators for those possibilities.

In this chapter, the research and practices associated with preparing special educators to teach literacy to students with disabilities are reviewed. In the first section, we describe what we currently know about literacy development for students with disabilities and knowledge of effective intervention. Next we highlight challenges associated with literacy teacher preparation. Finally, given the available research base, we examine possible approaches teacher educators could consider for crafting special education teacher preparation in literacy. The chapter concludes with directions for further research on preparing teachers to provide literacy instruction for students with disabilities.

Research on Teaching Literacy to Students With Disabilities

In the past two decades, researchers paid unprecedented attention to raising literacy achievement for U.S. students (e.g., Bryant, Goodwin, Bryant, & Higgins, 2003; Gersten, Fuchs, Williams, & Baker, 2001; Swanson, 2008; Taft & Mason, 2011). To better understand the literacy needs of students with disabilities and how to provide instruction that is responsive to those needs, researchers completed several research syntheses of effective literacy instruction for students with disabilities. Scholars examined individual components of the reading process (Berkeley, Scruggs, & Mastropieri, 2010; Berninger et al., 2003; Gajria, Jitendra, Sood, & Sacks, 2007; Klingner, Urbach, Golos, Brownell, & Menon, 2010; Sencibaugh, 2007) and writing processes (Graham & Harris, 2003; Graham & Harris, 2009; Santangelo, Harris, & Graham, 2008; Taft & Mason, 2011). They investigated combinations of components and ways disability affects cognitive processes (Berninger, Nielson, Abbott, Wijsman, & Raskind; 2008;

Spear-Swerling, 2006). Some scholars also looked at how literacy components interact with working memory (Carretti, Borella, Cornoldi, & De Beni, 2009; Swanson, Howard, & Sáez, 2006).

One major finding is that RD is one of the most common diagnoses for students with disabilities (Sze, 2010). RDs are grounded in students' inability to read words, either in isolation or in context, and/or to comprehend text (Swanson & Vaughn, 2010). RDs may be the direct result of cognitive processing abilities defined as working memory, executive functioning, phonological awareness and/or language processing and speed issues (Johnson, Humphrey, Mellard, Woods, & Swanson, 2010). These cognitive difficulties may interfere with students' abilities to accurately and fluently identify words (phonemic awareness, phonics, and fluency) or make meaning (vocabulary and comprehension). No matter what issues students with RD present, research findings converge to show the critical importance of reading literacy and writing literacy for students to gain access to the general education curriculum (Baker, Gersten, & Scanlon, 2002).

Intervention research provides guidelines for how teachers might go about preventing and remediating reading and writing disabilities. Several major syntheses and meta-analyses, including the well-known synthesis used to form the basis of the National Reading Panel Report (National Institute of Child Health and Human Development, 2000), establish that explicit and systematic instruction in the five major components of reading (e.g., phonemic awareness, phonics, vocabulary, fluency, and comprehension) benefit students who struggle with learning to read (Gersten et al., 2001). The most substantive of these findings are in the areas of phonemic awareness and decoding. When students with RD receive explicit instruction in blending, segmenting, and manipulating sounds in words, and when they receive instruction that helps them learn and apply the alphabetic principle to novel words, they improve their decoding skills.

Explicit systematic instruction is also important to developing reading fluency, reading comprehension, and vocabulary knowledge. Chard, Vaughn, and Tyler (2002) found that the most effective interventions for teaching fluency include explicit modeling of reading along with multiple chances to read text with feedback though such interventions seem to be less effective for older learners (Reed & Vaughn, 2010). Berkeley and colleagues (2010) confirm that comprehension interventions for students with learning disabilities have a greater positive effect on student skill development than comprehension instruction that is practiced typically in schools (i.e., reading text and responding to teacher questions), but ideas need to be taught explicitly and reviewed using a variety of texts. Finally, Bryant et al. (2003) suggest that students' vocabulary knowledge increases when provided with explicit instruction and extended opportunities for practice; however, Bryant et al. also acknowledge the limited research in this area.

Similar to reading instruction, effective writing instruction is based on teachers explicitly and systematically teaching writing strategies to students with disabilities (Taft & Mason, 2011). Graham and colleagues (Graham & Harris, 2003; Graham, & Harris, 2009; Graham & Perin, 2007; Santangelo et al., 2008) validate the benefits of teaching self-regulated strategy development (SRSD) for elementary, middle, and high school students with disabilities. Their findings show student improvement in writing when teachers explicitly model, teach, and repeatedly practice a six-part cycle that includes: (a) developing and activating background knowledge; (b) discussion of strategies; (c) modeling the strategies; (d) memorization of strategy steps; (e) scaffolding and support of students' strategy use; and (f) independent performance. Further, in a meta-analysis, Graham and Perin (2007), noted strong effects when researchers provide explicit instruction in (a) writing strategies; (b) teaching students to summarize text; (c) teaching students to collaboratively plan, draft, revise, and edit text; and (d) setting specific, reachable writing goals.

Based on the available reading and writing research we can draw several conclusions about what constitutes effective literacy instruction for students with disabilities. First and foremost, effective literacy instruction is explicit and systematic with multiple opportunities for students to practice and receive feedback. Second, in the area of reading, instruction is critical in phonemic awareness, phonics, fluency, vocabulary and comprehension. Finally, writing instruction should include specific writing strategies, goal setting, and attending explicitly to all aspects of the writing process. With this knowledge about effective literacy instruction for students with disabilities, one might assume that preparing special educators to deliver such instruction is a straightforward process. As we discuss in the following section, however, diverse student populations and instructional contexts add multiple layers of complexity to special education teacher preparation in literacy.

Challenges Associated With Preparing Teachers in Literacy

Effective special educators must know how to use key findings from research on literacy instruction to guide their instruction; however, simply knowing about research-based interventions and how to implement them is insufficient. First, not all students with disabilities respond equally well to evidence-based literacy interventions. Students with disabilities have diverse literacy needs, and these needs can be complicated by their cultural and linguistic backgrounds. Second, special education service delivery is complex, and special education teachers are required to play many roles within schools. Finally, special education teachers must figure out how to work with general education teachers to support students with disabilities in meeting challenging content area standards, and strategies for achieving such a goal are not entirely clear, particularly at the secondary level.

Student Diversity

The wide range of diversity among students with disabilities influences effective literacy practice. For instance, several studies show that poor readers are not all alike and that reading difficulties differ in their origins (Catts, Hogan, & Fey, 2003; Swanson et al., 2006). For example, some students have difficulty comprehending text because they have poor decoding skills. When these students decode words incorrectly, text meaning may be altered or lost (Ehri & Snowling, 2004). Poor decoding skills also compromises reading fluency causing students with RD to spend large amounts of time decoding text, which ultimately interferes with comprehension (O'Connor & Bell, 2004). Other students may struggle with comprehension because they (a) have limited sight word vocabularies (Ehri & Snowling, 2004); (b) lack sufficient background knowledge in relation to a text (Duke, Pressley, & Hilden, 2004; Mercer & Pullen, 2005); or (c) have limited oral vocabularies (Burns, Griffin, & Snow, 1999; Hart & Risley, 1995). Still other students have difficulties comprehending text because they have poor short term or working memories (Duke et al., 2004). Finally, some students are inactive readers and do not engage in metacognitive strategies that help self-monitor understanding (Gersten et al., 2001; Vaughn & Klingner, 2004).

In essence, students struggle to read for varying reasons. Thus, students who exhibit the most significant learning challenges will need literacy teachers who are considered "instructional experts" (Fuchs, Fuchs, & Compton, 2012). Using their extensive working knowledge of effective instructional approaches, these teachers will need to collect assessment data on individual students to determine the extent to which an approach is working for a particular student. Teachers will need to be able to interpret the assessment data and make instructional adjustments as needed (Fuchs et al., 2012). The process to find an instructional approach that will meet the needs of an individual student may take time, and teachers will need to demonstrate a certain level of persistence in finding an effective intervention. This illustrates the complex, comprehensive, and specialized working knowledge that special educators must possess to be able to select appropriate interventions and then monitor the student's response to the intervention (Fuchs et al., 2012).

Cultural and Linguistically Diverse (CLD) Students

Increasingly special educators work with students whose first language is not English. Research syntheses that summarize what good literacy instruction should look like for English Language Learners (ELLs;

August & Shanahan, 2006; Goldenberg, 2006, 2008; Teale, 2009) and specifically for ELLs with RD (Gersten & Baker, 2003; Gersten & Geva, 2003; Klingner & Soltero-González, 2009) indicate that, in many ways, effective literacy instruction for ELLs with RD is similar to effective literacy instruction for students with RD whose first language is English (Teale, 2009). Although effective literacy instruction is similar for these two student populations, there are some important adjustments that need to be made to adequately meet the needs of ELLs with disabilities. Experts recommend that special educators understand the second language acquisition process, how this process impacts literacy instruction, and how to incorporate students' native languages and cultures into literacy instruction (August & Shanahan, 2006; Klingner & Soltero-González, 2009).

Researchers suggest that strategically incorporating students' native languages into literacy instruction is beneficial (August & Shanahan, 2006; Klingner & Soltero-González, 2009). For example, it is best to use a student's native language to access prior knowledge about a topic or when explaining how to use a reading strategy (Klingner & Soltero-González, 2009). It is also important to capitalize on students' first-language literacy as many of these skills (i.e., decoding, fluency, and comprehension) will transfer and facilitate their acquisition of a second language (August & Shanahan, 2006; Francis, Rivera, Lesaux, Kieffer, & Rivera, 2006; Klingner & Soltero-González, 2009). Perhaps most important is the finding that developing oral proficiency in English is a critical but often overlooked component of effective literacy instruction for ELLs with RD. Underdeveloped oral proficiency in English is a large contributor to achievement differences between ELLs and their native English-speaking peers (August & Shanahan, 2006). ELLs with RD, therefore, will need extensive opportunities to develop their expressive language skills, vocabulary knowledge, listening comprehension skills, and metalinguistic skills throughout the entire sequence of literacy instruction (August & Shanahan, 2006; Francis et al., 2006). Finally, effective literacy instruction for ELLs with RD should incorporate high quality multicultural literature so that students can "see" their culture accurately represented in the texts they read (Klingner & Soltero-González, 2009). To support ELLs with RD special educators will have to have a strong command of all of these issues and be able to work collaboratively with general educators as well as ELL teachers.

Student Ages

Having a solid understanding of effective literacy instruction and ways to provide the individualized instruction that students with disabilities require is not limited to the elementary grades. A large proportion of secondary students with disabilities are reading below proficient levels, even reading on levels similar to elementary-aged students. Special educators, who often are trained to work with a broad range of student levels, must have awareness and understanding of the unique literacy needs of older students with disabilities. Older students are often embarrassed by the fact that they are reading on such low levels. Literacy instruction designed for elementary-aged students with disabilities will not meet the needs of older students with disabilities who do not want to be associated with instruction that appears "babyish" (Leko, Mundy, Kang, & Datar, 2013). Incorporating reading materials that are appropriate for older struggling readers is imperative. Such materials include high interest controlled readability texts and digital texts that provide embedded scaffolding and support (Leko et al., 2013).

When working with older students with disabilities, special educators should also be aware of students' affective needs. Because of repeated failure in the area of reading, adolescents with disabilities often lack motivation and avoid literacy instruction and reading-based activities (Biancarosa & Snow, 2006; Bulgren, Sampson Graner, & Deshler, 2013). Special educators will need to understand how to integrate effective, age-appropriate behavior management techniques with age-appropriate literacy instruction for older students with disabilities.

Special Educator Roles

The broad range of contexts in which special educators work influences the fluid nature of literacy knowledge and practice necessary to teach students with disabilities. Special educators often work across multiple instructional models and service delivery options. Each of these settings has unique challenges and requires special educators to draw on an array of skills. For example, special educators who provide reading interventions in resource rooms must be adept at maximizing instructional time, as they often work with students for only small amounts of time throughout the week. Special educators who support students with RD included in general education classrooms must work collaboratively with general educators in a variety of co-teaching models. In inclusive general education classrooms, special educators must balance multiple competing instructional goals including: (a) intensive literacy remediation; (b) access to the general education curriculum; and (c) preparation for high stakes assessments.

The implementation of Response to Intervention (RTI) models further complicates special educators' roles in schools. There is wide variation in how RTI models are implemented and even among experts there is no consensus on the degree to which special education is or should be a part of RTI models (Fuchs et al., 2012; Fuchs, Fuchs, & Stecker, 2010). The result is that special educators may be expected to assume a large number of roles in schools ranging from working with general educators to differentiate the core curriculum to providing highly intensive literacy interventions to students who exhibit the greatest learning challenges.

Challenging Content Area Standards

States' recent adoption of the Common Core State Standards (CCSS) has raised academic expectations for all students, including those with disabilities. Students are expected to engage in higher levels of reading, thinking, and reasoning within specific academic disciplines (Bulgren et al., 2013). To succeed, students must have advanced vocabulary, and must apply comprehension skills across a variety of text sources and formats. Thus, special educators must understand the complex literacy demands of challenging content area texts that are commonly used in history, mathematics, and science classes. Moreover, special educators must possess a deep working knowledge of evidence-based practices known to help students with disabilities access and comprehend content area texts (e.g., graphic organizers, outlining, note-taking) and be able to situate such strategies in a diverse array of content. The CCSS, however, provide little insight into how to further accommodate students with disabilities (Haager & Vaughn, 2013). Thus, special education teacher educators are left with many unanswered questions about the breadth and depth of knowledge that special educators need to help students with disabilities meet the literacy-related challenges posed by the CCSS.

Crafting Effective Teacher Education for Improving Literacy Instruction

Effective special education teachers must know how to use their knowledge to serve a diverse set of students in educational contexts that are increasingly demanding academically. Thus, effective special education teachers need to know how to apply their knowledge about interventions in flexible ways to solve the individual learning problems presented when teaching a diverse array of students. The research on expertise, however, informs us that such flexible strategic knowledge usually only evolves when professionals have acquired sufficient knowledge of their content and can implement that knowledge with a high degree of fluency. Although there is a strong and growing body of research related to literacy instruction for students with disabilities, what is less well researched is how to teach special educators to draw on and use literacy knowledge flexibly to adapt to a diverse range of students in demanding educational contexts. Instead, we must turn to the broader literature on how expertise develops and consider how our knowledge base in teacher education and professional development might inform development of this skill set.

Developing Special Education Teachers' Literacy Knowledge

Snow, Griffin, and Burns (2005) proposed a differentiated continuum for learning to teach reading that might be useful for understanding how special education teachers move from novice to expert status. Snow and colleagues hypothesized that preservice teachers were likely to have a good deal of *declarative knowledge* that comes from learning about reading theories and the content of literacy instruction. As teachers develop, they acquire and gain use of *situated procedural knowledge* or knowledge of how to implement strategies that is contextualized to the specifics of their classroom situations and *stable procedural knowledge* that enables teachers to implement strategies with fluency under usual circumstances. As teachers continually draw on their knowledge and receive feedback from students, other teachers, or administrators about how they are implementing their knowledge they begin to show a flexible, highly adaptive *reflective, organized, analyzed knowledge* that they can share with others through professional development and research activities.

This continuum, though woefully underresearched in education, has support in the literature on how professional expertise develops. As professionals acquire expertise, their knowledge becomes more detailed and differentiated and is characterized by principled abstractions; that is, they have elaborate knowledge schemas comprised of "detailed relationships among problem-relevant details" (Feldon, 2007, p. 93). Additionally, their knowledge is highly contextualized (Farrington-Darby & Wilson, 2006) and dependent on experiences they have acquired over time (Fadde, 2007). Their conceptual knowledge in a particular domain is well integrated with their experiences. For instance, medical doctors' knowledge of symptoms associated with disease is combined with their experiences treating patients manifesting different combinations of those symptoms. Well-integrated knowledge bases enable experts to rapidly recall information and recognize patterns or fundamental principles (Berliner, 2001; Ropo, 2004). Thus, experts can recognize problematic situations, such as a breakdown in student comprehension, more quickly and efficiently, and thereby devote more effort to finding solutions (Fadde, 2007).

Novices, in contrast, do not have the same well-integrated knowledge bases. They often fail to recognize the important features of a problem (Farrington-Darby & Wilson, 2006). Novices focus on more superficial features of instruction and generally require prompting to employ effectively their declarative or procedural knowledge. Further, researchers have established that novices and even many experienced teachers do not have some of the fundamental declarative and procedural knowledge needed to develop expertise in literacy. For instance, Spear-Swerling, Brucker and Alfano (2005) found that most teachers of elementary students were missing core knowledge about word study and language—knowledge that is essential to teaching students decoding skill (Brownell et al., 2007; McCutchen, Green, Abbott, & Sanders, 2009). Many teacher education programs that prepare these teachers have also come under fire for underemphasizing knowledge for teaching reading in their coursework (Moats, 2009). Thus, what can teacher educators do to ensure that beginning special education teachers have the knowledge needed to teach reading and the foundation analytical and problem-solving skills needed to solve the diverse array of learning problems they will encounter in practice? To answer this question, we turn to the research base and scholarly writings we have on initial teacher preparation and staff development.

Strategies for Improving Beginning Special Education Teachers' Knowledge and Practice

Although the research base on beginning teacher learning and professional development is incomplete and sometimes tenuous at best, there are some approaches to increasing knowledge and improving classroom practice among preservice and in-service teachers that could be considered. In this section, we describe those approaches and the research supporting them.

Approaches for Increasing Content Knowledge

Leko, Brownell, Sindelar, and Murphy (2012), in a review of the literature, indicated that few studies emphasize approaches for improving content knowledge for teaching special education. Instead, most studies focus on procedural knowledge for teaching students with disabilities (i.e., how to teach particular strategies that could be embedded in literacy instruction). For instance, Van Laarhoven, Munk, Lynch, Bosma, and Rouse (2007) used video tutorials to help preservice teachers understand how assistive technology could be used to support students with learning and physical disabilities in reading, writing, math, and communication. These tutorials were embedded into appropriate courses where preservice teachers watched the video and then completed a survey. Preservice teachers indicated that the tutorials helped them feel familiar and comfortable using the technology. Similarly, Dieker and colleagues (2009) used video modeling to help preservice teachers learn strategies for teaching reading, mathematics, and science. Specifically, the videos highlighted teachers demonstrating how to teach a strategy (e.g., Text Talk as a way of improving vocabulary instruction). For the Text Talk strategy, students were randomly assigned to the video-modeling condition and a lecture-based condition. Surveys provided before and after viewing the video model showed that preservice teachers in the video-modeling condition remembered more strategy steps than teachers in the lecture condition. Although video-modeling studies provide a glimpse of how technology might be used to help teachers acquire procedural knowledge, they provide little insight into how preservice educators might develop special education preservice teachers' content knowledge for teaching literacy.

Only one study focused on helping preservice teachers acquire content knowledge in literacy. Kennedy, Drive, Pullen, Ely, and Cole (2013) used a randomized control group design to determine the efficacy of Content Acquisition Podcasts (CAP) on education and noneducation majors' acquisition of knowledge about phonological awareness (PA) and interventions to support its development. One hundred and forty-eight university students were randomly assigned to watch a CAP or read a practitioner-friendly article about PA and PA interventions. Students were assessed prior to the intervention, immediately following intervention and then 3 weeks after intervention to determine changes in their knowledge of phonological awareness, phonemic awareness, and effective PA interventions. A 2×3 split-plot, fixed-factor repeated measures ANOVA showed CAP students profited substantially from the intervention; there was a significant effect for group favoring those in the CAP intervention. Moreover, 42% of the variance was explained by the treatment. Further, there was a significant interaction effect for group and time. Follow-up tests showed significant effects at posttest ($d = 0.86$) favoring the CAP condition that were greater at maintenance ($d = 0.97$); hence, the significant interaction. Although these effects on literacy knowledge have only been established in one study, other studies of the CAP technology have consistently demonstrated that they are useful tools for increasing preservice teachers' content knowledge (Kennedy, Hart, & Kellems, 2011; Kennedy et al., 2012). Thus, they should be considered strategies for helping teachers acquire content knowledge in literacy.

Practice-Based Approaches to Integrating Content and Pedagogy

In the professional development and preservice education literature, there are multiple studies showing the effectiveness of learning opportunities that enrich teachers' content knowledge for teaching reading and helping them to apply that knowledge using evidence-based strategies. At the preservice level, in three separate studies researchers examined how coursework combined with structured tutoring experiences enabled special education teachers to acquire more knowledge for teaching decoding and subsequently improve their student's achievement. In two separate studies, Spear-Swerling (2009) and Spear-Swerling and Brucker (2004) examined the impact of a language arts methods course combined with a tutoring experience on the knowledge gains of preservice special education teachers and the tutee's achievement gains. The language arts course focused on how reading develops, English word structure, struggles that students encounter in acquiring decoding and spelling skills, and reading assessments. Preservice teachers were then supported during a tutoring situation. Lesson plan formats that allocated time to specific instructional activities were provided to guide their planning. The course instructor attended all tutoring sessions, modeled strategies when necessary, and provided corrective feedback. In both cases, preservice teachers made pre to post gains in knowledge of phonemic awareness and English word structure. Additionally, their students demonstrated improved letter sound knowledge, reading and spelling of irregular words, and phonics concepts.

Al Otaiba, Schatsneider, and Silverman (2005) studied preservice teachers involved in a tutoring experience who had taken a language arts course that included content about phonics and the English word structure. Preservice teachers also participated in two practicum experiences prior to the tutoring experience. At the end of the tutoring experience, preservice teachers increased their knowledge of the English word structure from an average of 57.5% of the items correct prior to the tutoring experience to an average of 99.38% correct after the experience. Additionally, their students made impressive standard score mean gains in word identification, word attack, passage comprehension, vocabulary knowledge and phonemic awareness as measured by the Woodcock Reading Mastery Test—Revised, the Peabody Picture Vocabulary Test—Revised, and the Comprehensive Test of Phonological Awareness. Preservice teachers also demonstrated more skill in examining individual children's needs. All of these studies used AB designs and lacked the experimental control afforded studies that involve comparison groups. The consistent nature of their findings suggests, however, that coursework combined with well-structured tutoring or field experiences may be useful in helping preservice teachers integrate their content and pedagogical knowledge.

Studies of in-service teachers and early care providers have yielded similar findings. For example, Neuman and Cunningham (2009) studied how a 3-credit course in language and literacy combined with coaching impacted day-care providers' and family-care providers' knowledge of early literacy development and their early language and literacy practices in center- and home-based care and education settings. Using a stratified random sample Neuman and Cunningham assigned two types of providers to the course plus coaching condition, a course-only condition, and no treatment. A 45-item multiple choice test was developed to assess teacher knowledge and two previously validated classroom observations systems were used to assess the instructional and support strategies providers used to facilitate early language and literacy skill development and the literacy environment providers established. Providers participating in the course made modest, but significant gains in their knowledge compared to providers in the control group. When it came to early literacy practices, however, providers participating in the course plus coaching treatment demonstrated significant gains in their practices and the magnitude of that gain was large, with an effect size of 0.77 for day-care providers and 0.82 for home-care providers. There was no significant difference between providers in the course-only treatment and control group and the effect size was small 0.23. The authors concluded that coursework combined with coaching supported teachers in learning to implement effective reading practices—knowledge alone was insufficient.

McCutchen et al. (2009), in another study, also demonstrated the importance of combining intensive knowledge building experiences with opportunities for teachers to receive support during implementation. Researchers in this study provided 30 teachers working in grades three, four, and five with a 10-day summer institute focused on literacy instruction and related linguistic knowledge. The professional development (PD) institute focused exclusively on developing teachers' knowledge of phonology and phonemic awareness, and their role in balanced reading instruction that emphasizes both word-level and text-level instruction. For teachers of older students, researchers added content knowledge about teaching morphology, reading comprehension, and composition skills. During the PD institute, teachers developed lessons based on the content taught in the institute. Three 1-day follow-up sessions were convened in November, February, and May. Additionally, researchers visited classrooms regularly to provide consultation, observe instruction and provide feedback, and assess individual students. The purpose of these visits was to review content acquired in the PD institute.

Upon conclusion of the PD, teachers' posttest scores on the knowledge survey showed that the treatment had a moderate effect on teachers' linguistic knowledge (d =.50). In terms of time spent on instruction, the intervention only had an impact on teachers' vocabulary instruction. To analyze student growth, the researchers used hierarchical linear modeling analysis to assess student growth across three time points and relate change in performance to teacher group (intervention or no intervention). After holding constant teachers' entering linguistic knowledge, students' entering vocabulary knowledge, students' time 1 scores on all measures (scores on assessments after the PD begin), and time spent in vocabulary instruction, McCutchen et al. (2009) found that students of treatment teachers moderately outperformed students of control group teachers on the Gates-MacGinitie Test of Comprehension (d =0.47) and Test of Vocabulary (d =0.59). They also demonstrated moderate to large mean differences on narrative composition (d =0.74) and on the Wechsler Individual Achievement spelling subtest (d =0.44) and writing fluency subtest (d =0.48).

Other studies focused more on helping teachers integrate research-based vocabulary and comprehension strategies into their instruction. Gersten, Dimino, Jayanthi, Kim, and Santoro (2010) used Teacher Study Groups (TSG) to enhance the vocabulary and comprehension instruction of first-grade teachers participating in Reading First efforts. Control and treatment teachers attended a summer institute that was part of the Reading First effort and focused on scientifically based reading practices. All teachers attended follow-up PD sessions during the year. Teachers in the TSG also participated in 16 bimonthly follow-up sessions throughout the year. These teachers read chapters from *Bringing Words to Life: Robust Vocabulary Instruction* (Beck, McKeown, & Kucan, 2002) and discussed them in TSGs. The TSGs were structured to include the following: (a) debrief about efforts to implement strategies from previously read chapters; (b) walk through research explained in the assigned chapter; (c) review a lesson from the core curriculum that they would teach prior to the next TSG meeting and discuss how it could be improved using research strategies learned in the TSG; and (d) collaborative planning to incorporate research-based practices into the selected lesson.

Multilevel models were used to estimate TSG treatment effects on teaching practice, teacher knowledge, and teacher perceptions of professional culture. Teachers in schools implementing TSG scored significantly higher on observed comprehension practices (0.86 standard deviations higher), vocabulary practices (0.58 standard deviations higher), and assessments of vocabulary knowledge (0.73 standard deviations higher) than teachers in control schools. Additionally, teachers in treatment schools scored 0.32 standard deviations higher on assessments of comprehension knowledge compared to teachers in control schools, but this was not statistically significant. Although treatment teachers seemed to benefit from the TSG, the impact of their participation on student achievement was less remarkable. Oral vocabulary was the only area of reading in which students of treatment teachers significantly outperformed students of control teachers (0.44 effect size).

These studies demonstrate that deliberate, focused approaches to simultaneously improve teachers' knowledge and practice for teaching reading can be effective, and they raise questions about how teacher education programs currently are conceived. Most preservice teacher education programs do not align their reading coursework and field experiences so that preservice teachers have focused opportunities to learn about different aspects of reading instruction and receive considerable support in applying that knowledge (Smartt & Reschley, 2007) as are present in most professional development studies that yield effective results.

Strategies for Improving Strategic Knowledge

Far less is known about how teachers can improve their strategic knowledge (i.e., their ability to apply their conceptual and procedural knowledge to solve problems they confront in practice), a critical skill for special education teachers. Only two studies conducted with preservice special education teachers examined techniques for promoting teachers' strategic knowledge and evaluation of these techniques relied mostly on self-report. Al Otaiba et al. (2005) focused coursework on phonics and the English word structure combined with a tutoring experience. This helped preservice teachers become more reflective about their practice as indicated in comments about student performance made in weekly reflection logs. Specifically, preservice teachers described how they might individualize instruction based on student data, but the researchers did not collect data to validate that preservice teachers were individualizing in the ways they suggested in their logs.

Parker-Katz and Hughes (2008) helped mentor teachers learn to use artifacts as a way of helping preservice mentees learn about teaching literacy. Fifteen mentor teachers, recommended as excellent special education teachers by their district, taught in the program. Each mentor participated in eight professional development sessions that addressed how to: (a) select literacy artifacts; (b) work with adult learners; and (c) lead discussions with mentees. Artifacts were samples of classroom work (e.g., an activity or student work sample) that demonstrated teaching and learning about literacy in a special education classroom. Mentors completed reflection forms where they explained the artifact and why it was selected prior to engaging preservice teachers in a discussion about it. At completion of the experience, preservice teachers were asked to rate their experience and provide written comments. An analysis of written comments showed that preservice teachers felt mentors provided them with ideas and support for meeting students' needs and learning how to make instructional adaptations.

Since using knowledge strategically to solve problems of literacy practice is the ultimate key outcome of special education teacher preparation, it is concerning that more researchers have not examined how such knowledge can be taught to preservice teachers and developed in practica. Clearly, we need ways to teach these problem-solving skills and determine if our preparation provides the foundation needed so teachers can identify literacy learning difficulties, and respond to these difficulties appropriately using their conceptual and procedural knowledge. While we might expect that teachers' application of this knowledge base will become more sophisticated as they gain experience, it is critical that special education teachers exit preparation programs with a firm foundation that includes deep content knowledge in literacy, knowledge of evidence-based practices to teach literacy, and most importantly, the strategic skill set needed to monitor and carefully analyze student performance to inductively derive instructional programs that fit the individual literacy needs of students with disabilities (Fuchs et al., 2012).

Conclusion

Studies of initial preparation and professional development provide evidence that preservice teachers can acquire conceptual and procedural content knowledge, and, with sufficient training, can situate that knowledge in the classroom. These professional learning strategies must be focused and implemented for a substantial amount of time, something that is difficult to do in preparation programs that historically are diverse in terms of their course offerings and limited in their capacity to provide preservice teachers with opportunities to situate their content knowledge in authentic settings (Goe, 2006; Leko & Brownell, 2011). Further, even under the best professional learning conditions, researchers in teacher education and many other professions have not developed sufficient understanding about how strategic knowledge can be promoted no less hastened when certain learning conditions are present.

Future Research Directions

The knowledge we need to inform effective special education teaching and ensure its effective implementation in schools will require a research agenda of considerable magnitude in three major areas: (a) increased knowledge about how to improve the literacy skills of students with disabilities; (b) additional understanding about how knowledge and practice for literacy teaching develop and how to assess that knowledge and practice; and (c) research on effective teacher education practice that is founded in theoretically sound models of adult learning.

Although our knowledge of effective interventions for young students with reading disabilities is substantive, there are major gaps in this research. To establish a solid knowledge base for teaching literacy, our field needs more research on older students and those who are culturally and linguistically diverse. Researchers need to identify those strategies that help students access linguistically demanding and cognitively complex text specific to disciplines such as science and social studies. Additionally, researchers must determine the degree to which established evidence-based interventions are efficacious for students with disabilities who are also linguistically and culturally diverse or how these interventions might be modified to better address these students' needs. Further, we need implementation research that demonstrates how evidence-based programs can be incorporated into core content and intervention instruction to help students with disabilities meet Common Core State Standards for student learning. This understanding is critical for determining the specific knowledge about literacy content that special education teachers must acquire and the instructional contexts in which these teachers must practice and develop their skill and demonstrate competence.

Second, teacher educators in special education need a deeper understanding of how special education teachers' knowledge for teaching and instructional practice develops. We need to better understand how special education teachers move from novice understandings to more sophisticated understandings, and how these changes influence their instructional practice in literacy. This research should help teacher educators define the foundational knowledge that, with continued practice, application, and coaching, will lead to the refined diagnostic and instructional competence observed in expert, master teachers. For example, we need answers to the following types of questions. How much declarative knowledge should a novice special education teacher have about teaching reading? Is it critical that novice special education teachers respond successfully to rigorous surveys of content knowledge for teaching reading (e.g., survey of linguistic knowledge authored by Louisa Moats or the Survey of Content Knowledge for Teaching Reading authored by Geoffrey Phelps and Stephen Schilling)? Given the limited time available for initial preparation, what evidence-based programs for teaching reading and writing to small groups of students with disabilities should preservice teachers master? That is, what evidence-based reading and writing programs provide the best instructional foundation (i.e., core intervention components and underlying instructional principles) for engaging in the intensive strategic problem-solving skills needed to diagnose and develop individualized interventions for students with the most difficult literacy learning problems? Longitudinal research that describes how novice special education teachers, with various types of foundation training, develop expert skills will help us develop an understanding of the kinds of foundation knowledge, and induction and in-service programs that are most efficacious for developing expert practitioners. With this knowledge base we can design assessments to evaluate the development of special education teachers as they progress from novice to expert status. Chapter 26 in this handbook makes clear the need for additional well-executed research on teacher assessment that can inform our understandings of special education teacher knowledge and effective instructional practice.

Finally, research on special education literacy teacher education must be based on valid conceptual models of adult learning and knowledge development. We cannot design efficacious teacher education programs unless we know more about evidenced-based approaches for promoting teachers' knowledge and classroom practice (e.g., see Joyce & Showers, 2002). These approaches should be founded in theories of learning that have been validated through research, as these theories are likely to have the most to contribute to building a foundation for effective teacher education practice. In the broader literature on developing expertise, researchers have established that social learning theory has much to contribute to the development of expertise. The concept of "deliberative practice with feedback" (Bandura, 1986) assumes that novices learn best in the presence of expert models who provide specific feedback on performance (Ericsson, 2006). Similarly, in a meta-analysis of research on training teachers, Joyce and Showers suggest that efficacious training models are those that include understanding and discussion about the theory that underlies a desired instructional practice; demonstration, practice, and feedback during controlled applications of the desired practice; and classroom coaching that is aligned to theory and strategy implementation. Research is needed, however, to identify the most effective and efficient models for teaching teachers the relevant knowledge for teaching literacy (e.g., college classes; instruction embedded in professional development schools), and how to structure practica and student teaching that fosters application of that knowledge base in a diverse array of contexts.

References

Al Otaiba, S., Schatsneider, C., & Silverman, E. (2005). Tutor-assisted intensive learning strategies in kindergarten: How much is enough? *Exceptionality, 13*, 195–208. doi:10.1207/s15327035ex1304_2

August, D., & Shanahan, T. (2006). *Developing literacy in second-language learners: Report of the National Literacy Panel on language-minority children and youth.* Mahwah, NJ: Lawrence Erlbaum.

Baker, S., Gertsen, R., & Scanlon, D. (2002). Procedural facilitators and cognitive strategies: Tools for unraveling the mysteries of comprehension and the writing process, and for providing meaningful access to the general curriculum. *Learning Disabilities Research and Practice, 17*, 65–77. doi:10.1111/1540-5826.00032

Bandura, A. (1986). *Social foundations of thought and action: A social cognitive approach.* Upper Saddle River, NJ: Prentice Hall.

Beck, I. L., McKeown, M. G., & Kucan, L. (2002). *Bringing vocabulary to life: Robust vocabulary instruction.* New York, NY: The Guilford Press.

Berkeley, S., Scruggs, T. E., & Mastropieri, M. A. (2010). Reading comprehension instruction for students with LD, 1995–2006: A meta-analysis. *Remedial and Special Education, 31*, 423–436. doi:10.1177/0741932509355988

Berliner, D. C. (2001). Learning about and learning from expert teachers. *International Journal of Educational Research, 35*, 463–482. doi:10.1016/S0883-0355(02)00004-6

Berninger, V. W., Nielsen, K. H., Abbott, R. D., Wijsman, E., & Raskind, W. (2008). Writing problems in developmental dyslexia: Under-recognized and under-treated. *Journal of School Psychology, 46*, 1–21. doi:10.1016/j.jsp.2006.11.008

Berninger, V. W., Vermeulen, K., Abbott, R. D., McCutchen, D., Cotton, S., Cude, J., … Sharon, T. (2003) Comparison of three approaches to supplementary reading instruction for low-achieving second-grade readers. *Language, Speech and Hearing Services in Schools, 34*, 101–116. doi:10.1044/0161-1461(2003/009)

Biancarosa, C., & Snow, C. E. (2006). *Reading next—A vision for action and research in middle and high school literacy: A report to Carnegie Corporation of New York* (2nd ed.). Washington, DC: Alliance for Excellent Education.

Brownell, M. T., Haager, D., Bishop, A. G., Klingner, J. K., Menon, S., Penfield, R., & Dingle, M. (2007). Teacher quality in special education: The role of knowledge, classroom practice, and school environment. Paper presented at the annual meeting of the American Education Research Association, Chicago, IL.

Bryant, D. P., Goodwin, M., Bryant, B. R., & Higgins, K. (2003). Vocabulary instruction for students with learning disabilities: A review of the research. *Learning Disability Quarterly, 26*, 117–128. doi:10.2307/1593594

Bulgren, J. A., Sampson Graner, P., & Deshler, D. D. (2013). Literacy challenges and opportunities for students with learning disabilities in social studies and history. *Learning Disabilities Research & Practice, 28*, 17–27. doi:10.1111/ldrp.12003

Burns, M. S., Griffin, P., & Snow, C. E. (Eds.). (1999). *Starting out right: A guide to promoting children's success.* Washington, DC: National Academies Press.

Carretti, B., Borella, E., Cornoldi, C., & De Beni, R. (2009). Role of working memory in explaining the performance of individuals with specific reading comprehension difficulties: A meta-analysis. *Learning and Individual Differences, 19*, 245–251. doi:10.1016/j.lindif.2008.10.002

Catts, H. W., Hogan, T. P., & Frey, M. E. (2003). Subgrouping poor readers on the basis of individual differences in reading-related abilities. *Journal of Learning Disabilities, 36*, 151–164. doi:10.1177/002221940303600208

Chard, D. J., Vaughn, S., & Tyler, B.-J. (2002). A synthesis of research on effective interventions for building reading fluency with elementary students with learning disabilities. *Journal of Learning Disabilities, 35*, 386–406. doi:10.1177/00222194020350050101

Common Core State Standards Initiative. (2010). Retrieved from www.corestandards.org

Dieker, L. A., Lane, H. B., Allsopp, D. H., O'Brien, C., Butler, T. W., Kyger, M., … Fenty, N. S. (2009). Evaluating video models of evidence-based instructional practices to enhance teacher learning. *Teacher Education and Special Education, 3*, 180–196. doi:10.1177/0888406409334202

Duke, N. K., Pressley, M., & Hilden, K. (2004). Difficulties with reading comprehension. In C. A. Stone, E. R. Silliman, B. J. Ehren, & K. Apel (Eds.), *Handbook of language and literacy: Development and disorders*, New York, NY: The Guilford Press, 501–520.

Ehri, L., & Snowling, M. J. (2004). Developmental variation in word recognition. In C. A. Stone, E. R. Silliman, B. J. Ehren, & K. Apel (Eds.), *Handbook of language and literacy: Development and disorders*, New York, NY: The Guilford Press, 433–460.

Ericsson, K. A. (2006). The influence of experience and deliberate practice on the development of superior expert performance. In K. A. Ericsson, N. Charness, R. J. Hoffmann, and P. J. Feltovitch (Eds.), *The Cambridge handbook of expertise and expert performance*, New York, NY: Cambridge University Press, 683–703.

Fadde, P. J. (2007). Seeing is believing: Video mock-ups to evaluate and demonstrate multimedia designs. *TechTrends: Linking Research and Practice to Improve Learning, 51*(4), 32–38.

Farrington-Darby, T., & Wilson, J. R. (2006). The nature of expertise: A review. *Applied Ergonomics, 37*, 17–32. doi:10.1016/j.apergo.2005.09.001

Feldon, D. F. (2007). The implications of research on expertise for curriculum and pedagogy. *Educational Psychology Review, 19*, 91–110. doi:10.1007/s10648-006-9009-0

Francis, D., Rivera, M., Lesaux, N., Kieffer, M., & Rivera, H. (2006). *Practical guidelines for the education of English language learners: Research-based recommendations for instruction and academic interventions.* (Under cooperative agreement grant S283B050034 for U.S. Department of Education). Portsmouth, NH: RMC Research Corporation, Center on Instruction. Retrieved from http://www.centeroninstruction.org/files/ELL1-Interventions.pdf

Fuchs, D., Fuchs, L. S., & Compton, D. L. (2012) SMART RTI: A next generation approach to multilevel prevention. *Exceptional Children, 78*, 263–279.

Fuchs, D., Fuchs, L. S., & Stecker, P. M. (2010). The "blurring" of special education in a new continuum of general education placements and services. *Exceptional Children, 76*, 301–323.

Gajria, M., Jitendra, A. K., Sood, S., & Sacks, G. (2007). Improving comprehension of expository text in students with LD: A research synthesis. *Journal of Learning Disabilities, 40*, 210–225. doi:10.1177/00222194070400030301

Gersten, R., & Baker, S. (2003). English-language learners with learning disabilities. In H. L. Swanson, K. R. Harris, & S. Graham (Eds.), *Handbook of learning disabilities* (pp. 94–109). New York: The Guilford Press.

Gersten, R., Dimino, J., Jayanthi, M., Kim, J. S., & Santoro, L. E. (2010). Teacher study group impact of the professional development model on reading instruction and student outcomes in first grade classrooms. *American Educational Research Journal, 47*, 694–739. doi:10.3102/0002831209361208

Gersten, R., Fuchs, L. S., Williams, J., & Baker, J. (2001). Teaching reading comprehension strategies to students with learning disabilities: A review of research. *Review of Educational Research, 71*, 279–320. doi:10.3102/00346543071002279

Gersten, R., & Geva, E. (2003). Teaching reading to early language learners. *Educational Leadership, 60*(7), 44–49.

Goe, L. (2006). *The teacher preparation→teacher practices→student outcomes relationship in special education: Missing links and next steps.* Washington, DC: National Comprehensive Center for Teacher Quality. Retrieved from http://www.niusileadscape.org/docs/FINAL_PRODUCTS/LearningCarousel/NCCTQResearchSynthesis.pdf

Goldenberg, C. (2006). Improving achievement for English learners: What the research tells us. *Education Week, 25*(43), 34–36.

Goldenberg, C. (2008). Teaching English language learners: What the research does—and does not—say. *American Educator, 33*(2), 8–44.

Graham, S., & Harris, K. R. (2003). Students with learning disabilities and the process of writing: A meta-analysis of SRSD studies. In L. Swanson, K. R. Harris, & S. Graham (Eds.), *Handbook of research on learning disabilities* (pp. 383–402). New York, NY: The Guilford Press.

Graham, S., & Harris, K. R. (2009). Almost 30 years of writing research: Making sense of it all with *The Wrath of Khan*. *Learning Disabilities Research and Practice, 24*, 58–68. doi:10.1111/j.1540-5826.2009.01277.x

Graham, S., & Perin, D. (2007). A meta-analysis of writing instruction for adolescent students. *Journal of Educational Psychology, 99*, 445–476. doi:10.1037/0022-0663.99.3.445

Haager, D., & Vaughn, S. (2013). The Common Core State Standards and Reading: Interpretations and implications for elementary students with learning disabilities. *Learning Disabilities Research & Practice, 28*, 5–16. doi:10.1111/ldrp.12000

Hart, B., & Risley, T. R. (1995). *Meaningful differences in the everyday experience of young American children.* Baltimore, MD: Paul H. Brookes Publishing.

Johnson, E. S., Humphrey, M., Mellard, D. F., Wood, K., & Swanson, H. L. (2010). Cognitive processing deficits and students with specific learning disabilities: A selective meta-analysis of the literature. *Learning Disabilities Quarterly, 22*, 3–18.

Joyce, B., & Showers, B. (2002) *Student achievement through staff development* (3rd ed.). Alexandria, VA: Association for Supervision and Curriculum Development.

Kennedy, M. J., Driver, M. K., Pullen, P. C., Ely, E., & Cole, M. T. (2013). Improving teacher candidates' knowledge of phonological awareness: A multimedia approach. *Computers & Education, 64*, 42–51. http://dx.doi.org/10.1016/j.compedu.2013.01.010

Kennedy, M. J., Ely, E., Thomas, C. N., Pullen, P. C., Newton, J. R., Ashworth, K., … Lovelace, S. P. (2012). Using multimedia tools to support teacher candidates' learning. *Teacher Education and Special Education: The Journal of the Teacher Education Division of the Council for Exceptional Children, 35*, 243–257. doi:10.1177/0888406412451158

Kennedy, M. J., Hart, J. E., & Kellems, R. O. (2011). Using enhanced podcasts to augment limited instructional time in teacher preparation. *Teacher Education and Special Education: The Journal of the Teacher Education Division of the Council for Exceptional Children, 34*, 87–105. doi:10.1177/0888406410376203

Klingner, J., & Soltero-González, L. (2009). Culturally and linguistically responsive literacy instruction for English language learners with learning disabilities. *Multiple Voices, 12*, 1–17.

Klingner, J. K., Urbach, J., Golos, D., Brownell, M., & Menon, S. (2010). Teaching reading in the 21st century: A glimpse at how special education teachers promote reading comprehension. *Learning Disability Quarterly, 33*, 59–74.

Leko, M. M., & Brownell, M. T. (2011). Special education preservice teachers' appropriation of pedagogical tools for teaching reading. *Exceptional Children*, 77, 229–251.

Leko, M. M., Brownell, M. T., Sindelar, P. T., & Murphy, K. (2012). Promoting special education preservice teacher expertise. *Focus on Exceptional Children, 44*(7), 1–16.

Leko, M. M., Mundy, C. A., Kang, H.-J., & Datar, S. D. (2013). If the book fits: Finding appropriate texts for adolescents with disabilities. *Intervention in School & Clinic, 48*, 267–275. doi:10.1177/1053451212472232

McCutchen, D., Green, L., Abbott, R. D., & Sanders, E. A. (2009). Further evidence for teacher knowledge: Supporting struggling readers in grades three through five. *Reading and Writing, 22*, 401–423. doi:10.1007/s11145-009-9163-0

Mercer, C. D., & Pullen, P. C. (2005). *Students with learning disabilities* (6th ed.). Upper Saddle River, NJ: Merrill-Prentice Hall.

Moats, L. (2009). Knowledge foundations for teaching reading and spelling. *Reading and Writing, 22*, 379–399. doi:10.1007/s11145-009-9162-1

National Institute of Child Health and Human Development. (2000). *Report of the National Reading Panel. Teaching children to read: An evidence-based assessment of the scientific research literature on reading and its implications for reading instruction* (NIH Publication No. 00-4769). Washington, DC: U.S. Government Printing Office.

Neuman, S. B., & Cunningham, L. (2009). The impact of professional development and coaching on early language and literacy instructional practices. *American Educational Research Journal, 46*, 532–566. doi:10.3102/0002831208328088

O'Connor, R., & Bell, K. (2004). Teaching students with reading disability to read words. In C. A. Stone, E. R. Silliman, B. J. Ehren, & K. Apel (Eds.), *Handbook of language and literacy: Development and disorders* (pp. 479–496). New York, NY: The Guilford Press.

Parker-Katz, M., & Hughes, M. T. (2008). Preparing special education mentors: Classroom artifacts as a vehicle for learning about teaching. *Teacher Education and Special Education, 31*, 268–282. doi:10.1177/0888406408330646

Phelps, G., & Schilling, S. (2004). Developing measures of content knowledge for teaching reading. *The Elementary School Journal, 105*, 31–48.

Reed, D., & Vaughn, S. (2010). Reading interventions for older students. In T. Glover & S. Vaughn (Eds.) *The promise of response to intervention: Evaluating current science and practice* (pp. 143–186). New York, NY: The Guilford Press.

Ropo, E. (2004). Teaching expertise: Empirical findings on expert teachers and teacher development. In H. P.A. Boshuizen, R. Bromme, & H. Gruber (Eds.), *Professional learning: Gaps and transitions on the way from novice to expert* (pp. 159–179). Dordrecht: Kluwer Academic. doi:10.1007/1-4020-2094-5_9

Santangelo, T., Harris, K. R., & Graham, S. (2008). Using self-regulated strategy development to support students who have "trubol giting thangs into werds." *Remedial and Special Education, 29*, 78–89. doi:10.1177/0741932507311636

Sencibaugh, J. M. (2007). Meta-analysis of reading comprehension intervention for students with learning disabilities: Strategies and implications. *Reading Improvement, 44*, 6–22.

Smartt, S. M., & Reschley, D. J. (2007). *Barriers to the preparation of highly qualified teachers in reading.* Washington, DC: National Comprehensive Center for Teacher Quality. Retrieved from http://www.gtlcenter.org/sites/default/files/docs/June2007Brief.pdf

Snow, C. E., Griffin, P., & Burns, M. S. (Eds.). (2005). *Knowledge to support the teaching of reading: Preparing teachers for a changing world.* San Francisco, CA: Jossey-Bass.

Spear-Swerling, L. (2006). Children's reading comprehension and oral reading fluency in easy text. *Reading & Writing: An Interdisciplinary Journal, 19*, 199–220. doi:10.1007/s11145-005-4114-x

Spear-Swerling, L. (2009). A literacy tutoring experience for prospective special educators and struggling second graders. *Journal of Learning Disabilities, 42*, 431–443. doi:10.1177/0022219409338738

Spear-Swerling, L., & Brucker, P. O. (2004). Preparing novice teachers to develop basic reading and spelling skills in children. *Annals of Dyslexia, 54*, 332–364. doi:10.1007/s11881-004-0016-x

Spear-Swerling, L., Brucker, P., & Alfano, M. (2005). Teachers' literacy-related knowledge and self-perceptions in relation to preparation and experience. *Annals of Dyslexia*, *55*, 266–296. doi:10.1007/s11881-005-0014-7

Swanson, E. A. (2008). *Observing reading instruction provided to elementary students in resource rooms* (Doctoral dissertation, The University of Texas at Austin). Retrieved from http://www.lib.utexas.edu/etd/d/2008/swansone92290/swansone92290.pdf

Swanson, E. A., & Vaughn, S. (2010). An observation study of reading instruction provided to elementary students with learning disabilities in the resource room. *Psychology in the Schools*, *47*, 481–492.

Swanson, H. L., Howard, C. B., & Sáez, L. (2006). Do different components of working memory underlie different subgroups of reading disabilities? *Journal of Reading Disabilities*, *39*, 252–259. doi:10.1177/00222194060390030501

Sze, S. (2010). Teaching reading to students with learning disabilities. *Reading Improvement*, *47*, 142–150.

Taft, R. J., & Mason, L. H. (2011). Examining effects of writing interventions: Highlighting results for students with primary disabilities other than learning disabilities. *Remedial and Special Education*, *32*, 359–370. doi:10.1177/0741932510362242

Teale, W. H. (2009). Students learning English and their literacy instruction in urban schools. *The Reading Teacher*, *62*, 699–703. doi:10.1598/RT.62.8.9

Van Laarhoven, T. R., Munk, D. D., Lynch, K., Bosma, J., & Rouse, J. (2007). A model for preparing special and general education preservice teachers for inclusive education. *Journal of Teacher Education*, *58*, 440–455. doi:10.1177/0022487107306803

Vaughn S., & Klingner J. (2004). Teaching reading comprehension to students with learning disabilities. In C. A. Stone, E. R. Silliman, B. J. Ehren, & K. Apel (Eds.), *Handbook of language and literacy: Development and disorders*, New York, NY: The Guilford Press, 541–558.

16

Teacher Preparation

Mathematics

Cynthia C. Griffin
UNIVERSITY OF FLORIDA

Delinda van Garderen
UNIVERSITY OF MISSOURI

Tracy G. Ulrich
UNIVERSITY OF FLORIDA

Things to Think About

- While policy reforms in content and pedagogy have been significant, there are striking differences in mathematics performance between students with disabilities and their nondisabled peers.
- Persuasive research evidence reveals that a substantial part of the variability in student achievement gains in mathematics is due to the teacher, so the field must seriously consider how special education teachers are prepared in this content area.
- Standards in mathematics education and special education inform what these two fields expect teachers to know about mathematics content and related pedagogy and allow us to evaluate the mathematics content and pedagogy in studies included in the teacher preparation literature in special education.
- Many preservice and in-service teachers do not have an adequate understanding of essential mathematics concepts, and what preservice teachers learn in teacher preparation courses (e.g., evidence-based practices) often is not applied in classroom practice for teaching mathematics to students with disabilities.
- Recommendations for further research include (but are not limited to) a need to understand how students with disabilities learn mathematics, determine what special educators must know to effectively teach mathematics to students with disabilities, and learn how special education teacher preparation programs improve teachers' knowledge and skills in mathematics.

The National Context

National efforts to reform teaching and learning in America's K–12 schools have produced influential legislation, academic and professional standards, and a myriad of responses from colleges of education and state and local education agencies. Of note are federal accountability mandates designed to ensure that all students, including students with disabilities, meet high academic standards through shared responsibility among general and special education for student progress (No Child Left Behind Act [NCLB], 2001; Individuals with Disabilities Education Act [IDEA], 2004). In mathematics education, reforms in both content and pedagogy also have been significant. Both policy and professional groups have advocated that all students achieve mathematical preparedness for employment and/or postsecondary education. As a nation, our economic competitiveness, national security, and quality of life depend on it (National Council of Teachers of Mathematics [NCTM], 2000; 2006; National Mathematics Advisory Panel [NMAP], 2008).

Although enhancing the academic performance of students with disabilities has been a national priority and important progress has been made (e.g., Schiller, Sanford, & Blackorby, 2008), data from the National Assessment of Educational Progress (NAEP; National Center for Education Statistics [NCES], 2011) reveal deficiencies in mathematics learning pointing to numerous areas of instructional need for students with disabilities. Specifically, differences in mathematics performance on the NAEP between students with disabilities and their nondisabled peers are striking. While 86% of fourth-grade students not identified with a disability scored above *Basic* in 2011, only 55% of students with disabilities achieved this minimal standard. For eighth graders, the differences were even greater. More than three fourths (78%) of students not identified with a disability scored above *Basic*, compared to only 36% of students with disabilities. Persuasive research evidence reveals that a substantial part of the variability in student achievement gains in mathematics is due to the *teacher* (NMAP, 2008). Studies reviewed in the NMAP report suggest that student learning is negatively affected by teachers' lack of mathematical content knowledge and pedagogy. Moreover, school districts overemphasize materials, such as textbooks, and underestimate the skill required for teachers to deliver effective mathematics instruction (NMAP, 2008). If mathematics instruction is to be robust enough to improve the achievement of students with disabilities and close the gap between them and their nondisabled peers, the field must seriously consider how special education teachers are prepared in this content area.

Scope and Purpose of the Chapter

The purpose of this chapter is to explore the literature related to the preparation of special educators to teach mathematics. We will use a formative piece by Brownell, Sindelar, Kiely, and Danielson (2010) on special education teacher quality and teacher preparation to frame our review of what teachers should know and be able to do. Brownell et al. (2010) remind us that the research base on teaching and learning suggests broad areas of teacher knowledge, including: (a) content and how to teach it; (b) specific interventions and assessments for providing more intensive, explicit instruction, including evidence-based intervention strategies that address disability-specific learning needs; (c) specific problems that students with disabilities may experience in particular content areas; and (d) technology for avoiding learning concerns and supporting access to more sophisticated learning. These four areas will each be addressed to provide a context for interpreting the literature. We will then turn to a discussion of the research found in teacher preparation in special education and mathematics, and conclude with implications for preparing teacher educators and recommendations for further research.

To find the research pertaining to preparing special educators to teach mathematics, the following strategies were used to search the literature. First, several databases (Academic Search Premier, EBSCO Host, Education Full Text, ERIC, Google Scholar, and Psych Abstracts) were searched using the following keywords: *teacher education*, *mathematics*, *special education*, *inservice teacher education*, and *professional preparation*. In addition, ancestral searches for all articles selected were conducted to expand the base of studies. However, conference papers, dissertations, newsletter articles, or other unpublished documents were not included in the search.

This search yielded a total of 20 studies that met these criteria: Studies included in the review were peer-reviewed, had a relatively complete discussion of methodology, had either an acceptably high return rate for surveys or a detailed discussion characterizing the representativeness of the sample, and had a clear sense of purpose with regard to inquiring into some aspect of preparation or professional development of special education teachers in mathematics. Although general education teachers participated in some of the studies we reviewed, literature that focused solely on general education teachers was excluded from this review. Collectively, the studies reviewed fell into two categories: survey studies and studies of program components. In addition to the 20 studies, we also reviewed two pertinent program descriptions that included pilot data.

The discussion of the *content and how to teach it* (Brownell et al., 2010) begins with the relevant professional standards in mathematics education and special education to understand what these two fields expect teachers to know about mathematics content and related pedagogy. This discussion of the standards also allows us to evaluate the mathematics content and pedagogy in studies included in the teacher preparation literature in special education.

Content and How to Teach It

The sixth edition of the Council for Exceptional Children (CEC) professional standards and ethics for the field of special education (i.e., *What Every Special Educator Must Know*, 2008) provides direction from the field for what special educators should know and be able to do (knowledge and skill), as well as more specific recommendations related to mathematics teaching. CEC advises preparation programs to ensure that preservice special educators "possess a solid base of understanding of the content areas of the general curricula … sufficient to collaborate with general educators" (p. 10). Because special educators are expected to teach or co-teach students with disabilities across a range of grade levels, they must also know how to design accommodations and modifications across all academic subject areas. If special educators are teaching the secondary-level general education curriculum to students with disabilities, they must also have adequate content knowledge "to assure individuals with exceptional learning needs can meet state general curriculum standards" (p. 10). For knowledge and pedagogy needed by special educators who teach mathematics content to students with mild disabilities in the general education curricula, *Standard 4: Instructional Strategies* addresses (a) knowledge of "methods for increasing the accuracy and proficiency in math calculations and applications" (p. 55) and (b) the use of methods "to teach mathematics appropriate to [students'] needs" (p. 56).

Although these two statements of knowledge and skill provide additional detail for determining what special educators might need to know and be able to do to support the mathematics learning of students with disabilities, they offer minimal guidance for deciding what mathematics content special educators must know and be able to teach (e.g., addition, multiplication, rational number concepts, algebra). In addition, the statements may be understood by general education professionals as contradictory to some of the fundamental goals of mathematics pedagogy put forth by the National Council of Teachers of Mathematics (NCTM, 2000).

The *Professional Standards for Teaching Mathematics* document (*Principles and Standards for School Mathematics* [PSSM]) is produced by the National Council of Teachers of Mathematics (NCTM, 2000) and based on surveys of curriculum materials in the U.S. and abroad, education research, and publications put forth by government agencies such as the National Science Foundation. The PSSM outlines mathematics goals and standards for all students from prekindergarten through 12th grade and serves as a guide and resource in the areas of curricula, teaching, and assessment. Collectively, all 10 standards provide "descriptions of what mathematics instruction should enable students to know and do" (p. 29). Five *Content Standards* address all grade levels and include (a) numbers and operations, (b) measurement, (c) data analysis and probability, (d) geometry, and (e) algebra. The five *Process Standards* offer ways of teaching and applying the *Content Standards*. The five *Process Standards* are: (a) problem solving, (b) reasoning and proof, (c) connections, (d) communication, and (e) representation. In each of four grade-level bands (i.e., pre-K through grade 2, grades 3–5, grades 6–8, and grades 9–12) more detailed expectations for each standard are aligned with the grade-level bands.

The PSSM emphasis on *conceptual understanding* is key. Although traditional goals of mathematics learning (e.g., the CEC standard noted above regarding methods to *increase the accuracy and proficiency in math calculations and applications*) remain important, they are no longer sufficient as end goals of mathematics education. Instead, students must develop well-connected conceptual knowledge as a foundation underlying mathematical procedures. They must also develop productive views toward learning and behaving mathematically including positive opinions of themselves as mathematics learners, as well as learning and carrying out a variety of strategies while continuing to develop more efficient retrieval and reasoning strategies over time (Carpenter, Fennema, Franke, Levi, & Empson, 1999; Siegler, 2005).

Interestingly, the field of special education has long called for more attention to be paid to the content of teaching provided by special educators. For example, Parmar and Cawley (1997) argued for preparing special educators who held strong knowledge and skills competencies in mathematics. Based on their analysis of 1,200 KeyMATH scores of students with learning disabilities (LD), Cawley, Parmar, and Smith (1995) found that the performance of students with LD continued to fall further and further behind over a 6-year period when their scores were compared to test norms. Unfortunately, a similar lack of progress is evident in the recent NAEP data reported above, where the performance gap widened from 4th to 8th grades. Parmar and Cawley (1997) attributed this lack of student progress to teachers' poor content and curriculum decisions and to the use of instructional practices not designed to meet the unique learning needs of students with LD. Their solution was to recommend the careful alignment of the professional standards for teaching mathematics (NCTM, 1991) with the knowledge and skills competencies (Graves, Landers, Lokerson, Luchow, & Horvath, 1993). The Division for Learning Disabilities (DLD) developed the knowledge and skills competencies to guide the preparation of teachers of students with LD. Eleven of these competencies focus on mathematics. Parmar and Cawley proposed an approach to teacher professional development that would draw upon an integrated set of these standards from both general and special education. Even today, the design of teacher preparation programs and professional development efforts that integrate standards across disciplines remains an innovative approach with potential for addressing special educators' knowledge and skill needs. However, to our knowledge, little systematic work has created integrated learning standards or experiences like these for teachers, with one exception (i.e., the work of Greer & Meyen, 2009; Meyen & Greer, 2009), to be discussed later in this chapter.

Some might suggest that the *Common Core State Standards* (CCSS), sponsored by the National Governors Association and the Council of Chief State School Officers (2010) were developed to provide a clear and consistent understanding of what *all* K–12 students are expected to learn across content areas, including mathematics. The development of the CCSS occurred in response to concerns about a lack of focus and coherence in the curriculum. The mathematics standards focus on enhancing conceptual understanding of key ideas and defining what students should be able to comprehend and do for key mathematical domains (e.g., number and operations) and related specific standards (e.g., use place value understanding and properties of operations to perform multidigit arithmetic). The standards are organized by grade level.

Embedded within the CCSS for Mathematics document are Six Standards for Mathematical Practice (see pp. 6–8). These processes and proficiencies reflect the NCTM Process Standards (problem solving, reasoning and proof, communication, representation, and connections) and the five strands of mathematical proficiency as spelled out in the National Research Council's (2001) report "Adding It Up" (i.e., conceptual understanding, procedural fluency, adaptive reasoning, strategic competence, and productive disposition). The practices described in the CCSS for Mathematics include: (a) making sense of problems and persevering in solving them, (b) reasoning abstractly and quantitatively, (c) constructing viable arguments and critiquing the reasoning of others, (d) modeling with mathematics, (e) using appropriate tools strategically, (f) attending to precision, (g) looking for and making use of structure, and (h) looking for and expressing regularity in repeated reasoning.

Although the CEC is cautiously optimistic about the roll out of the CCSS, it has expressed some uncertainty about how students with disabilities will be supported to meet these new standards—an uncertainty undoubtedly shared by many special education professionals.

> CEC views the CCSS as providing the opportunity to continue the trend of greater access to the general curriculum while enhancing successful transition opportunities and improving results for all students with disabilities. That positive outlook, however, does not camouflage the very real challenges inherent in teaching to these more rigorous standards or the accountability of schools and, now, teachers in moving students to mastery of them.
>
> *(CEC, 2010, p. 3)*

With what appears to be an overabundance of published and adopted professional standards, an apparent lack of detail remains for discerning the mathematics content needed by special educators to support high levels of mathematics competence in students with disabilities. Yet, associations between teachers' content knowledge in mathematics, their classroom teaching, and student learning have emerged in the literature as researchers study the notion that "teachers who possess a deep and broad understanding of fundamental math provide more rigorous instruction for their students, which in turn leads to higher student achievement in math" (Koency & Swanson, 2000, p. 3). In general education, the view that teacher content knowledge of mathematics influences the quality of mathematics teaching thereby impacting student performance has been the subject of influential studies for over a decade (e.g., the work of Ball et al. at the Learning Mathematics for Teaching [LMT] Project at the University of Michigan). In particular, Hill, Rowan, and Ball (2005) found that teachers' mathematical knowledge for *teaching* (not simply teachers' mathematics computation and problem-solving abilities) was significantly related to student achievement gains in both first and third graders from low SES and minority backgrounds. Again, the connections between teachers' knowledge of mathematics, their classroom teaching, and the learning of students with disabilities remain elusive.

We return to what is known from the research in special education teacher quality and teacher preparation (i.e., Brownell et al., 2010) by discussing interventions and assessments for providing more intensive, explicit instruction in mathematics. Compared to the other three areas noted by Brownell and her colleagues, the bulk of the research in mathematics lies here.

Specific Interventions and Assessments for Providing More Intensive, Explicit Instruction

Gersten et al. (2009) noted that research on mathematics instruction for students with LD has been "treated as an afterthought" (p. 1203) for decades. For example, in a review of studies conducted from 1996–2005, Gersten, Clarke, and Mazzocco (2007) found a ratio of 5 : 1 when the number of studies conducted in reading were compared to those in mathematics with students with LD. Recently, Gersten et al. conducted a meta-analysis of 44 published experimental studies aimed at enhancing the mathematics performance of students with LD. The authors identified a series of evidence-based practices for special educators that have been shown to positively impact mathematics performance in school-aged students with LD:

1. *explicit instruction*—a step-by-step solution strategy for a specific problem type that leads to student use of the same process to solve similar problems;
2. *heuristics*—general approaches for organizing information and solving any problem type, such as, *Read the problem. Highlight the key words. Solve the problem. Check your work.* Heuristics instruction usually involves student discussion and solution evaluation to allow for multiple ways of problem solving;

3. *student verbalizations*—interventions that promote mathematics reasoning by teaching students to think aloud by verbalizing how they solved a problem (e.g., talking about the solution steps used, asking oneself a predetermined list of questions);
4. *visual representations to solve problems*—visual representations or demonstrations used while introducing or solving problems to build understanding and reasoning;
5. *a range or specified sequence of examples*—interventions that focus on the selection of teaching examples during concept instruction through the use of a specified sequence or pattern of examples (e.g., concrete to abstract, easy to difficult), or by systematically using a variation in the range of examples provided during instruction (e.g., teaching only proper fractions instead of initially teaching both proper and improper fractions);
6. *feedback on student progress*—occurs when teachers are given feedback on student progress or progress plus options for addressing instructional needs (e.g., instructional recommendations);
7. *assessment data and feedback to students*—occurs when a teacher, peer, or computer program provides a student with feedback on mathematics performance or effort, or feedback on performance or effort tied to a specific performance goal; and,
8. *cross aged peer tutoring*—occurs when a student's peer from a higher grade level provides instruction or assistance in a one-on-one tutoring situation (usually in the form of practicing a skill or problem type that has been introduced previously by the teacher).

Browder, Spooner, Ahlgrim-Delzell, Harris, and Wakeman (2008) conducted a comprehensive literature review and meta-analysis on teaching mathematics to students with severe cognitive disabilities (autism; developmental disabilities; and moderate, severe, or profound mental retardation) focusing on the prevalence of the five NCTM Content Standards discussed previously and the identification of effective instructional practices for this population of students. The authors found that 94% of all published mathematics studies that included students with severe disabilities focused on teaching only two of the five NCTM Content Standards (i.e., numbers and operations, and measurement) and that systematic instruction produced moderate to strong effects for these students. Systematic instruction involves a teacher in defining a desired response and then teaching that response until a student masters it through the use of prompting, explicit feedback, and eventually prompt fading. The authors noted that this type of instruction is usually a compilation of multiple components and as a result recommended the use of specific prompt fading procedures and the provision of opportunities to learn to apply mathematics skills in vivo and within real-world settings.

Overall, results of these research syntheses suggest that the field of special education knows much more about effective instructional practices in mathematics than about the specific mathematics content teachers should know and be able to teach to students with disabilities. Furthermore, the finding by Browder et al. (2008) that much of the research in severe disabilities is focused on only two of the five NCTM Content Standards suggests that special education researchers have not examined instructional strategies that complement the full range of mathematics topics students with disabilities may need to learn. In its place, researchers (e.g., Swanson, Geary, L. Fuchs, D. Fuchs) have focused their attention on the specific problems these students experience when learning mathematics.

Specific Problems That Students With Disabilities May Experience

Accumulated evidence suggests that teachers need to understand how underlying cognitive mechanisms, such as memory and monitoring processes, influence mathematical learning (Swanson & Jerman, 2006). In particular, students with LD characteristically display significant memory, attention, and self-regulation problems that adversely affect their performance in both reading and mathematics (Swanson & Sáez, 2003). These problems may interfere with their ability to retrieve basic facts quickly and disregard irrelevant features of a concept or problem (Geary, 2004). Interestingly, third-grade students' attentive behavior has been found to be a strong predictor of mathematics competence (Fuchs et al., 2006). Students with LD may also have (a) background knowledge deficits that stem from a lack of number sense typically acquired in early childhood, (b) linguistic and vocabulary difficulties that may pose challenges because of the distinctiveness of mathematical vocabulary, and (c) difficulties distinguishing important symbols in mathematics that represent key concepts and principles such as the symbols for addition and multiplication (e.g., Geary, 2004). In short, teachers who lack understanding of the cognitive processes involved in mathematics learning and the associated deficits students with disabilities experience may be ineffective at improving student performance.

Technology for Avoiding Learning Concerns and Supporting Access to More Sophisticated Learning

A number of research syntheses have been published over the past 20 years documenting the overall positive effects of the use of technology, including computer-assisted instruction (CAI), on the mathematics learning of students with LD (Kroesbergen & Van Luit, 2003; Mastropieri, Scruggs, & Shiah, 1991; Miller, Butler, & Lee, 1998; Swanson, Hoskyn, & Lee, 1999). In a more recent review, however, Seo and Bryant (2009) noted limitations in prior research and called for more rigorously designed and theory-driven studies in this area. Moreover, it appears that special education teacher preparation programs are not adequately integrating assistive technology (AT) competencies into their programs to ensure their graduates exit with the knowledge, skills, and dispositions necessary to address the AT needs of their students with disabilities (Judge & Simms, 2009; Michaels & McDermott, 2003).

Reflecting on this overview of the research base in mathematics and students with disabilities as aligned with the four broad areas of teacher knowledge (i.e., content, interventions, students' learning problems, and technology), we find only modest guidance for understanding what special educators need to know and be able to do to teach mathematics to students with disabilities. Generally, the overview suggests that teachers will need a fairly well-developed knowledge base about how effective instruction can be used to support students' access to demanding content standards. The literature also indicates that teachers should understand how to address the particular mathematics learning needs of students with disabilities. Clearly, researchers and teacher educators in special education must expand the literature base with the goal of ensuring that both general and special education teachers attain the knowledge and skill needed to help students with disabilities reach high academic standards. In the meantime, teachers must be skilled at using recursive, data-based approaches to assessment and instruction that allow them to determine which existing evidence-based practices are effective for improving students' learning (e.g., Fuchs, Fuchs, & Stecker, 2010). We now turn to a more focused discussion of the literature that specifically addresses the preparation of special educators to teach mathematics to students with disabilities.

Research on Teacher Preparation in Special Education and Mathematics

The review of the research literature that follows includes 20 studies and two program descriptions that address teacher education in special education and mathematics; only two of these studies evaluated student learning. We cluster discussions of these studies into two topical areas: (a) teachers' preparation in mathematics and their instructional practices; and (b) mathematics instructional practices in teacher education programs and professional development.

Teacher Preparation for Teaching Mathematics

We identified eight studies focused on the number of methods courses or hours or credits in mathematics education taken by special educators as a part of their teacher preparation programs or the professional development activities they completed related to mathematics. In one survey study of 139 preservice and in-service deaf education teachers, most respondents reported receiving no professional development in mathematics content and teaching (Pagliaro, 1998). Many of these teachers held no related degrees or certifications, with less than 61% completing fundamental courses in mathematics content and pedagogy, such as calculus, geometry, and methods of high school teaching. In particular, the author noted a lack of preparation received by deaf education teachers at the secondary level (grades 9–12) whose primary responsibility was teaching mathematics.

When assessments of teacher confidence were of interest, study results revealed that many special education teachers do not feel confident teaching mathematics. In a survey conducted by Pagliaro and Kritzer (2005), 290 deaf education teachers reported having unfamiliarity with discrete mathematics topics (e.g., matrices, logic problems, Venn diagrams), the terminology related to these topics, and the pedagogy for teaching them. The vast majority of teachers also reported that they did not include these topics in instruction as they considered them to be too complicated for their students. Teachers, even those who did teach discrete mathematics, rarely took advantage of opportunities for real-world mathematics problem solving and rarely involved students in discussions or presentations during instruction. Perhaps teacher unfamiliarity with mathematics content and pedagogy was due to the fact that only 6% of participants had taken a course that included information about discrete mathematics.

Fitzmaurice (1980) surveyed in-service teachers to determine how prepared they felt to teach CEC's DLD professional standards in mathematics. In only seven of the 35 areas did 90% or more of the teachers declare themselves to be competent at teaching various mathematics topics. Teachers reported having little or no competence for teaching: (a) concepts and operations involving conversions from one base to another; (b) concepts of prime and composite numbers; (c) computing the area or volume of geometric figures; (d) all concepts related to measurement (e.g., time, linear planes, weight, liquids, temperature); and (e) the metric system. Interestingly, the correlation between the number of course credits taken in mathematics or math methods and teachers' perceived levels of competence was not statistically significant. This finding was also evident in Carpenter's (1985) study discussed below.

Also using the DLD competencies, Carpenter (1985) surveyed 101 elementary and secondary resource room teachers to determine the amount of time they spent teaching mathematics, the amount of formal preparation they received in mathematics and mathematics education, their perceptions of their confidence to assess and teach math, and the importance they assigned to their knowledge, assessment practices, and teaching of mathematics. Findings revealed that despite taking, on average, more credit hours in mathematics and math methods than the minimum requirements set by the state, teachers rated themselves as inadequate in terms of their content knowledge and ability to teach the DLD competencies. Another related finding was that the time special educators allocated to mathematics instruction in their resource rooms did not differ from the time scheduled in general education classrooms.

More recently, Maccini and Gagnon (2002, 2006; Gagnon & Maccini, 2007) have conducted several survey studies involving hundreds of practicing general and special education secondary teachers to examine teacher perceptions of their knowledge of mathematics content, instructional strategies, and their teaching of mathematics to students with disabilities. Several useful findings reflect the breadth and depth of preparation and professional development these teachers' received in mathematics. First, Maccini and Gagnon (2006) found that special educators took significantly fewer mathematics methods courses than general educators and that teachers' confidence in their ability to teach mathematics relative to the NCTM standards increased with the number of such courses taken. Further, both general and special education secondary teachers reported taking few methods courses focused on teaching mathematics to students with disabilities (e.g., average of 1.27 courses for special educators [2006]). Although special educators typically felt somewhat better prepared than general education secondary teachers to teach students with disabilities and reported using more evidence-based instructional practices, the special educators also described feeling less well prepared or knowledgeable about mathematics content (Maccini & Gagnon, 2002, 2006; Gagnon & Maccini, 2007).

Despite the finding that special educators report using more evidence-based practices, related survey studies (Kelly, Lang, & Pagliaro, 2003; van Garderen, 2008) and one study that involved classroom observations (Swanson, Solis, Ciullo, & McKenna, 2012) suggest that special education teachers across elementary, middle, and high school classroom settings offer their students few opportunities for mathematics problem solving, a foundational practice within standards-based teaching (NCTM, 2000). Perhaps the lack of problem solving instruction is due to teachers' perceptions of their inadequate mathematical content knowledge and pedagogy, particularly at the secondary level, and these perceptions persist even if special education teachers have taken at least some mathematics coursework (Maccini & Gagnon, 2002).

Only Thibodeau and Cebelius (1987) found that special education teachers perceived themselves to be adequately prepared to teach mathematics. Of the 141 special education teachers surveyed, 83% indicated feeling prepared to teach mathematics, and this finding was relatively stable regardless of disability category taught. However, 74.2% of teachers also perceived themselves as needing additional mathematics education coursework, and this declared need declined only slightly with experience. This anomalous finding of adequate preparedness among special educators may be explained by problems inherent in the use of perceptions of competence as a proxy for actual knowledge. For example, recall bias is well known as a major threat to the internal validity of survey studies (Hassan, 2006).

Four studies were designed to examine more directly preservice or in-service teachers' content knowledge of mathematics for teaching of students with disabilities. In general, these studies revealed that both types of teachers possessed low levels of mathematics knowledge. In a study conducted by Rosas and Campbell (2010), 26 graduates preparing to become special education intervention specialists scored 60% or less on the eighth-grade Ohio Achievement Test, indicating that they lacked basic proficiency in mathematics. The teacher participants also had, on average, lower mathematical grade point averages (GPAs) compared to their overall undergraduate GPAs. However, despite lower levels of knowledge, most participants (78%) reported possessing the content knowledge needed to teach mathematics in grades K through 3, while 60% reported having enough knowledge to teach mathematics in grades 4 through 8. By contrast, only 25.4% of these graduate students reported possessing the mathematics content knowledge necessary to teach students in grades 9 through 12.

Similarly, Glidden (2008) examined 381 preservice elementary, early childhood, and special education teachers' knowledge of the order-of-operations. Although the majority (79.6%) viewed themselves as having average or above average mathematical ability, less than one tenth (7.1%) of these prospective teachers answered all four order-of-operations problems correctly, and more than half answered fewer than 50% of the problems correctly. Clearly, these findings suggest a superficial understanding of the topic.

Humphrey and Hourcade (2010) studied two in-service special educators taking a graduate-level mathematics methods course, "Mathematics and Content Area Learning for Students with Disabilities." These special education teachers disliked mathematics and mathematics-related activities and had a self-reported history of difficulties learning and applying mathematics. Based on interviews, student journaling, and instructor observations during course activities (e.g., solving problems in small groups), the researchers found that these teachers dealt with math phobia in dissimilar ways. "Athena" avoided delivering mathematics instruction based on the school's high standards. Instead of teaching the prescribed curriculum content, Athena reported that she "pulled stuff off the Internet" (p. 30) and had her students complete math puzzles independently. "Angela," in contrast, discussed a more empowering approach to contend with her math fears (i.e., collaborating with a knowledgeable colleague). However, the researchers caution that both teachers found mathematics exceedingly difficult and lacked essential knowledge and skills, which could negatively impact their instructional practices for teaching mathematics to students with disabilities.

In a study focused on the classroom practices of five preservice special educators while they were completing their internship experience, Griffin, Jitendra, and League (2009) examined the communication practices and teacher content knowledge during mathematics lessons, and tracked their students' learning with curriculum-based measures. Based on observations and interviews, several interesting conclusions were drawn. First, preservice teachers were characterized by two sets of instructional practices, communication patterns, and teacher perspectives that coincided with improved student performance or the lack thereof. Preservice teachers who offered more opportunities for students to elaborate ideas, asked more questions, achieved repetition in lessons using a variety of teacher-made materials and games, and supplemented the published curriculum with manipulative materials to represent abstract concepts in more concrete ways also had students who improved their learning of mathematics. Practices that were tied to the textbook in large group teaching arrangements, involved limited use of supplementary materials, and lacked clarity and understanding of critical concepts were observed in teachers with students who made limited progress over the 6-week study. Further these teachers did not realize the weaknesses in their mathematics instruction as they indicated they would continue this kind of instruction when they became in-service teachers; teachers' mathematical content knowledge did not necessarily translate into sound practices. Of the two teachers who used inferior practices, one demonstrated inadequate mathematics content knowledge during observations but the other did not. Finally, all preservice teachers provided few opportunities for peer interactions, a practice recommended by NCTM.

Taken together, findings across these four studies suggest that mathematics content knowledge, whether for a specific topic or across multiple topics, appears to be low among study participants who were either preservice or in-service special educators. In the next section, we discuss studies of mathematics practice in special education teacher education. Although limited research exists in this area, findings demonstrate that special education teachers' knowledge and skill for teaching mathematics can be improved. Of relevance is a recent, large-scale study by Feng and Sass (2010) linking teacher preparation and professional development to the mathematics achievement of students with disabilities. Two pertinent findings reveal that (a) achievement gains for students who received some or all of their mathematics instruction from a special education teacher were higher when the teacher had an advanced degree and (b) a small but positive and statistically significant relationship existed between preservice preparation and mathematics achievement, but only if students received their instruction in both regular and special education classes. Findings suggested that under these two conditions, students with disabilities may have access to more intensive instruction that positively influences their learning. However, this study does not reveal much about what can be done when special educators do not have adequate knowledge of content and pedagogy to teach mathematics well. The following discussion of effective teacher education practices provides more insight.

Effective Teacher Education Practices in Special Education

Six studies and two program descriptions of instructional practices within a teacher preparation course, field placement, or professional development experience provide useful information about how special teachers' content knowledge and instructional practices for teaching mathematics might be improved. Babbitt and Van Vactor (1993) used a case-study approach to demonstrate how one preservice special education teacher with a mathematics learning disability (i.e., "Kathy") was able to increase her knowledge using an intervention designed to help her successfully complete the required mathematics courses in the preparation program. The instructional intervention was conducted in one-to-one sessions and contained two primary components: adaptive strategies and the use of a problem-solving approach to mathematics teaching. For example, the teacher was taught to verbalize her understanding of mathematical concepts and procedures. She was also taught to ask for verbal clarifications during course demonstrations and to manipulate models to understand transformations (e.g., the rotation of geometric shapes). Colored manipulative materials were also used to discriminate between different variables and to explain place value concepts. With this intense intervention provided by a combination of researchers, graduate assistants, and mathematics instructors, the teacher was able to complete the required mathematics coursework successfully. The authors emphasized that Kathy's success was dependent on the interventionists' knowledge of mathematics, mathematics learning, and learning disabilities, and the importance of matching the intervention to the learning characteristics of individual teachers. However, one has to wonder if supporting teacher candidates who require the type of intensive assistance described above is feasible or practical.

The second study conducted by Halverson, Wolfenstein, Williams, and Rockman (2009) involved the development of a computer-based instructional program for special education teachers who had been teaching mathematics at the middle school and secondary levels. The Remembering Math Learning Objects (RMLOs) are online learning tools designed specifically to assist teacher participants in passing mathematics items on the PRAXIS II exam used for teacher licensure and certification. Results of a pre- and posttest taken by 59 pre- and in-service special education teachers indicated improvement in content knowledge as well as improved confidence in solving the problem types presented.

To foster preservice teachers' ability to transfer knowledge of content and skills learned in coursework to classroom practice, Alexander, Lignugaris/Kraft, and Forbush (2007) included an application-to-practice component in an online mathematics methods course they studied. The researchers examined the effects of this course on preservice teachers' knowledge of instructional planning, classroom instructional planning performance, and mathematics outcomes for their students. The six preservice teachers who participated in the study taught 26 pupils with disabilities and six students without.

The online instruction focused on an eight-step instructional planning process that could be used to plan mathematics curriculum that involved preservice teachers in: (a) analyzing the curriculum domain, (b) creating a survey curriculum-based assessment (CBA), (c) administering CBA, (d) analyzing test results, (e) defining the instructional program, (f) developing a focused CBA, (g) creating a monitoring system, and (h) implementing effective instruction. Examinations of preservice teachers' instructional planning knowledge, application of their knowledge to the school setting, and views of the course were conducted. Further, preservice teachers were asked to provide documentation that their students were improving in mathematics performance.

Results revealed remarkable improvements in teacher knowledge on pre to post assessments. However, even though preservice teachers increased their knowledge, they did not uniformly apply what they learned to the classroom setting (as evidenced in a classroom application measure that required teachers to submit written products generated for each section of the eight-step instructional planning process). In the course evaluations, teachers recommended that more instruction be provided on how to use the specific instructional strategies taught. Nonetheless, their students' average score exceeded an 80% mastery criterion on the curriculum-based measures. Overall, the use of the online instruction was considered a promising approach for developing both teacher knowledge for instructional planning and pedagogical skills.

Gerretson and Alvarez McHatton (2009) also conducted a study within the context of a semester-long methods course. The authors set out to determine what impact the required elementary mathematics methods course might have on teacher perceptions of themselves as teachers of mathematics. Specifically, the authors used a protocol in this study that prompted teachers to draw and narrate their "most vivid recollections of a mathematics classroom from their K–12 experiences" (p. 31). These drawings and narratives were collected from 18 alternative-entrant special education teachers at the beginning and end of the semester, and examined using a method of content analysis.

Findings indicated that these special education teachers had similar memories of their experiences as children in mathematics classrooms; teachers recalled that a majority of the time their teachers lectured and students worked independently. However, by the end of the semester, the data revealed that teachers' perceptions shifted from viewing their own teaching in ways comparable to how they were taught as children, to ones more aligned with the NCTM (2000) Standards. The authors noted shifts in teachers' understanding about the importance of active student participation in the learning of strategies, the use of manipulative materials, and group discussions centered on mathematics problem solving. Whether teachers would translate this shift in their understanding to actual classroom practice was not examined.

Dieker et al. (2009) developed and evaluated web-based video models of evidence-based practices for teacher learning. One video focused on Dynamic Assessment in Mathematics, and the other two addressed reading and science. The evaluation of the Dynamic Assessment in Mathematics video involved 22 preservice teachers. All of these students received the same instruction and handouts pertaining to mathematics dynamic assessment; however, students were then randomly assigned to video (12 students) and no-video (10 students) groups. Based on pre- and posttest data, findings revealed that although all students improved in knowledge about dynamic assessment, the video group demonstrated greater gains than the no-video group in identifying important features of the assessment strategy. Participants in both groups, however, revealed little ability to describe how they would apply the assessment process to the classroom context.

Although few study details are included in the three articles discussed below, their descriptions of practices are worth noting as these researchers have been involved in the design, development, and pilot testing of several promising approaches to mathematics teaching in special education. Meyen and Greer (2009a; Greer & Meyen, 2009) reported that over 300 schools over 5 years have been involved in pilot tests of the Blending Assessment With Instruction Program (BAIP) (Meyen & Greer, 2009). BAIP is "designed to assist teachers in aligning instruction with curriculum and instruction standards" (Meyen & Greer, 2009, p. 3). Specifically, BAIP involves teaching mathematics content to students with disabilities through the alignment of mathematics instruction with the NCTM standards focusing on deeper mathematics content knowledge for special education teachers. BAIP involves the use of instructional planning to ensure that teachers understand evidence-based instructional practices, develop knowledge of curriculum standards and instructional alignment, and learn to appreciate the time and effort needed to enact instructional planning. Specifically, these researchers recommend that special education teachers:

1. understand the mathematic concepts they will be responsible for teaching;
2. translate curriculum standards (or concepts) into lesson scripts;
3. align instruction with curriculum standards;
4. identify required prior knowledge of students for learning specific new concepts;
5. understand the relationship between curriculum standards, instruction, and state assessments; and,
6. apply the elements of effective instruction (e.g., review, presentation, guided practice, corrections and feedback, independent practice, and weekly and monthly reviews) (Meyen & Greer, 2009, p. 11).

In addition, Paulsen (2005) described how nine master's level students and two project staff served as tutors using mathematics instruction deemed effective in a large-scale study of first-grade students. The instruction was based on the CEC-DLD Knowledge and Skills Competencies in Math (Parmar & Cawley, 1997) and included five teaching standards: (a) *Modeling Good Mathematics Teaching*, characterized by explicit instruction and teaching behaviors found to increase student achievement; (b) *Knowledge of Mathematics*, including familiarity with K–12 curriculum standards and teaching methods aligned with mathematics content; (c) *Knowing Students as Learners of Mathematics*, including assessment practices designed to monitor student progress; (d) *Mathematics Pedagogy*, understanding the sequence of computational mathematics and problem solving in grades K–12; and (e) *Developing as a Teacher of Mathematics*, including an understanding a theories that facilitate mathematics learning. Based on data gleaned from the larger study that included 840 students, results suggested that at-risk students who received instruction characterized by the five standards performed significantly better on weekly CBM probes (computation and concepts/applications) than students who did not receive the tutoring. In addition, tutors provided the researchers with feedback on the lessons at the end of the 20 weeks of intervention. Tutors had positive comments about the lesson activities and scripts, and reported that the children enjoyed the use of the manipulative materials. The tutors also appreciated receiving practice opportunities before conducting the lessons. Yet, across all three programs described above, the impact of these practices on teachers' knowledge and skill was not assessed.

Summary

Although research studies related to special education teacher preparation in mathematics are small in number and somewhat scattered in focus, a few key themes related to teacher preparation can be drawn. First, studies reveal that many preservice and in-service teachers do not have an adequate understanding of essential mathematics concepts, including the mathematics they are expected to teach. This finding is disconcerting given the link between teacher content knowledge for teaching mathematics and student achievement gains (Hill et al., 2005). Second, researchers noted that what preservice teachers learn in teacher preparation courses (e.g., evidence-based practices) often is not applied in classroom practice for teaching mathematics to students with disabilities. In addition, beliefs, perceptions, and past experiences appear to have a strong influence on teachers' current practices and the levels of confidence teachers possess. Finally, the use of technology shows promise for providing models and cases of expert, evidence-based practice for preparing teachers.

Recommendations for Further Research for Improving Teacher Preparation

We suggest further research based on findings from the extant research reviewed in this chapter focusing on (a) mathematics instruction for students with disabilities, (b) teacher content knowledge, and (c) preparing special education teachers to effectively teach students with disabilities in mathematics. Suggestions are detailed in the following sections.

Mathematics Instruction for Students With Disabilities

To provide direction for improving special education teacher education in mathematics, we suggest building on what is currently known from the research on effective mathematics interventions for teaching students with disabilities (e.g., Gersten et al., 2009; Montague & Jitendra, 2012). Although a number of interventions have been developed (e.g., Montague & Jitendra, 2012), most research involves only number and operations (van Garderen, Scheuermann, Jackson, & Hampton, 2009) or number and operations and measurement (Browder et al., 2008). Clearly, a need exists to continue widening the scope of exploration into other topical areas of mathematics.

Second, continued work is needed to understand how students with disabilities learn mathematics and the extent to which the deficits they demonstrate can be supported through technology or remediated through interventions to allow them to learn more sophisticated mathematical concepts. Currently, 46 states have adopted the CCSS. These standards set high expectations for all students but "do not define the intervention methods or materials necessary to support students who are well below or well above grade-level expectations" (National Governors Association, 2010, p. 4). Developing effective intervention strategies that allow students with disabilities to reach high academic standards is critical.

Third, there is a need to determine the best way to provide remedial instruction to students with disabilities. Over the past few years, special education service delivery has increasingly moved into the general education classroom rather than outside it (Brownell et al., 2010; Kloo & Zigmond, 2008). However, many students with disabilities who require instruction targeted to their needs may benefit from specialized, intensive, small group instruction provided outside the general education classroom

(Montague & Jitendra, 2012). Further research focused on the effectiveness of individualized instruction in mathematics is indicated. In sum, we believe that if the field more fully understands the instructional approaches that best support students with disabilities to comprehend and apply a variety of mathematics topics, the implications for teacher education in this area will become clearer.

Teacher Content Knowledge for Teaching Mathematics

In general, research suggests that teachers' subject matter knowledge is a critical component of effective teaching (e.g., Hill et al., 2005) and that preparing teachers in pedagogical practices alone may be insufficient for improving student achievement (e.g., NMAP, 2008; Wayne & Youngs, 2003). Further, effective teachers not only have knowledge of content and pedagogy, but also have a "knowledge of how the discipline is structured and how students build knowledge within it" (Brownell et al., 2010, p. 368). Therefore, a need exists to determine what special educators must know to effectively teach mathematics to students with disabilities.

A starting point for future studies may be to explore the kind of knowledge special education teachers need to know (i.e., topic areas such as calculus) and at what levels (e.g., fundamental, advanced) in order to support students with disabilities in achieving content standards in mathematics. For example, studies might address the question of whether or not all special education teachers need advanced knowledge of mathematics or is knowledge that is foundational to teaching elementary and middle school mathematics sufficient for realizing adequate progress in student learning?

Preparing Special Education Teachers to Teach Mathematics

Once more is known about how best to teach mathematics to students with disabilities and the extent and kind of mathematics knowledge effective special education teachers need, studies of teacher education programs may be appropriate. Findings from the NMAP (2008) review of teacher education preparation for teaching mathematics revealed little evidence for the "impact of any specific form of, or approach to, teacher education on either teachers' knowledge or students' learning" (p. 40). More systematic and focused research and evaluation should be conducted in this area after a stronger database about mathematics teaching and teacher content knowledge is achieved in special education.

Other possible teacher preparation questions remain unanswered and are in need of further investigation. For example, in what ways do special education teacher preparation programs improve teachers' knowledge and skills in mathematics? And, how do these improvements translate into the mathematics learning of the students with disabilities they teach? What combination of coursework and practicum experiences is most effective and/or efficient in helping special education teachers acquire important mathematics knowledge and skills? How does technology enhance teacher preparation in special education and mathematics? How should special educators be prepared for the role(s) they assume (e.g., mathematics specialists) to ensure that students with disabilities reach high academic standards?

Final Thoughts

Paulsen (2005) noted that, "Regardless of the subject matter, becoming an effective, highly qualified teacher is complicated and usually not intuitive" (p. 28). We contend that preparing special education teachers to teach mathematics to students with disabilities is also a complex and challenging endeavor. Unfortunately, there is little research available offering clear guidance for how best to prepare them. However, "one critical component of any plan to improve mathematics learning is the preparation and professional development of teachers" (National Research Council, 2001, p. 428). A critical goal of any preparation program, therefore, should be to help teachers develop proficiency in mathematics teaching for students with disabilities. At a minimum, such preparation involves attending to the:

(a) mathematics content and how to teach it; (b) specific interventions and assessments for providing more intensive, explicit instruction in mathematics, including evidence-based intervention strategies that address disability-specific learning needs; (c) specific problems that students with disabilities may experience learning mathematics; and (d) technology for avoiding learning concerns and supporting access to more sophisticated mathematics learning (Brownell et al., 2010).

Note

Items in the references list marked ** are studies and program descriptions included in the review

References

**Alexander, M., Lignugaris/Kraft, B., & Forbush, D. (2007). Online mathematics methods course evaluation: Student outcomes, generalization, and pupil performance. *Teacher Education and Special Education, 30*, 199–216. doi:10.1177/088840640703000401

**Babbitt, B. C., & Van Vactor, J. C. (1993). A case study of mathematics learning disability in a prospective teacher. *Focus on Learning Problems in Mathematics, 15*(1), 23–37.

Browder, D., Spooner, F., Ahlgrim-Delzell, L., Harris, A. A., & Wakeman, S. (2008). A meta-analysis on teaching mathematics to students with significant cognitive disabilities. *Exceptional Children, 74*, 407–432.

Brownell, M. T., Sindelar, P. T., Kiely, M. T., & Danielson, L. C. (2010). Special education teacher quality and preparation: Exposing foundations, constructing a new model. *Exceptional Children, 76*, 357–377.

**Carpenter, R. L. (1985). Mathematics instruction in resource rooms: Instruction time and teacher competence. *Learning Disability Quarterly, 8*, 95–100. doi:10.2307/1510411

Carpenter, T. P., Fennema, E. Franke, Levi, M. L., & Empson, S. B. (1999). *Children's mathematics: Cognitively guided instruction*. Portsmouth, NH: Heinemann.

Cawley, J. F., Parmar, R. S., & Smith, M. A. (1995). An analysis of the performance of students with mild disabilities on KEY-MATH and KEYMATH-R. Unpublished manuscript, State University of New York at Buffalo.

Council for Exceptional Children. (2008). *What every special educator must know: Ethics, standards, and guidelines* (6th ed.). Arlington, VA: Author.

Council for Exceptional Children. (2010, May). Common core standards: What special educators need to know. *CEC Today*. Retrieved from http://www.broward.k12.fl.us/studentsupport/ese/PDF/CCSS-WhatSPED-ShouldKnow.pdf

**Dieker, L. A., Lane, H. B., Allsopp, D. H., O'Brien, C., Wright Butler, T., Kyger, M., ... & Fenty, N. S. (2009). Evaluating video models of evidence-based instructional practices to enhance teacher learning. *Teacher Education and Special Education, 32*, 180–196. doi:10.1177/0888406409334202

**Feng, L., & Sass. T. R. (2010). *What makes special-education teachers special? Teacher training and achievement of students with disabilities* (Working Paper No. 49). Washington DC: National Center for Analysis of Longitudinal Data in Education Research. Retrieved from http://www.urban.org/publications/1001435.html

**Fitzmaurice, A. M. (1980). LD teachers' self-ratings on mathematics education competencies. *Learning Disability Quarterly, 3*(2), 90–94. doi:10.2307/1510513

Fuchs, D., Fuchs, L. S., & Stecker, P. M. (2010). The "blurring" of special education in a new continuum of general education placements and services. *Exceptional Children, 76*, 301–323.

Fuchs, L. S., Fuchs, D., Compton, D. L., Powell, S. R., Seethaler, P. M., Capizzi, A. M., ... & Fletcher, J. M. (2006). The cognitive correlates of third-grade skill in arithmetic, algorithmic computation, and arithmetic word problems. *Journal of Educational Psychology, 98*, 29–43. doi:10.1037/0022-0663.98.1.29

**Gagnon, J. C., & Maccini, P. (2007). Teacher-reported use of empirically validated and standards-based instructional approaches in secondary mathematics. *Remedial and Special Education, 28*, 43–56. doi:10.1177/07419325070280010501

Geary, D. C. (2004). Mathematics and learning disabilities. *Journal of Learning Disabilities, 37*, 4–15. doi:10.1177/00222194040370010201

**Gerretson, H., & Alvarez McHatton, P. (2009). Learning to teach school mathematics: Perceptions of special education teachers. *Action in Teacher Education, 31*, 28–40. doi:10.1080/01626620.2009.10463526

Gersten, R., Chard, D. J., Jayanthi, M., Baker, S. K., Morphy, P., & Flojo, J. (2009). Mathematics instruction for students with learning disabilities: A meta-analysis of instructional components. *Review of Educational Research, 79*, 1202–1242. doi:10.3102/0034654309334431

Gersten, R., Clarke, B., & Mazzocco, M. M. (2007). Historical and contemporary perspectives on mathematical learning disabilities. In D. B. Berch & M. M. Mazzocco (Eds.), *Why is math so hard for some children? The nature and origins of mathematical learning difficulties and disabilities*. Baltimore, MD: Brookes.

**Glidden, P. L. (2008). Prospective elementary teachers' understanding of order of operations. *School Science and Mathematics, 108*, 130–136. doi:10.1111/j.1949-8594.2008.tb17819.x

Graves, A., Landers, M. F., Lokerson, J., Luchow, J., & Horvath, M. (1993). The development of a competency list for teachers of students with learning disabilities. *Learning Disabilities Research & Practice, 8*, 188–199.

**Greer, D. L., & Meyen, E. L. (2009). Special education teacher education: A perspective on content knowledge. *Learning Disabilities Research and Practice, 24*, 196–203. doi:1540-5826.2009.00293.x

**Griffin, C. C., Jitendra, A. K., & League, M. B. (2009). Novice special educators' instructional practices, communication patterns, and content knowledge for teaching mathematics. *Teacher Education and Special Education, 32*, 319–336. doi:10.1177/0888406409343540

Halverson, R., Wolfenstein, M., Williams, C. C., & Rockman, C. (2009). Remembering math: The design of digital learning objects to spark professional learning. *E-Learning and Digital Media, 6*(1), 97–118. doi:10.2304/elea.2009.6.1.97

Hassan, E. (2006). Recall bias can be a threat to retrospective and prospective research designs. *The Internet Journal of Epidemiology, 3*, 339–412. doi:10.5580/2732

Hill, H. C., Rowan, B., & Ball, D. L. (2005). Effects of teachers' mathematical knowledge for teaching on student achievement. *American Educational Research Journal, 42*, 371–406. doi:10.3102/00028312042002371

**Humphrey, M., & Hourcade, J. J. (2010). Special educators and mathematics phobia: An initial qualitative investigation. *The Clearing House, 83*, 26–30. doi:10.1080/00098650903267743

Individuals With Disabilities Education Improvement Act of 2004, Pub. L. No. 108-446 (2004).

Judge, S., & Simms, K. A. (2009). Assistive technology training at the pre-service level: A national snapshot of teacher preparation programs. *Teacher Education and Special Education, 32*, 33–44. doi:10.1177/0888406408330868

Kelly, R. R., Lang, H. G., & Pagliaro, C. M. (2003). Mathematics word problem solving for deaf students: A survey of practices in grade 6–12. *Journal of Deaf Studies and Deaf Education, 8*, 104–119. doi:10.1093/deafed/eng007

Kloo, A., & Zigmond, N. (2008). Coteaching revisited: Redrawing the blueprint. *Preventing School Failure, 52*, 12–20. doi:10.3200/PSFL.52.2.12-20

Koency, G., & Swanson, H. L. (2000, April). *The special case of mathematics: Insufficient content knowledge a major obstacle to reform*. Paper presented at the annual meeting of the American Educational Research Association, New Orleans, LA. (ERIC Document Reproduction Service No. ED444943).

Kroesbergen, E. H., & Van Luit, J. E. H. (2003). Mathematics interventions for children with special needs: A meta-analysis. *Remedial and Special Education, 24*, 97–114. doi:10.1177/07419325030240020501

**Maccini, P., & Gagnon, J. C. (2002). Perceptions and application of NCTM standards by special and general education teachers. *Exceptional Children, 68*, 325–344.

**Maccini, P., & Gagnon, J. G. (2006). Mathematics instructional practices and assessment accommodations by secondary special and general educators. *Exceptional Children, 72*, 217–234.

Mastropieri, M. A., Scruggs, T. E., & Shiah, S. (1991). Mathematics instruction for learning disabled students: A review of research. *Learning Disabilities Research and Practice, 6*, 89–98.

**Meyen, E., & Greer, D. (2009). The role of instructional planning in math instruction for students with learning disabilities. *Focus on Exceptional Children, 41*(5), 1–12.

Michaels, C. A., & McDermott, J. (2003). Assistive technology integration in special education teacher preparation: Program coordinators' perceptions of current attainment and importance. *Journal of Special Education Technology, 18*(3), 29–41.

Miller, S. P., Butler, F. M., & Lee, K. (1998). Validated practices for teaching mathematics to students with learning disabilities: A review of literature. *Focus on Exceptional Children, 31*(1), 1–24.

Montague, M., & Jitendra, A. K. (2012). Research-based mathematics instruction for students with learning disabilities. In H. Forgasz and R. Rivera (Eds.), *Towards equity in mathematics education: Gender, culture, and diversity* (pp. 481–502). New York, NY: Springer.

National Center for Education Statistics (2011). *The Nation's Report Card: Mathematics 2011* (NCES 2012-458). National Center for Education Statistics, Institute of Education Sciences. Washington, DC: U.S. Department of Education.

National Council of Teachers of Mathematics. (1991). *The curriculum and evaluation standards for school mathematics*. Reston, VA: NCTM.

National Council of Teachers of Mathematics. (2000). *Principles and standards for school mathematics*. Reston, VA: NCTM.

National Council of Teachers of Mathematics. (2006). *Curriculum focal points for prekindergarten through grade 8 mathematics: A quest for coherence*. Reston, VA: NCTM.

National Governors Association Center for Best Practices, Council of Chief State School Officers. (2010). *Common Core State Standards*. Washington, DC: National Governors Association Center for Best Practices, Council of Chief State School Officers.

National Mathematics Advisory Panel. (2008). *Foundations for success: The final report of the National Mathematics Advisory Panel*. Washington, DC: U.S. Department of Education.

National Research Council. (2001). Adding it up: Helping children learn mathematics. In J. Kilpatrick, J. Swafford, & B. Findell (Eds.), *Mathematics Learning Study Committee, Center for Education, Division of Behavioral and Social Sciences and Education*. Washington, DC: National Academy Press.

No Child Left Behind Act of 2001, Pub. L. No. 107-110 (2002).

**Pagliaro, C. M. (1998). Mathematics preparation and professional development of deaf education teachers, *American Annals of the Deaf, 143*, 373–379. doi:10.1353/aad.2012.0137

**Pagliaro, C. M., & Kritzer, K. L. (2005). Discrete mathematics in deaf education: A survey of teachers' knowledge and use. *American Annals of the Deaf, 150*, 251–259. doi:10.1353/aad.2005.0033

Parmar, R. S., & Cawley, J. F. (1997). Preparing teachers to teach mathematics to students with learning disabilities. *Journal of Learning Disabilities, 30*, 188–197. doi:10.1177/002221949703000206

**Paulsen, K. J. (2005). Infusing evidence-based practices into the special education preparation curriculum. *Teacher Education and Special Education, 28*, 21–28. doi:10.1177/088840640502800103

**Rosas, C., & Campbell, L. (2010). Who's teaching math to our most needy students? A descriptive study. *Teacher Education and Special Education, 33*, 102–113. doi:10.1177 0888406409357537

Schiller, E., Sanford, C., & Blackorby, J. (2008). *A national profile of the classroom experiences and academic performance of students with LD: A special topic report from the Special Education Elementary Longitudinal Study*. Menlo Park, CA: SRI International. Retrieved from http://www.seels.net/seels_textonly/info_reports/national_profile_students_learning_disabilities_txt.htm

Seo, Y., & Bryant, D. (2009). Analysis of studies of the effects of computer-assisted instruction on the mathematics performance of students with learning disabilities. *Computers and Education, 53*, 913–928. doi:10.1016/j.compedu.2009.05.002

Siegler, R. S. (2005). Children's learning. *American Psychologist, 60*, 769–778. doi:10.1037/0003-066X.60.8.769

Swanson, E., Solis, M., Ciullo, S., & McKenna, J. W. (2012). Special education teachers' perceptions and instructional practices in response to intervention implementation. *Learning Disability Quarterly, 35*, 115–126.

Swanson, H. L., Hoskyn, M., & Lee, C. (1999). *Interventions for students with learning disabilities: A meta-analysis of treatment outcomes*. New York, NY: Guilford Press.

Swanson, H. L., & Jerman, O. (2006). Math disabilities: A selective meta-analysis of the literature. *Review of Educational Research, 76*, 249–274. doi:10.3102/00346543076002249

Swanson, H. L., & Sáez, L. (2003). Memory difficulties in children and adults with learning disabilities. In H. L. Swanson, S. Graham, & K. R. Harris (Eds.), *Handbook of learning disabilities* (pp. 182–198). New York, NY: Guildford Press.

**Thibodeau, G. P., & Cebelius, L. S. (1987). Self perceptions of special educators toward teaching mathematics. *School Science and Mathematics, 87*, 136–143. doi:10.1111/j.1949-8594.1987.tb11685.x

van Garderen, D. (2008). Middle school special education teachers' instructional practices for solving mathematical word problems: An exploratory study. *Teacher Education and Special Education, 31*, 132–144. doi:10.1177/088840640803100206

van Garderen, D., Scheuermann, A., Jackson, C., & Hampton, D. (2009). Supporting collaboration between general educators and special educators to teach students who struggle with mathematics: A review of recent empirical literature. *Psychology in the Schools, 46*, 56–77. doi:10.1002/pits.20354

Wayne, A. M., & Youngs, P. (2003). Teacher characteristics and student achievement gains: A review. *Review of Education Research, 73*, 89–122. doi:10.3102/00346543073001089

17

Special Education Teacher Preparation in Classroom Organization and Behavior Management

Regina M. Oliver
UNIVERSITY OF NEBRASKA—LINCOLN

Daniel J. Reschly
VANDERBILT UNIVERSITY

Things to Think About

- How do we define classroom organization and behavior management?
- What are the core components of classroom organization and behavior management?
- What is the most effective way to increase teacher competencies in classroom organization and behavior management?
- How can teacher preparation programs provide not only classroom management theory and content but supervised field experience in applying those skills?
- How can teacher preparation programs evaluate course syllabi to determine the extent to which critical components of classroom organization and behavior management are taught?

There may be no greater need and challenge in the area of teacher preparation than developing pre-service and in-service teachers' competencies with establishing and executing proactive classroom management plans; plans that not only meet the behavioral needs of all students but also enhance teacher opportunities to teach and student opportunities to learn from effective instruction. Teacher competencies in classroom organization and behavior management have far-reaching effects for student social, emotional, and academic outcomes (Freiberg, Connell, & Lorentz, 2001; Kellam, Rebok, Ialongo, & Mayer, 1994; Leflot, van Lier, Onghena, & Colpin, 2010; van Lier, Vuijk, & Crijnen, 2005). Moreover, a lack of effective classroom management competencies has a deleterious effect on teacher stress and burnout (Brouwers & Tomic, 2000), teacher retention (Coggshall, 2006; Ingersoll & Smith, 2003), and inclusive practices for students with challenging behavior (Baker, 2005). Targeting improvement in teacher preparation programs to better prepare special and general education teachers' ability to effectively manage the classroom can affect a wide range of educational issues faced in schools.

The purpose of this chapter is to provide a review of the research on classroom organization and behavior management and identify core components pertinent to the preparation of preservice and in-service special education teachers. This will lead to a review of the research on teacher preparation in classroom organization and behavior management where gaps in teacher preparation will be identified. Based on these gaps in teacher preparation, we conclude the chapter with recommendations for improving teacher preparation and professional development. The Things to Think About are provided to guide the reader's process for thinking about barriers and solutions to the preparation of special education teachers in the area of classroom organization and behavior management.

Defining Classroom Management

Classroom management has taken on various meanings and definitions over the years, typically based on the current trends in ideology and theory at the time. Early definitions of classroom management focused on classroom control mirroring the common thinking at the time that the role of the teacher was to maintain control and order. More recent definitions have become much broader, encompassing multiple aspects of the complex nature of teaching. Evertson and Weinstein (2006) define classroom management as "the actions teachers take to create an environment that supports and facilitates both academic and social-emotional learning" (p. 4). While we acknowledge the critical role effective instruction plays in supporting and maintaining an environment that supports students' academic and behavioral learning, we are restricting our definition of classroom management to "a collection of nonacademic instructional classroom procedures implemented by teachers in classroom settings with all students for the purposes of teaching prosocial behavior as well as preventing and reducing inappropriate behavior" (Oliver, Wehby, & Reschly, 2011, p. 7). This definition is the basis for our review of the literature on the principles of effective classroom organization and behavior management.

Components of Effective Classroom Organization and Behavior Management

An extensive research base exists for individual classroom management practices used to modify student behavior; however, research on classroom management as a comprehensive system is less defined (Oliver et al., 2011). Observations of teachers identified as effective were the impetus for much of the early work in classroom management. Classroom management practices were deemed important or effective when teachers who were successful at improving student academic outcomes used them (Anderson & Evertson, 1978). Other early research in classroom management examined teachers' attitudes and concerns about classroom control and described leadership and management styles of teachers deemed better classroom managers (e.g., Kounin, 1970; Ryans, 1952). Behavioral theory and experimental research prominent in the 1960s and 1970s prompted applied experimentation in educational settings. Specific behavior change procedures emerged as researchers began identifying effective classroom management practices (e.g., Hall, Panyan, Rabon, & Broden, 1968; Strain, Lambert, Kerr, Stagg, & Lenkner, 1983). Subsequently researchers explored the use of multiple behavior strategies in combination as part of managing classrooms (e.g., Madsen, Becker, & Thomas, 1968; Musser, Bray, Kehle, & Jenson, 2001). The importance of student–teacher interactions that prompt appropriate behavior and reduce inappropriate behavior became a focus of later research (e.g., Anderson, Evertson, & Emmer, 1979; Shores, Jack et al., 1993). These and other examples have contributed to an extant research base of various classroom management practices.

The expansiveness of research on classroom management has prompted researchers to conduct literature reviews and systematic evaluations in an effort to determine which classroom management practices have sufficient evidence to make recommendations for their adoption and use in classroom management plans. In a meta-analysis, Oliver and colleagues (2011) found statistically significant reductions in inappropriate behavior when universal classroom management programs were implemented (e.g., Classroom Organization and Management Program—Evertson, 1988). Mean student-level effect sizes of .18 and .22 were found for classrooms using highly structured classroom management programs (e.g., The Good Behavior Game—Barrish, Saunders, & Wolf, 1969; Classroom Organization and Management Program—Evertson, 1988) compared to classrooms using typical classroom management procedures (i.e., classroom management as usual). These effect sizes indicate significant practical results for teachers because teachers who use effective classroom management procedures can expect to see significant reductions in inappropriate student behavior above and beyond what typical classroom management practices produce. Unfortunately, the authors were unable to determine which components of classroom management were more or less effective due to the low number of studies available for the analysis (Oliver et al., 2011).

Emmer and Stough (2001), in a review of the literature, identified several effective classroom management practices including: (a) structuring the physical environment to accommodate traffic patterns and minimize distractions as well as structuring instructional time and transitions; (b) establishing a few positively stated behavioral expectations; (c) identifying rules that provide behavioral examples of the expectations; (d) establishing routines for classroom tasks such as turning in homework; (e) actively teaching the rules and routines; (f) establishing procedures to reinforce appropriate behavior; (g) utilizing effective procedures to reduce and respond to inappropriate behavior; and (h) collecting data to monitor student behavior and modify the classroom management plan as needed. In addition to identifying these effective classroom management practices, Emmer and Stough suggest that effectively managed classrooms focus on prevention rather than reactive approaches. Moreover, teachers explicitly teach students desirable behaviors rather than expecting these behaviors to occur naturally.

Other researchers have found similar findings to Emmer and Stough (2001). In a more recent best-evidence review Simonsen and colleagues identified five broad areas important to effective classroom management (Simonsen, Fairbanks, Briesch, Myers, & Sugai, 2008). Out of the 81 studies identified, there were 20 general practices that met researchers' criteria for evidence-based. These 20 general practices fell into five broad categories: (a) maximize structure and predictability; (b) post, teach, review, and provide feedback on expectations; (c) actively engage students in observable ways; (d) use a continuum of strategies to acknowledge appropriate behavior; and (e) use a continuum of strategies to respond to inappropriate behavior (Simonsen et al., 2008). A range of two to six practices were classified under each broad category and the empirical studies supporting each practice ranged from three to eight studies per practice. This review synthesized and reported the empirical support of classroom management practices falling into each of these five broad categories.

Common categories or themes of classroom management competencies can be found in other reviews of the literature as well. In a What Works Clearing House Practice Guide, panel members reviewed the research on prevention and intervention strategies to promote appropriate student classroom behavior in elementary classrooms, made recommendations for practice, and indicated the quality of the evidence supporting each recommendation (Epstein, Atkins, Cullinan, Kutash, & Weaver, 2008). The first recommendation is that teachers need to understand why problem behavior is occurring through careful observations and develop interventions that are tied to the conditions that prompt and reinforce problem behavior within the classroom context. The second recommendation to decrease problem behavior is that teachers should adjust and structure classroom environments by carefully arranging physical classroom space, and developing schedules and learning activities that promote student engagement. Not surprisingly, in the third recommendation Epstein and colleagues indicated that teachers should teach and reinforce new skills or behaviors that replace inappropriate behaviors. Fourth, teachers should consult with colleagues and families for guidance and support and finally school-wide strategies should be used to prevent problem behavior and increase positive interactions among students and staff. The moderate to strong research evidence supporting each recommendation further underscores the value of core components of effective classroom management.

Finally, research on teacher preparation in classroom management has also provided insight into the common elements or components of effective classroom management. Gilberts and Lignugaris-Kraft (1997) reviewed the literature to identify the classroom management and instructional competencies expected of elementary and special education teachers. While the authors found differences between what was expected of each, the required competencies across teachers were categorized into four broad categories:

> (a) arrangement of the physical environment to facilitate student management; (b) formulation of a standard for student behavior in the classroom; (c) implementation of strategies to increase appropriate behavior or to reduce inappropriate behavior; and finally (d) assessing or measuring the effectiveness of the implemented strategies.
>
> *(Gilberts & Lignugaris-Kraft, 1997, p. 598)*

Although the language may be different, the features of each are representative of previous reviews.

Table 17.1 Critical Components of Classroom Organization and Behavior Management

Component	*Key Features*
Structured Environment	• Daily schedule is posted and designed to maximize student engagement. • Environment is arranged for ease of flow of traffic and distractions minimized.
Active Supervision and Student Engagement	• Teacher scans, moves in unpredictable ways, and monitors student behavior. • Teacher uses more positive to negative teacher–student interactions. • Teacher provides high rates of opportunities for students to respond. • Teacher utilizes multiple observable ways to engage students (e.g., response cards, peer tutoring).
Classroom Rules and Routines	• A few, positively stated behavioral rules linked to school-wide expectations. • Posted, systematically taught, reinforced, and monitored. • Classroom routines are systematically taught, reinforced and monitored within the context of the classroom (e.g., turning in homework, requesting assistance).
Increasing Appropriate Behavior	• Procedures to acknowledge appropriate behavior at the group level (e.g., specific, contingent praise, tokens, activities, group contingencies, "Good Behavior Game"). • Procedures to encourage appropriate behavior at the individual student level (e.g., specific, contingent praise, behavior contracts). • Data collection on frequency of appropriate behavior within classroom environment.
Decreasing Inappropriate Behavior	• Antecedent strategies to prevent inappropriate behavior (e.g., precorrection, prompts, environmental arrangements). • Multiple procedures to respond to inappropriate behavior. • Procedures to teach replacement behaviors and to reteach appropriate behavior (e.g., overcorrection). • Differential reinforcement (e.g., reinforcing other, competing behaviors) effective use of consequences (e.g., planned ignoring, time-out from positive reinforcement, reinforcing around target student).
School-Wide Behavioral Expectations	• A few, positively stated behavioral expectations, posted, systematically taught, reinforced, and monitored within a school-wide system of support.

Source: Adapted from Oliver & Reschly, 2007.

Based on these reviews and our search of the empirical research associated with classroom management we identified several principles of effective classroom organization and behavior management. Each principle, while important in and of itself, is part of a more comprehensive, and effective, approach to classroom management. Although researchers have not fully answered the question of which components are more or less effective within a comprehensive classroom management plan (Oliver et al., 2011), it is our recommendation that teacher preparation programs present these principles together as a packaged approach to classroom management, rather than scattered throughout coursework as is more typical of teacher preparation programs (Oliver & Reschly, 2010). These components might then be briefly reviewed in methods classes to illustrate how the principles might be integrated into various instructional contexts. The components outlined in Table 17.1 were the basis for the current review of special education teacher preparation (Oliver & Reschly, 2010) and are what is detailed in the next part of this chapter.

Structured Environment

The first critical element of effective classroom organization and behavior management is structuring the classroom environment to prompt appropriate student behavior and reduce the occurrence of inappropriate student behavior. Structuring the environment can be defined as the arrangement of furniture to facilitate the ease of traffic and teacher access to students, scheduling instructional activities to maximize student engagement and learning, and reducing transition time. Structuring a classroom so that it supports positive student behavior requires forethought and planning (Paine, Radicci, Rosellini, Deutchman, & Darch, 1983). The value of structuring the classroom environment should not be underestimated although it appears intuitively simple. Highly effective teachers structure the classroom environment to proactively decrease inappropriate behavior and increase desirable student interactions (Emmer & Stough, 2001). Teachers should receive adequate preparation in the various approaches to structuring the classroom environment not only as a means to organize the classroom setting and the flow of the day, but as a tool to set students up for success.

Organizing classroom space is necessary for ease of traffic flow, minimizing distractions, and providing the teacher access to students for questions and proximity control. The physical arrangement of the classroom should be flexible and based on the type of instructional task while addressing visibility, accessibility, and distractibility (Evertson & Neal, 2005; Sprick, Garrison, & Howard, 1998). Visibility refers to whether students are able to adequately see instruction and whether the teacher is able to see students in order to monitor their behavior. Similarly, accessibility refers to student access to materials and teacher access to students such as being responsive to student questions and using proximity control to help students maintain attention to task. The physical arrangement of the classroom is also important to reduce student distractions (e.g., windows, computers, other students). Structuring the environment, however, goes beyond structuring the physical space. Structure also involves managing instructional time, transitioning from various activities, and clearly communicating behaviors that are appropriate for particular classroom activities (Paine et al., 1983; Sprick et al., 1998). For example, students may be expected to interact with one another during cooperative learning activities, but not during independent seatwork activities. Teachers need to clearly communicate these expectations ahead of time and carefully monitor student behavior.

Active Supervision and Student Engagement

Beyond structuring the classroom environment teachers need to actively supervise, monitor student behavior, and provide frequent opportunities for students to respond to academic tasks to ensure that students are engaged in appropriate tasks. Active supervision and student engagement are actions performed by the teacher to monitor student behavior and maximize the amount of time students spend on-task. Monitoring student behavior during instructional and noninstructional times is important to prevent minor misbehavior from escalating. It requires active supervision by the teacher such as scanning and moving around the room in unpredictable patterns (Colvin, Sugai, Good, & Lee, 1997; De Pry & Sugai, 2002). Effective classroom managers are aware of everything happening in the environment and react quickly and efficiently to prevent behaviors from escalating through prompting and redirection (Kounin, 1970). Similarly, the use of precorrection (correcting the behavior before it happens) is an effective strategy to prevent problem behaviors that have previously been a concern under certain circumstances or settings from occurring (Colvin et al., 1997). The teacher provides a prompt indicating the behavioral expectations just prior to the transition or circumstance identified as problematic.

Keeping students academically engaged and on-task is not only effective teaching, but a preventive strategy to reduce disruptive behavior in the classroom. It is recommended that at least 80% of students should be on-task and engaged at any point during instructional times (Carnine, 1976; Coyne, Kame'enui, & Carnine, 2007). Active engagement in academic tasks is incompatible with disruptive behavior, that is, students who are actively engaged cannot at the same time be disruptive. When students are provided high rates of opportunities to respond to academic tasks, they are less disruptive and perform better on academic tasks (Sutherland & Wehby, 2001). Response cards, choral responding, and peer tutoring are all examples of ways to increase opportunities to respond to academic tasks (Christle & Schuster, 2003; Greenwood, Delquadri, & Hall, 1989; Lambert, Cartledge, Heward, & Yo, 2006).

Classroom Rules and Routines

The importance of clear and consistent classroom rules and routines as part of the primary classroom management system cannot be overstated. Classroom rules and routines are defined as the identified standards for student behavior in the classroom and for particular activities. Rules establish the teacher's expectations for appropriate behavior in the classroom and routines provide students with a clear and consistent process for handling classroom activities such as turning in homework, using the restroom, working in small groups, or asking for assistance (Sprick et al., 1998). Ineffective teachers do not have clearly identified classroom rules and routines and therefore tend to spend more time addressing inappropriate behavior and student questions regarding classroom procedures (Cameron, Connor, & Morrison, 2005). Transition time between activities or locations is also higher when teachers do not have established rules and routines and increases in inappropriate behavior are common (Fudge et al., 2008). Establishing classroom rules and routines is foundational to an effective classroom and behavior management plan as these elements provide students the roadmap to being successful in the classroom and increase opportunities for learning to occur.

Identifying classroom rules and routines alone are ineffective unless they are explicitly taught to students. Proactively teaching classroom rules in the actual setting with frequent opportunities to practice the skills, and reinforcement for skill attainment significantly reduces inappropriate behavior in the classroom and leads to reduced transition time (Cameron et al., 2005; Langland, Lewis-Palmer, & Sugai, 1998). On-task behavior can be increased during transitions with the use of specific rules and procedures taught prior to those activities and transitions (Fudge et al., 2008). Despite the pivotal role classroom rules and routines play in a well-designed and executed classroom management plan, additional procedures such as the use of behavior-specific praise are necessary to establish and maintain appropriate student behavior while minimizing student behaviors that interfere with learning (Madsen et al., 1968).

Increasing Appropriate Behavior

Arranging consequences to increase desired behavior is a critical component for effective classroom organization and management. Increasing appropriate behavior is defined as the specific procedures and practices teachers use to target prosocial behaviors and increase student use of appropriate classroom behavior. The use of behavioral procedures such as specific and contingent praise, differential reinforcement, token economies, and group contingencies are well-documented strategies to increase behavior (Alberto & Troutman, 2009; Conyers et al., 2004; Landrum & Kauffman, 2006; Mayer, Sulzer-Azaroff, & Wallace, 2011; Stage & Quiroz, 1997). Behavior-specific praise in particular is a powerful strategy teachers can use to increase desired behaviors. Behavior-specific praise is praise that specifies the particular behavior being reinforced (Sutherland, Wehby, & Copeland, 2000). Observations in classrooms with students identified with learning disabilities or emotional/behavioral disorders indicate behavior-specific praise is rarely used or at very low rates (Gable, Hendrickson, Young, Shores, & Stowitscek, 1983; Shores, Jack et al., 1993). Fortunately teachers can use a number of self-monitoring strategies to increase their use of behavior-specific praise. These include audio recording classroom instruction, graphing rates of behavior-specific praise, and setting goals for increased use of behavior-specific praise (Sutherland & Wehby, 2001). When behavior-specific praise is used appropriately, teachers are likely to see decreases in disruptive student behavior and increases in appropriate behavior such as student time on-task (Sutherland et al., 2000; Sutherland & Wehby, 2001).

Decreasing Inappropriate Behavior

Decreasing inappropriate classroom behavior is often a high priority for teachers. Decreasing inappropriate behavior is defined as the specific procedures and practices teachers use to reduce the reinforcing value of inappropriate behavior and increase the use of appropriate behavior. A concept that is central to arranging consequences that decrease inappropriate behavior is that teacher-selected consequences that are intended to stop or reduce negative behavior may or may not produce the desired outcomes. If over time targeted negative behaviors do not decrease or stop, then the consequences are not effective and may even be inadvertently reinforcing the inappropriate behavior (Cooper, Heron, & Heward, 2007). It is not uncommon for educators to engage in a cycle in which removal of the student from the classroom has positive effects for both the teacher and the student (Shores, Gunter, & Jack, 1993). By sending the student to the office, the teacher's behavior is reinforced with the removal of the disruptive student. At the same time the student's disruptive behavior is reinforced with removal of the aversive task (i.e., instruction). Research by Patterson and colleagues on the *coercive interactive process* or *negative reinforcement trap* suggests in the future, the student will be more likely to escalate his or her behavior in order to be sent to the office and the teacher will be more likely to react by sending the student to the office (Patterson, Reid, & Dishion, 1992; Sidman, 2001). Changing the consequences of classroom behavior that interfere with learning and stopping the negative reinforcement trap requires teachers to have knowledge and skills in the use of multiple strategies to reinforce, teach, and prompt appropriate behavior while reducing inappropriate behavior.

Strategies that target groups of students are an efficient approach to increasing appropriate behavior and decreasing inappropriate behavior as part of a comprehensive classroom management plan. In this way, teachers maximize support provided to students while at the same time minimizing the effort necessary to carry out the interventions (Litow & Pumroy, 1975; Skinner, Skinner, & Sterling-Turner, 2002). Group contingencies are highly effective to reduce disruptive behaviors and increase on-task or academic behaviors (Stage & Quiroz, 1997). Group contingencies are behavioral techniques in which contingent reinforcement is applied to groups of students based on the behavior of one or more members of the group (Litow & Pumroy, 1975). The "Good Behavior Game" from the original work of Barrish, Saunders, and Wolf (1969) is well documented in longitudinal randomized control studies as an evidence-based universal classroom management practice to prevent aggressive, disruptive behaviors particularly for children at-risk for later aggression and conduct problems (Bradshaw, Zmuda, Kellam, & Ialongo, 2009; Kellam, Ling Merisca, Brown, & Ialongo, 1998; van Lier, Muthén, van der Sar, & Crijnen, 2004). Other effective strategies to reduce inappropriate behavior include differential reinforcement, response cost, and time out from reinforcement (Conyers et al., 2004; Simonsen et al., 2008; Wright-Gallo, Higbee, Reagon, & Davey, 2006).

School-Wide Positive Behavior Interventions and Support

Classroom organization and behavior management can be more effective when it is embedded within a highly efficient school-wide system of behavior support. School-wide positive behavior interventions and support can be defined as a systematic continuum of procedures to proactively address the needs of all students through the integration of data to support decision making, systems to support staff behavior, and practices to support student behavior (Lewis & Sugai, 1999). Classrooms are not isolated entities but rather microsystems situated within the greater context of schools. The school environment greatly influences student behavior and teachers' ability to establish and maintain well-managed classrooms that support student academics and social behavior (Epstein et al., 2008). As such, it is important for preservice and in-service teachers to have a greater understanding of school-wide behavioral systems and how they may or may not support student behavior in the classroom. A brief overview of school-wide positive behavior interventions and support (SW-PBIS) follows within the context of this chapter; however, Lewis and Newman Thomas (Chapter 22, this volume) provide a more comprehensive treatment of this topic.

The pivotal purpose of school-wide behavioral systems is to prevent and reduce the occurrence of behavioral incidences across the school by creating environments that are predictable, consistent, positive, and engaging (Lewis & Sugai, 1999). Inherent to achieving these outcomes is an instructional approach to behavior. An instructional approach to behavior is adopted when adults in the school proactively teach prosocial behaviors, provide opportunities to practice them in the natural environment, and reinforce their occurrence (Colvin, Sugai, & Patching, 1993). Misbehavior is viewed as a behavioral error that requires reteaching rather than a deliberate attempt to undermine adult authority that requires some form of negative consequence intended to punish behavior. The effect on the school environment can be powerful; however, this does not occur by chance (Sugai & Horner, 2006). Schools that establish school-wide positive behavior interventions and support do the following:

1. Identify three to five positively stated behavioral expectations that apply to all students and staff in all settings (e.g., be respectful).
2. Identify behavioral examples for each expectation that replace inappropriate behavior (e.g., keep hallways clean; use polite language).
3. Teach and practice the expectations at the beginning of the school year and then periodically throughout the year (e.g., before or after school breaks).
4. Use effective procedures that encourage and reinforce prosocial behavior (e.g., specific, contingent praise; token economy).
5. Use evidence-based practices to discourage and reduce inappropriate behavior (e.g., precorrection; differential reinforcement; time out from positive reinforcement).
6. Monitor the effectiveness of the school-wide plan using data.

Schools that establish effective school-wide systems of behavioral support report improvements in important outcomes such as reductions in office referrals, suspensions, and absenteeism (Horner, Sugai, Todd, & Lewis-Palmer, 2005; Nelson, Martella, & Marchand-Martella, 2002; Taylor-Greene et al., 1997). When schools create the infrastructure to support student behavior and thereby reduce school-wide behavior concerns, teachers' classroom management is also supported. Well-designed and executed classroom management plans that are aligned with the school's system of positive behavior support can be more successful when the school-wide approach has reduced overall levels of inappropriate behavior and established systems to support teacher behavior (Sugai & Horner, 2006). Despite the importance of school-wide approaches to behavior, it is neither a focus of teacher preparation programs (Oliver & Reschly, 2010) nor state teacher certification requirements (Doolittle, Horner, Bradley, Sugai, & Vincent, 2007).

Preservice and In-Service Teacher Preparation

Preservice and in-service teachers alike indicate a high degree of concern with their ability to manage student behavior (Adams & Krockover, 1997; Meister & Melnik, 2003; Mergler & Tangen, 2010; Siebert, 2005) and issues with classroom management are one of the most frequently cited reasons for requesting assistance (Hertzog, 2002). Preservice teacher preparation programs play a critical role in preparing teachers to establish effective and well-managed classroom environments while supporting students with challenging behavior (Alvarez, 2007). When preservice teachers are asked their perceptions on how prepared they are to effectively manage the classroom environment, teachers typically feel unprepared and receive little specific instruction in classroom management (Baker, 2005; Siebert, 2005). The course work that is provided on classroom management in teacher preparation programs tends to be too theoretical or broad, and inadequate to prepare teachers to handle significant antisocial behavior (Siebert, 2005). In addition to feeling inadequately prepared, preservice teachers attribute only 41% of the influence of effective classroom management to the teacher and experienced teachers attribute only 49% of the influence of successfully managed classrooms to themselves (Long & Biggs, 1999). If teachers feel that they are inadequately prepared and have low self-efficacy regarding classroom management, it may contribute to their perceptions that they do not have a high level of influence on the success of classroom management and provide little motivation to change ineffective management strategies.

Students who are at-risk or participate in special education are disproportionately affected by teachers' inability to effectively manage the classroom environment. A national longitudinal survey regarding the education of students with emotional disturbance indicates a lack of teacher preparation to handle the challenges of this population (Wagner, Kutash, Duchnowski, Epstein, & Sumi, 2006). Of the national sample of students with emotional and behavior disorders, only one fourth to one third had teachers that reported receiving at least 8 hours of in-service training on topics regarding students with disabilities. Of the teachers in the sample only 22.9% of elementary, 30% of middle, and 13.1% of high school teachers "strongly agreed" they had adequate training to manage challenging student behavior (Wagner et al., 2006). In addition, when teachers feel unprepared to handle classroom management challenges, they are also less willing to implement individualized behavior support plans and reinforcement strategies, vary reinforcement schedules, or document student progress for systematic evaluation (Baker, 2005). This has implications for inclusive practices and teachers' ability to meet the legal mandates of IDEA to address the academic and behavioral needs of all students.

Another indication of the lack of teacher preparation in classroom and behavior management is research reviewing course syllabi at institutes of higher education (IHE) that prepare teachers. Although imperfect indices, course syllabi provide an indication of content taught during teacher preparation and what is prioritized. Our review of course syllabi from 26 universities suggests teachers' reports of inadequate preparation are quite founded (Oliver & Reschly, 2010). In this study, we reviewed the course syllabus for each course required for special education teacher licensure at each of the 26 IHEs. Surprisingly, only seven IHEs had a course on classroom management. The other 19 IHEs had classroom management content dispersed throughout multiple courses. When content on classroom management was taught, the focus was on reactive strategies (e.g., behavior reduction strategies) rather than preventive strategies (e.g., classroom rules and routines). In fact, nearly half (42%) of course syllabi did not even mention the topic of establishing classroom rules (Oliver & Reschly, 2010). The notable lack of emphasis on prevention is problematic considering the large body of research attesting to the necessity of preventive strategies to reduce the progression of challenging behavior (Kellam et al., 1998).

Improving Teacher Preparation and Continuing Education

Improving special education teachers' knowledge and competencies in the use of classroom organization and behavior management requires a two-prong approach: (a) address these issues in teacher preparation prior to and during induction, and (b) increase in-service teachers' knowledge and competencies through continuing education and professional development activities. IHEs play a fundamental role in preparing teachers to be highly effective classroom managers (Emmer & Stough, 2001). We cannot afford to assume that beginning teachers will eventually learn how to manage their classroom, and leaving them to learn valuable classroom management skills informally from colleagues—sometimes a useful strategy—is a tenuous gamble at best. Teacher education programs should place greater emphasis on classroom organization and behavior management by providing at least one course on managing the classroom and student behaviors along with supervised field experience in which teachers practice and receive feedback on their use of classroom management skills (Oliver & Reschly, 2007).

One way special education teacher preparation programs can evaluate how well they are preparing their teachers in the area of classroom organization and behavior management is through a critical review of their course syllabi. By using a tool called "The Classroom Organization and Behavior Management Innovation Configuration" (COBM IC—Oliver & Reschly, 2007), IHEs can apply the COBM IC to their course syllabi and determine the degree to which special education teachers are receiving preparation in the area of classroom organization and behavior management. An innovation configuration (or IC Map), similar to a rubric, identifies and describes the major components of a practice or innovation along with the range of possible levels of implementation (Hall & Hord, 2001). IC maps have been most notably used as professional development tools to guide implementation of an innovation within a school and to facilitate the change process but they can also be used for research, assessment, and evaluation. Innovation configurations have been developed and used to evaluate teacher preparation programs in a wide range of areas like reading (Smartt & Reschly, 2007), classroom management (Oliver & Reschly, 2007), inclusive practices (Holdheide & Reschly, 2008), mathematics (McGraner, VanDerHeyden, & Holdheide, 2010), English Language Learners (McGraner & Sanez, 2009), problem-solving competences (Reschly & Wood-Garnett, 2009), learning strategies instruction (Schumaker, 2009), and direct and systematic instruction (Oliver & Reschly, forthcoming). After the COBM IC is used to identify potential areas for improvement in teacher preparation, IHE faculty can ensure that the core content is taught systematically and that preservice teachers have adequate opportunities to practice these skills under careful supervision with feedback.

Another area for improving special education teachers' knowledge and use of effective classroom organization and behavior management is through high quality continuing education and professional development. At the district level, a decision-making team should analyze the current resources in the district and professional development needs of staff members related to behavior and classroom management. Once staff needs in the area of classroom management are identified, the use of high quality professional development methods such as the Teacher Study Group (Gersten, Dimino, Jayanthi, Kim, & Santoro, 2010) can facilitate the transfer of conceptual knowledge and practical application into practice. Partnerships with higher education to develop Professional Development Schools is another recommendation to provide additional training opportunities for both preservice and in-service teachers alike (Emmer & Stough, 2001; Siebert, 2005). Schools might also use prevention strategies to establish school-wide behavior support systems and then link class-wide, targeted group, and individualized behavior plans to the school-wide plan. Finally, schools can utilize internal experts to provide collaborative consultation to teachers experiencing difficulty with classroom management and student behavior.

Summary

Preparing special education teachers to be highly effective classroom managers has far-reaching implications in the areas of teacher retention (Coggshall, 2006; Ingersoll & Smith, 2003), teacher stress and burnout (Brouwers & Tomic, 2000), teacher quality (Oliver & Reschly, 2007), inclusive practices (Baker, 2005), and student social, emotional, and academic outcomes (Freiberg et al., 2001; Kellam et al., 1994; Leflot et al., 2010; van Lier et al., 2005). Whether managing their own class or assisting general education teachers through inclusive practice efforts, special education teachers require not only the theoretical and empirical content knowledge associated with effective classroom organization and behavior management but supervised field experience applying these skills as well. The research is clear. Teachers who are effective in proactively addressing classroom management and responding to student behavior also have increased instructional and student time on-task time with subsequent lower rates of disruptive behavior. The payoff for improving teacher preparation in the area of classroom organization and behavior management is large considering the policy mandates in the areas of teacher quality and student achievement (Duncan, 2009; Ingersoll & Smith, 2003; Yell & Drasgow, 2005). The challenge facing teacher preparation programs is to adapt to the needs of new teachers who will be required to meet the behavioral needs of a diverse student population. We are optimistic that these challenges can be met.

References

Adams, P. E., & Krockover, G. H. (1997). Concerns and perceptions of beginning secondary science and mathematics teachers. *Science Education*, *81*, 29–50. doi:10.1002/(SICI)1098-237X(199701)81:1<29::AID-SCE2>3.0.CO;2-3

Alberto, P. A., & Troutman, A. C. (2009). *Applied behavior analysis for teachers* (8th ed.). Upper Saddle River, NJ: Pearson.

Alvarez, H. K. (2007). The impact of teacher preparation on responses to student aggression in the classroom. *Teaching and Teacher Education*, *23*, 1113–1126. doi:10.1016/j.tate.2006.10.001

Anderson, L. M., & Evertson, C. M. (1978). *Classroom organization at the beginning of school: Two case studies*. Chicago, IL: Research and Development Center for Teacher Education. Retrieved from ERIC database (ED166193).

Anderson, L. M., Evertson, C. M., & Emmer, E. T. (1979). *Dimensions in classroom management derived from recent research*. R&D Report No. 6006. Austin, TX: Research and Development Center for Teacher Education (ERIC Document Reproduction Service No. ED175860).

Baker, P. H. (2005). Managing student behavior: How ready are teachers to meet the challenge? *American Secondary Education*, *33*, 51–64.

Barrish, H. H., Saunders, M., & Wolf, M. M. (1969). Good behavior game: Effects of individual contingencies for group consequences on disruptive behavior in a classroom. *Journal of Applied Behavior Analysis*, 2, 119–124. doi:10.1901/jaba.1969.2-119

Bradshaw, C. P., Zmuda, J. H., Kellam, S. G., & Ialongo, N. S. (2009). Longitudinal impact of two universal preventive interventions in first grade on educational outcomes in high school. *Journal of Educational Psychology*, *101*, 926–937. doi:10.1037/a0016586

Brouwers, A., & Tomic, W. (2000). A longitudinal study of teacher burnout and perceived self-efficacy in classroom management. *Teaching and Teacher Education*, *16*, 239–253. doi:10.1016/S0742-051X(99)00057-8

Cameron, C. E., Connor, C. M., & Morrison, F. J. (2005). Effects of variation in teacher organization on classroom functioning. *Journal of School Psychology*, *43*, 61–85. doi:10.1016/j.jsp.2004.12.002

Carnine, D. W. (1976). Effects of two teacher-presentation rates on off-task behavior, answering correctly, and participation. *Journal of Applied Behavior Analysis*, *9*, 199–206. doi:10.1901/jaba.1976.9-199

Christle, C. A., & Schuster, J. W. (2003). The effects of using response cards on student participation, academic achievement, and on-task behavior during whole-class, math instruction. *Journal of Behavioral Education*, *12*, 147–165. doi:1053-0819/03/0900-0147/0

Coggshall, J. G. (2006). *TQ Research & Policy Brief. Prospects for the profession: Public opinion research on teachers*. Washington DC: National Comprehensive Center for Teacher Quality.

Colvin, G., Sugai, G., Good, R. H., III, & Lee, Y.-Y. (1997). Using active supervision and precorrection to improve transition behaviors in an elementary school. *School Psychology Quarterly*, *12*, 344–363. doi:10.1037/h0088967

Colvin, G., Sugai, G., & Patching, B. (1993). Precorrection: An instructional approach for managing predictable problem behaviors. *Intervention in School and Clinic*, *28*, 143–150. doi:10.1177/105345129302800304

Conyers, C., Miltenberger, R., Maki, A., Barenz, R., Jurgens, M., Sailer, A., Haugen, M., & Kopp, B. (2004). A comparison of response cost and differential reinforcement of other behavior to reduce disruptive behavior in a preschool classroom. *Journal of Applied Behavior Analysis*, 37, 411–415. doi:10.1901/jaba.2004.37-411

Cooper, J. O., Heron, T. E., & Heward, W. L. (2007). *Applied behavior analysis*. Upper Saddle River, NJ: Pearson Education, Inc.

Coyne, M., Kame'enui, E., & Carnine, D. (2007). *Effective teaching strategies that accommodate diverse learners* (3rd ed.). Upper Saddle River, NJ: Merrill/Prentice Hall.

De Pry, R. L., & Sugai, G. (2002). The effects of active supervision and pre-correction on minor behavioral incidents in a sixth grade general education classroom. *Journal of Behavioral Education, 11*, 255–267. doi:1053-0819/02/1200-0255/0

Doolittle, J. H., Horner, R. H., Bradley, R., Sugai, G., & Vincent, C. G. (2007). Importance of student social behavior in the mission statements, personnel preparation standards, and innovation efforts of state departments of education. *The Journal of Special Education, 40*, 239–245. doi:10.1177/00224669070400040501

Duncan, A. (2009, October 22). *Teacher preparation: Reforming the uncertain profession—Remarks of Secretary Arne Duncan at Teachers College, Columbia University*. Retrieved from http://www2.ed.gov/news/speeches/2009/10/10222009.html

Emmer, E. T., & Stough, L. M. (2001). Classroom management: A critical part of educational psychology, with implications for teacher education. *Educational Psychologist, 36*, 103–112. doi:10.1207/S15326985EP3602_5

Epstein, M., Atkins, M., Cullinan, D., Kutash, K., and Weaver, R. (2008). *Reducing behavior problems in the elementary school classroom: A practice guide* (NCEE #2008-012). Washington, DC: National Center for Education Evaluation and Regional Assistance, Institute of Education Sciences, U. S. Department of Education. Retrieved from http://ies.ed.gov/ncee/wwc/PracticeGuide.aspx?sid=4

Evertson, C. M. (1988). *Improving elementary classroom management: A school-based training program for beginning the year*. Nashville, TN: Peabody College, Vanderbilt University. Retrieved from ERIC database (ED302528).

Evertson, C. M., & Neal, K. W. (2006). *Looking into learning-centered classrooms: Implications for classroom management*. Washington, DC: National Education Association.

Evertson, C. M., & Weinstein, C. (2006). Classroom management as a field of inquiry. In C. M. Evertson & C. Weinstein (Eds.), *Handbook of classroom management: Research, practice, and contemporary issues* (pp. 3–15). Mahwah, NJ: Lawrence Erlbaum Associates, Inc.

Freiberg, H. J., Connell, M. L., & Lorentz, J. (2001). Effects of Consistency Management® on student mathematics achievement in seven chapter I elementary schools. *Journal of Education for Students Placed at Risk, 6*, 249–270. doi:10.1207/S15327671ESPR0603_6

Fudge, D. L., Skinner, C. H., Williams, J. L., Cowden, D., Clark J., & Bliss, S. L. (2008). Increasing on-task behavior in every student in a second-grade classroom during transitions: Validating the Color Wheel system. *Journal of School Psychology, 46*, 575–592. doi:10.1016/j.jsp.2008.06.003

Gable, R. A., Hendrickson, J. M., Young, C. C., Shores, R. E., & Stowitscek, J. J. (1983). A comparison of teacher approval and disapproval statements across categories of exceptionality. *Journal of Special Education Technology, 6*, 15–22.

Gersten, R., Dimino, J., Jayanthi, M., Kim, J. S., & Santoro L. E. (2010). Teacher study group: Impact of the professional development model on reading instruction and student outcomes in first grade classrooms. *American Educational Research Journal, 47*, 694–739. doi:10.3102/0002831209361208

Gilberts, G. H., & Lignugaris-Kraft, B. (1997). Classroom management and instruction competencies for preparing elementary and special education teachers. *Teaching and Teacher Education, 13*, 597–610. doi: http://dx.doi.org/10.1016/S0742-051X(97)80003-0

Greenwood, C. R., Delquadri, J. C., & Hall, R. V. (1989). Longitudinal effects of classwide peer tutoring. *Journal of Educational Psychology, 81*(3), 371–383. doi:10.1037/0022-0663.81.3.371

Hall, G. E., & Hord, S. M. (2001). *Implementing change: Principles, patterns and potholes*. Needham Heights, MA: Allyn and Bacon.

Hall, R. V., Panyan, M., Rabon, D., & Broden, M. (1968). Instructing beginning teachers in reinforcement procedures which improve classroom control. *Journal of Applied Behavior Analysis, 1*, 315–322. doi:10.1901/jaba.1968.1-315

Hertzog, H. (2002). "When, how, and who do I ask for help?": Novices' perceptions of problems and assistance. *Teacher Education Quarterly, 29*(3), 25–41.

Holdheide, L. R., & Reschly, D. J. (2008). *Teacher preparation to deliver inclusive services to students with disabilities*. Washington DC: Learning Point Associates, National Comprehensive Center on Teacher Quality.

Horner, R., Sugai, G., Todd, A., & Lewis-Palmer, T. (2005). School-wide positive behavior support. In L. Bambara & L. Kern (Eds.), *Individualized supports for students with problem behaviors: Designing positive behavior plans* (pp. 359–390). New York: Guilford Press.

Ingersoll, R. M., & Smith, T. M. (2003). The wrong solution to the teacher shortage. *Educational Leadership*, 60, 30–33.

Kellam, S. G., Ling, X., Merisca, R., Brown, C. H., & Ialongo, N. (1998). The effect of the level of aggression in the first grade classroom on the course and malleability of aggressive behavior into middle school. *Development and Psychopathology, 10*, 165–185. doi:10.1017/S0954579498001564

Kellam, S. G., Rebok, G. W., Ialongo, N., & Mayer, L. S. (1994). The course and malleability of aggressive behavior from early first grade into middle school: Results of a developmental epidemiologically-based preventive trial. *Journal of Child Psychology, 35*, 259–281. doi:10.1111/j.1469-7610.1994.tb01161.x
Kounin, J. (1970). *Discipline and group management in classrooms*. New York: Holt, Rinehart & Winston.
Lambert, M. C., Cartledge, G., Heward, W. L., & Lo, Y.-Y. (2006). Effects of response cards on disruptive behavior and academic responding during math lessons by fourth-grade urban students. *Journal of Positive Behavior Interventions, 8*, 88–99. doi:10.1177/10983007060080020701
Landrum, T. J., & Kauffman, J. M. (2006). Behavioral approaches to classroom management, In C. M. Evertson & C. S. Weinstein (Eds.), *Handbook of classroom management: Research, practice, and contemporary issues* (pp. 47–71). Mahwah, NJ: Lawrence Erlbaum Associates, Inc.
Langland, S., Lewis-Palmer, T., & Sugai, G. (1998). Teaching respect in the classroom: An instructional approach. *Journal of Behavioral Education, 8*, 245–262. doi:10.1023/A:1022839708894
Leflot, G., van Lier, P. A., Onghena, P., & Colpin, H. (2010). The role of teacher behavior management in the development of disruptive behaviors: An intervention study with the good behavior game. *Journal of Abnormal Child Psychology, 38*, 869–882. doi:10.1007/s10802-010-9411-4
Lewis, T. J., & Sugai, G. (1999). Effective behavior support: A systems approach to proactive schoolwide management. *Focus on Exceptional Children, 31*, 1–24.
Litow, L., & Pumroy, D. K. (1975). A brief review of classroom group-oriented contingencies. *Journal of Applied Behavior Analysis, 8*, 341–347. doi:10.1901/jaba.1975.8-341
Long, J., & Biggs, J. (1999). Perceptions of education majors and experienced teachers regarding factors that contribute to successful classroom management. *Journal of Instructional Psychology, 26*(2), 105–110.
Madsen, C. H., Jr., Becker, W. C., & Thomas, D. R. (1968). Rules, praise, and ignoring: Elements of elementary classroom control. *Journal of Applied Behavior Analysis, 1*, 139–150. doi:10.1901/jaba.1968.1-139
Mayer, G. R., Sulzer-Azaroff, B., & Wallace, M. (2011). *Behavior analysis for lasting change* (2nd ed.). Cornwall-on-Hudson, NY: Sloan Publishing.
McGraner, K. L., & Sanez, L. (2009). *Preparing teachers of English language learners*. Washington DC: Learning Point Associates, National Comprehensive Center for Teacher Quality. Retrieved from http://www.gtlcenter.org/sites/default/files/docs/issuepaper_preparingELLteachers.pdf
McGraner, K. L., VanDerHeyden, A., & Holdheide, L. R. (2010). *Preparation of effective teachers in mathematics*. Washington DC: Learning Point Associates, National Comprehensive Center for Teacher Quality. Retrieved from http://www.gtlcenter.org/sites/default/files/docs/TQ_IssuePaper_Math.pdf
Meister, D. G., & Melnick, S. A. (2003). National new teacher study: Beginning teachers' concerns. *Action in Teacher Education, 24*, 87–94. doi:10.1080/01626620.2003.10463283
Mergler, A. G., & Tangen, D. (2010). Using microteaching to enhance efficacy of pre-service teachers. *Teaching Education, 21*, 199–210. doi:10.1080/10476210902998466
Musser, E. H., Bray, M. A., Kehle, T. J., & Jenson, W. R. (2001). Reducing disruptive behaviors in students with serious emotional disturbance. *School Psychology Review, 30*, 294–304
Nelson, J. R., Martella, R. M., & Marchand-Martella, N. (2002). Maximizing student learning: The effects of a comprehensive school-based program for preventing problem behaviors. *Journal of Emotional and Behavioral Disorders, 10*, 136–148. doi:10.1177/10634266020100030201
Oliver, R. M., & Reschly, D. J. (2007, December). *Effective classroom management: Teacher preparation and professional development*. Washington, DC: Learning Point Associates, National Comprehensive Center for Teacher Quality. Retrieved from http://files.eric.ed.gov/fulltext/ED543769.pdf
Oliver, R. M., & Reschly, D. J. (2010). Teacher preparation in classroom management: Implications for students with emotional and behavioral disorders. *Behavioral Disorders, 35*, 188–199.
Oliver, R. M., & Reschly, D. J. (forthcoming). *Specifying direct and systematic instruction: An innovation configuration to improve teacher preparation*. Washington DC: National Comprehensive Center on Teacher Quality (Manuscript in Preparation).
Oliver, R. M., Wehby, J. H., & Reschly, D. J. (2011). *Teacher classroom management practices: Effects on disruptive or aggressive student behavior*. Campbell Systematic Reviews 2011:4. doi:10.4073/csr.2011.4
Paine, S. C., Radicci, J., Rosellini, L. C., Deutchman, L., & Darch, C. B. (1983). *Structuring your classroom for academic success*. Champaign, IL: Research Press.
Patterson, G. R., Reid, J. B., & Dishion, T. J. (1992). *Antisocial boys*. Eugene, OR: Castalia.
Reschly, D. J., & Wood-Garnett, S. (2009). *Teacher preparation for response to intervention in middle and high schools*. Washington DC: National Comprehensive Center for Teacher Quality. Retrieved from http://files.eric.ed.gov/fulltext/ED520724.pdf
Ryans, D. (1952). A study of criterion data—A factor analysis of teacher behaviors in the elementary school. *Educational and Psychological Measurement, 12*, 333–344. doi:10.1177/001316445201200301

Schumaker, J. B. (2009). *Teacher preparation and professional development in effective learning strategy instruction.* Washington DC: Learning Point Associates, National Comprehensive Center for Teacher Quality.

Shores, R. E., Gunter, P. L., & Jack, S. L. (1993). Classroom management strategies: Are they setting events for coercion? *Behavioral Disorders, 18*, 92–102.

Shores, R. E., Jack, S. L., Gunter, P. L., Ellis, D. N., DeBriere, T. J., & Wehby, J. H. (1993). Classroom interactions of children with behavior disorders. *Journal of Emotional and Behavioral Disorders, 1*, 27–39. doi:10.1177/106342669300100106

Siebert, C. J. (2005). Promoting preservice teacher's success in classroom management by leveraging a local union's resources: A professional development school initiative. *Education*, 125, 385–392.

Sidman, M. (2001). *Coercion and its fallout* (revised ed.). Boston, MA: Authors Cooperative.

Simonsen, B., Fairbanks, S., Briesch, A., Myers, D., & Sugai, G. (2008). Evidence-based practices in classroom management: Considerations for research to practice. *Education and Treatment of Children, 31*, 351–380. doi:10.1353/etc.0.0007

Skinner, C. H., Skinner, A. L., & Sterling-Turner, H. E. (2002). Best practices in utilizing group contingencies for intervention and prevention. In A. Thomas & J. Grimes (Eds.), *Best practices in school psychology* (4th ed., pp. 817–830). Washington, DC: National Association of School Psychologists.

Smartt, S. M., & Reschly, D. J. (2007). *Barriers to the preparation of highly qualified teachers in reading.* Washington, DC: National Comprehensive Center on Teacher Quality. Retrieved from http://eric.ed.gov/?id=ED520775

Sprick, R., Garrison, M., & Howard, L. M. (1998). *CHAMPS: A proactive and positive approach to classroom management for grades K–9.* Longmont, CA: Sopris West.

Stage, S., & Quiroz, D. (1997). A meta-analysis of interventions to decrease disruptive behavior in the public education setting. *School Psychology Review, 26*, 333–368.

Strain, P. S., Lambert, D. L., Kerr, M. M., Stagg, V., & Lenkner, D. A. (1983). Naturalistic assessment of children's compliance to teachers' requests and consequences for compliance. *Journal of Applied Behavior Analysis, 16*, 243–249. doi:10.1901/jaba.1983.16-243

Sugai, G., & Horner, R. R. (2006). A promising approach for expanding and sustaining school-wide positive behavior support. *School Psychology Review, 35*, 245–259.

Sutherland, K. S., & Wehby, J. H. (2001). The effect of self-evaluation on teaching behavior in classrooms for students with emotional and behavioral disorders. *Journal of Special Education, 35*(3), 161–171. doi:10.1177/002246690103500306

Sutherland, K. S., Wehby, J. H., & Copeland, S. R. (2000). Effect of varying rates of behavior-specific praise on the on-task behavior of students with EBD. *Journal of Emotional and Behavior Disorders, 8*, 2–8. doi:10.1177/106342660000800101

Taylor-Greene, S., Brown, D., Nelson, L., Longton, J., Gassman, T., Cohen, J. … Hall, S. (1997). School-wide behavioral support: Starting the year off right. *Journal of Behavioral Education*, 7, 99–112. doi: 10.1023/A:1022849722465

van Lier, P. A. C., Muthén, B. O., van der Sar, R. M., & Crijnen, A. A. M. (2004). Preventing disruptive behavior in elementary schoolchildren: Impact of a universal classroom-based intervention. *Journal of Consulting and Clinical Psychology, 72*, 467–478. doi:10.1037/0022-006X.72.3.467

van Lier, P. A. C., Vuijk, P., & Crijnen, A. A. M. (2005). Understanding mechanisms of change of antisocial behavior: The impact of a universal intervention. *Journal of Abnormal Child Psychology, 33*, 521–535. doi:10.1007/s10802-005-6735-7

Wagner, M., Kutash, K., Duchnowski, A. J., Epstein, M. H., & Sumi, W. C. (2006). The children and youth we serve: A national picture of the characteristics of students with emotional disturbances receiving special education. *Journal of Emotional and Behavioral Disorders, 13*, 79–96. doi:10.1177/10634266050130020201

Wright-Gallo, G. L., Higbee, T. S., Reagon, K. A., & Davey, B. J. (2006). Classroom-based functional analysis and intervention for students with emotional/behavioral disorders. *Education and Treatment of Children, 29*, 421–436.

Yell, M. L., & Drasgow, E. (2005). *No Child Left Behind: A guide for professionals.* Upper Saddle River, NJ: Pearson/Merrill/Prentice Hall.

Part V

Preparation for Specific Student Populations

18

Research on the Preparation of Teachers of Students With Severe Disabilities

David L. Westling

WESTERN CAROLINA UNIVERSITY

Charles Salzberg

UTAH STATE UNIVERSITY

Belva C. Collins

UNIVERSITY OF KENTUCKY

Robert Morgan

UTAH STATE UNIVERSITY

Victoria Knight

VANDERBILT UNIVERSITY

Things to Think About

- Instructional approaches for students with severe disabilities have varied over the years. In the past 30 years emphasis was placed on teaching functional skills, but most recently, teaching academic skills that parallel the general curriculum has become a dominant curriculum model. Regardless of the instructional approach, most authorities have supported inclusion of students with severed disabilities.
- Authorities have identified important skills for teachers of students with severe disabilities, but there are no broadly accepted uniform professional preparation curricula or standards for teacher preparation.
- Objective evaluation of the performance of teachers of students with severe disabilities is problematic because there are few instruments designed to measure their performance and the existing instruments have not been shown to have adequate validity or reliability.
- Although no studies were found that examined the performance of teachers of students with severe disabilities as an outcome of preservice preparation, several follow-up reports relied on input from former students to assess the value of preparation programs.

- Available research, although limited, suggests that distance learning models, when accompanied by in-classroom coaching and feedback to teachers, may be a viable form of preservice preparation as well as useful for staff development.

Although not universal, instruction for individuals with severe disabilities began more than two centuries ago in Western Europe and then in the United States. However, in U.S. public schools, instruction for many of these students did not begin until well into the 20th century, and instruction for individuals with the *most* severe disabilities was not legally required until 1975. During the last 50+ years, the focus of instructional curricula for students with severe disabilities has varied, with the variation being related both to the degree of the disability and to what authorities have maintained should be critical learning outcomes.

In the 1950s and 1960s, students with moderate to severe intellectual disabilities were provided educational programs well into their adolescent years that were largely based on kindergarten curricula. Later, when students with more severe disabilities began to receive instruction, the focus of this instruction tended to be on achieving small, targeted gains based on typical human developmental milestones (Westling, 1986). In the 1970s, instruction for most students with severe disabilities shifted and became more clearly focused on *age-appropriate, functional* skills. Using teaching methods heavily based on the principles of Applied Behavior Analysis (ABA; Baer, Wolf, & Risley, 1968), students were provided with instruction that ranged from learning basic daily living skills to basic academic skills. As the trend toward functional curricula continued, the *ecological inventory* model, which identified learning content based on current and future environments, emerged (Brown, Branston et al., 1979; Brown, Branston-McLean et al., 1979). With this, there was an increase in the 1980s in nonschool, community-based instruction (Ford et al., 1989; Wilcox & Bellamy, 1987). Also during this time, there was an increase in placements of students with severe disabilities in integrated settings that allowed limited interaction with students without disabilities, primarily for the purpose of developing language and social skills. In contrast to being totally segregated in special schools, students were often housed in separate wings of elementary schools.

The functional movement continued into the 1990s, but self-determination also came to be seen as a valued educational outcome (Wehmeyer, 1992, 1996). Students were taught how to make choices and decisions and how to manage their own behavior, and longitudinal curricula were developed (e.g., Doll, Sands, Wehmeyer, & Palmer, 1996). Also during this period, a growing recognition occurred that being *integrated* was not the same as being *included*, so came a call by various leaders for *full inclusion* (e.g., Sailor et al., 1989; Stainback & Stainback, 1990; Villa & Thousand, 2000; York, Vandercook, MacDonald, & Wolff, 1989).

Toward the end of the 1990s and into the 2000s, advocates for students with severe disabilities emphasized access to the general curriculum with special focus on literacy skills (Katims, 2000; Spooner & Browder, 2006). This movement was reinforced by the 1997 and 2004 IDEA amendments and by the No Child Left Behind Act passed in 2001. Under this curriculum emphasis, students with severe disabilities were to be instructed in content that reflected the general curriculum with adaptations necessary for the curriculum to be consumable and meaningful to them (Browder, Spooner, Wakeman, Trela, & Baker, 2006). Hand in hand with participation in the general curriculum was a need for students with severe disabilities to participate in end of year alternate assessments. However, evidencing the difficulty of making the transition in instructional practice, Browder, Spooner, Wakeman et al. (2003) reported that several states continued to evaluate functional skills in their alternate assessments.

Preparation of Teachers for Students With Severe Disabilities: Current Practices and Issues

A number of writers have addressed issues related to preparing teachers with appropriate skills for these students. Whitten and Westling (1985) documented the recommended competencies for teachers of students with severe disabilities. They identified 59 competency statements in the literature that fell into nine categories: (a) general knowledge, (b) planning, (c) assessment, (d) curriculum, (e) behavior management, (f) instruction, (g) physical/medical, (h) other personnel, and (i) parents. Whitten and Westling also examined the level of empirical evidence supporting each desired skill, which they sorted into four classes: (a) opinion without empirical support; (b) opinion supported by one or more citations from the literature—in some cases these only represented the opinion of the cited author; (c) professional consensus (i.e., statements supported by surveys of professionals' opinions); and (d) student gains (i.e., statements supported by data that showed student learning increased in the presence of, or demonstration of, this competency). Unfortunately, Whitten and Westling found that only four of 59 competency statements were supported by data reflecting gains in student learning: (a) use of task analyses, (b) amount of time in teaching, (c) use of appropriate behavior management techniques, and (d) use of successive approximation. Thirty-five of the 59 competency statements were supported by surveys of professionals' opinions.

In a later study, Ryndak, Clark, Conroy, and Holthaus Stuart (2001) surveyed 20 nationally recognized master's degree programs to identify areas of expertise considered essential for teachers to work with students with severe disabilities and to examine configurations of teacher preparation programs. Respondents confirmed the critical nature of nine areas of knowledge/skills: (a) collaboration and technical assistance; (b) inclusion (e.g., facilitating social relationships between students with severe disabilities and peers without disabilities); (c) advocacy and self-advocacy; (d) assessment and curriculum content; (e) effective instruction (e.g., data collection on student's learning and ability to make changes in instruction based on analysis of student data); (f) functional assessment and behavior intervention; (g) transition across ages and settings; (h) physical and sensory disabilities; and (i) research in the field of severe disabilities. Respondents in the Ryndak et al. (2001) survey described how their programs provided coursework with didactic knowledge and field experiences to strengthen classroom performance skills. Although considerable range and diversity was noted across nationally recognized master's degree programs, most allocated credit hours for content courses and field experiences.

Other writers and researchers have focused on other key issues and have often lamented the fact that programs sometimes lack critical components. For example, Fox and Williams (1992) maintained that teacher education programs must be values-based and must focus on supporting students with disabilities to be more included and accepted by society. Unfortunately, there are often insufficient practicum models that allow inclusive instruction to be practiced. This fact inspired Rainforth (2000) to describe the development of a course that would teach inclusive practices despite "contextual constraints" (p. 83), that is, without having inclusive classrooms in which to apply the practices. Snell (2003) pointed out that the field has not done well in translating research into practice. She expressed the need for teacher educators and researchers to work more closely with teachers and to discover better mechanisms for implementing research-validated practices in the schools. More recently, Harmon, Kasa-Hendrickson, and Neal (2009) argued for the need to inculcate more culturally responsive ideology and pedagogy into the preparation of teachers for students with severe disabilities and recommended several ways to do so. In regard to assistive technology (AT), Judge and Simms (2009) documented the lack of training in this area, while Connor, Snell, Gansneder, and Dexter (2010) found that teacher preparation was the most essential predictor of the use of AT in the classroom.

The Council for Exceptional Children (CEC, 2009) provided a rather extensive list of teacher knowledge and skills appropriate for teaching students with severe disabilities. In the section titled "Initial Special Education Teachers of Individuals With Exceptional Learning Needs With Developmental Disabilities and/or Autism" (p.113), CEC presents 165 discrete knowledge or skill statements divided across ten standards. While these statements provide a useful reference for preparing teachers of students with severe disabilities, they often state a desired outcome but lack specificity with regard to how to reach that outcome. For example, one instructional strategy is "Use strategies to facilitate integration into various settings," (p. 115), and another is "Use specialized teaching strategies matched to the need of the learner" (p. 115). Although it is hard to argue with the importance of such skills, their lack of specificity could make it difficult to evaluate the appropriateness of specific teacher actions.

In a comprehensive paper, Delano, Keefe, and Perner (2008–2009) pointed out that there is little consensus as to what should constitute preservice preparation for teachers of students with severe disabilities, how programs should be structured, or the areas of expertise that teachers should have. They noted that certification requirements varied widely in different states and that there are still areas of instruction, such as accessing the general curriculum, where additional research is needed to find effective practices in order to inform teacher education. In a call to action, Delano et al. proposed that several proactive steps be taken to improve teacher education including:

1. Identify what is meant by a highly qualified teacher of students with severe disabilities and work within states to assure that appropriate standards are included in preservice preparation programs, whether they are traditional or alternative route programs. The standards, they suggested, should be based on skills that have been demonstrated through research to lead to student progress.
2. Examine and improve the use of technology to provide distance education programs including the use of online collaborative software, Internet-based phone systems, interactive videoconferencing, and the use of webcams in classrooms.
3. Study the structure of teacher education programs and conduct research to identify characteristics of effective programs. With regard to program structure, they suggested teacher education programs should increase collaboration with school districts and consider various alternative approaches to increasing the quantity and quality of personnel.
4. Increase collaboration between general and special education, both in higher education, for the purpose of preparing teachers, and in public schools for the purpose of increasing learning in the general curriculum.

Evaluating the Instructional Performance of Teachers of Students With Severe Disabilities

One important issue, related both to teacher education and to determining the impact of teacher education, is the ability to identify effective teachers of students with severe disabilities. Put succinctly, how do we know if a teacher is truly effective? In the case of teachers of students with severe disabilities, there are a limited number of classroom performance measurement tools that may give us an indication of the quality of a teacher.

Generally, most authorities would agree that teachers of students with severe disabilities should demonstrate competencies such as many of those identified by Whitten and Westling (1985), Ryndak et al. (2001) or CEC (2009). However, capturing appropriate teacher performance requires that relatively clearly stated, valid activities and actions be identified so that they can be reliably observed and recorded using either direct observation or rating scales. Further, after initial development, such observation instruments should be assessed to determine their adequacy in terms of psychometric properties and, most ideally, their relation to student progress. Unfortunately, after an extensive search of the existing literature, only a limited number of evaluation instruments were found that allowed such skills to be observed and documented in classrooms and schools (i.e., Abell et al., 2010; Clark, Cushing, & Kennedy, 2004; Demchak & Browder, 1987; Louisiana Department of Education, 2004). Two of these, which were recently designed to evaluate teachers or interns teaching students with severe disabilities, are relatively comprehensive (Abell et al., 2010; Louisiana Department of Education, 2004). We should note that several other observation instruments were found that targeted specific, but not comprehensive, teaching skills (e.g., Horrocks & Morgan, 2011; Kim & Hupp, 2007; Stephenson, Carter, & Arthur-Kelly, 2011).

The system created by Abell et al. (2010), the *Kentucky Teaching Standards and Individualized Independence Curriculum Alignment Document*, allows formative evaluation of a teacher's or intern's performance in a classroom working with students with severe disabilities. The document is based on CEC standards (2009). Using this instrument, a supervisor may score knowledge or skill items as *standard demonstrated, standard partially demonstrated*, or *standard not demonstrated.*

Similarly, the *Louisiana Teacher Assistance and Assessment Program* (Louisiana Department of Education, 2004) includes best practices checklists for teachers of low-incidence disabilities in multiple areas including physical setting, social climate, curriculum, positive behavior support, general support, Individualized Education Program (IEP) review, IEP transition services, and general safety checklist. Examples of checklist items include "Have modifications/accommodations for access to the curriculum been utilized and clearly documented?" and "Is functional assessment of behavior an ongoing process?" Items are checked *yes, no*, or *unclear.* The checklists are used in conjunction with a program called *Strategies for Effective Teaching for Special Educators* designed to proactively improve skills of in-service teachers (Louisiana Department of Education, 2004).

Although these teacher observation instruments represent comprehensive measures of a teacher's classroom performance, limitations and shortcomings are noteworthy. First, they have not been subjected to reliability or validity research, so users have no information on the psychometric features of the instruments. Second, although the Kentucky document is tied to CEC standards, neither instrument is based on empirically derived teaching practices or those known to predict improved student performance. Third, although the Louisiana program includes strategies allowing teachers to gain knowledge and practice teaching skills, no data are provided indicating that those strategies are effective.

As mentioned previously, the lack of having adequate measures to assess the performance of teachers of students with severe disabilities means these measures cannot be used to evaluate the impact of teacher education programs. Another somewhat related problem is that we have no good way to measure the performance of teachers in a pay for performance or merit pay system (Education Commission of the States, 2010). In such a system, three agreements must be reached: the definition of teacher performance, the definition of student performance, and, the purpose of schooling (Gratz, 2010). Implementing pay for performance is hindered by the fact that we cannot adequately measure a teacher's performance. Furthermore, valid and reliable assessment of student learning presents another challenge. Although formative assessment has been a mainstay in the education of students with severe disabilities (Westling & Fox, 2009), summative assessments of learning, such as through alternate assessments, has been problematic (Browder, Spooner, Algozzine et al., 2003; Browder, Wakeman & Flowers, 2006; Flowers, Wakeman, Browder, & Karvonen, 2009).

The Influence of Preservice Preparation on the Effectiveness of Teachers of Students With Severe Disabilities

As can be seen from the previous sections, there are several variations in programs providing preservice preparation for teachers of students with severe disabilities and a few observation instruments that might be used to study the relationship between preservice preparation and teacher performance, or teacher performance and student learning. Research that would be relevant to determining the influence of preservice preparation on teaching performance would use the observation instruments, as limited as they are in number and quality, to determine if preparation programs resulted in differential outcomes. For example, we could compare performance of teachers who were not initially certified, certified through an alternate route preparation program, or certified through a traditional undergraduate program. However, our search of the literature did not yield any such studies. Using the ERIC database, we searched for publications (including journals and documents between 1982 and 2012) using the following terms: *severe disabilities* and *teacher education, severe disabilities* and *teacher performance*, and *severe disabilities* and *teacher education research.* Although we found studies that focused on learning and implementing specific teaching skills (e.g., Courtade, Browder, & Spooner, 2010; Horrocks & Morgan, 2011), we found none that used holistic measures of teachers' performance as outcome measures. However, we found several program evaluation reports, but they used less direct measures and did not use experimental or quasi-experimental designs.

In order to evaluate the preparation of teachers of students with severe disabilities, course instructors or project directors have often used survey research procedures to determine the following: (a) the views of learners toward the value of individual courses or instructional programs, (b) the views of learners toward the instructional methods or procedures, and (c) the impact of the course or program on the learner's values, attitudes, or teaching skills. The identified reports are discussed below.

Wertlieb and Place (1984) documented the effects of a Massachusetts program that offered preservice preparation and staff development that focused on improving services for young children with severe and multiple disabilities. The authors reported that 20 teachers completed the program and received bachelor's or master's degrees and certification in early education for children with disabilities and 19 of its 20 graduates were successfully employed. During the third year of their project, they sent lengthy surveys to the supervisors of their first four graduates and received three responses. The supervisors were generally very positive about the performance of the graduates, giving them relatively high scores communicating with children, curriculum design and instructional skills, behavior management, and communication with adults. Comparatively lower ratings were given in the fifth area, evaluation procedures.

In another evaluation report, Snell, Martin, and Orelove (1995) described a multiuniversity program in Virginia developed to provide endorsements for teachers employed to teach students with severe disabilities but unendorsed to do so. Three universities each offered 15 graduate credit hours to 75 participants in the program, 50 of whom completed all of the requirements for the endorsement. As part of their project evaluation, in a follow-up survey, the project directors asked whether the program changed or influenced *thinking* and whether the program changed or influenced *practice* in 10 skill areas: inclusion, working with families, transition, communication, transdisciplinary teaming, functional and age-appropriate skills, positioning and handling, nonaversive techniques, peer support networks, and student performance data. The surveys were sent to 58 participants and returned by 48 (83%). The responses indicated that 62% to 75% of the respondents reported changing their thinking about inclusion, transition, communication, transdisciplinary teaming, and functional and age-appropriate skills *quite a lot* to *very much*. However, the authors reported that "Practices ... appear to have been somewhat less influenced by the program" (p. 24). In all but one area, working with families, thinking was reportedly more influenced by the program than was practice.

In one of the most extensive follow-ups, Grisham-Brown and Collins (2002) reported the effects of three 3-year cycles of OSEP-funded professional preparation programs for teachers of students with severe disabilities during which distance learning technology was used. The project, Training Rural Educators in Kentucky (TREK), focused on preparing teachers for students with moderate to severe intellectual disabilities and preparing teachers for early childhood special education (ECSE). For best practices information and skills to be made available to educators in remote areas of the state, courses were delivered through a variety of distance learning formats. At the end of the third cycle, the authors collected data on a wide range of information including students' satisfaction with program content, the use of distance education courses, and impact of the program on the use of best practices. Although their response rate was low (n=28/128; 21.8% return), the results were generally positive. Ratings on all courses were between 4.4 and 5.0 (on a 5-point scale). With regard to course delivery, on-site courses were favored by 12%, satellite was favored by 28%, 15% preferred interactive video, 28% preferred a combination approach, and 25% had no opinion. Finally, the respondents were asked to compare their use of best practices before and after program courses. The majority of participants reported increases in the use of best practices and also reported the specific number of students affected by best practices, a number that ranged from 20 to 68 students per practice.

From these reports we might conclude that preservice preparation for teachers can impact their knowledge, attitudes, and to some extent their teaching performance. However this conclusion is based on self-reports from a select group of program completers. Although we can say programs were rated well by the participants in them, we cannot draw any conclusions about the impact of the program on the performance of the teachers or the resultant impact on students' learning.

Effectiveness of Using Distance Learning Technology to Prepare Teachers of Students With Severe Disabilities

More than 15 years ago, Spooner (1996) discussed the difficulties of attracting and preparing special educators to teach students with severe disabilities and suggested that distance learning tools could be an important asset in addressing these needs. Subsequent research by Spooner and his colleagues (Beattie, Spooner, Jordan, Algozzine, & Spooner, 2002; Spooner, Jordan, Algozzine, & Spooner, 1999) found that student evaluations of courses taught through distance education had been about equal to evaluations of courses taught through traditional lectures.

Recently, Jones (2010) discussed the benefits of an online course for teachers of students with severe disabilities intended to foster interactions and discussions among the participants. After the course, 10 of the 12 teachers in the course completed an open-ended survey that allowed them to express their views about different components and learning activities. With regard using an online medium, Jones reported that there were 33 comments, 30 of which were positive. For example, one teacher wrote, "Although I have taken online courses before, this is the first one with live chat and this introduction helped me feel comfortable" (p. 691). Negative comments conveyed concerns about technical difficulties. Jones concluded, "Teacher responses to this course reveal that it is possible to engage teachers in new knowledge, skills and applications through an online medium of learning" (p. 694).

In a comprehensive study, McDonnell et al. (2011) compared the effectiveness of a distance and an on-campus graduate level preservice program for teachers of students with severe disabilities. The distance group included 15 participants, and the on-campus group included 17. On the whole, the groups were similar, although the on-campus group was younger on average and had fewer years of experience. The groups had essentially the same program, including the same course and practicum requirements, assignments, and many of the same learning activities. Courses were taught at the same time of day and in the same sequence. The on-campus group received instruction in a traditional class format, whereas the distance group received their courses through Internet videoconferencing. Several measures were used to assess candidates' acquisition of content and their ability to apply the knowledge and skills acquired through the program of study. The results indicated that there were no significant differences between students in the distance and on-campus groups in several areas including gains in knowledge of course content, IEP development skills, instructional program development skills, grade point average in specialization courses, and Praxis II scores. McDonnell et al. concluded "this study suggests that the use of videoconferencing technology paired with other Internet tools and on-site field supervision is an effective approach to preparing teachers of students with severe disabilities in rural and remote communities" (p. 116).

The work by Jones (2010) and McDonnell and his colleagues (2011) does not suggest any more to us about the impact of their courses or programs on teacher performance than do the previously cited reports. What they indicate, however, is that distance learning may be a worthy contributor to improving teacher skills. This premise is further buttressed by the available literature discussed in the following section.

The Influence of Staff Development and Coaching on the Performance of Teachers of Students With Severe Disabilities

Teachers of students with severe disabilities tend to fall into three distinct groups: teachers who enter the classroom immediately following traditional preservice preparation, teachers who enter the classroom via an alternate route often without any specialized preparation, and experienced teachers. Regardless of which group teachers are in, it is important to realize that because of the heterogeneity of the students they teach, many of the skills they need must be individualized to meet their student needs. This implies that one-to-one or small group mentoring will often be preferred to large group professional development sessions.

In-Service Professional Development and On-Site Mentoring

Often in-service teachers receive professional development through one-day workshops. Based on an extensive analysis, Yoon, Duncan, Lee, Scarloss, and Shapley (2007) concluded that this approach has generally shown no significant effects on student achievement. Not surprisingly, some authorities suggest that instead of one-shot training sessions, that experience, coaching, and practice are more effective, especially for teachers of students with severe disabilities (Lang & Fox, 2004). There is a small body of research that supports this position.

Arthur, Butterfield, and McKinnon (1998) conducted a brief, but targeted in-service program consisting of three meetings lasting 3 hours each that focused on specific communication activities. The program resulted in increased communicative partner skills by teachers and aides of students with severe disabilities in applied settings. Similarly, Lerman, Tetreault, Havanetz, Strobel, and Garro (2008) conducted an intense 5-day summer training program on preference assessments and direct teaching that included lectures, discussion, role-playing, modeling, and practice with feedback. All teachers met criteria during professional development, and all but one teacher generalized and maintained the skills during follow-up observations.

When follow-up coaching is added to the instruction of specific skills, the fidelity of skill implementation is increased (Kretlow & Bartholomew, 2010). Based on their analysis, Kretlow and Bartholomew reported that there are three critical components of coaching: (a) highly engaged, instructive group training sessions; (b) follow-up observation(s); and (c) specific feedback. However, because teachers of students with severe disabilities often are not clustered in large groups, focused group instruction with follow-up coaching may be a problem. One solution might be to group these teachers at the regional or state level. For example, Browder et al. (2012) conducted a 3-day statewide professional development for teachers of students with severe disabilities on general curriculum access and followed up with required product submission.

Emerging Practices in In-Service Development and Coaching

Another approach to teaching and coaching teachers of students with severe disabilities may be through the use of technology, local mentors, and learning communities. Using technology for communication and observation can allow interactions between distant consultants and teachers in the field. For example, Jung, Galyon-Keramidas, Collins, and Ludlow (2006) described a model program at West Virginia University in which local mentors were trained to support the in-service field experiences of teachers of students with severe disabilities working under emergency certificates. Overall, a hierarchy of professionals was used for support during practica. For example, the cooperating professional (i.e., local mentor) had the most contact with the teacher, including completing observations, modeling best practices, providing feedback, offering suggestions, and acting as a resource. On fewer occasions, a university supervisor monitored the cooperating professional and the teacher.

Another method to employ regional mentors to support rural learners is through the use of learning communities. In their report of a program at Utah State University, Glomb, Midenhall, Mason, and Salzberg (2009) described the use of 2-day workshops to prepare and employ successful graduates as mentors at distant sites. The mentors spent 2 to 3 hours per week working with students for $20 per hour. Using mentors, Glomb et al. increased graduation rates of their program participants from 53% to 75%.

If regional mentors are unavailable, technology may be an alternative means to provide supervision and coaching. For example, Hager (2011) supervised five teachers of students with severe disabilities at the University of Kentucky who were enrolled in the alternate certificate program and required to them to use Skype each week to participate in web conferences. Student teachers scheduled four to six conferences per semester, in which they set the agenda items for discussion (e.g., instruction, data collection, graphing data, IEPs, alternate portfolios) in an effort to perform their jobs better.

Reporting on another use of technology, Glomb, Lignugaris/Kraft, and Menlove (2009) implemented a model of support that included a videoconferencing network (i.e., EnVision, Polycom), Second Life virtual reality system, and discussions via Moodle. The benefits to this increased use in technology were that it decreased travel for supervision time, allowed for supervision and feedback from qualified professionals over time, and was cost effective (i.e., <$200); however, the use of technology increased troubleshooting time.

Dymond, Renzaglia, Halle, Chadsey, and Bentz (2008) also experimented with technology in providing support for and coaching teachers of students with a variety of disabilities and found that supervision via technology (i.e., Polycom system) can be as reliable as on-site supervision. Specifically, interobserver reliability was found to be 86% between on- and off-site supervisors. According to Dymond et al., the advantages of using technology include cost effectiveness, more frequent and longer observations, ability to use more distant sites, and less disruption by observers. There are, however, disadvantages that include equipment costs, necessary technology expertise, disruptive influence of cameras and microphones, poor Internet connections, and a limited visual field.

Impact of Staff Development on Teacher Behavior and Student Learning or Behavior

Perhaps ironically, we have more empirical evidence to support some forms of staff development than we have to support preservice learning. For example, there is evidence that on-site coaching, if done well, can have an effect on the behavior of both teachers and students with severe disabilities. Ingham and Greer (1992) found an increase in targeted responses of four master's level experienced teachers and 16 of their students in a private school for students with multiple disabilities following weekly 10–20 minute observations in which observers rated the teachers on the rate and accuracy of targeted skills. Whether or not the ratings were accompanied by written or verbal feedback, the act of rating the teachers increased the skills of both teachers and students, and the skills of both generalized throughout the day.

Because feedback is a crucial component of coaching, Scheeler, Ruhl, and McAfee (2004) conducted a comprehensive literature review on the attributes of feedback delivered to teachers to determine which contribute to teacher effectiveness. Based on the review, the authors offered three general implications for practice: (a) feedback is better than no feedback, (b) immediate feedback is better than delayed feedback, and (c) feedback that is immediate, specific, positive, and corrective is the most beneficial for changing and maintaining teaching behavior. Scheeler, McAfee, Ruhl, and Lee (2006) noted that immediate feedback delivered via technology can be nonintrusive and does not interrupt lesson flow. Furthermore, Goodman, Brady, Duffy, Scott, and Pollard (2008) found that immediate feedback using technology (e.g., SKYPE, Bluetooth, webcam) increased rate and accuracy of new special education teachers delivering elements of a specific teaching protocol. Likewise, Rock et al. (2009) found immediate feedback improved the instructional behavior of graduate students as well as the on-task behaviors of their students with disabilities during reading lessons.

Recommendations for Preservice Preparation of Teachers for Students With Severe Disabilities

What does the research allow us to conclude about how best to initially prepare teachers of students with severe disabilities? Obviously, we need to acknowledge that research on this topic is scant. Additionally, in so many ways, this area of special education has evolved and been modified so extensively that any recommendations must be based not only on the evidence that is available, but also on our own perceptions and experiences in this field. With these caveats, we propose the following:

1. Although there have been changes over the years, there is a generally accepted skill-set that preservice teachers of students with disabilities should acquire. These have been recognized in scholarly papers, textbooks, and professional manuals (e.g., CEC, 2009; Fox & Williams, 1992; Ryndak et al., 2001; Westling & Fox, 2009; Whitten & Westling, 1985). Preparation programs should recognize the need for these learning areas and assure that they are addressed in the preservice curriculum.
2. Aligned with the need for a degree of curricular consistency across programs is the need for a commonly used knowledge assessment to test graduates' knowledge about teaching students with severe disabilities. According to the National Comprehensive Center for Teacher Quality (2007), a Praxis II content area test is required for certification requirements to teach students with severe disabilities in 14 states (Delaware, Hawaii, Indiana, Kentucky, Louisiana, Maine, Maryland, Mississippi, Missouri, North Carolina, Ohio, South Carolina, Tennessee, and West Virginia), but it is not clear whether this is the specialization test for teaching students with severe disabilities (i.e., 0544: Education of Exceptional Students: Severe to Profound Disabilities) or another content area test. For example, to be certified to teach students with severe disabilities, Rhode Island requires the Praxis II in elementary content. In addition to the use of the Praxis II in some states, several other states require their own test for certification (i.e., Arizona, Florida, Georgia, Massachusetts, and Oklahoma). Other states had either no reported testing policy or did not require knowledge tests. This finding supports our contention that there is a need for consistent assessment to evaluate the knowledge of teachers of students with severe disabilities.
3. Similarly, there is the need for a valid and reliable classroom observation instrument to assure graduates are able to demonstrate skills in the classroom. Although observation instruments exist (e.g., Abell et al., 2010; Louisiana Department of Education, 2004), there is no indication that such instruments are widely used, or are valid, or reliable, or that their derived scores in any way correlate with gains in student learning. Instruments or systems that might meet these conditions should be developed, evaluated based on utility and reliability, and distributed to other programs.
4. Notwithstanding the need for knowledge and observation instruments, program evaluations have shown that some teacher education practices for teachers of students with severe disabilities are worthwhile. However, although these evaluations have documented the importance of a number of professional preparation curricular areas, they are limited in several ways. They are often flawed by low return rates and, thus, biased samples and the lack of independent observations to corroborate self-reports. If program evaluations are to continue to be based on survey methods, these shortcomings must be addressed.
5. The use of distance education technology seems to be both a valuable and promising practice for preparing teachers of students with severe disabilities. Taken together, findings from several studies (Beattie et al., 2002; McDonnell et al., 2011; Spooner et al., 1999) suggest that the outcomes for graduates of distance and face-to-face preparation programs are comparable. Although we might question the validity of the dependent measures used in these studies, distance education at least holds important potential because, as noted by Spooner (1996), given the low incidence of students with severe disabilities, the need to be able to prepare teachers from a distance could be a great benefit. Therefore, distance education models should continue to be developed, improved, and evaluated.
6. Although not clearly reflected in the literature on preservice preparation of teachers of students with severe disabilities, other literature and observations in the field suggest there are other areas that should be addressed in preservice preparation. One of these areas is the supervision and

management of paraeducators. These individuals play key roles in the education of students with severe disabilities (Giangreco, Edelman, Broer, & Doyle, 2001), but their supervision is rarely considered an important aspect of personnel preparation programs. This is an especially important issue with regard to inclusion, because there is some evidence that the overuse of paraeducators to support students in general education classrooms can be detrimental to their social and instructional inclusion (Giangreco, Smith, & Pinckney, 2006).

Recommendations for In-Service Education, Consultation, and Coaching

Although our research base is limited, the knowledge we have about effective in-service education, consultation, and coaching also can lead to meaningful suggestions. We believe that there are several key recommendations that can be made.

1. Because the needs of teachers of students with severe disabilities may vary, in-service education may require personalization. A one-size-fits-all approach to staff development is likely to result in limited usefulness for teachers and should generally be eschewed. Instead, practicing teachers should be asked to determine areas in which they need further instruction and then that instruction should be provided with targeted, one-to-one mentoring or small group instruction and support. As was discussed, this will be challenging due to the geographical dispersion of the teachers, but regional staff-development sessions and online instruction may address this problem.
2. All in-service professional development should be followed by in-classroom consultation and coaching. Without follow-up, effective instructional practices may not be implemented with a satisfactory degree of fidelity. Classroom coaching allows for demonstration, practice, and, most importantly, specific feedback to teachers. To be most effective, the feedback should be immediate (although delayed feedback may also be effective), positive, and corrective when necessary.
3. Emerging practices hold promise but lack a strong research base. These include the use of local mentors and communities of support, especially for new teachers or those in rural or remote areas who are not fully licensed. Along with local mentors, or in lieu of them if none are available, interactive technology, such as Skype or videoconferencing, can be used to provide supervision and coaching. Such approaches have been found to decrease the time required for face-to-face interactions and to be cost effective.

Recommendations for Future Research on the Preparation of Personnel for Students With Severe Disabilities

Virtually all of the recommendations listed in the previous sections call for empirical research. Although we have experience, program evaluations, and limited amounts of research to guide us, within a paradigm of empirical research, we are a field that has many independent variables, few dependent variables, and little knowledge about the relationship between them. Thus, one could create an extensive compendium of research needs, but we feel that answers to these questions are most important:

1. *What is the essential body of knowledge and skills needed by entry-level teachers of students with severe disabilities?* As a starting point, we need to review and extend the work of Ryndak et al. (2001) to establish consensus. This finding should then be widely disseminated and become a standard against which programs can be developed and evaluated.
2. *How well do graduates acquire the essential knowledge and skills, and how well do they demonstrate them in classrooms, including inclusive classrooms?* This requires, first, that there be valid and reliable instruments to assess teachers' knowledge and skills and their application in classrooms and, then, that these assessment instruments be applied to program graduates.

3. *What is the relation between preparation program features and demonstrated teacher performance?* Evaluations of projects have consistently found that certain aspects of programs are rated well and others less so. If these evaluations are to be meaningful, correlational research should be conducted to determine if valued program components are related to demonstrated teacher knowledge and skills.
4. *What is the relationship between demonstrated teacher knowledge and skills and gains in learning by students with severe disabilities?* Assuming we can identify and measure important teacher knowledge and skills, these should be further validated through determining their relationship to student gains. Correlational or quasi-experimental research could provide at least tentative answers to this question.
5. *How do various forms and features of distance education affect teacher knowledge and skill development and subsequent learning of their students with severe disabilities?* As we increase the use of distance education models, these forms of instruction, like traditional face-to-face instruction, call for at least correlational or quasi-experimental research to evaluate their effectiveness.
6. *What models of in-service development, consultation, and coaching increase teacher knowledge and skills and result in concomitant learning by students with severe disabilities?* In this area, there are many promising practices, some with supportive research but many with only anecdotal support. Because of the need for more specific forms of instruction to meet unique teacher needs, this question may often be addressed through more single subject research designs.

Conclusion

Preparing teachers of students with severe disabilities has a relatively brief history. Although we have a great deal of research on instructional and behavioral interventions that can be used successfully with students, we have much less research on how to initially prepare teachers or how to continue to educate them once they become practitioners. More knowledge in this area would be helpful to a field that must be sensitive to cost effectiveness because of the low incidence of students and teachers. Further, because of the unique nature of this field, teachers of students with severe disabilities often work in isolated settings, often with administrators and supervisors who have little understanding of the practices they use. This means that teachers may not be subjected to the same level of scrutiny or evaluation that occurs for general classroom teachers or teachers of students with less severe disabilities. The truth is, we do not really know the quality of education that students with severe disabilities are receiving; nor do we have a consensus even on how to measure that. It is essential then, that at least we know that teachers in this field are adequately prepared and that their repertoire of instructional skills is sufficient to affect the learning of their students.

In this paper, we have noted the heterogeneity and complexity of students referred to as having severe disabilities, the history of educational programs and curricular emphases, and elements and features of preservice and in-service education programs, including mentoring and coaching. We have enough knowledge to guide us to develop and offer initial and continuing training and support, but we do not have enough research to assure us that what we are doing is the most effective and efficient approach to doing so. The research that exists, and that which we recommend, is intended to help us move in this direction.

References

Abell, M., Brown, R., Collins, B., Kleinert, H., Robey, T., & Whetstone, P. (2010). KTS/IIC Alignment Document. Retrieved from http://asc-hdi.com/IHE/SitePages/Home.aspx

Arthur, M. Butterfield, N., & McKinnon, D. H. (1998). Communication intervention for students with severe disability. *International Journal of Disability, 45*(1), 97–115.

Baer, D. M., Wolf, M. M., & Risley, T. R. (1968). Some current dimensions of applied behavior analysis. *Journal of Applied Behavior Analysis, 1*, 91–97. doi:10.1901/jaba.1968.1-91

Beattie, J., Spooner, F., Jordan, L., Algozzine, B., & Spooner, M. (2002). Evaluating instruction in distance learning classes. *Teacher Education and Special Education, 25*, 124–132. doi:10.1177/088840640202500204

Browder, D. M., Jimenez, B. A., Mims, P. J., Knight, V. F., Spooner, F., Lee, A., & Flowers, C. (2012). The effects of a "tell-show-try-apply" professional development package on teachers of students with severe developmental disabilities. *Teacher Education and Special Education, 35*, 212–227. doi:10.1177/0888406411432650

Browder, D., Spooner, F., Ahlgrim-Delzell, L., Flowers, C., Algozzine, B., & Karvonen, M. (2003). A content analysis of the curricular philosophies reflected in states' alternate assessment performance indicators. *Research and Practice for Persons with Severe Disabilities, 28*, 165–181. doi:10.2511/rpsd.28.4.165

Browder, D. M., Spooner, F., Algozzine, R., Ahlgrim-Delzell, L., Flowers, C., & Karvonen, M. (2003). What we know and need to know about alternate assessment. *Exceptional Children, 70*, 45–61.

Browder, D. M., Spooner, F., Wakeman, S., Trela, K., & Baker, J. N. (2006). Aligning instruction with academic content standards: Finding the link. *Research and Practice for Persons with Severe Disabilities, 31*, 309–321.

Browder, D. M., Wakeman, S., & Flowers, C. P. (2006). Assessment of progress in the general curriculum for students with disabilities. *Theory Into Practice, 45*, 249–259. doi:10.1207/s15430421tip4503_7

Brown, L., Branston, M. B., Hamre-Nietupski, S., Pumpian, I., Certo, N., & Gruenewald, L. (1979). A strategy for developing chronological age appropriate and functional curricular content for severely handicapped adolescents and young adults. *The Journal of Special Education, 13*, 81–90. doi:10.1177/002246697901300113

Brown, L., Branston-McLean, M., Baumgart, D., Vincent, L., Falvey, M., & Schroeder, J. (1979). Using the characteristics of a variety of current and subsequent least restrictive environments as factors in the development of curricular content for severely handicapped students. *AAESPH Review, 4*, 407–424.

Clark, N. M., Cushing, L. S., & Kennedy, C. H. (2004). An intensive onsite technical assistance model to promote inclusive educational practices for students with disabilities in middle school and high school. *Research and Practice for Persons with Severe Disabilities, 29*, 253–262. doi:10.2511/rpsd.29.4.253

Connor, C., Snell, M., Gansneder, B., & Dexter, S. (2010). Special education teachers' use of assistive technology with students who have severe disabilities. *Journal of Technology and Teacher Education, 18*, 369–386.

Council for Exceptional Children. (2009). *What every special educator must know: Ethics, standards, and guidelines* (6th ed.). Arlington, VA: Author.

Courtade, G. R., Browder, D. M., & Spooner, F. (2010). Training teachers to use an inquiry-based task analysis to teach science to students with moderate and severe disabilities. *Education and Training in Autism and Developmental Disabilities, 45*, 378–399.

Delano, M. E., Keefe, L., & Perner, D. (2008–2009). Personnel preparation: Recurring challenges and the need for action to ensure access to general education. *Research and Practice for Persons with Severe Disabilities, 33/34*, 232–240.

Demchak, M., & Browder, D. M. (1987). Data-based teacher supervision: Evaluating task analytic instruction. *Journal of Special Education Technology, 9*, 9–18.

Doll, B., Sands, D. J., Wehmeyer, M. L., & Palmer, S. (1996). Promoting the development and acquisition of self-determined behavior. In D. J. Sands & M. L. Wehmeyer (Eds.), *Self-determination across the lifespan: Independence and choice for people with disabilities* (pp. 65–90). Baltimore, MD: Paul H. Brookes.

Dymond, S. K., Renzaglia, A., Halle, J. W., Chadsey, J., & Bentz, J. L. (2008). An evaluation of videoconferencing as a supportive technology for practicum supervision. *Teacher Education and Special Education, 31*, 243–256. doi:10.1177/0888406408330645

Education Commission of the States (2010). Pay for performance proposals in race to the top round II applications. *Briefing Memo*. Retrieved from http://www.ecs.org/clearinghouse/87/06/8706.pdf

Flowers, C., Wakeman, S., Browder, D. M., & Karvonen, M. (2009). Links for academic learning (LAL): A conceptual model for investigating alignment of alternate assessments based on alternate achievement standards. *Educational Measurement: Issues and Practice, 28*(1), 25–37.

Ford, A., Schnorr, R., Meyer, L., Davern, L., Black, J., & Dempsey, P. (Eds.). (1989). *The Syracuse community-referenced curriculum guide for students with moderate and severe disabilities*. Baltimore, MD: Paul H. Brookes.

Fox, L., & Williams, D. G. (1992). Preparing teachers of students with severe disabilities. *Teacher Education and Special Education, 15*, 97–107. doi:10.1177/088840649201500205

Giangreco, M. F., Edelman, S. W., Broer, S. M., & Doyle, M. B. (2001). Paraprofessional support of students with disabilities: Literature from the past decade. *Exceptional Children, 68*, 45–63.

Giangreco, M. F., Smith, C. S., & Pinckney, E. (2006). Addressing the paraprofessional dilemma in an inclusive school: A program description. *Research and Practice for Persons with Severe Disabilities, 31*, 215–229.

Glomb, N., Lignugaris/Kraft, B., and Menlove, R. R. (2009). The USU mild/moderate distance degree and licensure program: Where we've been and where we're going. *Rural Special Education Quarterly, 28*(3), 18–22.

Glomb, N., Midenhall, T., Mason, L., & Salzberg, C. (2009) Reducing isolation through regional mentors and learning communities: A way to support rural learners. *Rural Special Education Quarterly, 28*(4), 31–35.

Goodman, J. I., Brady, M. P., Duffy, M. L., Scott, J., & Pollard, N. E. (2008). The effects of "Bug-in-Ear" supervision on special education teachers' delivery of learn units. *Focus on Autism and Other Developmental Disabilities, 23*, 207–216. doi:10.1177/1088357608324713

Gratz, D. B. (2010). Looming questions in performance pay. *Phi Delta Kappan, 20(8)*, 16–21.

Grisham-Brown, J., & Collins, B. C. (2002). Training rural educators in Kentucky through distance learning: Impact with follow-up data. *Rural Special Education Quarterly, 21*(4), 12–20.

Hager, K. D. (2011). Web conferencing with distant alternate certificate student teachers. *Rural Special Education Quarterly, 30*(1), 49–55.

Harmon, C., Kasa-Hendrickson, C., & Neal, L. I. (2009). Cultural competencies for teachers of students with significant disabilities. *Research and Practice for Persons with Severe Disabilities, 34*, 137–144.

Horrocks, E. L., & Morgan, R. L. (2011). Effects of inservice teacher training on correct implementation of assessment and instructional procedures for teachers of students with profound multiple disabilities. *Teacher Education and Special Education, 34*, 283–319. doi:10.1177/0888406410397556

Ingham, P., & Greer, R. D. (1992). Changes in student and teacher responses in observed and generalized settings as a function of supervisor observations. *Journal of Applied Behavior Analysis, 25*, 153–164. doi:10.1901/jaba.1992.25-153

Jones, P. (2010). My peers have also been an inspiration for me: Developing online learning opportunities to support teacher engagement with inclusive pedagogy for students with severe/profound intellectual and developmental disabilities. *International Journal of Inclusive Education, 14*, 681–696. doi:10.1080/13603111003778452

Judge, S., & Simms, K. A. (2009). Assistive technology training at the pre-service level: A national snapshot of teacher preparation programs. *Teacher Education and Special Education, 32*, 33–44. doi:10.1177/0888406408330868

Jung, L. A., Galyon-Keramidas, C., Collins, B. C., & Ludlow, B. L. (2006). Distance education strategies to support practica in rural settings. *Rural Special Education Quarterly, 25*(2), 18–24.

Katims, D. S. (2000). Literacy instruction for people with mental retardation: Historical highlights and contemporary analysis. *Education and Training in Mental Retardation and Developmental Disabilities, 35*, 3–15.

Kim, O., & Hupp, S. C. (2007). Instructional interactions of students with cognitive disabilities: Sequential analysis. *American Journal on Mental Retardation, 112*, 94–106. doi:10.1352/0895-8017(2007)112[94:IIOSWC]2.0.CO;2

Kretlow, A. G., & Bartholomew, C. C. (2010). Using coaching to improve the fidelity of evidence-based practices: A review of studies. *Teacher Education and Special Education, 33*, 279–299. doi:10.1177/0888406410371643

Lang, M., & Fox, L. (2004). Breaking with tradition: Providing effective professional development for instructional personnel supporting students with severe disabilities. *Teacher Education and Special Education, 27*, 163–173. doi:10.1177/088840640402700207

Lerman, D. C., Tetreault, A., Havanetz, A., Strobel, M., & Garro, J. (2008). Further evaluation of a brief, intensive, teacher-training model. *Journal of Applied Behavior Analysis, 41*, 243–248. doi:10.1901/jaba.2008.41-243

Louisiana Department of Education. (2004). *Strategies for effective teaching in the twenty-first century: Louisiana teacher assistance and assessment program.* Baton Rouge, LA: Author. Retrieved from http://www.zacharyschools.org/departments/personnel/ZIP/Strategies%20for%20Effective%20Teaching_Special%20Ed.pdf

McDonnell, J., Jameson, J. M., Riesen, T., Polychronis, S., Crockett, M. A., & Brown, B. E. (2011). NA comparison of on-campus and distance teacher education programs in severe disabilities. *Teacher Education and Special Education, 34*, 106–118. doi:10.1177/0888406410380424

National Comprehensive Center for Teacher Quality. (2007). *Special education teacher certification and licensure.* Retrieved from http://mb2.ecs.org/reports/Reporttq.aspx?id=1542&map=0

Rainforth, B. (2000). Preparing teachers to educate students with severe disabilities in inclusive settings despite contextual constraints. *Research and Practice for Persons with Severe Disabilities, 25*, 83–91. doi:10.2511/rpsd.25.2.83

Rock, M. L., Gregg, M., Thead, B. K., Acker, S. E., Gable, R. A., & Zigmond, N. P. (2009). Can you hear me now? Evaluation of an online wireless technology to provide real-time feedback to special education teachers-in-training. *Teacher Education and Special Education, 32*, 64–82. doi:10.1177/0888406408330872

Ryndak, D. L., Clark, D., Conroy, M., & Holthaus Stuart, C. (2001). Preparing teachers to meet the needs of students with severe disabilities: Program configuration and expertise. *Research and Practice for Persons with Severe Disabilities, 26*, 96–105. doi:10.2511/rpsd.26.2.96

Sailor, W., Anderson, J. L., Halvorsen, A. T., Doering, M. A., Filler, J., & Goetz, L. (1989). *The comprehensive local school: Regular education for all students with disabilities.* Baltimore, MD: Paul H. Brookes.

Scheeler, M. C., McAfee, J. K., Ruhl, K. L., & Lee, D. L. (2006). Effects of corrective feedback delivered via wireless technology on preservice teacher performance and student behavior. *Teacher Education and Special Education, 29*, 12–25. doi:10.1177/088840640602900103

Scheeler, M. C., Ruhl, K. L., & McAfee, J. K. (2004). Providing performance feedback to teachers: A review. *Teacher Education and Special Education, 27*, 396–407. doi:10.1177/088840640402700407

Snell, M. E. (2003). Applying research to practice: The more pervasive problem? *Research and Practice for Persons with Severe Disabilities, 28*, 143–147. doi:10.2511/rpsd.28.3.143

Snell, M. E., Martin, K., & Orelove, F. P. (1995). *Virginia statewide program to endorse students with severe and profound handicaps—the endorsement project: Final report* (ERIC No. ED379877). Charlottesville, VA: University of Virginia.

Spooner, F. (1996). Personnel preparation: Where we have been and where we may be going in severe disabilities. *Teacher Education and Special Education, 19*, 213–215. doi:10.1177/088840649601900309

Spooner, F., & Browder, D. M. (2006). Why teach the general curriculum? In D. M. Browder & F. Spooner (Eds.), *Teaching language arts, math, & science to students with significant cognitive disabilities* (pp. 1–13). Baltimore, MD: Paul H. Brooks.

Spooner, F., Jordan, L. Algozzine, B., & Spooner, M. (1999). Student ratings of instruction in distance learning and on-campus. *Journal of Educational Research, 92*, 132–140. doi:10.1080/00220679909597588

Stainback, S., & Stainback, W. (1990). Inclusive schooling. In W. Stainback & S. Stainback (Eds.), *Support networks for inclusive schooling* (pp. 3–23). Baltimore, MD: Paul H. Brookes.

Stephenson, J., Carter, M., & Arthur-Kelly, M. (2011). Professional learning for teachers without special education qualifications working with students with severe disabilities. *Teacher Education and Special Education, 34*, 7–20.

Villa, R. A., & Thousand, J. S. (2000). *Restructuring for caring and effective education: Piecing the puzzle together.* Baltimore, MD: Paul H. Brookes.

Wehmeyer, M. L. (1992). Self-determination and the education of students with mental retardation. *Education and Training in Mental Retardation, 27*, 302–314.

Wehmeyer, M. L. (1996). Self-determination as an educational outcome: Why is it important to children, youth, and adults with disabilities. In D. J. Sands & M. L. Wehmeyer (Eds.), *Self-determination across the life span: Independence and choice for people with disabilities* (pp. 17–36). Baltimore, MD: Paul H. Brookes.

Wertlieb, D., & Place, P. (1984). *Multidisciplinary training for educators of young (3–7) severely handicapped children: Project CoNECT (Collaborative Network for Early Childhood Training). Final Report, October, 1981–September, 1984* (ERIC No. ED254970). Medford, MA: Tufts University.

Westling, D. L. (1986). *Introduction to mental retardation.* Englewood Cliffs, NJ: Prentice-Hall.

Westling, D. L., & Fox, L. (2009). *Teaching students with severe disabilities* (4th ed.). Columbus, OH: Pearson/Merrill/Prentice-Hall Publishers.

Whitten, T., & Westling, D. L. (1985). Competencies for teachers of the severely/profoundly handicapped: A review. *Teacher Education and Special Education, 8*, 104–111. doi:10.1177/088840648500800207

Wilcox, B., & Bellamy, G. T. (1987). *The activities catalog: An alternative curriculum for youth and adults with severe disabilities.* Baltimore, MD: Paul H. Brookes.

Yoon, K. S., Duncan, T., Lee, S. W.-Y., Scarloss, B., & Shapley, K. L. (2007). *Reviewing the evidence on how teacher professional development affects student achievement* (Issues & Answers Report, REL 2007-No. 033). Washington, DC: U.S. Department of Education, Institute of Education Sciences, National Center for Education Evaluation and Regional Assistance, Regional Educational Laboratory Southwest. Retrieved from http://ies.ed.gov/ncee/edlabs/projects/project.asp?ProjectID=70

York, J., Vandercook, T., MacDonald, C., & Wolff, S. (1989). *Strategies for full inclusion.* Minneapolis, MN: University of Minnesota, Institute on Community Integration.

19

Teacher Preparation for Students Who Demonstrate Challenging Behaviors

Maureen A. Conroy

UNIVERSITY OF FLORIDA

Peter J. Alter

SAINT MARY'S COLLEGE OF CALIFORNIA

Brian A. Boyd

UNIVERSITY OF NORTH CAROLINA—CHAPEL HILL

Elizabeth Bettini

UNIVERSITY OF FLORIDA

Things to Think About

- Teachers, regardless of content or certification area, need to have a wealth of knowledge and skills for working with students who present challenging behaviors.
- The 1997 reauthorization of IDEA included requirements directly related to providing appropriate educational services (i.e., Functional Behavioral Assessment, Behavioral Intervention Plan) for students with challenging behaviors.
- High-quality teacher preparation program should be based on three key elements: (a) research, (b) theory, and (c) practice.
- Since many students who demonstrate challenging behavior also have difficulties with academic content, effective academic instruction may serve as an effective classroom and behavior management strategy.
- Several innovations to better prepare and mentor teachers of students who demonstrate challenging behaviors include family-centered practices, service-learning, and e-mentoring and support.

Working with students who demonstrate challenging behaviors is one of the most significant problems facing teachers in our schools today. Exacerbating this problem is the scarcity of teachers who are available and qualified to work with these students (Oliver & Reschly, 2010; Van Acker, 2004). When teachers are found to work with these students, they often lack the necessary skills and are more likely to leave their jobs after a relatively short period of time (Adera & Bullock, 2010). Thus, teacher turnover and attrition are common. Whether teachers are certified in a categorical area (e.g., Emotional/Behavioral Disorders [E/BD], Autism Spectrum Disorders [ASD]) is somewhat irrelevant when it comes to successfully working with these students. Rather, teachers need to have a high level of knowledge and skills for preventing and ameliorating students' challenging behaviors in their classrooms while teaching the appropriate content knowledge.

Challenging behaviors include behavioral excesses (e.g., defiance, disruption, verbal and physical aggression) as well as behavioral deficits (e.g., off-task, disengagement from work completion) and are typically defined by the contexts in which they occur and, in educational settings, the impact they have on student learning and the classroom environment (Kauffman & Landrum, 2009). Of all the students served under the Individuals with Disabilities Educational Improvement Act (IDEA), children and youth who demonstrate challenging behaviors have the poorest life outcomes of any exceptionality (Kauffman & Landrum, 2009). In part, this may be due to the lack of highly qualified teachers available that have the skills to effectively work with these students. In the next section, we discuss a number of historical and current trends that have influenced teacher preparation of students with challenging behaviors. Following this section, we present an overview of the necessary skills and competencies teachers must attain to meet the complex needs of these students.

Historical and Current Legislative and Service Trends

Similar to many students with disabilities, children and youth with challenging behaviors were excluded from public education for many years. Due to extreme behaviors that were often unmanageable in school and home settings, these individuals were often housed in institutional settings, which provided limited access to appropriate educational opportunities (Brigham & Hott, 2011). Fortunately, this trend began to change in the first half of the 20th century, as educators and policy makers became increasingly invested in educating all students with disabilities. With the federal initiative to provide publicly funded appropriate educational services for students with disabilities, including students with challenging behaviors, legislation in the early 1960s supported funding for categorical teacher education programs, including the category of "Emotional Disturbance" (Kauffman & Landrum, 2006).

At the time, the literature on effective educational practices for working with students with challenging behaviors was limited and a wide variety of theories, ranging from psychoanalytic to behavioral models, drove educational practices. In fact, several model schools designed to address the needs of students with E/BD and other behavioral challenges began to appear in select locations throughout the country. Although these programs were often inaccessible to most students due to their locations (Brigham & Hott, 2011), their underlying theoretical approaches became the foundation for teacher preparation programs designed to prepare trainees to address the needs of students with challenging behaviors. Along with model programs, federal legislation provided the impetus for expanding teacher preparation programs in this area. The most significant piece of legislation impacting teacher preparation for all students with disabilities, including those with challenging behaviors, was the Education for all Handicapped Children Act of 1975, now known as the Individuals with Disabilities Education Improvement Act (IDEA).

Individuals With Disabilities Education Improvement Act

The 1960s and 1970s witnessed an explosion of legislation related to educating all students with disabilities, culminating with the Education for all Handicapped Children Act in 1975. The original legislation primarily addressed *access* to public education, with limited attention to the *quality* of education (Brownell, Sindelar, Kiely, & Danielson, 2010; Jameson & Huefner, 2006). Historically, educational practices (and subsequent teacher preparation programs) for students with behavioral challenges was primarily targeted at ameliorating existing behavioral excess or deficits with little attention for addressing academic deficits (Butler, 2004; Steinberg & Knitzer, 1992; Wehby, Lane, & Falk, 2003). As research expanded indicating the importance of high-quality academic instruction as well as behavior management practices (Gunter et al., 1994; Wehby et al., 2003), policy began to shift and educational services began to target both academic and behavioral needs of students with challenging behaviors. Unfortunately, this trend did not always translate into teacher preparation programs, as many teachers who were trained to work with this population reported feeling unprepared for teaching academics (Sutherland, Denny, & Gunter, 2005). Nevertheless, through our expansion of the research literature and revision of policies stemming from the subsequent reauthorizations of IDEA, a number of changes in our approaches toward educating students with challenging behaviors and preparing the teachers who work with them have occurred.

The IDEA 1990 and 1997 reauthorizations both made a significant impact on services and subsequently personnel preparation programs for students with challenging behaviors. With the 1990 reauthorization of IDEA, two new disability categories were included: Autism and Traumatic Brain Injury. Included within both of these disabilities are students who demonstrate challenging behaviors. Also, with inclusion of autism as an educational disability and the increasing prevalence of ASD came an increase in a number of personnel preparation programs focused in this area. This resulted in many states initiating state endorsements and training designed to increase the knowledge and skills of pre- and in-service teachers working with students with ASD.

In 1997, the most relevant changes of the reauthorization for students with challenging behaviors was the requirements of a functional behavioral assessment (FBA), behavioral intervention plan (BIP), and manifestation determination for any student who engaged in chronic problem behavior. All three of these initiatives have had a significant impact on personnel preparation. As a result of these changes, a dramatic increase in training current and future personnel in FBA and BIP (including manifestation determination) was initiated and remains. The most recent reauthorization (2004) amended and reauthorized IDEA to align with the mandates in the No Child Left Behind Act. In terms of personnel preparation, the largest impact came in defining "highly qualified" teachers and the routes to obtaining competence in a specific instructional area, such as E/BD or ASD.

No Child Left Behind

The No Child Left Behind Act (NCLB, 2002), designed to ensure that all students meet academic performance standards, played a major role in shifting the focus of special education services away from access and more toward student academic outcomes (Fitzsimons & White, 2004). This aspect has impacted teacher preparation and service for students with challenging behaviors in three ways: (a) making educators *accountable* for all students' progress, (b) requiring all teachers to be *highly qualified*, and (c) easing entry into the teaching profession through *alternative routes to certification* (AR).

Although teachers are ultimately responsible for student learning and outcomes, NCLB increased the schools' (and teachers') accountability for the academic progress of all students, including those with behavioral challenges (e.g., E/BD and ASD; Fitzsimons & White, 2004; Van Acker, 2004). NCLB also requires teachers to be *highly qualified* in all subjects they teach. Unfortunately, this requirement has exacerbated a problem that has plagued special education for many years. There has always been a significant shortage of teachers to work with students with challenging behaviors and the regulations in NCLB resulted in increased shortages of highly qualified teachers in this area (Henderson, Klein, Gonzalez, & Bradley, 2005; Thornton, Peltier, & Medina, 2007). Even though there is ample evidence that demonstrates highly qualified teachers make a significant difference in educational outcomes for students with disabilities (McLeskey & Billingsley, 2008), many states have had to allow exceptions to this requirement (Jameson & Huefner, 2006). Given the shortage of teachers in the area of E/BD, not surprisingly, teachers of students with E/BD are more than twice as likely as other special educators to hold certificates from alternate routes of certification (Henderson et al., 2005).

Paradoxically, NCLB holds teachers to higher standards, while simultaneously easing entry into the profession through AR (Sindelar, Brownell, & Billingsley, 2010). Although alternative routes to certification have many drawbacks (see Hardman & Mulder, 2004), they do hold some promise for addressing both the quality and the quantity of personnel working with students who have challenging behaviors. Longer and more rigorous AR prepare their students to have skills equal to graduates of traditional teacher education programs. AR also attracts more culturally and linguistically diverse teachers, which may help reduce the gap between the demographics of students and teachers (Billingsley, Fall, & Williams, 2006; Sindelar et al., 2010; Van Acker, 2004).

The Inclusion Movement

Since 1975, when PL 94–142 was first enacted, access to an appropriate education in least restrictive settings has been a consistent theme in the education of all students with disabilities. As the movement to include more students with disabilities in general education classrooms has continued to evolve, teacher preparation initiatives have responded by creating noncategorical teacher certification (Brownell et al., 2010; Cooley-Nichols, 2004; Oliver & Reschly, 2010). Since teachers in inclusive settings are likely to teach students with a wide variety of disabilities (Hardman & Mulder, 2004), noncategorical certification allows greater administrative flexibility and, theoretically, ensures that all special educators are trained in practices to address challenging behavior; a critical competency for successful teaching in inclusive settings (Butler, 2004).

Noncategorical teacher certification may train teachers in many of the necessary skills; however, this level of training is not necessarily sufficient for working with students with challenging behaviors. Simply put, teaching students with challenging behavior requires additional behavior management skills beyond the common special education teacher competencies and cross-categorical preparation programs (Bullock, Gable, & Melloy, 2004; Van Acker, 2004). Without supplementary coursework in strategies to address challenging behaviors, graduates from cross-categorical programs may be unprepared to teach students with the most severe challenging behaviors, such as students with E/BD or ASD (Oliver & Reschly, 2010). This may be one factor that contributes to the lack of successful inclusion of students with challenging behaviors in general education settings (Smith, Katsiyannis, & Ryan, 2011). If teachers in inclusive settings lack the appropriate preparation and skills for working with challenging behaviors, these students are less likely to be successful in these settings. One recent trend to address the need for more in-depth training and skills to work with students with challenging behaviors is the addition of behavior specialists in schools and support staff who are certified in Applied Behavior Analysis (ABA). Even though specialized training in ABA is not required of all teachers, this initiative suggests that specialized skills in behavior analysis are still warranted to address these students' behavioral challenges (Henderson, 2011).

Prevention and Response to Intervention

Along with the shift toward inclusive models of service delivery, a parallel shift exists which focuses on preventive approaches toward identification and intervention of students with disabilities, including prevention of challenging behaviors. With the increasing evidence indicating the effectiveness of early identification and intervention in the prevention of challenging behaviors in high risk children (Cheney, Flower, & Templeton, 2008; Corsello, 2005; Gresham, 2007) and the Response to Intervention (RTI) initiative to guide intervention and determine eligibility for special education (Salend & Garrick Duhaney, 2011; Smith et al., 2011), a more proactive approach toward preventing and ameliorating challenging behaviors has influenced teacher preparation and services for students with challenging behaviors. The use of RTI (in concert with positive behavior supports; PBS) is becoming more common for diagnosing and treating students with E/BD (Fairbanks, Sugai, Guardino, & Lathrop, 2007). To date, RTI has not been widely used for students with ASD (Allen, Robins, & Decker, 2008); however, as more and more students with Asperger syndrome or High Functioning Autism (HFA) are served, this may change.

Although the utility of RTI and PBS for diagnoses is unclear, substantial evidence demonstrates that PBS is extremely useful for preventing and managing challenging problems (McCurdy, Mannella, & Eldridge, 2003; Scott & Barrett, 2004), and teachers who work with these students must be trained appropriately.

In summary, the services for students with challenging behaviors have changed considerably over the past several decades. Likewise, preparing personnel to be highly qualified to meet the needs of these students has also come a long way. In the following section, we provide an overview of the core components and competencies that should comprise a high-quality personnel preparation program.

Components and Competencies of a High Quality Teacher Preparation Program

There is little margin for error when teaching students who engage in challenging behavior. Ineffective instruction that fails to engage the learner can have disastrous results. This group of students is unlikely to sit quietly while a teacher tries to salvage a lesson that is not going well. Similarly, poorly thought-out and/or culturally inappropriate responses to challenging behavior only serve to exacerbate situations. For these reasons teacher preparation programs for this population must be outstanding. We believe all components and competencies of a high-quality teacher preparation program should be set in the center of the triangle created by these three elements: (a) research (why the strategy should or should not be used); (b) theory (where the strategy came from and how it fits into an overarching model); and (c) practice (how do I implement this strategy in the classroom). For example, a token economy has been identified as an effective, evidence-based practice for students with E/BD (Naughton & McLaughlin, 1995). Within a model program, teacher candidates would be able to identify the research supporting this practice (Hackenberg, 2009; Kazdin, 1982), the theoretical framework that it is grounded in (behaviorism, applied behavior analysis, and operant conditioning) and the critical features that make it effective (tokens are dispensed immediately, consistently, and contingent upon the demonstration of desired behaviors) (Scott, Anderson, & Alter, 2011).

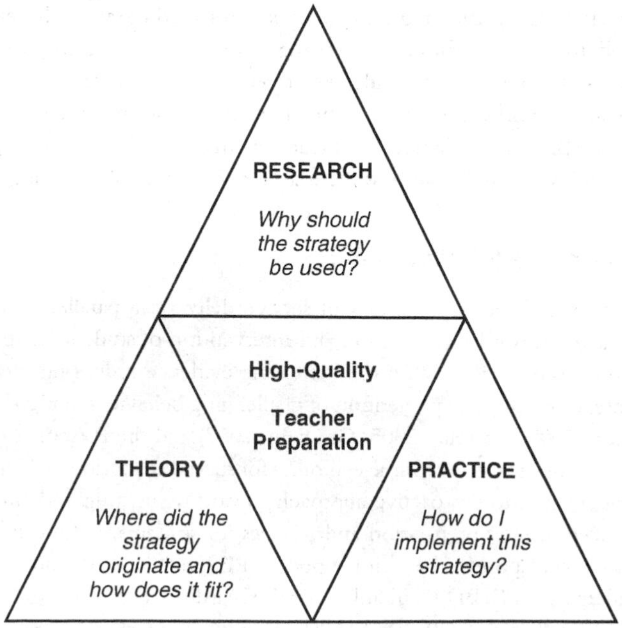

Figure 19.1 Components and Competencies of a High-Quality Teacher Preparation Program

This necessitates adequate instructional time and clinical and field experiences, a clear understanding of challenging behaviors in the classroom, and knowledge of the broad-based characteristics of students who engage in them. Within the proposed model, teacher candidates would become familiar with characteristics that may include students living in poverty, parents with limited education and a negative attitude toward schooling, harsh or inconsistent parenting styles and exposure within the community to gang membership, and drug and alcohol abuse (Karnick, 2004; Walker & Sprague, 1999). Understanding these characteristics as being discrepant with the school context and leading to challenging behavior is critical for candidates in teacher preparation programs.

In consideration of the components and competencies of high-quality teacher preparation programs, we view effective preparation as preparing teachers who are equipped with competencies in three key areas. These are areas facilitating: (a) academic success, (b) social/behavioral success, and (c) classroom/behavior management skills. This section operates on the assumption that teacher preparation programs are already providing high-quality training in basic pedagogy; thus, the three aforementioned areas are in addition to this basic pedagogical instruction.

Facilitating Academic Success

Remediating academic difficulties for students who demonstrate challenging behavior is a critical element for effective teacher preparation (Anderson, Kutash, & Duchnowski, 2001; Lane, 2004; Reid, Gonzalez, Nordness, Trout, & Epstein, 2004; Sabornie, Cullinan, Osborne, & Brock, 2005). Because behavior (rather than academics) is the identified problem area for the students, teacher preparation tends to focus primarily on classroom and behavior management (Wehby et al., 2003). This is unfortunate because research has suggested that by improving academic performance, a valuable proposition alone, we may also serve to improve social and behavioral difficulties (Witt, VanDerHeyden, & Gilbertson, 2004). In other words, effective academic instruction may serve as an effective classroom and behavior management strategy. For example, researchers have found that improving reading skills has decreased problem behavior (DuPaul, Ervin, Hook, & McGoey, 1998; Locke & Fuchs, 1995). In order to prepare teachers to address these difficulties, training to work with students with challenging behaviors must focus on both *what* they teach (content), and *how* they teach (instructional behaviors).

While we acknowledge the importance of all content areas in a balanced curriculum, the severe academic deficits that have been documented for many students with challenging behavior (Wagner et al., 2003) suggest that a more focused approach on basic skills in reading and math could be more appropriate. Researchers have established a powerful correlation between instructional time and student achievement and the diffusion of a curriculum attempting to cover all content areas may only serve to frustrate students and exacerbate a pattern of failure. Attention to reading difficulties may be the most important content area for teachers of students with challenging behavior to consider. Reading difficulties are a well-chronicled attribute of students with E/BD (Rivera, Al-Otaiba, & Koorland, 2006) and ASD (Whalon, Al Otaiba, & Delano, 2009). Reading is also an essential gateway skill for all content areas. Teachers of students with challenging behavior should be well-prepared to address all elements of reading phonemic awareness, phonics, vocabulary, fluency, and comprehension (Coyne, Kame'enui, & Carnine, 2011). However, phonemic awareness, alphabetic understanding, and automaticity with the code are identified as minimum building blocks for competent readers (Simmons & Kame'enui, 1998). By preparing teachers to address these basic components, they will be in a better position to remediate basic needs of learners.

The focus of mathematics instruction should be undergirded by the five strands put forward by the National Research Council in 2001: (a) conceptual understanding, (b) procedural fluency, (c) strategic competence, (d) adaptive reasoning, and (e) a productive disposition. However, while the so-called Math Wars rage over the importance of direct instruction versus inquiry-based teaching, for students who engage in challenging behavior and likely struggle academically, priority should be on achieving functional understanding (Cole & Washburn, 2010). This emphasis needs to be translated into teacher preparation programs so that teachers are prepared to guide students through skill acquisition to fluency and strategic competence. This also may include the use of research-supported assessment practices outlined by Allsopp and colleagues (2008) such as concrete–representational–abstract assessment and error pattern analysis. This content is best delivered through strategies that mirror effective instructional practices in reading including direct instruction, connecting to prior knowledge and preconceptions and use of metacognitive strategies.

Research has indicated that the best methods for teaching across all content areas includes the use of systematic, explicit instruction, schema-based instruction, and providing the appropriate use of scaffolded lessons that systematically give students who struggle with learning the necessary skills to become proficient in both reading and math (Barton-Arwood, Wehby, & Falk, 2005; Cole & Washburn, 2010). Other teacher behaviors that have empirical support include adequate opportunities to respond, clear instructional goals, and the use of effective prompts and cues (Scott et al., 2011). Therefore, teacher preparation programs must focus on preparing their candidates to deliver direct instruction effectively, identify problem areas, and brainstorm adequate supports to remediate difficulties. Finally, this should include the use of accurate assessment techniques possibly in the form of curriculum-based measurements, which allow for constant progress monitoring and guide necessary remediation.

Facilitating Social and Behavioral Success

Beyond addressing academic needs, it is imperative that teacher preparation programs provide instruction in the social/emotional domains. By definition students with E/BD (Kauffman & Landrum, 2009) and students with ASD (APA, 2013) have difficulty making and maintaining satisfactory relationships with teachers and peers because of poor social functioning. Therefore, instruction should focus on two critical areas. First, instruction will need to focus on social skills and self-determination (Carter, Lane, Crnobori, Bruhnk, & Oakes, 2011; Miller, Lane, & Wehby, 2005). This includes preparing current and future teachers to conduct role-plays of spontaneous social interactions, model metacognitive strategies to recognize emotions and display them appropriately, and recognize the relationships between students' actions and outcomes. Second, teachers need to be prepared in how to teach the rules, routines and procedures of daily school life (Witt et al., 2004). The end goal is to use instruction to address both the unpredictable social/behavioral elements of school life such as peer and adult interactions and the more structured components of a school such as how to turn in papers, transition between settings or activities, and even how and when to raise a hand before speaking. While the curricula for teaching these skills, especially social skills, are myriad, their basic structure should approach instruction in the social/emotional domain in a four-step process that includes: identifying potential problem areas in social interaction; developing solutions for these problems and various strategies to teach them effectively; providing judicious reviews to maintain consistency of implementation; and assessing to insure that strategies are being used and are effective.

Classroom and Behavior Management

Finally, criticism has been leveled at preparation programs for not providing adequate preparation in effective classroom management. Oliver and Reschly (2010) noted that only 27% of special education programs surveyed had an entire course dedicated to classroom and behavior management. Teacher preparation programs need to include a variety of strategies to deal with challenging behavior in both a preventative and a responsive fashion. Ducharme and Shecter (2011) propose a keystone approach that recommends that teachers first focus on a circumscribed set of skills including compliance, social skills and on-task skills and then use effective teaching practices and reinforcement to elicit and maintain these behaviors. Additionally, teachers should be prepared to move up and down a ladder of intensiveness when intervening (O'Neill, Johnson, Kiefer-O'Donnell, & McDonnell, 2001). This may include self-monitoring (e.g., behavior contracts), positive reinforcement and positive reinforcement systems (e.g., token economies), environmental room and material arrangements, functional behavior assessment, and strategies for managing escalating behavior (Scott et al., 2011). High skill and fluency with the implementation of these strategies is critical for two reasons. First, they will be essential for teacher candidates to use in order to provide effective instruction in their own classroom. Second and perhaps more importantly, teachers who work with students who exhibit challenging behavior often become the resource for schools and districts to provide coaching and assistance to other teachers who are dealing with challenging behavior. Thus, the goal is to not only train teachers; but also, teacher-leaders, with a high level of skill and efficiency in implementing these strategies.

Providing quality instruction and experiences that entail appropriate content and the necessary skills for delivery of instruction are essential components of a high-quality teacher preparation program. In addition, there are many factors that may influence teachers' abilities to deliver high-quality instruction in the context of real world situations. Students with challenging behaviors have a number of needs beyond the classroom. In the following section, we highlight several issues regarding personnel preparation with suggestions for future directions.

Personnel Preparation: Issues and Future Directions

As we have previously discussed, teachers believe their preservice and in-service educational experiences do not adequately prepare them to meet the needs of students who demonstrate challenging behaviors (Buysee, Wesley, Keyes, & Bailey, 1996; Hemmeter, Corso, & Cheatham, 2006; Westling, 2010). Additionally, these teachers are at an increased risk of experiencing stress, burnout and leaving the profession altogether (Abidin & Robinson, 2002; Nelson, Maculan, Roberts, & Ohlund, 2001). As a result, there have been a number of national initiatives to identify the competencies as well as knowledge and skills needed for teachers to work with students who demonstrate challenging behaviors (Council for Exceptional Children, 2003; Manning, Bullock, & Gable, 2009). For example, the Council for Exceptional Children identified 10 standards and 162 individual knowledge and skill areas (e.g., teaching students to use self-assessment) that relate to teaching students with challenging behaviors. However, if teachers feel ill-prepared to work with these students, then why would we expect them to be able to successfully implement these identified skill areas? In order to better prepare future (and current) teachers of students who have challenging behaviors, we must first reflect on the current state of practice to determine what is and is not working, and how to move forward to infuse innovation into our current models of personnel preparation.

Current State of Preservice and In-Service Preparation

In a recent study, Hemmeter, Santos, and Ostrosky (2008) surveyed faculty members from 2- and 4-year Institutions of Higher Education (IHEs) across nine states to determine how they prepare teachers to meet the social-emotional needs, and address the challenging behaviors, of young children. As the authors point out, currently there are different models for preparing early childhood educators with some programs having separate early childhood and early childhood special education programs, and other universities offering blended programs that allow students to receive concurrent training in both fields. Further, the strategies for infusing content on social-emotional development and challenging behavior can greatly vary across preservice preparation programs, with some programs addressing these content areas within a single course, infusing the content across multiple courses, and/or providing field-based experiences focused on these specific areas. The field of early childhood also is complicated by the fact that teachers can have a variety of training and certification requirements (e.g., a 2-year certificate in early childhood versus a 4-year degree) depending upon the type of setting in which they plan to teach, for example, in a community-based preschool classroom versus a public preschool classroom. Even with the variety of personnel preparation programs across IHEs, Hemmeter and her colleagues found that early childhood faculty believed their programs adequately prepared teachers to implement strategies designed to *prevent* challenging behavior; however, they believed their program graduates were less prepared to *implement* behavioral interventions once children started to demonstrate challenging behaviors. That is, early childhood faculty believed they were inadequately preparing teachers on what to do once a student started to exhibit behavior problems. Further, across both 2-year and 4-year programs faculty reported that preservice teachers were less likely to have direct field experiences focused on implementing interventions with children who demonstrate challenging behaviors.

In contrast to the Hemmeter et al. (2008) study, Westling (2010) directly surveyed teachers (38 special education, 32 general education) about their views on how prepared they felt to address students' challenging behaviors. Yet, the findings of Westling do parallel those of Hemmeter and her colleagues. The majority of teachers reported that they learned to address the problem behaviors of students while in practice, but their preservice and in-service experiences had not adequately prepared them to address behavioral challenges. Importantly, Westling also found that teachers' self-reported *confidence* in their ability to effectively manage challenging behaviors was most related to how well they felt their preservice education and training had addressed this topic. In addition, the types of *strategies* teachers used to address problem behaviors, such as reinforcing appropriate behavior, were most related to in-service experiences on challenging behavior. Thus, research both from the perspective of teacher educators as well as from teachers in the field confirm that teachers feel underprepared to work with students who demonstrate challenging behaviors. Further, they receive few direct field experiences with these students during their preservice preparation, and primarily learn through "trial and error" once in practice when there is often less ongoing support.

Moving Forward to Innovate Teacher Preparation

Changing teacher beliefs and practices is not an easy feat, nor is changing the ways in which teacher educators at IHEs prepare and continue to provide meaningful professional development opportunities to teachers once they begin to practice. We will focus on three concrete ways teacher educators can innovate and change teacher preparation to better prepare and mentor teachers of students who demonstrate challenging behaviors.

Family-Centered Practices

First, teacher educators who prepare teachers of students with challenging behaviors could adopt and infuse effective practices from other fields into their preservice curriculum; specifically, the use of family-centered practices, which often are used in the field of early childhood education (Dunst, 2002). Given that challenging behaviors occur in the context of students' home environments and the impact that these challenging behaviors have on the family, there is a need to more directly integrate family-centered practices into our preservice programs. Simply put, challenging behaviors do not occur in isolation. A vital component of many effective intervention programs is the inclusion of a family-based intervention so that supports can be provided to the children across settings. Whether students have an E/BD or ASD, challenging behaviors can have a substantial impact on family members and family functioning. Hemmeter and her colleagues (2008) developed the *Teaching Pyramid Model*, a tiered model of support, for preparing early childhood educators to meet the social-emotional and behavioral needs of young students. The universal strategies they suggest are effective at preventing challenging behaviors include providing teachers with strategies to build positive relationships with children and families as well as putting prevention strategies (e.g., the use of praise and encouragement) into place in both classroom and home settings. In order for teachers to be able to effectively implement these prevention strategies across contexts once they begin to practice, they must have multiple and meaningful opportunities to partner with families to address children's challenging behaviors as part of their preservice preparation.

Service-Learning

Second, given the complex characteristics and needs of students with challenging behaviors and their need for wrap-around services, teachers must be provided service-learning opportunities as part of their professional preparation. Service-learning opportunities would allow preservice teachers to collaborate with community stakeholders to identify and address specific community-based needs. McHatton, Thomas, and Lehman (2006) described the use of service-learning with a cohort of 19 students enrolled in their special education or communication disorders program who were working with children in urban and high-poverty areas. McHatton and colleagues introduced the concept of service-learning to a cohort of students through professional development trainings, course readings and discussions, with specific attention placed on differentiating service-learning opportunities from volunteer experiences or charity work. Subsequently, in conjunction with a community-based agency that focused on family support as well as children from the actual community, the students developed service-learning projects. These service-learning projects were not directly related to student achievement in school, but rather designed to address the identified needs of the community. For example, one service-learning project cogenerated by the preservice professionals and children from the community was to establish a community lending library. McHatton and her fellow researchers concluded that these service-learning projects increased the preservice professionals' awareness of the surrounding multicultural diversity of the community, and helped them to begin to understand how to address issues of educational inequality and social justice, which they may face in the future as practicing teachers. Providing preservice teachers with such family- and community-oriented experiences during their initial training should help them to build important relationships with family members and key community stakeholders, as Hemmeter and her colleagues suggest, so that preventative strategies could be implemented across settings. Further, it should facilitate family buy-in and support for any future intervention recommendations designed to reduce children's challenging behaviors.

E-mentoring and Support

Finally, we must be innovative in the ways in which we provide ongoing mentorship and in-service opportunities to practicing teachers. One strategy is to increase our use of online or web-mediated instruction to provide more individualized and specific feedback to teachers on the types of challenging behaviors students in their classrooms are demonstrating. There are increasing calls for the use of such technology to address the limited access students and teachers in rural communities may have to high-quality educational programs and training opportunities (Koch, 2007). Pianta and colleagues' development and use of MyTeachingPartner (MTP) is one example of an effective web-mediated support system that has been found to increase the quality of interactions teachers have with students, in particular those from socioeconomically disadvantaged households (Pianta, Mashburn, Downer, Hamre, & Justice, 2008), and in turn, to promote positive student outcomes (Hamre et al., 2010). The MTP system uses a combination of static media, such as providing teachers access to video exemplars of high-quality interactions with students, and interactive media, whereby teachers share video footage of their own interactions with students and an expert consultant provides web-mediated feedback on how to improve those interactions. The use of technology potentially allows teacher educators or other professionals to both provide more individualized feedback and to serve more practicing teachers, while also being a more cost-effective solution.

Summary

In summary, students who display challenging behaviors are some of the most difficult students for our schools to educate due to their complex behavioral and social needs. These are precisely the students that need to be taught by the most highly qualified and skilled teachers who can prevent and ameliorate their behavioral challenges. With high quality, effective instruction, the outcomes for these students can be quite promising. Unfortunately, as we discussed there are a shortage of teachers who are highly skilled and available to work with these students. This may be one factor that contributes to the continued negative trajectory that plagues so many of these students.

High-quality teacher preparation programs and in-service training programs (including behavioral coaching and consultation) that increase the knowledge and skills of future and current educators to meet the needs of these students are critically needed. Although there is a trend toward noncategorical teacher preparation, we highly recommend that all teachers working with students with challenging behaviors need a strong foundation in classroom-wide and individual behavioral practices that can prevent and remediate challenging behaviors. Fortunately, the fields of E/BD and ASD have a strong research-base that provides guidance for teachers in the use of effective practices and strategies that can be used when teaching these students. The challenge is to develop teachers' competence in these practices and provide them the supports needed for implementation in classroom settings.

References

Abidin, R. R., & Robinson, L. L. (2002). Stress, biases, or professionalism: What drives teachers' referral judgments of students with challenging behaviors. *Journal of Emotional and Behavioral Disorders, 10*, 204–212. doi:10.1177/10634266020100040201

Adera, B. A., & Bullock, L. M. (2010). Job stressors and teacher job satisfaction in programs serving students with emotional and behavioral disorders. *Emotional and Behavioural Difficulties, 15*(1), 5–14.

Allen, R. A., Robins, D. L., & Decker, S. L. (2008). Autism spectrum disorders: Neurobiology and current assessment practices. *Psychology in the Schools, 45*, 905–917. doi:10.1002/pits.20341

Allsopp, D. H., Kyger, M. M., Lovin, L., Gerretson, H., Carson, K. L., & Ray, S. (2008). Mathematics dynamic assessment: Informal assessment that responds to the needs of struggling learners in mathematics. *Teaching Exceptional Children, 40*(3), 6–16.

APA (American Psychiatric Association). (2013). *Diagnostic and statistical manual of mental disorders* (5th ed.). Arlington, VA: American Psychiatric Publishing.

Anderson, J., Kutash, K., & Duchnowski, A. J. (2001). A comparison of the academic progress of students with EBD and students with LD. *Journal of Emotional and Behavioral Disorders*, 9, 105–115. doi:10.1177/106342660100900205

Barton-Arwood, S., Wehby, J. H., & Falk, K. B. (2005). Reading instruction for elementary-age students with emotional and behavioral disorders: Academic and behavioral outcomes. *Exceptional Children, 72*, 7–27.

Billingsley, B. S., Fall, A. M., & Williams, T. O., Jr. (2006). Who is teaching students with emotional and behavioral disorders? A comparison to other special educators. *Behavioral Disorders, 31*, 252–264.

Brigham, F. J., & Hott, B. L. (2011). History of emotional and behavioral disorders. In A. F. Rotatori, F. E. Obiakor, & J. P. Bakken (Eds.), *History of Special Education (Advances in Special Education, Volume 21)*, (pp. 151–180). Bingley, United Kingdom: Emerald Group Publishing Limited.

Brownell, M. T., Sindelar, P. T., Kiely, M. T., & Danielson, L. C. (2010). Special education teacher quality and preparation: Exposing foundations, constructing a new model. *Exceptional Children, 76*, 357–377.

Bullock, L. M., Gable, R. A., & Melloy, K. J. (2004). Forward. In A. F. Peck, S. Keenan, D. Cheney, & R. S. Neel (Eds.), *Establishing exemplary personnel preparation programs for teachers of students with emotional and behavioral disorders: Partnerships with schools, parents, and community agencies* (v–vii). Arlington, Virginia: Council for Exceptional Children.

Butler, L. L. (2004). Key issues in the preparation of teachers of students with emotional and behavioral disorders. In L. M. Bullock & R. A. Gable (Eds.), *Quality personnel preparation in emotional and behavioral disorders* (pp. 100–104). Denton, TX: University of North Texas.

Buysee, V., Wesley, P., Keyes, L., & Bailey, D. B. Jr. (1996). Assessing comfort zone of child care teachers in serving young children with disabilities. *Journal of Early Intervention, 20*, 189–204. doi:10.1177/105381519602000301

Carter, E. W., Lane, K. L., Crnobori, M., Bruhnk, A. L., & Oakes, W. P. (2011). Self-determination interventions for students with and at risk for emotional and behavioral disorders: Mapping the knowledge base. *Behavioral Disorders, 36*, 100–116.

Cheney, D., Flower, A., & Templeton, T. (2008). Applying response to intervention metrics in the social domain for students at risk of developing emotional or behavioral disorders. *Journal of Special Education, 42*(2), 108–126. doi:10.1177/0022466907313349

Cole, J. E., & Washburn, L. H. (2010). Going beyond "The Math Wars." *Teaching Exceptional Children, 42*, 14–20.

Cooley-Nichols, S. M. (2004). Generic special education teacher preparation. *Emotional and Behavioral Difficulties, 9*, 28–40. doi:10.1177/1363275204041961

Corsello, C. M. (2005). Early intervention in autism. *Infants & Young Children, 18*, 74–85. doi:10.1097/00001163-200504000-00002

Coyne, M. D., Kame'enui, E. J., & Carnine, D. W. (2011). *Effective teaching strategies that accommodate diverse learners.* Upper Saddle River, NJ: Pearson.

Council for Exceptional Children (2003). *What every educator must know: Ethics, standards, and guidelines for special educators.* (5th ed.). Arlington, VA: Author.

Ducharme, J. M., & Shecter, C. (2011). Bridging the gap between clinical and classroom intervention: Keystone approaches with students with challenging behavior. *School Psychology Review, 40*, 257–274.

Dunst, C. J. (2002). Family-centered practices: Birth through high school. *The Journal of Special Education, 36*, 141–149. doi:10.1177/00224669020360030401

DuPaul, G. J., Ervin, R. A., Hook, C. L., & McGoey, K. E. (1998). Peer tutoring for children with attention deficit hyperactivity disorder: Effects on classroom behavior and academic performance. *Journal of Applied Behavior Analysis, 31*, 579–592. doi:10.1901/jaba.1998.31-579

Fairbanks, S., Sugai, G., Guardino, D., & Lathrop, M. (2007). Examining classroom behavior support in second grade. *Exceptional Children, 73*, 288–310.

Fitzsimons, A., & White, C. (2004) The impact of No Child Left Behind on the quality for special education programs for students with emotional/behavioral disorders. In L. M. Bullock & R. A. Gable (Eds.), *Quality personnel preparation in emotional and behavioral disorders* (pp. 105–111). Denton, TX: University of North Texas.

Gresham, F. M. (2007). Response to intervention and emotional and behavioral disorders best practices in assessment for intervention. *Assessment for Effective Intervention, 32*, 214–222.

Gunter, P. L., Denny, R. K., Shores, R. E., Reed, T. M., Jack, S. L., & Nelson, C. M. (1994). Teacher escape, avoidance and countercontrol behaviors: Potential responses to disruptive and aggressive behaviors of students with severe behavior disorders. *Journal of Child and Family Studies, 3*, 211–223. doi:10.1007/BF02234068

Hackenberg, T. D. (2009). Token reinforcement: A review and analysis. *Journal of the Experimental Analysis of Behavior, 91*, 257–286. doi:10.1901/jeab.2009.91-257

Hamre, B. K., Justice, L., Pianta, R. C., Kilday, C., Sweeney, B., Downer, J. T., & Leach, A. (2010). Implementation fidelity of MyTeachingPartner literacy and language activities: Association with preschoolers' language and literacy growth. *Early Childhood Research Quarterly, 25*, 392–347. doi:10.1016/j.ecresq.2009.07.002

Hardman, M. L., & Mulder, M. (2004). Federal education reform: Critical issues in public education and their impact on students with disabilities. In L. M. Bullock & R. A. Gable (Eds.), *Quality personnel preparation in emotional and behavioral disorders* (12–36). Denton, TX: University of North Texas.

Hemmeter, M. L., Corso, R., & Cheatham, G. (2006, February). *Issues in addressing challenging behaviors in young children: A national survey of early childhood educators.* Paper presented at the Conference on Research Innovations in Early Intervention, San Diego, CA.

Hemmeter, M. L., Santos, R. M., & Ostrosky, M. M. (2008). Preparing early childhood educators to address young children's social-emotional development and challenging behavior: a survey of higher education programs in nine states. *Journal of Early Intervention, 30*, 321–340. doi:10.1177/1053815108320900

Henderson, K. (2011). Policies and practices used by states to serve children with autism spectrum disorders. *Journal of Disability Policy Studies, 22*(2). 106–115.

Henderson, K., Klein, S., Gonzalez, P., & Bradley, R. (2005). Teachers of children with emotional disturbance: A national look at preparation, teaching conditions, and practices. *Behavioral Disorders, 31*(1), 6–17.

Jameson, J. M., & Huefner, D. S. (2006). "Highly qualified" special educators and the provision of a free appropriate public education to students with disabilities. *Journal of Law and Education, 35*(1), 29–50.

Karnick, N. S. (2004). The social environment. In H. Steiner (Ed.), *Handbook of mental health interventions in children and adolescents* (pp. 51–72). San Francisco, CA: Jossey-Bass.

Kauffman, J. M., & Landrum, T. J. (2006). *Children and youth with emotional and behavioral disorders: A history of their education.* Austin, TX: PRO-ED Inc.

Kauffman, J. M., & Landrum, T. J. (2009). *Characteristics of emotional and behavioral disorders of children and youth* (9th ed.). Boston, MA: Pearson/Merrill.

Kazdin, A. E. (1982). The token economy: A decade later. *Journal of Applied Behavior Analysis, 15*, 431–445. doi:10.1901/jaba.1982.15-431

Koch, S. P. (2007). Training rural special educators online to teach social skills. *Rural Special Education Quarterly, 26*(4), 16–20.

Lane, K. (2004). Academic instruction and tutoring interventions for students with emotional and behavioral disorders 1990–present. In R. Rutherford, M. M. Quinn, & S. Mathur (Eds.), *Handbook of Research in Emotional and Behavioral Disorders*. New York, NY: Guilford Press.

Locke, W. R., & Fuchs, L. S. (1995). Effects of peer-mediated reading instruction on the on-task behavior and social interaction of children with behavior disorders. *Journal of Emotional and Behavioral Disorders, 3*, 92–99. doi:10.1177/106342669500300204

Manning, M. L., Bullock, L. M., & Gable, R. A. (2009). Personnel preparation in the area of emotional and behavioral disorders: A reexamination based on teacher perceptions. *Preventing School Failure, 53*, 219–226. doi:10.3200/PSFL.53.4.219-226

McCurdy, B. L., Mannella, M. C., & Eldridge, N. (2003). Positive behavior support in urban schools: Can we prevent the escalation of antisocial behavior? *Journal of Positive Behavior Interventions, 5*, 158–170. doi:10.1177/10983007030050030501

McHatton, P. A., Thomas, D., & Lehman, K. (2006). Lessons learned in service-learning: Personnel preparation through community action. *Mentoring and Tutoring, 14*, 67–79. doi:10.1080/13611260500432665

McLeskey, J., & Billingsley, B. S. (2008). How does the quality and stability of the teaching force influence the research-to-practice gap? A perspective on the teacher shortage in special education. *Remedial and Special Education, 29*, 293–305. doi:10.1177/0741932507312010

Miller, M. J., Lane, K. L., & Wehby, J. (2005). Social skills instruction for students with high-incidence disabilities: A school-based intervention to address acquisition deficits. *Preventing School Failure, 49*, 27–39. doi:10.3200/PSFL.49.2.27-39

National Research Council. (2001). *Adding it up: Helping children learn mathematics.* J. Kilpatrick, J. Swafford, & B. Findell (Eds.). Mathematics Learning Study Committee, Center for Education, Division of Behavioral and Social Sciences and Education. Washington, DC: National Academies Press.

Naughton, C., & McLaughlin, T. F. (1995). The use of a token economy system for students with behaviour disorders. *B.C. Journal of Special Education, 19*(2), 29–38.

Nelson, J. R., Maculan, A., Roberts, M. L., & Ohlund, B. J. (2001). Source of occupational stress for teachers of students with emotional and behavioral disorders. *Journal of Emotional and Behavioral Disorders, 9*, 123–130. doi:10.1177/106342660100900207

No Child Left Behind Act of 2001, Pub. L. No. 107-110 (2002).

Oliver, R. M., & Reschly, D. J. (2010). Special education teacher preparation in classroom management: Implications for students with emotional and behavioral disorders. *Behavioral Disorders, 35*(3), 188–199.

O'Neill, R. E., Johnson, J. W., Kiefer-O'Donnell, R., & McDonnell, J. J. (2001). Preparing teachers and consultants for the problems of challenging behavior. *Journal of Positive Behavior Interventions, 3*, 101–108. doi:10.1177/109830070100300207

Pianta, R. C., Mashburn, A. J., Downer, J., Hamre, B. K., & Justice, L. (2008). Effects of web-mediated professional development resources on teacher–child interactions in pre-kindergarten classrooms. *Early Childhood Research Quarterly, 23*, 431–451. doi:10.1016/j.ecresq.2008.02.001

Reid, R., Gonzalez, J. E., Nordness, P. D., Trout, A., & Epstein, M. H. (2004). A meta-analysis of the academic status of students with emotional/behavioral disturbance. *The Journal of Special Education, 38*, 130–143. doi:10.1177/00224669040380030101

Rivera, M. O., Al-Otaiba, S., & Koorland, M. A. (2006). Reading instruction for students with emotional-behavioral disorders and at-risk of antisocial behaviors in primary grades: Review of literature. *Behavioral Disorders, 31*, 323–339.

Sabornie, E. J., Cullinan, D., Osborne, S. S., & Brock, L. B. (2005). Intellectual, academic, and behavioral functioning of students with high-incidence disabilities: A cross-categorical meta-analysis. *Exceptional Children, 72*, 47–63.

Salend, S. J., & Garrick Duhaney, L. M. (2011). Historical and philosophical changes in the education of students with exceptionalities. In A. F. Rotatori, F. E. Obiakor, & J. P. Bakken (Eds.), *History of Special Education (Advances in Special Education, Volume 21)*, (pp. 1–20). Bingley, United Kingdom: Emerald Group Publishing Limited.

Scott, T. M., Anderson, C., & Alter, P. J. (2011). *Managing classroom behavior using positive behavior support.* Longmont, CO: Sopris.

Scott, T. M., & Barrett, S. B. (2004). Using staff and student time engaged in disciplinary procedures to evaluate the impact of school-wide PBS. *Journal of Positive Behavior Interventions, 6*, 21–27. doi:10.1177/10983007040060010401

Simmons, D. C., & Kame'enui, E. J. (1998). *What reading research tells us about children with diverse learning needs: Bases and basics*. Mahwah, NJ: Erlbaum.

Sindelar, P. T., Brownell, M. T., & Billingsley, B. (2010). Special education teacher education research: Current status and future directions. *Teacher Education and Special Education, 33*, 8–24. doi:10.1177/0888406409358593

Smith, C. R., Katsiyannis, A., & Ryan, J. B. (2011). Challenges of serving students with emotional and behavioral disorders: Legal and policy considerations. *Behavioral Disorders, 36*(3), 185–194.

Steinberg, Z., & Knitzer, J. (1992). Classrooms for emotionally and behaviorally disturbed students: Facing the challenge. *Behavioral Disorders, 17*(2), 145–156.

Sutherland, K. S., Denny, R. K., & Gunter, P. L. (2005). Teachers of students with emotional and behavioral disorders reported professional development needs: Differences between fully licensed and emergency-licensed teachers. *Preventing School Failure, 49*, 41–46. doi:10.3200/PSFL.49.2.41-46

Thornton, B., Peltier, G., & Medina, R. (2007). Reducing the special education teacher shortage. *The Clearing House, 80*, 233–238. doi:10.3200/TCHS.80.5.233-238

Van Acker, R. (2004). Current status of public education and likely future directions in teacher preparation for students with emotional and behavioral disorders. In L. M. Bullock & R. A. Gable (Eds.), *Quality personnel preparation in emotional and behavioral disorders* (79–93). Denton, TX: University of North Texas.

Wagner, M., Marder, C., Blackorby, J., Cameto, R., Newman, L., Levine, P., & Davies-Mercier, E. (with Chorost, M., Garza, N., Guzman, A., & Sumi, C.). (2003). *The achievements of youth with disabilities during secondary school. A report from the National Longitudinal Transition Study-2 (NLTS2)*. Menlo Park, CA: SRI International.

Walker, H. M., & Sprague, J. R. (1999). The path to school failure, delinquency, and violence: Causal factors and some potential solutions. *Intervention in School and Clinic, 35*, 67–73. doi:10.1177/105345129903500201

Wehby, J. H., Lane, K. L., & Falk, K. B. (2003). Academic instruction for students with emotional and behavioral disorders. *Journal of Emotional and Behavioral Disorders, 11*, 194–197. doi:10.1177/10634266030110040101

Westling, D. L. (2010). Teachers and challenging behavior: Knowledge, views, and practices. *Remedial and Special Education, 31*, 46–63. doi:10.1177/0741932508327466

Whalon, K. J., Al Otaiba, S., & Delano, M. E. (2009). Evidence-based reading instruction for individuals with autism spectrum disorders. *Focus on Autism and Other Developmental Disabilities, 24*, 3–16. doi:10.1177/1088357608328515

Witt, J. C., VanDerHeyden, A. C., & Gilbertson, D. (2004). Troubleshooting behavioral interventions. A systematic process for finding and eliminating problems. *School Psychology Review, 33*, 363–383.

20

Preparation of Teachers for Children Who Are Deaf or Hard of Hearing

Lauri H. Nelson

UTAH STATE UNIVERSITY

Susan Lenihan

FONTBONNE UNIVERSITY

Karl R. White

UTAH STATE UNIVERSITY

Things to Think About

- Programs to educate deaf children have existed since at least the 1500s and systematic deaf education teacher preparation programs have existed in the United States since the late 1800s.
- The number of deaf education teacher preparation programs continues to decline (28% fewer programs since 1986), fewer students are graduating (half as many graduates in 2009 as in 1982) and programs have difficulty hiring and retaining qualified faculty.
- Federal legislation affecting special education, the widespread implementation of newborn hearing screening programs, and advances in hearing technology have changed which and where children who are deaf or hard of hearing (DHH) are educated. Compared with 30 years ago, children who are DHH are identified younger, more have secondary disabilities, more are in public schools with peers who have normal hearing, and fewer are using American Sign Language (ASL) as a primary mode of communication.
- According to recent graduates, some deaf education teacher preparation programs are not adequately preparing their graduates to teach children in mainstream settings, participate in interdisciplinary collaboration, teach children who are DHH who have additional disabilities, and take advantage of current hearing technology to teach children who are DHH to listen and talk.
- There is an increasing need for teachers of the deaf to serve children in early-intervention settings which requires a different skill set than has traditionally been provided in deaf education teacher preparation programs.

An average of 33 babies who are deaf or hard of hearing (DHH)[1] are born every day in the United States, making it the nation's most frequent major birth disorder (Leonard, Shen, & Howe, 1999; White, 1997; Stierman, 1994). Before 1990, most of these children were not identified until they were 2–3 years old (The Commission on Education of the Deaf, 1988). According to the U.S. Department of Health and Human Services (1990, p. 460), such late identification meant that it was:

> difficult, if not impossible, for many [children with congenital hearing loss] to acquire the fundamental language, social, and cognitive skills that provide the foundation for later schooling and success in society. When early identification and intervention occur, hearing impaired children make dramatic progress, are more successful in school, and become more productive members of society. The earlier intervention and habilitation begin, the more dramatic the benefits.

Beginning in the late 1980s, the widespread implementation of newborn hearing screening, diagnosis, and intervention programs (commonly referred to now as Early Hearing Detection and Intervention or EHDI programs) in the United States, dramatically reduced the age at which children who are DHH are identified. As a result of earlier identification, coupled with significant advances in hearing technology, the educational process and outcomes for children who are DHH have also changed in major ways (White, Forsman, Eichwald, & Munoz, 2010).

As emphasized in a 2006 joint letter sent to all state early-intervention programs from officials at the U.S. Department of Education and the U.S. Department of Health and Human Services (cited in White & Munoz, 2008, p. 150), the importance of early and appropriate educational services for children who are DHH is not limited to children with severe or profound degrees of hearing loss. This letter stated that there was a

> growing national crisis in the provision of essential early intervention and health care services for infants and toddlers with hearing loss. ... Studies have demonstrated that when hearing loss of any degree, including mild bilateral or unilateral hearing loss, is not adequately diagnosed and addressed, the hearing loss can adversely affect the speech, language, academic, emotional, and psychosocial development of young children. Although efforts to identify and evaluate hearing loss in young children have improved, there is still anecdotal evidence to suggest that many young children with hearing loss may not be receiving the early intervention or other services they need in a timely manner that will enable them to enter preschool and school ready to succeed.

Given the importance of providing early and continuing educational services to all children who are DHH, this chapter discusses the implications of changes in technology and pedagogy for teacher preparation programs for children who are DHH. Beginning with an overview of how deaf education has been provided historically, we summarize how teacher preparation programs for children who are DHH are changing, what can be concluded from research about the effectiveness of such programs, and suggest ways in which programs should continue to evolve to best meet the needs of children who are DHH.

History of Deaf Education and Teacher Preparation

Historical accounts of deaf education recognize the Mission of San Salvador in Madrid, Spain founded by Pedro Ponce de Leon in 1550 as the first school for children who were DHH (Benderly, 1990; Marvelli, 2010). By the end of the 18th century deaf education schools had been established throughout Western Europe with schools in France, England, and Germany having the greatest influence on deaf education in America.

The foundations of deaf education in the United States can be traced to several key historical events beginning in the 1800s. Thomas Hopkins Gallaudet, a minister from Hartford, Connecticut travelled to Europe to learn about teaching children who were DHH. There he met Laurent Clerc, a young teacher of the deaf from Paris. After studying the French approach that relied primarily on sign language, Gallaudet returned to Hartford with Clerc and established the first school for students who were DHH, the Connecticut Asylum for the Education and Instruction of Deaf Persons, in 1817. Fifty years later, there were 22 schools for the deaf using a sign language approach. The programs were funded by public funds and the teachers were mostly male college graduates. Gallaudet's son, Edward, established what is now known as Gallaudet University in Washington, DC in 1857 as the first college for students who were DHH (Marvelli, 2010).

In 1864, Bernard Englesmann, a teacher from Germany who used a spoken language approach rather than sign language, began teaching children who were DHH in New York City. By 1873, the school had grown to more than 90 students and eventually became known as the Lexington Avenue School for the Deaf. Through the efforts of parents who had children who were DHH, a program providing education using spoken language was started in Massachusetts in the 1860s. John Clarke provided an endowment to establish the school in Northampton in 1867. That school is now known at the Clarke School for Hearing and Speech.

Most people know Alexander Graham Bell as the scientist credited with inventing the telephone. However, he also played a pivotal role in deaf education through his advocacy for teaching children who are DHH to use listening and spoken language. The AG Bell Association, which supports spoken language development for children and adults who are DHH, was founded in 1890. Bell provided support as well as formal and informal training to teachers of the deaf, including the Clarke School in Northampton, Massachusetts.

Early Deaf Education Teacher Preparation Programs

In the early years of these programs, when teachers were needed, training was usually provided using an apprentice or in-service model (Marvelli, 2010). At the Connecticut Asylum, the primary professional training was conducted by Clerc and focused on learning sign language. The schools in New York and Northampton also used an in-service approach that focused on strategies for developing listening and spoken language skills. These in-service classes became more formal over time and by the late 1880s Lexington had started a "teacher in training" program. The Clarke teacher preparation program was a twice-a-week program taught by Caroline Yale that included comprehensive exams at the end of the school year. Clarke School also offered month-long summer programs that included observation and instruction for teachers throughout the United States beginning in 1904 (Marvelli, 2010).

During this time of establishing formal training programs, Alexander Graham Bell and Edward Miner Gallaudet were debating the effectiveness of sign language versus oral education (referred to now as listening and spoken language), culminating in an international conference of deaf educators (the Second International Congress on Education of the Deaf, often referred to as "The Milan Conference of 1880"). At the conclusion of the conference, participants passed resolutions declaring that oral education was superior to sign language and called for a ban on the use of sign language in schools. Many of the controversies and arguments in the field today about what mode of communication should be used in deaf education programs stem from the issues discussed and the conclusions reached at this conference (Monaghan, Schmaling, Nakamura, & Turner, 2002). The only countries opposed to the ban were the United States (represented by Edward Miner Gallaudet, Thomas Gallaudet, Isaac Peet, James Denison, and Charles Stoddard) and Great Britain. After the Milan Conference, the National Association of the Deaf (NAD) was formed with a primary focus of preserving sign language. The president of Gallaudet College (now University) decided to retain sign language on the Gallaudet campus, a move lauded by many as a pivotal point in ensuring the continuation of sign language instruction in the United States.

The next year, in 1891, Gallaudet University began a teacher preparation program that focused primarily on using sign language. This was the first teacher preparation program that used a college-based preservice model rather than an in-service model. Within a few decades several additional teacher preparation programs were established, often involving collaboration between a state school for the deaf and a nearby college. By the 1930s, the program at Clarke School had a formal affiliation with Smith College in Northampton and the program at Lexington had partnered with New York University and Teachers College at Columbia University. Other private schools, including Central Institute for the Deaf in St. Louis and the John Tracy Clinic in Los Angeles also established teacher preparation programs in cooperation with nearby universities. During much of the 19th century and into the early 20th century, professionals held the general view that individuals with disabilities were best treated in residential facilities, away from the general public. Consistent with that philosophy, teacher of the deaf preparation programs focused primarily on preparing teachers to instruct small groups of school-age children in residential or self-contained special schools.

A major shift in teacher preparation programs came during the 1960s when federal legislation, in an effort to increase the number of special education teachers (including teachers of the deaf), provided funds for teacher preparation in special education. A few years later, the passage of Public Law 94-142, the predecessor to IDEA (Individuals with Disabilities Education Act) required that school districts provide a free and appropriate public education to all children with disabilities. This law impacted preservice training programs for teachers of the deaf because it began gradually changing the focus from teaching children primarily in self-contained special schools (where many of the children were in residential programs), to more and more children who were DHH being educated in neighborhood schools.

Other developments during this time period had a significant effect on teacher preparation programs. For example, the total communication approach, developed during the 1960s, focused on using sign language that was based on English grammar and syntax while simultaneously using spoken language. Many teacher preparation programs embraced this approach (Schwartz, 2007; Stewart, 1992), which had the effect of increasing the use of sign language in teacher preparation programs and reducing the number of programs that focused primarily on listening and spoken language. A few years later, the Deaf Culture movement became well established (Padden & Humphries, 2005), which led to even more emphasis on using ASL in teacher preparation programs, or what is now often referred to as the Bilingual-Bicultural (or Bi-Bi) approach (LaSasso & Lollis, 2003; Strong, 1988). The Bi-Bi approach emphasizes teaching ASL—a language distinct from English with its own linguistic morphology, syntax, rules for pronunciation, word order, and complex grammar (Stokoe, 2005)—as the child's first language. English is taught as a second language with most of the emphasis on writing. The Bi-Bi approach does not advocate presenting English through a signed modality (Moores, 2008) as was typical in the Total Communication approach. As cochlear implants and more sophisticated digital hearing aids became more widely available in the 1990s, a relatively small number of teacher preparation programs revised curriculum to include more emphasis on listening and spoken language.

By the end of the 1990s the widespread implementation of universal newborn hearing screening and the attendant reduction in age of identification, increase in number of children who were DHH enrolled in early-intervention programs, and the change in focus from intervener-centered to family-centered services had major implications for the skills needed by teachers of the deaf (Sass-Lehrer & Bodner Johnson, 2003). These developments, which are discussed in more detail later in this chapter, led to shifts in the philosophical approach, curriculum, and field experiences for many teacher preparation programs. At the International Congress on Education of the Deaf (ICED) in Vancouver, Canada in July 2010, the Committee rejected all resolutions passed at the Milan Conference of 1880 that called for banning sign language and resolved "to ensure that educational programs for the Deaf accept and respect all languages and all forms of communication" (ICED, 2010).

Legislation That Has Impacted Teacher Preparation Programs

Three legislative initiatives over the past 40 years have had a major impact on teacher preparation programs in deaf education. First, the passage of the Education of All Handicapped Children Act in 1975 (Public Law 94-142) required states to provide a free and appropriate public education to all children with disabilities. The law supported providing education in the least restrictive environment, which meant that students had to be given opportunities to the greatest extent appropriate to be educated with peers who did not have disabilities and to participate in general education. As a result of PL 94-142 and other societal factors, there has been a significant shift from self-contained deaf education settings to inclusive general education settings (Mitchell & Karchmer, 2006; Moores, 2006). According to Mitchell and Karchmer (2006) the percentage of students who are DHH attending special deaf education schools has declined by more than half over the past 25 years as many more students are receiving itinerant services in general education settings.

In 1986, Congress amended the Education of All Handicapped Children Act with PL 99-457, which created statewide, coordinated, multidisciplinary, interagency programs for the provision of appropriate early-intervention services for all infants and toddlers with disabilities. This section of the law, known now as Part C (formerly known as Part H), did not require states to provide early-intervention services, but provided partial reimbursement of the costs of early-intervention services to states that wished to participate. All states have established Part C programs for birth to 3-year-old children (White, 2006).

The third key legislative activity is often referred to as the Walsh Act (after Congressman James Walsh of New York who was the primary proponent). It is actually a series of legislative initiatives and appropriations beginning in the early 1990s. In 2000 the Children's Health Act contained language Walsh introduced in 1999 as a separate piece of legislation that was never enacted. This language (included under Title VII of the Children's Health Act—"Early Detection, Diagnosis, and Treatment Regarding Hearing Loss in Infants") provided funds to the Department of Health and Human Services to have the Maternal and Child Health Bureau support statewide newborn and infant hearing screening, diagnosis, and intervention programs as well as funds for the Centers for Disease Control and Prevention to provide technical assistance for data management and applied research. This legislation accelerated the implementation of newborn hearing screening and intervention programs which resulted in many more children who are DHH being identified as infants and young children and enrolled in early-intervention programs (White, 2003). For example, in 1993, only 3% of newborns in the United States were screened for hearing loss, compared to over 95% today (White et al., 2010). The increase in the number of children being identified at ever-younger ages created challenges for teacher preparation programs to train teachers to meet the needs of infants and young children who are DHH and their families.

Deaf Education Teacher Preparation Programs

There are 63 colleges and universities in the United States that have teacher preparation programs in deaf education[2] with 35 states having at least one program (*American Annals of the Deaf*, 2011; Lenihan, 2010). Although research on teacher preparation programs in deaf education is somewhat limited, a number of studies have explored several key aspects of the challenges and trends facing deaf education graduate training programs, including critical teacher shortages that exist in deaf education, demographics of university faculty in teacher preparation programs, and the effectiveness of teacher preparation programs to adequately prepare deaf education teachers for the roles and responsibilities they will face in teaching this generation of children who are DHH (Andrews & Covell, 2006/2007; Benedict, Johnson, & Antia, 2011; Dodd & Scheetz, 2003; Dolman, 2008, 2010; Johnson, 2004; Jones & Ewing, 2002; Lenihan, 2010; Luckner, Muir, Howell, Sebald, & Young, 2005).

Shortages of Deaf Education Teacher Preparation Programs and Graduates

A critical shortage of deaf education teachers has been reported for many years (American Association of Employment in Education, 2008; Johnson, 2004). Dolman (2008) reported that the number of teacher preparation programs in deaf education declined by 17%, from 83 programs in 1986 to 69 programs in 2006. Since then, the *American Annals of the Deaf* (2011) reports that six more programs have been discontinued. In addition to lamenting the decline in the number of programs, Jones and Ewing (2002) questioned the strength of many of the remaining programs by noting in an analysis of 46 teacher preparation programs approved at that time by the Council on Education of the Deaf (CED) that there was only a median of two full-time faculty members in these programs who taught 75% of the courses. In a more recent analysis, Benedict et al. (2011) pointed out that 80% of the deaf education teacher preparation programs employed only one or two full-time tenured faculty, more than half the faculty were in nontenure track, part-time positions, and almost 20% of the current faculty are expected to retire by 2019.

Given the declining number of programs, it is not surprising that Dolman (2008, 2010) reported similar declines in the number of students graduating with a deaf education degree. In 1982, there were 1,680 deaf education graduates, yet there were just 737 graduates in 2009. There were less than half as many graduates in 2009 as there were in 1982, even though the total number of children identified as DHH rose slightly during that time. Dolman suggested that it is possible that fewer children are being identified with hearing loss, primarily because of a reduction of children born with hearing loss due to the rubella epidemic of the early 1960s, resulting in the need for fewer deaf education professionals. Although it is true that the number of children with hearing loss due to congenital rubella has declined dramatically since the 1960s, it does not account for the decline in deaf education graduates. Furthermore, the fact that more and more children who are DHH are being educated in mainstream settings makes these children harder to identify, in which case Dolman's conclusions about the declining ratio of deaf education professionals to the number of children who are DHH may be worse than it appears (Mitchell & Karchmer, 2006).

Demographics of University Faculty in Deaf Education Teacher Preparation Programs

Benedict et al. (2011) conducted surveys and interviews with faculty and administrators at existing deaf education teacher preparation programs and concluded that universities face serious challenges in filling faculty vacancies, including applicants who lack a doctoral degree and who do not possess appropriate teaching and research qualifications. Of existing faculty in deaf education teacher preparation programs, more than half are not in full-time positions, resulting in their primary responsibilities being teaching and practicum supervision, with little time or priority for research. Because of budget constraints faced by most institutions, tenured and tenure-track faculty in these programs often carry heavy teaching loads and administrative responsibilities, further impeding the ability to engage in research. Benedict et al. documented that language and literacy development, teacher preparation, and early intervention were the most frequently identified areas of research interest, but that the majority of faculty had little time to do more than teach classes, supervise practica, and advise students.

With the premise that graduate training programs with faculty who conduct high-quality research will mentor new faculty, thus perpetuating healthy programs that contribute evidence-based recommendations to the field, Schirmer (2008) reported on the scholarly productivity of 127 teacher educators in deaf education. She found that more than half had published little over the course of their careers, raising the concern that if the majority of teacher educators are not productive scholars, it is unlikely that the next generation of teacher educators will be productive researchers.

Effectiveness of Deaf Education Teacher Preparation

In the last 50 years the role of a teacher in deaf education has changed dramatically due to social, educational, and technological developments. In the 1960s, most teachers of the deaf taught language, literacy and academic content to small groups of children between the ages of 3 and 18 years in self-contained settings or residential schools for the deaf. Many teacher preparation programs have been slow to recognize the changing role of teachers of the deaf toward providing itinerant services in mainstream educational settings. Many programs continue to require coursework based on a model of instruction in self-contained or residential schools. Thus, many teachers are simply unprepared for the job requirements they will face (Dolman, 2010).

In a survey of deaf educators teaching in the Pacific Northwest, Harrison (2008) evaluated how well teachers felt their graduate training program had prepared them for teaching children who are DHH. Harrison reported that the majority of respondents, who graduated from 12 different teacher preparation programs across the United States, indicated that their college preparation programs were ineffective in preparing them to:

- serve children in mainstream settings (p. 66)
- teach children who have additional disabilities (p. 65)
- obtain and interpret assessment data for effective instructional programming (p. 66)
- effectively communicate with colleagues, supervisors, and other professionals (p. 67)
- participate in interdisciplinary collaboration (p. 66)
- develop appropriate Individualized Family Service Plans and Individualized Education Programs using a team approach (p. 67)
- teach children with cochlear implants how to "listen" and understand what they are hearing (p. 66).

In a similar study, Dodd and Scheetz (2003) surveyed 110 teachers of the deaf and found that only about half judged their teacher preparation program to be appropriate. Over 80% of the teachers indicated that professional education courses such as educational assessment, corrective reading skills, classroom management and teaching critical thinking skills would have been valuable, but were not present in their training program.

Using a different approach, Teller and Harney (2005/2006) surveyed program directors about the skills they expected in new teachers and the types of teaching positions they anticipated in the future. The program directors indicated they would need more itinerant teachers of the deaf and that teachers needed to have more experience in itinerant and resource settings, better understanding of the general curriculum, more experiences in techniques for developing listening and spoken language, more experience with children who are DHH who have additional disabilities, better signing skills, and more skills in working with children with cochlear implants.

In a survey of itinerant teachers serving children in deaf education, Luckner and Howell (2002) determined that the knowledge and skills required to meet the needs of the students in a general education setting were different than the knowledge and skills needed for teachers in a self-contained deaf education program. Since most teacher preparation programs focus on training preservice teachers to work in self-contained classrooms, the beginning teachers felt unprepared for the job responsibilities of the itinerant setting.

Key Influences on the Changing Face of Deaf Education

Much of the challenge for deaf education teacher preparation programs lies in the charge to ensure curriculum that reflects current educational and technological needs. As noted above, recent events have altered the course of deaf education. With the advent of early identification through newborn hearing screening, family-centered early intervention, more choices in communication options, and advances in hearing technology, deaf education has a different role than in previous decades.

The Effects of Universal Newborn Hearing Screening on Teacher Preparation Programs

Twenty-five years ago, most children with permanent hearing loss were not identified until they were 2½ to 3 years of age (The Commission on Education of the Deaf, 1988) and most experts concluded that one child per 1,000 was born with permanent hearing loss severe enough to require special education services (Northern & Downs, 1991). As a consequence, most children who were DHH were not enrolled in early-intervention programs that served birth to 3-year-old children and most of these programs were not designed to serve young children who were DHH. Furthermore, hearing technology for children was primitive by today's standards—pediatric digital hearing aids were not widely available and cochlear implants could not be done in the United States for children under 2 years of age. The implementation of newborn hearing screening has changed that situation dramatically (White 2004), and those changes have major implications for teacher preparation programs.

Currently, every state in the United States has implemented either a mandatory or voluntary newborn hearing screening program due to the documented benefit in speech and language acquisition when the loss is identified and intervention begins within the first few months of life (Kennedy et al., 2006; Moeller, 2000). In 1995, the percentage of newborns screened for hearing loss was just 3%. A decade later that number had increased to 95% (White, 2006). In those states where newborn hearing screening programs have been effectively implemented, the age of hearing loss identification has been reduced from an average of about 30 months of age to an average of 2–3 months of age (White et al., 2010). As a result, many more children who are DHH are enrolled in early-intervention programs and an increased number of early interventionists are needed to provide services to those children. The skills needed by early-intervention providers serving children who are DHH are quite different than those needed by teachers in self-contained, elementary, or secondary school settings and this has major implications for deaf education teacher preparation programs. Unfortunately, most college and university training programs have not yet adjusted their curricula to provide teachers of the deaf with the specific knowledge and skills needed for the important and growing population of birth to three-year-old children (Lenihan, 2010).

The Joint Committee on Infant Hearing (JCIH, 2007) recommends that infants should be screened before 1 month of age, hearing loss identified before 3 months of age, and that early intervention should be in place before 6 months of age to maximize linguistic competency and literacy development for children who are DHH. The JCIH also recommended that:

- All families of infants with any degree of bilateral or unilateral permanent hearing loss should be considered eligible for early-intervention services.
- There should be recognized central referral points of entry to ensure specialty services for infants with confirmed hearing loss.
- Early-intervention services for infants with confirmed hearing loss should be provided by professionals who have expertise in hearing loss.
- Both home-based and center-based intervention options should be available.

Training programs for teachers of the deaf need to be sure that graduates who will be working with young children are knowledgeable about and have the skills to implement these goals.

Family-Centered Early Intervention and the Impact on Teacher Preparation

According to the Report and Recommendations of the 2004 National Consensus Conference on Effective Educational and Health Care Interventions for Infants and Young Children with Hearing Loss (Marge & Marge, 2005), hearing health care and early-intervention services for children who are DHH should be accessible, family centered, comprehensive, continuous, coordinated, compassionate, and culturally sensitive. The need for well-trained early interventionists is significant, placing a tall order on deaf education teacher preparation programs to ensure that teachers gain the skills to address the linguistic, communication, academic, cognitive, and social needs of children who are DHH (Hands and Voices, 2010; Yoshinaga-Itano, 2003). Broadly defined, early-intervention services are specialized health, educational, and therapeutic services designed to meet the needs of infants and toddlers, birth to 36 months, and their families. Early intervention is concerned with the basic skills of typical development during the first three years of life, such as physical growth, cognitive development, communication skills, social/emotional development, and self-help (National Dissemination Center for Children with Disabilities, 2010; Nelson, Bradham, & Houston, 2011).

Part C of IDEA is designed to enhance the development of infants and toddlers with disabilities, reduce the education costs to society by minimizing the need for special education services when they reach school age, increase the potential for independent living in society, facilitate the ability of families to maximize their child's development in the child's natural environment, and meet the needs of underrepresented populations. For a state to participate in the Part C program, it must assure that early intervention will be available to every eligible child and family. The 2007 national newborn hearing screening report from the Department of Health and Human Services Centers for Disease Control and Prevention (CDC) reported that 83% percent of infants diagnosed with hearing loss were referred to Part C early-intervention programs. However, just 61% of children identified with hearing loss actually had documented enrollment in a Part C early-intervention program before 6 months of age (CDC, 2008). This means that nearly 40% of children with hearing loss may not be receiving the services available to them, jeopardizing the benefits of early identification.

These statistics provide an illustration of the paradigm shift that must occur to affect functional change in developmental outcomes for children who are DHH. No longer does "Teacher of the Deaf" mean just those serving school-age children in the classroom. Teachers and early interventionists play a critical role in educating parents and other professionals about the importance of appropriate and intensive early-intervention services. Since the majority of deaf education teacher preparation programs historically have prepared teachers for self-contained programs in elementary and secondary schools, many training programs have not incorporated sufficient coursework and hands-on practicum experiences to adequately prepare educators for serving this important population. For example, deaf educators should be knowledgeable about typical and atypical infant development, infant assessment, family-support and parent-coaching models, the importance of family/caregiver relationships in culturally competent services, cognition and the impact of hearing loss on early brain development, and language development in the child's natural environment. Through graduate-level coursework and hands-on practical experiences, deaf education teacher preparation programs have an opportunity to improve early-intervention services by preparing teachers who understand early-intervention challenges and who have the skills and strategies to support parents and other professionals to facilitate age-appropriate development in children who are DHH.

Choices in Communication Options

When parents learn their child is DHH, they must determine whether their child's primary mode of communication will be sign language or spoken language. This is a very personal choice that must often be made during a time in which parents have many questions, concerns, and likely have very little knowledge of deafness and all the accompanying medical and educational terminology. Throughout history, the debate as to which mode of communication is the most appropriate has continued, often with passionate views favoring one method or another. Deaf education teacher preparation programs may choose to emphasize either sign language or spoken language, or may elect to provide a program that focuses on both. Whatever the area of focus, the goal should be for training programs to produce teachers that have depth and expertise in a given area adequate to facilitate strong language and cognitive development in the children being served. For example, because of early identification, early intervention, and advances in hearing technology, most children who are DHH can develop listening and spoken language skills similar to their same-aged hearing peers and be successfully integrated into mainstream educational settings (Cole & Flexer, 2007; Robertson, 2009). It is important however, that training programs in both sign language and spoken language exist so that families have viable choices in their child's communication methodology.

Because of newborn hearing screening programs (which have resulted in earlier identification of hearing loss), combined with early intervention and availability of advanced hearing technology, more and more families are choosing to use listening and spoken language with their child who is DHH. For example, North Carolina has had a well-developed early-intervention program for DHH children for many years that includes a full range of listening and spoken language and sign-language-based options. Alberg (2011) and Brown (2006) reported and compared data on the choices made by families in 1995 with the choices made in 2010. In 1995, 40% of families chose listening and spoken language options compared to 60% who chose sign-language-based options. In 2010, 90% of families chose listening and spoken language options compared to 10% who chose sign-language-based options. Similar trends are being reported in other states such as New Jersey, Utah, and Arizona (Utah Schools for the Deaf and Blind [USDB], 2011).

Given that more and more parents are choosing listening and spoken language options, it is concerning that Dolman's (2008) analysis of the requirements and coursework in deaf education teacher preparation programs concluded that many programs are placing much less emphasis on course work related to speech and hearing and more emphasis on sign language courses. The declining number of programs and shift in emphasis to less content in speech and hearing is a mismatch with the current trends in educational placements for students with hearing loss.

Interdisciplinary Collaboration

It is typical for a child who is DHH to receive services from at least a deaf educator, a general educator, a special educator, a speech/language pathologist, and an audiologist. Children who are DHH and have other disabilities often need additional professionals. In providing excellent family-centered services, it is essential for these professionals to effectively communicate with one another and to follow protocols and practices for interdisciplinary collaboration. Bronstein (2003) describes interdisciplinary collaboration as "an effective interpersonal process that facilitates the achievement of goals that cannot be reached when individual professionals act on their own" (p. 299). Teaching students how to participate in and promote interdisciplinary service delivery is crucial for deaf education teacher preparation programs so that students realize the breadth of services that must be available to children who are DHH and their families. In cases where families want their children to learn listening and spoken language skills, teachers of the deaf need to have skills to work with general education, special education, speech language pathology and other professionals to help these children experience full integration into the general education experience. Likewise, for families who choose an ASL/English communication and educational approach, teachers of the deaf need to develop interdisciplinary collaboration with general education, special education, deaf mentors, and others to meet the educational needs of the child and family.

Most children who are DHH who are identified in the first months of life, and who receive consistent, ongoing, comprehensive services, will be able to perform academically and socially at the same level as their peers with normal hearing. For decades, researchers have reported that children who are deaf often do not achieve higher than a third to fourth grade reading level by the time they graduate from high school (Traxler, 2000). Regardless of the communication modality the child is using, this level of performance should no longer be the expectation or the norm. In fact, when children who are DHH are identified early and provided with appropriate, comprehensive family-centered early-intervention services from properly trained professionals, many are able to progress at age-appropriate rates and require very few special education services by the time they enter elementary school (Cole & Flexer, 2007; Geers, Moog, Biedenstein, Brenner, & Hayes, 2009; Kennedy et al., 2006; Moeller, 2000; Nicholas & Geers, 2007; Robertson, 2009; Yoshinaga-Itano, Sedey, Coulter, & Mehl, 1998). Positive outcomes have been documented for earlier compared with later-identified children, including better language, speech, and social-emotional development than later-identified children; more typical rates of cognitive development; and lower parental stress as the child acquires language and increases communication (Yoshinaga-Itano & Gravel, 2001). Given the myriad of research documenting the speech, language, academic, and social development skills of children with hearing loss, the goal should be for them to attain educational achievement similar to children with normal hearing. However, for children who are DHH to achieve at high levels, they require specialized services by professionals who are trained in how to promote the development of language and literacy and how to effectively collaborate with other invested colleagues who will work together for optimal child outcomes.

Advances in Auditory Technology and the Impact on Teacher Preparation

Approximately 95% of children who are DHH are born to parents with normal hearing (Mitchell & Karchmer, 2004). With the availability of better hearing technology, coupled with earlier identification, most families of children who are DHH choose to use some type of hearing technology. For example, an unprecedented number of infants are being fitted with hearing aids as young as four weeks of age and more than 25,000 children in the United States have received cochlear implants (National Institute on Deafness and Other Communication Disorders, 2009). If such hearing technology is to be most beneficial, it is critical that teachers know how the technology works, how to structure educational programs to take full advantage of hearing technology, and how to ensure that it is functioning correctly.

Hearing aids are the most commonly used technology for children who are DHH because they are appropriate for most types and degree of hearing loss. Hearing aid styles vary, but most hearing aids for children fit over the top of the ear and are connected with an ear mold that fits into the canal to direct the flow of sound into the ear. All hearing aids have similar core components, such as a microphone to capture sounds, an amplifier to make sounds louder, and a receiver that sends the amplified sound into the ear (American Speech and Hearing Association, 2011). Even with advances in hearing aid technology, the successful use of a hearing aid requires at least some residual hearing. For children with little or no residual hearing who do not benefit from hearing aids, cochlear implants may be the technology of choice for accessing sound. A cochlear implant consists of external components as well as surgically implanted internal components. A cochlear implant differs from a hearing aid because rather than amplifying sounds to make them louder, the cochlear implant captures sound, and then using complex algorithmic processing, stimulates the auditory nerve to send signals into the auditory centers of the brain. The cochlear implant user must learn how to utilize this input so that sounds become linguistically meaningful for the development of spoken language.

Deaf education teacher preparation programs should ensure that teachers are familiar with the basic components and functions of hearing technology. Historically, as many as a quarter to over half the children in a classroom had a malfunctioning hearing aid on any given day (Elfenbein, Bentler, Davis, & Niebuhr, 1988; Potts & Greenwood, 1983; Zink, 1972). Reichman (1986) found that teachers of children who are DHH in a national sample reported that they did daily hearing aid listening checks only 54% of the time. Elfenbein et al. (1988), reported that only 15% of the itinerant teachers serving school-age children who were DHH reported monitoring hearing aid functioning on a daily basis. Unfortunately, more than two decades after these statistics were reported, the situation has shown little improvement. Burkhalter, Blalock, Herring, and Skaar (2011) reported that less than half of the hearing technology in a sample of preschool children was functioning properly.

With proper training, teachers can complete basic troubleshooting measures, such as making sure the hearing technology is turned on with the controls placed in the proper position, determining if the battery needs to be changed, and identifying if the volume control or other programming switches need to be adjusted. A listening check and general monitoring of hearing technology should be completed on a daily basis with each child in the classroom. Otherwise, the child runs the risk of spending precious instructional time with insufficient or even no access to sound. For families who wish for their child to develop listening and spoken language skills, improvements in technology have resulted in dramatically improved success in communication, language acquisition, and educational achievement in mainstream classroom settings (Cole & Flexer, 2007; Geers et al., 2009; Robertson, 2009). However, such success is dependent on having professionals who are well trained in the specialized auditory skills, hearing technology, and teaching strategies necessary for optimal child outcomes (Estes, 2010; Lenihan, 2010).

Professional Standards and Teacher Competencies

The Council of Exceptional Children and the Council on the Education of the Deaf (CEC/CED) have established standards for Deaf Education Teacher Preparation Programs. The CED is comprised of representatives from seven member organizations: The Alexander Graham Bell Association for the Deaf, the Conference of Educational Administrators of Schools and Programs for the Deaf, the Convention of American Instructors of the Deaf, Association of College Educators—Deaf and Hard of Hearing, the National Association of the Deaf, CEC Division of Communication Disorders and Deafness, and the American Society for Deaf Children. The professional standards were developed with input from representatives of these organizations, including university professors, deaf education teachers, school administrators, parents, and consumers. The standards were originally developed in 1977, with periodic updates (CEC-CED, n.d.). The CED standards are in addition to the standards of practice for all special educators (CEC, 2008).

The CED standards were written predominantly for training programs that focus on elementary and secondary service delivery. As noted by the Joint Committee on Infant Hearing (2007), early-intervention services to children who are DHH also need to be provided by professionals with expertise in hearing loss. Because of the recent need for teacher preparation programs to train teachers to provide services to birth to 5-year-old children, the Office of Special Education Programs (OSEP) funded a project to identify the set of knowledge and skills needed to effectively serve young children who are DHH that may not be typically addressed in K–12 teacher education programs (Collaborative Early Intervention National Training e-Resource [CENTe-R], 2002; Proctor, Niemeyer, & Compton, 2005). In a similar effort, Rice and Lenihan (2005) also identified competencies needed by early interventionists in deaf education through surveys to professionals and focus group interviews with parents, professionals and preservice teachers. The broad categories of professional standards and competencies identified through these projects include the understanding of infant and toddler development, family-centered services, collaboration, assessment, curriculum development, program administration, special education legal issues, and the ability to advocate for high-quality services in the least restrictive environment.

Professional standards and competencies are very important for guiding the curriculum in deaf education teacher preparation programs if those standards are kept up to date and are consistent with evidence-based practice. Moreover, it is important that CED standards are carefully reviewed and updated frequently, given the dynamic changes in the field including recent increases in number of children who are DHH educated in mainstream settings, earlier identification and advances in technology, the number of children who are DHH with other disabilities, and the need for more itinerant teaching. To be effective, standards must also be accompanied by regular monitoring and evaluation of program impact including systematic feedback from employers of graduates, parents of children who are DHH, and present and former students.

Serving Children Who Are DHH With Additional Disabilities

According to Luckner and Carter (2001), 25% to 33% of the school-age population of children who are DHH have one or more additional disabilities. Mitchell and Karchmer (2006) identified a trend for an increasing proportion of children who are DHH to have additional disabilities, with the overall percentage likely exceeding 40%. In the *State Summary of Data from the 2009–10 Annual Survey of Deaf and Hard of Hearing Children and Youth*, the Gallaudet Research Institute (2011) reported that just 61.1% of students indicated hearing loss as their sole disability. This suggests that nearly 40% of students were identified with an additional disability.

With estimates of the incidence of children who are DHH to have an additional disability ranging from 25% to 40%, it is important to train educators to effectively work with this population. Luckner and Carter (2001, p. 7) reported that "the presence of a disability in addition to a hearing loss does not merely add to students' problems; it compounds them exponentially, making these students' special needs qualitatively different." Through a survey in 2001 sent to program supervisors across the United States, Luckner, and Carter identified 67 specific competencies needed for working with children who are DHH, and who have additional disabilities. Survey respondents identified the need for deaf education teacher preparation programs to ensure that graduates are skilled in modifying instructional methods for children with a variety of special needs, creating positive learning environments using authentic experiences, helping children use critical thinking and problem-solving skills, and providing services using an interdisciplinary team approach. They reported that the three fundamental barriers to effectively serving children who are DHH with additional disabilities included the difficulty of completing an appropriate assessment, challenges with accessing and implementing appropriate intervention strategies, and the shortage of well-trained personnel to provide effective and appropriate services. The broad set of 67 competencies identified in the Luckner and Carter survey were formulated into categories of:

- *General Knowledge of Serving Children with Special Needs* (e.g., learning environment, use of assistive devices, teaching children self-advocacy, authentic experiences, classroom modifications, research-supported instructional strategies).
- *Consultation and Collaboration* (e.g., transdisciplinary team models, parent support, educating other team members about hearing loss).
- *Behavior Management* (effective behavior support plans, classroom routines, nonaversive behavior management techniques, collaboration with parents).
- *Learning Difficulties* (conditions and psychological characteristics, social/emotional aspects of learning disabilities, instructional strategies).
- *Cognitive Development* (psychological characteristics of cognitive and perception development, appropriate assessment tools, alternative and augmentative communication systems).
- *Physical and Health* (materials, equipment, and technology appropriate for physical and health disabilities).
- *Vision* (impact of visual disorders on learning, individualized instruction, instruction modifications).
- *Deaf-Blindness* (combined effects of vision and hearing loss, nonlinguistics forms of communication and communication partnerships, incidental learning, use of technology).
- *Transition* (transition-focused educational programming, accessing services and resources).
- *Gifted and Talented* (development of specialized materials and programming).

Nearly a decade after Luckner and Carter identified competencies needed to serve children who are DHH with additional disabilities, Bruce, DiNatale, and Ford (2008) noted that most deaf education teacher preparation programs still do not sufficiently prepare preservice teachers to meet the needs of children who are DHH with additional disabilities and suggested that educators would benefit from preservice and in-service training related to serving these children. In a review of the literature on students who are DHH with additional disabilities, Guardino (2008) described the identification, incidence and placement for students who are DHH with autism, emotional/behavior disorders, attention deficit disorders, or mental retardation and suggested that more evidence-based research on intervention approaches is needed.

Needs of Present Deaf Education Teacher Preparation Programs

Teacher preparation programs need to train teachers who are prepared to adapt to changing roles and educational settings to best meet the needs of children who are DHH. In addition, these programs should include a foundation of content and experiences that provide preservice teachers with the knowledge and skills needed to become effective professionals. Assuming that the current CEC/CED standards provide a complete, up-to-date, evidence-based framework for training programs, currently only 36 teacher preparation programs are approved by the CED (*American Annals of the Deaf*, 2011; Easterbrooks, 2008; Easterbrooks & Putney, 2008). Research is needed to determine if programs that are not approved by CED produce teachers who are as skilled or less skilled than programs that meet CED standards. For teachers to become certified or licensed they must also meet the requirements of the states in which they will be teaching. These requirements vary dramatically leading to the possibility of inconsistent quality of teachers in deaf education.

Beyond the foundational requirements, some programs emphasize a particular aspect of deaf education and need to include that focus in the curriculum and practicum experiences of the preservice teachers. Programs that focus on listening and spoken language need to ensure that they are preparing students to complete the AG Bell Academy Listening and Spoken Language Specialist certification (Goldberg, Dickson, & Flexer, 2010). Teachers are eligible to apply for this certification after meeting several rigorous requirements including experience teaching in a listening and spoken language setting for 3–5 years. Some programs require extensive coursework and experience in ASL to prepare teachers for settings in which ASL is the primary mode of communication. For example, one of the key goals of the Center for ASL/English Bilingual Education and Research (CAEBER) at Gallaudet University is the development of a proficiency standard for ASL (Gallaudet University, 2011). Moreover, CAEBER provides bilingual professional development services to foster improved academic achievement in DHH students.

Other factors can impact the quality of graduates of teacher preparation programs in deaf education. For example, the challenge of recruiting and retaining an academically strong and diverse group of students impacts the quality of future teachers. The departmental structure of the university also influences the outcomes of the program. Deaf education programs need close collaboration with programs in education, special education, and speech and hearing sciences to provide preservice teachers with the academic content needed to be effective deaf education professionals. Another challenge faced by deaf education programs is acquiring and sustaining university support for programs that typically have a small student population. Some programs include distance learning to provide teacher preparation to individuals who would not otherwise be able to participate in teacher preparation (McGinnis, 2010). Some programs include a peer mentoring component as an effective means of increasing learning for preservice teachers (Trautwein & Ammerman, 2010).

Conclusions and Recommendations

Although it is cliché to say that deaf education teacher preparation programs are at an important crossroads, it is nonetheless an accurate and important description of the situation in which we find ourselves.

Because of the widespread implementation of newborn hearing screening programs and the resultant earlier identification of children who are DHH, coupled with dramatic advances in hearing technology and our understanding of how to teach language to young children, the prospects for success in school and society for children who are DHH have never been greater. Because these advances in teaching language are enabling children to be successful regardless of the communication mode they use, there is even the potential for reducing and perhaps eliminating the acrimonious debate that has raged for centuries about whether listening and spoken language or sign language is "best" for children who are DHH.

However, realizing the potential of these advances depends on having an adequate supply of well-trained educators of the deaf who know how to take advantage of these advances, have the skills to work with an increasingly heterogeneous group of children, can work collaboratively with other professionals, and are prepared to work in the settings where most children who are DHH are being educated. Unfortunately, as we stand on the cusp of success, this critical resource of well-trained teachers of the deaf is disappearing. More and more deaf education teacher preparation programs are closing, remaining programs are having trouble replacing faculty who retire, many of the remaining faculty are not involved doing research to advance knowledge, the number of students enrolled in deaf education teacher preparation programs has dropped by 50%, and many recent graduates report that they are not well prepared for the available deaf education jobs.

What is the solution? Clearly there is no quick fix, but it is evident that deaf education teacher preparation programs that train teachers to educate children who are DHH must include training across domains of deaf education, special education, early intervention, general education, audiology, and speech pathology. Teachers must also understand local, state, and federal laws and policies that regulate educational services. They must also learn to collaborate with other professionals who have a variety of perspectives, backgrounds, and expertise. Furthermore, the ability to partner with parents to deliver optimal services to children cannot be overstated.

The impact of federal legislation related to educational services for children, including infants and toddlers with disabilities, the development of various approaches including total communication, bilingual-bicultural and listening and spoken language, and the development of technology for cochlear implants and newborn hearing screening has changed the expectations and outcomes of children who are DHH and has altered the nature, roles, responsibilities, and work settings for many deaf educators. The availability of strong settings for practicum, student teaching and field experience is key to the successful development of a teacher in deaf education. Many deaf education teacher preparation programs establish professional development partnerships with private or public schools to provide quality experiences working with children. Programs need to require sufficient hours of hands-on experience in a variety of settings so that preservice teachers are prepared for the various responsibilities that may be needed. These experiences should be under the supervision of teachers who have kept up to date on the developments in deaf education and who have the skills needed to mentor beginning professionals.

Many challenges continue to exist for deaf education teacher preparation programs and the need to implement the empirically based recommendations that currently exist. A significant responsibility for those engaged in teacher preparation for teachers of children who are DHH is the need to continue to conduct high-quality research to guide new and emerging practice. Importantly, with the advent of early identification, early intervention, advanced hearing technology, and implementation of effective language and academic instructional strategies, never before have so many options existed for children who are DHH to reach their full potential.

Notes

1 Many different terms are used to refer to children with permanent hearing loss (e.g., deafness, hearing impairment, auditory disorders). Recognizing that there are limitations to any single term, this chapter will use the term "children who are deaf or hard of hearing (DHH)" to refer to children who have permanent hearing loss that is

serious enough to interfere with their success in educational programs. Educational services that are designed to meet the needs of these children and their families will be referred to as "deaf education" and teachers who serve these children will be referred to as "teachers of the deaf" or "deaf educators" except in those cases where another source is being quoted.

2 For data about the number of deaf education teacher preparation we have relied on the *American Annals of the Deaf* which is a professional journal published by Gallaudet University Press under the direction of the Council of American Instructors of the Deaf (CAID) and the Conference of Educational Administrators of Schools and Programs for the Deaf (CEASD). First published in 1847, the *Annals* is the oldest and most widely read English-language journal dealing with deafness and the education of deaf persons. Each year the *Annals* publishes a "reference" issue that lists, to the best of its ability, deaf education teacher preparation programs. Although we know the list is never 100% accurate, it is widely acknowledged as the best available list and consistently used for analyses of this type (see for example, Andrews & Covell, 2006/2007; Benedict, Johnson, & Antia, 2011; Dolman, 2008 and 2010; and Mitchell & Karchmer, 2006). It is also the only source of information that goes back at least 40 years using the same criteria and data collection methods.

References

Alberg, J. (2011, Summer). BEGINNINGS report: Change in communication choice over 10 years. *FYI-First Years Info*. Retrieved from http://firstyears.org/fyi/2011-summer.htm

American Annals of the Deaf. (2011). Programs for training teachers. *American Annals of the Deaf, 156*, 169–176.

American Association for Employment in Education. (2008). *Educator supply and demand in the United States* [2007 executive summary]. Columbus, OH: Author.

American Speech and Hearing Association. (2011). *Hearing aids*. Retrieved from http://www.asha.org/public/hearing/Hearing-Aids-Overview/

Andrews, J. F., & Covell, J. A. (2006/2007). Preparing future teachers and doctoral-level leaders in deaf education: Meeting the challenge. *American Annals of the Deaf, 151*, 464–475. doi:10.1353/aad.2007.0000

Benderly, B. L. (1990). *Dancing without music: Deafness in America*. Washington DC: Gallaudet University Press.

Benedict, K. M., Johnson, H., & Antia, S. D. (2011). Faculty needs, doctoral preparation, and the future of teacher preparation programs in the education of deaf and hard of hearing students. *American Annals of the Deaf, 156*, 35–46. doi:10.1353/aad.2011.0012

Bronstein, L. R. (2003). A model for interdisciplinary collaboration. *Social Work, 48*, 297–306. doi:10.1093/sw/48.3.297

Brown, C. (2006). *Early intervention: Strategies for public and private sector collaboration*. Paper presented at the Convention of the Alexander Graham Bell Association for the Deaf and Hard of Hearing, Pittsburgh, PA.

Bruce, S., DiNatale, P., & Ford, J. (2008). Meeting the needs of deaf and hard of hearing students with additional disabilities through professional teacher development. *American Annals of the Deaf, 153*, 368–375. doi:10.1353/aad.0.0058

Burkhalter, C. L., Blalock, L., Herring, H., & Skaar, D. (2011). Hearing aid functioning in the preschool setting: Stepping back in time? *International Journal of Pediatric Otorhinolaryngology, 75*, 801–804. doi:10.1016/j.ijporl.2011.03.011

Centers for Disease Control and Prevention (CDC). (2008). *Summary of 2006 national EHDI data*. Retrieved from http://www.cdc.gov/ncbddd/hearingloss/ehdi-data2006.html

Cole, E., & Flexer, C. (2007). *Children with hearing loss: Developing listening and talking, birth to six*. San Diego, CA: Plural Publishing.

Collaborative Early Intervention National Training e-Resource (CENTe-R). (2002). *Standards for professionals serving families with infants and toddlers who are deaf/hard of hearing*. Retrieved from http://center.uncg.edu/standards.pdf

Council for Exceptional Children. (2008). *What every special educator must know: Ethics, standards, and guidelines* (6th ed.). Arlington, VA: Author.

CEC-CED (Council of Exceptional Children and the Council on the Education of the Deaf). (n.d.). CEC-CED joint knowledge and skill statements for all beginning teachers of students who are deaf or hard of hearing. Retrieved from http://deafed.net/activities/ixb4.htm

Dodd, E. E., & Scheetz, N. A. (2003). Preparing today's teachers of the deaf and hard of hearing to work with tomorrow's students: A statewide needs assessment. *American Annals of the Deaf, 148*, 25–30. doi:10.1353/aad.2003.0002

Dolman, D. (2008). College and university requirements for teachers of the deaf at the undergraduate level: A twenty-year comparison. *American Annals of the Deaf, 153*, 322–327. doi:10.1353/aad.0.0049

Dolman, D. (2010). Enrollment trends in deaf education teacher preparation programs, 1973–2009. *American Annals of the Deaf, 155*, 353–359. doi:10.1353/aad.2010.0013

Easterbrooks, S. R. (2008). Knowledge and skills for teachers of individuals who are deaf or hard of hearing. *Communication Disorders Quarterly, 30*, 12–36. doi:10.1177/1525740108324043

Easterbrooks, S. R., & Putney, L. L. (2008). Development of initial and advanced standards of knowledge and skills for teachers of children who are deaf or hard of hearing: initial set revalidation. *Communications Disorders Quarterly 30*, 5–11. doi:10.1177/1525740108323857

Elfenbein, J. L., Bentler, R. A., Davis, J. M., & Niebuhr, D. P. (1988). Status of school children's hearing aids relative to monitoring practices. *Ear and Hearing, 9*, 212–217.

Estes, E. L. (2010). Listening, language, and learning: Skills of highly qualified listening and spoken language specialists in Educational settings. *The Volta Review, 110*, 169–178.

Gallaudet Research Institute. (2011). *State Summary of Data from the 2009–10 Annual Survey of Deaf and Hard of Hearing Children and Youth.* Washington, DC: GRI, Gallaudet University. Retrieved from http://research.gallaudet.edu/Demographics/

Gallaudet University. (2011). *Language Planning Institute: Center for ASL/English Bilingual education & research.* Retrieved from http://vl2.gallaudet.edu/initiatives_and_projects.php?id=initiative.4&preview=1

Geers, A. E., Moog, J. S., Biedenstein, J., Brenner, C., & Hayes, H. (2009). Spoken language scores of children using cochlear implants compared to hearing age-mates at school entry. *Journal of Deaf Studies and Deaf Education, 14*, 371–385. doi:10.1093/deafed/enn046

Goldberg, D. M., Dickson, C. L., & Flexer, C. (2010). AG Bell Academy certification program for listening and spoken language specialists: Meeting a world-wide need for qualified professionals. *The Volta Review, 110*, 129–144.

Guardino, C. A. (2008). Identification and placement for deaf students with multiple disabilities: Choosing the path less followed. *American Annals of the Deaf, 153*, 55–64. doi:10.1353/aad.0.0004

Hands and Voices. (2010). *Early identification and intervention: The journey starts here.* Retrieved from http://www.handsandvoices.org/articles/early_intervention/early_id_journey.html

Harrison, L. E. (2008). *Perceived efficacy of teacher preparation programs among teachers of the deaf/hard-of-hearing.* Unpublished dissertation, George Fox University, Newberg Oregon. (ProQuest #3301468)

International Congress on Education of the Deaf. (2010). *A new era: Deaf participation and collaboration.* Retrieved from http://www.milan1880.com/Resources/iced2010statement.pdf

Johnson, H. A. (2004). U.S. deaf education teacher preparation programs: A look at the present and a vision for the future. *American Annals of the Deaf, 149*, 75–91. doi:10.1353/aad.2004.0020

Joint Committee on Infant Hearing. (2007). *Updates in the Year 2007 position statement: Principles and guidelines for early hearing detection and intervention programs.* Retrieved from http://www.asha.org/aud/articles/EHDI.htm

Jones, T. W., & Ewing, K. M. (2002). An analysis of teacher preparation in deaf education: Programs approved by the Council on Education of the Deaf. *American Annals of the Deaf*, 147, 71–78. doi:10.1353/aad.2012.0246

Kennedy, C. R., McCann, D. C., Campbell, M. J., Law, C. M., Mullee, M., Petrou, S., … Stevenson, J. (2006). Language ability after early detection of permanent childhood hearing impairment. *New England Journal of Medicine, 354*, 2131–2141. doi:10.1056/NEJMoa054915

LaSasso, C., & Lollis, J. (2003). Survey of residential and day schools for deaf students in the United States that identify themselves as bilingual-bicultural programs. *Journal of Deaf Studies and Deaf Education, 8*, 79–91. doi:10.1093/deafed/8.1.79

Lenihan, S. (2010). Trends and challenges in teacher preparation in deaf education. *The Volta Review, 110*, 117–128.

Leonard, D. R., Shen, & T., Howe, H. L. (Eds). (1999). *Trends in the prevalence of birth defects in Illinois and Chicago 1989 to 1997: Epidemiologic Report Series 99:4.* Springfield, IL: Illinois Department of Public Health.

Luckner, J. L., & Carter, K. (2001). Essential competencies for teaching students with hearing loss and additional disabilities. *American Annals of the Deaf, 146*, 7–15. doi:10.1353/aad.2012.0065

Luckner, J. L., & Howell, J. (2002). Suggestions for preparing itinerant teachers: A qualitative analysis. *American Annals of the Deaf, 147*, 54–61. doi:10.1353/aad.2012.0210

Luckner, J. L., Muir, S. G., Howell, J. J., Sebald, A. M., & Young, J. (2005). An examination of the research and training needs in the field of deaf education. *American Annals of the Deaf, 150*, 358–368. doi:10.1353/aad.2005.0042

Marge, D. K., & Marge, M. (2005). *Beyond newborn hearing screenings: Meeting the educational and healthcare needs of infants and young children with hearing loss in America. Report and recommendations of the National Consensus Conference on Effective Educational and Health Care Interventions for Infants and Young Children with Hearing Loss.* Syracuse, NY: SUNY Upstate Medical University, Department of Physical Medicine and Rehabilitation.

Marvelli, A. L. (2010). Highlights in the history of oral teacher preparation in America. *The Volta Review, 110*, 89–115.

McGinnis, M. (2010). John Tracy Clinic/University of San Diego Graduate Program: A distance learning model. *The Volta Review, 110*, 261–270.

Mitchell, R. E., & Karchmer, M. A. (2004). Chasing the mythical ten percent: Parental hearing status of deaf and hard of hearing students in the United States. *Sign Language Studies, 4*(2), 138–163. doi:10.1353/sls.2004.0005

Mitchell, R. E., & Karchmer, M. A. (2006). Demographics of deaf education: More students in more places. *American Annals of the Deaf, 151*, 95–104. doi:10.1353/aad.2006.0029

Moeller, M. P. (2000). Early intervention and language development in children who are deaf and hard of hearing. *Pediatrics, 106*, e43-e43. doi:10.1542/peds.106.3.e43

Monaghan, L., Schmaling, C., Nakamura, K., & Turner, G. H. (Eds). (2002). *Many ways to be deaf: International variation in deaf communities.* Washington, DC: Gallaudet University Press.

Moores, D. F. (2006). Professional training emphasis. *American Annals of the Deaf, 151*, 3–4. doi:10.1353/aad.2006.0016

Moores, D. F. (2008). Research on bi-bi instruction editorial. *American Annals of the Deaf, 153*, 3–4. doi:10.1353/aad.0.0003

National Dissemination Center for Children with Disabilities. (2010). *Overview of early intervention.* Retrieved from http://www.nichcy.org/babies/overview/

National Institute on Deafness and Other Communication Disorders. (2009). *Cochlear implants.* Retrieved from http://www.nidcd.nih.gov/health/hearing/coch.asp

Nelson, L., Bradham, T. S., Houston, K. T. (2011). The EHDI and early intervention connection. *The Volta Review, 111*, 133–149.

Nicholas, J. G., & Geers, A. E. (2007). Will they catch up? The role of age at cochlear implantation in the spoken language development of children with severe to profound hearing loss. *Journal of Speech, Language, & Hearing, 50*, 1048–1062. doi:10.1044/1092-4388(2007/073)

Northern, J. L., & Downs, M. P. (1991). *Hearing in children* (4th ed.). Baltimore, MD: Williams and Wilkins.

Padden, C., & Humphries, T. (2005). *Inside Deaf culture.* Cambridge, MA: Harvard University Press.

Potts, P. L., & Greenwood, J. (1983). Hearing aid monitoring: Are looking and listening enough? *Language Speech Hearing Services in Schools, 14*, 157–163.

Proctor, R., Niemeyer, J. A., & Compton, M. V. (2005). Training needs of early intervention personnel working with infants and toddlers who are deaf or hard of hearing. *The Volta Review, 105*, 113–128.

Reichman, J. (1986). *Procedures used by educational agencies to monitor and maintain amplification systems worn by hearing impaired students.* Retrieved from http://hdl.handle.net/10150/183968

Rice, G. B., & Lenihan, S. (2005). Early intervention in auditory/oral deaf education: Parent and professional perspectives. *The Volta Review, 105*, 73–96.

Robertson, L. (2009). *Literacy and deafness: Listening and spoken language.* San Diego, CA: Plural Publishing, Inc.

Sass-Lehrer, M., & Bodner-Johnson, B. (2003). Early intervention: Current approaches to family-centered programming. In M. Marschark & P. E. Spencer (Eds.), *Oxford handbook of deaf studies, language, and education* (pp. 65–81). New York: Oxford University Press.

Schirmer, B. R. (2008). How effectively are we preparing teacher educators in special education? The case of deaf education. *American Annals of the Deaf, 153*, 411–419. doi:10.1353/aad.0.0056

Schwartz, S. (2007). *Choices in deafness: A parents' guide to communication options* (3rd ed.). Bethesda, MD: Woodbine House.

Stewart, D. A. (1992). Initiating reform in Total Communication programs. *The Journal of Special Education, 26*, 68–84. doi:10.1177/002246699202600105

Stierman, L. (1994). *Birth defects in California: 1983–1990.* Emeryville, CA: The California Birth Defects Monitoring Program, California Department of Health Services.

Stokoe, W. C., Jr. (2005). Sign language structure: An outline of the visual communication systems of the American Deaf (10th Anniversary Classic). *Journal of Deaf Studies and Deaf Education 10*, 3–37. doi:10.1093/deafed/eni001

Strong, M. (1988). A bilingual approach to the education of young deaf children: ASL and English. In M. Strong (Ed.), *Language learning and deafness* (pp. 113–132). New York, NY: Cambridge University Press. doi:10.1017/CBO9781139524483.007

Teller, H., & Harney, J. (2005/2006). Views from the field: Program directors' perceptions of teacher education and the education of students who are deaf or hard of hearing. *American Annals of the Deaf, 150*, 470–479. doi:10.1353/aad.2006.0011

The Commission on Education of the Deaf. (1988, February). *Toward equality: Education of the deaf.* Washington, DC: U.S. Government Printing Office.

Trautwein, B., & Ammerman, S. (2010). From pedagogy to practice: Mentoring and reciprocal peer coaching for preservice teachers. *The Volta Review, 110*, 191–206.

Traxler, C. B. (2000). The Stanford Achievement Test, 9th edition: National norming and performance standards for deaf and hard-of-hearing students. *Journal of Deaf Studies and Deaf Education, 5, 337–348.* doi:10.1093/deafed/5.4.337

U.S. Department of Health and Human Services. (1990). *Healthy People 2000: National health promotion and disease prevention objectives*. Washington, DC: Public Health Service.

Utah Schools for the Deaf and the Blind (USDB). (2011). *Annual Report for the Legislative Education Interim Committee*. Retrieved from http://www.usdb.org/pr/Shared%20Documents/Interim%20Final%20Report%202011.pdf

White, K. R. (1997). Realities, myths, and challenges of newborn hearing screening in the United States. *American Journal of Audiology, 4*, 90–94.

White, K. R. (2003). The current status of EHDI programs in the United States. *Mental Retardation and Developmental Disabilities Research Reviews, 9*, 79–88. doi:10.1002/mrdd.10063

White, K. R. (2004). Early hearing detection and intervention programs: Opportunities for genetic services. *American Journal of Medical Genetics, 130A*, 29–36. doi:10.1002/ajmg.a.30048

White, K. R. (2006). Early intervention for children with permanent hearing loss: Finishing the EHDI revolution. *The Volta Review, 106*, 237–258.

White, K. R., Forsman, I., Eichwald, J., & Munoz, K. (2010). The evolution of early hearing detection and intervention programs in the United States. *Seminars in Perinatology, 34*, 170–179. doi:10.1053/j.semperi.2009.12.009

White, K. R., & Muñoz, K. (2008). Screening for mild and unilateral hearing loss. *Seminars in Hearing, 29*, 149–158. doi:10.1055/s-2008-1075822

Yoshinaga-Itano, C. (2003). Early intervention after universal neonatal hearing screening: Impact on outcomes. *Mental Retardation and Developmental Disabilities Research Reviews, 9*, 252–266.

Yoshinaga-Itano, C., & Gravel, J. S. (2001). The evidence for universal hearing screening. *American Journal of Audiology, 10*, 62–64. doi:10.1044/1059-0889(2001/013)

Yoshinaga-Itano, C., Sedey, A. L., Coulter, D. K., & Mehl, A. L. (1998). Language of early-and later-identified children with hearing loss. *Pediatrics, 102*, 1161–1171. doi:10.1542/peds.102.5.1161

Zink, G. D. (1972). Hearing aids children wear: A longitudinal study of performance. *The Volta Review, 74*, 41–51.

21

Personnel Preparation in Visual Impairment

Laura Bozeman

UNIVERSITY OF MASSACHUSETTS BOSTON

Kim Zebehazy

THE UNIVERSITY OF BRITISH COLUMBIA

Things to Think About

- Personnel preparation programs in visual impairment have faced common challenges across the country including struggles to meet teacher shortages, particularly in rural areas.
- The vitality of personnel preparation programs depends on faculty-renewal and innovative practices.
- Quality and effective services for students with visual impairment depend on sustained collaboration and shared goals between stakeholders, including personnel preparation programs and corresponding universities, regional agencies, school districts, and departments of education.
- Recent discussions by personnel preparation programs in visual impairment to establish common, skill-based, standards for beginning teachers may promote future collaborations and focused outcomes.
- Future research in personnel preparation programs in visual impairment should include more direct investigations of the relationship between chosen methodologies, teacher outcomes, and progress for the student with visual impairment.

We envision a future world in which each individual is valued by society. In this society, the needs of each individual are respected and addressed. Individuals from diverse language, cultural, ethnic, and disability backgrounds are perceived and see themselves as contributing members of society. They have high expectations for leading fulfilling lives.

(Mason, Davidson, & McNerney, 2000, p. 9)

Unique Preparation for Unique Needs

Children With Visual Impairment

Children with visual impairment are a diverse group. Some children are congenitally blind and access the environment through senses other than vision. Other children have varying degrees of low vision and may use vision functionally for many tasks as well as in conjunction with other senses. There are children who have visual impairment as a singular disability while others (at least 60%) may have additional disabilities (Kirchner & Diament, 1999; Hyvärinen, 2011). Regardless of the amount of functional vision a child with visual impairment has and whether s/he has multiple disabilities, attention to the child's specialized needs within the school, home, and community environment is important to ensure equal opportunities to acquire concepts, to access the general curriculum in the most effective manner, and to develop independence in school and daily life.

Supporting the needs of children with visual impairment goes beyond simply providing accommodations. Vision is a distance sense and sensory loss impacts the way that information is gathered. Without proper instruction and opportunities for direct, interactive experience, children with visual impairment may miss critical concepts. Incidental learning, by which all children acquire knowledge about many concepts (through observation and imitation), is inhibited when vision is not sufficient to observe effectively from a distance (Barraga & Erin, 2001; Pogrund, 2002). Direct exposure to these concepts and a mediated learning environment to provide experiences that promote exploration, thinking skills, and understanding are important for all children, but particularly important for children with visual impairment. Another difference in the way children with visual impairment learn involves the approach to learning. Sighted children initially view an object in its entirety then learn about the parts of the object (e.g., a table as the whole concept, then the legs and pieces that make up the table). Children who do not use vision as a primary sense, view pieces of an object and then must understand those parts in the Gestalt—an abstract task (Fazzi & Klein, 2002; Skellenger & Sapp, 2010). Professionals who work with children with visual impairment and their families need to be knowledgeable about the potential impact of visual impairment on development, the specialized skills and techniques that children use to access the learning environment, and the teaching techniques that will be effective in promoting learning and the development of independence, competence, and a fulfilling life.

Roles of Professionals in Visual Impairment

Professionals within the education and rehabilitation fields who have specialized preparation in visual impairment include: teachers of students with visual impairment (TSVIs), orientation and mobility specialists (O&M), vision rehabilitation therapists (VRT), and low vision therapists (LVT). Personnel preparation of TSVIs and O&M specialists will be the focus of this chapter as these two are mandated by the Individuals with Disabilities Education Improvement Act (IDEIA) and are generally the most involved vision professionals within the special education environment (Koenig & Holbrook, 2000).

The vast majority of TSVIs are itinerant and provide support to general and special education teachers in several schools or districts. TSVIs who work in specialized schools are typically responsible for a class of students in both academic and nonacademic areas (Lewis & Allman, 2000). The TSVI serves in several roles. One role is to conduct assessments related to visual impairment. These assessments include the functional vision assessment (FVA), which evaluates how a child uses his/her vision and other senses in familiar and unfamiliar environments. The FVA serves as a basis for making recommendations for accommodations, adaptations, and instructional programming needs. In addition, TSVIs also conduct learning media assessments (LMA), which consider a child's use of sensory channels, help determine an initial learning medium for a child (print, braille, or both), and serve as a way to continue to monitor and assess a child's progress with his or her primary medium as well as assess other tools needed to give access to literacy across situations (assistive technology, low vision devices, etc.). Also, TSVIs may administer developmental tests and other evaluations that support psychological assessment of the child with visual impairment.

Other main roles include supporting the general education teacher to make appropriate adaptations to instruction and accommodations to learning materials, as well as to provide direct instruction to children with visual impairment. Direct instruction can occur within the context of the core and expanded core curricula. Within the core curriculum, TSVIs may teach concepts related to the general curriculum that are impacted by vision loss (e.g., understanding graphs and fractions via tactile methods, working on reading comprehension in braille, etc.). This instruction does not replace the general classroom instruction the child is receiving; it supplements it. The expanded core curriculum (ECC) is the term used to describe nine disability-specific areas of instructional needs that students with visual impairment may have. These areas are: compensatory skills (concept development, organization, communication, etc.), daily living skills, social skills, assistive technology, self-determination, recreation and leisure, career education, sensory efficiency skills, and O&M.

While the TSVI supports the development of O&M, it is the O&M specialist who provides the bulk of instruction in this area. Sometimes, the professional serving a child is dually certified as a TSVI and O&M specialist, in which case that professional may provide instruction in both specialty areas. O&M refers to the travel skills and concepts that students with visual impairment learn in order to move safely and efficiently through the environment. For the young child, instruction may target sensory motor development and integration (Rosen, 2010). For the child with additional disabilities, the O&M specialist may be integrating wheelchair travel or lessons with an emphasis on daily living skills (Rosen & Crawford, 2010). Using remaining vision, using the long cane, remaining oriented while traveling between destinations, learning how to problem-solve, using public transportation systems, and planning alternate routes are just a few of the many skills students with visual impairment learn through O&M instruction over the course of their school years as they work toward becoming interdependent/independent travelers.

Low-Incidence Population

TSVIs and O&M specialists work with a low-incidence population of students. The prevalence of visual impairment in children under the age of 15 in the United States was estimated by the World Health Organization to be less than one tenth of 1% (0.03%) in 2002. For all age categories, prevalence of blindness in the United States was estimated to be 0.2% and prevalence of low vision to be 1.2% (Resnikoff et al., 2004). In 2009, the CDC estimated that 1 in every 1,000 children in the United States has low vision or is legally blind. In 2010, the American Printing House (APH) for the Blind's federal quota number was 59,341 nationwide. This number reflects students, including adult students in rehabilitation programs, eligible for federal money to access APH educational materials based on the definition of legal blindness or visual performance reduced by brain injury or dysfunction determined by a doctor.

The low-incidence nature of visual impairment has implications for the services provided to students with visual impairment and the preparation of professionals who work with these students. First, it is difficult to get an accurate count of all children who could benefit from services for visual impairment. The APH count mentioned above excludes children with visual impairment who do not meet the federal quota definition, and the Office of Special Education Programs (OSEP) reporting process is based on primary disability. Many students with multiple disabilities who also have a visual impairment will not be included in the visual impairment count. Due to the low incidence and lack of exposure to children with reduced vision, most professionals in the public school setting do not understand the unique educational needs of children with visual impairment, making the need for qualified professionals to support these students even more important.

National Agenda

Given the unique educational needs of children with visual impairment and the low-incidence nature of visual impairment, a National Agenda for the Education of Children and Youths with Visual Impairments, Including Those with Multiple Disabilities was created in the United States in 1995 and revised in 2004 to highlight 10 goals important to improving the services for and attention to the educational needs of this population (Corn, Hatlen, Huebner, Ryan, & Siller, 1995; Huebner, Merk-Adam, Stryker, & Wolffe, 2004). Individual states have also created their own State Agendas that highlight state-specific efforts within the 10 National goals. While teacher preparation is inherently linked to the success of all 10 goals, several have direct implications for the work needed in personnel preparation. Goals one and six both reference the need for qualified TSVIs and O&M specialists to provide appropriate and quality services, including assessments. Goal three focuses directly on personnel preparation programs, stating, "Universities with a minimum of one full-time member in the area of visual impairment will prepare a sufficient number of teachers and orientation and mobility (O&M) specialists for students with visual impairments to meet personnel needs throughout the country" (Huebner et al., 2004, p. 8).

Visual Impairment Preparation Challenges

The need for the National Agenda as a strategic document to improve educational services to children and youth with visual impairment highlights the challenges that the field of visual impairment experiences in finding and preparing qualified professionals. The National Plan for Training Personnel to Serve Children with Blindness and Low Vision (NPTP), created over a 2-year time frame (1997–1999), estimated a need for an additional 5,000 TSVIs and 10,000 O&M specialists, with an increase in recruitment of underrepresented groups, to meet the shortage demands and provide manageable caseloads (Mason et al., 2000). However, Ferrell (2007) reported that on average, personnel preparation programs in the United States collectively prepare 250 professionals yearly. This level of preparation is well below the estimated shortage; also, the numbers of teachers in the field of visual impairment from culturally and linguistically diverse backgrounds appear to remain low (Correa-Torres & Durando, 2011; Milian & Ferrell, 1998).

While the goal of expanding and enhancing services to students with visual impairment through the preparation of highly qualified individuals is a top priority for personnel preparation programs in visual impairment, a multitude of factors have cocontributed over the years to the challenges programs encounter. These factors include: the size and characteristics of low-incidence programs, shortages in leadership in visual impairment, access to programs, funding and resources, and state and district policies (Ambrose-Zaken & Bozeman, 2010; Ferrell, 2007; Walker & Bozeman, 2002).

Size and Characteristics of Low-Incidence Programs

Low-incidence personnel preparation programs struggle to find a permanent home at a university. This conflict impacts the preparation of vision professionals and, ultimately, the outcomes for children with vision loss.

Personnel preparation programs in visual impairment are typically smaller than other teacher preparation programs. Certain coursework, like O&M blindfold technique courses, require small student to instructor ratios (1 : 6) in order to be effective, ensure safety, and to meet University Review Core Standard II. e. iii (Association for Education and Rehabilitation of the Blind and Visually Impaired [AERBVI], 2010). From the perspective of a university, small programs are expensive and typically bring in less money, making low-incidence programs vulnerable, particularly in tough financial times.

In addition, programs in visual impairment often have higher course credit amounts because of the specialized skills a future TSVI or O&M specialist must learn (CEC, 2011; Academy for Certification of Vision Rehabilitation and Education Professionals [ACVREP], 2011). For TSVI programs, the ECC, as mentioned earlier, has nine disability-specific instructional areas for which future teachers must learn assessment and best-practice teaching strategies to be effective (Sapp & Hatlen, 2010). These specialized skills are in addition to learning foundational information and procedural components (e.g., writing Individualized Education Plans [IEPs] and Individualized Family Service Plans [IFSPs]) of being a special educator. It is a challenge to effectively incorporate all the skills a beginning TSVI or O&M needs into a program, especially with pressure to keep the total credit load low or to create shorter programs.

Leadership Shortages

Related to the unique characteristics of visual impairment are challenges that faculty report in running a personnel preparation program and in maintaining a rigorous research agenda at the same time (Ambrose-Zaken & Bozeman, 2010; Corn & Spungin, 2002). Many programs in visual impairment are run by one or two faculty members, and shortages of current and future leadership are a main concern. In 2002, Corn and Spungin noted the dearth of faculty to fill special education positions, including faculty for personnel preparation in visual impairment. The shortage continues to be a concern per the 2010 research by Ambrose-Zaken and Bozeman. Respondent data in that research reported 35 doctoral students in visual impairment. That number falls far short of the current and anticipated need of 49 to fill the 25 vacant positions and 24 projected vacancies due to retirement in 2009–2013. For small, specialized programs that are often understaffed, a wide range of tasks fall on the shoulders of faculty: recruitment, advising, program evaluation, community support and networking, supervision of students during internship, licensure and certification paperwork, etc. This, coupled with the fact that students with visual impairment are widely spread across geographical areas (only a couple of students might be in a school or district), conducting research directly with students with visual impairment becomes challenging. In general, there is a heavier burden on many personnel preparation programs in visual impairment to demonstrate their viability and contribution within the university environment, unless the university embraces the social responsibility of serving a region in a specialty area not found in other locations.

Access to Programs

Access to programs in the area of visual impairment is more limited than in most other specialty areas. Not all states have a program in visual impairment. In fact, 46% of states do not have any TSVI programs and fewer than two thirds of states have programs in other specialty areas such as O&M (Ambrose-Zaken & Bozeman, 2010). One of the challenges personnel preparation programs face in providing access to areas without programs is the logistical issue of certification granted to individuals attending an out-of-state visual impairment program. A regional collaboration between UMass Boston and the six New England states has succeeded because of collaboration among and financial commitments from the parties involved, and agreements about licensure requirements.

In addition, programs need to consider the best program delivery method that will uphold high standards while providing access to a greater range of students in wider geographical areas. For example, although distance education methods provide greater access, participants in rural areas may have fewer professional colleagues with whom to network or from whom to seek mentoring. The availability of professional peers should be considered when planning program instructional methodologies. One solution that integrates local mentors into the university curriculum is to designate state or area liaisons. Liaisons recruit candidates, provide links to local vision professionals for observations and practicum supervision, and provide support to first-year teachers. Accessibility, particularly for individuals with disabilities, may also be enhanced by technologies such as Universal Design for Learning (UDL; CAST, 2011), which make distance education materials and software available and usable for all.

A further challenge to recruitment is obtaining student funding. Many programs, particularly those without scholarship money to offer, struggle to launch effective recruitment efforts to entice prospective teachers into programs. Many programs recruit nontraditional students—professionals interested in changing careers, teachers already working as TSVIs on emergency certifications, and older students—who are likely to have families and financial obligations. Furthermore, although the diversity and range of experiences that nontraditional students bring to a program are welcomed, the stresses these students feel to balance work, school, and family can be more challenging than is seen with more traditional students. Some students may drop out or take leave, which impacts program enrollment and the ultimate effectiveness of filling shortages.

Funding and Resources

To keep programs running, fund instructors and faculty, and provide support for students to improve recruitment potential, most personnel preparation programs in visual impairment are dependent on outside grants, particularly from the OSEP and the Rehabilitation Services Administration (RSA). Some programs also benefit from state grants. Securing federal personnel preparation funding is becoming more and more of a challenge with financial cuts reducing the amount and number of awards. Furthermore, funding agencies and foundations are demanding evidence about the effectiveness of programs based on outcomes for students taught by our graduates. For a host of reasons, such research is difficult if not impossible to do; nonetheless, it is a well-known fact that these data are sorely needed.

The urgency to secure funding has other negative consequences. In a field like visual impairment where collaboration is important, the need to secure funding for survival creates a level of competition among personnel preparation programs that can undermine collaboration within regions. In addition, the OSEP low-incidence competition to which visual impairments (VI) programs apply continues to include the burgeoning area of autism, which increases the number of submissions and competition for grants.

State and District Policies

Even with better recruitment and the preparation of more qualified TSVIs and O&M specialists, improved services for children who are blind or visually impaired require collaboration on the part of the education system as well. State Departments of Education and districts must embrace the unique needs of students with visual impairment (Erin, Holbrook, Sanspree, & Swallow, 2006). Additional positions for professionals must be created when current caseloads grow too large.

In many areas of the country, TSVI and O&M caseloads are too large to adequately serve students. Research published in 2000 by Mason et al. noted the need for caseload ratios of 1 : 8 for adequate instruction and student learning. In determining caseloads, the geographical region covered, travel time, an accurate identification of children with visual impairment in the district, and the needs of those children based on assessment are just some of the factors that must be considered (Toelle & Blankenship, 2008). Large caseloads led to the trend of consult-only or sporadic services from a TSVI or O&M. In addition, needed positions were not created or remained unfilled. This trend must change for students to be properly served.

Rural districts struggle to find TSVIs and O&M specialists to provide services. Continued collaborative efforts between these areas, State Departments of Education, and institutes of higher education (the university program covering that region) are critical to developing solutions so that students with visual impairment receive the services they require.

Current Approaches

Current approaches, through individual program and collaborative efforts, attempt to address the many challenges faced by personnel preparation programs in visual impairment. Noteworthy current practices include the diversity of program delivery methods; collaborative endeavors between programs, leadership, research, and materials-sharing; as well as review of personnel preparation programs for quality and consistency.

Current Delivery Methods

A majority of the TSVI and O&M programs utilize some form of distance education methodologies to reach out to more students, to address the absence of programs in many states, and to increase program viability within the university environment. However, the types of methodologies and the structure of different programs in visual impairment vary. There are basically three main ways programs in visual impairment are organized: traditional on-campus programs (all classes face to face); hybrid programs with some form of distance education classes (e.g., online, video, traveling instructor) and some face-to-face courses such as during summer terms or on weekends; and completely distance education programs (e.g., all courses online). Currently the hybrid model is the most utilized (Ambrose-Zaken & Bozeman, 2010).

The distance education methods and tools used within these main models vary as well. For example, many programs utilize some sort of Internet Learning Platform (Blackboard, WebCT, Moodle) to deliver content and foster discussions and interaction within the class. The advent of audio, text, and visual chat tools such as Skype, WIMBA, Adobe Connect, and tcConference provide additional opportunities to connect with students in real time at little or no expense. Some programs have the instructor travel to the student to teach a cohort. Some programs send videos to students for the lectures and weekly content. Others deliver instruction via Smart Rooms that connect virtually with other Smart Rooms or stream real-time face-to-face classroom content to students' individual computers at a distance. Many programs use a combination of approaches to best meet the needs of the students.

Collaborative Approaches

Personnel preparation programs in visual impairment have engaged in different collaborative approaches to support the needs of teacher preparation as well. Through AERBVI's Personnel Preparation Division, representatives from a majority of the university programs have a vehicle to discuss common issues. Other regional forums for discussion of needs in personnel preparation are present. The Consortium of TVI/O&M Personnel Preparation Programs in Western United States and Canada and the Northeast Regional Center for Vision Education (NERCVE) are examples. Through these vehicles as well as individual program efforts, collaborative projects (VIPrep Share, Delphi studies on Literary and Nemeth Braille code) have emerged.

Regional Approaches

In the area of program delivery, some communities have found a regional approach to personnel preparation in visual impairment to be a viable option. For example, this approach works, geographically, in New England with all six states served by UMass Boston (Bozeman, 2009). A regional approach can help alleviate some of the financial challenges, through diversification of funding sources by having all regions served contribute financially or in kind (by providing mentors, teacher volunteers, etc.) to the running of the program. State Liaisons in each of the six New England states, for instance, serve as mentors, practicum supervisors, and provide networking opportunities for the students across the region.

Collaboration between some universities and/or schools for the blind and visually impaired are used as well for the delivery of course content and internships. An area within a larger state or province can also be considered a region (Griffin-Shirley, Almon, & Kelley, 2002). And, there are some nontraditional examples where the region is located far away from the university serving the area. One example is the Pacific Visual Instruction Program (Pacific VIP). This program is funded by OSEP to prepare TSVIs and O&Ms to meet the needs of children with visual impairment living in the islands of Micronesia (*Saipan Tribune*, 2012). The curriculum is provided through the UMass Boston Vision Studies program. Additional regional efforts have set up targeted cohorts in an effort to address the shortage of culturally and linguistically diverse individuals in the field. Again, meeting the needs of the community can be accomplished with creative delivery systems that maintain quality and offer highly qualified preparation (Bozeman, 2011).

Materials-Sharing

Over the years, through federal funding, personnel preparation programs have created materials that could be shared across programs. These projects have enriched the instructional materials readily available for dynamic, multimedia content without programs having to reinvent the wheel. For example, materials produced by Project SLATE (Supporting Literacy Achievement and Teacher Effectiveness for Students who are Blind and Visually Impaired) include videos of teachers working with students with visual impairment on literacy acquisition as well as assessing a student's learning media (Holbrook, Croft, & Koenig, 2005; Koenig et al., 2005). Another example is Project Math Access. These materials include videos of mathematics adaptations for students with visual impairment (Kapperman & Sticken, 2006). Early intervention training materials through the Early Intervention Training Center for Infants and Toddlers with Visual Impairments include videos, PowerPoints, and handouts related to early intervention topics (Anthony, Lowry, Brown, & Hatton, 2004; Gleason, Wheeler, Murphy, & Hatton, 2006; Hatton, McWilliam, & Winton, 2006; Sapp & Hatton, 2005; Topor, Rosenblum, & Hatton, 2004). The APH offers field representatives for guest lectures on the vital role of the APH and lends materials to universities to enhance and supplement instruction. A more informal material-sharing effort, VIPrepShare, is also in place. This server space allows individuals at university programs to post materials they are willing to share with colleagues in other university programs. VIPrepShare is a renewed effort of a similar past attempt at material-sharing. The current effort began slowly, and widespread sharing of materials has yet to be realized due to various factors. Intellectual property rights and university regulations can be impediments, as can the time required of faculty to post materials.

Creative efforts by individual universities to meet instructional needs in distance formats also hold future promise for other universities. For example, a project to bank teaching videos clips that demonstrate best practices is being developed by Hunter College (Gale, Trief, & Lengel, 2010). Other programs have developed online tools such as an interactive abacus, and Literary and Nemeth braille tutorials.[1]

Leadership Collaboration

An innovative and collaborative step to improve the numbers of vision leaders occurred in 2006 when then Pennsylvania College of Optometry (now Salus University) announced the National Center for Leadership in Visual Impairment (NCLVI, 2010). The NCLVI collaboration through a consortium of 14 universities was funded by OSEP and offered support for doctoral students pursuing leadership roles in visual impairment. The fellows in this program had opportunities to interact with each other through institute courses, meetings at conferences, and joint research projects. Leaders in the consortium as well as in other personnel preparation programs, related agencies, and stakeholders contributed to the leadership institute in various ways, including serving as guest discussants in online courses and mentoring projects undertaken by the fellows. As of October 2010, there were 19 doctoral graduates. Other low-incidence groups recognized this leadership effort as successful. Currently there is a new leadership institute underway called the National Leadership Consortium in Sensory Disabilities (NLCSD). Fellows in this institute specialize in the areas of deaf/hard of hearing, blind/visually impaired or deaf-blindness.

Research Efforts

As mentioned earlier, VI scholars struggle to maintain consistent lines of research and replication due to the low-incidence of visual impairment. Some efforts have begun to look at solutions to this problem. One larger effort was in the creation, in 2001, of a National Center on Low Incidence Disabilities (NCLID) through the University of Northern Colorado, now called the National Center on Severe and Sensory Disabilities (NCSSD; Ferrell, 2009). Supporting doctoral students, offering "Research in the Rockies" summits as a vehicle for researchers to collaborate and discuss issues, and research efforts to summarize and document progress within the field are among the many projects undertaken by this center. The Center also endeavored to strengthen the voice of low-incidence disabilities by having a center that allowed for collaboration between specialty areas and to serve as a center for information, training, and technical assistance. In addition to the Center's efforts, several grant-funded collaborative efforts in visual impairment have allowed multiple universities to investigate a common question and accomplish more in the area of research. Two examples would be a collaborative longitudinal study in braille literacy (i.e., ABC Braille Study), and a multiple-university research effort in O&M in the area of roundabout crossings.

Levels of Review

There are several avenues by which personnel programs in visual impairment could be reviewed for quality. Programs in visual impairment at universities that engage in the National Council for Accreditation of Teacher Education or Teacher Education Accreditation Council use the Council for Exceptional Children (CEC) competencies for visual impairment. A more vision-specific review process is also available through AERBVI, the professional organization, which recently upgraded its University Review Process. University review is a method whereby programs in TSVI, O&M, and VRT are examined for adherence to administrative and curricular standards, use of best practices, and consistency across university programs. The university review process is another layer of accountability and provides opportunities for improvement.

Graduates of O&M programs are vetted for initial certification by ACVREP through transcript review, practicum performance, and examination. Certification is granted for 5 years and requires professional development and improvement to be demonstrated for renewal. One current barrier to the strength of ACVREP certification is that not all agencies and schools hiring O&M professionals require certification.

Recent progress toward state licensure for vision rehabilitation professionals was seen in New York. Collaborating agencies, the Hunter College program in visual impairment, and the New York State Chapter of AERBVI are among the many supporters of this bill. Other states are interested in pursuing licensure as a way to validate O&M and ensure that highly qualified professionals are hired in the state.

Research in Personnel Preparation

Literature in personnel preparation for visual impairment includes anecdotal and case study-based information, with programs describing creative efforts and successes in innovative practices (use of multimedia, video analysis, increased attention to cortical/cerebral visual impairment and traumatic brain injury) to address regional and rural shortages, expand distance education efforts, and infuse important content within their programs (e.g., Bozeman, 2009; Buckley & Smith, 2008; Gale et al., 2010; Griffin-Shirley et al., 2002; Griffin-Shirley & Pogrund, 2010; Hatton, 2010; Jacobson, 2005; Lejeune, 2010; McKenzie, 2010; Parsons, 1990; Sanspree & Kelley, 1991). The documentation of efforts in the field, some with supporting survey or interview evidence (Linehan, 2000; Milian & Ferrell, 1998), provides a picture of collaborative efforts and ingenuity in attempts to address the persistent challenges in personnel preparation over the years. In addition to this literature base, the field has engaged in research to closely analyze the problems and potential solutions in preparing personnel, document the status of personnel preparation programs and faculty, and consider common standards among personnel preparation programs.

National Plan for Training Personnel (NPTP)

As mentioned earlier in this chapter, the NPTP was a two-year strategic planning process, funded by OSEP, and undertaken from 1997–1999. Key stakeholders came together to create a plan to address challenges in training personnel to serve children with blindness and visual impairment. The combination of personnel shortages for direct service and leadership, underidentification of children with visual impairment, geographical dispersion of students needing services, underfunded personnel preparation programs, and complacency and lack of accountability within the systems that influence services offered to students with visual impairment were all noted as barriers to quality education of children who are blind or visually impaired (Mason et al., 2000). The ultimate vision of the NPTP project was to work toward a future where children with visual impairment were valued by society, envisioned themselves as contributing members, and had access to high-quality and comprehensive programs and services.

Research to arrive at this national plan included interviews and surveys with state vision consultants, direct service personnel, and university faculty; surveys of key stakeholders in 17 states and 50 state directors of special education; focus groups with key stakeholders; national stakeholder dialogues; and case studies of state training models. As part of this data collection, a comprehensive needs assessment was conducted to determine well-informed assumptions about the number of children requiring services, a standard for ensuring quality services, the need for additional direct service personnel, and the ability of personnel preparation programs to prepare enough teachers to meet the projected needs now and in the future. To determine the number of TSVIs and O&M specialists needed, the NPTP project used an estimate of 93,600 children needing services—a number higher than any single source estimates due to differing criteria for reporting—in conjunction with a recommended average caseload size of eight.

The data collection procedures resulted in a three-goal plan with corresponding objectives that would need to involve sustained collaboration between institutions of higher education, key stakeholders, and OSEP to be fully accomplished. Goal one focused on increasing the number of qualified personnel and included implementation plans to create a Personnel Preparation Technical Assistance Network and to increase the impact of OSEP-funded personnel preparation projects. This network would promote collaborative efforts to meet national personnel preparation needs including application of national standards and giving technical assistance to new and existing programs. OSEP funding periods would be extended to 5-year terms to stabilize programs, and award sizes would increase. Goal two focused on leadership development with implementation plans to include a Leadership Development Institute and Research to Practice Institute in Blindness and Low Vision. The concept of the Research to Practice Institute was to design studies to collect and disseminate data regarding personnel needs, including empirical studies of program methodologies and educational outcomes for students, and annual counts of children and service providers. Goal three focused on recruitment and retention with plans for a Recruitment and Retention Project that would create a cohesive recruitment campaign (Mason et al., 2000).

Success in these goal areas over the past 10 plus years has been quite variable, and no literature is actually available that directly measures and summarizes the success achieved with the goals and initiatives specifically in the NPTP. However, regional program examples, the NCLID leadership endeavor, and the NCLID/NCSSD center are examples of ways in which the NPTP has been embraced. OSEP grants are 4–5 year awards, but the monetary amount and number of awards has decreased. Some programs have been able to create diversified funding streams that have improved program stability. In addition, for many years the NCLID collected annual data on student graduates from personnel preparation programs in visual impairment. However, this effort has subsided due to recent low response rates from the personnel programs themselves. So, the challenges for the field are how to best sustain successful and initial efforts and how to continue strong collaborations in the face of overwhelming workloads and strained financial situations.

Profiles in Personnel Preparation in Visual Impairment

Another collaborative effort by researchers in personnel preparation in visual impairment has been to investigate and document the status of personnel preparation programs. A series of five profiles have been published since 1989, with each profile analyzing trends from the previous profiles' data (Ambrose-Zaken & Bozeman, 2010; Corn & Silberman, 1999; Silberman, Ambrose-Zaken, & Corn, 1989; Silberman, Ambrose-Zaken, Corn, & Trief, 2004; Silberman & Corn, 1996). This series of studies is the main source of sustained data collection for personnel preparation program characteristics in the field of visual impairment. In the most recent profile, Ambrose-Zaken and Bozeman (2010), in a seven-part program director survey and a shorter faculty survey, collected demographic data for the 2007–2008 school year on characteristics of faculty and programs, doctoral students, instructional models, and funding.

Ambrose-Zaken and Bozeman (2010) identified a total of 48 confirmed active programs in the different specialty areas (TSVI, O&M, VRT, LVT) in 31 states, Puerto Rico, and three Canadian provinces. Program delivery methods were varied, but the most common model currently being used is a distance education model with on-campus summer semester(s). Other programs have on-campus weekends or off-campus locations to which instructors travel. Still others have students travel to satellite sites. In O&M, most survey respondents considered it important to offer blindfold instruction on-campus or face to face. Overall, 80% of programs use distance learning tools, with 13.9% of programs' content delivered completely through distance models (although all have a face-to-face component for the O&M lab). Internship requirements were not changed with the conversion to distance models, but, in addition to standard site visits, online check-ins and videotaped lessons were part of some programs' means for supervision.

In terms of funding, 30 of the 47 programs returning the survey obtain partial or full external funding to support and maintain their programs, with OSEP and RSA personnel development grants and state grants as key sources of funding. Tenure-track faculty were not necessarily assigned full-time to the visual impairment program. Thirty-five doctoral students were expected to graduate between 2009–2011, with 22 expressing interest in personnel preparation. Of the current full-time faculty in personal preparation programs, 35 of 83 had tenure, and 13 were in tenure-track positions. Thus, approximately 42% of faculty were not in tenure-track positions. Programs established for longer periods of time were more strongly correlated with having tenure-track positions compared to newer programs.

Ambrose-Zaken and Bozeman's (2010) analysis of the trends of these data for personnel preparation programs in visual impairment unfortunately show few improvements. Fewer universities opened programs in visual impairment than in the three previous periods covered in the other profiles. Federal funding remains critical to the survival of many programs in visual impairment with OSEP and RSA competitions remaining the largest source for grants, followed by state grants. The percentage of personnel who are paid 100% from hard money sources continues to decline, with only 58% of faculty with that financial arrangement in the 2008 reporting period. The number of doctoral students between 2004 and 2008 remained about the same, and was about the same number of current doctoral students reported in Corn and Spungin's leadership study (2002). These findings suggest a nationwide trend toward understaffing programs in visual impairment. The field continues, however, to explore distance education models and to update as technologies and resources allow.

Standards and Quality

Along with research to document and analyze the status of personnel preparation programs, program standards have been discussed. While personnel preparation programs for TSVIs adhere to CEC standards for beginning teachers and O&M programs cover content identified by the ACVREP, these standards are not specific about minimum requirements for beginning instructors. Additionally, interest in quality and consistency among programs preparing TSVIs and O&Ms prompted AERBVI to completely restructure and strengthen the University Review process (AERBVI, 2010). There is similar interest in specific areas such as competency in teaching braille and assistive technology.

Some survey and interview evidence highlights variation in the confidence and perceived skill level of practitioners as well as how well prepared individuals felt by their personnel preparation programs in specific skill areas like Nemeth code (mathematics braille), assistive technology, and other job-specific skills such as working with children from culturally and linguistically diverse backgrounds (e.g., Correa-Torres & Durando, 2011; Griffin-Shirley, Pogrund, Smith, & Duemer, 2009; Rosenblum & Amato, 2004; Zhou, Parker, Smith, & Griffin-Shirley, 2011). In a review of survey studies about teacher use and knowledge in the ECC (e.g., Lohmeier, Blankenship, & Hatlen, 2009), Sapp and Hatlen (2010) found that teachers are not providing adequate instruction in the ECC and called for personnel preparation programs to evaluate how to better prepare teachers to implement the ECC. Suggestions included developing additional knowledge of methods and implementation strategies for a range of vision levels and abilities, and skills and knowledge about the ECC, as well as advocating for and incorporating the ECC into IEPs.

Discussions and efforts around establishing minimum proficiency levels and standards have begun in the areas of assistive technology, literary braille and Nemeth code, and other special codes (computer, foreign language, music braille). Based on findings about what personnel preparation programs were and were not covering in the area of assistive technology (Smith & Kelley, 2007), Smith, Kelley, Maushak, Griffin-Shirley, and Lan (2009) conducted a Delphi study of university faculty in visual impairment, direct service providers, assistive and educational technology specialists, and consumers to create a set of 111 assistive technology standards.

Similarly, a working group of the Personnel Preparation Division of AERBVI revisited the question about braille standards for beginning TSVIs. Rosenblum, Lewis, and D'Andrea (2010) collected information about personnel preparation programs' current practices in teaching the braille code. They found similar outcomes to Amato's (2002) findings, with wide variations between programs in length of assignments, policies for resubmissions, time allotted to different topics, and allowable errors. These data prompted a Delphi study with faculty in personnel preparation programs on minimum standards for beginning TSVIs in literary braille code and how to develop and implement consistent standards across all programs. Similarly, another working group from the Personnel Preparation Division of AERBVI is currently conducting a standards study to establish minimum standards for Nemeth code (mathematics braille), computer, music, and foreign language braille codes. Next steps for all of these efforts are to continue to discuss feasibility and willingness of programs to adopt common sets of specific standards in the various areas of the ECC. These issues have fostered international collaboration among programs to improve quality and consistency. These studies also encouraged introspective program evaluations that resulted in improved modules and curriculum.

Future Research Needs

Scholars of personnel preparation in visual impairment have generated useful data through survey research on several topics and have engaged in a consolidated effort to analyze the multifaceted issues around personnel preparation. Continued documentation of personnel preparation progress as well as innovation is important. However, in addition, a closer analysis of outcomes of personnel preparation programs in visual impairment is warranted and currently missing from the research. Programs have been innovative in creating distance education in order to reach a broader potential student base, rural areas, and a wider region. However, how effective these chosen methodologies have been in creating effective beginning TSVIs and O&M specialists has been on the field's radar as a research need for some time without notable advancement (e.g., DeMario & Heinze, 2001). For example, few research studies were currently found that attempt to analyze the success of instructional methodologies or assessments to evaluate preservice TSVI or O&M skill levels (e.g., Zebehazy, Zimmerman, & Fox, 2005). One way some programs are beginning to address outcomes beyond student self-report is to survey graduates' employers to determine how the hiring districts and agencies view the preparation of the TSVI and O&M and to ask whether the person would be rehired. Also, with the emphasis on outcomes, OSEP is requiring that programs study the progress of the children taught by graduates. These trends should produce telling, outcome-based, data, so on.

Future Directions

As is evident in trends in personnel preparation in visual impairment, available research, and documented efforts, the field strives to continually improve programs and creatively address significant challenges. However, in some areas, personnel preparation has remained fairly stagnant with relatively no growth in the total number of programs available nationwide, equal or increasing dependence on personnel development grant funding, and continued struggles in sustaining university positions. Recruitment, shortages (particularly in rural areas), and the lack of an adequate number of TSVI and O&M positions in school districts to effectively serve students with visual impairments are continual challenges that will require advocacy, creativity, and collaboration.

Many other ideas about how to improve the effectiveness of personnel preparation have surfaced in discussions among colleagues over the years. The following list suggests some avenues the field may want to discuss, revisit, and/or pursue:

1. Collaborate across programs on research efforts that evaluate instructional methodologies, including distance technologies to supervise students in internship, and their relationship to preservice skill development and outcomes for students with visual impairments.
2. Conduct a reanalysis of old ideas and current models and supports in the light of a new economic era: regional programs, liaisons, national standards and certification for TSVI, course- and content-sharing between programs, maintenance of established centers, funding models, etc.
3. Work collaboratively to improve program effectiveness to tap into diversified funding opportunities and to promote sustained buy-in from a variety of resources (departments of education, agencies, etc.).
4. Brainstorm efforts to preserve tenure-track positions in personnel preparation programs.
5. Brainstorm ways to create stronger mentorship programs for beginning TSVIs and O&M specialists.
6. Engage in a strategic planning process regarding sustained collaboration and strengthening of the field.
7. Consider creative programming options such as: (a) specializations (vision plus another specialty) to expand viability and interest especially in small rural areas where a full-time position as TSVI or O&M specialist may not be available, and (b) tiered programs where more direct access to advanced skill building and professional development is available with the university.
8. Advocate for reasonable caseloads that allow TSVIs to attend to the ECC and other assessed needs and goals of children with visual impairment.
9. To help with recruitment, maintain a range of program options, including undergraduate, graduate, certificate, master's, etc.

10. Brainstorm new and innovative recruitment ideas to which all programs could contribute.
11. Collaboration is noted in the research as a key to successful projects. As a low-incidence field, collaboration may prove to be strongest method by which personnel preparation programs in visual impairment can improve and remain strong. Sustained partnerships are crucial for programs to be flexible with the changing needs of communities.

Note

1 http://www.nercve.org/professional-development/sustaining-braille-proficiency

References

Academy for Certification of Vision Rehabilitation and Education Professionals (ACVREP). (2011). *O&M body of knowledge: O&M certification handbook.* Retrieved from: http://www.acvrep.org/Certified-Orientation-and-Mobility-Specialist-Scope-of-Practice.php

Amato, S. (2002). Standards for competence in braille literacy skills in teacher preparation programs. *Journal of Visual Impairment & Blindness, 96*(3), 143–153.

Ambrose-Zaken, G., & Bozeman, L. (2010). Profile of personnel preparation programs in visual impairment and their faculty. *Journal of Visual Impairment & Blindness, 104*(3), 148–169.

American Printing House for the Blind. (2010). *Distribution of eligible students based on the federal quota census of January 05, 2009.* Retrieved from: http://www.aph.org/fedquotpgm/dist10.html

Anthony, T. L., Lowry, S. S., Brown, C. J., & Hatton, D. D. (2004). *Developmentally appropriate orientation and mobility.* University of North Carolina at Chapel Hill, NC: Early Intervention Training Center for Infants and Toddlers with Visual Impairments.

Association for the Education and Rehabilitation of the Blind and Visually Impaired (AERBVI). (2010). University Review Curricular Standards. Retrieved from: http://www.aerbvi.org/modules.php?name=News&file=article&sid=1851

Barraga, N. C., & Erin, J. N. (2001). *Visual impairments and learning* (4th ed.). Austin, TX: Pro-Ed.

Bozeman, L. A. (2009). Maximizing resources: Meeting the critical need for highly-qualified teachers in visual impairment. *AER Journal: Research and Practice in Visual Impairment and Blindness,* 1(2), 35–36.

Bozeman, L. A. (2011, October). *Changing lives: A regional approach to change outcomes for children with visual impairment in the Pacific region.* Proceedings of the AERBVI Regional Conference, Cleveland, OH.

Buckley, W., & Smith, A. (2008). Application of multimedia technologies to enhance distance learning. *RE: View: Rehabilitation Education for Blindness and Visual Impairment, 39,* 57–65. doi:10.3200/REVU.39.2.57-65

CAST (Center for Applied Social Technology). (2011). *Universal Design for Learning Guidelines Version 2.0.* Wakefield, MA: Author.

Corn, A. L., Hatlen, P., Huebner, K. M., Ryan, F., & Siller, M. A. (1995). *The national agenda for the education of children and youths with visual impairments, including those with multiple disabilities.* New York: AFB Press.

Corn, A. L., & Silberman, R. K. (1999). Personnel preparation programs in visual impairments: A status report. *Journal of Visual Impairment & Blindness, 93*(12), 755–769.

Corn, A. L., & Spungin, S. J. (2002). Graduates and current students in leadership programs in visual impairments. *Journal of Visual Impairment & Blindness, 96*(10), 736–740.

Correa-Torres, S. M., & Durando, J. (2011). Perceived training needs of teachers of students with visual impairments who work with students from culturally and linguistically diverse backgrounds. *Journal of Visual Impairment & Blindness, 105*(9), 521–532.

Council for Exceptional Children. (2011). *Council of Exceptional Children performance-based standards.* Retrieved from: http://higherlogicdownload.s3.amazonaws.com/SPED/d2199768-679e-41f6-aa2a-e9d3b5b748c8/UploadedImages/CEC%20Initial%20Special%20Education%20TVI%20Knowledge%20and%20Skills%20(1).pdf

DeMario, N. C., & Heinze, T. (2001). The status of distance education in personnel preparation programs in visual impairment. *Journal of Visual Impairment & Blindness, 95*(9), 525–532.

Erin, J. N., Holbrook, C., Sanspree, M. J., & Swallow, R. M. (2006). *Professional preparation and certification of teachers of students with visual impairments.* Reston, VA: Council for Exceptional Children.

Fazzi, D. L., & Klein, M. D. (2002). Cognitive focus: Developing cognition, concepts, and language. In R. L. Pogrund, & D. L. Fazzi (Eds.), *Early focus: Working with young children who are blind or visually impaired and their families* (2nd ed.) (pp. 107–153). New York: AFB Press.

Ferrell, K. A. (2007). *Issues in the field of blindness and low-vision*. Greeley, CO: The National Center on Severe and Sensory Disabilities, University of Northern Colorado. Retrieved from http://www.unco.edu/ncssd/resources/issues_bvi.shtml

Ferrell, K. A. (2009). *Prospectus: National Center on Severe and Sensory Disabilities*. Retrieved from: http://www.unco.edu/ncssd/NCSSD%20UNCFoundation%20Prospectus%20Jan-09.pdf

Gale, E., Trief, E., & Lengel, J. (2010). The use of video analysis in a personnel preparation program for teachers of students who are visually impaired. *Journal of Visual Impairment & Blindness, 104*(11), 700–704.

Gleason, D., Wheeler, A. C., Murphy, J. L., & Hatton, D. D. (2006). *Assessment for infants and toddlers with visual impairments*. University of North Carolina at Chapel Hill: Early Intervention Training Center for Infants and Toddlers with Visual Impairments.

Griffin-Shirley, N., Almon, P., & Kelley, P. (2002). Visually impaired personnel preparation program: A collaborative distance education model. *Journal of Visual Impairment & Blindness, 96*(4), 233–244.

Griffin-Shirley, N., & Pogrund, R. (2010). Inclusion of CVI in Texas Tech University's personnel preparation program. *Journal of Visual Impairment & Blindness, 104*(10), 660–661.

Griffin-Shirley, N., Pogrund, R. L., Smith, D. W., & Duemer, L. (2009). A three-phase qualitative study of dual-certified vision education professionals in the southwestern United States. *Journal of Visual Impairment & Blindness, 103*(6), 354–366.

Hatton, D. D. (2010). Personnel preparation and CVI at Vanderbilt University. *Journal of Visual Impairment & Blindness, 104*(10), 661–663.

Hatton, D. D., McWilliam, R. A., & Winton, P. J. (2006). *Family-centered practices for infants and toddlers with visual impairments*. University of North Carolina at Chapel Hill, NC: Early Intervention Training Center for Infants and Toddlers with Visual Impairments.

Holbrook, M. C., Croft, J. E., & Koenig, A. J. (2005). *Project SLATE: Supporting literacy achievement and teacher effectiveness for students who are blind or visually impaired: Facilitator's manual*. Lubbock, TX: Texas Tech University

Huebner, K. M., Merk-Adam, B., Stryker, D., & Wolffe, K. (2004). *The national agenda for the education of children and youths with visual impairments, including those with multiple disabilities, revised*. New York: AFB Press.

Hyvärinen, L. (2011). *Visually impaired children with multiple disabilities*. Retrieved from: http://drleahyvarinen.com/2011/01/14/visually-impaired-children-with-multiple-disabilities/

Jacobson, W. H. (2005). Transforming a traditional personnel preparation program in orientation and mobility into an online program at the University of Arkansas at Little Rock. *Journal of Visual Impairment & Blindness, 99*(11), 707–711.

Kapperman, G., & Sticken, J. (2006). *Project math access*. Sycamore, IL: Research and Development Institute.

Kirchner, C., & Diament, S. (1999). Estimates of the number of visually impaired students, their teachers, and orientation and mobility specialists: Part 1. *Journal of Visual Impairment & Blindness, 93*, 600–606.

Koenig, A. J., & Holbrook, M. C. (2000). Professional practice. In M. C. Holbrook, & A. J. Koenig (Eds.), *Foundations of education volume I: History and theory of teaching children and youths with visual impairments* (2nd ed.) (pp. 260–276). New York: AFB Press.

Koenig, A. J., Holbrook, M. C., Edmonds, A. R., White, D., Wang, Q., & Martindale, T. (2005). *Project SLATE: DVD and CD-ROM sets*. Lubbock, TX: Texas Tech University.

Lejeune, J. (2010). Brain injury and personnel preparation at Mississippi State University. *Journal of Visual Impairment & Blindness, 104*(10), 658–660.

Lewis, S., & Allman, C. B. (2000). Educational programming. In M. C. Holbrook & A. J. Koenig (Eds.), *Foundations of education volume I: History and theory of teaching children and youths with visual impairments* (2nd ed.) (pp. 218–259). New York: AFB Press.

Linehan, P. (2000). *Selected state strategies for addressing personnel shortages in the area of VI: Quick turn around (QTA)*. Alexandria, VA: National Association of State Directors of Special Education (ED442246).

Lohmeier, K., Blankenship, K., & Hatlen, P. (2009). Expanded core curriculum: 12 years later. *Journal of Visual Impairment & Blindness, 103*(2), 103–112.

Mason, C., Davidson, R., & McNerney, C. (2000). *National plan for training personnel to serve children with blindness and low vision*. Reston, VA: The Council for Exceptional Children.

McKenzie, A. R. (2010). Personnel preparation for training professionals to work with individuals with CVI at Florida State University. *Journal of Visual Impairment & Blindness, 104*(10), 655–656.

Milian, M., & Ferrell, K. A. (1998). *Preparing special educators to meet the needs of students who are learning English as a second language and are visually impaired: Final Report*. Greeley, CO: University of Northern Colorado, College of Education. (ED466072).

NCLVI. (2010, October 10). *Completed doctorates*. Retrieved from http://www.salus.edu/nclvi/completed/completedDoc.htm

Parsons, A. S. (1990). A model for distance delivery in personnel preparation. *Journal of Visual Impairment and Blindness, 84*(9), 445–450.

Pogrund, R. L. (2002). Refocus: Setting the stage for working with young children who are blind or visually impaired. In R. L. Pogrund & D. I. Fazzi (Eds.), *Early focus: Working with young children who are blind or visually impaired and their families* (pp. 1–15). New York: AFB Press.

Resnikoff, S., Pascolini, D., Etya'ale, D., Kocur, I., Pararajasegaram, R., Pokharel, G. P., & Mariotti, S. P. (2004). Global data on visual impairment in the year 2002. *Bulletin of the World Health Organization, 82*, 844–851.

Rosen, S. (2010). Improving sensorimotor functioning for orientation and mobility. In W. R. Wiener, R. L. Welsh, & B. B. Blasch (Eds.), *Foundations of orientation and mobility, Volume II: Instructional strategies and practical applications* (3rd ed.) (pp.118–159). New York: AFB Press.

Rosen, S., & Crawford, J. S. (2010). Teaching orientation and mobility to learners with visual, physical, and health impairments. In W. R. Wiener, R. L. Welsh, & B. B. Blasch (Eds.), *Foundations of orientation and mobility Volume II: Instructional strategies and practical applications* (3rd ed.) (pp. 564–623). New York: AFB Press.

Rosenblum, L. P., & Amato, S. (2004). Preparation in and use of the Nemeth braille code for mathematics by teachers of students with visual impairments. *Journal of Visual Impairment and Blindness, 98*(8), 484–498.

Rosenblum, L. P., Lewis, S., & D'Andrea, F. M. (2010). Current practices in instruction in the literary braille code university personnel preparation programs. *Journal of Visual Impairment & Blindness, 104*(9), 523–532.

Saipan Tribune. (2012, January 20). Graduate students pass Braille literacy exam. Retrieved from http://www.saipantribune.com/newsstory.aspx?cat=1&newsID=115865

Sanspree, M. J., & Kelley, P. (1991). Preparing personnel to serve students with visual handicaps in rural areas: Two preservice alternatives. In *Reaching Our Potential: Rural Education in the 90's, Proceedings of the Rural Education Symposium*, Nashville, TN. (ED342564).

Sapp, W., & Hatlen, P. (2010). The expanded core curriculum: Where we have been, where we are going, and how we can get there. *Journal of Visual Impairment & Blindness, 104*(6), 338–348.

Sapp, W. K., & Hatton, D. D. (2005). *Communication and emergent literacy: Early intervention issues*. University of North Carolina at Chapel Hill, NC: Early Intervention Training Center for Infants and Toddlers with Visual Impairments.

Silberman, R. K., Ambrose-Zaken, G., & Corn, A. L. (1989). A profile of teacher educators and the future of their personnel preparation programs for serving visually handicapped children and youth. *Journal of Visual Impairment and Blindness, 83*(3), 150–155.

Silberman, R. K., Ambrose-Zaken, G., Corn, A. L., & Trief, E. (2004). Profile of personnel preparation programs in visual impairments and their faculty: A status report. *Journal of Visual Impairment & Blindness, 98*(12), 741–756.

Silberman, R. K., & Corn, A. L. (1996). Teacher educators and the future of personnel preparation programs for serving students with. *Journal of Visual Impairment & Blindness, 90*(2), 115–124.

Skellenger, A. C., & Sapp, W. K. (2010). Teaching orientation and mobility for the early childhood years. In W. R. Wiener, R. L. Welsh, & B. B. Blasch (Eds.), *Foundations of orientation and mobility, Volume II: Instructional strategies and practical applications* (3rd edition) (pp.163–202). New York: AFB Press.

Smith, D. W., & Kelley, P. (2007). A survey of assistive technology and teacher preparation programs for individuals with visual impairments. *Journal of Visual Impairment & Blindness, 101*(7), 429–433.

Smith, D. W., Kelley, P., Maushak, N. J., Griffin-Shirley, N., & Lan, W. Y. (2009). Assistive technology competencies for teachers of students with visual impairments. *Journal of Visual Impairment & Blindness, 103*(8), 457–469.

Toelle, N. M., & Blankenship, K. E. (2008). Program accountability for students who are visually impaired. *Journal of Visual Impairment & Blindness, 102*(2), 97–102.

Topor, I., Rosenblum, L. P., & Hatton, D. D. (2004). *Visual conditions and functional vision: Early intervention issues.* University of North Carolina at Chapel Hill, NC: Early Intervention Training Center for Infants and Toddlers with Visual Impairments.

Walker, B. R., & Bozeman, L. A. (2002). A successful grass-roots endeavor to develop a permanent university program for vision professionals: The North Carolina model. *Journal of Visual Impairment and Blindness, 96*(6), 429–434.

Zebehazy, K. T., Zimmerman, G. J., & Fox, L. A. (2005). Use of digital video to assess orientation and mobility observational skills. *Journal of Visual Impairment & Blindness, 99*(10), 646–658. Retrieved from EBSCO*host.*

Zhou, L., Parker, A. T., Smith, D. W., & Griffin-Shirley, N. (2011). Assistive technology for students with visual impairments: Challenges and needs in teachers' preparation programs and practice. *Journal of Visual Impairment & Blindness, 105(4)*, 197–210.

Part VI
Preparation for Specific Roles

22

Educator Preparation Within the Context of School-Wide Positive Behavior and Academic Supports

Timothy J. Lewis and Cathy Newman Thomas

UNIVERSITY OF MISSOURI

Things to Think About

- Teachers are called upon to implement EBPs with fidelity to improve student outcomes. Yet the field is faced with an ongoing struggle to educate, retain, and continually renew an education workforce that can implement EBPs. The challenge of continually recruiting, updating, and maintaining a well-qualified workforce, coupled with the poor professional development outcomes to date, leave schools largely unprepared for sweeping systemic reforms mandated by current educational policies.
- Reforms such as SW-PBS insist on the leveraging of best practices recommended across the pre- and in-service professional development literature, and require that schools, districts, states, and higher education institutions rethink professional development at the pre- and in-service level in order to bridge the research-to-practice gap and create sustainable practice at scale.
- There is a disconnect between how in-service educators are solving complex problems using the logic of SW-PBS. Traditional professional development methods are often compartmentalized and target specific personnel within schools, perpetuating instability and failing to make either significant or sustained impacts in educator practices. Substantive changes in professional development—both pre- and in-service—are necessary, but high-quality professional development will require dedicated resources and a long-term commitment to change.
- To support educators' use of effective practices and improve student outcomes requires clearly identifying the key segments that constitute effective instruction situated within complex classroom environments and developing a culture of education that adopts and sustains research-based instructional strategies.
- Given the positive evidence to date for capacity building systems like SW-PBS to improve student outcomes and support implementation of EBPs, professional development models and practices should be examined to promote such educational reforms. Professional development that is implemented in light of SW-PBS places an emphasis on developing skill sets that allow the school and/or district to use existing resources to address their challenges, focuses on building team capacity.

Preparing educators to impact a wide range of academic and social behavior challenges from preschool to high school is a complex enterprise that is unfortunately characterized as lacking a unified set of recommendations with regard to best practices within and across disciplines. The challenging task of preparing professionals is compounded by the need to ready them to work within today's educational framework and service delivery model while simultaneously preparing them with strategies to apply skills and knowledge to solve future problems. Fortunately, recent work addressing social behavior challenges, and emerging work addressing academic challenges among at-risk students provides a framework in which a universal problem-solving strategy can assist teams of educators in taking on these complex problems. Specifically, the recent work in developing School-Wide Positive Behavior Support (SW-PBS) and Response to Intervention (RTI) has profound implications for both pre- and in-service professional development. As you read this chapter, we encourage you to focus on the disconnect between how in-service educators are solving complex problems using the logic of SW-PBS and RTI while most professional development, especially at the preservice level, continues to emphasize an inefficient model of education service delivery. Likewise, we encourage you to challenge our recommendation calling for substantive changes in professional development to follow the empirically validated SW-PBS logic model through a parallel process of training and technical assistance.

The link between implementation of effective teaching practices and student learning and behavioral outcomes is firmly established among students with and without disabilities. Startling outcomes such as Lyon and colleagues (2001) reporting up to 70% of students who were identified as having learning disabilities would not have needed specialized instruction had effective early reading intervention been in place and Sanders and Rivers (1996) reporting up to a difference of 50 percentile points on standardized tests among students who experienced successive years of poor instruction at the elementary level place an exclamation point on the need for effective instruction. As Rivers and Sanders (2002) have reported, regardless of risk factors found among students in schools today, "research indicate(s) that the academic growth rate of student populations is primarily a function of the effectiveness of school districts, schools, and, most important, teachers" (p. 14).

While it is easy to point to the teacher as the "weak link" leading to educational failure, the issue is not that simple. In fact, a compelling case can be made that the failure is not on the part of the classroom teacher, rather, the failure lies within the larger educational system to provide the classroom teacher with the knowledge, skills, and ongoing supports necessary to adopt and sustain use of effective practices. Equal responsibility for the failure to create effective systems lie both in teacher preparation programs and traditional in-service professional development. To support educator's use of effective practices and improve student outcomes, two pressing challenges to the educational system must be addressed: (a) clear identification of the key segments that constitute effective instruction situated within complex classroom environments, and (b) development of a culture of education that adopts and sustains research-based instructional strategies. Both challenges are especially acute within the area of serving students with, and those at-risk for, emotional/behavioral disorders (E/BD) given that these students present both significant academic and social problems (Scott, Nelson, & Liaupsin, 2001).

The literature is replete with examples of effective instructional practices and the simultaneous failure within the field to adopt such practices (e.g., Kauffman, 1996), evidence of the significant and enduring "research-to-practice" gap (Burns & Ysseldyke, 2009; Kauffman, 1996). The professional literature calls for specific actions among the research community to ameliorate this gap (Kauffman, 1996); yet, there are no such calls for specific actions among the practice community. Furthermore, in practice, the vehicle for change relies on traditional professional development practices, which according to the literature have continually failed to make either significant or sustained impacts in educator practices (Guskey, 2000). This failure is compounded by large shortages of certified teachers across all areas of special education. A lack of qualified teachers, however, is particularly acute for students with E/BD (Henderson, Klein, Gonzalez, & Bradley, 2005), forcing most states to allow provisionally or alternatively certified educators to fill positions. Adding to this pressure are current mandates (e.g.,

Individuals with Disabilities Education Act [IDEA]; U.S. Department of Education, Office of Planning, Evaluation and Policy Development [U.S. DOE, OPEPD], 2010) that all districts employ "highly qualified" teachers.

The purpose of this chapter is to provide an overview of the necessary features of educator professional development within the context of school-reform efforts designed to support all students along a continuum of social and academic behavior supports. Specifically, an overview of essential features of School-Wide Positive Behavior Support (SW-PBS) and Response to Intervention (RTI) provides the context for these frameworks within which evidence-based practices (EBPs) are successfully implemented and sustained within schools. Following, a review of current professional development practices for pre- and in-service teachers is provided with an eye toward disconnects in current practice and what educators need to implement school reform. Finally, based on the success of scaling up and sustaining SW-PBS efforts across the United States, recommendations are offered for needed changes in both pre- and in-service professional development.

Creating Systems of Support for Students and Educators

Over the past two decades, work focusing on creating school environments that prevent significant behavioral challenges and provide environments that incorporate EBPs to address existing problem behavior has resulted in the establishment of SW-PBS (Horner & Sugai, 2005; Sugai et al., 2000).

SW-PBS is best characterized as a problem-solving approach in which teams of educators use a standard process to examine commonly collected school data (e.g., office referrals, suspensions) to determine what practices would be appropriate to support students. Data (e.g., intervention checks) are then used to monitor implementation fidelity and student progress, continually informing next steps (see Figure 22.1). The use of data to guide and monitor intervention selection and implementation then follows a continuum of supports, allowing educators to place increasingly intensive and individualized supports based on student need (see Figure 22.2). In response to current behavioral challenges, school teams typically start by clearly defining a set of positively stated expectations, and then develop strategies

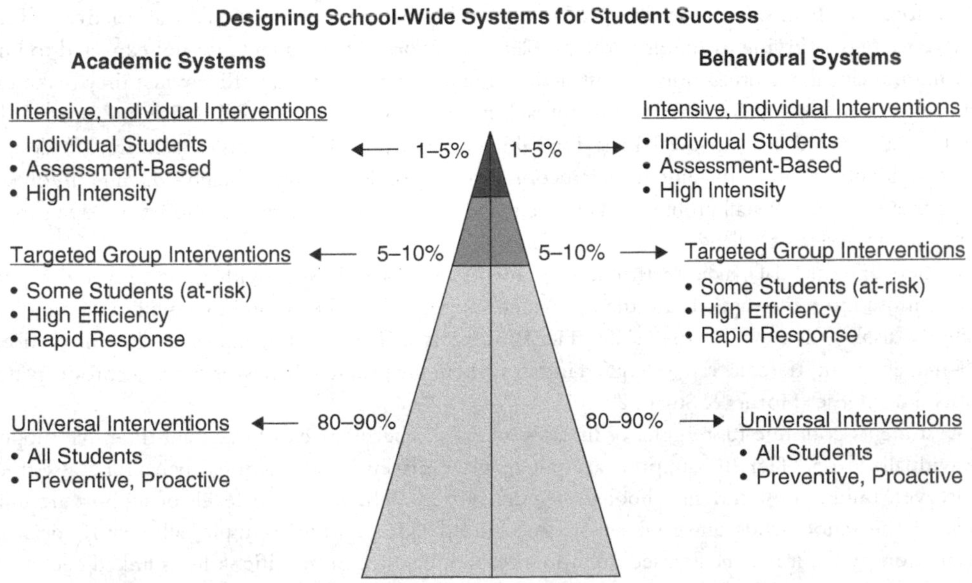

Figure 22.1 The Continuum of Academic and Behavioral Supports Within a SW-PBS and RTI Framework

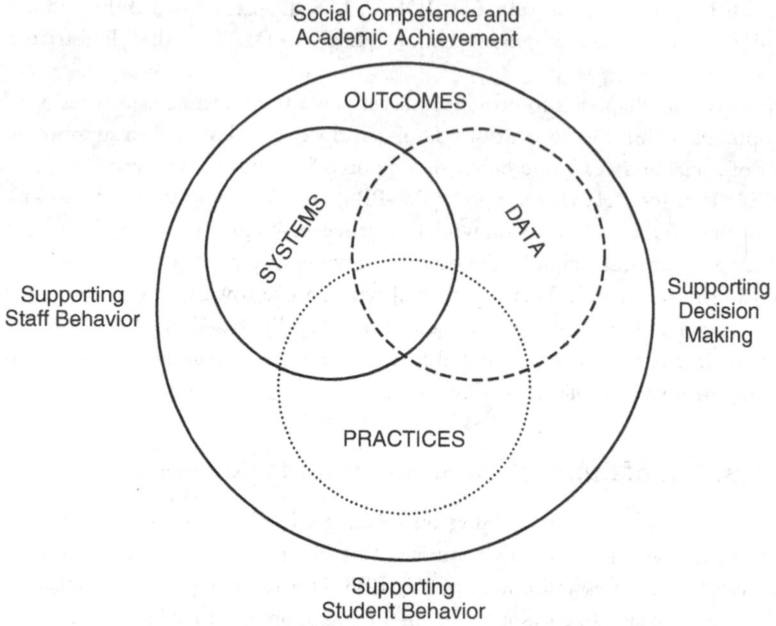

Figure 22.2 SW-PBS Problem Solving Logic Model

to teach, practice, and acknowledge mastery of these prosocial behaviors providing a set of "universal" or "Tier 1" supports. Universal supports are implemented by all school faculty and staff, across all school settings and are designed to support all students. For example, in response to widespread name-calling, "bullying," and social exclusion found within a school, the team may create the expectation that students are "respectful" and carefully identify behaviors that are reflective of respectful behavior that can be taught (e.g., "treat others like you want to be treated," "include others in your activities"), creating conditions which allow staff to acknowledge appropriate behavior versus the typical reactive and ineffective strategy of trying to "punish" the problem behavior. Just as students are not expected to know key mathematical constructs prior to instruction, nor are they sent to the office when they make math errors, the emphasis of SW-PBS is on approaching social behavior as a skill deficit and needed skills are taught: (a) staff assesses social/behavioral skills currently in the students' repertoire, (b) desirable skills are identified and a timeline for instruction is set, (c) skills are taught, practiced, and reinforced to build fluency, and (d) staff problem solve when students struggle, bringing in more intensive supports as needed to address challenges.

When ongoing data indicate that some students are not successful with these universal supports alone, more intensive supports are then provided to increase the likelihood they will master and consistently display the newly learned skills. Tier II supports such as small-group social skill instruction or self-management strategies can be applied in cases where the problem behavior shows a chronic pattern, but is not intense (Horner & Sugai, 2005).

If students continue to struggle, or in cases where the behavior clearly warrant intensive supports, individualized or "Tier III" supports are put in place driven by a functional behavioral assessment. However, unlike most current school service delivery models, all tiers or levels of support are linked back to the school-wide universal set of expectations (Tier 1). For example, all Tier II social skill instruction, while it may be focused on more in-depth practice on specific skills, is linked back to key school-wide expectations (e.g., "Respect," "Responsible," "Safe"). Likewise, all individual plan goals/objectives, including objectives on student's Individualized Education Plans, are linked back to and use the language of the school's universal expectations. The goal is to create a seamless continuum of supports by having *all* staff use a common language, prompt appropriate behavior, and provide high rates of positive feedback when students demonstrate prosocial behavior, regardless of how many or how few additional supports individual students require to be successful. SW-PBS emphasizes data-based decision making matching the intensity of environmental supports to the intensity of student need.

Systems (see Figure 22.2), the third critical feature and a hallmark of SW-PBS, has led to the success of schools who implement SW-PBS with fidelity. The system feature of SW-PBS refers to the training and supports adults require to implement and sustain the targeted behavioral support strategies with fidelity (Horner & Sugai, 2005; Sugai et al., 2000). SW-PBS incorporates key evidence-based professional development strategies directly within the process, thereby avoiding typical failures of transfer to practice and lack of sustainability common in professional development (Guskey, 2000). Prior to implementation of any intervention, or in relation to key changes in school policy relative to SW-PBS efforts (e.g., revising how behavioral infraction data are coded and reported), SW-PBS teams provide (a) brief training on key features for the entire school staff, (b) model the practice as part of the training where appropriate, (c) provide a written summary of the practice in concise bulleted steps, (d) plan for follow-up training, and (e) provide ongoing technical assistance through peer coaching once the practice is put in place (Fixsen, Naoom, Blase, Friedman, & Wallace, 2005; Guskey, 2000).

SW-PBS also includes additional levels of system support within the foundational materials of its framework. If individual schools are going to be successful, district, regional, and state support relative to professional development must also be reconceptualized to employ the basic SW-PBS problem-solving logic. At its simplest, professional development from the district through state level must shift its focus from preparing individual teachers and specialists to engage in compartmentalized tasks, to providing skill sets to school *teams*, allowing them to best use their collaborative resources to solve current, and future, challenges (Lewis, Barrett, Sugai, & Horner, 2010). In other words, all professional development should be focused on increasing the capacity of the school team made up of cross-discipline professionals versus giving individual school faculty, or related professionals (e.g., mental health workers, school psychologists), isolated skill sets. Given high rates of teacher mobility and attrition, particularly in high need areas (McLeskey & Billingsley, 2008), the current model of "experts" consulting with individual teachers on a case-by-case basis is both ineffective and fails to build capacity within the school. SW-PBS places the emphasis of all professional development on building "expertise" among and across the school-based team, training staff to use skills, tools, and structures that allow them to address current and future challenges (Lewis et al., 2010). In addition, SW-PBS professional development also considers the phases of implementation schools go through in adopting reform (Fixsen et al., 2005). By clearly identifying what phase of implementation the school is in, professional development can be tailored to ensure a good contextual fit, rather than overwhelming school teams or hindering their progress.

To date, implementation of the SW-PBS process has been associated with decreases in overall levels of problem behavior of at-risk students in a number of randomized control trial (e.g., Bradshaw, Reinke, Brown, Bevans, & Leaf, 2008) and quasi-experimental studies (e.g., Barrett, Bradshaw, & Lewis-Palmer, 2008). Evidence is also emerging that Tier II or small-group supports delivered as part of a SW-PBS continuum are altering potential trajectories toward more chronic and intense behavior patterns (e.g., McIntosh, Campbell, Carter, & Dickey, 2009).

Response to Intervention: A Framework for Academic Supports

Using the same data-based problem-solving logic, recent work providing a continuum of academic supports through a "Response to Intervention" (RTI; Sugai, 2001; see Figure 22.1) process also employs similar essential features to produce positive student outcomes (i.e., data–practices–systems) and reveals the need to rethink professional development (National Association of State Directors of Special

Education [NASDSE], 2008). As defined in IDEA (2004), RTI is an alternate method for identifying students with learning disabilities. Interestingly, based on the effectiveness of SW-PBS, there are increasing calls for the development of a social behavioral RTI protocol to identify students with emotional/behavioral disorders (Gresham, 2007; Maag & Katsiyannis, 2008). The broader application of RTI as a tool for systematically identifying at-risk learners and providing early intervention supports along a continuum (e.g., Tier II and III) has been ongoing and focuses on altering the poor school outcomes among students at-risk for early learning failure (Jimerson, Burns, & VanDerHeyden, 2007). Given the positive evidence to date for capacity building systems like SW-PBS and RTI to improve students outcomes and support sustainable EBPs, professional development models and practices should be examined to promote such educational reforms.

Current Professional Development Models and Practices

Teachers form the largest workforce in the U.S., with nearly 7.2 million teachers employed in 2008 (U.S. Census Bureau, 2010), with special education teachers numbering nearly half a million (Bureau of Labor Statistics, 2012). More than 1,300 preservice teacher preparation programs are currently in existence (Ball & Forzani, 2010), and every year "schools, districts and the federal government spend millions, if not billions, of dollars on in-service seminars and other forms of professional development" (Borko, 2004, p. 3). The central purpose of preservice and in-service professional development is to improve student outcomes. Professional development is the primary avenue for improving teachers' pedagogical knowledge, and may encompass all aspects of teaching, including but not limited to "knowledge of learners," learning theory, content knowledge, skill development, and fidelity to EBPs (Darling-Hammond, 2006). To bridge the gap between research and practice, professional development must help teachers to understand the importance of using EBPs as well as support them in implementing the practices as they were designed, preserving the critical attributes that make them effective (Kretlow & Blatz, 2011).

Due to the perennially high demand for teachers in the U.S., teaching is one of the easiest professions to enter; yet teaching is not a simple profession to learn. Ball and Forzani (2010) note that, "if teaching were so simple, all veteran teachers would perform uniformly skillfully" (p. 10). For newly graduated teachers, six or more years of classroom experience seem to be required for expert knowledge and skills to fully develop (Lopez, 1995). Teacher education researchers (e.g., Dray & Thomas, 2010) report that in other performance-based professions like medicine, law, engineering, and aviation, novitiates are required to demonstrate sufficient mastery of critical skills before they are permitted to practice independently. Yet teaching is an "un-staged" profession, one in which brand-new teachers have the same responsibilities as their experienced colleagues. Unfortunately this leads to a common situation in which the students with the highest need most often have the least prepared and least experienced teachers (Darling-Hammond, 2006). Ball and Forzani (2010) report, "In no other domain do we allow trainees to assume so much responsibility" (p. 11). In many cases, teachers are not even certified for the content or demographic for which they are hired to teach (Billingsley, 2004). Temporary and emergency licenses are issued by the majority of states, with varying degrees of rigor (Darling-Hammond, 1999). As an example, for students with E/BD, some of the most challenging students to teach, about 12% of teachers were certified through alternative routes (McLeskey & Waldron, 2004). In 2002–2003, 12.38% of teachers serving special education students were not fully licensed for their primary teaching assignment (McLeskey & Billingsley, 2008). In simpler terms, that equals 830,000 students with special needs were served by nearly 50,000 teachers who would not be considered "highly qualified" by even minimal standards.

Lack of preparedness paired with the significant challenges faced in placing new teachers in the most challenging classrooms has resulted in persistently high rates of early career attrition for special educators. The cycle is perpetuated when novice teachers are placed in the vacated positions (McLeskey &

Billingsley, 2008). In response to these challenges, new avenues such as professional learning communities (PLCs) and mentoring to support novice educators during induction are being investigated (Brownell, Adams, Sindelar, Waldron, & Vanhover, 2006) while at the same time, to meet demands for supply, new programs that may reduce exposure to pedagogy, methods, clinical experiences, and supervision levels are also being widely implemented (Darling-Hammond, 2006; McLeskey & Billingsley, 2008).

At the in-service level, teachers of high need students are at-risk for burnout (Schlichte, Yssel, & Merbler, 2005). Special education teachers have higher mobility rates than general educators, and many remain in education, but leave their special education classrooms for other, perhaps, easier positions (McLeskey & Billingsley, 2008). Research on teacher mobility suggests that teachers make transitions for a variety of reasons (e.g., low self-efficacy, lack of certification for their assigned position, lack of administrative support, workload demands, and challenging students; Billingsley, 2004). Teaching is a mobile workforce, and teacher education, particularly special education teacher education, struggles to produce an adequate supply to meet the demand.

Legislation, Policy, and Teacher Reform Movements

Current legislation and policy (IDEA, 2004; NCLB, 2002; U.S. DOE, OPEPD, 2010) call for all teachers to be *highly qualified* and to receive *high-quality* professional development. Highly qualified teachers are then called upon to implement EBPs with fidelity to improve student outcomes. For professional development, NCLB is very specific; schools that receive NCLB Title 1 funds are required to

> devote sufficient resources to effectively carry out high-quality and ongoing professional development for teachers, principals, and paraprofessionals and, if appropriate, pupil personnel services, parents, and other staff to enable all children in the school *to meet the State's student academic achievement standards* (NCLB 1114[1]).
>
> *(Kratchowill, Volpiansky, Clements, & Ball, 2007, p. 621, original emphasis)*

However, the term *high quality* is not operationally defined in a way that crosses programs and contexts (Brownell, Hirsch, & Seo, 2004; Darling Hammond, 2006) and researchers have not clearly identified the best ways to reliably train teachers, at either the pre- or in-service levels (Ball & Forzani, 2010).

Professional development research is labor intensive, and is often conducted with a small number of teachers. These efforts often lead to results that are not predictable because some practices are harder and take longer to develop or change than others, and individual teachers make differential rates and degrees of change (Brownell et al., 2006). What we do know is that the teacher is the greatest single factor that affects students outcomes (Darling-Hammond, 1999; McLeskey & Billingsley, 2008). In addition, the accumulating literature suggests that professional development can affect teacher behaviors, and that positive changes in teacher behaviors result in improvements in student achievement and behavior (Brownell et al., 2006; Joyce & Showers, 2002; Kratchowill et al., 2007; McLeskey & Billingsley, 2008). Furthermore, current policies mandating standards-based reforms and accountability have begun to generate data that link teacher education to teacher performance and student outcomes (Darling-Hammond, 1999), although for populations like students with disabilities and English language learners, the challenges of measuring the relationship among teacher education, teacher performance, and student outcomes are complex (Holdheide, Goe, Croft, & Reschly, 2010).

Unfortunately, the simultaneous challenge of continually recruiting, updating, and maintaining a well-qualified workforce, coupled with the poor professional development outcomes to date, leave schools largely unprepared for sweeping systemic reforms mandated by current educational policies (e.g., IDEA, 2004; NCLB, 2002; U.S. DOE, OPEPD, 2010). The emerging reforms that are considered best practice (e.g., SW-PBS and RTI) require schools, districts, states and higher education to rethink professional development at the pre- and in-service level in order to bridge research and practice and create sustainable practice at scale.

Effective Preservice Professional Development

High-quality preservice education programs are those that demonstrate high rates of retention for their graduates over time and link the teaching performance of their graduates to student learning (Darling-Hammond, 1999; Holdheide et al., 2010). The majority of preservice education still takes place in university classrooms, although alternative programs have increased over the years (Grossman & Loeb, 2010). In their university-based programs, preservice educators need to develop skills in what Ball and Forzani (2010) refer to as the "curriculum of practice" and Bransford, Brown, and Cocking (2000) call "conditionalized knowledge"; knowing how to apply knowledge effectively in authentic contexts in situations where that particular learning will be helpful in solving authentic problems of practice. Following a comparative review of the critical features of high-quality preservice special and general teacher education, Brownell and her colleagues (Brownell, Ross, Colón, & McCallum, 2003) concluded that there were seven specific qualities that distinguished successful university-based preparation programs. These defining characteristics include:

- a well-articulated vision of the program;
- coursework designed to develop pedagogical knowledge, subject specific/content knowledge, and disciplinary knowledge, including facts about learning theory, learners themselves, and methods;
- field experiences of adequate duration with an expert mentor and model, and active and expert university supervision;
- clear standards that define and evaluate quality teaching;
- active pedagogy, including explicit modeling and opportunities for reflection and dialogic feedback;
- focus on how to meet the needs of the increasingly diverse learners in today's classrooms; and
- a collaborative structure that supports the development of professional learning communities.

Furthermore, in this digital age, for diverse learners, mastery of technological innovations is key (Brownell, Sindelar, Kiely, & Danielson, 2010). In addition, preservice teachers must become well-versed in classroom and behavior management (Oliver & Reschly, 2007), and prepared to participate in and contribute to systemic school reforms (Schaughency & Ervin, 2006).

However, the reality is that most new teachers report that their programs did not sufficiently prepare them to meet these challenges (Baker, 2005; Blanton, Pugach, & Florian, 2010; Oliver & Reschly, 2010). Oliver and Reschly conducted a syllabus review of special education program coursework for 26 institutions in a single state and found that only 27% of these included an entire course devoted to behavior management. For preservice general education teachers, 73% of elementary programs and 67% of secondary programs require a single course about students with disabilities (Blanton et al., 2010). Blanton and her colleagues advocate for a continuum of professional development that begins in preservice teaching, provides extended, high quality, situated and supervised clinical practice, and that candidates become good teachers *before* they are independently responsible for a classroom. In addition, these authors suggest that preservice teacher education for special education must also be reframed, providing a strong foundation in core curriculum and sufficient practice in teaming to develop competence in a variety of collaborative teaching approaches and formats. Collaboration at the preservice level between general and special educators and specialist staff is needed to prepare future teachers to work in systemic frameworks such as RTI and PBS. Finally, Blanton et al. call attention to the need for robust and sustained funding for research into preservice teacher education and program development. Well-funded, university-based preservice teacher education programs with an extensive clinical component, situated in local schools with established partnerships with universities, would then transition into well-designed induction supports.

Effective Induction Programs

Successful induction programs are adequately funded and well organized (Brownell et al., 2004). These programs are characterized by access to dedicated mentoring by an expert (McGlamery, Fluckinger, & Edick, 2006; Smith & Ingersoll, 2004) and evaluation practices that examine growth toward clearly specified objectives (Brownell et al., 2004). Collaborative partnerships between the preparation program and schools with careful alignment between university content and methods and school-based practice are critical features needed to promote generalization from preservice preparation into the first years of practice (Scheeler, Bruno, Grubb, & Seavey, 2009), along with a collaborative culture of lifelong learning established in the schools.

Data documenting positive outcomes for such collaborations between universities and schools does exist, including improved retention, enhanced skills for novice teachers, leadership growth experienced by mentors, and improved student outcomes. For example, the induction program at the New Teacher Center housed at the University of California at Santa Cruz has an 88% retention rate over a 6-year period, with approximately another 6% of teachers remaining in the field of education but moving to other positions (Strong & St. John, 2001). Furthermore, the experienced teachers who served as mentors also remained in the field and professional growth toward leadership was a positive byproduct of their mentoring role (Villar & Stobbe, 2004). For participating teacher preparation programs in the Comprehensive Teacher Induction Consortium, Gilles, Davis, and McGlamery (2009) report retention rates of 91% up to 8 years postgraduation for graduates of the University of Missouri, 82% for graduates of Texas State University over a 10-year period, and 89% for graduates from the University of Nebraska five years postgraduation. This teaching fellows induction model was established in 1984. Hallmarks of the program include selectivity of mentors, training for mentors, release time to engage in induction activities, a full year of induction support for mentees including coursework leading to a master's degree, inclusion in a cohort of beginning teachers, participation in action research, and recognition of the personal nature and complexity of mentor/mentee relationships (Gilles et al., 2009; McGlamery et al., 2006). In an evaluation of the CADRE project at the University of Nebraska, McGlamery and colleagues (2006) matched teaching fellows participants with first-year teacher nonparticipants as controls. Trained observers assessed participants on 27 teaching skills. Each observation lasted approximately 1 hour, and each participant was observed four times each year. Data were collected over a 6-year period and 38 to 42 teachers were observed each year. As first-year teachers, there were few skill differences observed between groups. Over the course of the study significant differences emerged, with the CADRE group outperforming peers on all 27 skills by 30% or better. By the fifth year of the study, only 37% of the control group remained in the field (Gilles et al., 2009). While there is limited research reporting student outcomes in response to induction, Wong (2004) reported that following implementation of a 3-year induction program in Islip, New York, Regents Diploma rates for the district increased from 40% to 70% and more students participated in Advanced Placement coursework. While early career teachers require some specialized supports, there are a core set of critical components of in-service professional development that support positive changes in teachers' instructional behaviors and result in improved student outcomes.

To benefit from professional development, in-service faculty must learn about theory, see explicit modeling of new skills, have sheltered and scaffolded opportunities for practice, and receive expert coaching during initial implementations (Joyce & Showers, 2002; Kretlow & Bartholomew, 2010). When these components are in place, Joyce and Showers report that 95% of the teachers in their research practiced and sustained innovations. Other characteristics of successful professional development include sufficient duration (Kratchowill et al., 2007), observable and measurable improvements in student outcomes (Joyce & Showers, 2010; Waldron & McLeskey, 2010), collaborative learning communities (Borko, 2004; Kratchowill et al., 2007), congruence with local values and stakeholder buy-in (Kratchowill et al., 2007; Waldron & McLeskey, 2010), and the practicality and utility of the interventions (McLeskey & Waldron, 2004). High-quality professional development requires dedicated resources and a long-term commitment to change.

School Reform Within Current Models of Professional Development

Preparing pre- and in-service educators within existing professional development models to participate in systemic multitiered school reform at its simplest shares characteristics with the reforms themselves. Just as with students in these models, staff respond differentially to the same intervention/instruction, with some requiring more intensive supports to make and sustain change (Brownell et al., 2006). At the first tier, professional development should be system-wide and focus on essential features for all educational professionals (e.g., teachers, administrators, specialists). There must be stakeholder buy-in, and strong leadership (Handler et al., 2007). The professional development must be of sufficient intensity, frequency, and duration to create learning and sustain change (Kratchowill et al., 2007). Teachers (and others) must acquire a sufficient knowledge base and skill set to participate effectively in the process (Blum & Cheney, 2009). At the second tier, scalability and sustainability are dependent upon the development and effective functioning of new systems such as collaborative teams, teacher networks, teacher study groups, and professional learning communities to provide ongoing support (Borko, 2004; Waldron & McLeskey, 2010). In the third tier, most if not all teachers will need opportunities for internal and external expert consultation and collaboration at the individual level, and those might include co-teaching, coaching, modeling, and observation (Joyce & Showers, 2002; Kretlow & Bartholomew, 2010). Active staff participation and developing expert capacity to provide coaching and consultation are key (Handler et al., 2007). Evaluation is critical at all stages, and in many forms, including professional reflection, self-reported performance, and direct observation of fidelity (Kratchowill et al., 2007). Ultimately, the measure of successful systemic reforms is demonstrable improvements in the student outcomes that drove the reforms, whether behavioral or academic (Borko, 2004; Darling-Hammond, 1999). To meet these challenges, educators will require intensive and sustained supports to create comprehensive system-wide changes.

New Directions in Professional Development Within the Context of SW-PBS and RTI

Comprehensive school-wide reform, such as SW-PBS and RTI, require leveraging best practices recommended across the pre- and in-service professional development literature. In addition, "lessons learned" through scaling up efforts provide insight into successful and sustainable implementation. Key to the success of implementing SW-PBS, which is currently being implemented with fidelity in over 19,000 schools and supported by 46 state initiatives across the United States (see www.pbis.org) is building parallel iterative problem-solving processes. District, region, and state professional development efforts are needed that use the same data–practices–systems problem-solving process. This process includes data that indicate what supports school teams need, tools and examples to assist with practice implementation, and ongoing skill-based professional development with technical assistance providing systemic support (Horner & Sugai, 2005). Especially critical to success within the SW-PBS implementation framework are two levels of technical assistance. First, "external coaches," are personnel who have fluent knowledge of the SW-PBS framework and are fluent in all procedures at each tier of this multicomponent process (see Figures 22.1 and 22.2). These external coaches are available to provide on-site technical assistance to school teams based on need. Second, "internal coaches," are within-building personnel who receive additional training on SW-PBS implementation allowing them to serve as a team resource as well as serving as the link between school needs and the district or state initiative. "Lessons learned" in working with in-service educators through the Centers work to date highlights key aspects of this successful professional development, including (a) schools teams as central to success, (b) a focus on team functions rather than individual titles or roles of members, and (c) the use of data in an iterative process to guide decision making. Readers are encouraged to download the "Implementers Blueprint" and the "Professional Development Blueprint" (www.pbis.org) for more detailed recommendations on implementation of SW-PBS.

School Teams as Focal Point

Three key realities underscore the need to focus all SW-PBS professional development activities on building team capacity versus supporting the individual educator. First, the expectation that we can prepare any one teacher or specialist within a school building to address all behavioral challenges is simply unreasonable. Second, even among teachers and specialists who are highly skilled, the current education system precludes wide-scale impact. Third, the mobility within education precludes reliance on individuals to sustain practice. The highly skilled teacher is bound by the obligations of the classroom and the specialist through an inefficient case-by-case process. In addition, the high exit rate of educators who often times have advanced skills and experience also exacerbates the problem. By focusing both training and ongoing technical assistance (i.e., external and internal coaches) on teaching teams of educators to solve their own challenges, and by focusing on function rather than roles, professional development will potentially have both a more efficient immediate impact as well as capacity to apply the same process to future challenges. Likewise, the focus on working with teams of educators provides a de facto network of mentoring and coaching for new educators.

Function Within Process Versus Traditional Roles

SW-PBS places an emphasis on developing skill sets that allow the school and/or district to use existing resources to address their challenges. Traditional professional development is often compartmentalized and targets specific personnel within schools, thus providing limited impact and perpetuating instability. For example, general and special educators often attend and are supported by separate professional development activities and personnel. The same holds true for administrators, school psychologists, or school counselors leading to the perception across the various educational professionals that they must have access to specialized personnel. SW-PBS professional development encourages school and district leadership teams to think about what "function" different professionals traditionally assume with an eye toward providing those skill sets to existing personnel within the school or district. For example, the school may traditionally rely on the school counselor to teach small-group social skills or the school psychologist to conduct individualized functional behavioral assessments. Both of these "functions" are composed of skill sets that can be taught to others. Instead of seeking out more counselor or school psychologist time, which may not be an option, training is focused on current school personnel (e.g., an assistant principal, general and special educators, paraprofessionals) with the support of the school team who provide ongoing technical assistance to build capacity to carry out key functions in the SW-PBS process, independent of which personnel may or may not be available.

Start and Finish With Clearly Measurable Outcomes

Education professional development is replete with examples of targeting "hot topics" and "noted speakers" versus focusing on measurable outcomes that should be observable following any and all professional development. SW-PBS professional development starts with a desired outcome, identifies a tool or strategy to measure the outcome, then works backward to identify materials, examples, training and technical assistance to reach the outcome (Lewis et al., 2010). The training incorporates effective adult learning practices. For example, an essential feature of SW-PBS is the development of a matrix of school-wide expectations with examples of each expectation across all school settings (e.g., classroom, bus, lunchroom, etc.) along with a set of developed teaching strategies to teach each example (Horner & Sugai, 2005). The OSEP Center on Positive Behavioral Interventions and Supports has developed several tools to measure implementation of these two features including the *School Assessment Survey*, the *School-Wide Evaluation Tool*, and *Benchmarks of Quality* (available at www.pbis.org). By referencing the measures, clear and observable markers of essential features of the matrix and lesson plans are evident. Starting at the outcome, trainers and coaches should then delineate key steps in development of targeted features, gather examples, and outline a teaching strategy such as face to face in-service for staff, podcast, vodcast, or on-site training of the school team. At the completion of training, the measures are put in place to assess skill acquisition and track maintenance. In instances where teams do not meet minimum criteria on the measure, targeted technical assistance is put in place.

Skill Sets of Trainers and Coaches

While the SW-PBS process emphasizes a measurable outcome approach across all professional development activities, success will require a skilled set of trainers and technical assistance providers/coaches. As stressed throughout this chapter, a hallmark of the SW-PBS initiative is to pay equal attention to the parallel processes put in place to support school leadership teams. An additional parallel process is recommended in the development of trainers and coaches. That is, training for professional development providers follows the same outcome based approach with accompanying measures (Lewis et al., 2010). For example, in preparing trainers and coaches to develop universal supports among school teams, trainers are referred to whole school implementation outcome measures such as the School-Wide Evaluation Tool and the School Assessment Survey with the provision that they will be responsible for all schools attending training and receiving support achieving minimal scores related to implementation fidelity (e.g., 80% or better on the School-Wide Evaluation Tool). Likewise, trainers and coaches understand that all professional development activities must lead to school implementation that results in improved student behavior. Corresponding to school team training that results in positive student outcomes, trainer and coach professional development focuses on core content and professional development skills on which all are expected to demonstrate mastery (see "Professional Development Blueprint").

Implications and Recommendations for Teacher Education

As noted within the opening paragraph of this chapter, the importance of educators implementing EBPs with integrity is essential for short- and long-term success for all students, especially students at-risk for social and academic failure. Also emphasized throughout this chapter is the ongoing struggle to educate, retain, and continually renew an education workforce that can implement and sustain EBPs. Many barriers and challenges to bridging the research-to-practice gap are outside the control of the professionals on whom the responsibility of preparing the education workforce falls. Ultimately, higher education, state, and district professional development providers control whether this system will continue to rely on a fractured, fragmented, decontextualized and dated model of "train and hope" pre- and in-service professional development, or embrace this new model that emphasizes school teams and measureable student outcomes.

At the preservice level, candidates require coursework designed to explicitly prepare them with the requisite knowledge to participate in SW-PBS systems. Furthermore, fieldwork and coursework should be directly linked, interactive, and provide scaffolded opportunities for candidates to apply the theory, principles, and procedures that are foundational to functioning school-wide systems (Gettinger, Stoiber, & Koscik, 2008). Preservice teachers benefit from opportunities for observation and practice, whether virtual and simulated or field-based and supervised. To transition effectively into systemic reforms, preservice educators will need knowledge of behavior analytic theory, including knowledge of functional assessment (Gettinger et al., 2008). Candidates should receive explicit training in collaborative processes to prepare them for active participation in school-wide systemic reforms (Allen & Blackstone, 2003). Specialist candidates, such as special educators and school psychologists must be prepared to implement EBPs, and to serve as a resource in their schools. Preservice educators must be knowledgeable and skilled in using data to make instructional decisions, including identifying data collection procedures, collecting data using direct and indirect measures, and then displaying data using graphs to demonstrate student outcomes (Riccomini & Fish, 2005). Preservice educators must be supported in developing strong self-efficacy for managing student behavior as self-efficacy translates into both a readiness and willingness to meet student needs, and furthermore, lowers teacher stress (Baker, 2005).

Recommendations

Throughout this chapter, we have called for two key reforms in educator preparation. The first is to ensure that pre- and in-service professional development follows current and emerging recommendations with respect to best practice (e.g., skill-based instruction, opportunities to practice and receive performance feedback). The second is to begin an overall examination of how professional development is implemented in light of current reform movements such as SW-PBS and RTI that shift the focus from reliance on experts to building expertise within school leadership teams, enabling schools to solve learning and behavior challenges through a standard problem-solving process. This process begins with the desired outcome and builds a continuum of student supports in response to careful progress monitoring while simultaneously building a school environment that develops, supports, retains, and promotes master educators.

The field of education, and, in particular higher education, can ill afford to stand by and perpetuate ineffective professional development practices while schools, districts and states have moved to embrace and implement effective reforms such as SW-PBS and RTI in light of the empirical student outcomes evidenced by such reforms. At minimum, the field as a whole must embrace current best practices to ensure the following skill sets are common across all professionals who work within the P–12 educational system:

Preservice Educators

- Develop knowledge of the basic problem-solving process of SW-PBS and RTI (i.e., data, practices, and systems).
- Develop beginning mastery of the basic problem-solving process of SW-PBS and RTI (i.e., data, practices, and systems).
- Learn to work collaboratively within multidisciplinary teams.
- Understand the need to alter and/or supplement core curriculum and learning environments, including classrooms, to increase academic and behavior success of at-risk learners.
- Understand the different "functions" within the SW-PBS and RTI process (e.g., the need to teach small groups, differentiate instruction based on data), versus the traditional roles of various personnel.
- Understand the essential features of SW-PBS and RTI and how the process works within the school setting, including district and state level supports to ensure schools are successful.

In-Service Educators

- Develop knowledge of the basic problem-solving process of SW-PBS and RTI (i.e., data, practices and systems).
- Develop a high level of mastery of the basic problem-solving process of SW-PBS and RTI (i.e., data, practices, and systems).
- Understand the essential features of SW-PBS and RTI and how the process works within the school setting including district and state level supports to ensure schools are successful.
- Understand their role in carrying out traditional responsibilities (e.g., classroom instruction) and as a member of the larger school community (e.g., assist with tier II interventions and implement connect points across more intensive supports and the universal supports within their classroom).
- Understand how to access assistance within the school-wide system.
- Become well informed consumers with respect to quick fix interventions and competing initiatives with respect what data are present in their school that indicate new practices are warranted and how it will, or will not, align with the current school efforts.

References

Allen, S. J., & Blackstone, A. R. (2003). Training preservice teachers in collaborative problem solving: An investigation of the impact on teacher and student behavior change in real-world settings. *School Psychology Quarterly, 18*, 22–51. doi:10.1521/scpq.18.1.22.20878

Baker, P. H. (2005). Managing student behavior: How ready are teachers for the challenge? *American Secondary Education, 33*(3), 51–64.

Ball, D. L., & Forzani, F. M. (2010). What does it take to make a teacher? *Phi Delta Kappan, 92*(2), 8–13.

Barrett, S. B., Bradshaw, C. P., & Lewis-Palmer, T. (2008). Maryland statewide PBIS initiative. *Journal of Positive Behavior Interventions, 10*, 105–114. doi:10.1177/1098300707312541

Billingsley, B. S. (2004). Promoting teacher quality and retention in special education. *Journal of Learning Disabilities, 37*, 370–376. doi.10.1177/00222194040370050101

Blanton, L. P., Pugach, M., & Florian, L. (2011). *Preparing general education teachers to improve outcomes for students with disabilities.* Washington, DC: American Association of Colleges for Teacher Education, National Center for Learning Disabilities.

Blum, C., & Cheney, D. (2009). The validity and reliability of the Teacher Knowledge and Skills Support Survey for Positive Behavior Support. *Teacher Education and Special Education, 32*, 239–256. doi:10.1177/0888406409340013

Borko, H. (2004). Professional development and teacher learning: Mapping the terrain. *Educational Researcher, 33*(8), 3–15. doi:3102/001318X03308003

Bradshaw, C., Reinke, W., Brown, L., Bevans, K., & Leaf, P. (2008). Implementation of school-wide positive behavioral interventions and supports (PBIS) in elementary schools: Observations from a randomized trial. *Education and Treatment of Children, 31*, 1–26.

Bransford, J. D., Brown, A. L., & Cocking, R. R. (2000). *How people learn: Brain, mind, experience, and school.* Washington, DC: National Academies Press.

Brownell, M. T., Adams, A., Sindelar, P. T., Waldron, N. L., & Vanhover, S. (2006). Learning from collaboration: the role of teacher qualities. *Exceptional Children, 72*, 169–185.

Brownell, M. T., Hirsch, E., & Seo, S. (2004). Meeting the demand for highly qualified special education teachers during severe shortages: What should policymakers consider? *The Journal of Special Education, 38*, 56–61. doi:10.1177/00224669040380010501

Brownell, M. T., Ross, D. R., Colón, E. P., & McCallum, C. L. (2003). *Critical features of special education teacher preparation: A comparison with exemplary practices in general teacher education* (COPSSE Document Number RS-4). Gainesville, FL: University of Florida, Center on Personnel Studies in Special Education.

Brownell, M. T., Sindelar, P. T., Kiely, M. T., & Danielson, L. C. (2010). Special education teacher quality and preparation: Exposing foundations, constructing a new model. *Exceptional Children, 76*, 357–377.

Bureau of Labor Statistics, U.S. Department of Labor. (2012). *Occupational outlook handbook, 2012–13 edition, teachers—special education.* Retrieved from http://www.bls.gov/ooh/education-training-and-library/special-education-teachers.htm

Burns, M. K., & Ysseldyke, J. E. (2009). Reported prevalence of evidence-based practices in special education. *The Journal of Special Education, 43*, 3–11. doi:10.1177/0022466908315563

Darling-Hammond, L. (1999). *Teacher quality and student achievement: A review of state policy evidence.* Seattle, WA: Center for the Study of Teaching Policy, University of Washington.

Darling-Hammond, L. (2006). Constructing 21st-century teacher education. *Journal of Teacher Education, 57*, 300–314. doi:10.1177/0022487105285962

Dray, B. J., & Thomas, C. N. (2010). Teaching is NOT a profession: How general and special education teacher education have failed. In F. E. Obiakor, J. P. Bakken, & A. F. Rotatori (Eds.), *Current issues and trends in special education: Research, technology, and teacher preparation, Advances in Special Education, Vol. 20.* (pp. 187–203). United Kingdom: Emerald Group Publishing.

Fixsen, D. L., Naoom, S. F., Blase, K. A., Friedman, R. M., & Wallace, F. (2005). *Implementation Research: A Synthesis of the Literature.* Tampa, FL: University of South Florida, Louis de la Parte Florida Mental Health Institute, The National Implementation Research Network (FMHI Publication #231).

Gettinger, M., Stoiber, K., & Koscik, R. (2008). Effects of a preparation program focused on accommodating children with challenging behaviors. *Teacher Education and Special Education, 32*, 164–181. doi:10.177/0888406408330624

Gilles, C., Davis, B., & McGlamery, S. (2009). Induction programs that work. *Kappan, 91*(2), 42–47.

Gresham, F. M. (2007). Response to intervention and emotional and behavioral disorders: Best practices in assessment for intervention. *Assessment for Effective Intervention, 32*, 214–222. doi:10.1177/15345084070320040301

Grossman, P., & Loeb, S. (2010). Learning from multiple routes. *Educational Leadership, 67*(8), 22–27.

Guskey, T. R. (2000). *Evaluating professional development.* Thousand Oaks, CA: Corwin Press.

Handler, M. W., J. Rey, J., Connell, J., Thier, K., Feinberg, A., & Putnam, R. (2007). Practical considerations in creating school-wide positive behavior support in public school. *Psychology in the Schools 44*, 29–39. doi:10.1002/pits.20203

Henderson, K., Klein, S., Gonzalez, P., & Bradley, R. (2005). Teachers of children with emotional disturbance: A national look at preparation, teaching conditions, and practices. *Behavioral Disorders, 30*, 6–17.

Holdheide, L. R., Goe, L., Croft, A., & Reschly, D. J. (2010). *Challenges in evaluating special education teachers and English language learner specialists.* Washington, DC: National Comprehensive Center for Teacher Quality.

Horner, R. H., & Sugai, G. (2005). School-wide positive behavior support: An alternative approach to discipline in schools. In L. Bambara & L. Kern (Eds.) *Positive behavior support* (pp. 359–390). New York: Guilford Press.

Individuals With Disabilities Education Improvement Act of 2004, Pub. L. No. 108-446 (2004).

Jimerson, S., Burns, M. K., & VanDerHeyden, A. M. (2007). Response to intervention at school: the science and practice of assessment and intervention. In S. R. Jimerson, M. K. Burns, & A. M. VanDerHeyden (Eds.), *Handbook of response to intervention: The science and practice of assessment and intervention* (pp. 3–9). New York: Springer. doi:10.1007/978-0-387-49053-3_1

Joyce, B., & Showers, B. (2002). *Student achievement through staff development* (3rd ed.). Alexandria, VA: ACSD.

Kauffman, J. M. (1996). Research to practice issues. *Behavioral Disorders, 22*, 55–60.

Kratchowill, T. R., Volpiansky, P., Clements, M., & Ball, C. (2007). Professional development in implementing and sustaining multitier prevention models: Implications for response to intervention. *School Psychology Review, 36*, 618–631.

Kretlow, A. G., & Bartholomew, C. C. (2010). Using coaching to improve the fidelity of evidence-based practices: A review of studies. *Teacher Education and Special Education, 33*, 279–299. doi:10.1177/0888406410371643

Kretlow, A. G., & Blatz, S. L. (2011). The ABCs of evidence-based practices for teachers. *Teaching Exceptional Children, 43*(5), 8–19.

Lewis, T. J., Barrett, S., Sugai, G., & Horner, R. H. (2010). *Blueprint for school-wide positive behavior support training and professional development.* Eugene, OR: National Technical Assistance Center on Positive Behavior Interventions and Support. Retrieved from http://www.pbis.org/common/pbisresources/publications/PBIS_PD_Blueprint_v3.pdf

Lopez, O. S. (1995). *The effect of the relationship between classroom student diversity and teacher capacity on student performance: Conclusions and recommendations for educational policy and practice.* Austin, TX: The Strategic Management of the Classroom Learning Enterprise Research Series.

Lyon, G. R., Fletcher, J. M., Shaywitz, S. E., Shaywitz, B. A., Torgeson, J. K., Wood, F. B., … Olson, R. (2001). Rethinking learning disabilities. In C. E. Finn, A. J., Rotherham, & C. R. Hokanson (Eds.), *Rethinking special education for a new century* (pp. 259–287). Washington, DC: Thomas Fordham Foundation.

Maag, J. W., & Katsiyannis, A. (2008). The medical model to block eligibility for students with EBD: A response-to-intervention alternative. *Behavioral Disorders, 33*, 184–194.

McGlamery, S., Fluckinger, J., & Edick, N. (2006). The CADRE Project: Looking at the development of beginning teachers. *Educational Considerations, 33*(2), 42–50.

McIntosh, K., Campbell, A. L., Carter, D. R., & Dickey, C. R. (2009). Differential effects of a tier two behavior intervention based on function of problem behavior. *Journal of Positive Behavior Interventions, 11*, 82–93. doi:10.1177/1098300708319127

McLeskey, J., & Billingsley, B. S. (2008). How does the quality and stability of the teaching force influence the research-to-practice gap? A perspective on the teacher shortage in special education. *Remedial and Special Education, 29*, 293–305. doi:10.1177/041932507312010

McLeskey, J., & Waldron, N. L. (2004). Three conceptions of teacher learning: Exploring the relationship between knowledge and the practice of teaching. *Teacher Education and Special Education, 27*, 3–14. doi:10.1177/088840640402700102

National Association of State Directors of Special Education (NASDSE). (2008). *Response to intervention blueprints: School building level.* Alexandria, VA: Author.

No Child Left Behind Act of 2001, Pub. L. No. 107-110 (2002).

Oliver, R., & Reschly, D. (2007). *Effective classroom management: Teacher preparation and professional development.* Washington, DC: National Comprehensive Center for Teacher Quality.

Oliver, R., & Reschly, D. (2010). Special education teacher preparation in classroom management: Implications for students with emotional and behavioral disorders. *Behavioral Disorders, 35*(3), 188–199.

Riccomini, P. J., & Fish, R. (2005). Supervising a struggling student teacher: A midterm action plan. *Essays in Education, 15*, 1–13. Retrieved from http://www.usca.edu/essays/vol15fall2005.html

Rivers, J. C., & Sanders, W. L. (2002). Teacher quality and equity in educational opportunity: Findings and policy implications. In L T. Izumi & W M. Evers (Eds.), *Teacher quality* (pp. 13–23). Stanford, CA: Hoover Institution Press.

Sanders, W. L., & Rivers, J. C. (1996). *Cumulative and residual effects of teachers on future student academic achievement* (Research Progress Report). Knoxville, TN: University of Tennessee Value-Added Research and Assessment Center.

Schaughency, E., & Ervin, R. (2006). Building capacity to implement and sustain effective practices to better serve children. *School Psychology Review 35*, 155–166.

Scheeler, M. C., Bruno, K., Grubb, E., & Seavey, T. L. (2009). Generalizing teaching techniques from university to K–12 classrooms: Teaching preservice teachers to use what they learn. *Journal of Behavioral Education, 18*, 189–210. doi:10.1007/s10864-009-9088-3

Schlichte, J., Yssel, N., & Merbler, J. (2005). Pathways to burnout: Case studies in teacher isolation and alienation. *Preventing School Failure, 50*, 35–40. doi:10.3200/PSFL50.1.35-40

Scott, T. M., Nelson, C. M., & Liaupsin, C. (2001). Effective instruction: The forgotten component in preventing school violence. *Education and Treatment of Children, 24*, 309–322.

Smith, T. M., & Ingersoll, R. M. (2004). What are the effects of induction and mentoring on beginning teacher turnover? *American Educational Research Journal, 41*, 681–714. doi:10.3102/00028312041003681

Strong, M., & St. John, L. (2001). *A study of teacher retention: The effects of mentoring for beginning teachers.* Santa Cruz, University of California, Santa Cruz.

Sugai, G. (2001, June 23). *School climate and discipline: School-wide positive behavior support.* Paper presented at the National Summit on Shared Implementation of IDEA, Washington, DC.

Sugai, G., Horner, R. H., Dunlap, G., Hieneman, M., Lewis, T. J., Nelson, C. M., ... Ruef, M. (2000). Applying positive behavioral support and functional behavioral assessment in schools. *Journal of Positive Behavioral Interventions, 2*, 131–143. doi:10.1177/109830070000200302

U.S. Census Bureau. (2010, June. 15). *Back to school 2010–2011* (CB10-FF.14). Washington, DC: U.S. Department of Commerce.

U.S. Department of Education, Office of Policy, Evaluation, and Policy Development. (2010). *A blueprint for reform: The reauthorization of the Elementary and Secondary Education Act.* Retrieved from http://www2.ed.gov/policy/elsec/leg/blueprint/publicationtoc.html

Villar, A., & Stobbe, C. (2004). *Researching the domains of mentor development: The transition from veteran classroom teacher to formal mentor status.* Paper presented at the American Educational Research Association, San Diego.

Waldron, N. L., & McLeskey, J. (2010). Establishing a collaborative school culture through comprehensive school reform. *Journal of Educational and Psychological Consultation, 20*, 58–74. doi:10.1080/104744109035364

Wong, H. K. (2004). Induction programs that keep new teachers teaching and improving. *NASSP Bulletin, 88*(638), 41–58. doi:10.1177/019263650408863804

23

Teacher Preparation

Early Intervention/Early Childhood Special Education

Peggy A. Gallagher
GEORGIA STATE UNIVERSITY

Elizabeth A. Steed
UNIVERSITY OF COLORADO—DENVER

Katherine B. Green
GEORGIA STATE UNIVERSITY

Things to Think About

- This chapter on personnel preparation in Early Intervention (EI) and Early Childhood Special Education (ECSE) provides an overview of themes specific to young learners.
- Partnerships with families, a wide variety of child placements available in natural environments, an emphasis on interdisciplinary work, and the importance of collaboration with family members and other caregivers are central to EI/ECSE.
- Standards have been developed by different professional organizations to guide personnel preparation in EI/ECSE.
- Various types of programs have been established in EI/ECSE to prepare personnel, such as blended programs.
- The research in personnel preparation in EI/ECSE specific to preservice education and professional development is growing and includes recent trends in EI/ECSE, such as emergent literacy and infant mental health.

Introduction

Teacher preparation in Early Intervention (EI) and Early Childhood Special Education (ECSE) encompasses the preparation of teachers and other personnel who work with young children, birth through age eight, with special needs and their families. Early Intervention teachers and related personnel, such as service coordinators or special instructors, work with children from birth through age two and their families in programs guided by Part C of the Individuals with Disabilities Education Act (IDEA; 2004), while teachers in ECSE work with young children from ages three through eight in programs guided by Part B of IDEA. There are four overarching themes that distinguish EI and ECSE that must be considered in personnel preparation including: (a) close partnerships with the family, (b) a wide variety of natural settings where young children play and interact, (c) the inherent interdisciplinary nature of EI/ECSE settings, and (d) the necessity of collaboration in working with family members and other caregivers who interact with the child.

One main overarching theme for teachers in EI/ECSE is the importance of close partnerships with the child's family. Indeed, in many EI programs, the special instructor is seen as working with the parents or other family members such as grandparents, as much as or more, than with the individual child. This structure allows the child's caregivers the opportunity to give input on what the child should learn or what supports the child needs to function in his or her natural environment and supports the caregiver in working with the child across the day and weeks, rather than in individual or group sessions alone. A family-centered perspective takes into account the needs, resources, and desires of a family regarding their child (Bernheimer & Weisner, 2007; Dunst, 2002). Working in partnership with families continues through the ECSE years as children transition to school services. Honoring and valuing a family's cultural and linguistic attributes is an important part of partnering with families and should be taught in teacher preparation programs (Fults & Harry, 2012).

Another overarching theme in EI/ECSE is the wide variety of settings that make up the natural environment where young children are served (IDEA, 2004). This becomes especially important in the context of early childhood. After all, children are developmentally still very close in age during early childhood and learning gaps are not as wide as they may be later; serving children with disabilities with their typical peers is "natural" at this age. This means, however, that there are a wide variety of people and settings that the child will interact with in natural environments; each of whom should be prepared in how to teach the child. Children, for instance, may be placed in family childcare homes, Head Start, or other childcare settings or they may be served in preschool special education classrooms in public schools. It is important to note that the new Race to the Top—Early Learning Challenge Program grants mandate a broad definition of "early childhood educators" including professionals who work in centers and family childcare homes, home visitors, teacher assistants, infant and toddler specialists and importantly, early interventionists and early childhood special educators (Race to the Top—Early Learning Challenge, 2011). Personnel preparation programs in EI/ECSE must include attention to these myriad personnel in various settings.

Another unique feature of EI and ECSE programs is the inherent interdisciplinary nature of working with babies, toddlers, and preschoolers. Many of the children who have been identified with disabilities at such a young age have multiple or severe issues that demand the involvement of personnel from various disciplines. The adults involved must learn to work together so as not to overwhelm the child or family and to focus on important interventions. As Stayton, Whittaker, Jones, and Kersting (2001) noted, professionals who work with young children with disabilities should "possess a core set of competencies while mastering their own discipline specific competencies" (p. 395). Disciplines such as occupational therapy, physical therapy, speech and language pathology, or social work, for instance, are often involved with young children with disabilities and each discipline has its own disciplinary standards. Stayton et al. urged personnel preparation programs to model interdisciplinary approaches so that students practice such approaches when they are in the field. With the involvement of such a variety of persons from different agencies and with different backgrounds and education, comes a challenge in teacher preparation in EI/ECSE. While our focus in this chapter is on the preparation of those working as special instructors or teachers in EI/ECSE, the context in which they work is an important feature they need to be prepared for. With these three overarching themes of working with families as partners and serving children in regular early childhood environments that are by nature interdisciplinary, collaboration becomes imperative.

Thus, collaboration with family members and other caregivers is a final area where EI/ECSE preparation programs must put a special focus. EI and ECSE teachers must have excellent skills in collaboration to partner with families and interact positively with the adults from a wide variety of disciplines who are involved in working with the young child (Friend & Cook, 2010; Kampwirth & Powers, 2012). A historical perspective has shown that personnel preparation in EI/ECSE is the only area of special education that demonstrated a broad-based and systematic effort to support and coordinate services across disciplines and settings (Pugach, Blanton, & Correa, 2011). With these overarching themes of partnering with families, involving personnel from a wide variety of settings and disciplines, as well as the importance of collaboration, in mind, we now turn to the standards that have been developed in the field of EI and ECSE to guide the preparation of teachers and other personnel. We will next provide an overview of personnel preparation in EI/ECSE; then a review of research on personnel preparation in EI/ECSE, including preservice education and professional development; and finally, highlight recent trends that should be addressed in EI/ECSE personnel preparation programs in order to prepare the best qualified teachers.

Standards and Accountability in EI/ECSE

There is a growing emphasis on the use of standards as a means of increasing educational accountability that has evolved from the No Child Left Behind legislation (NCLB; 2001). Both NCLB and IDEA (2004) specify that a highly qualified teacher be in every classroom. NCLB (2002) required that all teachers be "highly qualified", including preschool teachers in federally funded prekindergarten programs. There are also increasing qualifications for Head Start teachers. The Good Start, Grow Smart Initiative (Bush Administration's Early Childhood Initiative, 2002) promoted early learning standards and professional development and began emphasizing quality rating systems to assess the quality of programs, systematically document improvements to program quality, and communicate information about program quality to consumers such as parents. The competencies and skills needed by teachers are reflected in early learning standards that increasingly guide how early interventionists and early childhood special educators deliver instruction to children with special needs (Scott-Little, Kagan, Frelow, & Reid, 2009). Scott-Little et al. (2009) found that as of 2009, more than half of states in the U.S. had developed early learning guidelines for infants and toddlers. Some have cautioned against relying too heavily on standards when planning instruction for young children with disabilities because the standards are not comprehensive and may not fully address the adaptations and needs of young children with disabilities (e.g., Grisham-Brown, Pretti-Frontczak, Hawkins, & Winchell, 2009). While the accountability movement has extended to EI/ECSE, early interventionists and early childhood special educators may be ill-equipped to address learning across all domains (e.g., cognitive, social/emotional, adaptive) due to limited program hours, the diverse demographics of young children and families, and a lack of training in standards-based instruction (Winton, McCollum, & Catlett, 2008).

Teacher education programs in EI/ECSE use at least three sets of professional standards to guide the preparation of their candidates and provide the foundation for the development of competent personnel in EI/ECSE. These include the general standards from the Council for Exceptional Children (CEC), the specialized standards from the Division of Early Childhood (DEC) of CEC, and the standards from the National Association of the Education of Young Children (NAEYC), which govern regular early childhood programs. Pugach et al. (2011), in a historical review of collaborative efforts, note Bredekamp's (1993) plea to find common ground between the fields of early childhood education (ECE) and ECSE. Indeed, the 15 years that followed saw much collaboration between the fields primarily through the professional organizations, DEC and NAEYC, with position papers on licensure, inclusion, and alignment of standards.

DEC has been a leader in promoting best practices in EI/ECSE personnel preparation. Major contributions include the development of a DEC Recommended Practices book (Sandall, Hemmeter,

Smith, & McLean, 2005) and the formation of a Special Interest Group on Personnel Preparation, which developed the DEC specialized standards at both initial and advanced levels (Lifter et al., 2011). The DEC standards place emphasis on the specialized knowledge providers need to work with children from birth through age eight who are at-risk for or have developmental delays or disabilities, and their families. These standards were developed for faculty to use in guiding course content, field experiences, and evaluating program effectiveness in EI/ECSE as well as by accrediting agencies. It is important to note that practitioners and researchers from both DEC and NAEYC validated the DEC EI/ECSE standards (Cochran et al., 2012) and that they are supported by research. Paralleling the development of the DEC specialized EI/ECSE standards was the revision of the NAEYC standards to be more attentive and inclusive of all children, including those with special needs. A DEC/NAEYC workgroup has aligned the EI/ECSE standards with the NAEYC standards (Chandler et al., 2012) so that programs can utilize both sets of standards as needed for their blended or combined teacher education programs in ECE, Birth to Five, or ECSE.

Though we have national standards for personnel preparation through NAEYC and DEC, Stayton et al. (2009) found that state standards for early childhood special educators were not necessarily aligned with the national standards of either NAEYC or DEC. In the Stayton et al. study, data on state models of certification were gathered by the Center to Inform Personnel Preparation Policy and Practice in Early Intervention and Preschool Education through web searches and interviews with state representatives. The authors found that most of the certification guidelines reviewed did not include the DEC, CEC, or NAEYC core standards, though some of the teacher education programs did use these standards. The authors recommended further alignment among the three sets of standards and increasing adoption of the standards by state certification agencies. It is important, too, to think about how these standards can be used in 2-year and technical college programs that offer the Child Development Associate (CDA) or paraprofessional training for those working at child development centers in inclusive settings since these personnel are vital to the implementation of inclusive programs in EI/ECSE.

Personnel Preparation in EI/ECSE

There are several options and pathways for individuals interested in becoming EI/ECSE educators in the United States (Maxwell, Lim, & Early, 2006). First, there are blended or unified undergraduate programs (e.g., Birth to Five programs) that offer a baccalaureate degree with certification and prepare practitioners to work with children with and without disabilities in a range of educational environments (Stayton & McCollum, 2002). Likewise, most early intervention professionals who work with very young children with disabilities in natural settings have at least a bachelor's degree in a social services field. There are also postbaccalaureate programs specific to EI or ECSE that offer advanced degrees (e.g., master's) with certification or nondegree, certification only programs. More states are offering certification programs that are specific to working with young children with disabilities from birth to age eight (Geiger, Crutchfield, & Mainzer, 2003). Approximately 33 states offered some type of ECSE certification, either dual (Early Childhood Education and ECSE) or single certification covering typically developing children and children with special needs (Stayton et al., 2009). There are also alternatives to traditional university-based preservice training in EI/ECSE, such as Teach for America. These alternative programs have increased in their size and number across the country with some federal funding targeted specifically for alternative pathways to education.

Personnel preparation for teachers who work with infants, toddlers, and very young children with disabilities is different than personnel preparation for teachers who work with older students since the content and practices of early interventionists and ECSE teachers must reflect the developmental needs of infants, toddlers, and preschoolers (Winton, McCollum, & Catlett, 1997). Early interventionists and early childhood special educators must also be trained on the components of service delivery that are different for Part C and Part B 619, such as the programmatic requirements under Part C to provide intervention in natural environments. Building upon these ideas, Macy, Squires, and Barton (2009) outlined several areas where EI/ECSE teacher preparation programs differ philosophically from more traditional special education personnel preparation programs that focus on teaching older students. These include a developmental focus, a situated learning perspective that emphasizes authentic activities and Piagetian constructivist models (Piaget, 1970), a transactional perspective (Sameroff & Chandler, 1975), and empirically based research practices that include behavioral technologies.

The preparation of early interventionists and early childhood special educators does not end after they have finished their formal training regardless of their pathway to teaching. In-service professional development occurs once educators begin working with young children and families. Professional development for EI/ECSE personnel in the workforce is integral to high-quality programs for young children with disabilities (Buysse & Hollingsworth, 2009). The National Professional Development Center on Inclusion (NPDCI, 2011) describes professional development for early educators as including three key components: (a) characteristics and contexts of the learners (the "who"), (b) content (the "what"), and (c) organization and facilitation of learning experiences (the "how"). States should have comprehensive systems of personnel development (CSPDs) for early interventionists and early childhood special educators that include these three components. Such professional development should focus on particular instructional practices rather than general topics related to the EI/ECSE field. Professional development for practicing teachers should also align with standards or specific instructional goals and provide feedback and guidance to educators that are intensive, collaborative, and sustained (Buysse & Hollingsworth, 2009).

New standards for in-service training established by The National Education Association, the Public Education Network, and the National Staff Development Council specifically mention the use of individualized, intensive, and sustained training that is grounded in practice. These suggestions are mirrored in NCLB (2002) guidelines that indicate that in-service training must be sustained, intensive, and connected to the classroom and include instruction on how to use data and assessments to inform classroom practices.

The federal Office of Special Education Programs' (OSEP) funding has had a great influence on unifying the preparation of EC and ECSE teachers. Since 1989 there has been a stand-alone funding stream to prepare personnel in EI/ECSE, which has encouraged blended and unified program development. EI and ECSE are fortunate to have had ongoing federal support starting with demonstration projects that grew to include technical assistance centers and research institutes. The major technical assistance center in EI/ECSE, currently known as ECTA (Early Childhood Technical Assistance Center), has provided national guidance for over 40 years. While technical assistance in EI/ECSE started out focused on services to children, it has since expanded to include personnel development (Fixsen & Blase, 2009), particularly for in-service professionals.

General Research Findings on Personnel Preparation in EI/ECSE

While the field has compiled literature that includes recommendations for personnel preparation for EI/ECSE educators, there are few comprehensive studies to validate certain approaches to personnel preparation or the use of certain components of preservice or in-service technical assistance. Educator preparation research is in its infancy, especially in the field of EI/ECSE (Winton & McCollum, 2008). There are a multitude of factors that have hindered professional preparation research in EI/ECSE and the field of education in general. First, the program and teacher variables and student outcomes that are measured are often complex, poorly defined in the field, and separated by a time lag (Cochran-Smith, 2005). Further, professional preparation research is typically limited in scope and does not use rigorous experimental designs due to inadequate funding dollars for this type of research (Cochran-Smith & Zeichner, 2005).

Research specific to EI/ECSE professional preparation is limited. However, we will review the studies and reports that have been conducted regarding key components of the two primary areas of personnel preparation for EI/ECSE educators: (a) preservice education, and (b) professional development (or in-service training). Preservice education includes learning that occurs through coursework and field experiences prior to entering the field of teaching. These experiences may include university degree and nondegree programs in EI/ECSE as well as alternative pathways to EI/ECSE teacher education. Professional development includes participation in in-service training opportunities once in a paid teaching position in order to hone skills and/or learn new models or approaches (Winton & McCollum, 2008).

Preservice Education

As previously noted, there is some guidance from the literature about the key components that should appear in preservice training programs for individuals who will provide educational services to young children with disabilities. These components include training in linked systems of assessment, a focus on teaching strategies that are play- or routine-based, a connection between research-based practices and standards, training and practice developing Individualized Family Service Plans (IFSPs) and Individualized Education Plans (IEPs), and training and practice collaborating with families and professionals from other disciplines in coursework and field experiences (Bruder & Dunst, 2005; NPDCI, 2011; see the Appendix to this chapter for a list of resources to promote these and other components of personnel preparation in EI/ECSE).

Field experiences are an essential component of preservice personnel preparation (Macy et al., 2009). Some key features of quality practicum experiences include a match between the philosophy and approach of the preservice program with that of the practicum setting, a match of expected student competencies to the activities asked of the practicum student in the field setting, and a multitude of diverse experiences across children, families, and related services personnel (Macy et al., 2009). "Staged" learning opportunities are helpful to move students from observing to demonstrating more skilled strategies and competencies. Hemmeter, Santos, and Ostrosky (2008) also recommended using graduated coursework, supervised fieldwork, and reflection to practice effective strategies for preventing challenging behaviors.

We know less about how preservice programs are addressing other recommended components in their curriculum (Winton & McCollum, 2008). A 1999 survey found that courses covering disability-related content in undergraduate programs was inadequate; 40% of bachelor's degree programs that had a mission to prepare ECE educators did not offer a single course regarding working with young children with disabilities (Chang, Early, & Winton, 2005). Only 60% of associate's degree programs that included infants and toddlers actually had a required course on the topic and 63% had a required field experience with infants and toddlers (Early & Winton, 2001). Further, Bruder and Dunst (2005) found that most preservice programs for early interventionists focused on family-centered practices with less emphasis on service coordination and teaming. Another study analyzed ECSE preservice teachers' field experiences journals to uncover that they were most focused on child-related practices, followed by assessment, and then family-based practices (Hanline, 2010). Preservice teachers seldom mentioned interdisciplinary models, technology, personnel preparation, or more systemic policies or systems change (Hanline, 2010). An earlier qualitative study of teachers' perspectives indicated that they felt they needed more preservice training in how to work with families and other professionals (Butera, 1993). Finally, a survey by Hemmeter et al. (2008) found that faculty members in nine states reported that their graduates were prepared in working with families, preventive practices, and supporting social-emotional development, but were not as well prepared to work with children with challenging behaviors. Other surveys of EI/ECSE practitioners have also indicated training needs in the areas of family systems, assessment, and program evaluation (e.g., Gallagher, Malone, Cleghorne, & Helms, 1997).

These studies on preservice training indicate that there is a schism between recommendations for personnel preparation and how EI/ECSE personnel are actually prepared. The dearth of literature in this area points to the need for conducting more research to fully understand what occurs during preservice training, including field experiences/practicum, and the impact on EI/ECSE teachers' use of recommended practices in the field. Research that compares traditional teacher preparation programs to alternative pathways to teaching, such as Teach for America, to assess if there are differences in how individuals are prepared to work with young children with special needs and their families and how that preparation affects outcomes for young children is also needed. We also need to know more about how preservice programs address current issues, such as the use of technology in EI/ECSE settings and how to best support students and families from diverse cultural and linguistic backgrounds (Lee, Ostrosky, Bennett, & Fowler, 2003). Specific preservice training strategies such as the case study approach also have some initial research to support their use in EI/ECSE training programs (Kilgo & Aldridge, 2011; Snyder & McWilliam, 2003) but we need to know much more about teacher education strategies.

Professional Development

Research in on-the-job personnel preparation (or in-service training), also known as professional development, for EI/ECSE educators has primarily focused on the most effective methods of delivery of information. The most often used method of professional development is the workshop model with groups of teachers participating in brief trainings at a central location (e.g., school cafeteria, hotel conference room; Guskey, 2003). While it is the most utilized, we also have fairly conclusive evidence that the workshop model is ineffective as a way to improve teachers' use of recommended practices (Fixsen, Naoom, Blase, Friedman, & Wallace, 2005; Joyce & Showers, 2002). In one study 50% of teachers reported that in-service trainings made no difference in their professional development (Farkas, Johnson, & Duffett, 2003).

Research indicates that alternative forms of in-service training may be more effective for influencing EI/ECSE teachers' behavior once they are on the job (Whitebrook & Ryan, 2011). Indeed, Dunst and Trivette's (2009) meta-analysis of studies using adult learning principles including accelerated learning, coaching, guided design, and just-in-time training confirmed the importance of these approaches. Professional development approaches that include collaboration with other teachers (e.g., mentoring, peer study groups), and on-site training and individualized consultation with teachers in the form of coaching or consultation show promise but, still lack sufficient evidence to consider them research-based approaches (Winton, 2006). The research that currently exists suggests that teachers find these alternative approaches more appealing. For example, one study found that teachers favored time to collaborate with other teachers over workshop trainings (Sunderman, Tracey, Kim, & Orfield, 2004). Another study found that 255 early childhood teachers preferred on-site training in their classrooms rather than conference presentations and workshops (Dunst & Raab, 2010).

In addition to teacher satisfaction, collaborative and on-site professional development has been shown to be effective in improving teacher and child outcomes. Pairing a novice teacher with a mentor can provide modeling of evidence-based practices, feedback on use of newly learned strategies, and guided reflection on the use of strategies and their impact on young children (Whitebrook & Ryan, 2011). This approach has been supported in studies such as Gallagher, Abbott-Shim, and VandeWiele (2011), in which mentor teachers in Head Start classrooms improved the perceived competence of new or less experienced teachers through a mentoring program which included a 50-hour mentor seminar, ongoing mentoring of protégés by mentors, and support for mentors by a mentor coordinator. Further, the cognitive, language, and social skills of young children increased in participating teachers' classrooms. Applequist, McLellan, and McGrath (2010) described an apprenticeship model for early interventionists as part of one state's CSPD, required under Part C of the IDEA (1997). They define an apprentice as one who learns through "guided practice from someone who has mastered the trade or practice" (p. 24). Though the model was effective in establishing standards of practice for individuals, it was costly in terms of time and personnel resources.

In order to provide more effective professional development, and to bridge the gap between research and teacher consumers, many schools and service providers have implemented coaching models. There are a variety of ways to implement professional development models of coaching, from in-class coaching to online coaching to peer mentoring. For example, in a study of teachers of preschoolers at-risk for school failure, Landry, Anthony, Swank, and Monseque-Bailey (2009) found mentoring, with detailed, instructionally linked feedback produced greater teacher and child improvement than mentoring or feedback alone. Professional development in the areas of positive behavioral supports and emergent literacy has utilized on-site coaching and mentoring models to build teacher knowledge in the classroom context. For example, in an assessment of the effects of in-classroom coaching on early childhood teachers' use of emergent literacy teaching strategies, Hsieh, Hemmeter, McCollum, and Ostrosky (2009) found that in-class coaching consisting of (a) initial group meetings to introduce new teaching strategies, (b) semi-weekly observations with follow-up discussions of the data collected during the observation, and (c) a booster component when the teacher did not achieve preestablished criteria was successful in increasing the number of teaching strategies. Many professional development programs implement coaching as just one component of the professional development plan. Neuman and Cunningham (2009) found that coaching along with coursework demonstrated higher quality practices than professional development workshops or coursework alone.

Some of the research on in-service personnel preparation has suggested areas for improvement. For example, Campbell and Sawyer (2009) trained home visitors to use the participation-based approach with families. The authors utilized PowerPoint and picture and video examples over two time periods and three activities to train home visitors on the collaborative approach to working with families of young children with disabilities. They found that 60% of home visitors implemented the recommended approach following training, but that 40% continued to use a traditional approach with families (Campbell & Sawyer, 2009). The authors suggested that home visitors should have received more intensive training (i.e., more time periods) and more frequent feedback between sessions. They also recommended the use of a needs assessment and follow-up application activities in the participants' work settings as part of their professional development approach for training home visitors. Current practice suggests that the field of EI/ECSE has far to go to implement these recommendations.

Policy and professional development oversight in EI/ECSE systems of service delivery will need to respond to growing evidence that workshop trainings, in isolation, are insufficient methods of improving EI/ECSE educators' skills and improving child outcomes. Professional development for EI/ECSE educators will need to become more connected and integrated across systems so that these efforts can be monitored and evaluated for effectiveness.

Technology

We shift now to a discussion of how personnel preparation is delivered, and the use of technology in personnel preparation activities such as online preservice training or online modules for professional development, and remote/online video-based coaching or feedback on teachers' performance. Technology's use in professional development has received increased attention given its availability and reduced costs and the advantages of using technology to break free of geographical and/or time constraints (see Smith & Kennedy, Chapter 11, this volume).

Various models of personnel preparation now incorporate different forms of technology into instructional delivery. For example, some preservice programs have utilized technology to deliver instruction online in university-based programs for early interventionists (e.g., Lifter et al., 2005). These preservice training programs are able to reach greater numbers of future practitioners and interventionists in more remote/rural areas where services for young children with disabilities are often needed. In another example, Chen, Klein, and Minor (2008) describe the development and successful implementation of an online course to train EI personnel to work with family members to promote interactions with their infants with multiple disabilities. Researchers have found that special education online courses have no significant differential outcomes from on-campus courses (e.g., Caywood & Duckett, 2003; Steinweg, Davis, & Thompson, 2005). Online course programs have also allowed colleges and universities to collaborate with faculty and students from a variety of locations. Caro, McLean, Browning, and Hains (2002) evaluated a collaborative distance education ECSE course for preservice teachers from six colleges and universities taught by eight faculty members from different institutions. This course was designed to address current issues and innovative practices in ECSE through videoconferencing, electronic mail, listservs, web-based discussions, and a web-based course management program, resulting in shared expertise and increased skills in distance learning technology.

Other recent work has compared the use of video-based online professional development with more traditional in-person coaching (e.g., Powell, Diamond, Burchinal, & Koehler, 2010). In a controlled evaluation of a language and literacy professional development intervention, Powell et al. found that when 88 Head Start teachers were randomly assigned to either remote (online) or in-person (on-site) professional development, no significant results on teaching practices or children's outcomes were noted between the two delivery types. All participants had attended a 2-day workshop on language and literacy skills and strategies, and each condition had access to additional resources and video exemplars. The on-site coaching group received individualized coaching after a scheduled observation session, whereas the remote group turned in 15-minutes video clips of their teaching practices and got video feedback from the coach. This research demonstrated that online professional development can be as effective as in-person coaching models. Mashburn, Downer, Hamre, Justice, and Pianta (2010) examined an online language and literacy professional development program, MyTeachingPartner (MTP), with teachers of young children considered at-risk for school failure. The 134 prekindergarten teachers in their study were randomly assigned to three study conditions: language and literacy activities only; language and literacy activities and access to the MTP video library which included annotated video exemplars of language and literacy instruction; or language and literacy activities, access to the video library, and participation in the MTP consultancy program (one-on-one web-based consultation on teacher-recorded interactions and instruction with students). Mashburn et al. (2010) found that children whose teachers utilized all elements of MTP had greater success in receptive language progress (particularly in vocabulary development) in their prekindergarten year than children whose teachers participated in the language and literacy activities or video exemplars only. Positive associations were noted between the amount of time a teacher used the MTP resources and children's receptive language skill development. Although it is noted that online professional development may be a more scalable, cost-effective, and flexible approach to professional development, challenges arise when the locations do not have access to the technology.

Advances in technology may allow for increases in research dissemination, more collaboration between EI/ECSE faculty across universities (Caro et al., 2002), and outreach to EI/ECSE practitioners who live or work in remote areas. Continual research of technology is needed in personnel preparation to keep up with technological advances and discover the most appropriate and effective forms of technology in our field.

Trends in Personnel Preparation in EI/ECSE

As special education is an ever-changing field, there are several new areas in EI/ECSE preparation that researchers and practitioners are currently exploring that will be critical to future preservice and professional development efforts. These areas include, but are not limited to, emergent literacy strategies, emergent mathematics strategies, Response to Intervention (RTI), positive behavioral intervention and supports (PBIS), infant mental health, and the classroom environment. Each of these topics and their relevance for EI/ECSE personnel preparation is described in more detail in this section.

Emergent Literacy Strategies

Emergent literacy refers to the knowledge about reading and writing that children typically acquire before formal schooling (Justice & Pullen, 2003). Educators in EI/ECSE need to be aware of the precursors of reading (e.g., phonological awareness, alphabet knowledge, print and letter awareness) and the reading strategies used with typically developing children (e.g., shared storybook reading, decoding; National Early Literacy Panel [NELP], 2008). They must also be aware of the literature on emergent literacy strategies and characteristics of children with multiple risk factors for reading difficulties (e.g., Al Otaiba & Fuchs, 2006; Justice, 2006). For example, current research supports the importance of a home literacy environment (e.g., Briet-Smith, Cabell, & Justice, 2010; NELP, 2008), and strategies such as structured phonological awareness activities and literacy-enriched play (Justice & Pullen, 2003). While this area of research is still growing, personnel should be trained in the most successful practices of emergent literacy and how to adapt these specifically for young children with disabilities. This is particularly important given recent research that suggests that educators working with young children exhibit low levels of literacy instruction (e.g., Justice, Mashburn, Hamre, & Pianta, 2008) and have gaps in their knowledge of emergent literacy content and skills (e.g., Powell, Diamond, Bojczyk, & Gerde, 2008).

Emergent Mathematics Strategies

With the recent emphasis on science, technology, engineering, and mathematics (STEM) at the elementary and secondary levels, researchers are turning to focus on math for young children, including those with disabilities. Greary (2004) found that 5%–8% of school age children have a deficit that interferes with mathematical development. Further, 7% of students will be identified as having a math disability, and 10% will exhibit persistent math difficulties (Greary, Hoard, Nugent, & Bailey, 2011). On the other hand, it is well documented that young children are developmentally ready for mathematics instruction (Arnold, Fisher, Doctoroff, & Dobbs, 2002), and EI can help preschoolers build the foundation for mathematical knowledge (Clements & Sarama, 2008). Arnold et al. (2002) found that when Head Start teachers implemented mathematics activities throughout the day, preschoolers' interest in math increased, as well as their math skills. Further, when teachers simply increased the amount of "math talk" throughout the day, children exhibited mathematical growth in the classroom (Klibanoff, Levine, Huttenlocher, Vasiljeva, & Hedges, 2006).

Two important preschool predictors of later math achievement include number sense and counting (Aunola, Leskinen, Lerkkanen, & Nurme, 2004; Jordan, Kaplan, Locuniak, & Ramineni, 2007). Gersten, Jordan, and Flojo (2005) stressed that the goals for math instruction for young children with math difficulties should include increasing a child's fluency and accuracy with basic arithmetic combinations and developing mature and efficient counting strategies, as well as the foundational principles of number sense. Foundations in math and science will be important additions to future personnel preparation in EI/ECSE.

Response to Intervention

Response to Intervention (RTI) is designed to provide prevention and intervention as well as to provide an alternative assessment process for children with learning disabilities in elementary and secondary settings (National Center on RTI, 2012). RTI consists of tiered intervention at the universal (classroom-wide interventions), secondary (small group interventions), and tertiary (individualized interventions) levels and is being adapted for use at the preschool level. Those working in EI/ECSE have particular challenges with RTI for young children as assessments are not readily available and may not be sensitive to the academic growth of young children with disabilities (Brownell, Ross, Colón & McCallum, 2005). One example of current research on RTI for preschoolers is a study of Recognition and Response (R & R), a three-tiered pyramid model (Buysse & Peisner-Feinberg, 2010) designed to enhance the academic skills of children enrolled in center-based early childhood programs. In another example, a consortium is focusing on early intervening services based on RTI (Greenwood et al., 2011). The use of RTI is an area of emerging study in EI/ECSE and will be an important component of curricula for future EI/ECSE personnel preparation.

Positive Behavioral Intervention and Supports

The need for behavior support in early childhood settings is great (Hemmeter, Fox, Jack, & Broyles, 2007). The school-wide positive behavioral interventions and supports (SW-PBIS) model has been studied for over a decade in elementary and secondary settings as one way to reduce students' challenging behavior, teach appropriate social skills, and improve school safety and a sense of community (e.g., Sugai & Horner, 2006). Program-wide PBIS is the adaptation of the SW-PBIS model for early learning environments and it focuses on reducing young children's challenging behavior while teaching developmentally appropriate social skills (Hemmeter et al., 2007). Fox and colleagues (Fox, Dunlap, Hemmeter, Joseph, & Strain, 2003) developed a framework for understanding the application of PBIS to early childhood classrooms. Similar to RTI, their Teaching Pyramid model includes four tiers. The first tier includes high-quality supportive environments followed by the second tier of nurturing and responsive relationships. These two tiers involve universal practices that are directed at all children, families, and teaching staff. Caregivers provide positive, supportive relationships with the children that may result in children focusing on adult directions, seeking positive attention, and reducing challenging behavior (Fox et al., 2003). Children who do not respond to the universal tier may require small group or targeted support focused on social/emotional supports or secondary tier prevention. Secondary interventions require more focused, explicit interventions, and may target social and emotional competence behaviors such as friendship skills, problem solving, and identification of emotions (Fox & Hemmeter, 2009; Green, Mays, & Jolivette, 2011). The final tier—intensive interventions or tertiary prevention—is designed to support children who do not respond to the universal or secondary preventative PBIS tiers (Fox & Hemmeter, 2009). In EI/ECSE, these intensive tertiary supports may be developed for home, early education, and/or community settings (Fox et al., 2003), and a functional behavior assessment should be conducted to discover the function of the undesired behaviors. As the implementation of program-wide PBIS in early childhood settings becomes increasingly popular, early childhood practitioners will need to have knowledge of the framework and associated implementation strategies.

Infant Mental Health

Infant mental health (IMH) has emerged as an important area of multidisciplinary study and treatment research in fields such as genetics, basic neuroscience, developmental psychopathology, and clinical disorders (Zeanah & Zeanah, 2009). Within the first five years of life, children are the most vulnerable to violence, neglect, and accidents, resulting in death or injury, as the emotional well-being, environment, and circumstances of life profoundly affect family relationships (Osofsky & Lieberman, 2011). The definition of IMH includes the developing capacity for young children to form close and secure relationships, experience and express emotions, and learn and explore within a caring family and community environment (Parlakian & Seibel, 2002; Zero to Three, 2001). Risk and protective factors for infants and young children's social-emotional and cognitive competence include individual child characteristics (e.g., genetic predispositions; cognitive strengths and limitations), parent characteristics (e.g., parental mental health; sense of efficacy; levels of education), family factors (e.g., quality of relationships between parent and child; emotional climate), community connectedness (e.g., social resources and support), and neighborhood factors (e.g., availability of resources; housing; crime and violence; Sameroff & Fiese, 2000).

Osofsky and Lieberman (2011) proposed a focus on collaboration between psychologists and EI intervention disciplines in personnel preparation (within didactic courses, practicum experiences, and internships) in order to serve children and families, focusing on intervention and prevention with children at-risk as early as possible. As risk factors for infants and young children are influenced by their own predispositions, as well as family, community, and neighborhood characteristics (Sameroff & Fiese, 2000), Osofsky and Lieberman suggested educating professionals with the theoretical perspective of an ecological–transactional model of development (e.g., Bronfenbrenner & Morris, 2006). Personnel preparation courses that focus on collaboration in EI should not only prepare educators to work with other professionals, but also with families, caregivers, and service systems.

Classroom Environment

As young children move into classrooms, the quality of the classroom environment and teacher–child relationships influences children's social-emotional and academic outcomes. Classroom environments deemed positive by assessment tools have been associated with improved academic performance, less challenging behaviors (Rimm-Kaufman, LaParo, Downer, & Pianta, 2005), better cognitive and behavioral self-control and work habits (Rimm-Kaufman, Curby, Grimm, Nathanson, & Brock, 2009), and positive effects on language and literacy skills (Dickinson, McCabe, & Essex, 2006). Conversely, poorer classroom environments have been linked to a lack of academic focus, poor peer relationships, and challenging behaviors (Barth, Dunlap, Dane, Lochman, & Wells, 2004).

Validated assessment tools are now being used to determine the quality of EI/ECSE classrooms. The Classroom Assessment Scoring System (CLASS; LaParo, Pianta, & Stuhlman, 2004) was developed in order to measure classroom quality in three domains of emotional support, classroom organization, and instructional climate. This observational tool measures the nature and form of the emotional and instructive climate while assessing the prekindergarten classroom as a learning environment (Pianta et al., 2005). Researchers have found the CLASS to be applicable for assessing interactions in classrooms with ethnic and language diversity (Downer et al., 2012), as well as for classrooms outside the U.S. (Pakarinen et al., 2010). The Early Language Literacy Classroom Observation Tool (ELLCO; Smith & Dickinson, 2002) focuses on the quality of literacy in the preschool classroom using observation, a literacy checklist, and rating scale while the Early Childhood Environment Rating Scale-Revised (ECERS-R; Harms, Clifford, & Cryer, 1998) and the Infant/Toddler Environment Rating Scale-Revised, Updated (ITERS-R; Harms, Cryer, & Clifford, 2006) measure the classroom environment encompassing the physical environment, materials, and child–teacher interactions. The ECERS-R has widespread use in childcare settings and is currently the primary assessment for measuring classroom quality in early childhood education (Tout, Zaslow, Halle, & Forry, 2009). Personnel preparation programs in EI/ECSE will need to assure that students are well trained in the use of such instruments.

Conclusions

Personnel preparation in EI/ECSE is at an exciting crossroads. There is important national attention on the vital importance of working with children at very young ages. Standards have been developed and validated, program models have been tested, and content and instructional strategies at the preservice and in-service levels are understood; however there are few comprehensive studies to validate certain approaches or components and in fact, there seems to be a schism between best practice recommendations and how teachers in EI/ECSE are actually prepared. Now more research to fully understand what occurs during preservice training, including field experiences; the impact on use of recommended practices in the field; and how EI/ECSE personnel are prepared to work on current issues is needed. We must also extend the research beyond preservice training to professional development in order to understand how to effectively promote EI/ECSE educators' ongoing skills in improving child and family outcomes since we know that practices such as coaching appear to be much more effective than traditional workshop approaches. Indeed, Snyder, Hemmeter, and McLaughlin (2012) urge us to fully define the structural and process features of professional development and analyze components of professional development interactions to understand how and when and for whom professional development is best delivered.

Appendix: Resources for Personnel Preparation in Early Childhood Special Education

1. *Center on the Social and Emotional Foundations for Early Learning (CSEFEL)*
   CSEFEL, a national resource center funded by the Office of Head Start and the Child Care Bureau, focuses on the promotion of social emotional and school readiness of children ages birth to five. CSEFEL disseminates research and evidence-based practices on social and emotional competence in infants and young children through training materials, videos, and print resources provided to faculty, professional development providers, and practitioners. These materials and information are available on the CSEFEL website: http://csefel.vanderbilt.edu/
2. *CONNECT*
   CONNECT, the Center to Mobilize Early Childhood Knowledge, is a web-based resource for faculty and professional development providers designed to build early childhood practitioners' abilities to make evidence-based decisions. Online modules are designed using a problem-solving process with a dilemma commonly found in EI/ECSE. Topics include, but are not limited to, embedded interventions, transitions, communication for collaboration, family and professional partnerships, and assistive technology. These online modules are available on the CONNECT website: http://community.fpg.unc.edu/connect
3. *Division of Early Childhood (DEC) Monographs*
   DEC of the Council for Exceptional Children provides monographs related to topics in EI/ECSE. These include, but are not limited to, supporting and working with families, inclusion, autism, early literacy, interdisciplinary teams, and working with children with challenging behaviors. DEC Monographs are available through the DEC website: http://www.dec-sped.org
4. *International Society on Early Intervention (ISEI)*
   Composed of researchers, clinicians, policy makers, and individuals from biomedical and behavioral disciplines, ISEI, in partnership with the Association of University Centers on Disabilities (AUCD), provides a framework and forum for professionals from around the world to communicate about advances in EI. The ISEI website includes a Professional Training Resource Library (PTRL), a searchable, web-based library with a wide range of free materials to support professional training in EI. The types of materials located in the library include, but are not limited to, assessment tools, internship guidelines, course syllabi, modules, and case studies. These resources can be found at the ISEI website: http://depts.washington.edu/isei/
5. *Personnel Preparation in Early Childhood Special Education: Implementing the DEC Recommended Practices (Stayton, Miller, & Dinnebeil, 2003)*
   This resource provides guidance in the application of DEC's personnel preparation recommended practices for young children ages birth to five. Including case studies and assessment checklists, this tool is designed for faculty and practitioners to guide special educators with the knowledge they need in order to meet their job requirements. It is available to purchase from the DEC website: http://www.dec-sped.org/Store/Recommended_Practices
6. *Technical Assistance Center on Social Emotional Intervention for Young Children (TACSEI)*
   TACSEI creates free products and resources using current research that shows improved social emotional outcomes for young children with, or at-risk for, delays or disabilities. These products and resources are designed to help decision makers, caregivers, and service providers apply best

practices in their work. These resources are available on the website: http://www.challengingbehavior.org/

7. *Center for Response to Intervention in Early Childhood (CRTIEC)*
   CRTIEC is a consortium of researchers looking at early intervening services that are based on the RTI model. They share research and presentations that focus on progress monitoring measures and validated interventions in language and early literacy at the Tier 2 and 3 levels. The information is available on the website: http://www.crtiec.org

References

Al Otaiba, S., & Fuchs, D. (2006). Who are the young children for whom best practices in reading are ineffective: An experimental and longitudinal study. *Journal of Learning Disabilities, 39*, 414–431. doi:10.1177/00222194060390050401

Applequist, K. L., McLellan, M. J., & McGrath, E. R. (2010). The apprenticeship model: Assessing competencies of early intervention practitioners. *Infants and Young Children, 23*, 23–33. doi:10.1097/IYC.0b013e3181c975d5

Arnold, D. H., Fisher, P. H., Doctoroff, G. L., & Dobbs, J. (2002). Accelerating math development in Head Start classrooms. *Journal of Educational Psychology, 94*, 762–770. doi:10.1037/0022-0663.94.4.762

Aunola, K., Leskinen, E., Lerkkanen, M. K., & Nurmi, J. E. (2004). Developmental dynamics of math performance from preschool to grade 2. *Journal of Educational Psychology, 96*, 699–713. doi:10.1037/0022-0663.96.4.699

Barth, J. M., Dunlap, S. T., Dane, H., Lochman, J. E., & Wells, K. C. (2004). Classroom environment influences on aggression, peer relations, and academic focus. *Journal of School Psychology, 42*, 115–133.

Bernheimer, L. P., & Weisner, T. S. (2007). "Let me just tell you what I do all day…": The family story at the center of intervention research and practice. *Infants and Young Children, 20*, 192–201. doi:10.1097/01.IYC.0000277751.62819.9b

Bredekamp, S. (1993). The relationship between early childhood education and early childhood special education: Healthy marriage or family feud? *Topics in Early Childhood Special Education, 13*, 258–273. doi:10.1177/027112149301300305

Briet-Smith, A., Cabell, S. Q., & Justice, L. M. (2010). Home literacy experiences and early childhood disability: A descriptive study using the National Household Education Surveys (NHES) program database. *Language, Speech, and Hearing Sciences, 41*, 96–107. doi:10.1044/0161-1461(2009/08-0048)

Bronfenbrenner, U., & Morris, P. A. (2006). The bioecological model of human development. In R. M. Lerner (Ed.). *Handbook of child psychology: Vol. 1. Theoretical models of human development* (6th ed., pp. 793–828). New York, NY: Wiley.

Brownell, M. T., Ross, D. D., Colón, E. P., & McCallum, C. L. (2005). Critical features of special education teacher preparation: A comparison with in general teacher education. *Journal of Special Education, 38*, 242–252. doi:10.1177/00224669050380040601

Bruder, M. B., & Dunst, C. J. (2005). Personnel preparation in recommended early intervention practices: Degree of emphasis across disciplines. *Topics in Early Childhood Special Education, 25*, 25–33. doi:10.1177/02711214050250010301

Bush Administration's Early Childhood Initiative. (2002). Good Start Grow Smart: The Bush Administration Early Childhood Initiative. Retrieved from http://georgewbush-whitehouse.archives.gov/infocus/earlychildhood/toc.html

Butera, G. (1993). *Practitioner perspectives of early childhood special educators: Implications for personnel preparation.* (ERIC ED358998)

Buysse, V., & Hollingsworth, H. L. (2009). Program quality and early childhood inclusion: Recommendations for professional development. *Topics in Early Childhood Special Education, 29*, 119–128. doi:10.1177/0271121409332233

Buysse, V., & Peisner-Feinberg, E. (2010). Recognition and response: Response to intervention for PreK. *Young Exceptional Children, 13*, 2–13. doi:10.1177/1096250610373586

Campbell, P. H., & Sawyer, L. B. (2009). Changing early intervention providers' home visiting skills through participation in professional development. *Topics in Early Childhood Special Education, 28*, 219–234. doi:10.1177/0271121408328481

Caro, P., McLean, M., Browning, E., & Hains, A. (2002). The use of distance education in a collaborative course in early childhood special education. *Teacher Education and Special Education, 25*, 333–341. doi:10.1177/088840640202500402

Caywood, K., & Duckett, J. (2003). Online vs. on-campus learning in teacher education. *Teacher Education and Special Education, 26*, 98–105. doi:10.1177/088840640302600203

Chandler, L. K., Cochran, D. C., Christensen, K. A., Dinnebeil, L. A., Gallagher, P. A., Lifter, K., ... Spino, M. (2012). The alignment of CEC/DEC and NAEYC personnel preparation standards. *Topics in Early Childhood Special Education, 32*, 52–63. doi:10.1177/0271121412437047

Chang, F., Early, D. M., & Winton, P. J. (2005). Early childhood teacher preparation in special education at 2- and 4-year institutions of higher education. *Journal of Early Intervention, 27*, 110–124. doi:10.1177/105381510502700206

Chen, D., Klein, M. D., & Minor, L. (2008). Online professional development for early interventionists. *Infants and Young Children, 21*, 120–133. doi:10.1097/01.IYC.0000314483.62205.34

Clements, D. H., & Sarama, J. (2008). Experimental evaluation of the effects of a research-based preschool mathematics curriculum. *American Educational Research Journal, 45*, 443–494. doi:10.3102/0002831207312908

Cochran, D. C., Gallagher, P. A., Stayton, V. D., Dinnebeil, L. A., Lifter, K., Chandler, L. K., & Christensen, K. A. (2012). Early Childhood Special Education and Early Intervention personnel preparation standards of the Division for Early Childhood: Field validation. *Topics in Early Childhood Special Education, 32*, 38–51. doi:10.1177/0271121412436696

Cochran-Smith, M. (2005). Studying teacher education: What we know and need to know. *Journal of Teacher Education, 56*, 301–306. doi:10.1177/0022487105280116

Cochran-Smith, M., & Zeichner, K. (2005). *Studying teacher education: The report of the AERA panel on research and teacher education*. Mahwah, NJ: Lawrence Erlbaum.

Dickinson, D. K., McCabe, A., & Essex, M. (2006). A window of opportunity we must open to all: The case for preschool with high-quality support for language and literacy. In S. B. Neuman & D. K. Dickinson (Eds). *Handbook of early literacy, Volume 2* (pp. 11–28). New York, NY: Guilford Press.

Downer, J. T., Lopez, M. L., Grimm, K. J., Hamagami, A., Pianta, R. C., & Howe, C. (2012). Observations of teacher-child interactions in classrooms serving Latinos and dual language learners: Applicability of the Classroom Assessment Scoring System in diverse settings. *Early Childhood Research Quarterly, 27*, 21–32.

Dunst, C. J. (2002). Family centered practices: Birth through high school. *Journal of Special Education, 36*, 141–149. doi:10.1177/00224669020360030401

Dunst, C. J., & Raab, M. (2010). Practitioners' self-evaluations of contrasting types of professional development. *Journal of Early Intervention, 32*, 239–254. doi:10.1177/1053815110384702

Dunst, C. J., & Trivette, C. M. (2009). Let's be PALS: An evidence-based approach to professional development. *Infants and Young Children, 22*, 164–176. doi:10.1097/IYC.0b013e3181abe169

Early, D., & Winton, P. (2001). Preparing the workforce: Early childhood teacher preparation at 2- and 4-year institute of higher education. *Early Childhood Research Quarterly, 16*, 285–306. doi:10.1016/50885-2006(01)00106-5

Farkas, S., Johnson, J., & Duffett, A. (2003). *Stand by me: What teachers say about unions, merit pay, and other professional matters*. New York: Public Agenda.

Fixsen, D. L., & Blase, K. A. (2009). Technical assistance in special education: Past, present, and future. *Topics in Early Childhood Special Education, 29*, 62–64. doi:10.1177/0271121409333795

Fixsen, D. L., Naoom, S. F., Blase, K. A., Friedman, R. M., & Wallace, F. (2005). *Implementation research: A synthesis of the literature*. Tampa, FL: University of South Florida, Louis de la Parte Florida Mental Health Institute.

Fox, L. Dunlap, G., Hemmeter, M. L., Joseph, G., & Strain, P. (2003). The Teaching Pyramid: A model for supporting social competence and preventing challenging behavior in young children. *Young Children, 58*, 48–52.

Fox, L., & Hemmeter, M. L. (2009). A program-wide model for supporting social emotional development and addressing challenging behavior in early childhood settings. In W. Sailor, G. Dunlap, G. Sugai, & R. Horner (Eds.), *Handbook of positive behavior support* (pp. 177–202). New York, NY: Springer.

Friend, M., & Cook, L. (2010). Families. (184–208). *Interactions: Collaboration skills for school professionals*. Boston, MA: Pearson.

Fults, R. M., & Harry, B. (2012). Combining family centeredness and diversity in early childhood teacher training programs. *Teacher Education and Special Education, 35*, 27–48. doi:10.1177/0888406411399784

Gallagher, P. A., Abbott-Shim, M., & VandeWiele, L. (2011). An evaluation of the Individualized Learning Intervention: A mentoring program for early childhood teachers. *NHSA Dialog, 14*, 57–74.

Gallagher, P., Malone, D. M., Cleghorne, M., & Helms, K. A. (1997). Perceived inservice training needs for early intervention personnel. *Exceptional Children, 64*, 19–30.

Geiger, W. L., Crutchfield, M., & Mainzer, R. (2003) *The status of licensure of special education teachers at the beginning of the 21st century* (COPSSE Document No. RS-7E). Gainesville, FL: Center on Personnel Studies in Special Education.

Gersten, R., Jordan, N. C., & Flojo, J. R. (2005). Early identification and interventions for students with mathematical difficulties. *Journal of Learning Disabilities, 38*, 293–304. doi:10.1177/00222194050380040301

Greary, D. C. (2004). Mathematics and learning disabilities. *Journal of Learning Disabilities, 37*, 4–15. doi:10.1177/00222194040370010201

Greary, D. C., Hoard, M. K., Nugent, L., & Bailey, D. H. (2011). Mathematical cognition deficits in children with learning disabilities and persistent low achievement: A five-year prospective study. *Journal of Educational Psychology, 104*, 206–223. doi:10.1037/a0025398

Green, K. B., Mays, N. M., & Jolivette, K. (2011). Making choices: A proactive way to improve behaviors for young children with challenging behaviors. *Beyond Behavior, 20*, 25–31.

Greenwood, C. R., Bradfield, T., Kaminski, R., Linas, M. W., Carta, J. J., & Nylander, D. (2011). The response to intervention (RTI) approach in early childhood. *Focus on Exceptional Children, 43*(9), 1–22.

Grisham-Brown, J., Pretti-Frontczak, K., Hawkins, S. R., & Winchell, B. N. (2009). Addressing early learning standards for all children within blended preschool classrooms. *Topics in Early Childhood Special Education, 29*, 131–142. doi:10.1177/0271121409333796

Guskey, T. R. (2003). What makes professional development effective? *Phi Delta Kappan, 84* (10), 748–750.

Hanline, M. F. (2010). Preservice teachers' perceptions of field experiences in inclusive preschool settings: Implications for personnel preparation. *Teacher Education and Special Education, 33*, 335–351. doi:10.1177/0888406409360144

Harms, T., Clifford, R. M., & Cryer, D. (1998). *Early Childhood Environment Rating Scale-R (Revised)*. New York: Teachers College Press.

Harms, T., Cryer, D., & Clifford, R. M. (2006). *Infant/Toddler Environment Rating Scale-Revised, Updated (ITERS-R)*. New York:Teachers College Press.

Hemmeter, M. L., Fox, L., Jack, S., & Broyles, L. (2007). A program-wide model of positive behavior support in early childhood settings. *Journal of Early Intervention, 29*, 337–355. doi:10.1177/105381510702900405

Hemmeter, M. L., Santos, R. M., & Ostrosky, M. M. (2008). Preparing early childhood educators to address young children's social-emotional development and challenging behavior: A survey of higher education programs in nine states. *Journal of Early Intervention, 30*, 321–340. doi:10.1177/1053815108320900

Hsieh, W. Y., Hemmeter, M. L., McCollum, J. A., & Ostrosky, M. M. (2009). Using coaching to increase preschool teachers' use of emergent literacy teaching strategies. *Early Childhood Research Quarterly, 24*, 229–247. doi:10.1016/j.ecresq.2009.03.007

Individuals with Disabilities Education Act Amendments, 20 U.S.C. & 1400 *et seq.* (1997).

Individuals with Disabilities Education Improvement Act of 2004. Pub. L. No. 108-446 (2004).

Jordan, N. C., Kaplan, D., Locuniak, M. N., & Ramineni, C. (2007). Predicting first grade math achievement from developmental number sense trajectories. *Learning Disabilities Research and Practice, 22*, 36–46. doi:10.1111/j.1540-5826.2007.00229.x

Joyce, B., & Showers, B. (2002). *Student achievement through staff development* (3rd ed.). Alexandria, VA: Association for Supervision and Curriculum Development.

Justice, L. M. (2006). Evidence-based practice, response to intervention, and the prevention of reading difficulties. *Language, Speech, and Hearing Services in Schools, 37*, 284–297. doi:10.1044/0161-1461(2006/033)

Justice, L. M., Mashburn, A., Hamre, B., & Pianta, R. (2008). Quality of language and literacy instruction in preschool classrooms service at-risk pupils. *Early Childhood Research Quarterly, 23*, 51–68. doi:10.1016/j.ecresq.2007.09.004

Justice, L. M., & Pullen, P. C. (2003). Promising interventions for promoting emergent literacy skills: Three evidence-based approaches. *Topics in Early Childhood Special Education, 23*, 99–113. doi:10.1177/02711214030230030101

Kampwirth, T. J., & Powers, K. P. (2012). Consulting with parents and families (p. 58–62). In T. J. Kampwirth & K. P. Powers, *Collaborative consultation in the schools: Effective practices for students with learning and behavior problems* (4th ed.). Boston, MA: Pearson.

Kilgo, J., & Aldridge, J. (2011). Using cases to teach teams of professionals: Lessons learned from transdisciplinary early intervention/education seminars. *Focus on Inclusive Education, 8*, 4–7.

Klibanoff, R. S., Levine, S. C., Huttenlocher, J., Vasiljeva, M., & Hedges, L. V. (2006). Preschool children's mathematical knowledge: The effect of teacher "Math Talk". *Developmental Psychology, 42*, 59–69. doi:10.1037/0012-1649.42.1.59

Landry, S. H., Anthony, J. L., Swank, P. R., & Monseque-Bailey, P. (2009). Effectiveness of comprehensive professional development for teachers of at-risk preschoolers. *Journal of Educational Psychology, 101*, 448–465. doi:10.1037/a0013842

LaParo, K., Pianta, R. C., & Stuhlman, M. (2004). Classroom Assessment Scoring System (CLASS): Findings from the pre-k year. *The Elementary School Journal, 10*, 409–426.

Lee, H., Ostrosky, M. M., Bennett, T., & Fowler, S. A. (2003). Perspectives of early intervention professionals about culturally-appropriate practices. *Journal of Early Intervention, 25*, 281–295. doi:10.1177/105381510302500404

Lifter, K., Chandler, L. K., Cochran, D. C., Dinnebeil, L. A., Gallagher, P. A., Christensen, K. A., & Stayton, V. D. (2011). DEC Personnel preparation standards: Revision 2005–2008. *Journal of Early Intervention, 33*, 151–167. doi:10.1177/1053815111418975

Lifter, K., Kruger, L., Okun, B., Tabol, C., Poklop, L., & Shishmanian, E. (2005). Transformation to a web-based preservice training program: A case study. *Topics in Early Childhood Special Education, 25*, 15–24. doi:10.1177/02711214050250010201

Macy, M., Squires, J. K., & Barton, E. E. (2009). Providing optimal opportunities: Structuring practicum experiences in early intervention and early childhood special education preservice programs. *Topics in Early Childhood Special Education, 28*, 209–218. doi:10.1177/0271121408327227

Mashburn, A. J., Downer, J. T., Hamre, B. K., Justice, L. M., & Pianta, R. C. (2010). Consultation for teachers and children's language and literacy development during pre-kindergarten. *Applied Developmental Science, 14*, 179–196. doi:10.1080/10888691.2010.516187

Maxwell, K. L., Lim, C., & Early, D. (2006). *Early childhood teacher preparation programs in the United States: National Report*. Chapel Hill, NC: University of North Carolina, FPG Child Development Institute.

National Center on RTI. (2012). *American Institutes for Research launch new RTI Center*. Retrieved from www.air.org/focus-area/education

National Early Literacy Panel (NELP). (2008). *Developing early literacy: Report of the National Early Literacy Panel*. Washington, DC: National Institute for Literacy.

National Professional Development Center on Inclusion. (2011). *Competencies for early childhood educators in the context of inclusion: Issues and guidance for states*. Retrieved from http://npdci.fpg.unc.edu/

Neuman, S. B., & Cunningham, L. (2009). The impact of professional development and coaching on early language and literacy instructional practices. *American Educational Research Journal, 46*, 532–566. doi:10.3102/0002831208328088

No Child Left Behind Act of 2001, Pub. L. No. 107-110 (2002).

Osofsky, J. D., & Lieberman, A. F. (2011). A call for integrating a mental health perspective into systems of care for abused and neglected infants and young children. *American Psychologist, 66*, 120–128. doi:10.1037/a0021630

Pakarinen, E., Lerkkanen, M. K., Poikkeus, A. M., Kiuru, N., Siekkinen, M., Rasku-Puttonen, H., & Nurmi, J. E. (2010). A validation of the Classroom Assessment Scoring System in Finnish kindergartens. *Early Education and Development, 21*, 95–124. doi:10.1080/10409280902858764

Parlakian, R., & Seibel, N. L. (2002). *Building strong foundations: Practical guidance for promoting the social-emotional development of infants and toddlers*. Washington, DC: Zero to Three.

Piaget, J. (1970). Piaget's theory. In P. Mussen (Ed.), *Carmichael's manual of child psychology* (Vol. 1, pp. 703–732). New York, NY: John Wiley.

Pianta, R., Howes, C., Burchinal, M., Bryant, D., Clifford, R., Early, D., & Barbarin, O. (2005). Features of pre-kindergarten programs, classrooms, and teachers: Do they predict observed classroom quality and child-teacher interactions? *Applied Developmental Science, 9*, 144–159. doi:10.1207/s1532480xads0903_2

Powell, D. R., Diamond, K. E., Bojczyk, K. E., & Gerde, H. K. (2008). Head Start teachers' perspectives on early literacy. *Journal of Literacy Research, 40*, 422–460. doi:10.1080/10862960802637612

Powell, D. R., Diamond, K. E., Burchinal, M. R., & Koehler, M. J. (2010). Effects of an early literacy professional development intervention on Head Start teachers and children. *Journal of Educational Psychology, 102*, 299–312. doi:10.1037/a0017763

Pugach, M. C., Blanton, L. P., & Correa, V. I. (2011). A historical perspective on the role of collaboration in teacher education reform: Making good on the promise of teaching all students. *Teacher Education and Special Education, 34*, 183–200. doi:10.1177/0888406411406141

Race to the Top—Early Learning Challenge Grant Application. (2011). Retrieved from www2.ed.gov/programs/racetothetop-earlylearningchallenge/

Rimm-Kaufman, S. E., Curby, T. W., Grimm, K. J., Nathanson, L., & Brock, L. L. (2009). The contribution of children's self-regulation and classroom quality to children's adaptive behaviors in the kindergarten classroom. *Developmental Psychology, 45*, 958–972. doi:10.1037/a0015861

Rimm-Kaufman, S. E., LaParo, K. M., Downer, J. T., & Pianta, R. C. (2005). The contribution of classroom setting and quality of instruction to children's behavior in kindergarten classrooms. *The Elementary School Journal, 105*, 377–394. doi:10.1086/429948

Sameroff, A. J., & Chandler, M. J. (1975). Reproductive risk and the continuum of caretaking casualty. In F. D. Horowitz, E. M. Hetherington, S. Scarr-Salapatek, & G. M. Siegel (Eds.), *Review of child development research* (Vol. 4, pp. 187–244). Chicago, IL: University of Chicago Press.

Sameroff, A. J., & Fiese, B. H. (2000). Transactional regulation: The developmental ecology of early intervention. In J. P. Shonkoff & S. J. Meisels (Eds.), *Handbook of early childhood intervention* (pp. 135–159). New York, NY: Cambridge University Press. doi:10.1017/CBO9780511529320.009

Sandall, S., Hemmeter, M. L., Smith, B. J., & McLean, M. E. (2005). *DEC Recommended practices: A comprehensive guide for practical application*. Longmont, CO: Sopris West.

Scott-Little, C., Kagan, S. L., Frelow, V. S., & Reid, J. (2009). Infant-toddler early learning guidelines: The content that states have addressed and implications for programs serving children with disabilities. *Infants and Young Children, 22*, 87–99.

Smith, M., & Dickinson, D. (2002). *Early language and literacy classroom observation*. Baltimore, MD: Paul Brookes Publishing Co.

Snyder, P., Hemmeter, M. L., & McLaughlin, T. (2012). Professional development in early childhood intervention: Where we stand on the silver anniversary of PL 99-457. *Topics in Early Childhood Special Education, 33*, 357–370.

Snyder, P., & McWilliam, P. J. (2003). Using the case method of instruction effectively in early intervention personnel preparation. *Infants and Young Children, 16*, 284–295.

Stayton, V. D., Deitrich, S. L., Smith, B. J., Bruder, M. B., Mogro-Wilson, C., & Swigart, A. (2009). State certification requirements for early childhood special educators. *Infants and Young Children, 22*, 4–12.

Stayton, V. D., & McCollum, J. (2002). Unifying general and special education: What does the research tell us? *Teacher Education and Special Education, 25*, 211–218. doi:10.1177/088840640202500302

Stayton, V. D., Miller, P. S., & Dinnebeil, L. A. (Eds.). (2003). *DEC personnel preparation in early childhood special education: Implementing the DEC recommended practices*. Denver, CO: Sopris West.

Stayton, V. D., Whittaker, S., Jones, E., & Kersting, F. (2001). Interdisciplinary model for the preparation of related services and early intervention personnel. *Teacher Education and Special Education, 24*, 395–401. doi:10.1177/088840640102400414

Steinweg, S. B., Davis, M. L., & Thompson, W. S. (2005). A comparison of traditional and online instruction in an introduction to special education course. *Teacher Education and Special Education, 28*, 62–73. doi:10.1177/088840640502800107

Sugai, G., & Horner, R. R. (2006). A promising approach for expanding and sustaining school-wide positive behavior support. *School Psychology Review, 35*, 245–259.

Sunderman, G. L., Tracey, C. A., Kim, J., & Orfield, G. (2004). *Listening to teachers: Classroom realities and No Child Left Behind*. Cambridge, MA: The Civil Rights Project at Harvard University.

Tout, K., Zaslow, M., Halle, T., & Forry, N. (2009). Issues for the next decade of Quality Rating and Improvement Systems. OPRE Issue Brief #3, Publication #2009-014. Washington, DC: Child Trends.

Whitebrook, M., & Ryan, S. (April,2011). Degrees in context: Asking the right questions about preparing skilled and effective teachers of young children. *Preschool Policy Brief, 22*, New Brunswick, NJ: National Institute for Early Education Research.

Winton, P. J. (2006). The evidence-based practice movement and its effect on knowledge utilization. In V. Buysse & P. Wesley (Eds.), *Evidence-based practice in the early childhood field* (pp. 71–115). Washington, DC: Zero to Three.

Winton, P. J., & McCollum, J. A. (2008). Preparing and supporting high quality early childhood practitioners: Issues and evidence. In P. J. Winton, J. A. McCollum, & C. Catlett (Eds.), *Practical approaches to early childhood professional development: Evidence, strategies, and resources* (pp. 1–12). Washington, DC: Zero to Three.

Winton, P. J., McCollum, J. A., & Catlett, C. (Eds.). (2008). *Practical approaches to early childhood professional development: Evidence, strategies, and resources*. Washington, DC: Zero to Three.

Winton, P. J., McCollum, J. A., & Catlett, C. (Eds.). (1997). *Reforming personnel preparation in early intervention: Issues and practical strategies*. Baltimore, MD: Paul Brookes Publishing Co.

Zeanah, C. H., & Zeanah, P. D. (2009). The scope of infant mental health. In C. H. Zeanah (Ed.). *The handbook of infant mental health* (pp. 5–21). New York: Guilford.

Zero to Three. (2001). *Definition of infant mental health*. Washington, DC: Zero to Three Infant Mental Health Screening Committee.

24

Preparing Secondary Special Educators and Transition Specialists

Mary E. Morningstar and Beth Clavenna-Deane

UNIVERSITY OF KANSAS

Things to Think About

- Transition planning is a legally mandated part of secondary special education students, yet many secondary special educators are underprepared to plan and implement transition services.
- Preparation programs and content are often enhanced with support of federal funding.
- There are agreed upon transition-related competencies for both secondary special educators and transition specialists that are incorporated in preservice preparation and professional development programs with great variability.
- Preparation programs are likely to place appropriate emphasis on transition services when led by state certification and licensure requirements.
- More research is needed to determine the impact of transition-related teacher preparation on postschool outcomes for students with all types of disabilities.

Since 1990, and with subsequent amendments in 1997 and 2004, the transition provisions of the Individuals with Disabilities Education Act (IDEA) have been a strong impetus for special educators to assume a coordinated approach to delivering transition services. The mandate contains language identifying special education teachers as having primary responsibility for overseeing the planning and facilitation of school to adulthood transitions. Despite such requirements, students with disabilities continue to face postschool outcomes in which they are less prepared for adulthood than their peers without disabilities (Newman, Wagner, Cameto, & Knokey, 2009). One reason students with disabilities may face challenges during transition could be due in part to secondary special education teachers' feeling unprepared to plan for and deliver transition services (Li, Bassett, & Hutchison, 2009; Wolfe, Boone, & Blanchett, 1998). Effectively preparing transition educators requires focusing on knowledge and skills that are often beyond what is currently included in most special education teacher preparation programs (Anderson et al., 2003). Studies have revealed that special education teachers report a lack of knowledge of transition competencies and that this hinders their abilities to implement effective practices (Benitez, Morningstar, & Frey, 2009; Knott & Asselin, 1999). Consequently, teachers who are unprepared to plan and deliver transition services may be contributing to poor outcomes for students with disabilities.

Over the past three decades, a major focus of advocates, policy makers, educators, and parents has been to increase the adult opportunities and quality of life for students with disabilities. Given the changing roles of secondary special educators, it stands to reason that teacher education programs would respond accordingly. Unfortunately, this has not yet proven to be the case. In fact, findings from a national survey of special education personnel preparation programs revealed that less than half of the special education programs offered a stand-alone course devoted to transition (Anderson et al., 2003). Whether special education teacher education programs offer transition content and coursework is often dependent on state licensure requirements as well as federal and state funding and incentives promoting specialized content. Personnel development has been recognized as a central strategy for systems change and improvement among state educational agencies (Blalock et al., 2003); yet clear guidance has yet to emerge for ensuring high quality methods.

This chapter provides a foundation for rethinking current practices in preparing special education teachers to provide transition services. As such, it examines (a) the current state of practice in preparing teachers for transition teacher education, (b) the degree to which current preparation practices are resulting in secondary teachers who can deliver effective transition practices, (c) the factors influencing the delivery of effective transition, (d) research supporting comprehensive preparation programs, and (e) implications for future practice and research.

Transition Teacher Education Content and Delivery

Consensus exists that teacher education programs must ensure instructional content that addresses evidence-based transition practices. The Division of Career Development and Transition (DCDT) recommended that transition teacher education emphasize both instructional content as well as unique delivery systems:

1. Transition planning must provide a framework for aligning secondary curriculum and transition services for the individual student.
2. Quality preparation for P–16 instructional programs must include principles, models, and strategies proven to support career development and transition.
3. Higher education must increase inclusion of appropriate transition content across all personnel preparation programs.
4. Quality programs for transition specialists and secondary special educators are critical for creating improved outcomes for students.
5. Education systems must align efforts in order to improve quantity, quality, and diversity of personnel so that appropriate supports and services are available to reach postschool goals (Blalock et al., 2003).

Morningstar and Clark (2003) describe five broad content areas for teacher education programs targeting transition. The first area focuses on principles and concepts of transition education and services. This includes possessing thorough knowledge and application of the transition services requirements under the IDEA, as well as the emerging evidence-based practices that impact transition planning and the development of the IEP (e.g., student-directed IEP planning, family collaboration during transition planning).

The second content area targets transition evidence-based practices, pertaining to specific interventions for student-focused planning. This includes specific methods of instruction for certain disability groups, as well as cross-categorical approaches. Transition assessment methods used to determine postsecondary goals and track student progress is considered within this content area. Also considered are programmatic models that use student-centered planning for determining programs and services.

Strategies for developing, organizing, and implementing transition education and services make up the third major domain. This includes strategies for community-referenced curriculum and instruction, particularly targeting identified evidence-based practices (Alwell & Cobb, 2006; Kohler & Field, 2003; Test, Fowler, Kohler, & Kortering, 2010). Content focused on career development curriculum and work-based experiences, community-referenced instruction, preparation for postsecondary education and independent living, and planning and support for transition within general education classes are all subsumed under this area.

Interagency collaboration forms the basis of the fourth content area. Learning about community agencies, programs, services, and organizational and eligibility requirements are included. Maintaining professional ethics when interacting with outside agencies as well as families and other stakeholders is also considered in this domain. In addition, working with employers and the business community is essential.

The fifth area of focus is related to addressing systemic problems in transition service delivery. This involves the barriers inherent in planning, developing, and implementing transition services at the local, state, and federal levels. Examples include how governmental systems work and how to work within such systems; funding sources and skills in grant writing; policy issues and how to effect change; skills in promoting individual student and program interests within the school and in the community; child and labor laws regarding employment; and skills for participating in systemic change.

These five areas are consistent with research in the field regarding effective practices and research toward positive postschool outcomes (Alwell & Cobb, 2006; Kohler & Field, 2003; Test, Fowler et al., 2009). In addition, they reflect identified national transition training needs (Lattin, Dove, Morningstar, Kleinhammer-Tramill, & Frey, 2004). Most recently, efforts are underway to reexamine the national standards articulated in the CEC Advanced Standards for Transition Specialists, which are included in the publication, *What Every Special Educator Must Know* (Council for Exceptional Children, 2008) to better reflect both emerging research and the realities of secondary programs (Morningstar, Wade, & Benitez, 2012).

Even a brief look at the content areas demonstrates that special education teacher education programs do not sufficiently prepare transition knowledge and skills (Anderson et al., 2003). This is particularly evident when examining the typical methods for delivering transition content, in which programs that prepare special education teachers across all grade levels (K–12) are less likely to adequately cover even the essentials of secondary education, let alone transition planning.

Delivering Transition Content

Transition-specific content for teacher education has been validated by research over the past two decades (Benitez et al., 2009; Blalock et al., 2003; DeFur & Taymans, 1995; Severson, Hoover, & Wheeler, 1994), yet how content is delivered is varied. Morningstar and Clark (2003), describe four types of transition personnel preparation programs:

1. Transition master's programs (30 or more hours toward an advanced degree)
2. Transition-specialization programs (15 or fewer credit hours; focusing on a state endorsement or licensure program for transition specialists)
3. Transition class or classes
4. Transition content infused within existing courses.

Facilitative factors for *transition master's programs* have included both federal support for personnel preparation programs, as well as higher education institutional commitment to faculty specialization. Albeit very limited in numbers, long-standing transition master's programs are case examples of the importance of both federal and institutional support for training and preparation of graduate students in transition.

Transition specialization programs are most likely to emerge as a direct response to federal support for personnel preparation, or as a result of state transition certification programs. At this point in time, there is minimal information that systematically describes how programs are developed, what courses and competencies are included, and how programs are sustained. Anecdotally, however, it appears that transition specialization programs typically consist of three to four classes and are based on the CEC standards for transition specialists (Council for Exceptional Children, 2009). In states such as Ohio, Georgia, and Michigan, a critical factor is strong support for transition within state departments of education. In such states, teacher competencies for transition have been developed and incorporated into a stand-alone transition certification.

Offering a *transition course* is the third delivery method, and approximately half (45%–47%) of institutions of higher education (IHEs) responding to national surveys offer this option (Anderson et al., 2003; Hu, 2001). Establishing a specific course allows instructors to devote sufficient time to transition competencies. Opportunities to offer single courses in transition are often tied to faculty interest and knowledge of transition, as well as transition-specific state teaching standards embedded within traditional special education licensure requirements.

Finally, *infusing transition content within existing courses* is the most common approach to offering transition content when training special education teachers (Anderson et al., 2003). As states move toward K–12 noncategorical teacher standards, the increased pressures on higher education faculty to cover the breadth of information will mean that less time can be devoted to transition content. In addition, faculty who have limited knowledge are less likely to embed transition content into existing coursework. To illustrate, Anderson et al. found that content such as "collaboration among multiple agencies in transition planning" was not taught when transition content was infused within other classes. An earlier study found that faculty were not comfortable teaching this content because of limited knowledge (Becker-Staab & Morningstar, 1995). Transition assessment competencies are also commonly neglected primarily because faculty lack this expertise (Thoma, Held, & Saddler, 2002). Kohler and Greene (2004) provide guidelines for effective infusion of transition content within existing characteristics, assessment, methods, and collaboration courses. They argue that infusing content underscores the relationship between secondary education and transition services, as well as reinforcing the importance of a longitudinal approach to transition skills development and career awareness; however, research suggests that embedding content into existing coursework is ineffective (Anderson et al., 2003).

The range of transition preparation approaches has led to varied results. Offering a single transition class, the most common approach, provides an overview of transition content, but potentially without sufficient depth. Additionally, embedding transition content into existing coursework has drawbacks including limited instructor expertise and lack of time. Currently, there is not a definitive record of the actual number of transition master's programs or transition specialists programs in existence. However, we do know that 18 university programs providing advanced training in transition are currently receiving funding from the Office of Special Education programs.[1] Even with these pockets of excellence, it is highly probable that insufficient opportunities exist for intensive transition preparation. It stands to reason that limited transition preparation will lead to unprepared secondary educators who are not able to fully implement transition practices. In the next section, we will discuss the transition-related roles of secondary special educators and transition specialists and then review research findings regarding how prepared these professionals are to carry out these critical roles.

What Do We Know About Secondary Special Educators and Transition Specialists?

Two types of school personnel are involved with transition education and services: (a) secondary special education teachers engaged in IEP transition planning and instruction, and (b) transition specialists who ensure a coordinated set of activities as specified in the transition requirements of IDEA. Whereas

IDEA articulates that any special educator holding a valid special education credential and working in a secondary school is responsible for transition planning, the most effective programs have transition specialists who provide coordination and support across students, families, teachers, and outside systems (Noonan, Morningstar, & Gaumer Erickson, 2008). Most local education agencies use certified special education teachers in the role of transition specialists; however, a few rely on related services personnel (e.g., school social workers, guidance counselors).

The Role of Secondary Special Educators

Secondary special educators are responsible for individual student skill development and planning activities, rather than program development or service coordination. Identifying secondary special educators as transition "specialists" misrepresents the complexity of the transition process. In working with individual students, special educators teach specific skills (e.g., self-determination, social, learning strategies, academics, career/vocational). They also help identify and support accommodations students will need in school and community (Blalock et al., 2003).

In most high school settings, secondary special educators provide curriculum and instruction addressing students' academic and functional IEP goals. As IEP case managers, teachers are also required to ensure that students receive transition planning and services. It would seem that secondary special education teachers feel most comfortable with the competencies related to planning and developing transition IEPs. However, a wider range of knowledge and skill is needed to create effective transition programs for students with disabilities in order to assure improved postsecondary outcomes. Indeed, preparing qualified transition personnel is recognized as one of the critical factors to improving the outcomes of students with disabilities (Blalock et al., 2003; Kohler & Greene, 2004). However, knowledge and skills extend well beyond what many teachers receive (Anderson et al., 2003; Hu, 2001; Wolfe et al., 1998). Given such critical needs, one approach used by school districts has been to create the position of a transition specialist.

The Role of Transition Specialist

The position of transition specialist has emerged with the advent of transition-focused education and related legislation. This specialized position consists primarily of coordinating transition services, rather than providing direct services to students for which secondary special educators are most qualified to do (Blalock et al., 2003). Transition specialists ensure that teachers are informed of current information and methods for facilitating transition planning (e.g., identifying students' postschool interests, preferences, strengths, and needs). In this respect, most transition specialists are engaged in professional development activities within specific high schools or districts. Furthermore, transition specialists work as liaisons between students, parents, administrators, and staff to connect postsecondary goals with curriculum decisions that drive course content. According to Blalock and colleagues, transition specialists support:

1. *Student development* by developing and implementing career/vocational programs
2. *Student planning* by assisting to identify postsecondary options and coordinating with community agencies and services as well as monitoring the IEP transition services
3. *Interagency collaboration* by encouraging local interagency teams and by developing information and training about community resources
4. *Program evaluation* and strategic planning targeting transition program improvements.

Transition specialists are expected to possess certain knowledge and skills as reflected in the CEC *Advanced Content Standards for Transition Specialists* (Council for Exceptional Children, 2009). The CEC standards provide guidance to state educational agencies and teacher education programs of the core knowledge and skills a transition specialist should attain. The CEC standards address advanced knowledge of transition philosophy, practices, and legal requirements; in addition to competencies of knowledge and experience with transition assessment, diagnosis, and evaluation and instruction on community based activities, vocational experiences, and academic preparation for postschool environments. Transition specialists play a critical and meaningful role in promoting successful postschool outcomes for youth with disabilities. Their knowledge and skills focus on systems coordination, and they are instrumental in ensuring that secondary special educators are providing effective transition planning.

As previously described, teacher education programs offering specific transition preparation (i.e., individual courses, transition specialization, transition masters) are able to provide the depth of information needed to obtain the knowledge and skills to ensure effective transition practices. Without structured opportunities for learning, secondary professionals will not possess the skills or competencies to effectively implement transition practices. In the next section, we will review research finding regarding this issue.

How Well Do Secondary Special Educators and Transition Specialists Implement Transition Practices?

Since all secondary special educators should be involved in transition planning and service delivery, it is critical that they possess core knowledge and skills to enable them to effectively plan and deliver transition services. However, not all special educators possess, or believe that they possess, high levels of competence (Blanchett, 2001; Li et al., 2009; Wolfe et al., 1998). Possessing limited knowledge and skills impacts implementation of effective transition practices, in that teachers who are not confident of their transition skills are less likely to implement transition activities (Benitez et al., 2009; Knott & Asselin, 1999).

Delivering effective transition services is based upon the level of transition knowledge and skills teachers possess (Benitez et al., 2009). Research findings over the past decade indicate teachers are well aware of whether or not they have acquired in-depth transition knowledge. Schools expect special education teachers to assume the role of transition case managers, yet teachers report they do not have the time or training to do so (U.S. General Accounting Office, 2003). In fact, secondary special educators report feeling poorly prepared to address the transition needs of their students (Blanchett, 2001; Prater, Sileo, & Black, 2000; Wolfe et al., 1998). More importantly, only those secondary special educators who perceive that they are well prepared are likely to implement effective transition-related activities with any degree of frequency (Benitez et al., 2009).

In terms of actual practices, special education teachers have reported possessing a general understanding of transition planning and mandates. Teachers rated their level of involvement in transition and IEP planning as moderate to high (Knott & Asselin, 1999). However, they indicated they were not able to implement the myriad of activities required for effective transition education and services such as interagency collaboration, or how best to collaborate with families (DeFur & Taymans, 1995; Wolf et al., 1998).

More recently, a national study examined secondary special educators' abilities to implement transition practices (Benitez et al., 2009). The majority of the 557 participants were middle (23%) and high school (66%) special education teachers from 31 states. Using the Secondary Teachers Transition Survey (STTS; Benitez & Morningstar, 2005), teachers rated being most prepared to implement transition planning. However, as summarized in Table 24.1, secondary special education teachers were less likely to implement activities in other domains (e.g., transition assessment, interagency collaboration, transition-focused curriculum and instruction, and instructional planning). Relationships between level of teacher preparation and frequency of implementation were statistically significant. In other words, teachers who felt more prepared were more likely to implement transition activities. Such findings

Table 24.1 Preparedness and Frequency of Implementation Among National Sample of Secondary Special Educators and Transition Specialists

Ranking	*Domain*	*M*	*SD*
Preparedness			
1	Transition planning	3.15	0.74
2	Curriculum and instruction	2.96	0.63
3	Instructional planning	2.65	0.70
4	Assessment	2.52	0.79
5	Collaboration	2.49	0.83
6	Additional competencies	2.47	0.81
Frequency			
1	Transition planning	3.24	0.67
2	Curriculum and instruction	2.98	0.55
3	Instructional planning	2.53	0.72
4	Assessment	2.46	0.70
5	Collaboration	2.46	0.74
6	Additional competencies	2.44	0.83

suggest that typical teacher education programs have armed secondary special educators with the skills needed to plan, but not deliver effective transition services.

The study by Benitez and colleagues (2009) is the only published work to compare secondary educators and transition specialists. These researchers found that there were significant differences between transition specialists and secondary special education teachers who teach specific groups of students with disabilities (e.g., learning disabilities, emotional disabilities, intellectual disabilities). Across all groups, transition specialists reported significantly higher levels of preparation than secondary special educators, with no differences among the different groups of special education teachers. This study also found that transition specialists reported statistically higher levels of performing transition planning and services than their secondary special education colleagues. However, the results also indicated that teachers of students with intellectual disabilities reported higher rates of implementation than teachers of students with learning disabilities. Given the functional nature of programs for students with more significant disabilities, these results are not surprising. However, transition planning and services are equally critical for students with all types of disabilities, and ensuring that all secondary special education teachers have sufficient training to implement established practices should be a priority.

Differentiating the roles of secondary and transition educators is an essential element of offering teacher education programs that produce highly qualified transition practitioners. Such distinct competencies necessitate teacher education programs to respond accordingly. However, critical issues continue to impact the opportunities to provide specialized teacher training programs. Facilitative and hindering factors impacting transition teacher education will be described next, including federal support for transition preparation, state certification standards, and limited preparation programs.

Issues Impacting Transition Teacher Education

The issues and challenges of providing coordinated transition services are complex and pressing. Relatively few special education personnel preparation programs include even one course devoted to transition (Anderson et al., 2003). Furthermore, most secondary special educators report their transition training was on-the-job, rather than through comprehensive teacher education (Greene & Kochhar-Bryant, 2003). External factors influencing teacher education opportunities may cause inadequacies in preparation. In this section, we will first review federal support for transition personnel development and how priorities promote or limit transition teacher education. State policies and licensure standards also have a significant influence on teacher education, particularly with regard to transition content. The availability of transition teacher education programs or even stand-alone courses within teacher education impacts the quality and depth of transition knowledge and skills obtained by teachers. Finally, state priorities regarding personnel development and training can impact the acquisition of transition competencies among practicing special educators.

Federal Support for Transition Personnel Preparation

According to Kleinhammer-Tramill, Baker, Tramill, and Fiore (2003), federal funding specifically targeting transition personnel preparation began in 1984. At this time, model demonstration grants were an invitational priority that addressed the need to integrate services across education, health, and rehabilitation and to assist in the transition from school to employment in the community. Transition personnel preparation priorities soon followed, with the first being programs to prepare doctoral-level professionals. Subsequent competitions targeted transition services as a separate program for entry-level professionals (i.e., obtaining a license or master's degree).

With the reauthorization of IDEA in 1990 (P.L. 101-476), in which transition services for students age 16 and older were mandated, transition personnel preparation was emphasized (Kleinhammer-Tramill et al., 2003). Between the 1997 reauthorization of IDEA and 2010, decreased funding specifically for transition personnel preparation was the predominant trend. Beginning in 2011, the Department of Education, Office of Special Education Programs reinstituted a priority area in transition. These new personnel preparation priorities support programs offering a sequence of career, vocational, or secondary transition courses to meet either state requirements for a credential or endorsement in secondary transition services (U.S. Department of Education, 2011).

The renewed focus on transition personnel preparation signifies federal understanding that specialized transition knowledge and expertise is needed to promote effective services and programs leading to improved postsecondary outcomes. It is expected that the federal reinvestment in transition teacher preparation will expand the number of programs offering specialized content and, therefore, produce highly trained specialists who can improve services. The ultimate result, of course, is improved outcomes for youth in transition.

State Policies and Regulations Impacting Transition Personnel Development

While federal priorities encourage the expansion of transition professional development, state policies and certification standards maintain the most influence over teacher education programs. Kleinhammer-Tramill, Geiger, and Morningstar (2003) examined state special education credentials to identify transition licensure. Only three states had a specific transition credential in place. Thirty-five states (70%) had at least some transition-related standards or coursework within special education credential areas. While there appeared to be some structural framework for transition personnel preparation programs at the state level, gaps in transition licensure standards contributed to discrepancies in teacher education programs. Additionally, while some states had a transition credential structure in place, there was not necessarily a transition teacher education program operating within that state.

Clearly, state certification systems influence the content that teacher education programs offer (Geiger, Crutchfield, & Mainzer, 2003). Furthermore, states that do not require a transition-related certification or endorsement are least likely to influence teacher preparation programs. Teacher preparation programs in states with weak transition requirements did not include that content in special education curriculum at the preservice level (Kleinhammer-Tramill, Baker et al., 2003). These factors suggest that limited teacher education programs likely impact teachers' perceptions of how qualified they are to plan and deliver transition services (DeFur & Taymans, 1995; Hu, 2001; Li et al., 2009; Knott & Asselin, 1999).

Limited Teacher Education Programs Focused on Transition

In one of the few studies of transition preparation in special education, Anderson et al. (2003) found that a majority of teacher education programs addressed transition by embedding transition-related standards within existing courses. Findings from this national survey of 573 special education personnel preparation programs revealed that less than half of the programs addressed specific transition standards (Anderson et al., 2003). In terms of the method of delivery, the investigators found that 50% of the respondents indicated that transition content was infused into their existing courses; and about 45% devoted one or more courses to transition. Interestingly, almost 10% indicated that there was little or no transition content covered in their special education programs. When programs embedded transition within other courses, less time was devoted to specific transition content. These findings were consistent with earlier conclusions that embedding transition content does not allow for adequate emphasis or coverage of important transition-related content (Hu, 2001; Kohler & Greene, 2004; Severson et al., 1994).

While teacher education programs are addressing transition-related content to some degree, it is not sufficient for ensuring competent and confident secondary special educators when it comes to transition implementation. Supporting rigorous transition teacher education is an essential aspect of any comprehensive personnel preparation system. The next section reviews the impact of teacher education programs focused on transition.

Evaluating the Impact of Transition Teacher Education

If we consider the importance of training special educators in transition, then we recognize the need for results connecting teacher education programs to an increase in transition knowledge and expertise. To date, research has not sufficiently addressed the impact of personnel preparation programs on secondary special educators in relationship to specialized competencies needed to impact students during transition from school to adult life. Unfortunately, very few studies are published on this topic. In one of the few studies, Morningstar, Kim, and Clark (2008) evaluated transition competencies gained by secondary practitioners involved in a transition specialization program consisting of four transition-specific courses. Using a repeated-measures design, significant increases were found in knowledge and skills among graduates of the program with a large effect size ($t(71) = -11.734$, $p = .000$, $d = 2.79$). From focus group data, program graduates described the importance of the program content linking school and adult agency issues, leading to "real world" perspectives. In addition, all of the transition specialists indicated that they moved into their positions as a direct result of having completed the transition preparation program. In the only study evaluating multiple universities offering a single transition class, Wandry and colleagues (2008) found that among almost 200 preservice teachers, participants reported having received virtually no previous instruction regarding transition-related topics. A repeated-measures analysis of perceived competence revealed significant changes across the five major transition domains.

There is a prevailing concern of the limited number of studies that primarily focus on levels of competencies, rather than addressing impact of training on programmatic changes leading to students achieving successful postschool outcomes. To narrow this research gap, Morningstar and Clavenna-Deane (2009) completed a comprehensive study of the impact of an online transition-specialization program. The program provides 15 hours of graduate coursework in the area of transition services and planning; and was designed to scaffold learning from introductory knowledge to more detailed expertise in evidence-based practices (see Appendix to this chapter).

Seventy-seven educators from 18 states participated in the study with transition specialists (35%) and secondary special educators (40%) comprising the two largest groups of professionals. Participants completed two surveys using a repeated-measures design to determine changes in knowledge, expertise, and application of transition concepts. Approximately halfway through the program, participants identified a goal to improve specific transition activities in their classroom, district, or state (e.g., using transition assessments, implementing new planning strategies with students, collaborating with adult agencies; and including self-determination curricula). They completed a Goal Attainment Scale (GAS), and at the end of the program, rated their level of goal attainment and participated in a portfolio review and in-depth interview.

Analysis of pre- and posttest means generated from the KU Transition Competency Survey, produced a statistically significant difference ($t(91) = -13.258$, $p < .000$) indicating substantial increases in knowledge. The Secondary Teachers Transition Survey (Benitez & Morningstar, 2005), was also completed at the beginning and end of the program to determine frequency of implementing practices in transition. The results indicated statistically significant increases in the frequency with which participants reported implementing transition practices after completing the program ($t(68) = -6.170$, $p = .000$). Finally, the GAS results indicated that the participants sampled were likely to have met or surpassed their identified goal ($t(12) = 18.028$, $p = .000$) with a moderate effect size ($d = 0.45$). It is important to note that the use of a scaling instrument for goal attainment accounts for variance in achieving the expected and desirable result. For the individuals who rated their results below the expected level, they still achieved parts of their goal but had encountered time or administrative constraints and were still working on the goal when asked to rate attainment.

The researchers also conducted an artifact review of final reflection papers and portfolios as well as individual in-depth interviews; and this produced seven notable themes regarding professional growth and impact on students, parents, and programs:

1. increased self-determination and student involvement opportunities;
2. better parental involvement and engagement;
3. expanded use of age-appropriate transition assessments;
4. increased interagency collaboration;
5. development or enhancement of vocational and employment programs;
6. improved transition planning methods for the IEP; and
7. increased professional roles and responsibilities.

The themes demonstrated changes that the participants made in their classrooms, schools, and districts as a result of participating in the specialized transition program.

It is evident that the research examining transition teacher education is limited and narrow in scope. The results from the study by Morningstar and Clavenna-Deane (2009) lend credibility to the need for transition-specific teacher education programs that lead to significantly improved transition professional knowledge, expertise, and programmatic changes. Certainly there is a need for research to produce results of the impact of transition teacher education on improved practices in secondary special education settings, and ultimately student outcomes. The increased sophistication of emergent research lends support to innovative approaches to evaluating teacher education; and such methods should be carefully considered for the future.

Future Implications for Transition Teacher Education Practice and Research

Throughout the chapter, observations have been made regarding a paucity of research related to increased and purposeful preparation of teachers and transition specialists that directly impacts the transition of secondary students with disabilities. Given the environments within which secondary special educators and transition specialists are operating, and the high stakes impact on future adult lives of students, it stands to reason that intensive personnel preparation for transition must be taken seriously.

A case for quality personnel preparation programs in transition should not be made simply on the basis of logic and rhetoric. The research reported in this chapter frames the current understanding of critical issues and research involved in transition teacher preparation. As with most complex areas of interest, implications for practice and research are warranted. The following issues will be described next: (a) enhancing transition course content, (b) revising standards for transition specialists, and (c) evaluating transition teacher education.

Including Transition Evidence-Based Practices in Course Content

While general consensus has been reached regarding the domains for teaching transition content, research related to transition evidence-based practices offer continued enhancements to what should be taught. The steady increase in the volume of research targeting evidenced-based interventions associated with positive postschool outcomes (Test, Fowler et al., 2009) should guide content enhancement efforts. For example, the What Works in Transition Research Synthesis Project analyzed over 100 studies and found that student-focused planning strategies and student skill development were directly related with improved transition-related outcomes (Alwell & Cobb, 2006). Test and colleagues have also compiled a large research base of predictors of transition success, such as academic and functional skill development, student self-advocacy, interagency collaboration, family involvement, transition planning, and school program structures (Test, Mazzotti et al., 2009). Taken together, these research syntheses provide direction for training secondary special educators and transition specialists in practices exhibiting at least moderate effects on postschool outcomes, as well as important areas that predict future success.

We acknowledge the challenge to support teachers to not only gain knowledge, but to change their practices. The results from meta-analyses identifying transition interventions showing evidence of effectiveness should be carefully considered when constructing transition coursework. It is clear that research should continue to address the impact of transition teacher education on changing practices. Current methods have just touched the surface by evaluating distal indicators (e.g., perceived competencies and frequency of implementation) as proxy measures of impact on student outcomes. The next generation of research must directly examine student postschool outcomes in relationship to teacher training. In addition, teacher education programs must carefully examine what are believed to be essential components of transition, but for which there is limited research (e.g., interagency collaboration, family involvement). Finally, future research should consider examining the degree to which current transition programs include evidence-based practices in their coursework. To date, this important area of research has yet to be undertaken.

Revising Standards for Transition Specialists

It is not surprising that as new interventions and evidence of effectiveness emerge, long-established standards may be in need of revision. Recently, an effort to update the CEC Transition Specialist standards was undertaken through a systematic review and content analysis of research and established frameworks documenting transition competencies (Morningstar et al., 2012). The review identified over 600 items that first, aligned with the CEC standards, and second, included additional competencies incorporated within a matrix of domains. After an expert review and follow-up pilot test with transition specialists, approximately 70 transition specialist competencies have been identified. Interestingly, the broader domains historically associated with transition remain intact (e.g., transition planning, assessment, curriculum and instruction, program development, interagency collaboration). However, emergent issues and research were identified at the competency level. For example, the role transition specialists play with regard to culturally responsive transition planning (Morningstar & Nix, 2012); or the implementation of specific evidence-based practices such as dropout prevention interventions (Test, Fowler et al., 2009).

A research implication of improving standards for transition specialists is determining not only the knowledge and skills of such positions, but identifying what these professionals do on a day-to-day basis, and the impact of their roles on transition services. Unfortunately, this endeavor may be difficult to accomplish, as the position of transition specialist is not accredited in most states (i.e., only a handful of states have a specialization or endorsement in this area). From our work over the past decade with transition specialists from across the country, we do know that there is significant variance in their configurations and therefore, their roles. For example, some may be full-time positions and others may be part-time with added classroom responsibilities. Even in states without a formal credential for transition, districts may have created the position. Understandably, identifying who serves as a transition specialist and identifying what they do can be a challenge.

Currently, a study is underway to better understand the role of the transition specialist (Morningstar et al., 2012). With over 1,600 respondents representing all 50 states and U.S. territories, this research has the potential to provide a national picture of the preparation and activities of this position. Understanding the roles and responsibilities of transition specialists will be an important step toward consistency of implementation. Once established, further research is needed to determine the impact of transition specialists on programs and practices and ultimately student outcomes.

Evaluating Transition Teacher Education

Researchers have called for better and more effective methods for evaluating the acquisition of competencies among transition practitioners (Blalock et al., 2003; Flexer, Baer, Simmons, & Shell, 1997; Kohler & Greene, 2004; Morningstar & Clark, 2003; Morningstar & Kleinhammer-Tramill, 2005). However, moving beyond rudimentary research establishing knowledge gains and perceived increases in implementation are certainly needed. As evidenced by the phases of the evaluation methods shared in this chapter, research efforts are becoming increasingly more sophisticated, with the intent of identifying the impact of training on school programs as well as student outcomes. However, there is room for an expansion of initial efforts.

Continuing to refine and expand the evaluation efforts across transition teacher education is a necessary first step. While the results of research point toward a better understanding of the efficacy of personnel preparation, it is not yet clear what really matters when it comes to preparing special education teachers for the complexities of transition education and services. In other words, future research should begin to systematically evaluate content and delivery methods of personnel preparation, as well as impact of training. Still to be answered are questions articulated by Morningstar & Clark (2003):

1. How effective are current delivery methods?
2. What is the critical mass needed to make infused content effective?
3. What are the courses into which transition content can and should be infused?
4. How do we ensure consistency of content and implementation?
5. Does specific content instruction make a difference in terms of outcomes for students with disabilities and postschool indicators of success?

Summary

Federal efforts for improving postsecondary opportunities and adult-life outcomes for students with disabilities are at the forefront of educational reform efforts. With increased attention placed on improving outcomes, the roles of secondary special educators are clearly shifting. It stands to reason that teacher education programs would respond accordingly with expanded transition training. Unfortunately, changes in teacher preparation are slow (Anderson et al., 2003). The few programs offering comprehensive transition teacher preparation do so with support from multiple sources, including federal incentives, state licensure policies, and institutional support within teacher education programs.

Much is known about the roles and responsibilities of secondary special educators and transition specialists as district and school level coordinators of programs, services, and planning. Special educators play a critical role in student-level planning and service delivery. The impact of transition specialists is often improved planning and transition services, communication with families, and interagency collaboration, ultimately leading to better postschool outcomes for students. Unfortunately, both secondary special educators and transition specialists have acknowledged that their training and preparation is often minimal, thereby impacting their abilities to implement effective transition practices.

Such concerns should compel teacher educators to consider critical transition content that should be included within teacher preparation programs, as well as the methods of delivering training. National standards for transition specialists have been in place for almost two decades; however, only recently have we seen efforts to review and update critical knowledge and skills necessary to effectively implement transition practices. Current efforts to incorporate evidence-based interventions, as well as culturally responsive transition practices, into teacher preparation is at the forefront of change. Finally, evaluating the impact of transition preparation on the ability of practitioners to improve services and practices that will impact student outcomes is a critical initiative for the future.

Appendix: Online Transition Course Descriptions

Course Title	*Description*
Transition Education and Services	Emphasis on IDEA requirements related to transition services Foundation in background, history, and evidence supporting the use of effective transition practices with students with disabilities
Vocational Training and Employment	• Review various vocational and employment models for adolescents and young adults with disabilities Highlight tools to build employment experiences into high school settings Provide effective strategies for job placement, building natural supports, and school-business partnerships
Assessment for Transition Planning	• Establish a foundation for conducting formal and informal assessments Using assessments effectively to inform transition services and planning Hands-on exposure to various types of assessments used to measure the transition preparation and experiences of students with disabilities
Interagency and Community Services for Transition to Adulthood	• Provide a well-planned combination of theory and practice Support increases in positive and smooth transitions for students with disabilities from school supportive environments to the various supports found in the community (e.g., adult service agencies, postsecondary training environments, etc.) Conduct activities that increase students' awareness of and engagement with community agencies
Secondary Curriculum and Academic Instruction for Transition	• Provide information about teaching academic content (that is, the general education curriculum) and evidence based practices for teaching that content to youth Use an instructional framework, Universal Design for Transition, to link academic and transition education Implement a universal design for learning approach to academic planning, instruction, and assessment

Note

1 At http://www.personnelcenter.org/get2.cfm

References

Alwell, M., & Cobb, B. (2006). A systematic review of the effects of curricular interventions on the acquisition of functional life skills by youth with disabilities. *What works in transition: Systematic review project*. Ft. Collins, CO: Colorado State University.

Anderson, D., Kleinhammer-Tramill, P. J., Morningstar, M. E., Lehman, J., Bassett, D., Kohler, P., ... Wehmeyer, M. (2003). What's happening in personnel preparation in transition? A national survey. *Career Development for Exceptional Individuals, 26*, 145–160. doi:10.1177/088572880302600204

Becker Staab, M. J., & Morningstar, M. E. (1995). *Report of survey of institutions of higher education in Kansas on preservice training in transition*. Lawrence, KS: Department of Special Education, University of Kansas.

Benitez, D. T., & Morningstar, M. E. (2005). *The secondary teachers transition survey*. Lawrence, KS: University of Kansas.

Benitez, D. T., Morningstar, M. E., & Frey, B. B. (2009). A multi-state survey of special education teachers' perceptions of their transition competencies. *Career Development and Transition for Exceptional Individuals, 32*, 6–16. doi:10.1177/0885728808323945

Blalock, G., Kocchar-Bryant, C. A., Test, D. W., Kohler, P., White, W., Lehman, J., ... Patton, J. (2003). The need for comprehensive personnel preparation in transition and career development: A position statement of the Division on Career Development and Transition. *Career Development and Transition for Exceptional Individuals, 26*, 207–226. doi:10.1177/088572880302600207

Blanchett, W. J. (2001). Importance of teacher transition competencies as rated by special educators. *Teacher Education and Special Education, 24*, 3–12. doi:10.1177/088840640102400103

Council for Exceptional Children. (2008). *What every special educator must know: Ethics, standards, and guidelines* (6th ed.). Arlington, VA: Author.

Council for Exceptional Children. (2009). *CEC advanced standards for transition specialists*. Arlington, VA: Author.

DeFur, S. H., & Taymans, J. M. (1995). Competencies needed for transition specialists in vocational rehabilitation, vocational education, and special education. *Exceptional Children, 62*, 38–52.

Flexer, R. W., Baer, R. M., Simmons, T. J., & Shell, D. (1997). Translating research, innovation and policy: Interdisciplinary transition leadership training. *Career Development and Transition for Exceptional Individuals, 20*, 55–67. doi:10.1177/088572889702000105

Geiger, W. L., Crutchfield, M. D., & Mainzer, R. (2003). *The status of licensure of special education teachers in the 21st century* (COPSSE document No. RS-7E). Gainesville, FL: University of Florida, Center on Personnel Studies in Special Education. Retrieved from http://copsse.education.ufl.edu/docs/RS-7E/1/RS-7E.pdf

Greene, G. A., & Kochhar-Bryant, C. A. 2003. *Pathways to successful transition for youth with disabilities: A developmental Process*. Columbus, OH: Merrill Prentice Hall.

Hu, M. (2001). *Preparing preservice special education teachers for transition services: A nation-wide survey*. Unpublished doctoral dissertation. Kansas State University, White, Kansas.

Kleinhammer-Tramill, P. J., Baker, B. C., Tramill, J. L., & Fiore, T. A. (2003). The history and status of OSEP personnel preparation policy for transition. *Career Development and Transition for Exceptional Individuals, 26*(2), 131–143. doi:10.1177/088572880302600203

Kleinhammer-Tramill, P. J., Geiger, W. L., & Morningstar, M. (2003). Policy contexts for transition personnel preparation: An analysis of transition-related credentials, standards, and course requirements in state certification and licensure. *Career Development and Transition for Exceptional Individuals, 26*(2), 185–206. doi:10.1177/088572880302600206

Knott, L., & Asselin, S. B. (1999). Transition competencies: Perception of secondary education teachers. *Teacher Education and Special Education, 22*, 55–65. doi:10.1177/088840649902200106

Kohler, P. D., & Field, S. (2003). Transition-focused education: Foundation for the future. *Journal of Special Education, 37*, 174–183. doi:10.1177/00224669030370030701

Kohler, P. D., & Greene, G. (2004). Strategies for integrating transition related competencies into teacher education. *Teacher Education and Special Education, 27*, 146–162. doi:10.1177/088840640402700206

Lattin, D. L., Dove, S. M., Morningstar, M. E., Kleinhammer-Tramill, P. J., & Frey, B. (2004). *Transition professional development needs: Preliminary report of a multi-state survey*. Lawrence, KS: University of Kansas, Transition Coalition.

Li, J. Y., Bassett, D. S., & Hutchinson, S. R. (2009). Secondary special educators' transition involvement. *Journal of Intellectual & Developmental Disability, 34*, 163–172. doi:10.1080/13668250902849113

Morningstar, M. E., & Clark, G. M. (2003). The status of personnel preparation for transition education and service: What is the critical content? How can it be offered? *Career Development and Transition for Exceptional Individuals, 26*, 227–237. doi:10.1177/088572880302600208

Morningstar, M. E., & Clavenna-Deane, E. (2009, April). *Effective practices during transition: Does preparation make a difference?* Presented at the Division of Career Development and Transition International Conference, Savannah, GA.

Morningstar, M. E., Kim, K.-H., & Clark, G. M. (2008). Evaluating a transition personnel preparation program: Identifying transition competencies of practitioners. *Teacher Education and Special Education, 31*, 47–58. doi:10.1177/088840640803100105

Morningstar, M. E., & Kleinhammer-Tramill, J. (2005). Professional development for transition personnel: Current issues and strategies for success. *National Center on Secondary Education and Transition Information Brief.* Minneapolis, MN: University of Minnesota.

Morningstar, M. E., & Nix, T. (2012, May). *Culturally responsive transition planning: Transforming transition course curriculum.* Presented at the National Secondary Transition Technical Assistance Center Annual Capacity Building Institute. Charlotte, NC.

Morningstar, M. E., Wade, D., & Benitez, D. T. (2012). *The transition coordinator survey: Content analysis procedures.* University of Kansas, Lawrence, KS. Lawrence, KS: University of Kansas.

Newman, L., Wagner, M., Cameto, R., & Knokey, A. (2009). *The post-high school outcomes of youth with disabilities up to 4 years after high school: A report from the National Longitudinal Transition Study-2 (NLTS2).* Menlo Park, CA: SRI International.

Noonan, P. N., Morningstar, M. E., & Gaumer Erickson, A. (2008). Improving interagency collaboration: Effective strategies used by high performing local districts and communities. *Career Development for Exceptional Individuals, 31*, 132–143. doi:10.1177/0885728808327149

Prater, M. A., Sileo, T. W., & Black, R. S. (2000). Preparing educators and related school personnel to work with at-risk students. *Teacher Education and Special Education, 23*, 51–64. doi:10.1177/088840640002300108

Severson, S. J., Hoover, J. H., & Wheeler, J. J. (1994). Transition: An integrated model for the pre- and in-service training of special education teachers. *Career Development for Exceptional Individuals, 17*(2), 145–158. doi:10.1177/088572889401700204

Test, D. W., Fowler, C., Kohler, P., & Kortering, L. (2010). *Evidence-based practices and predictors in secondary transition: What we know and what we still need to know.* Charlotte, NC: National Secondary Transition Technical Assistance Center.

Test, D. W., Fowler, C. H., Richter, S. M., White, J., Mazzotti, V., Walker, A. R., … Kortering, L. (2009). Evidence-based practices in secondary transition. *Career Development for Exceptional Individuals, 32*, 115–128. doi:10.1177/0885728809336859

Test, D. W., Mazzotti, V. L., Mustian, A. L., Fowler, C. H., Kortering, L., & Kohler, P. (2009). Evidence-based secondary transition predictors for improving postschool outcomes for students with disabilities. *Career Development and Transition for Exceptional Individuals, 32*, 160–181. doi:10.1177/0885728809346960

Thoma, C. A., Held, M. F., & Saddler, S. (2002). Transition assessment practices in Nevada and Arizona: Are they tied to best practices? *Focus on Autism and Developmental Disabilities, 26*, 242–250. doi:10.1177/10883576020170040701

U.S. Department of Education. (2011, May). *Application for new grants under the Individuals with Disabilities Act (IDEA). Personnel development to improve services and results for children with disabilities (CFDA 84.325).* Washington, DC: Author.

U.S. General Accounting Office. (2003, July). *Special education: Federal actions can assist states in improving postsecondary outcomes for youth.* Washington, DC: Author.

Wandry, D. L., Webb, K. W., Williams, J. M., Bassett, D. S., Asselin, S. B., & Hutchinson, S. R. (2008). Teacher candidates' perceptions of barriers to effective transition programming. *Career Development and Transition for Exceptional Individuals, 31*, 14–25. doi:10.1177/0885728808315391

Wolfe, P. S., Boone, R. S., & Blanchett, W. J. (1998). Regular and special educators' perceptions of transition competencies. *Career Development and Transition for Exceptional Individuals, 21*, 87–106. doi:10.1177/088572889802100108

Part VII
Teacher Quality

25

Dimensions of Teacher Quality in General and Special Education

Mary T. Brownell

UNIVERSITY OF FLORIDA

Trisha Steinbrecher

UNIVERSITY OF NEW MEXICO

Jenna Kimerling

UNIVERSITY OF FLORIDA

Yujeong Park

UNIVERSITY OF TENNESSEE

Jungah Bae and Amber Benedict

UNIVERSITY OF FLORIDA

Things to Think About

- Teachers are believed to be the most valuable resource in improving students' outcomes, and researchers have thus tried to define what constitutes effective or highly qualified teachers. Despite these efforts, however, there is little consensus on the meaning and the features of high-quality teachers because of the complexity of this phenomenon.
- Measuring teacher quality for special education teachers is particularly complicated because of its highly contextual nature. There are several substantial challenges to understanding effective teaching for students with disabilities, including the difficulty of securing valid metrics of teacher effectiveness, the limited nature of standardized achievement data available for students, and multiple problems with using state assessments to determine teachers' effectiveness for students with disabilities.
- The research on teacher qualifications, knowledge, and classroom practice in general education and special education enable us to draw limited conclusions about teacher expertise generally and more specifically in special education. Many studies of the relationship of teacher qualifications and student achievement, as well as those of classroom performance and teacher content knowledge, have been fueled by political agendas, which have also funded research to determine the knowledge and practices that characterize highly effective teachers.

- It is commonly held that teachers' subject matter knowledge influences their teaching effectiveness. The existing research in general education and special education provides some clarity about the role that knowledge for teaching content and classroom practice plays in improving student outcomes, particularly in the area of reading. However, much of the research capturing teachers' knowledge for teaching is focused on general education teachers or general education teachers and special education teachers without disaggregating data by teacher type.
- What teachers do in the classroom seems to have the strongest impact on student achievement. Over the past decade, researchers have studied what constitutes effective classroom practice and how it can be measured. There is strong evidence that classroom practice can be measured and related to important student outcomes.
- To improve teacher education or professional development efforts and determine their effectiveness, more fine-grained measurements of teacher knowledge and classroom performance are needed. Measurement that captures the multidimensional nature of instruction for different content and types of learners will need to be explored further.

The quality of a school's teaching staff is its most important instructional resource, and teacher effects account for the largest variance in student achievement. Multiple studies have demonstrated that teachers account for approximately 7%–21% of the variance in student performance (Goldhaber, 2002; Nye, Konstantopoulos, & Hedges, 2004; Rivkin, Hanushek, & Kain, 2005). Over the past two decades, a large number of research studies have been undertaken to establish linkages between teacher characteristics, teacher knowledge, and observed classroom practice, on the one hand, and student achievement, on the other. The majority of these studies have focused on the value-added contribution teacher qualifications (e.g., experience, initial preparation, subject matter preparation, academic ability) make to student achievement, as teacher qualifications are easy to measure, are thought to constitute one dimension of teacher quality (i.e., credentials), and are accessible via state and national databases (Kennedy, 1992).

Many studies of the relationship of teacher qualifications and student achievement are borne out of a highly politicized agenda determined to prove or disprove that teacher preparation contributes to the quality of the teaching workforce. Studies of classroom performance and teacher content knowledge have also emerged for political reasons. Federal and state policy makers along with federal agencies and think tanks (e.g., Institute for Education Sciences, Carnegie Foundation) have a keen interest in understanding effective teacher development and teachers' implementation of evidence-based practices in literacy and mathematics. As a result, research funding exists for determining the knowledge and practices that characterize highly effective teachers.

Understanding what makes teachers effective in promoting student learning is no doubt a worthwhile endeavor, regardless of the motivations for doing so. Our efforts to ensure that each student has access to a quality teacher by providing the best teacher education experiences depend on our ability to define and validly assess the dimensions of effective teaching. Without a well-developed conception of what it means to be an effective teacher, we cannot design or focus our initial teacher preparation and professional development efforts.

Although all teacher effectiveness research is complex and challenging to conduct, measuring teacher quality in special education is especially so (Brownell et al., 2009). Students with disabilities are often taught by both general and special education teachers and sometimes receive direct services from related service personnel. Thus, how can achievement gains of these students be attributed to one teacher? Also, what should the individual contribution of both general and special education teachers be to the education of students with disabilities? Will general education teachers be responsible for certain aspects of instruction and special education teachers others? Further, academic achievement is not the only important outcome; positive behavioral, social, adaptive, communication, and transition outcomes are also considered goals for many students with disabilities. Thus, the concept of teacher effectiveness is much broader in scope and more difficult to articulate for students with disabilities than it is for students who do not receive special education services.

The purpose of our chapter is to develop a conceptual framework that articulates the defining features of teacher quality for students with disabilities and to review the research in both general and special education related to those features. A summary of the general education research is provided in each section of the conceptual framework for two reasons. One, the literature base in special education is quite small compared to general education. Two, general education research findings serve as a comparison for the special education research. An additional purpose of the chapter is to discuss the conceptual and measurement issues associated with conducting research on teacher quality for students with disabilities and provide some direction for how those issues might be resolved.

Conceptual Framework for Special Education Teacher Quality

Frameworks developed by Laura Goe (2008) and Mary Kennedy (2010) provide a foundation for conceptualizing teacher quality. Goe (2008) conceptualizes teacher quality as the result of several factors: teacher inputs, processes, and effectiveness. According to Goe, inputs include teacher qualifications (e.g., educational background, certification, and experience) as well as teacher characteristics (e.g., attitudes, beliefs, and gender). The third factor, effectiveness, focuses on those processes or teacher practices that influence teacher quality (e.g., planning, instructional delivery, classroom management, interactions with students). Although not mentioned specifically by Goe, teachers' knowledge for teaching content affects their instructional practice and, in turn, is influenced by curricular materials and students. Finally, the ability of teachers to be effective in producing desirable student outcomes is also a component of teacher quality. Thus, teacher quality affects student growth on important outcomes and the degree to which students make gains influences a teacher's quality.

Goe (2008) and Kennedy (2010) indicate that teacher practices are influenced by school and classroom contexts, though Kennedy places far more emphasis on contextual factors. She argues that the time teachers have for teaching, the curriculum materials they have to use, the support they have for learning on the job, their different roles and responsibilities in and outside of school, and the types of students they teach all affect the quality of teachers' instruction; therefore, evaluations of teachers' quality must simultaneously consider the quality of their work environments. In special education, context is likely to be especially important, as general education teachers often provide the majority of instruction to students with disabilities and the degree to which general and special education teachers effectively collaborate influences the quality of instruction these students receive.

Figure 25.1 portrays the influences on special education teacher quality described in this section. We have treated knowledge for teaching as a process variable and not an input because although special education teachers bring a certain amount of knowledge to the job as a result of their initial preparation, their knowledge also changes in response to their classroom and school environments.

Method for Reviewing the Literature

To gather the research on teacher quality, we conducted an electronic search of the Education Resources Information Center (ERIC), EBSCO, Wilson Web, and Google Scholar using combinations of terms related to each major area of interest (i.e., teacher qualifications, teacher knowledge, and classroom practice). We also only included studies from 2000 forward, since a major literature review in this area was published by Wayne and Youngs in 2003. In addition, we searched the literature according to the types of classroom practice assessments catalogued on the National

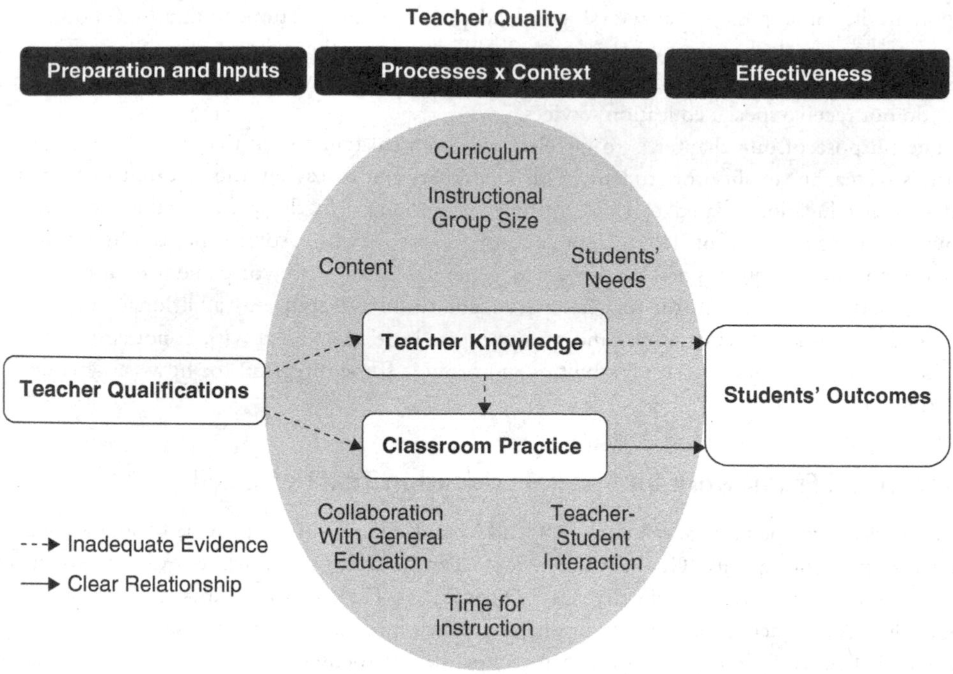

Figure 25.1 Teacher Quality and Its Influences

Comprehensive Center for Teacher Quality website. For the most part, we only selected published research studies where assessments of teacher variables were analyzed to determine their relationship with student achievement gains or classroom practice. Due to limited research in special education, however, we included two qualitative studies of classroom practice that were linked to student outcomes since 1990, as previous work was based on process-product approaches to classroom practice, which have been reviewed previously.

Most of the papers we identified were published in refereed journals; however, we did identify key papers published by authors on national center websites widely recognized for research in their respective areas. In total, we found 75 research papers that focused on teacher qualifications, teacher knowledge, and teacher practice in general education, whereas in special education, we found seven research papers. We do not include a section on professional collaboration in our review, as research designed to identify and assess special education teachers' collaborative skills was nonexistent. In the sections that follow, we outline our major conclusions from this research as well as the conceptual and methodological issues inherent in the work. Finally, we discuss implications for future research on teacher quality in special education.

Results

It is logical that teachers' qualifications, experience for teaching, and teaching knowledge would influence their classroom practices, and their practices in turn would influence the outcomes of their students. However, to what degree is such logic supported by the research? In the sections that follow, we summarize the research on teacher qualifications, knowledge, and classroom practice in general education and special education and draw conclusions about this research in terms of what it communicates about teacher expertise generally and more specifically in special education.

Teacher Qualifications

One's professional preparation to teach has been considered an important dimension of teacher quality (Kennedy, 1999, 2010). As such, teacher qualifications, at least in general education, have been targeted in many large-scale studies examining relationships among certification or preparation, hours of coursework, degrees earned, selectivity of institution, amount of professional development, and the contribution made to student achievement. Such studies have for the most part yielded mixed findings, with some teacher qualification variables demonstrating relationships with student achievement and others not. Since research specific to the achievement of students with disabilities, however, was sparse we widened our scope to include special education teacher classroom performance.

General Education

Teachers' academic ability, measured through SAT scores or university selectivity, is positively related to student achievement (Wayne & Youngs, 2003). Yet recent findings suggest that these differences are often mixed (Clotfelter, Ladd, & Vigdor, 2010) or nonsignificant with negligible effect sizes (Boyd, Grossman, Lankford, Loeb, & Wyckoff, 2008). The relationship between college coursework and student achievement is also mixed, and significant effects cannot be generalized to all content areas. One study (Clotfelter et al., 2010) and a comprehensive review of the literature (Wayne & Youngs, 2003) found that math content knowledge was significantly related to secondary students' achievement. In contrast, two studies performed at preschool and elementary levels found no significant relationships between student achievement and subject matter coursework (Early, Maxwell, Burchinal, Alva, Bender et al., 2007; Phillips, 2010), although in Guarino, Hamilton, Lockwood, and Rathbun (2006), pedagogical coursework moderated kindergarten teachers' instructional approaches and was related to kindergarten student achievement.

Analyses of the relationship between advanced degrees in teacher education and student achievement also have resulted in mixed findings. Of the eight studies examining level of educational attainment (i.e., master's degrees or higher), five found no statistical significance favoring teachers who held advanced degrees (Clotfelter et al., 2010; Early et al., 2007; Guarino et al., 2006; Huang & Moon, 2008; Phillips, 2010). This was true across subject matter (i.e., reading, math) as well as grade level (i.e., preschool, kindergarten, and elementary). In addition, Clotfelter et al. found that a Ph.D. yielded large negative effects on student achievement. Wayne and Youngs' (2003) literature synthesis obtained mixed results on the relationship of student achievement to teachers' advanced degrees. For the most part, only advanced degrees in mathematics seemed to have any consistent influence (on student gains in math). More recent evidence has shown that advanced degrees do seem to have some positive effects on reading achievement of students at-risk of failure. Phillips (2010) found that subject specific degrees (i.e., reading instruction versus curriculum) produced positive reading achievement gains for the disaggregated at-risk subpopulation in both early childhood and elementary programs.

Teacher certification also has been correlated with student achievement. Seven studies identified a significant relationship between certification and student achievement. This relationship was identified in math (Boyd, Lankford, Loeb, Rockoff, & Wyckoff, 2008; Clotfelter et al., 2010; Heck, 2007; Goldhaber & Brewer, 2000), English (Clotfelter et al., 2010), reading (Heck, 2007), and science (Neild, Farley-Ripple, & Byrnes, 2009). Marszalek, Odom, LaNasa, and Adler (2010) found that teachers who begin teaching without first gaining full certification negatively impacted student achievement in both math and communication arts and that the magnitude of this negative relationship increased from 3rd grade to 11th grade. Wayne and Youngs' (2003) synthesis of seven studies with measures of teacher test scores (i.e., licensure scores, verbal skills cores) provided mixed findings. Five studies yielded a positive relationship while the other two were negative. This led Wayne and Youngs to conclude that test scores do matter, but only if college ratings were not already controlled. Three studies found no statistical significance between licensing status and educational attainment and student achievement gains

(Huang & Moon, 2008; Guarino et al., 2006; Phillips, 2010). Five studies investigating the impact of National Board Certification found little to no significant impact and negligible effect sizes on student achievement in either high school (Cavalluzo, 2004) or elementary school (Goldhaber & Anthony, 2004; Stronge, Ward, Tucker, Hindman, McColsky, & Howard, 2007; Vandevoort, Amrein-Beardsley, & Berliner, 2004).

More experienced teachers are often posited to be more effective teachers. Four studies found a positive significant relationship between years of teaching experience and student achievement but this relationship plateaus after 3 to 5 years of experience (Boyd, Lankford et al., 2008; Clotfelter et al., 2010; Henry, Bastian, & Fortner, 2011; Huang & Moon, 2008). Huang and Moon (2008) differentiated between years of total teaching experience and years of teaching at the same grade level, finding only the latter to be significant. The remaining studies found no relationship between teachers' experience and student achievement (Heck, 2007; Phillips, 2010). In summary, general education researchers have found few direct relationships between some teacher inputs (i.e., aptitude, coursework) and student achievement. However, teacher certification and experience appear to have clear relationships with student achievement.

Special Education

Only one study specifically examining the relationship of teacher qualifications with the achievement of students with disabilities has been published. Feng and Sass (2010) found that special education coursework, certification status, and degree earned were all significantly related to the achievement of students with disabilities, but the effect size of this relationship was small. Their results indicate that, in math, for students who received all instruction in special education classrooms, achievement gains were higher when the teacher held an advanced degree in special education. In reading, positive significant relationships were observed between special education teacher certification and achievement of students who received reading instruction either in special education only or in both special and general education settings. By contrast, in math, the relationship between special education certification and achievement gains was limited to students receiving instruction in both regular and special education courses. Feng and Sass concluded that important differences exist between general and special education populations and special education teacher preparation appears more important for students with special needs. As a result, reduced preparation via alternate certification routes is counterintuitive.

Finally, special education students' reading gains were positively correlated with their teacher's experience, particularly in the teacher's first few years. In math, however, this relationship was less clear and was moderated by service delivery model. Teacher experience had less of a relationship to student math achievement in self-contained courses when compared to regular education courses. This may be due, however, to the student math ability level and the validity of the math achievement test for this subpopulation.

Two studies (Nougaret, Scruggs, & Mastropieri, 2005; Sindelar, Daunic, & Rennells, 2004) examined the impact of traditional versus alternative preparation of special education teachers on their classroom performance. Sindelar et al. (2004) compared graduates of traditional programs and two types of alternative programs (i.e., university-district partnership and district add-on) to determine if differences existed in overall effectiveness. Graduates were observed in their classrooms (using Praxis III), and they and their principals both rated their preparedness (on the Praxis criteria). While all three programs seemed to produce competent graduates, graduates of alternative programs reported higher average levels of preparedness than graduates of traditional programs. Similarly, average principals' ratings were higher for teachers from the two alternative programs than for those who entered through a traditional program on almost every Praxis criterion. On the other hand, on observations of classroom practice, graduates of traditional programs were rated higher on three of five Domain C criteria (Teaching for Student Learning), on the Domain C total score, and on the total Praxis score.

Nougaret et al. (2005) found that preservice training is important and trained teachers are more effective than untrained teachers. Large, significant effect sizes were observed when teachers who completed a state-approved special education teacher education program were compared to teachers with bachelor's degrees in a noneducation area. On the three measured domains of Charlotte Danielson's (1996) Framework for Teaching (i.e., planning and preparation, classroom environment, and instruction), teachers who were traditionally prepared out performed those who were not prepared.

In special education, the results of the Feng and Sass (2010), Sindelar et al. (2004), and Nougaret et al. (2005) studies suggest that preparation and years of experience have some impact on special education teachers compared to little or no preparation, but three studies hardly constitute a sufficient evidence base. We remain largely uninformed about the ways in which preparation, experience, or ability might matter in either general education or special education.

Teacher Knowledge

It is commonly held that teachers' subject matter knowledge influences their teaching effectiveness, and this belief undergirds major shifts in required teacher qualifications within both the No Child Left Behind Act and the reauthorization of the Individuals with Disabilities Education Act. For example, highly qualified special education teachers providing direct instruction to students with disabilities in middle and high school are those with demonstrated subject matter knowledge, a bachelor's degree, and full state certification, which can be secured in many states by simply passing tests in the content area they teach and in special education. State certification routes no longer require completion of a teacher education program or evidence of pedagogical knowledge even when special education teachers are providing direct instruction.

In the sections that follow, we summarize research examining the knowledge general education teachers have for providing instruction in mathematics and reading, as these are two of three areas where special education teachers are likely to provide instruction. (The knowledge needed for writing instruction has not been empirically examined.) We then examine the limited research available on special education teachers' pedagogical knowledge.

Teacher Knowledge for Math Instruction

Two studies have examined the knowledge teachers need for teaching mathematics and its relationship to classroom practice and student achievement. These studies have been conducted with elementary and middle schools students in mostly high-poverty schools using multilevel analyses. Both studies demonstrated that teachers' knowledge predicted a small to moderate proportion of variance in student achievement and that in both instances, the relationships were significant (Hill, Rowan, & Ball, 2005; Shechtman, Roschelle, Haertel, & Knudsen, 2010). Shechtman et al. also demonstrated that the professional development teachers participated in created positive changes in their knowledge, but these changes were minimal and short in duration. Finally, the impact of knowledge on classroom practice was mixed. In the larger scale study, there was no impact (Shechtman et al.); however, in a smaller study of 10 elementary teachers, Hill and her colleagues (2007) were able to demonstrate a positive relationship between teachers' classroom practice and knowledge by rank ordering teachers on both variables and comparing the two. Further, qualitative analysis of classroom observations revealed that teachers with lower knowledge exhibited more errors during mathematics instruction, while teachers with higher knowledge engaged in richer, error-free mathematics instruction.

Teacher Knowledge for Reading Instruction

Until the mid- to late 1990s, it was assumed that strong teachers of reading were those who had good reading skills themselves (Phelps, 2009). Mounting research validated the role that phonological awareness and decoding skill played in the development of early reading abilities, and scholars began to focus on the knowledge reading teachers should have to teach reading effectively. Mostly, these studies have focused on two different types of knowledge. One is the content knowledge teachers would need to teach decoding and structural analysis. Specifically, researchers have examined the knowledge teachers have of the English language (i.e., phonology, morphology, and orthography) and how that knowledge relates to either classroom practice or students' reading achievement. A smaller number of researchers have looked at the types of knowledge teachers might use while teaching reading, which includes not only content knowledge but also knowledge of how students learn to read and the struggles they might encounter while reading.

Findings from studies that focus on teachers' knowledge of the English language have been mixed and somewhat complex. Early studies employing Pearson correlations and multiple regression analytic techniques have demonstrated relationships among teachers' knowledge, their classroom practice, and student achievement in the elementary grades (Foorman & Moats, 2004; McCutchen, Abbot, Green, Beretvas, Cox, et al., 2002). Later studies, however, using more rigorous, multilevel analyses to study teacher knowledge have yielded more mixed results. One study demonstrated direct relationships between teacher knowledge and elementary students' reading achievement (McCutchen, Green, Abbot, & Sanders, 2009), whereas a second study (Carlisle, Correnti, Phelps, & Zeng, 2009; Cirino, Pollard-Durodola, Foorman, Carlson, & Francis, 2007) showed that teacher knowledge did not have a direct effect on students' reading achievement. Piasta, Connor, Fishman, and Morrison (2009) found that knowledge moderated the influence of classroom practice on student achievement such that high knowledge teachers who also provided the most direct instruction in phonics secured significant gains in first-grade reading achievement compared to low-knowledge teachers providing a high degree of direct instruction. Two studies, however, were unable to establish any relationship between teacher quality and student achievement.

Knowledge assessments designed to measure both content knowledge for teaching reading and the knowledge needed for teaching reading have been somewhat more consistent in predicting classroom reading practice and student achievement gains. Carlisle, Kelcey, Rowan, and Phelps (2011), using HLM analyses, showed a relationship between teachers' knowledge and first-grade students' comprehension scores, but not between teachers' knowledge and second- and third-grade students' achievement in decoding or comprehension. However, Carlisle, Kelcey, Berebitsky, and Phelps (2011) showed that second- and third-grade teachers' scores on the knowledge instrument were related to teachers' classroom reading practice, and teachers' knowledge modified the relationship between free and reduced-price lunch (FRL) status and student achievement, with higher knowledge teachers being more effective with students not on FRL. Finally, Lane et al. (2009) studied teachers' knowledge for providing fluency instruction. Using multilevel analyses, they demonstrated that teachers' knowledge scores predicted first- and second-grade students' scores on nonsense word fluency and oral reading fluency measures from the DIBELS. Results for third grade were not significant.

Teacher Knowledge for Teaching Students With Disabilities

Much of the research capturing teachers' knowledge for teaching is focused on general education teachers or general education teachers and special education teachers without disaggregating data by teacher type. Few studies have investigated the specialized knowledge needed for teaching students with disabilities. Some researchers claim to be focusing on knowledge of disability, technology, or accommodations, but instrumentation used in these studies often captures teachers' perspectives regarding knowledge they have or their dispositions toward using certain practices (Anderson & Hendrickson, 2007; Hollenbeck, Tindal, & Almond, 1998; Jackson, 1997–1998; Moody, 2003; Nabors, Little, Akin-Little, & Iobst, 2008; Weyandt, Fulton, Schepman, Verdi, & Wilson, 2009).

Four studies investigated the knowledge special education teachers had for teaching reading (Brownell et al., 2009; Brownell et al., 2007; Spear-Swerling, 2009; Spear-Swerling & Brucker, 2004).

Spear-Swerling and Brucker and Spear-Swerling investigated preservice special education teachers' knowledge of English word structure as well as their knowledge of reading related abilities and reading development and how this knowledge changed as a result of participating in coursework and field experiences. Knowledge of English word structure was taught in coursework and assessed using a test of teachers' knowledge of graphophonemic segmentation, syllable types, irregular words, morpheme segmentation, and general knowledge of reading. Alpha coefficients for the test scales ranged from .64 to .96. Special education preservice teachers implemented the knowledge they were acquiring in tutoring experiences or in the classrooms in which they were teaching. In both studies, preservice teachers demonstrated significant gains in knowledge, outperforming their peers who did not receive such experiences on tests of knowledge. Tutored students also made significant gains on selected reading achievement measures. Preservice teacher knowledge across both intervention and control groups was also correlated with student achievement gains, but significant Pearson correlations were found only in the Spear-Swerling and Brucker study. Spear-Swerling found it difficult to explain the different findings for these two studies; however, the larger sample size in the first study provided more power to establish significant correlations. Alternatively, Pearson correlations would not account for the nested nature of the data, which could have inflated results in the first study.

In one study, two separate analyses (Brownell et al., 2009) examined relationships among special education teachers' knowledge for teaching reading, teachers' classroom practices in reading, and student achievement gains among students with learning disabilities. The first analysis focused on 34 beginning special education teachers providing reading instruction to students with learning disabilities. Linear regression and HLM analyses were used to examine relationships between teachers' knowledge for teaching decoding, knowledge for teaching reading comprehension, and their classroom reading practices. Content knowledge for teaching decoding and comprehension did not account for a significant portion of the variance in any of the classroom practice scales.

In a second study, Brownell et al. (2007) assessed 90 beginning and experienced general and special education teachers' content knowledge for teaching reading. Their findings indicate that special education teachers' content knowledge for teaching reading was one third of a standard deviation above the mean of general education teachers with 15 years of experience. Additionally, content knowledge for teaching decoding predicted a significant but small to moderate portion of variance in six classroom practices variables. Although it seems surprising that content knowledge for teaching decoding predicted variance in classroom management practice and comprehension practice, teachers who performed well on one aspect of classroom reading practice tended to perform well on others. As a result, content knowledge for teaching decoding tended to be predictive of other aspects of instruction.

Conclusions

The positive relationship between teachers' knowledge for teaching content and either classroom practice or student achievement is more often significant than not, particularly when professional development has been provided or knowledge is related to classroom practice. The relative consistency of findings across studies suggests what many scholars have intuitively known—that is, the content knowledge teachers have for teaching is important to their ability to teach successfully. The research in special education is far more limited, but it does suggest a need for more research examining the role knowledge for teaching content plays in the instruction of special education teachers, and if that knowledge is different from the knowledge general education teachers need.

Further, the specific knowledge tapped in these studies varies, and relationships between knowledge and student achievement differ at various grade levels. More research is needed in special and general education to identify types of knowledge necessary for effective instruction at different grade levels, across varying student abilities, and for different content areas.

Role of Classroom Practice in Effective Instruction

What teachers do in the classroom seems to have the strongest impact on student achievement. Over the past decade, researchers have studied what constitutes effective classroom practice and how it can be measured. These studies have either focused on developing valid assessments of classroom practice that can be applied across content areas or are specific to reading and mathematics. Since reviews of previous decades of research are available in the published literature on effective classroom practice (Brophy & Good, 1986), we only focus on the past decade of research. We also include two qualitative studies in special education because the literature base is small in this area, and these two studies analyzed the practices of special education teachers who had achieved some quantitative outcome.

General Education Studies of Generic Classroom Practices

Two widely used observations systems have been developed to examine the classroom practice of general education teachers. Systems developed based on Danielson's Framework for Teaching (FFT) and Pianta's Classroom Assessment Scoring System (CLASS; Pianta, Belsky, Vandergrift, Houts, & Morrison, 2008) are being used across the country as part of teacher evaluation systems in Race to the Top states. The FFT is a "research-based set of components of instruction, aligned to the INTASC standards and grounded in a constructivist view of learning and teaching" (The Danielson Group, 2011). This framework provides standard knowledge and skills required for teachers' classroom practices and a rubric for scoring and assessing their teaching performance across all grade levels and content areas (Danielson, 1996; Milanowski & Kimball, 2003). It contains 22 component criteria in four interrelated domains of teacher responsibilities, including planning and preparation (Domain 1), classroom environment (Domain 2), instruction (Domain 3), and professional responsibilities (Domain 4).

Four research studies have been conducted using the Danielson framework in three different school districts (Borman & Kimball, 2005; Heneman, Milanowski, Kimball, & Odden, 2006; Kane, Taylor, Tyler, & Wooten, 2010; Milanowski, 2004). These studies used analyses that combined domain scores, treated domains separately, or used only Domains 2 and 3 to predict student achievement gains. In some cases, teacher performance on Danielson's framework accounted for a moderate and significant portion of the variance in student achievement (Kane et al., 2010), and in other cases the effect of classroom performance is significant but trivial (Borman & Kimball, 2005). Even within studies, the relationship between teacher practice and student achievement in math, reading, and science varies in terms of content and grade level taught and domain scores used to predict achievement (though performance on Domains 2 and 3 seem to have the greatest impact on student achievement).

The Classroom Assessment Scoring System (Pianta et al., 2008) assesses three major categories of classroom-level processes that have been related to student achievement, including emotional climate (e.g., positive classroom climate, teacher sensitivity, regard for student perspective), classroom organization (e.g., behavior management, productivity, instructional learning formats) and instructional support (e.g., concept development, quality of feedback, language modeling). Scores on the instructional support and emotional climate scales have been linked to a variety of outcomes for prekindergarten, kindergarten, and first-grade students, including reading and math achievement, language competence, reduced conflict with teachers, higher teacher-rated social competence, on-task behavior, and teacher-rated competence in mathematics and language (Connor, Son, Hindman, & Morrison, 2005; Hamre & Pianta, 2005; Howes et al., 2008; Mashburn et al., 2008; La Paro, Payne, Cox, & Bradley, 2002; Pointz, Rimm-Kaufmann, Grim, & Kirby, 2009; Ponitz, Rimm-Kaufman, Grimm, & Curby, 2009; Rimm-Kaufman, La Paro, Downer, & Pianta, 2005).

Both the CLASS and FFT have also been used in the Measuring Teacher Effectiveness (MET) Study (Bill and Melinda Gates Foundation, 2012) to determine their ability to predict teachers' value-added scores on state standardized assessments in mathematics and reading compared to subject specific observation systems. The correlation between the CLASS and FFT is high (.88) and the relationship between these instruments and subject specific observation systems in mathematics and reading are also high (.67 to .93). Overall scores on the classroom practice domains of both instruments were significantly different for teachers whose students' mean gains were in top quartile compared to those in the bottom quartile, and they were just as successful in predicting teachers' value-added as subject specific observation tools.

General Education Studies of Classroom Practices in Literacy

For more than a decade, researchers have been attempting to describe what effective reading teachers do to promote their students' achievement, particularly those at-risk for school failure (e.g., Connor et al., 2005, 2009; Taylor, Pearson, Peterson, & Rodriguez, 2001; Taylor, Peterson, Pearson, & Rodriguez, 2002). Most studies have created measurement systems that assess the content and quality of reading instruction, whereas only one study has assessed the quality of both reading and writing instruction (Grossman et al., 2010). These systems have assessed classroom practice using two main approaches: (a) time sampling and (b) Likert ratings.

Studies using time sampling instruments have attempted to understand the content effective teachers emphasize during instruction and the instructional practices they use. Multilevel analyses were used to demonstrate relationships between assessed reading instruction and students' gains in reading achievement. These studies identified a variety of teacher practices that were related to student achievement gains in reading. Many of these identified practices can be categorized under two main categories: (a) teacher-directed instruction that involved modeling and explanation, and (b) support for student learning that included such behaviors as asking students questions, prompting and cuing students, coaching them to apply strategies, and providing opportunities to practice with error correction. It is worth noting that two other effective teaching practices were identified in a smaller set of studies by Taylor and her colleagues, including cognitively engaging instruction and strategies for promoting high levels of on-task behavior. Additionally, teacher-directed instruction was identified as predictive of student achievement gains in all studies but one. Smolkowski and Gunn (2012) found that teacher demonstrations were not significant predictors of students' gains on decoding measures; only rate of practice opportunities and rate of opportunities without student error predicted achievement. These findings suggest that effective teaching practices may be unique to the content being taught.

Four other teams of researchers relied on Likert rating scales to assess the classroom reading instruction of kindergarten and first-grade teachers working with students who were identified as English Language Learners (ELL), the language arts instruction of fourth- and eighth-grade teachers, and the reading comprehension instruction of sixth- and seventh-grade teachers. With one exception, all of these studies used multilevel analyses to examine the relationship between classroom instruction and student achievement. In two of the studies (Baker, Gersten, Haager, & Dingle, 2006; Grossman et al., 2010), explicit instruction either predicted students' reading gains or characterized teachers whose students were in the top quartile on their value-added achievement scores. The studies focused on teachers of ELL students also showed that how teachers use language or teach it matters in affecting the achievement of these students. For instance, Baker et al. found that Sheltered English techniques (e.g., using visuals and manipulatives to teach content, providing explicit instruction in English language conventions) had a more beneficial effect on the reading achievement of Spanish-speaking students than those who were native English speakers. Further, Cirino et al. (2007) found that teachers' use of Spanish during instruction and their demonstrated oral language proficiency (i.e., quality of their fluency, pronunciation, grammar, and vocabulary when speaking) predicted students' reading achievement gains, whereas other indicators of instructional quality did not.

Other instructional practices were identified as effective but not consistently across studies. Baker et al. (2006) found positive, significant correlations among instruction geared toward low performers, interactive teaching, vocabulary development, and classroom reading composite gain scores; whereas Grossman et al. found that teachers in the top quartile of value-added scores performed better on student engagement items and spent more time teaching across content domains and emphasizing writing and speaking compared to low-quartile teachers. Finally, in the only study that did not use multilevel analyses, Matsumura Garnier, Slater, and Boston (2008) found that a combined teacher quality score composed of teachers' scores on classroom talk (e.g., teacher involves students in conversations about text, helps students link ideas), teacher expectations (e.g., provides clear expectations for student performance, expectations are rigorous), and cognitive demand of the task (e.g., text is rigorous, lesson activities provide opportunities for text analyses) predicted student achievement on SAT-10 reading comprehension scores.

Only two groups of researchers have used measurement approaches that capture the more individualized nature of special education instruction. Connor and her colleagues (Connor, Morrison, & Petrella, 2004; Connor, Morrison, & Underwood, 2007; Connor, 2009) have used a time sampling instrument to examine interactions between instruction and child characteristics on students' reading achievement gains. Their Individualizing Student Instruction (ISI) classroom observation system focuses on the content of instruction, how instruction is managed (e.g., teacher managed versus child managed), the content of instructional activities and subactivities (e.g., reading: decoding, fluency, comprehension), classroom management activities (e.g., organization, transitions), and duration of an activity within a content area. Multiple studies using the ISI have employed HLM analyses and demonstrated that prekindergarten through third-grade teachers use of instructional time interacts with students' entering reading abilities (Connor et al., 2004; Connor et al., 2007; Connor, 2009). Specifically, teacher-managed code instruction and teacher-managed meaning instruction had a greater impact on students whose initial letter word recognition, vocabulary, and comprehension skills were weaker than their peers. Additionally, younger students generally seemed to profit from more teacher-managed vocabulary and code-based instruction. Further, when teachers participated in an intervention designed to adjust the type and amount of instruction they provided to first- and third-grade students based on students' entering reading skills, they were more effective in promoting students' achievement (Connor et al., 2009).

Carlisle, Kelcey, Berebitsky, and Phelps (2011) used the Automated Classroom Observation System (ACOS-R) to analyze third-grade teachers' reading comprehension instruction. These researchers hypothesized that effective practices would depend on students' entering instructional needs, the content being taught, and duration of the lesson. Results of HLM analyses showed that teacher-directed instruction and support for students' learning were predictive of students' reading achievement gains, whereas pedagogical structure (e.g., reviewing material from previous lessons, stating lesson goals) was not. Moreover, teacher-directed instruction and support for students' learning allowed students on FRL and students with higher pretest reading comprehension scores to make stronger reading comprehension gains than students not on FRL and those with lower pretest scores. These researchers demonstrated that what defines effective instruction depends on students' needs, findings that seem at odds with those documented by Connor and her colleagues. Finally, lesson duration positively influenced the propensity of using instructional actions in pedagogical structure, teacher-directed instruction, and support for student learning. This later finding is illuminating for assessing the impact of special education teachers' instruction, as these teachers often work with students for short periods of time on focused aspects of reading instruction (e.g., decoding).

Special Education Studies of Classroom Practices in Reading

Within the last decade, three studies analyzed the reading instructional practices of beginning and experienced special education teachers (Brownell et al., 2007; Brownell et al., 2009; Seo, Brownell, Bishop, & Dingle, 2008). Reading instruction was analyzed using an adapted version of the ELL instrument developed by Gersten, Baker, Haager and Graves (2005). HLM analyses showed that overall classroom practice, general instructional environment (i.e., student engagement, student motivation and interest, and continuous and intensive instruction), and classroom management predicted gains in oral reading fluency (Brownell et al., 2009). Beginning teachers' classroom management scores also predicted gains in word identification. Both beginning and experienced teachers' decoding practices predicted students' word identification and word attack gains. Additionally, several practices (i.e., overall classroom practice, general instructional environment, classroom management, and comprehension practices) predicted students' reading comprehension scores after controlling for initial oral reading fluency scores (Brownell et al., 2007). Further, duration of lessons and instructional group size were significant moderators of the relationship between classroom practice and reading achievement. Longer lessons resulted in larger student word attack and oral fluency achievement gains, but student word identification gains were smaller when special education teachers served larger numbers of students.

Seo et al. (2008) qualitatively analyzed the observed practices of beginning special education teachers scored as capable of engaging their students during reading instruction. They selected engagement during reading instruction as an outcome, as it has been tied to student achievement in many studies. These authors distinguished the most engaging teacher from less engaging teachers on four instructional dimensions: instructional quality, responsiveness to student needs, socioemotional climate, and student autonomy. High-quality instruction was intensive, deliberate, cohesive, and capable of fostering student interest. Responsiveness to student needs described such behaviors as monitoring student learning, asking probing questions or providing prompts, reacting spontaneously to student input, and subtly redirecting student behavior. Socioemotional climate captured the teachers' ability to create a warm and engaging classroom where students were encouraged to help each other and persist in the face of challenging instruction. Finally, student autonomy was promoted when teachers provided student choice and promoted self-regulated behavior.

General Education Studies of Classroom Practice in Mathematics

Most research on general education math classroom practices has focused on developing assessments that can determine the degree to which teachers employ instructional practices that align with the Principles and Standards for School Mathematics produced by the National Council for Teachers of Mathematics (NCTM). These standards suggest that teachers should ensure that all students have access to mathematics instruction that is challenging, focuses on problem-solving and conceptual learning, encourages multiple ways of representing problems, and builds a collaborative culture for learning. The instruction intended to capture NCTM principles and standards is referred to as "reform-oriented" instruction, which embraces a constructivist and student-centered approach to learning.

The assessment systems designed to capture reform-oriented mathematics instruction involve mostly direct observation of classroom instruction that requires observers to rate teachers using Likert rating scales. These assessment systems rate a variety of classroom practices, but most focus on the teacher's ability to: (a) teach mathematical content accurately and in ways that further student understanding and reasoning, (b) use students' thinking during instruction, and (c) develop students' ability to make mathematical representations. Attempts to establish the reliability and validity of these systems have been reported in a seven studies involving elementary, middle school, and secondary mathematics. Many of these studies have involved urban districts and, with only two exceptions (Jong, Pedulla, Reagan, Salomon-Fernandez, & Cochran-Smith, 2010; Matsumura et al., 2008), all have used multilevel statistical techniques to analyze data (Gearhart et al., 1999; Bill and Melinda Gates Foundation, 2012; Saxe, Gearhart, & Seltzer, 1999; Tarr et al., 2008).

In all studies, assessed classroom practices were significant predictors of students' mathematics achievement, yet drawing conclusions about the dimensions of effective classroom mathematics instruction is difficult. Researchers either collapsed teachers' overall ratings and used them to predict student achievement (Matsumura et al., 2008; Bill and Melinda Gates Foundation, 2012; Muijs & Reynolds, 2003), or they did not define dimensions of classroom practice in ways that they could be easily compared (Gearhart et al., 1999; Saxe et al., 1999; Tarr et al., 2008). Despite these inconsistencies, there do seem to be some broad dimensions of classroom practice that are captured across these various instruments. These include teachers' ability to: (a) create instruction that is responsive to student thinking, (b) promote students' conceptual understanding during instruction, and (c) encourage student involvement in talking about or representing mathematical concepts.

Further, only one study seems to suggest that reform-oriented mathematics instruction, at least as defined and assessed currently, may not be effective for lower-performing students.

Saxe et al. (1999) used the same approach as Gearhart et al. (1999) to determine if fifth-grade students with a rudimentary understanding of fractions learned more than those who had little understanding when their teachers used practices that elicited and built on student thinking and addressed conceptual issues when problem-solving with fractions. Using HLM analyses, these researchers demonstrated a linear, positive relationship between more conceptual reform-oriented practices and student achievement for students with at least a rudimentary understanding. By contrast, teachers' practices were not related to achievement gains when students began instruction with weaker understandings of fractions. The authors suggest that direct, explicit instruction may be more useful for promoting computation skills and building conceptual understanding where none exists.

Special Education Studies of Classroom Practices in Mathematics

Only two studies have attempted to quantify the practices of teachers providing mathematics instruction to students with disabilities and link those practices to student achievement. Kurz, Elliott, Wehby, and Smithson (2009) used a survey to determine the degree to which 18 special and general education teachers offered students with disabilities opportunities to learn mathematics content articulated in state standards. The survey asked teachers to indicate the content to be learned by students (e.g., number sense, operations, measurement) and the level of cognitive demand required during instruction (e.g., memorize facts, demonstrate understanding of mathematical ideas). Teachers were required to complete the survey three times throughout the course of the year to assess alignment between state standards (or intended curriculum), planned curriculum, and enacted curriculum. Teachers' alignment scores for intended versus enacted curriculum at midyear and end of year were compared to students with disabilities' gain scores on three different achievement measures analyzed at the class level. Stronger alignment between intended and enacted curriculum correlated positively with students' with disabilities achievement scores for special education teachers, but the same was not true for general education teachers. Researchers concluded special education teachers' use of cognitively demanding instruction that addressed content covered in the state standards was likely responsible for student gains; however, they cautioned that a larger sample could produce different results, as correlations are often inflated in analyses that do not account for within classroom variance.

As an attempt to understand the dimensions of effective mathematics instruction in special education, Griffin, Jitendra, and League (2009) examined the classroom communication practices of five preservice special education teachers observed during mathematics lessons. The researchers examined the number of lower-order and higher-order teacher questions asked, teacher-to-student exchanges, student-to-teacher exchanges, student-to-student exchanges, and occurrence of teacher press (i.e., teacher requests for students to elaborate their ideas and reasoning behind problem solutions). Student achievement gains were calculated using researcher-constructed pretest and posttest measures aligned with content students were learning. The researchers noted that students made the most progress from pre- to posttest in mathematics classrooms where teachers employed more teacher press and asked many more lower-order than higher-order questions. Griffin et al. (2009) suggested that their findings raised questions about the efficacy of peer-mediated practices, heavily promoted by the NCTM, for students with disabilities, and suggested that teacher-directed explicit, interactive instruction that helps students justify their reasoning and solutions during problem-solving might be more effective.

Conclusions About Effective Classroom Practice

Findings from this review provide strong evidence that classroom practice can be measured and related to important student outcomes. The studies reviewed provide evidence of the reliability and validity of the instrumentation used, with more evidence being provided to support the different dimensions of effective reading instruction than effective mathematics instruction.

Classroom practice can also be assessed effectively using observation systems that are content-free as well as those that are content-specific. Results from these studies of general and special education teachers suggest that classroom management and climate are important for promoting language outcomes, reducing aggressive behavior, and promoting social competence, particularly in younger children. Classroom management and climate also seem to play a role in the achievement of older children. Further, the use of explicit instruction and the ability to support students during reading instruction seems important, particularly for low-achieving students. Because many of the studies examining effective reading instruction involve high-risk students, it is logical to conclude that findings relevant in these studies likely generalize to populations of students with disabilities, particularly those with high incidence disabilities.

How teachers spend their time in specific content areas depends on needs of particular students. Findings from Connor and her colleagues' research (2004, 2007, 2009) were particularly illustrative on this point; students with poor decoding skills need to spend more time on code-focused instruction, whereas students with strong skills in this area need a different type of instruction, more child-managed instruction. These results appear to generalize to math where lower-performing students appear to realize greater benefit from a combination of explicit instruction and reform-oriented teacher practices. In particular, students with disabilities may benefit from opportunities to learn state standards and the use of teacher press.

What seems less clear is exactly how the effectiveness of specific instructional practices (e.g., explicit instruction, opportunities to practice) varies with the content being taught. Carlisle, Kelcey, Rowan, & Phelps (2011) found that direct, explicit instruction and support for student learning significantly predicted student comprehension gains, whereas Smolkowski and Gunn (2012) found that opportunities to practice without errors were more predictive of gains in reading decodable words. Further, Connor and her colleagues established that teacher-directed comprehension instruction was more appropriate for struggling learners, whereas child-managed comprehension instruction was more appropriate for students scoring in the 90th percentile or higher. In mathematics, Saxe et al. (1999) demonstrated that teachers who provided more conceptual instruction in fractions and based their instruction on students' thinking were more likely to promote the achievement of students with a rudimentary understanding of fractions than students without such understanding. These findings suggest researchers should construct measurement systems in ways that recognize the multidimensional aspects of classroom instruction (i.e., how instructional practices vary according to type of content being taught, time available for instruction, type of students taught, and curricula available).

Finally, even though research in general education should be able to inform special education practice, the small number of studies focused on teachers working with students with disabilities suggests that more research is needed to better understand the instructional practices of special education teachers and their influence on student outcomes.

Conclusions, Challenges, and Future Research

The research on teacher qualifications in general education is so inconsistent that it is difficult to interpret, and thus, does little to inform work in special education. Although the Feng and Sass (2010) and

Nougaret et al. (2005) studies provide consistent evidence that initial teacher preparation influences achievement or the instructional practices of special education teachers, we do not know if future studies would achieve similar findings. Nor do we know about how the content or experiences in teacher preparation matter. Considering the diversity of coursework among U.S. universities, it is also difficult to equate knowledge gained from courses at one university with another. The Feng and Sass study, conducted wholly in Florida, will likely not compare to a national or multistate study because state standards for teacher preparation vary considerably. Policy makers seek global understanding of initial preparation and professional development; teacher educators and staff developers are more concerned with the exact processes.

The existing research in general education and special education provides some clarity about the role that knowledge for teaching content and classroom practice plays in improving student outcomes, particularly in the area of reading. Teachers' knowledge of English word structure and language appear important for teaching decoding to high-risk students and students with disabilities, especially when teachers have received some type of professional development that focuses on enacting knowledge or when the knowledge test attempts to measure the intersection of teachers' content knowledge and their knowledge for teaching. Only one study was found tying special education teachers' knowledge for teaching reading to classroom practice, and so our conclusions are based almost exclusively on the general education literature. Based on the general education math research, it is evident that teachers must be able to understand and apply both conceptual and procedural math, analyze and appropriately respond to student errors, and provide support for students' mathematical thinking. In both general and special education, more research is needed to more fully understand the knowledge underlying different aspects of instructional practice within a content area and across content areas.

With regard to effective classroom practice, researchers examining relationships among student outcomes and scores on Danielson's Framework for Teaching or the CLASS have demonstrated that well-managed environments supportive of student learning are helpful for improving academic and social outcomes for preschool and early elementary students. Additionally, instructional support as measured by Danielson's framework has been correlated with student achievement gains in reading and math. Instructional support as measured by the CLASS has been related to student gains in reading and math for young children, but not older children. Less clear is the role that classroom environment and instructional support, as measured by the CLASS or Danielson Framework, might play in the social or academic outcomes of students with disabilities.

Studies of classroom practice in reading instruction, far more so than math, seem to provide the most direction regarding effective teaching for students with disabilities, as most of these studies have addressed instruction for students at-risk for reading failure or students with disabilities. From these studies, we conclude that teacher-managed, explicit instruction in both decoding and comprehension that provides sufficient support (e.g., opportunities to practice with little error or give students opportunities to ask questions) and time for students to learn the appropriate skills or strategies is important in elementary school. Additionally, teachers that approach instruction in organized ways that maximize students' academic engagement and minimize student disruption also appear to promote the learning of students with disabilities and those at-risk for reading failure. Interestingly, these findings are well supported in the instructional intervention literature and are considered pillars of effective special education instruction (Swanson & Hoskyn, 2001). Moreover, we would be remiss if we did not point out that effective instruction must be conceptualized differently for different types of learners and for different content, both within and outside the area of reading. At least a handful of studies in this review make it clear that instruction has to be differentiated to meet the needs of students who are struggling in reading and math. Also, the instructional practices that promote decoding instruction appear different than the instructional practices that promote comprehension instruction, and the same might be true for computation versus problem-solving in mathematics. Thus, measurement that captures the multidimensional nature of instruction for different content and types of learners seems important to explore further.

Challenges

There are several substantial challenges to understanding effective teaching for students with disabilities. For one, valid metrics of teacher effectiveness are difficult to secure. States typically collect standardized achievement data on students, but this is only one important educational outcome for students with disabilities. Competence in the social, communication, and everyday living realms are also important for students with disabilities. Most states, however, do not measure these outcomes in any uniform way, so teachers cannot be compared on their ability to achieve these outcomes. Further, there are multiple problems using state assessments to determine teachers' effectiveness for students with disabilities. Perhaps one of the most perplexing challenges has to do with attributing the between-classroom variance (assumed to be the teacher effect) to the special education teacher when students with disabilities are served by general and special education teachers. State assessments present other problems for assessing the gains of students with disabilities and using them as value-added scores: (a) there are floor effects for at least 20% of students with disabilities participating in the assessments (Laitusis, Buzick, Cook, & Stone, 2011); (b) test accommodations are often not delivered consistently or in standardized ways (Shriner & DeStefano, 2003); (c) most state assessments measure proficiency and are not appropriate measures of academic achievement for students who are off grade; and (d) accuracy of the value-added score for a teacher depends on the number of students taking the test. Finally, the use of parametric statistics with an intentionally nonrandomized sample to measure teacher effectiveness is particularly concerning. Longitudinal modeling does help mitigate this effect but may be negated by the long-term delivery of services by the same special educator over multiple years.

Other validity challenges focus on issues of time spent in instruction, instructional group size, and students' opportunity to learn assessed content. Special education teachers spend varying amounts of time with students with disabilities and such variability influences both what a teacher can accomplish during instruction (e.g., Carlisle, Kelcey, Berebitsky, & Phelps, 2011) and the relationship between classroom practice and student achievement (e.g., Brownell et al., 2007). The size of a special education teachers' instructional group influences the intensity of instruction they are capable of providing (Brownell et al., 2007). Instructional group size, however, is rarely within the special education teachers' control. Finally, the access students with disabilities have to appropriate content (i.e., opportunity to learn) across both general and special education teachers likely influences their achievement (Kurz et al., 2009), but special education teachers may not have influence on what the general education teacher addresses or vice versa.

Future Research

Our review makes obvious the need for research to better understand all major dimensions of teacher quality in special education and how they might be assessed for different purposes. To improve teacher education or professional development efforts and determine if they are effective, our field will need more fine-grained measurements of teacher knowledge and classroom performance. To determine the impact of an innovation, such as a professional development effort designed to improve special education teachers' comprehension instruction, researchers need dependent measures that are well-aligned with the content of the innovation. In this particular case, researchers would need an instrument that captures the ways in which a teacher might move from less effective to more effective comprehension instruction. In contrast, more global assessments of special education teachers' classroom performance are desirable when making evaluative decisions, such as granting tenure or merit pay. In these instances, it is more helpful if assessment systems can be used in a more comprehensive way, such as across content areas, grade level, or types of students taught. In addition, key instructional practices will need to be defined and assessed more globally.

We also need to understand the ways in which different dimensions of special education teacher quality are related to each other and to student outcomes. Based on the results of several studies in this review, we anticipate that teacher knowledge will have a more direct effect on classroom practice and a more indirect effect on student outcomes, so the relationship between teacher knowledge and classroom practice should be relatively strong. Special education teachers' classroom practice, however, should be related to important student outcomes. Some of these outcomes will be linked directly to the special education teacher (e.g., IEP goal completion), but others will not (e.g., student gains on state achievement tests). It seems imperative then to determine the degree to which special education teachers' practice can be assessed reliably using value-added scores on either state assessments or other outcomes, such as performance on DIBELS or indicators of social competence. Although states are currently grappling with this issue in value-added assessments of special education teachers, we are a long way from understanding how the variance in student classroom performance can be attributed to the special and general education teacher.

Finally, our field needs to strengthen its infrastructure for doing this complex work. Studying the knowledge and classroom performance of special education teachers will require the collaboration of researchers with extensive knowledge of general and special education content and practice as well as those with sophisticated measurement and statistical analyses. Historically, special education doctoral programs have prepared their students to engage in intervention research; thus, many researchers are not prepared to engage in the sorts of creative measurement work needed to measure teacher quality in special education. Moreover, logistics associated with measuring special education teachers' knowledge and practice are enormous. The numbers of special education teachers working in one school is small; thus, researchers will be in the unenviable position of collecting data across many school sites. Such studies undoubtedly will require numerous research sites and personnel to conduct research; the costs of doing such research are beyond the current level of support provided by the Institute for Education Sciences. Clearly, if special education teacher quality is to become a focus of research efforts, more support from the U.S. Department of Education must be forthcoming.

References

Anderson, L. F., & Hendrickson, J. M. (2007). Early-career EBD teach knowledge, ratings of competency importance, and observed use of instruction and management competencies. *Education and Treatment of Children, 30*(4), 43–65. doi:10.1353/etc.2007.0019

Baker, S., Gersten, R., Haager, D., & Dingle, M. (2006). Teaching practice and the reading beginning special education teacher quality. *Exceptional Children, 75*, 391–411.

Bill and Melinda Gates Foundation. (2012). Gathering feedback for teaching: Combining high-quality observations with student surveys and achievement gains. Policy and practice brief. Retrieved from: http://www.metproject.org/downloads/MET_Gathering_Feedback_Practioner_Brief.pdf

Borman, G. D., & Kimball, S. M. (2005). Teacher quality and educational equality: Do teachers with higher standards-based evaluation ratings close student achievement gaps? *The Elementary School Journal, 106*(1), 3–20. doi:10.1086/496904

Boyd, D., Grossman, P., Lankford, H., Loeb, S., & Wyckoff, J. (2008). Measuring effect sizes: The effect of measurement error (CALDER Working Paper No. 19). Retrieved from: http://www.caldercenter.org/publications/upload/1001257_measuring_effect_sizes.pdf

Boyd, D., Lankford, H., Loeb, S., Rockoff, J., & Wyckoff, J. (2008). The narrowing gap in New York City teacher qualifications and its implications for student achievement in high-poverty schools. *Journal of Policy Analysis and Management, 27*, 793–818. doi:10.1002/pam.20377

Brophy, J., & Good, T. (1986). Teacher and student achievement. In M. Wittrock (Ed.), *The third handbook of research on teaching*. New York: Macmillan.

Brownell, M. T., Dimino, J., Bishop, A. G., Haager, D., Gersten, R., Menon, S., Klingner, J. K., Sindelar, P. T., & Penfield, R. D. (2009). The role of domain expertise in beginning special education teacher quality. *Exceptional Children, 75*, 391–411.

Brownell, M. T., Haager, D., Bishop, A. G., Klingner, J. K., Menon, S., Penfield, R., & Dingle, M. (2007, April).

Teacher quality in special education: The role of knowledge, classroom practice, and school environment. Paper presented at the annual meeting of the American Education Research Association, Chicago.
Carlisle, J. Kelcey, B., Berebitsky, D., & Phelps, G. (2011). Embracing the complexity of instruction: a study of the effects of teachers' instruction on students' reading comprehension. *Scientific Studies of Reading, 15*, 409–439. doi:10.1080/10888438.2010.497521
Carlisle, J. F., Correnti, R., Phelps, G., & Zeng, J. (2009). Exploration of the contribution of teachers' knowledge about reading to their students' improvement in reading. *Reading and Writing, 22*, 457–486. doi:10.1007/s11145-009-9165-y
Carlisle, J. F., Kelcey, B., Rowan, B., & Phelps, G. (2011). Teachers' knowledge about early reading: effects on students' gains in reading achievement. *Journal of Research on Educational Effectiveness, 4*(4), 289–321.
Cavalluzo, L. (2004). *Is National Board certification an effective signal of teacher quality?* Washington, DC: The CNA Corporation.
Cirino, P. T., Pollard-Durodola, S. D., Foorman, B. R., Carlson, C. D., & Francis, D. J. (2007). Teacher characteristics, classroom instruction, and student literacy and language outcomes in bilingual kindergartners. *Elementary School Journal, 107*, 341–364. doi:10.1086/516668
Clotfelter, C. T., Ladd, H. F., & Vigdor, J. L. (2010). Does teacher certification matter: Evaluating the evidence. *Journal of Human Resources, 45*, 655–681. doi:10.1353/jhr.2010.0023
Connor, C. M. (2009). Individualized reading instruction in early elementary classrooms. *Perspectives on Language and Literacy, Special Edition*, 33–38.
Connor, C. M., Morrison, F. J., & Petrella, J. N. (2004). Effective reading comprehension instruction: Examining child × instruction interactions. *Journal of Educational Psychology, 96*, 682–698. doi:10.1037/0022-0663.96.4.682
Connor, C. M., Morrison, F. J., & Underwood, P. S. (2007). A second chance in second grade? The independent and cumulative impact of first and second grade reading instruction and students' letter-word reading skill growth. *Scientific Studies of Reading, 11*, 199–233. doi:10.1080/10888430701344314
Connor, C. M., Piasta, S. B., Fishman, B., Glasney, S., Schatschneider, C., Crowe, E., ... Morrison, F. J. (2009). Individualizing student instruction precisely: Effects of child × instruction interactions on first graders' literacy development. *Child Development, 80*, 77–100. doi:10.1111/j.1467-8624.2008.01247.x
Connor, C. M., Son, S. H., Hindman, A., & Morrison, F. J. (2005). Teacher qualifications, classroom practices, family characteristics, and preschool experience: Complex effects on first graders' language and early reading. *Journal of School Psychology, 43*, 343–375. doi:10.1016/j.jsp.2005.06.001
Danielson, C. (1996). *Enhancing professional practice: A framework for teaching.* Alexandria, VA: Association for Supervision and Curriculum Development.
Early, D. M., Maxwell, K. L., Burchinal, M., Alva, S., Bender, R. H., Bryant, D., ... Zill, N. (2007). Teachers' education, classroom quality, and young children's academic skills: Results from seven studies of preschool programs. *Child Development, 78*(2), 558–580. doi:10.1111/j.1467-8624.2007.01014.x
Feng, L., & Sass, T. (2010). *What makes special education special? Teacher training and achievement of students with disabilities* (CALDER Working Paper No. 49). Retrieved from http://www.caldercenter.org/publications.cfm
Foorman, B. R., & Moats, L. C. (2004). Conditions for sustaining research-based practices in early reading instruction. *Remedial and Special Education, 25*, 51–60. doi:10.1177/07419325040250010601
Gearhart, M., Saxe, G. B., Seltzer, M., Schlackman, J., Ching, C. C., Nasir, N., ... Sloan, T. F. (1999). Opportunities to learn fractions in elementary mathematics classrooms. *Journal for Research in Mathematics Education, 30*, 286–315. Retrieved from http://www.jstor.org/stable/749837
Gersten, R., Baker, S. K., Haager, D., & Graves, A. W. (2005). Exploring the role of teacher quality in predicting reading outcomes for first-grade English learners: An observational study. *Remedial & Special Education, 26*, 197–206. doi:10.1177/07419325050260040201
Goe, L. (2008, May). *Key issue: Using value-added models to identify and support highly effective teachers.* Washington, DC: National Comprehensive Center for Teacher Quality.
Goldhaber, D. (2002). The mystery of good teaching. *Education Next, 2*(1), 50–55.
Goldhaber, D., & Anthony, E. (2004). Can teacher quality be effectively assessed? (Working Paper) Washington, DC: Urban Institute. Retrieved from www.urban.org/UploadedPDF/410958_NBPTSOutcomes.pdf
Goldhaber, D. D., & Brewer, D. J. (2000). Does certification matter? High school teacher certification status and student achievement. *Educational Evaluation and Policy Analysis, 22*, 129–145. Retrieved from http://www.jstor.org/stable/1164392
Griffin, C. C., Jitendra, A. K., & League, M. B. (2009). Novice special educators' instructional practices, communication patterns, and content knowledge for teaching mathematics. *Teacher Education and Special Education, 32*, 319–336. doi:10.1177/0888406409343540
Grossman, P. L., Loeb, S., Cohen, J., Hammerness, K., Wyckoff, J., Boyd, D., & Lankford, J. (2010). Measure for measure: The relationship between measures of instructional practice in middle school English language arts

and teachers' value-added scores (NBER Working Paper No. 16015). Cambridge, MA: National Bureau of Economic Research. Retrieved from: http://www.nber.org/papers/w16015

Guarino, C. M., Hamilton, L. S., Lockwood, J. R., & Rathbun, A. H. (2006). Teacher qualifications, instructional practices, and reading and mathematics gains of kindergartners: Research and development report (NCES 2006-031). Washington, DC: National Center for Education Statistics. Retrieved from http://nces.ed.gov/pubs2006/2006031.pdf

Hamre, B. K., & Pianta, R. C. (2005). Can instructional and emotional support in the first grade classroom make a difference for children at risk of school failure? *Child Development, 76*, 949–967.

Heck, R. H. (2007). Examining the relationship between teacher quality as an organizational property of schools and students' achievement and growth. *Educational Administration Quarterly, 43*, 399–432. doi:10.1177/0013161X07306452

Heneman, H. G., III, Milanowski, A., Kimball, S. M., & Odden, A. (2006). Standards-based teacher evaluation as a foundation for knowledge- and skill-based pay (CPRE Policy Briefs RB-45). Retrieved from http://files.eric.ed.gov/fulltext/ED493116.pdf?

Henry, G. T., Bastian, K. C., & Fortner, C. K. (2011). Stayers and leavers: Early-career teacher effectiveness and attrition. *Educational Researcher, 40*, 271–280. doi:10.3102/0013189X11419042

Hill, H. C., Rowan, B., & Ball, D. L. (2005). Effects of teachers' mathematical knowledge for teaching on student achievement. *American Educational Research Journal, 42*, 371–406.

Hollenbeck, K., Tindal, G., & Almond, P. (1998). Teachers' knowledge of accommodations as a validity issue in high-stakes testing. *The Journal of Special Education, 32*, 175–183. doi:10.1177/002246699803200304

Howes, C., Burchinal, M., Pianta, R., Bryant, D., Early, D., Clifford, R., & Barbarin, O. (2008). Ready to learn? Children's pre-academic achievement in pre-kindergarten programs. *Early Childhood Research Quarterly, 23*, 27–50.

Huang, F. L., & Moon, T. R. (2008). Is experience the best teacher? A multilevel analysis of teacher characteristics and student achievement in low performing schools. *Education, Assessment, Evaluation, and Accountability, 21*, 209–234. doi:10.1007/s11092-009-9074-2

Jackson, S. C. (1997–1998). Preservice special education teachers' knowledge of technology. *National Forum of Special Education Journal, 6*(1 & 2), 27–32.

Jong, C., Pedulla, J. J., Reagan, E. M., Salomon-Fernandez, Y., & Cochran-Smith, M. (2010). Exploring the link between reformed teaching practices and pupil learning in elementary school mathematics. *School Science & Mathematics, 110*(6), 309–326. doi:10.1111/j.1949-8594.2010.00039.x

Kane, T. J., Taylor, E. S., Tyler, J. H., & Wooten, A. L. (2010). Identifying effective classroom practices using student achievement data (NBER Working Paper 15803). Cambridge, MA: National Bureau of Economic Research. Retrieved from http://www.nber.org/papers/w15803

Kennedy, M. M. (1992). The problem of improving teacher quality while balancing supply and demand. In E. Boe & D. Gilford (Eds.), *Teacher supply, demand, and quality: policy issues, models, and data bases* (pp. 63–126). Washington, DC: National Academies Press

Kennedy, M. M. (1999). Approximations to indicators of student outcomes. *Educational Evaluation and Policy Analysis, 21*, 345–363. doi:10.3102/01623737021004345

Kennedy, M. M. (2010). Attribution error and the quest for teacher quality. *Educational Researcher, 39*(8), 591–598. doi:10.3102/0013189X10390804

Kurz, A., Elliott, S. N., Wehby, J. H., & Smithson, J. L. (2009). Alignment of the intended, planned, and enacted curriculum in general and special education and its relation to student achievement. *Journal of Special Education, 44*, 131–145. doi:10.1177/0022466909341196

Laitusis, C. C., Buzick, H. M., Cook, L. L., & Stone, E. A. (2011). Adaptive testing options for accountability assessments. In M. Russell (Ed.), *Assessing students in the margins: Challenges, strategies, and techniques*. Charlotte, NC: Information Age Publishing.

Lane, H. B., Hudson, R. F., Leite, W. L., Kosanovich, M. L., Strout, M. T., Fenty, N. S., & Wright, T. L. (2009). Teacher knowledge about reading fluency and indicators of students' fluency growth in reading first schools. *Reading and Writing Quarterly, 25*, 57–86. doi:10.1080/10573560802491232

Marszalek, J. M., Odom, A. L., LaNasa, S. M., & Adler, S. A. (2010). Distortion or clarification: Defining highly qualified teachers and the relationship between certification and achievement. *Education Policy Analysis Archives, 18*, 27. Retrieved from http://epaa.asu.edu/ojs/article/view/837

Mashburn, A. J., Pianta, R. C., Hamre, B. K., Downer, J. T., Barbarin, O. A., Bryant, D., ... Howes, C. (2008). Measures of classroom quality in pre-kindergarten and children's development of academic, language and social skills. *Child Development, 79*, 732–749.

Matsumura, L. C., Garnier, H. E., Slater, S. C., & Boston, M. D. (2008). Toward measuring instructional interactions "at-scale." *Educational Assessment, 13*, 267–300. doi:10.1080/10627190802602541

McCutchen, D., Abbott, R. D., Green, L. B., Beretvas, S. N., Cox, S., Potter, N. S., ... Gray, A. L. (2002). Beginning literacy: Links among teacher knowledge, teacher practice, and student learning. *Journal of Learning Disabilities*, *35*, 69–86. doi:10.1177/002221940203500106

McCutchen, D., Green, L., Abbott, R. D., & Sanders, E. A. (2009). Further evidence for teacher knowledge: supporting struggling readers in grades three through five. *Reading and Writing*, *22*, 401–423. doi:10.1007/s11145-009-9163-0

Milanowski, A. (2004). Relationships among dimension scores of standards-based teacher evaluation systems, and the stability of evaluation score: Student achievement relationships over time (CPRE-UW Working Paper Series TC-04-02). Retrieved from http://www.cpre-wisconsin.com/papers/AERA04Measurement.pdf

Milanowski, A., & Kimball, S. M. (2003). *The framework-based teacher performance assessment systems in Cincinnati and Washoe* (CPRE-UW Working Paper Series TC-03-07). Retrieved from http://cpre.wceruw.org/papers/CinciWashoe_TE.pdf

Moody, B. A. (2003). Juvenile corrections educators: Their knowledge and understanding of special education. *Journal of Corrections Education*, *54*, 105–107.

Muijs, D., & Reynolds, D. (2003). Student background and teacher effects on achievement and attainment in mathematics: A longitudinal study. *Educational Research and Evaluation*, *9*, 289–314. doi:10.1076/edre.9.3.289.15571

Nabors, L. A., Little, S. G., Akin-Little, A., & Iobst, E. A. (2008). Teacher knowledge of and confidence in meeting the needs of children with chronic medical conditions: Pediatric psychology's contribution to education. *Psychology in the Schools*, *45*, 217–226. doi:10.1002/pits.20292

Neild, R. C., Farley-Ripple, E. N., & Byrnes, V. (2009). The effect of teacher certification on middle grades achievement in an urban district. *Educational Policy*, *23*, 732–760. doi:10.1177/0895904808320675

Nougaret, A. A., Scruggs, T. E., & Mastropieri, M. A. (2005). Does teacher education produce better special education teachers? *Exceptional Children*, *71*, 217–229.

Nye, B., Konstantopoulos, S., & Hedges, L. V. (2004). How large are teacher effects? *Educational Evaluation and Policy Analysis*, *26*, 237–257. doi:10.3102/01623737026003237

Phelps, G. (2009). Just knowing how to read isn't enough! Assessing knowledge for teaching reading. *Education, Assessment, Evaluation, and Accountability*, *21*, 137–154. doi:10.1007/s11092-009-9070-6

Phillips, K. J. R. (2010). What does "highly qualified" mean for student achievement? Evaluating the relationships between teacher quality indicators and at-risk students' mathematics and reading achievement gains in first grade. *The Elementary School Journal*, *110*, 464–493. doi:10.1086/651192

Pianta, R. C., Belsky, J., Vandergrift, N., Houts, R., & Morrison, F. J. (2008). Classroom effects on children's achievement trajectories in elementary school. *American Educational Research Journal*, *49*, 365–397. doi:10.3102/0002831207308230

Piasta, S. B., Connor, C. M., Fishman, B. J., & Morrison, F. J. (2009). Teachers' knowledge of literacy, classroom practices, and student reading growth. *Scientific Studies in Reading*, *13*, 224–248. doi:10.1080/10888430902851364

Ponitz, C. C., Rimm-Kaufman, S. E., Grimm, K. J., & Curby, T. W. (2009). Kindergarten classroom quality, behavioral engagement, and reading achievement. *School Psychology Review*, *38*, 102–120.

Rimm-Kaufman, S. E., La Paro, K. M., Downer, J. T., & Pianta, R. C. (2005). The contribution of classroom setting and quality of instruction to children's behavior in kindergarten classrooms. *The Elementary School Journal*, *105*, 377–394. doi:10.1086/429948

Rivkin, S. G., Hanushek, E. A., & Kain, J. F. (2005). Teachers, schools, and academic achievement. *Econometrica*, *73*, 417–458. doi:10.1111/j.1468-0262.2005.00584.x

Saxe, G. B., Gearhart, M., & Seltzer, M. (1999). Relations between classroom practices and student learning in the domain of fractions. *Cognition and Instruction*, *17*, 1–24. doi:10.1207/s1532690xci1701_1

Seo, S., Brownell, M. T., Bishop, A. G., & Dingle, M. (2008). Beginning special education teachers' classroom reading instruction: Practices that engage elementary students with learning disabilities. *Exceptional Children*, *75*, 97–122.

Shechtman, N., Roschelle, J., Haertel, G., & Knudsen, J. (2010). Investigating links from teacher knowledge, to classroom practice, to student learning in the instructional system of the middle-school mathematics classroom. *Cognition and Instruction*, *28*, 317–359. doi:10.1080/07370008.2010.487961

Shriner, J. G., & DeStefano, L. (2003). Participation and accommodation in state assessment: The role of Individualized Education Programs. *Exceptional Children*, *69*, 147–16.

Sindelar, P. T., Daunic, A., & Rennells, M. S. (2004). Comparisons of traditionally and alternatively trained teachers. *Exceptionality*, *12*, 209–233. doi:10.1207/s15327035ex1204_3

Smolkowski, K., & Gunn, B. (2012). Reliability and validity of the Classroom Observations of Student–Teacher Interactions (COSTI) for kindergarten reading instruction. *Early Childhood Research Quarterly*, *27*, 316–328. doi:10.1016/j.ecresq.2011.09.004

Spear-Swerling, L. (2009). A literacy tutoring experience for prospective special educators and struggling second graders. *Journal of Learning Disabilities*, *42*, 431–443. doi:10.1177/0022219409338738.

Spear-Swerling, L., & Brucker, P. O. (2004). Preparing novice teachers to develop basic reading and spelling skills in children. *Annals of Dyslexia, 54*, 332–364. doi:10.1007/s11881-004-0016-x

Stronge, J. H., Ward, T. J., Tucker, P. D., Hindman, J. L., McColsky, W., & Howard, B. (2007). National board certified teachers and non-national board certified teachers: Is there a difference in teacher effectiveness and student achievement? *Journal of Personnel Evaluation in Education, 20*, 185–210. doi:10.1007/s11092-008-9052-0

Swanson, H. L., & Hoskyn, M. (2001). Instructing adolescents with learning disabilities: A component and composite analysis. *Learning Disabilities Research & Practice, 16*, 109–119. doi:10.1111/0938-8982.00012

Tarr, J. E., Reys, R. E., Reys, B. J., Chavez, O., Shih, J., & Osterlind, S. J. (2008). The impact of middle grades mathematics curricula and the classroom learning environment on student achievement. *Journal for Research in Mathematics Education, 39*, 247–280.

Taylor, B. M., Pearson, P. D., Peterson, D., & Rodriguez, M. C. (2001). *Year one of the CIERA school change project: Supporting schools as they implement home-grown reading reform.* Minneapolis, MN: University of Minnesota.

Taylor, B. M., Peterson, D. S., Pearson, P. D., & Rodriguez, M. C. (2002). Looking inside classrooms: Reflecting on the "how" as well as the "what" in effective reading instruction. *Reading Teacher, 56*, 270–279. doi:10.1598/RT.56.3.5

The Danielson Group. (2011). The Framework for Teaching. Retrieved from http://www.danielsongroup.org/article.aspx?page=frameworkforteaching

Vandevoort, L. G., Amrein-Beardsley, A., & Berliner, D. C. (2004, September 8). National Board certified teachers and their students' achievement. *Education Policy Analysis Archives, 12*, 46. Retrieved from http://epaa.asu.edu/ojs/article/view/201

Wayne, A. J., & Youngs, P. (2003). Teacher characteristics and student achievement gains: A review. *Review of Educational Research*, 73, 89–122. doi:10.3102/00346543073001089

Weyandt, L. L., Fulton, K. M., Schepman, S. B., Verdi, G. R., & Wilson, K. G. (2009). Assessment of teacher and school psychologist knowledge of attention-deficit/hyperactivity disorder. *Psychology in the Schools, 46*, 951–961. doi:10.1002/pits.20436

26

Qualitative Research on Special Education Teacher Preparation

Beth Harry and Miriam Lipsky

UNIVERSITY OF MIAMI

Things to Think About

- Qualitative research in special education is slowly gaining acceptance in a field that has deep roots in a positivist, quantitative tradition.
- Teacher preparation in special education has moved from preparation for work in residential facilities and specialized settings to preparation to work in inclusive settings, with an accompanying shift away from positivism toward more constructivist approaches.
- The shift toward more constructivist approaches to special education has fueled the need for more qualitative research in this field as qualitative methods lend themselves to exploratory research and may provide a deeper understanding of the topics in special education that are the focuses of these research protocols. There are three key aspects of qualitative methods that support the constructivist principle (Charmaz, 2006): the purpose and nature of the questions, the data collection procedures, and the data analysis procedures.
- Concerns about the use of qualitative methodologies in research have centered on issues related to objectivity and generalizability of findings. These challenges are faced by employing extensive triangulation of data sources, methods, and researchers, as well as by the expectation that researchers will engage in intensive self-examination regarding the presence of preconceived assumptions and biases toward particular aspects of the data (Harry, 1996).
- The themes in the research literature in special education indicate a focus on the following categories: inclusion and collaboration; field experience; specialized competencies; program philosophy and conceptual change (where conceptual change is sometimes related to program philosophy and at other times related to multicultural diversity).
- Given the period of development in which the field of special education now exists, inductive studies are particularly useful.

Epistemology and Qualitative Research in the Field of Special Education

The field of education has aspired to use the positivist tradition to attain the status of a social science. In order to attain this, great emphasis has been placed on quantitative research methods.

Further, the debate around evidence-based research in education has promoted and supported this view, despite some acknowledgement of the relevance of qualitative methods (Feuer, Towne, & Shavelson, 2002). The history of special education, based on a medical model of disability, has not only mirrored but has intensified a positivist epistemology. Indeed, Skrtic's (1991) analysis of special education concluded that the field has been grounded in a "functionalist paradigm," whose emphasis has been on the teaching of discrete skills and measureable, quantifiable outcomes, while Artiles (2011) emphasized that categorical thinking has reified beliefs about disabilities and racial inferiority.

The field, however, has come a long way since its early conceptualization. Brownell, Sindelar, Kiely, and Danielson (2010), in a review of special education teacher preparation, traced the field's development from "specialized, clinical preparation in residential facilities into an enterprise that now lacks clear conceptual boundaries" (p. 358). The authors highlight the movement from separate teacher preparation for specific categories, through the 1990s push for inclusive services, to the current requirement for full alignment with the general education curriculum, and the consequent emphasis on teachers being highly qualified in content areas. According to Brownell and her colleagues, along with the movement away from categorical thinking came a shift away from positivism toward constructivist approaches, which included the emergence of qualitative methods "as an alternative to traditional quantitative methods" (p. 365).

In this review we seek to determine the extent and utility of qualitative research on special education teacher preparation. Our review resulted in a total of 41 reports, of which we found 25 that used either qualitative or mixed methods. Specifically, 13 relied totally on qualitative methods, while 12 were mixed. Two of the studies in our review were reviews of the literature, and 14 relied on quantitative methods. We approached our review by searching the ERIC database for articles with the following keywords: teacher preparation, evaluation, special education, early intervention, and early childhood special education. Additionally, we conducted a search in the journal *Teacher Education and Special Education* for articles containing these keywords. We reviewed articles from this search that focused on the evaluation of teacher preparation programs, as well as ancestral searches of the articles that were found in the original search.

Qualitative Methods

If it is true that the field of special education is currently marked by a shift to constructivism and by considerable conceptual confusion, the need for and appropriateness of qualitative research methods should be evident. These methods are most useful for exploratory purposes, and for gaining a deep understanding of the fluid and nuanced meaning of disability and of special education. With a particular focus on perceptions and experiences of various stakeholders and on the social processes that drive and influence practice, qualitative methods have great power to guide both policy and practice decisions (Brantlinger, Jiminez, Klingner, Pugach, & Richardson, 2005).

Conceptually, the limitations of qualitative research represent the converse of its strengths. Pursuing fluid concepts requires personalized research methods and small research samples that prompt concerns about trustworthiness, which the positivist tradition refers to as objectivity, and about transferability of findings, which the positivist tradition refers to as generalizability (Lincoln & Guba, 1985). In terms of methods, information on perceptions of stakeholders often rely on self-report; the search for in-depth understanding and open-ended process relies on small sample sizes which cannot be broadly generalized; and the absence of standardized protocols for interviews and observations raises questions about trustworthiness. These challenges are faced by employing extensive triangulation of data sources, methods, and researchers, as well as by the expectation that researchers will engage in intensive self-examination regarding the presence of preconceived assumptions and biases toward particular aspects of the data (Harry, 1996). Additionally, in studies that evaluate educational programs, there may be the complication that the researcher is involved in the project being studied. In such cases, an external evaluator/researcher provides a balance.

There are three key aspects of qualitative methods that support the constructivist principle (Charmaz, 2006): the purpose and nature of the questions, the data collection procedures, and the data analysis procedures. We will discuss each briefly here and will return to these points as we report on the range of studies in our review.

The Purpose of Qualitative Methods and the Resulting Questions

These methods ask the "how" and "why" questions rather than the "what" and "how much" questions. We can use quantitatively constructed surveys to assess the range and extent of stakeholders' views of the success and relevance of a program. We can discover the size of the difference between pre and post mastery of concepts or skills. These methods can measure student achievement and outcomes (e.g., Adams & Wolf, 2008; Daunic, Correa, & Reyes-Blanes, 2004; Nougaret, Scruggs, & Mastropieri, 2005).

Quantitative methods, however, cannot adequately assess the beliefs and values underlying teacher candidates' responses, partly because respondents may not be fully aware of these influences and may need thoughtful, individualized, probing before underlying ideas will emerge. Another reason is that a survey is limited by the awareness and intent of its creator, so if a question is not asked explicitly, it will not be answered. To the contrary, an open-ended question, supported by appropriate probes, can elicit views that the researcher may never have thought of seeking. Thus, qualitative methods are particularly useful for understanding why and how a teacher preparation program is or is not effective.

Qualitative Data Collection

Qualitative data collection strives to be as naturalistic as possible. While quantitative approaches are concerned with controlling variables of interest, qualitative approaches most typically assume that all aspects of a setting are important and that in the real world control is not possible. What a quantitative researcher may see as "contaminating variables," the qualitative researcher sees as "data." Thus, the data collection methods should be as inclusive and open-ended as possible, positioning the researcher as a learner rather than a director. Patton (2001) has described the most common methods as: face-to-face interviews, which may range from semistructured to totally open-ended and ethnographic; focus groups, which seek a range of views on a specified topic; observations of naturalistic settings, with the observer deciding where to position him/herself on a spectrum from full participant to full observer; and examination of archival materials, such as school records, photographs, or journals, relevant to the topic being studied. While a given study may focus on one or more of these methods, high value is placed on the use of multiple sources, informants, and researchers, in order to provide adequate triangulation of data. In keeping with the constructivist nature of this work, a range of perspectives is thought to provide a more accurate, though often a more intricate picture of the complexity of social processes in naturalistic settings.

Qualitative Data Analysis

While it is beyond the scope of this chapter to go into depth on analytic procedures, we emphasize a couple of central points. Qualitative analysis, once more in keeping with the constructivist principle, is most often inductive in process. While some researchers advocate more deductive approaches (e.g., Yin, 2009), the inductive principle, which precludes a priori assumptions, is the most highly espoused (Charmaz, 2006; Denzin & Lincoln, 2005; Patton, 2001). Across several approaches the common core lies in starting with open-ended coding of discrete points of data, to a clustering process in which common properties are identified across codes, and underlying themes that interrelate the categories are then delineated a posteriori. The purpose of the process is to conclude with a cross-cutting statement that captures the main explanations for patterns in the data. With that said, it is also acceptable to proceed in a more deductive manner by specifying a priori categories into which data will be classified. In this approach it remains important for the researcher to stay open to the emergence of additional categories that may not have been preconceived.

We now turn to a review of the studies located for this chapter. We will connect this discussion of purpose and method to the review.

Review of Literature

Brownell, Ross, Colón, and McCallum (2005) described special education teacher preparation research as "almost nonexistent" (p. 248). Yet, in a review comparing this body of research to that in general education teacher preparation, the authors found 64 studies that met their criteria of being program descriptions and evaluations published between 1990 and 2003. Comparing the special education research to national studies of general education programs, the review was very useful in identifying commonalities and differences, and offered a helpful framework for examining teacher preparation research. Key features of the framework were: (a) the presence of a coherent vision; (b) a blend of theory; (c) disciplinary knowledge, subject-specific knowledge, and practice; (d) a strong base in field experience; (e) clear standards for quality teaching; (f) an active pedagogy; (g) attention to issues of inclusion and cultural diversity; and (h) collaboration. The special education literature examined by Brownell et al., shared a strong emphasis on three aspects of this framework—field experience, collaboration, and attention to diversity. Additionally, it emphasized systems in place for program evaluation and also paid attention to issues related to OSEP funding.

In light of the perspective of this chapter as explained in the introduction, perhaps the most revealing point of comparison by Brownell et al. (2005) was that, overall, the special education studies displayed a more mixed range of program philosophies compared to the predominant constructivist orientation in the general education studies. Specifically, the studies that focused solely on special education programs displayed a more positivist bent, while those examining merged or integrated programs were more likely to indicate a constructivist approach. Further, the special education studies showed noticeably less presence of a clear programmatic vision and less focus on subject-matter pedagogy, although the latter feature was more evident in merged/integrated programs.

In the introduction, we cited the arguments of critical scholars such as Skrtic (1991) and Artiles (2011) regarding the "functionalist" lens with which special education was originally framed. Brownell et al. (2005) described a "positivist view of knowledge" as "an epistemological stance that acknowledges a single, valid body of knowledge that teachers should acquire through training" (p. 247). This is seen in programs that place greatest emphasis on competencies to be mastered, as contrasted with more "constructivist epistemologies" that place greater emphasis on reflection and integration of research, practice, and prior cultural and social knowledge. In categorizing thus, the authors focused on the content of the program. They did not, however, connect this to the kinds of data collection and analysis methods used by researchers in evaluating the programs. In other words, we do not know, from that review, whether the research methods themselves were more or less "positivist" or "constructivist."

Brownell et al. (2005) offered four main recommendations for future research on special education teacher preparation: (a) the need to specify valued outcomes of programs and to determine how to assess them, including linking teacher knowledge to student outcomes and teacher retention; (b) to note what components of programs are effective in attaining program goals; (c) to determine the importance of subject matter knowledge; and (d) the impact of OSEP funding on special education teacher preparation programs. Once more, the authors did not address the issue of research methods except to say that evaluating outcomes will require the development of "valid and reliable measures of teacher knowledge and behavior that can be linked to student learning" (p. 249). Although the Brownell et al. (2005) review focused solely on content, with no comment on methods, we find their categorization of topics of study useful and will use it as the organizing basis of this chapter, while focusing on how qualitative methods have been used to address these topics.

As we pointed out in the introduction to the chapter, qualitative methods are most helpful for the study of stakeholder perceptions and also of individual and social learning processes. An analysis by Aksamit, Hall, and Ryan (1990) used naturalistic inquiry in the evaluation of one of the first merged special/general education programs in the country and highlighted the power of this approach to "evaluate the complex, ideographic, dynamic nature of a teacher preparation program" (pp. 224–225), as contrasted with a method that would reduce the program to a discussion of "variables which would be carefully controlled" and would miss "the more subtle, but important underlying themes" (p. 225). These authors also took on the thorny issue of generalizability, a criterion typically touted as a central strength of quantitative methods, and as a limitation of qualitative methods. The authors argued that quantitative studies are "frequently not realistically generalizable" (p. 225) because of the wide variability in the social, political, and human contexts surrounding each teacher preparation program. This is reminiscent of Lincoln and Guba's (1985) proposition that qualitative studies provide "transferability" in that the rich contextual detail allows for an understanding of which aspects of the findings can be transferred to the unique environment of a different setting. Similarly, Berliner (2002) argued that government funding of research should support qualitative methods because of their power to guide decision-making through detailed understanding of local contexts.

In categorizing the content of the studies in our review we found strong consonance with the typology presented by Brownell et al. (2005), but we emphasize the interrelatedness of all the topics. Most noticeably, the theme of collaboration cut across all the studies and was most explicit in studies that foregrounded inclusion and cultural diversity. We also noted two other issues highlighted by Brownell et al.—field experiences and program philosophy—although these also overlapped with attention to inclusion and diversity. Studies that highlighted program philosophy were mostly concerned with questions of conceptual change as a learning goal. In addition, there were some studies that, while tangentially addressing any of the topics above, had a primary focus on specialized competencies needed by special education teachers.

Since our concern in this chapter is with the use and effectiveness of qualitative methods, and since we believe that the most powerful application of these methods lies in documenting individual learning processes within specific social contexts, we address, first, the studies that focused on conceptual change and program philosophy. While it is true that many studies (e.g., Fullerton, Ruben, McBride, & Bert, 2011; Loreman, Earle, Sharma, & Forlin, 2007) use Likert scales and standardized instruments to study change, we believe that the results of such studies are limited by the static nature of the findings; that is, we can learn only what learners thought or felt at specific points in time. We do not learn how or why they moved from one point to another or what challenges they faced in the process. Second, we address the use of qualitative methods in studies that focus on the development of inclusive programs, in several cases of merged or integrated programs, and we note that the theme of collaboration is central to these studies. Third, we connect the topic of inclusion and collaboration to that of field experiences and, finally, we review studies that, while displaying many of the foregoing interests, focus on relatively discrete specialized competencies. These themes and the studies that relate to them are presented in Table 26.1.

Table 26.1 Themes of Reviewed Studies

Program Philosophy & Conceptual Change	*Inclusion & Collaboration*	*Field Experiences*	*Specialized Competencies*
• Trent, Pernell, Mungai, and Chimedza (1998)[a**] • Trent and Dixon (2004)[a**] • Pleasants, Johnson, and Trent (1998)[a*] • Blasi (2002)[a*] • Fults and Harry (2012)[a*] • Corbett, Kilgore, and Sindelar (1998)[b*] • Benner and Judge (2000)[b*]	• Fullerton, Ruben, McBride, and Bert (2011)** • Sobel, Iceman-Sands, and Basile (2007)** • Sobel, French, and Filbin (1998)** • Lombardi and Hunka (2001)** • Smith and Smith (2000)**	• O'Brian, Stoner, Appel, and House (2007)* • Hanline (2010)*	• Allsopp, McHatton, and Cranston-Gingras (2009)** • Welch and Brownell (2002)** • Rock, Gregg, Thead, Acker, Gable, and Zigmond (2009)** • Morningstar, Kim, and Clark (2008)** • Nevin, Malian, and Williams (2002)** • Bay and Lopez-Reyna (1997)** • Pavri (2004)* • Snell, Martin, and Orelove (1997)**

Notes
* = qualitative methods
** = mixed methods
a = conceptual change regarding multicultural diversity
b = conceptual change regarding program philosophy

Conceptual Change

Seven studies in our sample focused explicitly on conceptual change related to diversity as a key goal of teacher preparation. Five of these highlighted changes regarding multicultural diversity and two focused on changes regarding program philosophy as related to inclusion. As we would expect, these studies examining conceptual change among participants in teacher preparation programs relied heavily on qualitative methods. Of the seven, five used qualitative methods exclusively, while two used mixed methods. All found that the programs had succeeded to varying extents in effecting conceptual change regarding diversity.

Conceptual Change Regarding Multicultural Teacher Preparation

One approach to studying students' conceptual change is the construction of concept maps, which combine visual and verbal representations of individuals' perception of their own concept development. Stan Trent led two research teams in conducting and then replicating a pre/post design to assess student teachers' changes in attitudes toward cultural diversity before and after a course in multicultural issues in special education. Pointing out that the growing call for multicultural preparation for special education teachers was in need of empirical support, Trent, Pernell, Mungai, and Chimedza (1998) laid the groundwork for the application of the concept map methodology to special education teacher preparation, while Trent and Dixon (2004) replicated the study. Both studies used mixed methods, comparing pre and post conceptual maps of groups of students (30 and 26 respectively) who were enrolled in introductory classes on multicultural issues in special education. Students were required to write an explanatory paragraph to accompany their pre map and a retrospective essay to accompany their post map. It is interesting to note that, in both reports, the authors report the quantitative findings first, although the entire analysis rested on the qualitative categorization of the concepts present in the maps and writings. That is, qualitative analysis was used to identify the major categories of concepts appearing in the maps. The researchers then scored the concept map by classifying the responses into the following categories: examples of a concept, relationships between concepts, hierarchies among concepts, and cross-links indicating integration and synthesis of concepts. Further, they analyzed the extent to which concepts were well specified and were placed in a central role on the maps.

Findings revealed that the quantitative data, which had shown limited significant differences in conceptual changes in the first study, was stronger in the second study, especially in the area of increased synthesis and integration of concepts. The qualitative data corroborated that finding and went further—indicating that in the second study, course content was directly represented in the post maps, responses were more specific, and students attributed the changes in their thinking to effective instruction in new content. In these studies the quantitative and qualitative methods were mutually complementary, but we note the power of the latter to reveal nuances that are quite lost in the summary scores of "significant" differences. For example, in the second study, students' reflective essays at the end of the course were able to reveal the "why" of their conceptual development, such as their limited prior knowledge and social experience, the impact of specific aspects of instruction in the course, and the inclusion of Cultural-Historical Activity Theory (CHAT) as a theoretical framework in the second course. A particularly impressive aspect of this work was the importance of replication by the same researcher, by which Trent was able to learn which aspects of his own development as an instructor had actually resulted in improved outcomes for his students the second time around. Similarly, in the second study, he was able to implement some of the recommendations he had called for in the first study, specifically, more detail on course content, and a more explicit focus on using theory (i.e., CHAT) to help students integrate and synthesize their learning.

In both studies, the researchers pointed out the limitations of the design—self-report only without any performance data, and the limitations of a single case and only two instructors. Clearly, there is a need to strengthen confidence in such findings through more replication and or modification of such designs across the field. The authors called for longitudinal studies of cohorts, and the inclusion of a broader range of data collection methods, such as video and audio recording of instruction and conferences, reflexive journals kept by instructors, and a focus on student outcomes.

Pleasants, Johnson, and Trent (1998) also addressed the goal of conceptual change with a focus on one discrete aspect of a multicultural teacher education course—the development of a portfolio assignment worth 20% of students' grades. The researchers evaluated the assignment using a 15-item questionnaire, administered to a total of 115 students, and from which 60 were randomly selected for analysis. This procedure indicates a reasonable approach to the challenge in qualitative research of wanting to blend the advantages of a representative sample with those of in-depth analysis, which requires smaller numbers of participants. Once more, the qualitative nature of this study provided the opportunity for the researchers to document not only their students' growth, but also their own, as they described the difficulties with their first attempt at this assignment and the changes they implemented in a second iteration. This process was completed as a team and the report quotes at length some of the dialogue among the team members as they explained their approaches and challenged each other. The analysis was entirely qualitative, and the flexibility of the design allowed the researchers to focus on the findings emerging from a cluster of three questions that are typical of the best kinds of qualitative questions, which asked participants simply to identify what aspects were most important and why; what students learned about themselves; and what they learned about diversity. The analysis resulted in four themes: self-reflection, realization of bias and prejudice, career goal clarification, and application of material. The authors concluded that the greatest benefit of the study was the demonstration of the effects of "purpose-driven reflection and discourse" (p. 55). Arguing that "teacher thinking" must be extended by "teacher teaming," the researchers argued that this mutual purpose emerged over time rather than as a predetermined goal of the project. They concluded with a call for more of this "longitudinal, reflective, and dialogic perspective toward course and assignment development" (p. 56).

The process of conceptual change regarding cultural diversity was also addressed by two studies focusing on working with diverse families of young children with disabilities. One study (Blasi, 2002), examined a preservice course that involved coursework and a field site, while the other (Fults & Harry,

2012) focused on a master's degree course for practicing teachers. Both used a pre/post design relying exclusively on qualitative methods. Adhering to traditional principles of qualitative design, both studies utilized multiple sources of data for the purpose of triangulating information: pre/post questionnaires, student journals, and face-to-face interviews. However, the details of the methodologies were quite different. The Blasi study involved 26 students completing a 12-item open-ended questionnaire, writing weekly journal entries reflecting on readings and practicum experiences, and five volunteers from the group meeting twice a month for a one-hour reflective focus group. The study by Fults and Harry used a somewhat unusual format for the pre/post assessment, in which students: responded to a research-based case study of an African-American child designated with an Emotional/Behavior Disorder, wrote reflective papers on class readings and experiences, and also participated in individual face-to-face interviews regarding their perceptions of changes in their responses at the end of the semester. The analysis methods also differed, as Blasi used thematic analysis to examine the changes in participants' responses, while Fults and Harry compared pre/post responses using an a priori schema of four points on a spectrum of positive to negative attitudes. Both studies found that students' perceptions of families had become more positive as a result of the course, although Fults and Harry found that one student remained unchanged from his position of relatively negative views of the family in the vignette.

Conceptual Change Regarding Program Philosophy

There were two studies that focused on conceptual change in regard to program philosophy and epistemology. Although one program was an added-on inclusion model and the other offered students a choice of an alternative inclusion model, the concern of the researchers was very much related to the question of constructivist vs. positivist epistemology in teacher preparation.

Corbett, Kilgore, and Sindelar (1998) and Benner and Judge (2000), both relied totally on qualitative methods to examine student teachers' perceptions of the effects of the lack of coherence, even conflicting philosophies within a program. The methodologies in both studies exemplified one of the main advantages of qualitative research, wherein small samples allow for extensively triangulated data that enables an in-depth exploration of participant perspectives. Corbett et al. began their report by acknowledging that they expected to find that students were floundering because of the lack of thematic integrity between their traditional elementary education curriculum and the special education courses that were "added on" in response to federal funding. The authors described their university's elementary education program and special education program as being "grounded in different educational and research traditions," the former being committed to "inquiry-oriented teacher education" and the latter to an "eco-behavioral orientation" (p. 294). Students participating in the new "added on" program also took part in a three-semester seminar intended to help them reflect on and integrate their learning in the two parts of the program. Of the 11 students in that seminar, six volunteered to participate in a qualitative study of their perceptions. Data sources provided exemplary triangulation by the inclusion of three formal interviews with each participant, four hours of observation of teaching every week for 10 weeks, informal interviews following each observation, and analysis of documents including exams, papers, plan books, and unit plans, throughout the three years of the program. In addition, two teaching sessions were videotaped and followed by reflective discussions about students' teaching. Finally, the interns' cooperating teachers were interviewed. The researchers were surprised to find that the students did not seem to be fazed by the lack of congruence in their program. Rather, thematic analysis of the data indicated that the students felt they had benefitted by being exposed to a range of ideas, which provided them with a broader repertoire of teaching approaches. The students proved to be effective classroom managers and held an inclusive view of their responsibility to the full range of children.

In an interesting contrast to the Corbett et al. study, Benner and Judge (2000) found that students did flounder when exposed to a new program philosophy, but the longitudinal design revealed how these attitudes changed over the period of a year. Also using a totally qualitative design with strong triangulation and the benefit of a longitudinal view, these authors examined the effectiveness of a "talent development model" designed to prepare teachers for inclusive elementary-level settings, which was offered as an alternative to the traditional teacher preparation program at the university. The alternative model was explicit in its constructivist orientation; engaging students in a 16-credit block that focused on exploratory and inquiry-based activities as well as rotations to four different field experiences. An external evaluator, hired specifically to study the evolution of the program, conducted the research. Data collection included individual interviews, observations, study of artifacts, and the use of multiple focus groups, at two data collection periods—the first spring semester of the program, and again a year later during the students' internships. The data collected included the perspectives of all stakeholders including interns, mentoring teachers, and administrators. The preinternship data reflected two quite discrepant groups of views—those who were discomfited by the constructivist epistemology of the program and those who embraced it. The data from the internship year was more consistent, with many students reflecting on their development from dissonance and frustration to appreciation for a constructivist approach to learning. In this particular study, it was evident that the longitudinal qualitative approach was successful in capturing changing learning processes.

Preparing Teachers for Inclusion

The goal of conceptual change overlaps with several other studies that we will address next, since the issue of changing attitudes is also central to several of the studies focusing on inclusion. Our categorizing of the studies, however, reflects the predominant focus of this group as representing reflections on efforts to prepare students for inclusive classrooms, with attitude change being a part of each program to differing extents. We located five studies that used qualitative or mixed methods to study the views of teacher preparation for inclusion. Of these, one was a multiple case study of perceptions of six K–3 teachers in a "pro-inclusion" school district, while four investigated the actual process of developing inclusive teacher preparation programs. Of the latter group, two were evaluations of "merged" general/special education programs and one study evaluated, longitudinally, the impact of an "immersion" program on students and a range of other key stakeholders. The fifth used predominantly quantitative methods to investigate first- through fourth-year students' mastery of special education competencies in an inclusive preparation program.

The study of teacher perceptions by Smith and Smith (2000) was entirely qualitative, and sought to provide the field with in-depth views of practicing teachers regarding the need for better teacher preparation for inclusion. Participants were selected by an approach quite often used in qualitative research—that of casting a wide net as an initial screening device, from which to select participants for in-depth study. All K–3 general educators in the district ($n=75$) were sent a survey asking them to rate themselves as "successful" or "unsuccessful" with inclusion. From a responding group of 47, the researchers randomly selected three "successful" and three "unsuccessful" teachers who then participated in four audio-recorded interviews, writing of field memos, and a researcher journal. The first two interviews were open-ended, and were thematically analyzed to produce a semistructured guide for the final two interviews. Not surprisingly for a group of teachers who had received only school district in-service training for the inclusive settings in which they found themselves, the dominant theme across the interviews emerged as, "I believe in inclusion, but …" The "buts" related to the need for training, the challenge of large class size, inadequate support, and inadequate time for planning and collaborating.

As mentioned earlier, related to the findings of the Brownell et al. (2005) review, the issue of program philosophy received hugely variable treatment in special education reports, as contrasted with general education programs that seemed to hold quite consistently to a constructivist view. Although the foregoing study (Smith & Smith, 2000) reflects the perspectives of only six teachers, the qualitative report provides nuanced views of the need for extensive revamping not only of teacher preparation approaches, but also of thoughtful approaches to the provision of resources. The voices of the six teachers were essentially pragmatic in their assessment of what was needed and provided an interesting backdrop to the following two studies in our review, which were themselves mutually contrasting on the importance of program philosophy.

Two studies in this section provided evaluations of "merged" programs. Using predominantly qualitative methods, Fullerton, Ruben, McBride, and Bert (2011) studied a merged secondary and special education program, and Sobel, Iceman-Sands, and Basile (2007) examined a merged general and special education elementary program. The report by Sobel et al. was the culmination of a predominantly qualitative line of research evaluating a program redesign effort started in 2000, and summarized findings of three previous studies (not reviewed in this chapter) by Iceman-Sands, Duffield, and Anderson-Parsons (2007) and Taylor and Sobel (2001, 2006). As reported by Sobel et al. (2007), this series of studies included a mixture of methods, including qualitative analyses to examine the curriculum of the merged program and the perceptions of 12 lead instructors. The latter thematic analysis revealed that faculty felt the program successfully inculcated values of collaboration and diversity and also enhanced their own skills and content knowledge. In seeking the views of a larger number of teacher candidates (n = 88 in one study and 30 in another), the researchers used Likert-scale surveys. Like faculty, the teacher candidates and graduates also identified collaboration as one of the main learning assets in the program and reflected generally strong positive attitudes to including all children. In addition to these general trends, however, the qualitative data provided much detail on strengths and needs of the program.

Unique in this set of studies is a report by Sobel, French, and Filbin (1998) who described an intensive collaboration between the university and a large, urban school district. With shared funding for teacher interns, the collaboration featured a full-year, 25-hour per week "immersion" of teacher candidates in selected school sites, accompanied by coursework, exposure to multidisciplinary experiences, and supervision by faculty from both the school district and the university. Eight-question surveys were completed by 64 student interns, 16 mentor teachers, eight administrators, and two university supervisors. The responses were analyzed qualitatively and resulted in four strongly supported themes: the value of clear program expectations, mentorship styles and mentors' levels of expertise, level of involvement by interns, and adjusting to the specific needs of the teacher candidates. These findings assisted the program developers in their efforts at program improvement, the central theme being the need for collaboration in all aspects of the project from recruitment of quality candidates, to supervision and evaluation.

Although several of the foregoing studies employed excellent triangulation of methods and sources, the issue of self-report data remains a limitation in many cases. Even when stakeholder perceptions are included, they are not necessarily based on direct observation or assessment of teacher practice.

A study by Fullerton et al. (2011) provided a strong attempt to ground the findings in direct assessment of teachers' practice. Examining the outcomes of preparation in a merged special education/secondary education program, the research questions targeted collaboration, accommodation of diverse needs, and differentiation of instruction for a diverse range of students. Surveying 44 candidates and/or teacher graduates, four faculty, seven supervisors, and three principals who had hired graduates, the researchers utilized a self-assessment by graduates; a faculty review of teachers' work samples; a school-wide program evaluation; and interviews with graduates, university supervisors, and principals. Qualitative analysis of all the data yielded agreement among all stakeholders that the graduates were effectively practicing the targeted skills and that two key features of the program had contributed to its effectiveness: curricular coherence and a strong emphasis on collaboration.

We conclude this section on inclusive programs with a study by Lombardi and Hunka (2001), which used mixed methods, but with a greater reliance on quantitative methods. Using a six-item survey containing both closed and open-ended questions, the researchers focused their assessment on the extent to which students in their second, third, and fourth years felt they were acquiring specific special education competencies and outcomes. Of a total of 140 student questionnaires and 12 faculty questionnaires, 72 (51%) student and 11 (92%) faculty questionnaires were returned. Not surprisingly, the quantitative analysis yielded a significant difference between the positive responses of second-year and fourth-year students. It also showed greater, though not significant, levels of perceptions of self-competence and confidence among the fourth-year students, although 25% of the latter still did not feel adequately competent. For faculty, the findings revealed that only four of 11 members felt fully competent and confident in the special education content, and also that a rather small percentage of intended competencies were actually covered in the coursework. As we believe is common in mixed method studies, the quantitative results offer a clear-cut picture of the overall perspectives, while the qualitative data provided detail as to perceptions of what was needed to improve the program, specifically, more special education content and the need for more hands-on and less lecture style instruction.

Field Experience

The need for extensive experience in the field is well recognized as a crucial feature of effective teacher preparation programs (Brownell et al., 2005). We located two evaluations of this aspect, one of which focused on inclusive settings and the other on the "first" field experience. Both studies were predominantly qualitative, utilizing interviews, observations of conferences, and reflective journals, reflection on a critical event, and supervisors' observation notes.

O'Brian, Stoner, Appel, and House (2007) conducted a study utilizing two interviews with each of nine preservice teachers and nine cooperating teachers; observations of conferences between the candidates and teachers; and reflective logs written by both. Findings indicated that preservice teachers relied greatly on the development of a trusting relationship with their cooperating teachers, and that these relationships were dynamic, developing in a gradual process in which the roles of both parties were negotiated and became clearer. Three requirements for effective learning were hands-on classroom experience, support, and reflection. Very noticeable in the analysis was the ability of the qualitative data to capture the developmental process by which preservice teachers' roles emerged.

Similarly, Hanline (2010) used weekly reflective journals and written end-of-semester program evaluations by 15 preservice early childhood special education (ECSE) teachers, as well as the observation notes of their cooperating teachers to study the impact of field experiences on the preservice teachers' perceptions of ECSE practices. The journal material was extensive, including 13 entries by each preservice teacher, and cooperating teachers' observation notes included the responses and self-reflections of the preservice teacher. In total, the data included 182 journal entries and 45 supervision observations and 15 end-of-semester evaluations. Data were analyzed using seven CEC Division of Early Childhood (DEC) recommended practices as codes. Descriptive statistics revealed that data were most frequently coded as child-focused practices, next as assessment, and third as family-based practices. The coded data were then analyzed thematically. The study pointed to the importance of including effective intervention strategies in field experiences that are intentionally selected to provide a range of experiences and to assist preservice teachers in becoming comfortable with, and skilled in, family-centered interventions.

Specialized Competencies

The final cluster of eight articles we reviewed represents a range of quite diverse specialized competencies needed by teacher preparation programs. Three related to technology or technological applications, two to secondary students' transition and self-determination, one to bilingual special educators, one to preparation for teaching students with severe disabilities, and one to preparing teachers to provide social support for students in inclusive settings. All but one of the studies used mixed methods, with a tendency to focus on the quantitative findings and the extent to which the qualitative data supported those findings.

Technology

While technology is touted as a valuable learning tool, there is relatively little study of its effectiveness in preparing special education teachers. Studies by Allsopp, McHatton, and Cranston-Gingras (2009) and Welch and Brownell (2002) used mixed methods to evaluate preservice teachers' knowledge, perceptions, and attitudes regarding the integration of instructional technology. The former study focused on a program in which the provision of individual laptops to every student was supported by intensive and ongoing instruction in the use of technology in all course work. Quantitative analysis of a pre and post Likert-type survey of 13 students at the beginning and end of each of three semesters revealed increases, but not significant differences in students' positive response to technology use. However, qualitative analysis of open-ended questions seemed to raise more questions than it answered, including the fact that students did not seem interested in utilizing the technologies they were already familiar with (e.g., discussion boards, videoconferencing) in their teaching, but did increase their interest in the use of software packages for instruction. Further, the qualitative analysis reflected rather limited understanding of how they would integrate technology into their teaching. The study begs the question of whether follow-up interviews and/or focus groups could have provided better understanding of these limitations in the program outcomes.

The study by Welch and Brownell (2002) evaluated a program that used technology specifically to prepare teachers for collaborative practice. Students were self-selected into three groups—one receiving the traditional curriculum, one with an added CD-ROM feature, and one with the CD-ROM and a video feature. Results showed that the students participating in the full technology feature showed significantly higher mean scores on the cognitive and attitudinal measures related to collaboration. The qualitative responses, as in the Allsopp et al. (2009) study, brought some surprises and provided the researchers with information about students' preferences that resulted in helpful modifications to the use of the materials.

A third study, by Rock et al. (2009), relied heavily on quantitative methods to investigate 15 special education graduate students' perceptions of the use of an advanced, online, wireless form of "bug-in-ear" (BIE) technology. Based on video-recorded observations of student teachers, the researchers found significant differences in preintervention and intervention instructional practices of the trainees as well as in levels of student engagement during instruction. Written reflections by the trainees provided qualitative data that supported the quantitative findings.

Preparation of Secondary Teachers

Morningstar, Kim, and Clark (2008) and Nevin, Malian, and Williams (2002) examined the transition-related competence of preservice secondary special educators. Using a combination of survey methods and focus groups, Morningstar et al. found overwhelming mastery of transition competencies by program participants. In the Nevin et al. study, researchers investigated the effects on teacher advocacy skills of a five-course sequence, accompanied by supervised field experiences that focused on IEP development. Quantitative analysis of surveys completed by students showed that their post definitions more closely matched research-based definitions. Qualitative analysis of open-ended comments revealed strong support for the value of the field experience. Most interesting were the individual student case studies developed by teacher candidates to demonstrate the input their data-based instruction had on their students.

The Provision of Social Support to Students in Inclusive Settings

The only study in this cluster (Pavri, 2004), which relied totally on qualitative methods, was an investigation of 60 teachers' perceptions of the preparation they had received for facilitating social skills and social relationships among students in inclusive classrooms. Semistructured interviews with 30 special educators and 30 general educators indicated that the vast majority felt they had received minimal preparation on this topic and felt the need for more training. Ironically, special educators reported even less preparation than their general education colleagues. Despite noting the limitations of self-report, time lapse since the teachers' preparation programs, and the small relatively rural demographics of the schools in the study, the researchers concluded that the data did point to a real need for increased attention to this aspect of teacher preparation for inclusion.

Preparation of Bilingual Special Educators

We include briefly a report by Bay and Lopez-Reyna (1997) regarding a preparation program for bilingual special educators. In the absence of a clear research methodology, this report was essentially a qualitative summary of the feedback received from the program participants. However, the report showed the helpfulness of qualitative feedback. Small group advising conversations and written evaluations by students gave the program directors valuable information on the advantages of the cohort model, the students' appreciation of the research-based knowledge they gained, and the frustrations they experienced in their teaching settings regarding securing English Language Learner services for their students in the rigid mainstream settings in which they were practicing. The latter limitation revealed the need for such a program to provide practical support to in-service teachers who are trying to effect change in their school settings.

Preparation of Teachers of Students With Severe Disabilities

Finally, Snell, Martin, and Orelove (1997) used mixed methods to evaluate a federally-funded, endorsement-only training program for teachers of children with severe disabilities. The program combined 15 credits of coursework with supervised field experiences in the settings where the teachers worked. Of 60 teachers who completed the program, 58 responded to mailed surveys asking them to rate the degree to which they felt the program had changed their thinking about and their implementation of 10 best practices taught in the program. The respondents were divided into two groups—those who were teaching children with severe disabilities and those who were not. More than 50% reported change in six of the topics, with significantly greater influence of the program being evident among those who were teaching children with severe disabilities as compared to those who were not. In addition to the quantitative data, open-ended responses revealed insights into the difficulties teachers had in implementing some of the practices as well as concerns about inadequate support for the new practices. Further, a focus group discussion with seven participants (of 12 who were invited) was transcribed and analyzed thematically, and provided information about participants' views of problems with existing programs as well as recommendations for improvements in teacher preparation, specifically, the need for mentorship and for training in collaborative skills.

Conclusions and a Reflection on "Objectivity"

The previously discussed study by Snell et al. (1997) provides an appropriate ending for our chapter because of a comment by the researchers regarding the notion of "objectivity"—one of the traditional thorns in the side of qualitative research. We quote the following, in which the researchers state that the qualitative data provided insights on teachers' views of:

> how the program influenced their thinking about individuals with disabilities and their families, and the application of the best practices addressed by the program ... This finding is consistent with results from the more objective section of the survey in which teachers rated the influence of each of the areas addressed by the program.
>
> *(Snell et al., 1997, p. 227)*

Returning to our point at the beginning of this chapter, about the well-known arguments regarding objectivity and subjectivity, this statement highlights a common fallacy—that numbers equal objectivity. In responding to a Likert scale, study participants select a number that they believe represents the extent of their assessment of an item; their selection of this number is as subjective as is their verbal description of that same feeling. The application of a numerical value is in no way objective.

Indeed, an experience of the first author of this paper was very instructive in gaining this insight when, on reading evaluations by participants in a workshop she conducted, she noted one response in which the person gave a five out of five, indicating the highest score for the impact of the presentation, and then, in the open-ended section, commented, "I'm giving this a five—and I just about never give fives!" What does this mean? It seems that if one person seldom gives fives, it is likely that another often gives fives, while others may occasionally give fives. If this is true, then there is no way of knowing whether these "fives" are at all comparable, if some respondents are given to superlatives and others are not! It could be argued, rather, that a well-explained open-ended verbal response may give much more reliable information than the arbitrary choice of a numerical value. In either case, we do not have objectivity. We simply have a person's subjective judgment at a given point in time.

Another concept that has serious limitations is that of generalizability of large-scale statistical findings. Berliner (2002), referring to the "power of context" and the "ubiquity of interactions" (p. 19) in real classrooms, cited one large-scale study of 93 classroom contexts which, included a range of negative correlations from about −.80 to zero as well as positive correlations as high as +.45. Berliner argued that the study resulted in general scientific conclusions that "completely missed the particularities of each classroom situation" (p. 19).

In summary, this review of qualitative studies of special education teacher preparation programs highlights the relationship between the positivist assumptions of the field and the types of research we utilize. An overall pattern emerged, whereby the more constructivist the question, the greater the reliance on qualitative methods. That is, these methods were most consistently used in studies that focused on social processes, in particular, conceptual changes regarding program philosophies and regarding inclusion. For the other topics there was greater use of mixed methods.

We emphasize that the selection of methods must be related to the purpose of the investigation (Brantlinger et al., 2005). We believe that, given the period of development in which the field of special education now exists, inductive studies are particularly useful. Clearly, for the purpose of formative evaluation of teacher preparation programs, such methods seem to be a requirement if we are to understand how and why the programs are perceived as effective or ineffective. Overall, the main limitation we see in the existing body of research is not an absence of qualitative work, but rather the difficulty of balancing self-reported perceptions with verifiable data on how teacher candidates actually perform as a result of the preparation they receive. We believe that this issue can be addressed by direct observational methods, which can include both quantitative and qualitative analysis and should be enhanced by technological support such as video and audio recording of teacher practice. If there is to be a concern about objectivity then these methods will provide the kind of triangulation needed to balance self-reports. Similarly, if there is to be a concern about generalizability, thick description of settings and practices, along with richly documented interview data, will allow for transferability of findings between similar settings.

References

Adams, S. K., & Wolf, K. (2008). Strengthening the preparation of early childhood teacher candidates through performance-based assessments. *Journal of Early Childhood Teacher Education*, *29*, 6–29. doi:10.1080/10901020701878644

Aksamit, D. L., Hall, S. P., & Ryan, L. (1990). Naturalistic inquiry applied to the evaluation of a teacher education program. *Teaching & Teacher Education*, *6*, 215–226. doi:10.1016/0742-051X(90)90014-V

Allsopp, D. H., McHatton, P. A., & Cranston-Gingras, A. (2009). Examining perceptions of systematic integration of instructional technology in a teacher education program. *Teacher Education and Special Education, 32*, 337–350. doi:10.1177/0888406409346144

Artiles, A. (2011). Toward an interdisciplinary understanding of educational equity and difference: The case of the racialization of ability. *Educational Researcher, 40*, 431–445. doi:10.3102/0013189X11429391

Bay, M., & Lopez-Reyna, N. (1997). Preparing future bilingual special educators: The lessons we've learned. *Teacher Education and Special Education, 20*, 1–10. doi:10.1177/088840649702000102

Benner, S. M., & Judge, S. L. (2000). Teacher preparation for inclusive settings: A talent development model. *Teacher Education Quarterly, 27*(3), 23–38.

Berliner, D. C. (2002). Educational research: The hardest science of all. *Educational Researcher, 31*, 18–20. doi:10.3102/0013189X031008018

Blasi, M. W. (2002). An asset model: Preparing preservice teachers to work with children and families "of promise." *Journal of Research in Childhood Education, 17*, 106–122. doi:10.1080/02568540209595003

Brantlinger, E., Jiminez, R., Klingner, J., Pugach, M., & Richardson, V. (2005). Qualitative studies in special education. *Exceptional Children, 71*, 195–207.

Brownell, M. T., Ross, D. D., Colón, E. P., & McCallum, C. L. (2005). Critical features of special education teacher preparation: A comparison with general teacher education. *The Journal of Special Education, 38*, 242–252. doi:10.1177/00224669050380040601

Brownell, M. T., Sindelar, P. T., Kiely, M. T., & Danielson, L. C. (2010). Special education teacher quality and preparation: Exposing foundations, constructing a new model. *Exceptional Children, 76*, 357–377.

Charmaz, K. (2006). *Constructing grounded theory: A practical guide through qualitative analysis*. London: Sage.

Corbett, N. L., Kilgore, K. L., & Sindelar, P. T. (1998). "Making sense" in a collaborative teacher education program: Lessons from Project PART students. *Teacher Education and Special Education, 21*, 293–305. doi:10.1177/088840649802100405

Daunic, A. P., Correa, V. I., & Reyes-Blanes, M. E. (2004). Teacher preparation for culturally diverse classrooms: Performance-based assessment of beginning teachers. *Teacher Education and Special Education, 27*, 105–118. doi:10.1177/088840640402700203

Denzin, N. K., & Lincoln, Y. S. (2005). *Handbook of qualitative research* (3rd ed.). Thousand Oaks, CA: Sage.

Feuer, M. J., Towne, L., & Shavelson, R. J. (2002). Scientific culture and educational research. *Educational Researcher, 31*, 4–14. doi:10.3102/0013189X031008004

Fullerton, A., Ruben, B. J., McBride, S., & Bert, S. (2011). Evaluation of a merged secondary and special education program. *Teacher Education Quarterly, 38*(2), 45–60.

Fults, R. M., & Harry, B. (2012). Combining family centeredness and diversity in early childhood teacher training programs. *Teacher Education and Special Education, 35*, 27–48. doi:10.1177/0888406411399784

Hanline, M. F. (2010). Preservice teachers' perceptions of field experiences in inclusive preschool settings: Implications for personnel preparation. *Teacher Education and Special Education, 33*, 335–351. doi:10.1177/0888406409360144

Harry, B. (1996). "These families, those families": The impact of researcher identities on the research act. *Exceptional Children, 62*, 292–300.

Iceman-Sands, D. J., Duffield, J., & Anderson-Parsons, B. (2007). Evaluating infused content in a merged special education and general education teacher preparation program. *Action in Teacher Education, 28*(4), 92–103.

Lincoln, Y., & Guba, E. G. (1985). Establishing trustworthiness. In Y. S. Lincoln & E. G. Guba (Eds.), *Naturalistic inquiry*, pp. 289–331. Thousand Oaks, CA: Sage.

Lombardi, T. P., & Hunka, N. J. (2001). Preparing general education teachers for inclusive classrooms: Assessing the process. *Teacher Education and Special Education, 24*, 183–197. doi:10.1177/088840640102400303

Loreman, T., Earle, C., Sharma, U., & Forlin, C. (2007). The development of an instrument for measuring preservice teachers' sentiments, attitudes, and concerns about inclusive education. *International Journal of Special Education, 22*(2), 150–159.

Morningstar, M. E., Kim, K.-H., & Clark, G. M. (2008). Evaluation a transition personnel preparation program: Identifying transition competencies of practitioners. *Teacher Education and Special Education, 31*, 47–58. doi:10.1177/088840640803100105

Nevin, A., Malian, I., & Williams, L. (2002). Perspectives on self-determination across the curriculum: Report of a preservice special education teacher preparation program. *Remedial and Special Education, 23*, 75–81. doi:10.1177/074193250202300203

Nougaret, A. A., Scruggs, T. E., & Mastropieri, M. A. (2005). Does teacher education produce better special education teachers? *Exceptional Children, 71*, 217–229.

O'Brian, M., Stoner, J., Appel, K., & House, J. J. (2007). The first field experience: Perspectives of preservice and cooperating teachers. *Teacher Education and Special Education, 30*, 264–275. doi:10.1177/088840640703000406

Patton, M. Q. (2001). *Qualitative research and evaluation methods* (3rd ed.). Thousand Oaks, CA: Sage.

Pavri, S. (2004). General and special education teachers' preparation needs in providing social support: A needs assessment. *Teacher Education and Special Education, 27*, 433–443. doi:10.1177/088840640402700410

Pleasants, H. M., Johnson, C. B., & Trent, S. C. (1998). Reflecting, reconceptualizing, and revising: The evolution of a portfolio assignment in a multicultural teacher education course. *Remedial and Special Education, 19*, 46–58. doi:10.1177/074193259801900105

Rock, M. L., Gregg, M., Thead, B. K., Acker, S. E., Gable, R. A., & Zigmond, N. P. (2009). Can you hear me now? Evaluation of an online wireless technology to provide real-time feedback to special education teachers-in-training. *Teacher Education and Special Education, 32*, 64–82. doi:10.1177/0888406408330872

Skrtic, T. M. (1991). *Behind special education: A critical analysis of professional culture and school organization.* Denver, CO: Love Publishing.

Smith, M. K., & Smith, K. E. (2000). "I believe in inclusion, but ...": Regular education early childhood teachers' perceptions of successful inclusion. *Journal of Research in Childhood Education, 14*, 161–180. doi:10.1080/02568540009594761

Snell, M. B., Martin, K., & Orelove, F. P. (1997). Meeting the demands for specialized teachers of students with severe disabilities. *Teacher Education and Special Education, 20*, 221–233. doi:10.1177/088840649702000304

Sobel, D., French, N., & Filbin, J. (1998). A partnership to promote teacher preparation for inclusive, urban schools: Issues and strategies. *Teaching and Teacher Education, 14*, 793–806. doi:10.1016/S0742-051X(98)00031-6

Sobel, D. M., Iceman-Sands, D., & Basile, C. (2007). Merging general and special education teacher preparation programs to create an inclusive program for diverse learners. *The New Educator, 3*, 241–262. doi:10.1080/15476880701484113

Taylor, S. V., & Sobel, D. M. (2001). Addressing the discontinuity of students' and teachers' diversity: A preliminary study of preservice teachers' beliefs and perceived skills. *Teaching and Teacher Education, 17*(5), 487–503.

Taylor, S. V., & Sobel, D. M. (2006). Addressing the discontinuity of students' and teachers' diversity: A follow-up study of preservice teachers' beliefs and perceived skills. *Teaching and Teacher Education, 17*, 487–503. doi:10.1016/S0742-051X(01)00008-7

Trent, S. C., & Dixon, D. J. (2004). "My eyes were opened": Tracing the conceptual change of pre-service teachers in a special education/multicultural education course. *Teacher Education and Special Education, 27*, 119–133. doi:10.1177/088840640402700204

Trent, S. C., Pernell, E., Mungai, A., & Chimedza, R. (1998). Using concept maps to measure conceptual change in preservice teachers enrolled in a multicultural education/special education course. *Remedial and Special Education, 19*, 16–31. doi:10.1177/074193259801900103

Welch, M., & Brownell, K. (2002). Are professionals ready for educational partnerships? The evaluation of a technology-enhanced course to prepare educators for collaboration. *Teacher Education and Special Education, 25*, 133–144. doi:10.1177/088840640202500205

Yin, R. (2009). *Case study research: Design and methods.* Thousand Oaks, CA: Sage.

27

The "Wicked Question" of Teacher Education Effects and What to Do About It

Benjamin Lignugaris/Kraft

UTAH STATE UNIVERSITY

Paul T. Sindelar, Erica D. McCray, and Jenna Kimerling

UNIVERSITY OF FLORIDA

Things to Think About

- Special education teacher education presents "wicked problems" because of its inextricable connections to state licensing and education policy, the economic well-being of the children taught by graduates, the larger area of general education teacher preparation, and the varying perspectives on what our teachers and school leaders should know and be able to do to best serve students with disabilities.
- The difficulties of conducting high-quality teacher education research have resulted in a lack of both empirical inquiry and evidence. Not only is there a limited amount of research on teacher education in special education, but the quality of the research that exists often is suspect, and reliable assessments of teacher performance or student outcomes are rarely used as outcome measures.
- Research on the impact of program reforms may lead to redefining the preparation required for special educators, including the special educator's collaborative role at the classroom level, how general and special educators might effectively operate within the broader, emerging systems that support low-performing students, and special educators' roles in providing intensive, evidence-based interventions for students who struggle.
- Increased emphasis on accountability, a range of school-based innovations, implementation of the Common Core State Standards, and innovative technologies are changing the contexts in which special educators operate, the roles they assume, and the character of special education teacher preparation.
- Integrating evidence-based practices into special education teacher preparation programs and conducting research on the efficacy of those practices is critical for building an empirical foundation for special education teacher preparation.

Virtually all of the authors who contributed chapters to this *Handbook* expressed concern about how little research was available to them. Clearly, there is no solid empirical foundation on which to build special education teacher education. The work we do as teacher educators builds instead on professional consensus, which, to outsiders, may seem insular and self-serving—as the decade-long barrage of criticism leveled at teacher preparation would suggest (Sindelar, Wasburn-Moses, Thomas, & Leko, Chapter 1, this volume). By failing to establish a warrant for our work that is credible to policy makers and the public and by failing to solve the problems we recognize in our work, we remain an easy mark for critics. Adding to the complexity of the challenge we face is our inability to persuade policy makers about the difficulty of conducting high-quality research on teacher preparation.

In many respects these issues may be viewed as "wicked problems" (Rittel & Webber, 1973, p. 160). That is, assessing the impact of special education teacher education is a messy social problem, inextricably connected to state licensing and education policy, the economic well-being of the children our graduates teach, the larger area of general education teacher preparation, and the varying perspectives on what our teachers and school leaders should know and be able to do to best serve students with disabilities—and one whose resolution defies traditional methods of scientific inquiry. Historically, efforts to address wicked problems have led to short-term solutions whose shortcomings often necessitate a new cycle of reform. We believe—and believe that the chapters in this *Handbook* affirm—that the concept of wicked problems provides a helpful perspective on the state of the art of special education teacher preparation. Given that wicked problems resist resolution, we will forego conclusions in this final chapter and instead pose broader questions to consider. What can we do to get policy makers' attention? What can we do to persuade a skeptical public about the importance of our work? How can we solve the persistent problems that have plagued our field since its emergence in the 1970s? What research and policies are needed to shape the future of special education teacher preparation?

Teacher educators and teacher education scholars are well aware of the difficulty of conducting high-quality teacher education research. Teacher education is a complex, multifaceted and multiyear—if not career-long—independent variable (hence the term "wicked problem"). What should special education teacher preparation look like and how do we realize that vision? The answer to this question varies depending upon one's perspective. At the state level, that perspective is influenced by licensure policy, student outcome standards, and school practices that vary from state-to-state (Geiger, Mickelson, McKeown, Barton, Kleinhammer-Tramill, & Steinbrecher, Chapter 3, this volume). Further, the content and structure of special education teacher preparation varies from program to program with differences in faculty size, expertise, educational philosophy, and beliefs about how best to prepare school professionals. Furthermore, teacher education graduates, once employed in schools, are subject to powerful socialization processes that may dilute or obscure the effects of preparation. Yet, even if preparation effects were robust, we lack reliable and valid measures of what teachers know and do, and measures of special education teacher practice that align to the broad range of expected outcomes for students with disabilities are even scarcer (Brownell, Steinbrecher, Kimerling, Park, Bae, & Benedict, Chapter 25, this volume). Indeed, special education teaching presents a unique set of challenging problems for teacher assessment, with which our field has only begun to grapple.

Certain aspects of teacher preparation would seem to lend themselves readily to empirical inquiry. For example, although Boe (Chapter 5, this volume) makes use of large-scale databases, he laments the fact that a sample of teachers as large as that in the Schools and Staffing Survey includes too few SETs for powerful statistical analysis specific to our field. Field experiences offer another example of a potentially fruitful area of inquiry. A ubiquitous element of special education teacher preparation, field experiences would seem to be a ready target for researchers. Yet, as Maheady, Smith, and Jabot (Chapter 10, this volume) point out, the research on field experience lacks rigor, and student samples used in the research are idiosyncratic and seldom representative of any larger population. Furthermore, because these studies involve field experiences that vary substantially in quality, their overall effect is diluted when studies are aggregated. Maheady et al. also argue that we have not developed consensus about what constitutes high-quality field experiences and how to design them. As a result, we know too little about the design of effective field experiences and how to integrate them to maximize impact on teaching practice and pupil learning.

Reading provides a related example. Although many aspects of teaching reading have a sound empirical foundation, preparing teachers to teach reading does not. Besides, as Brownell and Leko (Chapter 15, this volume) argue, developing expertise at teaching reading is a career-long proposition, and we know little about structuring curriculum and practice in initial preparation to support advanced learning throughout a teacher's career. Pugach, Blanton, and Boveda (Chapter 9, this volume) make a similar argument about collaborative teacher preparation, noting that its research base, too, is limited and flawed. Most researchers have focused on a course, a small set of courses, or courses and field experiences. Few of them have addressed programmatic impact, and few have used credible measures of teacher outcomes. Pugach et al. acknowledge that the state of research on collaborative preparation may be the product of how difficult it is for teacher education to achieve and sustain programmatic reform. Generally speaking, finding sites at which a reform is implemented with fidelity is a difficult challenge for researchers seeking to evaluate programmatic reforms of any sort.

The research on recruitment and retention illustrates another shortcoming of teacher education research. Billingsley, Crockett, and Kamman (Chapter 6, this volume) point out that existing research does not emanate from well-developed conceptual frameworks. As a result, findings seem disjointed, and studies fail to generate new ideas about what preparation experiences promote commitment to and retention in special education teaching. Billingsley et al. conclude that too much is done in the name of recruitment that has little or no support in research. As a result, developing and sustaining a competent, qualified teaching workforce has been a "wicked problem" for special education teacher preparation that has persisted in our field for over 25 years.

Of course, the shortage of highly qualified special education teachers has fallen to 5% and, to all appearances, the problem seems to be resolving itself. Yet, as with most "wicked problems," solutions beget new problems. The original NCLB definition of *highly qualified* included individuals enrolled in alternative route programs and, in the OSEP data from which highly qualified percentages are derived, there is no way to differentiate the subset of SETs who have achieved highly qualified status simply by virtue of being enrolled in an alternative route program. Moreover, in spite of the increase in the percentage of highly qualified SETs, the performance of students with disabilities on high-stakes assessments is consistently poor. Taken together, consistently poor outcomes and increasing proportions of highly qualified teachers make clear that *highly qualified* and *highly competent* are far from synonymous.

There is a second "wicked problem" in SET shortage, which also has gone unresolved: the disproportionality between the diversity of the teaching force and the diversity of students (Correa, McHatton, McCray, & Baughan; Kozleski, Artiles, McCray, & Lacy, Chapters 12 and 7, both this volume). Like teacher shortage generally, the problem of recruiting, preparing, and retaining a diverse teaching workforce appears intractable and resistant to influence. Kozleski et al. reframe the issue by arguing that children attending high-poverty, highly diverse schools are likely to be taught by young, inexperienced teachers, particularly vulnerable to attrition and apt to relocate, even if they do not leave the field. Reframing the issue in this way suggests new potential solutions to some aspects of the problem. For example, embedding teacher preparation in the context of high-poverty schools may well attract more diverse students, willing to teach near home and endowed with more specific and location-specific human capital to invest in high-poverty schools (Dai, Sindelar, Denslow, Dewey, & Rosenberg, 2007). Correa and colleagues (Chapter 12, this volume) also reframed the issue in a manner that suggested new solutions. They propose that preparing all teachers to be culturally competent mitigates the issue even if it does not resolve it. Bolstering preservice preparation and professional development also puts the resolution to the issue in the hands of teacher educators, something that cannot be said about recruitment strategies, whose success depends largely on the actions of others.

Finally, some areas of special education teacher preparation are essentially void of empirical work. For example, in their chapter on the preparation of early childhood educators, Gallagher, Steed, and Green (Chapter 23, this volume) note that the research on early childhood special education teacher preparation is limited, particularly in terms of validating specific approaches. They describe research focused on trends in content emphasis (e.g., literacy) and delivery (e.g., distance learning) that parallels the larger body of general teacher education research but contributes little to our understanding of early childhood preparation. Similarly, Morningstar and Clavenna-Deane (Chapter 24, this volume) lamented the scarcity of research on the preparation of transition specialists. Transition content often is crammed into a curriculum that is otherwise undifferentiated for special educators with a secondary focus. It is small wonder, as these authors point out, that special education teachers do not feel adequately prepared to engage in effective transition practices.

We could cite more examples, of course, but suspect we have made our points: too little credible research on special education teacher preparation, too many flaws in the research that exists, and too many wicked—and important—problems unanswered for too long. Furthermore, high-quality research on teacher preparation generally is difficult to conduct in a compelling manner without substantial monetary support, and, in special education, scale compounds the need for research support. In spite of its longstanding commitment to and investment in personnel preparation (Kleinhammer-Tramill, Mickelson, & Barton, Chapter 2, this volume), OSEP lost its research authority and can no longer fund research of any kind. At the same time, the Institute for Education Sciences, the primary source of funding for education research, supports little research on preservice preparation (Brownell et al., Chapter 25, this volume). Lacking a solid foundation of empirical work renders special education teacher preparation vulnerable to external influences, ranging from the whimsy of legislatures to rapid and often unpredictable change in professional practice in schools. Credible and enduring or not, change in school practice will have significant impacts on teacher education curriculum and design.

Changing School Practice and the Role of Special Education Teachers

In this section, we describe how increased emphasis on accountability, a range of school-based innovations (e.g., RTI, SW-PBIS), implementation of the Common Core State Standards, and technology innovations (e.g., cochlear implants for students with hearing impairments) are changing the contexts in which special educators operate, the roles they assume, and the character of special education teacher preparation.

Accountability

More than ever before, teacher education programs are being held accountable for the quality of the teachers they prepare, and the standard to which they are being held is P–12 student achievement. Simply put, evaluating teacher preparation programs on the basis of their graduates' ability to produce student achievement gains has found political traction (Leko, Brownell, Sindelar, & Murphy, 2012). Nonetheless, studies linking student performance to teachers and teachers to their preparation suffer from a number of significant shortcomings. For one, many states are still in the process of developing valid and reliable systems to measure teacher effectiveness (Blanton, McLeskey, & Hernandez, Chapter 8, this volume). In addition, value-added methodology is problematic, particularly when used in assessing special education teachers, who often share responsibility for students' instruction with general education teachers and, often, curriculum specialists. Jones, Buzick, and Turkan (2013) describe a number of challenges when value-added scores are used to estimate teacher-specific effects on achievement of students with disabilities. For example, when used inconsistently, testing accommodations threaten the validity of inferences regarding academic progress, as does the broad heterogeneity of student characteristics and opportunities to learn. Also, the large proportion of students with disabilities who have extreme scores on state assessments introduces the possibility of high measurement error and lower score reliability.

Other options for program evaluation—including job placement and job retention, satisfaction surveys of graduates and their employers, and performance assessments—broaden the range of potential measures and provide useful and meaningful information to programs, policy makers, and the public. Yet, when attempting to link students to teachers and teachers to programs, no single approach yields fully valid, reliable, or useful information. Blanton et al. (Chapter 8, this volume), among many others, call for the use of multiple measures to assess both teacher quality and program effectiveness. They assert that only high-quality indicators and rigorous methodologies provide the understanding necessary to make improvements in teacher preparation that ultimately will result in effective classroom practice and positive outcomes for all students, including those with disabilities. In all likelihood, the problems associated with teacher evaluation will take years to resolve. In the meantime, in many places, decisions regarding teachers' employment, tenure, and salary will continue to be made on the basis of flawed evaluation processes. The dissonance created by the emphasis on accountability and absence of evaluation methodology may inadvertently bias classroom teachers against including students with disabilities and, perhaps, discourage individuals from becoming special education teachers.

School-Based Innovations

Federal policies requiring that students with disabilities be held to the same performance standards as students without disabilities have led to designing systems that support all students and reduce the need for special education services (Sindelar et al., Chapter 1, this volume), much like *inclusive education* as practiced in Great Britain and elsewhere in the world (and described by Florian, Chapter 4, this volume). In the U.S., fewer students are being identified as learning disabled, and more students with disabilities are spending more time in general education classrooms, possibly as a result of the success of school-based innovations such as Response to Intervention (RTI), School-Wide Positive Behavior Support (SW-PBIS), and more recently multitiered systems of support (MTSS; Algozzine et al., 2012). Sindelar, Brownell, and Billingsley (2010) discuss this as a "revolution in the interface between special and general education" (p. 14). As students with disabilities are included increasingly in general education classrooms, special educators will be charged with solving student learning problems as part of a team (Lewis & Thomas; Oliver & Reschly, Chapters 22 and 17, both this volume). Successful implementation of systems of support requires change in how we prepare special educators and general educators alike. Personnel preparation systems should be designed collaboratively with the primary goals of improving general education teachers' success with struggling students and students with disabilities, and redefining the preparation of special educators and other specialists (Pugach et al., Chapter 9, this volume). This approach is consistent with the foundational principles of the multitiered preventative intervention systems emerging in schools (Sailor, Doolittle, Bradley, & Danielson, 2009).

Although these goals are laudable, most general education and special education preparation programs have not adapted to fit the multitiered systems of support employed in many schools (Freeman et al., 2009; Lewis & Thomas, Chapter 22, this volume). Yet Pugach et al. (Chapter 9, this volume) found descriptions of 16 teacher education program redesigns in which general and special education teacher preparation were integrated. Integrated programs of this sort represent the standard in many places in the world (Florian, Chapter 4, this volume), particularly where few support services are available and teachers are expected to address all of their students' needs. The studies reviewed by Pugach et al. primarily address teacher interactions at the classroom level and document changes in preservice teachers' knowledge, their perceptions when given the opportunity to co-teach, and, in a few instances, improvement in student performance during practica or student teaching. There is little indication in these studies that teachers learned how to operate effectively within broader school frameworks such as RTI, SW-PBIS, or other MTSS. As Pugach et al. point out, the long-term goal of most collaborative program reform is to integrate special education content into elementary or secondary teacher preparation programs. Additional research clearly is needed to evaluate the impact of program reforms on general education teachers' knowledge and skills, and the achievement of the students with disabilities they teach. This work might then continue by redefining the preparation required for special educators. Redesign should reflect not only the special educator's collaborative role at the classroom level and how general and special educators might effectively utilize the broader, emerging systems that support low-performing students (Freeman et al., 2009), but also the special educator's role in providing intensive, evidence-based interventions for students who struggle (Brownell, Sindelar, Kiely, & Danielson, 2010).

Common Core State Standards

The third broad change in schools that is profoundly affecting the role of special education teachers is adoption of the Common Core State Standards (CCSS). These standards are being implemented in 46 states, the District of Columbia, and four territories with the introduction of state assessments tied to these standards scheduled for implementation during the 2014–2015 school year.[1] Historically, students with disabilities were taught basic skills in resource rooms and self-contained classrooms, and special education teacher preparation emphasized the pedagogical skills required to implement specialized strategies for basic skill instruction. Often this high degree of specialization resulted in students with disabilities learning only basic or foundational reading and math skills (e.g., learning to decode text, respond well to low-level questions, and develop basic math skills). Because the CCSS tap higher order skills and processes, special education's emphasis on basic skill instruction may no longer suffice.

Of course, this traditional role began to evolve with the movement to include students with disabilities in general education placements (and ultimately the general education curriculum). Inclusive school practice required more of special education teachers, including skill in collaborating with general education teachers and knowledge of the general education curriculum. For special education teachers, adoption of the Common Core State Standards has upped the ante again. These standards emphasize conceptual understanding and students' ability to respond to questions requiring analysis, synthesis, and application. Importantly, the available research indicates that teachers who can teach conceptual and higher level understanding effectively have powerful instructional repertoires, deep content knowledge, and the ability to represent content to meet student needs (Brownell et al., Chapter 25, this volume; Lignugaris/Kraft & Harris, Chapter 14, this volume). Unfortunately, few special education teacher preparation programs provide their students with the deep content knowledge required to diagnose a broad range of complex reading and mathematics problems (Griffin, van Garderen, & Ulrich, Chapter 16, this volume; Brownell & Leko, Chapter 15, this volume), and few provide sufficient practice in adapting evidence-based instructional routines to address these problems (Lignugaris/Kraft & Harris; Maheady, Smith, & Jabot, Chapters 14 and 10, both this volume).

It seems likely that redesigning teacher preparation in response to the CCSS roll-out will be idiosyncratic to individual states and guided by the state-to-state variation in special education teacher licensing requirements (Geiger et al., Chapter 3, this volume). Some possible directions that special education teacher educators might explore in redesign include (a) collaborating with liberal arts faculty to identify general education courses that provide deep content understanding in literacy and mathematics, (b) revising professional education requirements so coursework focuses on special educators' pedagogical content knowledge, (c) working closely with school districts to ensure that induction programs focus on deep content understanding in literacy and math and the application of teachers' foundational skill sets to that content, and (d) carefully evaluating special education coursework and practica to ensure that preservice teachers acquire a broad range of evidence-based practices and have opportunities to apply and adapt them to a range of instructional problems. These core elements were central to the 325T program improvement grants funded by the OSEP Personnel Development Program (Kleinhammer-Tramill et al., Chapter 2, this volume).

Although these approaches apply readily to traditional preparation, alternate preparation routes present a challenge. Colleges and universities offer most alternative routes, and such programs tend to be comparable in length and rigor to traditional, campus-based programs (Connelly, Rosenberg, & Larson, Chapter 13, this volume). However, some alternative route programs, including Teach for America and other politically popular routes, are streamlined and require fewer credit hours than traditional routes and less time to completion (Connelly et al.). For streamlined alternative route programs, expansion of content—even for as important a purpose as preparing teachers to teach the Common Core State Standards—undermines the less-is-more principle that underlies their design. Thus, for graduates of streamlined preparation, effective induction will be critical to their success and persistence (Billingsley, Griffin, Smith, Kamman, & Israel, 2009).

Technological Advances

The fourth broad change affecting special educators' role in schools and their preservice preparation is the rapid development of instructional technology. Smith and Kennedy (Chapter 11, this volume) explore how technology is used to engage students and the barriers to effective implementation, including the fact that few teachers have the skills required to effectively integrate instructional and assistive technologies into their teaching. They note that 48 of 50 states align their state technology with the National Educational Technology Standards for Teachers (NETS•T), in which there is only one indirect reference to learners with disabilities. Moreover, CEC's Knowledge and Skill Standards require few technology competencies for all special educators, and most technology requirements are included in CEC's Advanced Skill Standards. According to Smith and Kennedy, few special education programs require a specific assistive technology course and neither general educators or special educators have sufficient technology skills needed to develop technology-rich IEPs to meet the needs of students with disabilities. Without such preparation, neither special education nor general education teachers are learning about potentially powerful tools for the efficient design and delivery of effective instruction that benefits all students, especially those with disabilities.

In addition to learning about technologies that might be included in instruction, technological advances in treating some disabilities are changing the preparation requirements for teachers of students with disabilities. For example, the development and implementation of technologies for universal newborn hearing screening has led to increasingly earlier identification of young children who are deaf or have significant hearing loss. In addition, the development of advanced hearing technologies such as infant hearing aids and cochlear implants increases the need for early interventionists (Nelson, Lenihan, & White, Chapter 20, this volume). Thus, the emerging technology in the field is expanding the range of service providers needed to serve children with hearing impairments. Unfortunately, expansion of need for teachers is occurring at a time when the number of deaf education programs is decreasing (Programs are being discontinued in visual impairments, too, as Bozeman and Zebehazy note in Chapter 21, this volume).

The development of these technologies also requires an expanded knowledge base for teachers of children with hearing impairments. Hearing technologies benefit children most when early interventionists and teachers understand how advanced hearing technologies work and structure children's educational programs to take advantage of those technologies (Nelson et al.). Teacher preparation programs need to adapt to these changing technologies, particularly as they contribute to the increased inclusion of children with hearing disabilities. Thus, teachers of children who are deaf must have the skills needed both to help these children manage their technology and to work collaboratively with other teachers (Nelson et al.). Unfortunately, current graduates report that they are not well prepared for the new technological demands for the available deaf education jobs.

Innovative technologies are changing how special education teacher educators prepare future practitioners. Regional consortia are using distance education technologies to extend their reach across state lines and into rural areas. In the field of visual impairments, Bozeman and Zebehazy (Chapter 21, this volume) describe how regional consortia have grown increasingly important as the number of preparation programs has diminished. Importantly, as these technologies develop further, it will be critical to examine the effects of training on the skill development of practitioners who participate in such programs. Another emerging technology for preservice teacher preparation is the development of multimedia simulations that allow preservice teachers opportunities to analyze and practice responding to various academic and behavior scenarios they will face in the classroom (Smith & Kennedy). Finally, two OSEP-funded projects, the IRIS Center at Vanderbilt University[2] and MAST (Modules Addressing Special Education and Teacher Education) at East Carolina University[3] combine online learning technology and multimedia resources. Both of these projects provide teacher educators with a comprehensive set of case-based multimedia modules on topics that include basic classroom management practices, differentiated instruction, RTI, transition, and cultural/linguistic diversity among individuals with disabilities.

Evaluation of each IRIS STAR Legacy Module is conducted with college faculty, college students, professional development providers, and teachers who use the modules. Smith and Tyler (2011) report that college students and teachers consistently rate the modules highly and indicate that they benefit from the instruction. Moreover, in a field test with preservice teachers, the modules produced positive learning outcomes, whether used to enhance or replace course content, or as independently completed homework assignments (Smith & Tyler, 2011). Additional research is needed on the effects of these technologies on teacher knowledge, application in local classrooms, and the impact that teachers prepared using these technologies have on the lives of students with disabilities. In their discussion of distance technologies and simulations, Smith and Kennedy provide a clear outline for improving the quality of research on classroom simulations and online personnel preparation technologies. In the long run, these materials will enable teacher educators to upgrade their courses with high-quality content and, as more teacher education programs adopt the materials, will create more uniformity in how important topics are addressed.

In truth, special education teacher educators need to identify and evaluate personnel preparation approaches of all stripes through which teachers experience expanded opportunities to practice and apply skills in schools and, as a result, learn more in less time. In addition, we also need to infuse content into evidence-based practices. Integrating evidence-based practice into special education teacher preparation programs and conducting research on the efficacy of those practices is critical for building an empirical foundation for special education teacher preparation. Evidence-based practices are instructional and management interventions and programs that, in well-controlled research studies, reliably increase student performance (Cook & Odum, 2013). The general idea of evidence-based practice appears deceptively simple when applied to preparing effective teachers: Teacher preparation programs should focus on increasing teachers' proficiency with practices that through rigorous scientific research have been shown to produce increased performance with children with disabilities. Many of the foundational practices with strong research support are identified in various chapters in this *Handbook* (e.g., Brownell & Leko; Griffin et al.; Lewis & Thomas; Lignugaris/Kraft & Harris; Oliver & Reschly). For example, Oliver and Reschly describe a validated set of principles that provides a basis for effective classroom management. Similarly, Lignugaris/Kraft and Harris (Chapter 14); Conroy, Alter, Boyd, and Bettini (Chapter 19, this volume); and Westling, Salzberg, Collins, Morgan, and Knight (Chapter 18, this volume) identify instructional competencies and skill sets for effective teachers of students with high incidence disabilities, students with challenging behaviors, and students with significant cognitive impairments. These evidence-based practices provide a good starting place for preparing teachers who can effectively address the learning problems presented by students with disabilities. However, there is no guarantee that an evidence-based intervention will produce positive outcomes when applied in a particular instructional context to a particular learning problem (Brownell & Leko, Chapter 15, this volume; Cook & Odom, 2013; Maheady et al., Chapter 10, this volume). Special education teacher preparation needs to extend beyond the reliable implementation of evidence-based interventions to preparing teachers who can effectively engage in a recursive problem-solving process that includes intensive performance monitoring, evaluation, and, most importantly, making decisions about changing practice to improve outcomes for the most difficult to teach students. The fruit of this process is referred to as *practice-based evidence* (Maheady et al., Chapter 10, this volume; Smith, Schmidt, Edelen-Smith & Cook, 2013).

Special education teacher educators are in an ideal position to conduct this type of research. Systematic examinations are needed to address the effectiveness of evidence-based practices when implemented in the classroom and how preservice teachers adjust these practices in different instruction and management contexts (Maheady, Jabot, Rey, & Michielli-Pendl, 2007). This research may be conducted using a variety of research methodologies including single subject, quasi-experimental, case study, and qualitative research designs. The purpose of such research is to derive an empirically based model for teaching new teachers the knowledge base and decision-making strategies needed to adjust evidence-based instruction and management strategies to students' learning problems.

Baker, Gersten, Dimino, and Griffiths (2004) provide an example how this type of research might inform teacher education practice. Using a multimethod case study approach, Baker et al. examined the extent to which teachers trained to implement an evidence-based math program, Peer-Assisted Learning Strategies (PALS), continued to implement the program 4 years after training. One variable examined was the quality of teachers' implementation and their understanding of the program. The two teachers coded at the *mechanical* level of implementation had a good understanding of the day-to-day logistics for implementing the program. The three teachers coded at the *routine* level of implementation had the logistical understanding as well as an understanding of one or more key concepts in the program, such as how the program promotes positive student interactions through peer teaching. Finally, the three teachers coded at the *refined/integrated* level demonstrated understanding of the program logistics and one or more key elements, and had a deep conceptual understanding of the program as evidenced by their ability to apply the program strategies and techniques to other subject areas or other mathematics lessons. The deeper program understanding was evident in the teacher's responses in an interview as well as through classroom observations and in observers' field notes.

Baker et al.'s research suggests several strategies that may be readily applied to special education preservice preparation programs to develop the foundational skills needed to solve difficult and persistent instructional problems. First, preservice teachers must understand the content knowledge and underlying pedagogical principles that drive an evidence-based practice. Second, these principles must be directly linked to classroom implementation through rich clinical experiences. That is, university faculty supervisors must be available on-site to point out, discuss, clarify, and provide feedback to preservice teachers on the underlying principles as they are implemented. Finally, preservice teachers must be provided opportunities and encouraged to apply evidence-based strategies learned in one context to new content and to new instructional problems. Additional investigations are needed to document the processes required to prepare teachers who can identify potentially effective instruction and management interventions and collect and evaluate practice-based evidence to adjust instruction as needed (Maheady et al., 2007; Spencer, Detrich, & Slocum, 2012). This body of research might provide the empirical foundation needed to improve the design and implementation of special education preservice teacher preparation.

Next Steps

In addition to having a limited amount of research on teacher education in special education, the quality of the research that exists often is suspect. Much of the work reported in these chapters is descriptive, and teacher self-reports, trainee self-reports, program descriptions, and small-scale surveys predominate the literature. As we have noted, outcome measures used in existing research rarely include reliable assessments of teacher performance or student outcomes. As a result, preparation in its myriad forms is built upon convention and consensus more so than empirical inquiry. Yet, even if better measures were more readily available, rigorous quantitative research on preparation would be next to impossible to conduct.

Qualitative research represents an alternative with good potential, and in this volume, Harry and Lipsky (Chapter 26) review qualitative research on special education teacher preparation. They acknowledge special education's deep positivist roots but argue that qualitative methodology allows researchers to address questions rigorously that are essentially unanswerable using traditional quantitative methods. They find a rather substantial number of studies, 25 in all—13 qualitative and 12 mixed—method studies. In their critique of this literature, Harry and Lipsky note that its main limitations include overreliance on self-report data and surveys and failure to link findings to credible performance and outcome measures. Thus, the quality of both qualitative and quantitative research is undermined by the absence of adequate outcome measures. Yet, there seems to be a growing consensus in the field that future research must focus on linking teacher preparation, on the one hand, to teacher knowledge and practice, and ultimately to student performance. There is public and political pressure to establish such relationships, and we will remain vulnerable as a field if we cannot demonstrate the merits of what we do in this manner. We believe an initial step in linking preservice teacher education to student outcomes involves documenting growth in teacher candidates' knowledge and skills.

As we have seen, to develop knowledge and skills, it is important that candidates are given frequent and meaningful opportunities to practice with feedback. However, amassing opportunities to learn does not constitute evidence of effect. For teacher educators to build a credible evidence base for their programs, they must link candidates' performance in field experiences to growth in student outcomes. Some of the research reviewed by Lewis and Thomas, Lignugaris/Kraft and Harris, and Maheady et al. (Chapters 22, 14 and 10, this volume) meets this standard. Then, as findings of this sort accumulate, we can develop inductively an understanding of effective teacher education practice. To this end, we must commit to collecting more meaningful data in intentional, systematic, and consistent ways. This can happen only through collaboration across programs.

Just as we prepare teachers to use data to assess the impact of what they do, we need to assess the impact of what we do and to think about our work as inquiry. For guidance, there is a strong international tradition of self-study in teacher education (Loughran, 2007; Loughran & Russell, 2012) and an emerging tradition in general teacher education in the U.S. (Zeichner, 2007). We believe practice can be improved and a credible empirical foundation laid through the accumulation and organization of findings from inquiry about the work we do on a day-to-day basis. Of course, realizing this potential will require both an individual and collective commitment. An organization like TED, the Teacher Education Division of the Council for Exceptional Children, could be instrumental in moving this agenda forward. TED leadership could use its resources to foster self-study and collaboration among its members, to rally the troops, and to provide media and infrastructure with which information generated through self-study may be accumulated and organized. We conclude this *Handbook* by urging TED leadership to do so.

Notes

1 http://www.corestandards.org/

2 http://iris.peabody.vanderbilt.edu/

3 http://mast.ecu.edu/

References

Algozzine, B., Wang, C., White, R., Cooke, N., Marr, M. B., Algozzine, K., … Duran, G. Z. (2012). Effects of multitier academic and behavior instruction on difficult-to-teach students. *Exceptional Children, 79*, 45–64.

Baker, S., Gersten, R., Dimino, J. A., & Griffiths, R. (2004). The sustained use of research-based instructional practice: A case study of peer-assisted learning. *Remedial and Special Education, 25*, 5–24. doi:10.1177/07419325040250010301

Billingsley, B. S., Griffin, C. C., Smith, S. J., Kaman, M., & Israel, M. (2009). *A review of teacher induction in special education: Research, practice, and technology solutions.* (NCIPP Doc. No. RS-1). Retrieved from University of Florida, National Center to Inform Policy and Practice in Special Education Professional Development Web site: http://ncipp.education.ufl.edu/files_5/NCIPP%20Induction%20Exc%20Summ.pdf.

Brownell, M. T., Sindelar, P. T., Kiely, M. T., & Danielson, L. C. (2010). Special education teacher quality and preparation: Exposing foundations, constructing a new model. *Exceptional Children, 76*, 357–377.

Cook, B. G., & Odom, S. L. (2013). Evidence-based practices and implementation science in special education. *Exceptional Children, 79*, 135–144.

Dai, C., Sindelar, P. T., Denslow, D., Dewey, J., & Rosenberg, M. S. (2007). Economic analysis and the design of alternative-route teacher education programs. *Journal of Teacher Education, 58*, 422–439. doi:10.1177/0022487107306395

Freeman, R., Lohrmann, S., Irvin, L. K., Kincaid, D., Vossler, V., & Ferro, J. (2009). Systems change and the complementary roles of in-service and preservice training in schoolwide positive behavior. In W. Sailor, G. Dunlap, G. Sugai, & R. Horner (Eds.), *Handbook of positive behavior support: Issues in clinical child psychology* (pp. 603–629). New York: Springer.

Jones, N. D., Buzick, H. M., & Turkan, S. (2013). Including students with disabilities and English learners in measures of educator effectiveness. *Educational Researcher, 42*, 234–241. doi:10.3102/0013189X12468211

Leko, M., Brownell, M. T., Sindelar, P. T., & Murphy, K. M. (2012). Promoting special education preservice teacher expertise. *Focus on Exceptional Children, 44*(7), 1–16.

Loughran, J. (2007). Researching teacher education practices: Responding to the challenges, demands, and expectations of self-study. *Journal of Teacher Education, 58*, 12–20. doi:10.1177/0022487106296217

Loughran, J., & Russell, T. (Eds.). (2012). *Improving teacher education practices through self-study*. New York: Routledge.

Maheady, L., Jabot, M., Rey, J., & Michielli-Pendl, J. (2007). An early field-based experience and its impact on pre-service candidates' teaching practice and their pupils' outcomes. *Teacher Education and Special Education, 30*, 24–33. doi:10.1177/088840640703000103

Rittel, H. W. J., & Webber, M. M. (1973). Dilemmas in a general theory of planning. *Policy Sciences, 4*, 155–169. doi:10.1007/BF01405730

Sailor, W., Doolittle, J., Bradley, R., & Danielson, L. (2009). Response to intervention and positive behavior support. In W. Sailor, G. Dunlap, G. Sugai, & R. Horner (Eds.), *Handbook of positive behavior support: Issues in clinical child psychology* (pp. 729–753). New York: Springer.

Sindelar, P. T., Brownell, M. T., & Billingsley, B. (2010). Special education teacher education research: Current status and future directions. *Teacher Education and Special Education, 33*, 8–24. doi:10.1177/0888406409358593

Smith, D., & Tyler, N. (2011). Effective inclusive education: Equipping education professionals with necessary skills and knowledge. *Prospects, 41*, 323–339.

Smith, G. J., Schmidt, M. M., Edelen-Smith, P. J., & Cook, B. G. (2013). Pasteur's Quadrant as the bridge linking rigor with relevance. *Exceptional Children, 79*, 147–161.

Spencer, T. D., Detrich, R., & Slocum, T. A. (2012). Evidence-based practice: A framework for making effective decisions. *Education and Treatment of Children, 35*(2), 127–151. doi:10.1353/etc.2012.0013

Zeichner, K. (2007). Accumulating knowledge through self-study in teacher education. *Journal of Teacher Education, 58*, 36–46. doi:10.1177/0022487106296219

Appendix: Discussion Questions

Chapter 1: The Policy and Economic Contexts of Teacher Education

1. Discuss some of the issues involved in linking teacher education to student outcomes. What efforts have been made in this area?
2. Summarize the controversy over alternative routes to teacher education. What does the existing research say?
3. In what ways has it been difficult for Colleges of Education to "prove" their worth?
4. Identify the major differences between general and special education that have had implications for teacher preparation within the current policy context.
5. How has the recent recession impacted conditions in schools, and how have these conditions in turn impacted teacher preparation?
6. Describe the potential impact of RTI on teacher preparation, particularly in the area of special education?

Chapter 2: Federal Support for Personnel Development in Special Education: Where We've Been, Where We Are, and a Look to the Future

1. What purpose does the PDP currently fulfill and what should its purpose be in the future?
2. How does OSEP fulfill that purpose?
3. How are funding priorities influential in guiding the field of special education?
4. What are the barriers and supports inherent to the PDP program in its efforts to positively affect outcomes for children and youth with disabilities?
5. What do you think is the future of the PDP? Will it continue? What will be factors to watch?
6. Why should the PDP continue and how should it be structured? Should it continue? If so what advocacy efforts are needed? If not, what alternative should replace it?

Chapter 3: Patterns of Licensure for Special Education Teachers

1. What role should the federal government play in assuring the quality of special education teachers?
2. Have the "highly qualified teacher" provisions of NCLB and IDEIA improved the education of student with disabilities?
3. Does a lack of consistency in special education licensure patterns create problems in assuring adequate numbers of well-prepared special education teachers in the United States? If greater consistency is desired, what steps can be taken to reach that goal?
4. What are the benefits of categorical patterns of licensure for special education teachers? What are the benefits of noncategorical patterns of licensure for special educators?
5. What are the benefits and liabilities of PK/K/1–12 age/grade ranges for licensure of special education teachers? What are the benefits of narrower age/grade ranges?

6. Should each state put in place licensure standards for secondary special education teachers to promote the transition requirements of IDEA?
7. The field of early childhood special education is complex with great variation in age ranges served and licensure models for professionals. While national standards and recommendations exist, immense variability persists. How can the field move toward greater cohesiveness? Should it? What are the benefits? Barriers?
8. What are the unique proficiencies required of early childhood special educators? How does licensure promote these proficiencies? How does licensure interface with post-secondary degree programs for early childhood educators?

Chapter 4: Preparing Teachers to Work With Students With Disabilities: An International Perspective

1. What is "Education for All" and what does it mean for students with disabilities in different world regions?
2. Why are so many children with disabilities excluded from school? What is being done about it?
3. How do disparities in educational opportunity impinge on educational opportunity for students with disabilities?
4. What are the most pressing issues facing those who are responsible for ensuring that students with disabilities have an equal opportunity to participate in schooling with others of similar age? How does the UNCRPD define the educational rights of students with disabilities? What does this mean in different national contexts and what are the implications for how teachers should be prepared?
5. What approaches to teacher education for inclusive education are emerging in different parts of the world? What can be learned from developments elsewhere? Do all countries need both general and special education teachers? Why or why not?

Chapter 5: Teacher Demand, Supply, and Shortage In Special Education: A National Perspective

1. Identify the main issue in developing and maintaining the teaching force in special education.
2. Discuss the difference between total and annual demand as well as trends in teacher demand.
3. Discuss trends in teacher supply.
4. What are the opposing perspectives that persist in regards to teacher shortage, and how would each impact research and policy decision-making?
5. What are reasons and predictors of teacher turnover, and why is teacher turnover important to consider?
6. Describe why redistribution of teachers among various school types and locations would not eliminate the shortage problem.
7. Summarize explanations of teacher shortage as well as short- and long-term interventions to improve shortage.
8. What are some significant conclusions that can be made about teacher demand, supply, and shortage in special education?

Chapter 6: Recruiting and Retaining Teachers and Administrators in Special Education

1. Discuss the benefits of recruiting and retaining teachers and leaders in special education.
2. Summarize weaknesses in the literature base in regards to research and theory in recruitment and retention.

3. Describe the importance of the use of theoretical models to guide research on teacher and leader retention and turnover.
4. Identify contextual factors related to teachers' entry into the field and work-related conditions that matter for teacher and leader retention and turnover.
5. Why should more research be conducted to examine how special education leaders are recruited, prepared, and supported in their professional roles?

Chapter 7: Equity Challenges in the Accountability Age: Demographic Representation and Distribution in the Teacher Workforce

1. In what ways do teachers' cultures impact the ways in which classroom learning is facilitated?
2. In what ways have NCLB and IDEA influenced special educator recruitment and retention rates?
3. In what ways can teacher preparation programs prepare teachers for today's demographic shift in student population?
4. How do features of public school organization and curriculum impact teacher persistence over time?
5. Where should the responsibility of teacher recruitment, retention, and distribution lie?

Chapter 8: Examining Indicators of Teacher Education Program Quality: Intersections Between General and Special Education

1. What are the two dominating quality indicators of teacher preparation programs?
2. Summarize the stages of teacher education research and accompanying policy mandates that have influenced accreditation components.
3. Describe how expanding databases have provided the opportunity to establish the connection between a teachers' preparation and the performance of the students they teach.
4. Identify other indicators of teacher education program quality attempting to broaden the ways in which programs can demonstrate quality and comply with federal mandates.
5. How is special education teacher education addressed within the discussion of quality indicators for teacher preparation programs?

Chapter 9: Working Together: Research on the Preparation of General Education and Special Education Teachers for Inclusion and Collaboration

1. Why are efforts to redesign the preparation of general and special education teachers to improve collaboration increasing?
2. How are teacher education programs addressing the preparation of general education and special education teachers for inclusion and collaboration?
3. Identify specific teacher education program components for improving preservice teachers' knowledge and skills for inclusive practice.
4. What do existing studies of complete program redesign address?
5. Describe what is meant by *intentionality* and how it may improve research on the preparation of general education and special education teachers for inclusion and collaboration?
6. Discuss marker variables that could improve the overall quality of research on collaborative teacher education.
7. Summarize gaps in the research on collaboration teacher education.

Chapter 10: Field Experiences and Instructional Pedagogies in Teacher Education: What We Know, Don't Know, and Must Learn Soon

1. How do we move toward a model of clinically rich teaching experiences in which the quality of instruction delivered by preservice teachers is measured against important pupil outcomes?
2. How can preservice teachers learn to *select* evidence-based practices based on pupil needs; *implement* these practices with fidelity; and *assess* the efficacy of their practice on important pupil outcomes?
3. How might teacher education programs (or other agencies) develop coursework and field experiences based on the needs of P–12 schools?
4. What evidence can be gathered to show that preparation content (e.g., instructional pedagogies) is applied by prospective teachers during field-based experiences, and, if applied, has a positive impact on pupil learning?
5. What relationships, if any, exist between preservice field experiences and subsequent classroom practices during initial years of teaching?

Chapter 11: Technology and Teacher Education

1. To what extent can teacher preparation programs reorganize with the intent of adding additional emphasis for creating courses, and/or other experiences that may help teacher candidates prepare for working with students with disabilities? What are steps individual teacher educators can take within individual courses and practice that may help make positive steps toward further preparing teachers for working with students with disabilities using technology?
2. What are common and/or program-specific problems of practice faced by teacher educators (i.e., limited face-to-face instructional time) that may be resolved in whole or part through individual or combinations of technology applications?
3. Given the need to provide an individualized education to individuals with disabilities, what are implications for teacher educators as we embed technology-based applications within teaching at the university level, and then as we recommend specific tools and strategies for our future educators to use in the classroom?
4. What are unanswered research questions in the field of teacher education with respect to using technology to present content and create meaningful and engaging learning experiences for teacher candidates? What methodologies are appropriate for answering these questions?
5. As online learning becomes further embedded in teacher preparation, what tool considerations will further develop special education teacher competency? How can we alter our teacher preparation practices to further embed these tools and thus, improve on teacher effectiveness in the K–12 classroom?

Chapter 12: Preparing Teachers to Work With Diverse Populations

1. How are teacher educators preparing teachers for teaching diverse students and working with their families?
2. What do we know about the preparation of teachers working with a diverse population? Which approaches used by teacher preparation programs promote openness to diversity and deeper understanding in preservice teachers?
4. Faculty may not be prepared to address issues of culturally responsive teaching in their courses. Who is responsible for addressing this lack?
5. What are the challenges we face in preparing teachers and school personnel for the changing demographics of the population?

Chapter 13: Alternative Routes to Special Education Teacher Preparation: Context, Outcomes, and Implications

1. Identify what prior research has concluded about AR programs.
2. Describe the changes in AR programs since that research in terms of prevalence, purpose, and participants.
3. What are some differences between traditional and alternative general education programs? What factors are associated with successful outcomes of AR program graduates?
4. Summarize the results of a search of the empirical literature on special education AR programs.
5. Discuss the challenges in the study of AR programs in special education teacher preparation.
6. What are some significant conclusions that can be made about AR programs in special education teacher preparation?

Chapter 14: Teacher Preparation: Principles of Effective Pedagogy

1. Describe the relationship among teacher knowledge, pedagogical practice, and situated practice. What challenges does this framework pose for teacher educators in terms of designing teacher preparation programs?
2. Describe the foundation instructional practices identified for special educators that yield positive student outcomes. How can these practices be adapted to various content lessons?
3. Trace the development of effective instructional pedagogy from the 1970s to the present. Are there additional evidence-based foundation instructional skills that you would include?
4. The lesson cycle provides a useful general framework for designing lessons. How would you structure a reading, math, or content lesson using this framework?
5. Discuss how teacher-training programs might be redesigned to provide more opportunities for cross-content application of foundation instructional skills. How would you evaluate these experiences?
6. What challenges do teacher educators face when designing research that links teacher preparation, teacher practice, and student outcomes?

Chapter 15: Preparing Special Educators to Teach Literacy

1. What are some of the specific literacy needs of students with disabilities, and what has intervention research revealed about the types of instruction that is responsive to those needs? Specifically, what do guidelines say about how teachers can prevent and remediate reading and writing difficulties?
2. Recall the specific challenges associated with preparing teachers in literacy. Which of these presents the most pressing and urgent challenge for teachers, and why? How can teacher education programs better prepare preservice teachers to face these challenges?
3. We noted that effective special education teachers must possess knowledge about interventions and be able to apply that knowledge to solve individual learning problems presented when teaching a diverse array of students. According to research, what are some specific strategies that teacher education programs can use to help preservice teachers develop such knowledge and become proficient in applying it?
4. Snow, Griffin, and Burns (2005) proposed a continuum for learning to teach reading. What implications would the acceptance of this continuum have in terms of how teacher education programs are currently conceived?
5. We suggested three major areas in which future research must focus in order to inform effective special education teaching and ensure its effective implementation in schools. Which of these areas is most urgent? Which of these areas is currently receiving most attention? What are some specific research ideas that would move each of these areas along?

Chapter 16: Teacher Preparation: Mathematics

1. Describe the current national context in mathematics education.
2. Discuss standards in mathematics education and special education that inform what these two fields expect teachers to know about mathematics content and related pedagogy.
3. What is learned from studies included in the teacher preparation literature in special education about mathematics content and pedagogy?
4. Summarize research on teacher preparation in special education and mathematics.
5. Identify recommendations for further research.

Chapter 17: Special Education Teacher Preparation in Classroom Organization and Behavior Management

1. How does theory and epistemology hinder or facilitate the adoption of evidence-based classroom management practices by preservice and in-service teachers?
2. How can teacher preparation programs influence students in their programs regarding potentially counterproductive, previously held beliefs regarding student behavior?
3. What role does high-quality instruction play in effective classroom organization and behavior management?
4. How does state policy regarding teacher competencies in classroom organization and behavior management influence IHE requirements for teacher certification?
5. What resources are needed to reform teacher preparation in the area of classroom organization and behavior management?

Chapter 18: Research on the Preparation of Teachers of Students With Severe Disabilities

1. Given the relatively short history of educational programs for students with severe disabilities, why has there been so much fluctuation in instructional philosophies and approaches?
2. Various authorities and associations have attempted to describe the knowledge and skills necessary for teachers of students with severe disabilities. How would you go about this task determining necessary competencies for these teachers?
3. Let us assume that not all preservice teacher education programs for students with severe disabilities are at the same level of quality. Describe how you would undertake the task of evaluating these programs. And as a follow-up, how would you determine the values base of preservice programs?
4. Aside from the availability and common use of observation instruments and rating scales to evaluate the performance of teachers of students with severe disabilities, there is the problem that these teachers may teach in different settings. What skills might be more important for teachers who teach in inclusive classrooms as opposed to those who teach in separate classrooms and schools?
5. How would you demonstrate the importance of preservice teacher education for teachers of students with severe disabilities? Propose a correlational study that would allow you to make this demonstration.
6. Staff development for teachers of students with severe disabilities can be challenging because of the relatively low density of teachers in an area. What would be the benefits and the limitations to using online staff development programs for these teachers?

Chapter 19: Teacher Preparation for Students Who Demonstrate Challenging Behaviors

1. What are some of the factors that may dissuade teachers from working with students with challenging behaviors? What could be changed in our current approach toward teacher preparation to increase the retention of these teachers?
2. Noncategorical teacher preparation and inclusive services are educational trends. Yet, many students with challenging behaviors are provided educational services in self-contained settings. How could teachers who work across all educational settings, including general education teachers, be trained to work more proactively with students who demonstrate challenging behaviors?
3. What are some of the differences and similarities of students with E/BD and ASD and how may the nature of each disability impact teacher preparation for working with these students?
4. We suggested incorporating family-centered practices and service components into the preparation of teachers who work with students with challenging behaviors. Based on our discussion, what do you see as the benefits and potential challenges to these approaches?
5. As researchers reported, preservice and in-service education and training often does not adequately prepare teachers to successfully address the challenging behaviors of their students. How can we change our education and training practices to increase teachers' knowledge and skills in this area?

Chapter 20: Preparation of Teachers for Children Who Are Deaf or Hard of Hearing

1. What demographic characteristics of children who are DHH should be considered in deciding how to structure deaf education teacher preparation programs?
2. How have improvements in hearing technology changed the way in which deaf education programs are organized?
3. The fact that there are significantly fewer deaf education teacher preparation programs today than there were in the mid-1980s (yet approximately the same number of children who are DHH that need to be educated) has led to serious shortages of teachers of the deaf. What can be done about this problem?
4. Thirty years ago most children who were DHH were educated in small groups of children in self-contained classrooms or schools. Today, most are educated in neighborhood schools with their normal hearing peers. What implications does this have for deaf education?
5. The average age at which children who are DHH are identified has dropped dramatically in the last 25 years. What does this mean for deaf education teacher preparation programs?
6. Name three legislative initiatives during the last 40 years that have significantly affected the education of children who are DHH. And explain what changes have happened as a result of that legislation. How should deaf education teacher preparation programs be structured to respond to those changes?

Chapter 21: Personnel Preparation in Visual Impairment

1. What actions at the university level can personnel preparation programs in visual impairment take to promote the importance of their programs?
2. What might new regional collaborations in personnel preparation in visual impairment look like?
3. How can personnel preparation programs in visual impairment best balance use of multimedia technologies with universal accessibility to create effective distance education platforms within the confines of limited budgets and resources?

4. With decreasing availability of scholarship funds, what might be some new innovative ways to recruit individuals into personnel preparation programs in visual impairment?
5. What methodologies should be used to further the research base on outcomes? What factors need to be considered to make connections between preparation and effective services for students with visual impairments?
6. What role can personnel preparation programs in visual impairment play to promote appropriate caseloads for teachers of students with visual impairments and orientation and mobility instructors? What are some barriers to appropriate caseloads? What might be some solutions?
7. What might be the advantages and disadvantages of a national certification for teachers of students with visual impairment? What effects might this have on personnel preparation programs?

Chapter 22: Educator Preparation Within the Context of School-Wide Positive Behavior and Academic Supports

1. Provide a clear and well-elaborated definition of the foundational problem-solving systems used in these frameworks.
2. What are the characteristics of effective professional development for preservice teachers? For in-service teachers?
3. How can and should professional development outcomes be evaluated?
4. What basic knowledge and skill sets are required for preservice and in-service teachers to participate effectively within these frameworks?
5. What must schools do to develop functional and effective collaborative communities to support school-wide reforms?
6. How do the roles and responsibilities of teachers and other school personnel change within the RTI and SW-PBS frameworks?
7. What contextual barriers exist in schools that prevent reforms from improving student outcomes?
8. What contextual barriers exist in schools that prevent effective reforms from becoming sustainable?
9. What internal and external variables and supports must be in place for RTI and SW-PBS to be successful?
10. How are the impacts of RTI and SW-PBS measured?
11. How can schools identify, monitor and correct challenges to the efficacy of SW-PBS and RTI systems as they arise?

Chapter 23: Teacher Preparation: Early Intervention/Early Childhood Special Education

1. Describe what makes personnel preparation in EI/ECSE unique in contrast to the preparation of teachers for elementary and secondary special education.
2. There are several sets of standards used by personnel in EI/ECSE. Describe the organizations involved in developing these standards and discuss the importance of aligning the standards.
3. Based on the research for "on-the-job" training in EI/ECSE, describe the approaches to professional development and explain why they are more or less effective.
4. Why and how do RTI and PBIS differ in EI/ECSE from traditional general education and special education settings? How do these programs need to be modified for EI/ECSE settings?
5. What are some resources available for EI/ECSE personnel preparation faculty and practitioners? What resources can you find beyond those listed in this chapter?

Chapter 24: Preparing Secondary Special Educators and Transition Specialists

1. As states continue to develop common core standards related to preparing teachers to deliver high-quality academic instruction, what steps could be taken to ensure that specialists focused on secondary special education can be adequately prepared to deliver high-quality transition services and planning?
2. Considering the trend of most universities toward embedding transition content into current coursework, how can higher education instructors more effectively address transition content and critical domain areas noted in the research?
3. With evidence from this chapter acknowledging the impact full, transition-devoted graduate programs have on improving the knowledge, skills, and expertise of program participants, how would you map out a plan to improve your local university's special education program to include transition content?
4. A case has been made that transition content being embedded in university coursework and in general professional development has not made a significant impact. How would you design a professional development activity that increased secondary special educator's knowledge, skills, and expertise related to transition?

Chapter 25: Dimensions of Teacher Quality in General and Special Education

1. Drawing upon the evidence, which teacher qualifications have been demonstrated to be effective at impacting student learning in general education? To what degree is specialized training for special education teachers supported in the research?
2. It is important for teachers to have a strong underlying knowledge base. However, what should this knowledge base consist of, how should it be measured, and how does teachers' knowledge impact students' academic achievement? And, is the knowledge needed for teaching general education likely to be different for special education?
3. There is substantial evidence that teachers' practices can be linked to increases in student achievement. What instructional practices are most powerful for impacting student learning gains in reading and mathematics, and are there specific practices and strategies essential for special education teachers?
4. The multiple problems associated with measuring special education teacher quality make effectiveness difficult to measure. How can these dilemmas guide teacher effectiveness researchers as they engage in high-quality research?

Chapter 26: Qualitative Research on Special Education Teacher Preparation

1. As the field of special education increasingly focuses on the preparation of teachers to work in inclusive settings, rather than self-contained placements, what type of research will be needed to drive instructional practices?
2. This chapter provides evidence of the benefits of qualitative research in special education, a field that has historically adhered to a positivist tradition. What are the benefits, and the drawbacks, of qualitative vs. quantitative research?
3. Identify a topic related to special education research for which you think qualitative methods would be most appropriate. Provide an explanation of the topic and why you think qualitative methods would be appropriate for your research design.

4. When designing qualitative investigations of topics related to special education, how can researchers create study protocols that minimize the chance for bias?
5. Many quantitative research studies are concerned with "scaling up" or generalizing an intervention that has been successful in a particular population. How can qualitative studies inform researchers' or practitioners' efforts to "scale up" particular interventions?

Chapter 27: The "Wicked Question" of Teacher Education Effects and What to Do About It

1. Given the lack of an empirical foundation, on what is special education preparation built? How has such a foundation contributed to the lack of credibility the field faces from policy makers and the public? Discuss the specific ways this could be remedied according to this chapter.
2. What can be done to get policy makers' attention? And what can be done to persuade a skeptical public and skeptical policy makers about the importance of our work?
3. How can the persistent problems that have plagued the field of special education since its emergence in the 1970s be solved?
4. Discuss some of the factors that make conducting high-quality teacher education research so difficult. What types of research and policies are needed to shape the future of special education teacher preparation?
5. What are some of the unique challenges the field of special education faces regarding teacher assessment? What are some potential solutions?
6. Discuss the areas in which there are critical shortages of research (i.e., field experiences, collaborative preparation, literacy instruction, early childhood special education teacher preparation, transition specialist preparation, and recruitment and retention). Discuss which of these presents the most serious need, and provide support for your conclusion. Also discuss which research methodologies might be best suited to each of these areas.
7. Discuss the difference between *highly qualified* and *highly competent* as it relates to the performance of students with disabilities on high stakes assessments.
8. Discuss some potential solutions to the problem of recruiting, preparing, and retaining a diverse teaching workforce.
9. How has the evaluation of teacher preparation programs on the basis of their graduates' ability to produce student achievement gains influenced teacher education programs? Discuss the viability of some alternatives to student outcome measures.
10. Discuss the types of changes and reform that will be required in special and general education teacher preparation to successfully implement multitiered systems of support?
11. Discuss how the adoption of the Common Core State Standards will affect the role of special educators, the focus of special educator preparation, and alternative route preparation routes.
12. How can preparation programs work to prepare teachers to work amidst the continued and rapid development of technology? How can preparation programs themselves best put to use innovative technology as they prepare teachers?

Index